W9-BCE-822

MUSKINGUM COLLEGE
LIBRARY

SELECTIONS FROM THE SMUTS PAPERS

VOLUME VI

DT779.8
S6
A25
v. 6

SELECTIONS FROM THE
SMUTS PAPERS

VOLUME VI

DECEMBER 1934 – AUGUST 1945

EDITED BY

JEAN VAN DER POEL

CAMBRIDGE

AT THE UNIVERSITY PRESS

1973

JAN 3 1974

179551

Published by the Syndics of the Cambridge University Press
Bentley House, 200 Euston Road, London NW1 2DB
American Branch: 32 East 57th Street, New York, N.Y.10022

Original Smuts Papers © The Smuts Archive Trust 1973
Editorial material © Cambridge University Press 1973

Library of Congress Catalogue Card Number: 64–21586

ISBN: 0 521 08603 5

Printed in Great Britain
at the University Printing House, Cambridge
(Brooke Crutchley, University Printer)

CONTENTS OF VOLUME VI

PART XVI

THE FUSION GOVERNMENT

10 DECEMBER 1934–2 SEPTEMBER 1939

THE FUSION GOVERNMENT

Smuts's private papers provide valuable material on the working of the Fusion government and his own attitude to it. He did his best to make it work and had high hopes of the emergence, at last, of a united South African nation (438). His acceptance of Hertzog's Native policy, with amendments, is recorded (371, 374, 379, 380, 388, 414, 430) as is his support of the government even against some of his own followers (432, 439, 440, 443, 444, 464). On the other hand, the issue which was to smash fusion—neutrality or participation in a war involving the Commonwealth—can be seen moving from the merely 'academic' to dangerous actuality as international tensions grow (445, 462, 473, and see *infra*, pp. 190–1). Meanwhile Smuts kept a close watch on developments in neighbouring territories—East Africa, Rhodesia, the Protectorates, South West Africa (393, 395, 418, 427, 429, 431, 439, 448, 468).

Optimism about fusion was offset by pessimism about world politics. The whole headlong course to disaster, as seen by a passionately concerned statesman trying in vain to stop it, is vividly depicted in Smuts's correspondence. Letter after letter records his efforts to save the failing League, to induce the British government to take the initiative in Europe, to get some restitution for Germany, to draw the United States into a partnership of democracies. They record also increasing perplexity before intractable problems, growing awareness of the evil purposes of the dictators who are not open to fair settlement, anxiety lest British commitments on the Continent disrupt the Commonwealth. But he went on defending the causes he believed in—among them, the Zionist cause (401–3, 407, 419, 447, 459, 462, 463, 465).

In his personal life Smuts turned at this time to thought about religion and to what proved to be prolonged study of the Greek Testament. The 'struggle of the ideologies' seemed to him essentially 'a vast religious war' which could perhaps only be finally won through a new Christian vision—a fresh interpretation of the 'message of Jesus' (405, 410, 458, 460, 461, 469).

371   To M. C. Gillett   Vol. 52, no. 190

Doornkloof
Irene, Transvaal
10 December 1934

This, I suppose, will be the Christmas mail, as it will reach you after 20 December and the next will be the New Year mail. So I send you all best wishes for Christmas...I shall spend Christmas either here or somewhere on the eastern mountains, where Jannie [Smuts] and I may go. It could not be as good as that time up the Mauchberg, or that wonderful Christmas we spent on the Mount Anderson mountains above Lydenburg.[1] But if the weather is good we may still have a good time without scaling those cliffs and heights of Being...

Last week Isie and I spent some days at Bloemfontein at our new party's congress. It all went quite well and I hope the future will be all right. We eliminated the colour bar and left membership to be decided by the congress of each province. Of course this means that it will be possibly introduced in some of the provinces, but at the Cape we shall be able to keep it out. I hate these useless colour distinctions which are no good and simply act as pinpricks to the Coloured and Native people. But it seems to belong to the very framework of our South African outlook to put things into colour lines. It is once more the fear complex and largely has unconscious sources. But to me it is often very distressing. Nothing isolates me more from my kind than this sort of thing. It is often most difficult to know what to do when you live in such a pervasive atmosphere of thought and outlook. The Natives are getting more and more suspicious and they think that Fusion means that they are now without champions and that the Nationalist viewpoint has won. At present they look to the so-called Dominion party of Stallard, perhaps unconscious of the fact that Stallard is the most reactionary of all on the Native question. Such is our tangle.

I have been spending some days since my return from Bloemfontein in going through my London papers and documents, arrived by the last mail. It will take me some days more to sort them, destroy the useless and file those that have to be kept. I suppose my English visit is by now clean forgotten, and this five weeks' wonder has sunk into the limbo of the forgotten past. It often makes me wonder whether these exertions are really worth while. There is no time to put up a sustained fight and one can only just touch the edge of great issues and then return to the obscurity whence one has

---

[1] Mountains to the east of Lydenburg in the eastern Transvaal. Both Mauchberg and Mount Anderson are more than 7,000 ft.

for a moment emerged. And then a new stunt, and all is over and the ripples die away on the waters. But I have received a very large number of letters from old friends and unknowns to thank me most sincerely for what little I have been able to do to hearten them; and perhaps some lasting deposit remains from these floods of meetings and speeches and general busy-ness. I hope so, at least. But for me it means again very large numbers of letters that have to be answered, alas.

No mail letter from you last week. I suppose the letter failed to catch the air mail. No complaint, of course. It is always an event to get a letter from you or from Arthur. But sometimes (very seldom however) the routine is interrupted. I hope there is no bad news or worse cause. Everything here appears to be normal, and Doornkloof in its quiet, its natural movement and pleasant air of indifference is very soothing after all the strenuous and hectic days in London etc. I do love this sense of repose and absence of fuss and pressure. Life is too much with us.[1] And here—in my library or on the hills—I can be lonely in the sense of absence from the pressure of others. We had a huge crowd yesterday (Sunday; I write on Monday morning) but even that could be avoided by going to the bush. However, it is good to meet one's fellows once or twice a week. All from here send love and loving greetings to the dear ones at 102, of whom, alas, we have so little, so very little, nowadays. Ever yours,

Jan

372   To M. C. Gillett   Vol. 52, no. 191

Irene
[Transvaal]
14 December 1934

Your letter which arrived yesterday was doubly welcome because of a long silence. Thank you for it. I was most sorry to see that you and Arthur had been disappointed by not hearing from me *en route*. And he, poor dear, thought that I had parted at the Savoy Hotel with a severe look! As if I could ever look severely at him, my own dear soul's brother for whom I have nothing but unexpressed affection! I suppose I was a bit worried and strained by the final duties and calls of that hour of parting. You know from experience that I am a bad parter! I often awake at about 2 a.m. at night, filled with dismal thoughts and forebodings of failure and frustration. It is all nonsense as a rule, but there it is. Similarly at parting life always presents its most forbidding aspect to me, and I often feel as if the bottom has dropped out. I should never be judged by my

---

[1] 'The world is too much with us...' Wordsworth, *Miscellaneous Sonnets*, xxxiii.

parting mood! I had very little opportunity for letter writing on the way as days are long in the air, and nights were often spent with the hospitality of the great on the way, which it was difficult to avoid. Even so however I perhaps had no real excuse. But it was an enjoyable flight. The late afternoon at the Acropolis once more proved a glorious interval. And the long flight in one day from Nairobi to Salisbury was on the whole quite enjoyable. And there was lunch at Mpika with that good Mrs Smith at the new hotel. I hope we shall stay there for a few days at some future time. From the air it appears that Mpika is situated in a series of hills, which must be very good botanically. By the way my last parcels have arrived, including your botanical specimens, which with my own are housed in the boys' old tool-house, which now serves as a herbarium. The library is restored to its original spacious openness and opulence of size.

I was amused at what you report of Mrs Lionel Curtis's conversation.[1] I am much interested to see from my correspondence and vast masses of cuttings which reach Isie from Durrant that my last speech has made a real impression. Well, both Hungary and the Saar have gone well so far;[2] and perhaps my heartening optimism has done some good in high quarters. But I have no desire for office in England—or anywhere! Oh could I dream and wander about and shake off all worldly cares! Is there no time of life when one retires on the score of age? Is sixty-five not enough? My last experience in England was really frightening, and I shall not be over-anxious to go into that sort of ordeal again!

Yes, the L.N.U.[3] has got itself into a bad tangle which may seriously affect its future. It is correct to say that Cecil has always hankered after some form of military or some such sanction. I have explained to him again how fatal I think any such development will be. It may be that in the far future public opinion will be ripe for such a change. But I am convinced it will not work now, except in limited areas and for specific defensive purposes. I am not moved

[1] She had said to Margaret Gillett that, after Smuts's speech at the Royal Institute of International Affairs, her husband had had many letters asking why Smuts was not foreign secretary or prime minister of Great Britain. See Smuts Collection, vol. 51, no. 126.

[2] The assassination of King Alexander of Yugoslavia in Marseilles on 9 October 1934 led to tension between Yugoslavia and Hungary, which was suspected of encouraging terrorist organizations. When the matter came before the League of Nations in December, Hungary submitted to censure. On 4 June 1934 the council of the League fixed the date of the Saar plebiscite (see vol. v, p. 392, note 5) for 13 January 1935. In October the French threatened military intervention to stop the intimidating activities of the local Nazi organization. On 5 December, at the instance of Mr Anthony Eden, the council agreed that an international force should be sent to the Saar to ensure order until the plebiscite should be held. Both France and Germany accepted this.

[3] The League of Nations Union. See vol. v, p. 246, note 3.

by the call of France or the Little Entente[1] for sanctions. Their lack of statesmanship during the last sixteen years has nearly ruined our prospects of future peace. And I for one am not going a step further than we went in 1919—on the contrary. Even article 16 may have to be toned down to carry the U.S.A. with us into the League. Article 10 is a dead letter.[2] Fusion is through; my colleagues have dispersed to their homes for the holidays. We have won handsomely two test bye-elections.[3] And I am not going anywhere for Dingaan's Day this year. I remain at Pretoria to sign papers for myself and colleagues and to be near in case of need. And I am reading and generally pottering about. We have had wonderful rains and the air is cool and fresh. With good companions I would run to Zoutpansberg or [Mount] Anderson or Lydenburg. But not now...

373   To Lord Lothian   Vol. 53, no. 151

20 February 1935

My dear Philip, I was very pleased to get your last letter with your report of your German visit and of your interview with Hitler.[4] You have done very important work there, and have evidently paved the way for the direct negotiations which may now take place between the British and German governments. I understand from the cables that these negotiations are likely to be conducted in the first instance through diplomatic channels. That is where the risk comes in, as from long experience I know that diplomats correspond at arm's length, and no real progress in understanding is made.

I wish it could be possible for you to remain 'on tap', as it were, and to keep in touch with these negotiations so as to prevent unnecessary suspicions and misunderstandings. You have been a member of the government[5] and should be sufficiently trusted in high circles to do what is best in this case.

[1] The Little Entente consisted of Czechoslovakia, Yugoslavia and Rumania. It had been completed in April 1921. Its main purpose was to maintain the national integrity of its members against a possible Hapsburg restoration and aggression by Hungary.

[2] Article 16 obliged the members of the League to impose sanctions in certain circumstances. Under article 10 they undertook 'to respect and preserve...the territorial integrity and existing political independence' of all members.

[3] At Uitenhage on 14 November 1934 G. Dolley won the seat from the Labour candidate by 742 votes. At Queenstown on 12 December 1934 E. W. Douglas beat the Dominion party candidate by 2,373 to 1,752.

[4] This letter is not in the Smuts Collection. For the interview, which took place on 29 January 1935, see J. R. M. Butler, Lord Lothian, pp. 330–7.

[5] Lord Lothian became chancellor of the Duchy of Lancaster in August 1931 and under-secretary of state for India in October 1931. He resigned in 1932 on the issue of imperial preference.

I agree very much with Hitler where he says that no progress will be made by Franco-German conversations. The French are either too suspicious, or their government is too weak to come to any arrangement which requires courage and foresight. French policy has consistently queered the pitch ever since the peace. If any advance is to be made, it will have to be made by direct talks between England and Germany. It is only after a careful exploration of a possible settlement between these two, that a strong line can be taken with France, and she can be induced to acquiesce in a settlement. England has the advantage of support by Italy in any firm line that she might take, and I cannot believe that once there is the possibility of an advantageous settlement agreed on between England, Italy and Germany, that France will really stand out. But some such strong inducement will be needed by any French government to make them face up to public opinion which is manufactured by the Paris press. Any lead today will have to come from the British government. Her position is strong enough to weigh very heavily both with Germany and France, and if your initiative is followed up, the results may well be very far-reaching. I wish you not to leave your baby uncared for at this stage, but continue to hammer away, and push your effort a stage further on.

I received your letter in bed, to which I had been reduced by some troublesome gastric attack. This unfortunate illness prevented me from taking part in the reception to the Empire press conference, and all appointments I had made in that connection had to be cancelled. I had however written out the address which I was about to deliver to our local Institute of International Affairs, and as Curtis thought that this address might do a lot of good, I got Duncan to read it in my absence.[1] You will have seen from the cables that it was intended to reinforce the arguments which I used in my Chatham House speech,[2] and to promote solidarity between the Commonwealth and the U.S.A.

I have just received a letter from Mallory [W. H.][3] of the foreign affairs committee, saying that my timely intervention in the Chatham House speech has been very helpful in bringing about better understanding between the two groups, and adding that the feeling towards us is better in the States than it has ever been before. It is all to the good, and it would almost appear as if the pro-Japanese intrigue has been definitely scotched for the present. Evidently a good deal

[1] The address, read on 9 February 1935, is entitled 'Some Features of the International Situation'. *See* Smuts Collection, Box I, no. 94.   [2] **370.**

[3] Walter Hampton Mallory, born 27 July 1892, Newburgh, New York; executive director, Council on Foreign Relations from 1927; editor, *Political Handbook of the World* from 1930.

of spade work has to be done on both sides of the Atlantic before we shall be out of the wood. The lamentable decision of the senate in regard to the world court[1] shows that American opinion is still unripe for any real move forward. On the other hand, there must be a great deal of profound misgiving in America over developments in the Far East, and it may be that fundamentally the position is better than appears at first sight. Even from this point of view, a really friendly attitude of Great Britain towards Germany may have very far-reaching effects. The danger is that if Germany continues as a pariah in Europe, she may become associated with dangerous friendships in the Far East. But so long as Germany knows that England is really well-disposed towards her, she is not likely to become associated with England's opponents in the Far East. Of course there is a good deal in what Hitler says about Russia, and permanent lines of cleavage in the future. Still, he has always had a bee in his bonnet about Russia, and his fears may be very much exaggerated.

It is quite clear that world relations are in a fluid stage at present, and that resolute efforts by you and others may be most helpful in keeping the world out of dangerous developments in future. I think you have made a very good start, and hope that your initiative will be maintained.

I note what you say about the imperial conference next year. It will be an important occasion, and my mind is not quite free from fear about the whole matter. But it may be that by next year the position may have so far cleared up that the Commonwealth might be in a position to adopt a broad policy into which all can more or less fall into line. With kindest regards, and hoping to hear from you again, Yours ever sincerely,

s. J. C. Smuts

374   To M. C. Gillett   Vol. 53, no. 194

Tsalta
[Cape Town]
23 February 1935

I have just read your letter, this being Saturday morning when the weekly air mail arrives. There is now a second mail weekly, but

---

[1] In 1925 the senate adopted resolutions which prevented the adherence of the United States to the world court. In 1929, to re-open the matter, Senator Elihu Root submitted a compromise resolution but this was pigeon-holed by the committee on foreign relations until 1935 when it was rejected by 52 votes to 36.

I think this is the more convenient one for us. I receive my letters here on Saturday, answer that day or Sunday and post on Monday. Your letter is full of good things and was most acceptable. Its cheerfulness and interest helps to buck me up, as I still feel feeble and aimless after the gastric bout of two weeks ago. More and more it takes time to pick up after these set-backs, and this last one was by no means negligible. It is pleasant to read of you once more by the fireside at Millfield, of your drive to York, to Burford, of Olney and Cowper[1] and many other good things and places. And how near your letters bring you! It is the tragic feeling of so near and yet so far. Space the great uniter is also the great separator, and we talk at 6,000 miles apart. Marion, Helen[2]—it is all very dear to read about.

You refer to my recent address[3] and the space *The Times* has given it. Of course I don't know how much has been cabled, and I am somewhat out of touch with the most recent developments. The speech was written the Saturday when I began to feel upset (Sunday I did not get up at all). You will remember a similar case in December 1918 when I wrote the League of Nations pamphlet in bed in that upper room[4] with a mysterious 'flu attack. I hope the speech will help to keep the government out of the Japanese influence which I hear is still going very strong on the quiet. McKenna [R.][5] is now here and he says there is only one policy—to keep well with Japan.

You refer to my changed attitude on Locarno. Remember two points. Locarno[6] was a definite abandonment of diplomatic unity in the Empire, and made it impossible for the Dominions to continue as a brake on British foreign policy and keep Great Britain out of Continental entanglements. This seemed to me a bad business as I thought the Dominions were having a good influence on British foreign policy.

Then secondly, the original Locarno did at the time seem like a camouflaged Anglo-French alliance. Nobody ever took it seriously that England would fight for Germany against France: it was the *other* situation that was really contemplated. Here too a change has taken place in British feeling towards Germany which makes

---

[1] The English poet William Cowper lived at Olney in Buckinghamshire from 1767 to 1786.

[2] *See* vol. II, p. 255, note 2. The Gilletts' daughter, Helen, was then at school in York where Marion Wilkinson lived.

[3] *See supra*, p. 8, note 1.

[4] In the Gilletts' house, 102 Banbury Road, Oxford.

[5] Reginald McKenna (q.v. vol. IV) was then chairman of the Midland Bank.

[6] *See* vol. V, p. 258, note 2.

Locarno now appear less one-sided in fact. Also, Dominion influence has remained a powerful force with Great Britain in spite of the Locarno break. My qualms have thus been allayed. At the same time it is quite clear that Europeans will never come to rest until they have more of the old-fashioned security—and Locarno in a way helps them to feel more secure. Locarno has more and more appeared as a concession to this fear complex. So now I am a Locarno man. But at bottom I was originally right about the whole business. Briand's influence with Austen Chamberlain made me suspect the whole business and the underlying motives.

You write about the unemployment muddle. We have not heard much about it yet, as the air mail is so far ahead of the newspapers which will only arrive in two weeks' time. But I suspect it is not so much a change of policy as the difficulty of getting new machinery started without much upset and friction. It is quite likely that the new system will prove an improvement on the old.[1] Then again about India as a prospective Dominion. Here the whole difficulty is political. The Conservative party is already hopelessly broken over the bill,[2] and I daresay the formal mention of Dominion status had to be avoided to pass the bill at all. The whole Indian situation is becoming extremely confused. I gather from Willingdon's letters to me that he is far from optimistic. Indians have no practical political instincts or sense, and after all the new instrument is entirely one for their own handling. My own feeling is that the government should have gone farther and, in form at any rate, should have appeared bolder. But as a practical politician I know the sort of difficulty one is up against in these big matters. And the bill does really mean an enormous advance for India. If Indians can agree to work the new system, India will be a free Dominion at any time she likes. [C. F.] Andrews's letters and speeches about the Indian attitude almost seem to indicate that a great chance is going to be missed by India. Gandhi has for the moment turned to religious and social reforms, and perhaps he is wise there, and is taking the only line which will lead to solid results. The oriental mind is religious and real reforms will come along that path. Politics is a game which only Japan has so far learnt to play successfully. And I understand the Japs are not a religious people—but intensely political in their outlook.

Here we are again busy with the Native bills. It is clear that I am

[1] Under the Unemployment Act of 1934 the administration of relief to unemployed persons in Great Britain was transferred to the Unemployment Assistance Board. Widespread opposition to the board's scales of relief payments forced the government to suspend (5 February) the putting into effect of the scales.

[2] The Government of India Bill which became an Act in 1935.

going to be beaten and Hertzog will get his two-thirds majority in spite of my opposition. Many of my stalwarts are beginning to think that the mixed franchise will lead the Natives nowhere. The Native voters at the Cape have actually dwindled to about 10,000. As a constructive advance I have suggested a Native council or assembly for South Africa on the Bunga[1] type to which Natives will be elected and nominated, and which will deliberate on all matters of Native interest and advise parliament. This may become a body of real importance as a platform for intelligent Native opinion and give Natives that voice in their own affairs which it will be impossible for parliament to ignore. This, with a land bill and improved educational and health facilities, may make a real advance. Personally I shall have to stand by the Native franchise at the Cape and cannot compromise on that issue. But public opinion is growing the other way, even among really enlightened people like Duncan and others. We are now discussing my new proposals to which Hertzog has agreed but which many of his friends don't like. This is still confidential. But I thought you might like to have a general idea of what is going on behind the scenes. News about Daniel[2] is much better. But I don't like what you write about Tona.[3] Love,

Jan

375   From D. D. T. Jabavu   Vol. 52, no. 4

[1935]

Dear General, I wish, as a humble admirer, to compliment you on your wonderful achievement in arresting the tide of racialism which had overrun the politics of our country, a country which we Natives love as loyally as all others who belong thereto.

When your cabinet considers future policy with regard to the Native question I hope you will persuade your *confrères* to leave the vote or franchise question severely alone to remain as at present and to address themselves rather to the

(*a*) land question
(*b*) the Native conference legally established under the Native Affairs Act of 1920[4] as established by you yourself for the purpose of consultation with Natives; that this consultation be kept up regularly and annually instead of as now when it occurs spasmodically. This helps Natives to let out steam

---

[1] Under the Native Affairs Act of 1920 a general Native council, known as the 'Bunga' had been set up in the Transkei.

[2] Eldest son of Bancroft and Cato Clark; grandson of Smuts.

[3] A. W. Gillett.   [4] *See* vol. v, p. 372, note 4.

(as you so well said in parliament a few years ago) and keep quiet.

(c) the extension of Native local councils.

All this can be well done without the introduction of the vexed and contentious matter of the Native vote with which we are satisfied as it stands. Wishing you long life and happiness, I am, Yours sincerely,

D. D. T. Jabavu

376   To L. S. Amery   Vol. 53, no. 158

House of Assembly
Cape Town
15 March 1935

My dear Amery, I am very much obliged to you for your letter of 14 February in regard to young Mudie.[1] I did not expect you to take any particular action, but sometimes an opportunity occurs of saying a good word in the right quarter which proves helpful. I know how outside interference in these delicate matters of promotion is resented.

Since you wrote your letter, additional force has been added to what you say about the shaken position of your government. The White Paper looks like very bad staff work, however much may be said for the policy underlying the increases in the estimates.[2] Coming on top of the unemployment muddle, an incident like this creates a very damaging impression. The reconstruction of the government cannot be far off, and I sincerely hope that your doughty fighting in the ranks for the last couple of years, in addition to your other high claims, will be duly recognized.

There is really no argument about a small policy cabinet, and I hope it will come through. It is quite impossible to carry out great questions of policy unless there is this small 'super-cabinet' divorced from actual administration of departments.

The papers here are full of the come-back of Lloyd George.[3] I have no inside information, but in view of the feebleness of the

---

[1] Not identified.

[2] On 4 March 1935 the British government published a White Paper on Defence (Cmd. 4827) which stated that Germany was rearming and that expenditure on the British defence services must therefore be increased. The Paper appeared three days before the foreign secretary was to visit Berlin to try to arrive at an agreed settlement of the question of German armament. Hitler at once postponed the meeting.

[3] He had been asked to submit his proposals for ending unemployment to the cabinet and subsequently attended meetings of a cabinet sub-committee.

government, and the energy of the old 'wizard', I should not be surprised to see him stage a come-back, which would have been thought quite impossible a few years ago. Now it is as well that he is not throwing his great influence on the side of the Socialists as at one time seemed possible.

I hope that Simon and [Anthony] Eden will bring back the goods from Berlin and Moscow.[1] Europe is relapsing into a very sad state, which may soon be a very dangerous state. And a resolute policy of appeasement and reconstruction of the peace by Great Britain will have a very far-reaching effect.

Roosevelt seems to be getting deeper into his muddles on the financial side. I wonder what is going to come of it all! World recovery is so much dependent on the recovery of the United States that one wonders what will happen if things once more take a wrong turn there. I am not unduly pessimistic, but there is great work for you today and for other stalwarts who envisage a new world order to replace the present anarchy.

With very kind regards to you and Mrs Amery from an old friend and well-wisher, Ever yours sincerely,

s. J. C. Smuts

377   To A. B. Gillett   Vol. 53, no. 198

Cape Town
23 March 1935

I have just received air mail letters from you and Margaret, yours coming through the bank. I smiled to read that you were acting chairman of D.C.O.[2] But for certain heresies you would be chairman of Barclay's. But it is better as it is, and I should not like to see you add to your burdens.

I also smiled at the last sentence in your letter, that you 'see no cause for uneasiness in this difficult world!' And as I read I do not think [sic] whether it will be peace or war in a few days. The White Paper was a bad business, I mean the way it was published, apart from the merits of the case.[3] Then followed the French conscription.[4]

---

[1] The postponed visit to Berlin (see supra, p. 13, note 2) took place on 25 March. Nothing came of it. Sir John Simon was then foreign secretary and Mr Anthony Eden (later Earl of Avon) was lord privy seal. Eden also visited Moscow, Warsaw and Prague.

[2] The Dominion, Colonial and Overseas branch of Barclay's Bank.

[3] See supra, p. 13, note 2.

[4] On 12 March 1935, to make up a deficiency in conscripts caused by a decreased population, the French government decided to double the period of service and reduce the age of enlistment.

And *on top* has come Germany's army and air plans, with full conscription.[1]

The fat is of course in the fire, and the position is very bad. When this reaches you the crisis will have gone one way or the [other] way. I think it will be peace. But at the moment the French seem to have lost their heads, and one cannot say what will happen. I hope Simon will persuade Hitler partly to retrace his steps.[2] It may be that the French plan to frighten Hitler into such a course by their violent attitude. But with Germany in the mood of nationalistic exultation in which she has been for some time, the outcome of the Simon mission is in doubt. I have spoken some words backing up a peaceful settlement which express the sentiment of South Africa. But of course that does not amount to much. It is almost unthinkable that we should once more be precipitated into war. But the impossible sometimes happens when people are not normal, and people today are not normal on the Continent. The English have only one role and that is to be the peace-maker in this sad and dangerous development.

Margaret writes that you may come out somewhat earlier this year to South Africa. It is good news and you will make us all much happier the earlier you come. I still plan an East African visit for July-August if I can get away and you mad Europeans will leave us in peace. Whether the plan can be carried out I don't yet know. Perhaps you and Margaret could fly out to Kenya or Tanganyika and meet me there. That would be good fun and give us botanists and birders a good time. I still feel a bit shaken after my last illness, and a holiday to the wilds will do me good. And you too! Ever lovingly,

Jan

378   To M. C. Gillett   Vol. 53, no. 199

Cape Town
23 March 1935

I am in my office this Saturday morning for some business and in a free interval I am writing to you and Arthur, from both of whom I received letters this morning. I have written to Arthur about the gravity of the European situation and shall not trouble you about

---

[1] On 16 March 1935 the German government decreed conscription and planned an army of over half a million men. On 9 March they had announced the existence, in contravention of the treaty of Versailles, of a German air force.

[2] *See supra*, p. 14, note 1.

that. He raises however another point which I may refer to here in your letter. His suggestion is that some provision should be made in the League constitution which will make territorial arrangements more flexible and less rigid than they are today. Some have perhaps too much of the good things and others (like Japan and Germany) have too little. Unless the League has power to adjust such differences he thinks the existence of the League may be at stake. Of course it is an enormously difficult subject, and I do not see what could be done at the present stage of international opinion. My own view is that the colonial question as settled at Paris should be re-opened and that some real effort should be made to satisfy Germany. But what can be done to satisfy Japan? And there is the greedy Italy to reckon with. If we could reach a stage of international appeasement when these matters could be calmly and objectively considered in a judicial spirit, a solution is perhaps possible. But today, in these noises and in this atmosphere of constant crisis and deep-seated distrust one almost despairs of finding any way out. My only hope is in the British Empire—that we will keep out of these violent disputes and resist war at all costs and act as the peace-makers. Twice during the last couple of days I have spoken publicly in this sense,[1] but not with much conviction that my advice will be followed in London. We shall only save Europe from war if Great Britain declared herself out of it and exerts all her immense power and prestige as the peace-maker. I fear there is a section in the Conservative party that would advocate an opposite policy. But the effect of a really pacific policy on the part of the British Empire may be decisive for the maintenance of the peace of the world. But is John Simon strong enough for such a crisis? He has not come very well out of previous trials. Let us hope for the best...

379   To M. C. Gillett   Vol. 53, no. 204

Tsalta
[Cape Town]
28 April 1935

This is Sunday evening after supper. I am sitting on the sofa with my feet on that nice *riempies*[2] stool Arthur had made for me. And some music is going on on the wireless. This is the time to think of dear friends, and to think of those wonderful Sunday nights at 102, round the fire on the hearth, while pleasant prattle goes on among

---

[1] One of these speeches was made at a press conference dinner on 21 March 1935. *See* the *Cape Times*, 22 March 1935.   [2] Thongs cut from hide (Afrikaans).

the 102s and 111s.[1] Alas, it is a long time since I last enjoyed those delightful evenings. And it may be a long time before I can do so again...

Last night we were shocked to hear of the terrible accident to the Governor-General's son at Kimberley which cost him his life. They were hartbeest shooting, and in dismounting from his motor for a shoot he missed his step, fell and the bullet (a dumdum too) pierced him, and a couple of hours later he was dead. His wife was waiting for him here, and this afternoon Lady Clarendon had to break the sad news to her. She is expecting a baby next month. It is a heart-breaking business. This is now the third time in succession that our Governor-General loses his only or eldest son—Buxton, Athlone, Clarendon. Hyde was an accomplished shot and experienced huntsman. But that was not enough. I have not seen Lady Hyde, but the poor parents are quite broken.

The house feels empty. Sylma [Coaton] left yesterday with her two lively daughters[2] to spend a last week with the grandparents at Wellington...To me children are a pure delight, and grand- are a crowning glory. It is a curious thing how we change—and not for the better—as we get older. While we represent the power, children undoubtedly reproduce the loveliness of nature. Of such is the kingdom of Heaven.[3] Think of Helen [Gordon] and Nico [Gillett] as they were years ago—the most bewitching creatures imaginable. Not that they are not lovely still, but it is in quite another way. I love the trailing clouds of glory in which they come.[4]

I had a letter from Mrs Millin saying she had finished the first volume of her book about me. It brings me to the point before the Great War. I shall look through the MS when I go home. I wonder what she has made of me, knowing so little of me as she really does. The only people who could tell the truth about me and know me are Isie and you. And you are dumb oracles.[5] I suppose she has written about me as she has written about Rhodes. She has a real admiration for me, but is naturally critical and is certain to be discriminating. But in my case she will revive many forgotten episodes and memories and my opponents will no doubt rejoice to find me in the pillory once again. I think no book should be written about a living politi-

---

[1] 111 Banbury Road, the house of Dr Henry Gillett.

[2] Sybilla Margaret Smuts Strick and Lilian Elizabeth Smuts Dreyer.

[3] 'Suffer little children, and forbid them not to come unto me: for of such is the kingdom of Heaven.' St Matthew xix. 14.

[4]   But trailing clouds of glory do we come
        From God, who is our home.
                Wordsworth, Ode on the Intimations of Immortality, iv.

[5] 'The oracles are dumb...' Milton, Hymn. On the morning of Christ's Nativity, l. 173.

cian. She is most anxious for the next volume, which begins with the Great War, to have from you any letters written by me on big or critical occasions and showing my reactions. I have not encouraged her to trouble you. But she knows you are coming out this year, and thinks you can provide illuminating material. You will do as you like in the matter. If it is going to be a really valuable work one would like to help her. She has been through your letters to me, but that has only whetted her appetite for mine to you. The story of the inner life is of course hidden for her, and I don't know whether she is really interested in it. But she wishes naturally to have my reactions to the tremendous external events through which I have passed in a life which is no doubt very unusual. I shall tell her that I have put her request before you, without pressing you in any way.[1]

Tomorrow we shall lay on the table the report of the Native select committee.[2] Apart from the fundamental provision taking the Native vote away in future (and which I have opposed to the end) the new draft bills are great advances. The Natives get considerable additional land, and white representation in the senate, and Native representatives in a new Native council which will advise parliament on all aspects of Native interests. At the Cape Native representatives are also sent to the provincial council. The Natives will never acquiesce in the loss of their parliamentary franchise, but they will in time come to look upon the *quid pro quo* given them as from every practical point of view far more valuable. I would have left their franchise intact if the matter were in my discretion. But white opinion is firmly opposed to the continuance of the Native franchise. And the two-thirds majority required under the constitution will probably be forthcoming to make the change. Much as I sympathize with the Native point of view I am convinced the alternative now given them will in the end prove far more valuable to them. At present they have about 10,000 electors in a total of over half a million—a mere drop in the ocean. What is really valuable in the new bills is due to my individual efforts, and I cannot be blamed for the reactionary views of others. It is of course not certain yet that the new scheme will pass, as many consider it too liberal to the Natives. I only fear if it does not pass worse things will happen later.[3]

We are all rather at sea over MacDonald's attack on Germany in his recent article.[4] We do not know what has produced this un-

[1] Smuts's letters to M. C. Gillett were not made available to Mrs Millin.

[2] *See* vol. v, p. 453, note 1.

[3] On the legislation of 1936 *see* C. M. Tatz, *Shadow and Substance in South Africa*, chapters 6 and 7.

[4] For this article, entitled 'Peace, Germany and Stresa', *see The Times*, 26 April 1935, pp. 16, 18.

expected change in the British attitude. There may be good grounds for such a tirade against Germany. But it is not likely to bring Germany back to the League, which we all understood to be the British policy. I do not like the present look of things. But enough. I end with love to you all. Ever yours,

Jan

380   To M. C. Gillett   Vol. 53, no. 205

Tsalta
[Cape Town]
6 May 1935

This is written after 10 p.m. and will be my last letter from Tsalta this year. Parliament finished its session last Saturday and day after tomorrow we go home. I have spent a busy but futile day in all the jubilee celebrations,[1] starting at 8.45 in the morning, and I have only just come home from the last item in town. Thank goodness, it is all over. How I pity the King who has had to endure the full blast of it in London today. I listened to his final speech just now, and it was very good and human, as all he does and says. I wonder what you and Arthur have been doing this day? Of course there is something very significant about this jubilee, and the survival of the Empire after all the storms which have destroyed others. I referred to this significance and its explanation in my speech today.[2] The British Empire in spite of all its failures and shortcomings does still in some measure practise some of the ideas which lie at the basis of all good and lasting government. There is still far more real personal and political liberty in the British system than in any other; and that in large measure accounts for its comparative success. Let us draw some comfort from these things, in a world in which there is today not much to comfort us. But I don't want to write in a pessimistic strain, for I really don't feel in a pessimistic mood. I believe that even with disarmament gone by the board we shall not see war but rather what I have called equilibrium on a new basis. If we cannot get the nations to disarm, let us at least get them to maintain peace on an armed basis, as long as that is possible. I believe the grave danger now is not war but bankruptcy and the undermining of our economic civilization. If that goes it still is a question how much else of our civilization could be saved. But I don't see any war

---

[1] The twenty-fifth anniversary of the accession of George V.

[2] For this speech, entitled 'The King's Reign and the Commonwealth', see Smuts Collection, Box I, no. 97.

coming just yet, except in Abyssinia. There Italy seems determined to annexe a new colony, and a war there will be. Mussolini may yet burn his fingers badly. But after Manchukuo[1] why not Abyssinia? And so we go on in the old ways...

We have so far had no real criticism of the Native bills. I suppose people are still digesting what we have put before them. Today's paper contains a criticism from Ballinger [W. G.] which rather misses the point. But incidentally he attacks the English members on the select committee and points out that among those who stood by the Native vote at the Cape the Dutch were the majority. It is a great mistake they make in England to look upon the Dutch as trampling on British traditions and submerging the British in South Africa. I see no difference between them—both dear to me and both pretty full of the devil. But in these bills—apart from the Cape Native vote—we have not done so badly, and the Native representative council, which I could get agreed to this last session, is a great and I think a far-reaching advance. I only fear the Malanites and Stallardites will dislike it so much as to kill the whole scheme. Stallard in the committee resolutely fought the council scheme as going too far! And yet every Native voter at East London voted for his candidate who gave us in consequence a handsome beating.[2] Such is the contrariness of the world.

Now this has to be posted to catch the mail tomorrow. So goodnight. I don't know why but you and Arthur have been specially much in my thoughts today. Perhaps I was a bit in yours! I love to think of us botanising and roaming the wilds together. Ever lovingly,

Jan

381   From F. C. Kolbe   Vol. 53, no. 93

The Monastery
Sea Point
[Cape Town]
24 May 1935

My dear General Smuts, In sending you my three articles on the Collects[3] I am not intending to prod you with piety. It is just an art-study in a surely unique form of soul-expression—not an

---

[1] Manchukuo had been under the control of Japan, in defiance of the League of Nations, since 1932.

[2] In the bye-election at East London North on 17 April 1935 R. M. Christopher of the Dominion party beat the United party candidate by 3,135 votes to 2,586.

[3] These appeared in the *Southern Cross*, 24 April, 8 and 15 May 1934, under the title 'Our Treasury of Prayer'.

individual, but a corporate soul. You may not have had the opportunity of seeing the collects *in globo*.[1] And after all, prayer is an holistic phenomenon. I will not let you forget how your theory draws us together.

When you have read the articles, will you please return them. I have kept no other copy.

Let me write for you the definition of beauty I spoke to you about. I think it will hold water. It has the merit of emphasizing the δυναμις or prodding power, or suggestiveness, of things; and moreover it can with a word of alteration apply to everything in the same universe of discourse—sublime, interesting, charming, humorous, ridiculous, etc. and their opposites.

Beauty is that quality in things whereby, on mere presentation or representation, they excite in us, by congenial stimulation of our powers or by their own suggestiveness, a non-self-regarding feeling of delight.

The scholastic definition is simply *quod visum placet*:[2] but of course their *visio*[3] is spiritual as well as sensuous.

I have just heard that one of our scientists, E. K. du Plessis,[4] has become a Catholic,—and of course he is under the harrow. Why cannot people be large-hearted towards one another, even if they cannot be *concordes*?[5] I daresay you know his work on the tsetse etc. He lives at Brakpan. If you get an opportunity, do see that he gets fair play.

I did not have a chance to thank the Duchess for the fresh supply of *biltong*.[6]

I am glad that Hitler is beginning to justify your optimism. Yours affectionately,

F. C. Kolbe

382   To A. B. and M. C. Gillett   Vol. 53, no. 217

Doornkloof
[Transvaal]
5 July 1935

This letter is addressed to you jointly as I have several letters from both of you to answer. However all my letters to you separately are also meant for you jointly, so there is no difference in fact.

---

[1] As a whole.   [2] What pleases the sight.   [3] Vision.
[4] Fellow of the Royal Geographical Society; travelled widely in Africa making a study of its fauna; author of *Natal's Nature Sanctuaries in Zululand* (1934).
[5] Of one mind.
[6] Sun-dried strips of meat (Afrikaans).

Your letters are mostly over family affairs to which I shall first refer. I need not say anything more about Esther's passing away.[1] I knew it would be a most cruel blow, especially to Margaret. But she looked to me last year already as no longer of this world, though still in it. And it is better so—hard as it is to those who remain. She was one of the very best and leaves a memory of pure undiluted fragrance. She has been much in my mind these last weeks...

I have no desire to visit England or Europe in these days. The things I have worked for or hoped for are being defeated one after the other. I see no good that I could do by any visit. Nor do I see any opportunity of so doing in the near future. But we have no free choice in these matters. And 'they also serve who only stand and wait'.[2] So I am waiting. Perhaps the Lord will come; perhaps not. I see no clear course but waiting for developments. It may be that things must be worse before they become better. It may be that they will become worse without becoming better thereafter. The world is bigger than our view of it, and impatience does not become us poor mortals in the sort of situation confronting mankind today. We who believe in God must also believe that inner forces are working themselves out beyond our vision or understanding. In the end I am a mystic, believing in a world beyond this world, or rather *inside* and underneath this world, where is the moving Finger[3] whose scrawl we see on the wall of this world. Of course, if there is the clear call of duty one should be prepared to act; but at the moment I hear no such call. Rather I feel warned off. But of course a change may come at any moment. Just after the Boer War I felt that inaction was the only action called for. And I was right. I have the same feeling at the moment. But if the call to action comes and I have the strength I hope to do what lies in my power to help my world in its sore troubles.

This all sounds rather serious. But it puts my present view and mood. It would be a joy and a help to talk things over with you, but if the time for that also is not yet, then we must just bow to our fate. I shall accept without demur any decision you may come to in regard to your visit.

Yesterday—4 August—I was thinking a great deal of twenty-one years ago, when mankind took the great plunge into the abyss. I wonder whether we have been wrong about the way out. So many

---

[1] *See* vol. IV, p. 92, note 1.   [2] *See* vol. I, p. 45, note 1.

[3]   The Moving Finger writes; and, having writ,
              Moves on.
                        Edward Fitzgerald, *Omar Khayyám*, edition 1, lii.

think the League a failure, and there is so much to show its weakness and inadequacy to the needs of these times. And yet I can see no other way. Perhaps it is a deeper reform that is called for—something in the hearts of men. A change of heart, as the old phrase is. Perhaps we really need a new religion of the spirit, which will express itself in new institutions deeply rooted in new convictions and viewpoints. But little of this is forthcoming. I see a new paganism in Germany and Russia which runs counter to the fundamental spiritual doctrines in which I believe. But real Christianity seems to have gone underground, and its official spokesmen are just mumbling in the wind. The new world evidently is still to be born and there are no signs of birth except the sorrows and pains through which the whole world is passing.

This week I am leaving on an extended tour to Natal, the Transkeian Territories and the Eastern Province. I shall be away for a couple of weeks, speaking and conferencing, and carrying on in my little world. But my real mind will be elsewhere, where our fate is being decided without our taking any part in the decision.

We feel very happy over the arrival at Street of the little youngster[1] and rejoice with the parents and other members of the Street circle. Here we are all well and normally happy. I am waiting, while writing this, for Sarah Gertrude Millin who wants to talk to me about the Great War. So good-bye. My love to you and the dear children.

Jan

383 To F. C. Kolbe   Vol. 53, no. 174

Irene
[Transvaal]
16 July 1935

Dear Father Kolbe, I must apologize for having delayed so long in answering your letter of 24 May and in returning your papers on 'Our Treasury of Prayer'. I have been very much on the move politically and all private correspondence has had to suffer. Your letter was more than welcome, and 'Our Treasury' has been read and reread several times, as it deserves. I agree with you as to the significance of prayer. In many ways it is the most intimate and unique expression of our personality. Things we dare not say to our friends, not even to ourselves, we pour out in prayer to the Mother Soul of our soul. And although I am not acquainted with the

---

[1] The birth of Jan Smuts, son of Cato and Bancroft Clark.

Catholic prayers, I am deeply versed in the Psalms of the Old Testament, which seem to me the greatest and noblest outpourings of the human spirit ever put into language. The inexpressible finds expression there. Emotions almost too deep for utterance somehow find an outlet there. The soul is greatest when it returns to rest and solace in its primal source, and even language then transcends its ordinary range of expression. Of course it is all truly holistic. When the broken fragment returns to its niche in the whole it reaches a new consummation. I also agree with you as to the nobility of the language which Catholic Christianity has evolved. What could match the beauty of *De Imitatione Christi*.[1] Somehow it breathes a spirit which is beyond all language. It is curious how in such a case the human soul sets on fire its own earthly vesture, and language becomes a blaze of glory, which transcends all dictionary values. The soul literally pours itself out *through* language and the meaning and significance seem to pass beyond all language. You who have so intimate a knowledge of all this, must be able to appreciate far more than I can this wonderful way in which language transcends itself on the spiritual–emotional plane. I return your papers and hope you will continue your delightful *causerie* on this intimate subject.

Tomorrow I fly north to Tanganyika in order from there to motor south and spend a fortnight in the wilds, with plants and animals. No hunter am I, but I find much consolation and healing in nature. And so I hope to fossick round till the end of this month.

I hope you are continuing well and maintaining the progress you have recently made. My wife sends her dear love, and will follow it up with something more tangible in due course. Ever yours affectionately.

J. C. Smuts

384   To M. C. Gillett   Vol. 53, no. 227

Doornkloof
[Transvaal]
10 September 1935

I returned this morning from Bloemfontein after a day there at the party congress. Two bad nights in the train and a raw tummy without food made a stay for a second day undesirable. Then to my delight the office phoned just now that I need not come in this morning. So I can attend to correspondence. We had a very good congress, and my move three years ago is more and more being

---

[1] *The Imitation of Christ*, a devotional work by Thomas à Kempis (1380–1471).

justified by the new spirit of co-operation. Hertzog made a great attack on the parsons and teachers who abuse their positions for party purposes. You know what political parsons and teachers mean in the atmosphere of South Africa. He also told the congress that he had advised the king in favour of a South African as governor-general next time, and asked English and Dutch to come to agreement about the matter. We shall see. The risk is that such a step may start another movement towards the Dominion party with its colonial complex. I have warned him about the risk that is being run. But he is now committed.

Of course all news from here is more than overshadowed by the bad news from Geneva. Italy is definitely determined to go to war, and no half measures will satisfy her.[1] War there will be. The closing of the Suez canal as 'sanctions' would stop it—if Great Britain and France co-operate. And so another defeat for the good causes and another weakening of the League. Still, there are many possibilities. I need not mention them. But evil-doing carries its own judgment, and with public opinion dead against Italy, she may yet find out what awful blunders she has made, and it may become a flaming warning to others. I see indications that Germany sympathizes with Italy. I suppose if Italy is successful, they will go and do likewise as soon as there is an opening. We may therefore be in for a bad time—just at a moment too when the chances of world-recovery were definitely improving. But some evil destiny is bestriding Europe in these days. Still, the unpredictable may happen and things may be altered in ways we do not now foresee. It is a very discouraging outlook in any case. Of course European co-operation will really become impossible unless there is co-operation on this occasion. It is no use talking of a collective system and collective security if it breaks down every time it is tested. The League position will be unutterably bad if Italy gets off with it, as the saying goes. No, imperialism is not dead. It may even become a more active danger, judging from the cases of Japan and Italy, and indications elsewhere. If the system of liberty breaks down, I see no guarantee for any of our other great human principles. But I still have the feeling that something will happen to stay the rot and so justify our hopes and efforts of the

[1] Mussolini's decision to go to war with Abyssinia in order to extend Italian possessions in Africa was taken in 1933. On 5 December 1934 Italian and Abyssinian forces clashed at Walwal in disputed territory bordering Italian Somaliland. The Abyssinian government appealed to the League and protracted negotiations ensued. On 3 September a League commission of inquiry into the Walwal clash exonerated both parties and then went on to examine the whole question of Italo-Abyssinian relations. Before it could report further it had become clear that Italy would not accept any compromise and was bent upon war.

past. Some have suggested colonial revision. But what would be the use of it when the world is in such a temper? In a reign of law and order any revision would be open to consideration. But revision as between brigands takes you no farther and only increases the danger of further troubles. And yet mere isolation and each retiring to his own shell has become equally impossible as an international policy. The world is too close knit today to revert to the policies of the past. We can only move forward, but progress on the Japanese and Italian lines would mean a world in flames. I cannot believe that universal bankruptcy and anarchy is the goal towards which man is moving. But the way out of the tangle is today darker than ever. We must put on our thinking caps afresh. I think I have written to you in this strain before, but my mind keeps reverting to the fundamental situation and alternatives by which we are today faced. The danger would depart if there is genuine co-operation. But there is not. Hence the awful dilemma. What can we do to save our civilization from violence and shipwreck? I wish I could see more clearly into the future. Now enough. My love and kindest memories and thoughts to your dear ones at 102.

Jan

Later: 16 September 1935. The above was written last week, and subsequently came the news of the fine speech of Hoare's at Geneva[1] and of the way the other countries had rallied and responded to his lead, and finally of the speech of Laval [P.] in which he appeared to agree to what Hoare had said. It was all very heartening, although I am not even yet satisfied that Laval is not facing both ways. But Italy appears undeterred and determined to go on with her plan of campaign. We must now await events at Geneva. But the very fact that Great Britain has at last spoken clearly and given a firm lead is of inestimable value. World opinion will now crystallize round the British policy in support of the League. While I write we are awaiting the news of Hitler's speech, in which he is sure to refer to the League position; and he may even show his hand or at least his sympathies in this dispute. But it may take another week or even two before we know where we are. South Africa has backed up Great Britain in a very creditable way.

I leave for Cape Town tonight, and shall be away for a week. Politics and again politics.

[1] On 11 September 1935, Sir Samuel Hoare, the British foreign secretary, made a speech in the League assembly which declared his country's intention to 'stand for the collective maintenance of the covenant in its entirety, and particularly for... resistance to all acts of unprovoked aggression'.

26

The Campbell-Bannerman portrait[1] arrived duly per Patrick Duncan. Thank you for the noble and welcome gift. The case has however not yet been opened. Love,

Jan

385   To M. C. Gillett   Vol. 53, no. 229

Doornkloof
[Transvaal]
30 September 1935

Sunday night again—always a good time for a talk. I have a very busy week behind me, and even yesterday was tired out by these country functions. But I find it impossible at this stage in our politics to avoid them or to pass them on to younger members of the cabinet. I trust however that the call for my services will ease off in the near future, for I could not keep this up...

The Geneva news has been better last week. The firm line taken by Great Britain has had its effect on Italy, and reading between the lines one concludes that Mussolini is at last beginning to think of a way out. I don't however see what way out there is, after his refusal of the more than handsome compromise which was made and curtly refused at Paris.[2] I only hope your people will not weaken and abandon the fine lead they have at last given. It is quite clear that *this* is the vital test of the League, and failure here will be fatal for the League. Manchuria was too obscure a situation and too far away. But here the issue is clear and at our door. I should love to see Great Britain not only take but maintain the moral leadership to which her position in the world entitles her. It is not a case of Abyssinia so much as of the future of our whole civilization which cannot survive on the lines of the old imperialism now once more showing its horrid head.

No, I do *not* agree with Jan [Gillett] that there is some trickery on the part of Great Britain. I feel sure that your government must be profoundly impressed by the peace ballot which has been such a revelation to all.[3] And they also feel that their association with

---

[1] This portrait had formerly hung in Millfield, the house of the Clarks at Street. Smuts hung it above the desk in his study at Doornkloof.

[2] After a three-power conference (Great Britain, France, Italy) called by the council of the League compromise proposals were submitted to Mussolini and rejected with derision on 18 August.

[3] In the 'Peace Ballot' held in Great Britain in 1934 and closely associated with the League of Nations Union over $11\frac{1}{2}$ million people voted on a questionnaire. G. M. Gathorne-Hardy in *A Short History of International Affairs 1920–1938* (p. 407) sums up the result, announced on 27 June 1935, as follows: 'Regarded in the light of

Continental politics on the old alliance basis has become impossible. The position has been so clearly put by Hoare at Geneva that I am sure there is intellectual conviction behind the new policy. And the only question is whether there will be sufficient courage and persistence to see it through. Simon often made a good beginning, only to abandon it later. I hope Hoare and Eden will be tougher. There is of course the risk that Abyssinia may find it impossible to restrain her army and may precipitate the crisis by attacking. That of course would be fatal. But fate has played such pranks in recent history that one never knows whether the pitch may be queered once more.

But enough of all this politics. However there is nothing else specially to write about at the moment. All well here. My dear love to you all.

Jan

386   From L. S. Amery   Vol. 53, no. 4

3 October 1935

My dear Smuts, You speak of the favourable impression that Hoare's speech at Geneva made upon you.[1] As a speech I have no doubt it was admirable. As political action it filled me with dismay, as indeed does the whole policy of our government over this Abyssinian business. For ten years, since the rejection of the Geneva Protocol,[2] we have taken the line, so admirably expounded by yourself last November,[3] that the League exists as a conference table of the nations and not as an international war office, and that arrangements for actual support against aggression must be confined to the powers more directly concerned. That is a task beyond the capacities of the League, where unanimity precludes anything like prompt or decisive action. Even as recently as this year Austen [Chamberlain] laid it down, I think apropos of this very Italian question, that the League could only preserve peace between nations

a mandate to the British government, on a critical occasion, the voice of the plebiscite may fairly be said to have been: "Go as far as you can, in combination with other members, to secure and observe loyalty to the covenant, and to resist aggression; and we give no support at all to military measures which will fall exclusively or preponderantly on British shoulders."' A. J. P. Taylor in *English History 1914–1945* (p. 379) sums up as follows: 'The Peace Ballot had become undesignedly a ringing assertion of support for collective security by all means short of war, and more hesitant support even for war.' On military action against an aggressor the vote was roughly $6\frac{1}{2}$ million for, $2\frac{1}{2}$ million against, 2 million abstentions.

[1] In a letter of 17 September 1935. *See* Smuts Collection, vol. 53, no. 177.
[2] *See* vol. v, p. 239, notes 2 and 4.   [3] In the Chatham House speech (**370**).

already predisposed that way, and could not possibly stop a great nation bent on war.

In the last few months, with an election pending, and anxious to conciliate the strong pacifist vote, the government, pushed by young Eden, have increasingly identified themselves with the absurd theory that war is indivisible and that any war anywhere must be prevented by the League, but only by the League. The result is that we have dangerously inflamed the situation between Italy and ourselves, which she naturally and rightly regards as the protagonist in this whole business, and yet, when it comes to the point, the League is not likely to agree to anything but the mildest and most ineffective of sanctions. The best result to hope for now is that even ineffective sanctions, coupled with Abyssinian resistance, may wear out Mussolini. I regard that as extremely unlikely. The most probable result is a humiliating diplomatic defeat of this country in the eyes of the world and a complete failure to satisfy the pacifists here whose appetite for blood we have only whetted. Possible, though not probable, is a disastrous war for which we are in no way prepared materially or psychologically. Yours ever,

s. L. S. Amery

387   To L. S. Amery   Vol. 53, no. 181

Office of the Minister of Justice
Pretoria
2 December 1935

My dear Amery, I have two letters from you to answer for both of which I thank you very much.

I also thank you for your book[1] which I hope to read with deep interest as soon as the Christmas holidays arrive. Anything I can do in connection with the book I shall gladly do as soon as I get the opportunity to look it through.

Now with regard to your letters, let me just clear away what may be a misunderstanding. I have never been opposed to sanctions, nor have I ever expressed views to that effect. What I said in England last autumn and also on other occasions had reference to what appeared to me to be an attempt to endow the League with a defence force of its own and make it in that way a sort of super-state able to enforce its own decisions as apart from its constituent members. My critical remarks were directed against this development, which

---

[1] L. S. Amery, *The Forward View* (1935).

was deliberately vetoed in the discussions which led to the drafting of the covenant at Paris. But I am and remain a supporter to the fullest extent of the covenant as it stands, including clause 16.

And let me make this further point. If Italy had been allowed to get away with it on this occasion, not only would the League have been reduced to a position of futility, but I doubt whether it would have been possible to continue its activity even as a debating society for the future. From the purely British point of view, you know how Simon lost face over the Manchukuo affair. My feeling is that unless the British government and its representatives at Geneva had acted on the present occasion with much more energy and decision than Simon had done on the previous occasion, the stock of the government would have sunk very low indeed in foreign affairs. The way the British electorate has supported the attitude of the government is to my mind very strong proof that they were sick of the old dilly-dallying, and that they approved of the much more energetic action and firm attitude which Eden and Hoare had taken up.

As regards the more general situation, I have this feeling that as Great Britain cannot go in for a policy of isolation, she has either to strengthen the position of the League, or abandon it and go in for a policy of alliances. Now you know that British opinion is getting more and more opposed to the old alliance system, and I do not think that any government could have openly adopted it without jeopardizing its position.

Strengthening the League therefore remained the only practical alternative, and that again meant making a reality of the sanction clause. If this had not been done, the position might have become very serious indeed. Today it is a second-class great power like Italy, tomorrow it will be a first-class great power like Germany, trying to impose her will by high-minded action on other countries. The stand had to be made now, and I think has been rightly made, for fear of greater evils which might ultimately arise if Italy had got away with it. Such frankly is my opinion of the present difficulties, and my hope is that the League will survive its present trials in a strengthened form. In that case the position of Italy may become a very grave one, and she may become an additional heavy liability to our European system. Mussolini may have to go, with consequences which no one can foresee at the moment, but I think that we might face that more calmly if we knew that the collective system was functioning properly and that other greater calamities were not in store for us.

I am sorry that you are not in the government and that your views have been put with such force and insistence that you must have made Baldwin's position difficult in the matter. From the way he has repeatedly spoken to me, he has the highest regard for you, and your services, and I hope that your present difference of opinion with his policy may not be allowed to lead to permanent cleavage. I notice that Churchill has made his peace, and you yourself have been closer to the true Conservative position than Churchill, and should not allow the present difference of opinion to develop into something permanent. Your power for good is very great, and it is getting harder and harder for the dissident person to make his weight felt. There is no doubt that the world is becoming very much more difficult and the job of governments far more arduous than before, and a force like yours should not be confined to mere outside criticism. However this is just a bit of fatherly advice from one who has always admired you and been greatly attached to you. Do not let this difference go too far. I myself do not at present see what will hold, say, Germany in check in future unless we can make the collective system function effectively.

Christmas greetings and all good wishes to you and Mrs Amery. Ever yours sincerely,

s. J. C. Smuts

388   To M. C. Gillett   Vol. 54, no. 207

Tsalta
[Cape Town]
24 January 1936

I have just received a large batch of letters—from three continents (or four including Africa) but the most welcome was yours!...

Another interesting letter—a long and good one—was from Jan [Gillett], who explained to me his view of the British peace plan—you know it already. He thinks the next step will be a big loan to Germany to help German rearmament! Then Walter Elliott writes to explain all about Hoare's great mistake[1] in going much further than the cabinet had ever wished or authorized. He gibes at the pacifists become militarists, and pro-Boers become pro-Abyssinian!...

Jabavu is here but quite busy and has not yet been to see me, but I have arranged for him and his friends to meet Hertzog over Native

---

[1] On 7 December 1935 Hoare had agreed to a proposal by Laval to end the war in Abyssinia by offering Mussolini possession of about two-thirds of that country. When this became known public indignation in Great Britain forced the resignation of Sir Samuel Hoare who was succeeded by Anthony Eden. The Hoare–Laval plan lapsed.

bills. I view these bills in a detached spirit, as a matter decided for me in far-off days by my temperament and outlook which cannot now be affected by what passes or happens today. But of course I see the rocks ahead quite clearly. Love to you both. A letter has gone to Fort Hare already.

389   To M. C. Gillett   Vol. 54, no. 210

Tsalta
[Cape Town]
30 March 1936

Again Monday night, and again a few lines to bring you the news. David[1] left this morning for Fort Hare by the garden route...on the whole he has sampled this part of the Union quite well, and I hope his visit north will be equally successful...

In parliament we are now again busy with the Native Representation Bill, in which I cannot manage to feel any great interest. We shall be busy with it till next Tuesday when the third reading will take place. I cannot say that there is great excitement in parliament, and so I have stayed away tonight in order to read the mail papers which arrived this morning, and to write this letter.

Hitler's general election is over and once more the inevitable 100% majority has been recorded. And now the negotiations will be resumed. It is a cursed spite that we have (for the sake of European peace) to support the ruffianly policy of Hitler. That is to say we have to maintain peace with him and keep France in check, although we hate the internal policy of Hitler.[2] Fate makes strange company, and we cannot always choose ours. I hope however that Hitler and his friends have had a real fright over the dangers they have just escaped owing to the restraint of British public opinion, and that they have learnt a lesson which will be useful at the next critical stage in diplomacy which is now coming. I said some things at the Rhodes Memorial function[3] last Sunday for which the

[1] Son of Arthur B. Gillett's cousins, Ronald and Richenda Gillett; lecturer at Achimota College, near Accra.

[2] On 7 March 1936 German troops marched into the demilitarized zone of the Rhineland in contravention of the treaty of Versailles. Although this action should have brought the Locarno guarantees into force (*see* vol. v, p. 258, note 2), the powers did not take military action. On 14 March the council of the League declared Germany guilty of a breach of her international obligations but the powers merely began negotiations with her on the basis of Hitler's offer of a non-aggression pact for twenty-five years, an air agreement, and a hint that Germany might rejoin the League.

[3] The annual ceremony at the memorial on the slopes of Table mountain above Groote Schuur to commemorate Rhodes's death on 26 March 1902.

local German *chargé d'affaires* thanked me but I improved the opportunity by giving him a good bit of my mind over the folly and extravagances of German policy. I suppose the poor fellow in his heart of hearts agreed with me, but what could he say? My prayer nowadays is that Eden will keep out of the toils which France and Belgium are spreading for him. Any further Locarno commitments would be a dreadful mistake. The present Locarno lesson should surely be enough. But enough of all this business...

390 To M. C. Gillett

Vol. 54, no. 213

Tsalta
[Cape Town]
19 April 1936

...While we have been gently holidaying there has been great agitation in the international world. The German business seems somewhat in abeyance while French politicians are fighting their elections. But in Abyssinia the crisis is rapidly arriving—with Dessie occupied by the Italians and the Abyssinian forces melting away before aeroplanes and poison gas. Europe is getting an ocular demonstration of what the next great war will mean when it comes— as it is expected on the Continent to come within two or three years. If Italy succeeds in 'getting away with it' we are up against a crisis as grave as has ever been faced since 1914. For if she does, the thing will be repeated—on a much vaster scale than that of Abyssinia. I am for hanging on grimly to sanctions, even if it proves impossible to add further sanctions. Italy must not get away with it. If sanctions cannot end the war they could and should secure a decent peace— even if Italy goes burst in the process. Sanctions should, in my view, be continued till a peace is made 'within the framework of the League and in the spirit of the covenant' as the phrasing has been up to now. Sanctions must be bleeding Italy white and the process should be continued even if she annexes Abyssinia. Unless this happens the League is broken and Great Britain either retires from the Continent or remains in as a party to some military alliance. In my view economic sanctions—even without military or naval action—must prove effective if persisted in to the bitter end. And if they avail to rob Italy of the unholy fruits of her wrongdoing, the deterrent effect for the world would be almost more striking than if they had succeeded in stopping the war. The long arm of the law— international law—would at last have overtaken the aggressor.

Please discuss this matter with Gilbert Murray[1] as I believe it is important. I do not know what the official British view is and I don't know whether Geneva has the grit to see the thing through. But to me holding on to sanctions seems the right policy. If they could not prevent the war they could yet save the peace.

As regards the Franco-German business the danger of military sanctions against Germany seems definitely past. I only hope the British government, in its anxiety to secure a *quid pro quo* to France, which Germany will not give, will not make the fatal mistake of getting further entangled by promises of military assistance in future outside the covenant. I am also very sorry that the French have made such ridiculous counter-proposals for permanent settlement in answer to Germany's peace offer. This offer seems to me a big and feasible scheme while the French scheme (with its return to the Geneva Protocol, to an international League army and that sort of nonsense) appears well calculated to lead to nothing at all and to let things drift on to the next war. An air agreement, a twenty-five years firm peace agreement and Germany's return to the League is a good manageable programme, while the French programme is one for the Greek Kalends.[2] The French have missed *every* opportunity since Versailles. Will they miss this one too? That is the question before the world. The Soviet is a baneful influence under the present circumstances. Russia, knowing that in Hitler's policy *she* is a potential enemy, is straining every nerve to keep France from a permanent peace with Germany and conserving her as an ally in possible trouble. The Russian treaty[3] has really been a bad business from the point of view of Franco-German reconciliation. In the end it may weaken British restraining influence on French policy, as France may consider the Russian alliance sufficient for her in the last resort to go on with.

Perhaps this is not fit matter for a letter and I may appear to be writing a newspaper article. But you will understand how deeply I feel all that is passing abroad. The chance for peace at last is there; but some wicked fate seems to be spoiling that chance once again. And this time it may be the last chance. For the League cannot survive both an Abyssinian defeat and a miscarriage over the

[1] M. C. Gillett showed Gilbert Murray this letter. He asked Smuts's permission to publish it in part (*see* **391**). M. C. Gillett believed that its publication was one reason for 'the Conservative government's coolness to Smuts henceforth'.

[2] A locution for *never*. There were no Kalends in the Greek months.

[3] A treaty of mutual assistance between France and the Soviet Union was ratified by the chamber of deputies on 27 February 1936 but not finally concluded until 27 March. Hitler claimed that it was incompatible with the Locarno treaty and used this as a pretext to send his troops into the Rhineland on 7 March.

German peace offer. It may be that European civilization could not survive this double defeat. And hence my deep anxieties.

I do not share Jan's[1] view about British statesmen being pro-Hitler in order to down Bolshevism. Much more practical and menacing issues than Bolshevism are to the fore. Hitler's odious internal policy should not stand in the way of European peace and the prevention of a collapse of our civilization. Bolshevism simply is not in this picture at all. But enough. My pen is running dry although there is much more to say. Love from us all,

Jan

P.S. Both Arthur and Margaret have flowered—the dears![2]

391   To M. C. Gillett   Vol. 54, no. 216

Tsalta
[Cape Town]
10 May 1936

...On Monday morning I had a cable from Gilbert [Murray] asking permission to publish what I had written you about sanctions.[3] I was for a short moment in a quandary because my letters are mostly of a very colloquial character and scarcely fit for publication, and I feared the letter to you was no exception. However, if what I had written could serve a useful purpose, why not publish, even though it was expressed in slang? So I agreed, and in the afternoon I found my little epistle to you in the *Cape Argus*. But it was all right—to my great relief, although perhaps crudely put. And I note that it *has* helped to stay the rot started by the die-hards and other good enemies of the League and friends of Mussolini, and induced the government to go slow with the abandonment of sanctions at this stage—though Lord only knows what they will do a little later. I induced Hertzog also to make quite a firm and strong speech in the same sense in which I had written, and I added a short interview to dot the i's. So that on the whole South Africa was well to the fore in the cables and appeared to be the only people quite clear in their own minds that the League had to be firmly supported against the Italian sabotage, and that this was not a time for running away. Your discretion has been soundly exercised and some good, however temporary, has been done. Eden has spoken weakly, Baldwin has sat mum. It is a fair inference that they know not what they do. No

---

[1] Jan Gillett.
[2] Two shrubs—a red and a white pomegranate—which had been planted on either side of the entrance to 'Tsalta'.   [3] *See* **390**.

lead is given, no firm voice is heard, and the world is at sixes and sevens. Meanwhile I see that Mussolini has annexed Abyssinia and made his king the emperor of that country.[1] No hanging back there. *That* at any rate is the way things are *done*, right or wrong. Of course I don't mean to deny that the position is one of extreme difficulty and even of danger. But cowardice is always the worst way to face an awkward situation. And to run away from sanctions and thus yield Mussolini his reward would have been a fatal blunder and an invitation to Hitler to go and do likewise tomorrow. I wish the British government would follow our lead and take a firm stand and give Europe and the world a clear lead. I think a courageous line like that will make an enormous appeal and yet save the League from disaster at this stage. The issue is joined in this Abyssinian business. See it out to the end, and I think the League will emerge victorious whatever the consequences. No nonsense is so silly as that of the dear people who (like Austen Chamberlain) say that the League should be allowed to go down so that a stronger League could be built on firmer foundations. There will be no other League in our day if this one is allowed to perish.

This Abyssinian business is not only a test for the League but for the nations and the statesmen themselves. If they fail here, what confidence could one have in their good faith and loyalty in future? Why would they serve a new League better than the old League? Besides, I don't think the construction of a new League—if this one is now let down—will be a feasible proposition. The League was born in 1919 under the most extraordinarily favourable situation— with the U.S.A. leading and Wilson backing it to the utmost, and the others almost *coerced* to follow. Today the atmosphere is quite different, the idealism and enthusiasm of humanity are gone, and dictatorships sit on top of our hesitant democracies. I see no earthly hope of a new League now if this one perishes. But enough.

Sarah Gertrude [Millin] writes that she is leaving (has left) for Russia, that *General Smuts* has passed the censors and will appear next month. All to the good, for I think the story has its lesson for Europe today. She also writes that my place is in Europe at this moment and that the position looks very black from all she hears. Well, well. This doctor has not yet been called in, and if he is, his medicine will be too bitter for the palates in Europe.

Your last letter is most welcome and interesting. What a consolation your letters are these days. Love ever from

Jan

[1] On 2 May 1936 the Emperor Haile Selassie left his country. On 9 May Mussolini announced the annexation of Abyssinia and the king of Italy became an emperor.

392   To A. Einstein   Vol. 54, no. 167

Cape Town
15 May 1936

Dear Dr Einstein, Some months ago I received from a mutual friend, Mr Landau, *The World as I see It*,[1] with a kind inscription from you to me. I have now had time to look through the book and to be profoundly interested in the collection of your reflections and views of the world in general. I wish to thank you most sincerely for inscribing the book to me.

It is pleasant to contemplate the physical universe with its mystery and its immensity. And you are fortunate that that is the sphere which you have chosen for the exercise of your genius. As for me, and for many of us, who are for many years in the world of practical affairs, the world presents another aspect, and today a very sad one. The reign of reason in our western civilization seems to be in decay. Intolerance, persecution, denial of rights, dictatorships, threaten to become the order of the day. Statesmen are perplexed and do not know how to deal with the situations that face them.

And yet we dare not lose faith. In human affairs, just as in the physical universe, very long views have to be taken if one wishes to arrive at the truth. The curve of history is a long range one, and I have the feeling that mankind is not plunging into the night, but is passing through a phase, a very disheartening and trying phase, but one through which it will work to daylight beyond. In the end, the forces of good and right in human nature will prevail and mankind will settle down in a new society on a higher level of living and thinking.

Such is the faith which keeps one going in these difficult days. Reading your thoughts and reflections, I come to the conclusion that this is also your faith and your consolation. Just at present however the situation is extremely threatening. The League of Nations, on which such high hopes had been founded, is in extreme danger, and may not survive the shocks that have been delivered to it at Geneva and in Abyssinia. It would be a pitiable thing if at this moment the light which was lighted at the end of the Great War, is put out, and Europe is once again plunged into chaos.

You have immense authority; scientists and thinkers the world over look to you as a great leader. I hope you will find it possible in these days to raise your voice and to send some message to old Europe of encouragement, faith and enlightenment which may help and strengthen those who are labouring for a better world.

---

[1] Published in 1934.

I feel that all our resources ought now to be put into the field in the present grave crisis. I suggest this for your consideration, and hope that you will not make too humble an estimate of your influence on the thinking section of mankind. I know it is very great and far-reaching. With all good wishes, for you personally, and your work,

Ever yours sincerely,

s. J. C. Smuts

393   To L. S. Amery   Vol. 54, no. 168

Cape Town
18 May 1936

My dear Amery, Many thanks for your note of 4 May in regard to the Tanganyika mandate.[1]

With much of what you say I am in cordial agreement; at the same time I think it would be unwise of me to make a statement now as to the meaning of the mandates, and South Africa's interest in the maintenance of the *status quo* in Tanganyika. I noticed Senator [Sir George] Pearce's statement on behalf of Australia[2] some time ago, but did not consider it a particularly wise one to have made. You must bear in mind that [South] Africa is a mandate holder itself,[3] and must be particularly careful in the line it takes and the way it may appear to save its own skin by throwing responsibility on others. The view I take is that it is premature for us to launch on a discussion of this question of mandates. There has been a great deal of propaganda in Germany, but the German government itself has been pretty cautious and has only said that when a general settlement has been come to, and Germany has rejoined the League, they would expect the question of mandates also to be raised. I see no prospect at present of either of these conditions being fulfilled, and in the meantime, we must not play the game of the German propagandists, and create confusion among ourselves. Some time or other I think it would be wise to meet the German point of view, and concede them one or two mandates as a consequence or by-product of a general settlement. I do not for a moment dream of

[1] Tanganyika was a 'B' mandate, that is, the territory remained an entity under the administration of the mandatory power, Great Britain. Amery's letter is not in the Smuts Collection.

[2] The former German colonies in Australasia constituted a 'C' mandate, that is, the mandatory power, Australia, might administer them as part of its territory. In March 1936 Sir George Pearce, in emphasizing the strategic importance of New Guinea, said, 'The return of territories under Australian mandate is unthinkable.' See N. Mansergh, *Survey of British Commonwealth Affairs* (1952), p. 160.

[3] The Union of South Africa held a 'C' mandate over South West Africa.

Tanganyika being given away. Nor do I for a moment think that the British government would think of such a thing. There would be the very gravest opposition to any such solution of the difficulty.

To me the British government has appeared hitherto to have adopted an attitude only of reserve, and to have avoided making embarrassing declarations at this stage. I cannot for a moment think that they are in doubt as to the right course to pursue. What you say about the African position, the Indian position, and, in fact, the whole position of British communications eastwards, seems to me perfectly correct, and I think that that will be commonly accepted by all people who understand the matter at all.

Pirow, our minister of defence, is proceeding in a week or so to London, to have defence talks with the British government. You may like to get into touch with him and discuss the question with him too. He is very intelligent and able, and I think a talk might be mutually useful. With kindest regards, Ever yours sincerely,

s. J. C. Smuts

394   To H. M. L. Bolus   Vol. 54, no. 170

Cape Town
26 May 1936

My dear Lulu, I am most deeply grateful to you and Frank [Bolus] for that beautiful picture on my birthday. No gift could have been more happily conceived or more welcome. Many, many thanks for it.

We spent the day in most lovely weather up the mountains at French Hoek. I felt very happy. Even sixty-six years sat very lightly on me as I climbed the upper heights. And life is so good and so sweet.

You will be glad to hear that I have at last succeeded in arranging with the forestry division to clear Table mountain on top of all pines and eucalypts. I shall give such [two illegible words] as is required. Mr [J. D.] Keet thinks the work can be done in a couple of years and thereafter will be maintained until the mountain is safe once more for its original flora.

We have been particularly busy and so I have had no time to look you up. But I hope to do so before I go north in a couple of weeks. With love to you both, Ever yours,

J. C. Smuts

395   To E. F. C. Lane   Vol. 54, no. 171A

Cape Town
26 May 1936

My dear Lane, It was a great pleasure to get your long informative letter. Thank you for it and for your good wishes on my birthday. Sixty-six is quite a good age to be still in harness, after all we have passed through in our generation. But I am thankful to say that my health continues good, I still climb the mountains and find life full of deepest interest.

I am sorry that you have got into this farming tangle. You were not trained for it and much of your life experience is wasted in having to recondition farms in Dorsetshire! Still I suppose you had no option. There is very little in farming at best even when you are a Scotchman and have been a practical farmer all your life. But you grew up in the field of administration, far from barley and cabbages. In the end you will tire of it and return to a more congenial climate. So don't get too deeply into it. Even the thought of the county council does not thrill me.

The old world continues full of trouble and Great Britain has her share of it. The mistakes of the past have led Germany back to her old Prussian paths and so we have all to rearm, at ruinous expense. Even in South Africa we feel nervous, and Pirow has gone to London to consult about our defences and the world situation itself. We do not know what Germany has in mind about colonies; and if she gets one near us, you know what will happen to us from the air. Abyssinia has proved that against the air arm and poison gas of a great power there is no hope for a small country. I suppose Great Britain is arming both because of German rearmament and because of what is threatening in the Mediterranean. Italy has now become a new front, and one very dangerous for our Empire communications, and for Africa in general. France is unreliable and wobbly; fixed only in her fear of Germany. Devaluation is coming and may mean a Fascist reaction there. A Socialist government under a Jew[1] cannot be looked upon as a safe thing just now. The League is in heavy water and the future there is very dark. I wish I knew more and had materials for forming a judgment. But we know very little out here.

. . . In Rhodesia I am told quite a Union feeling is growing up. I am told it may soon become practical politics. The position of Southern

---

[1] The elections of 3 May 1936 had resulted in a victory for the Popular Front of Radicals, Socialists and Communists. On 5 June a Popular Front government under Léon Blum, leader of the Socialist party, was formed. The Communists supported but did not join it.

Rhodesia is of course quite untenable in the long run. Here things are going well. Everything is booming, except farming, which still causes some small anxiety. But Johannesburg is now more prosperous than ever before in her history and wealth pours out over all South Africa. My love to you and Jessie.[1] Kind remembrances to the dear old people. Ever yours affectionately,

J. C. Smuts

396   To M. C. Gillett   Vol. 54, no. 221

Tsalta
[Cape Town]
14 June 1936

Saturday night—after a day mostly of packing, as we leave for Doornkloof next Monday. I am glad to get away from parliament with its waste of good time and its atmosphere of friction. A week at Rooikop will do me good and heal me of my wounds![2]

I had this week two very interesting letters from you and Arthur and another from Lothian to whom Arthur had spoken. I am very glad and grateful to Arthur for the trouble he has taken in the matter.[3] The position is quite obscure, but Neville Chamberlain's calculated indiscretion[4] has thrown some light into the darkness of British policy. My own reading of that policy is as follows. Sanctions will be dropped and Italy conciliated. This with a view to the reconstitution of the Stresa front—that is, the collaboration of Britain, France and Italy in order to keep Germany in check.[5] In this way Italy and France will be placated and the tension for Britain in the Mediterranean will also be eased. At the same time Germany must also be placated and the negotiations with her will be continued. She must not feel aggrieved at being 'encircled'. As neither Italy nor Germany want sanctions article 16 must be eliminated from the covenant, which will be made as harmless and

---

[1] Born Jessie Maud Heys, daughter of George Heys of Pretoria; married E. F. C. Lane in 1911.

[2] '...and I will heal thee of thy wounds'. *Jeremiah* xxx. 17.

[3] Arthur Gillett had seen Lord Lothian and Walter Elliot in London to find out why the British government was dilatory with regard to sanctions against Italy. *See* Smuts Collection, vol. 54, no. 38.

[4] On 10 June 1936 Chamberlain, without consulting his cabinet colleagues, made a speech to the 1900 Club in which he said that to continue and to increase sanctions against Italy would be 'the very midsummer of madness'.

[5] The Stresa front had first been formed on 11 April 1935 but, in effect, broken when Great Britain made the naval agreement with Germany on 18 June 1935. *See infra*, p. 72, note 2.

toothless as the Kellogg Pact.[1] This spurious form of collective security having thus been done away with a policy of rearmament becomes the only alternative, and all the powers will be pleased. We shall be back again in the old system of the balance of power, and Britain will oscillate from one side to the other as her interests may dictate. Gone is the dream of world peace and the covenant as the basis and keystone of British foreign policy. The foreign office can work the balance machine so much better than the impracticable idealism enshrined in the covenant. I don't think I am unduly cynical in my reading of the situation. Others will be more cynical and say that the British government was never sincere about sanctions, that the brave speeches of Hoare and others were simply effective electioneering, and as soon as the British electorate had given the government a majority[2] the pretence of sanctions was dropped, first in the Hoare–Laval agreement, and then in the Chamberlain speech, and finally tomorrow officially at Geneva. Another ruse like the Zinovieff letter.[3] I do not say this is my opinion but many will take this view of the mysterious vacillations of the last few months and wait for the eyes of the British electorate to be opened at the next general election.

I am more concerned with the defeat of a brave effort to reform international diplomacy and the apparent disappearance of our vision of a better, safer, saner world. What can poor Geneva do but register the death sentence which is being prepared in the great capitals?

Lothian and others, while deeply deploring the balance system and all it means, are yet satisfied to weaken the covenant. They put their faith in the British Empire. But time may yet show that an efficient League was essential to the British system, and that without the covenant not even the Empire can endure. Certainly the states of the Commonwealth do not feel attracted by the policy of the balance of power and special alliances with powers for whom they feel no sympathy. Great Britain may be alone in entering into that dangerous circle, and what then will become of the Commonwealth

[1] *See* vol. v, p. 447, note 1.

[2] The election in November 1935 had resulted in a victory for the Conservatives who won 387 seats. With Liberal and Labour supporters of the National government they had a majority of 247 over the opposition parties.

[3] Four days before the general election of 29 October 1924 a letter signed 'Zinoviev' (president of the Communist International) and addressed to the executive of the British Communist party was published in *The Times*. It contained instructions for fomenting revolution in Great Britain and urged support for the trade treaty with Russia which the Labour government had negotiated. The authenticity of the letter was denied and remained in doubt but its publication was considered to have ensured a Conservative victory in the election.

as a whole? No, I fear the disappearance of the League as the basis of British policy may have after-effects which will astonish our imperialists who are today joining in the killing of the League. I shall tell my imperialist friends—Lothian and others—of my fears in this connection. I pray that they may never be justified. But I am certainly alarmed at the present tendencies and policies in London. The League was the greatest possible support for the British Commonwealth with its sovereign Dominions, but that has never been clearly realized by British leaders.

It is undoubtedly a time of the most profound discouragement and disappointment. My own course is in the deep shadows. I shall stand by the League to the end, but that will not mean anything against the forces ranged against it and the apparent failure of the League so far. Did we try too much? Was our faith in humanity too great? Is another long march through the night ahead of us? It almost looks like it. I feel dejected beyond words. And yet. And yet. I hear those brave words which Paul repeated: 'My strength is made perfect in your weakness.'[1] Can such great faith be practised in human affairs, or does it belong merely to the ideal religious sphere?...

397   From L. S. Amery   Vol. 54, no. 2

112 Eaton Square
S.W.1
22 June 1936

My dear Smuts, The government have decided to cry off sanctions[2] and so ends what I have always regarded as a disastrous experiment. You suggest in your letter[3] that the blame does not rest so much on the covenant as on disloyal members who did not act up to their duties. The trouble is they never will act up to their duties. Obviously the French could not afford to quarrel with Italy beyond a certain point. On Thursday Lloyd George, after an impassioned denunciation of the government for not living up to the letter of the covenant, declared that nothing would induce the people of this country to fight for Austria! If you try to place a hundredweight load on a cardhouse and it collapses it is no use saying that the cardhouse is all right and that it is only the cards which are at fault. If you could substitute entirely different nations for the nations that exist today

---

[1] 'And he said unto me, My grace is sufficient for thee: for my strength is made perfect in weakness.' 2 *Corinthians* xii. 9.

[2] This was announced on 18 June 1936.   [3] Not in the Smuts Collection.

you might perhaps have a covenant in which article 16 would be workable. But you have not.

The experiment has been tried in the easiest case conceivable and it is only because the case seemed so easy and obvious that the British government was tempted away from the attitude which it had taken up for ten years (and which no one stated so well as you did in your address to the Royal Institute),[1] and deserting the limitations of Locarno, attempted to enforce article 16. Just think. You had Italy deliberately preparing aggression for nine months, insulting the League and doing its best to work up general anti-Italian feeling over and above the specific anti-Italian feeling of Russia, the Little Entente[2] and the French Left. You had in Abyssinia a nation which had no enemies prepared to find it in the wrong whatever the merits of the case. I know of few nations in Europe of which the same can be said. You have the whole proceedings covered by the British navy so that nobody need fear Italian retaliation. Lastly you had a seven months war. When will so favourable a conjuncture occur again? And yet the thing collapsed.

When Germany jumps Czecho-Slovakia she will have some pretext of ill-treatment of the German minority which will create confusion at Geneva. Hungary for certain, Bulgaria probably, will declare that she was in the right. If by then Italy is not reconciled to the western powers she will do the same. The war will probably be over before the League can be convened, and the present Abyssinian situation[3] will have arisen before they have begun to discuss who was in the wrong.

Such a situation can clearly only be met by the immediate action of those who are directly concerned. If they can get the moral approval of the League, well and good, either before or after action.

That brings me to the fundamental issue on which I had hoped at one time that we were agreed, namely that the League exists to create an atmosphere of international understanding and improved machinery for conciliation always available, the influence and authority of which would grow gradually and exercise its moderating and restraining influences on the ordinary forces of international relations which would otherwise continue as before. After all, those forces of diplomacy, of defensive groupings etc. were all the result of experience in endeavouring to maintain peace, and did a great deal to maintain peace even if they were not always successful. I believe we should revert to them frankly but with the added idea

[1] *See* **370**.   [2] *See supra*, p. 7, note 1.
[3] Here the writer added a footnote which reads: 'i.e. the disappearance of the victims of aggression'.

that we should endeavour, wherever we can, to reduce even the possibility of conflict by making these groupings permanent and the basis of a common patriotism which would exclude all possibility of war within the group. Such a larger 'whole' is already given us in the British Commonwealth. A similar whole might be built up by the nations of western Europe. These things are all in the line of your own philosophy.

I have never felt happy about the identification of Empire foreign policy with League *policy*, though it has been a sound instinct which has identified Empire foreign policy with League principles and support of the League as an institution (*vide* Smuts R.I.I.A.).[1] If you do me the favour of re-reading my chapter on foreign policy in *The Forward View* you will see I have attempted to answer the question in your letter as to how the foreign policy of the Empire can be kept together. I quite agree that we here are so near Europe and perhaps to face such real dangers that we may not be able to consider complete detachment. But I would limit our obligation, whether by treaty, or by some sort of Monroe doctrine[2] of our own, to the narrowest limits, attempting to secure the Low Countries and France and the Mediterranean. Moreover, in the case of France, I would make it quite clear that our obligation to defend her against Germany would not arise if Russia were also at war with Germany.

Anyhow one thing seems clear to me now and that is that the British government cannot wobble back once more. Article 16 has gone for good and any reform of the League can only be in the direction of emphasizing the fact that it has gone, and that the League exists for other purposes than obligatory general coercion.

I know how badly all this has embarrassed your government and that was one of the reasons why from the very beginning I dreaded the line we began to take now more than a year ago. It has all been very unfortunate but we can at any rate profit by our experiences.

Pirow has made a very favourable impression here. What he has said about Tanganyika in particular has been very useful in stiffening up the government. Yours ever,

L. S. Amery

[1] *See* **370**.   [2] *See* vol. III, p. 639, note 2.

398   To S. G. Millin   Vol. 102, no. 66

Irene
[Transvaal]
27 June 1936

My dear Sarah, I have several letters of yours to answer, but indeed they don't call for any particular answer. Your book[1] has gone well and has, I suppose, captured the English market by this time. Thank you for the *Telegraph* serials. Those appearing here have been better than the excerpts from vol. 1 and have attracted more attention. I think you have been wise in insisting on immediate publication as much of the material is apposite to the times and the grave experiences through which we are passing.

The cowardly surrender of the British government to Mussolini has come as a grievous disappointment to me, and I don't know on what issue they could now be counted to stand firm. I warned Brodetsky [S.] that a surrender to the Arabs in Palestine is now not out of question. Why make a determined stand in favour of Jewish immigration to the national home if such a policy means the alienation of the Arab and perhaps the Mohammedan world? My confidence is deeply shaken, and I do not know at the moment where a solid foundation for hope and confidence remains. But the real issue now is the League and it is here that British policy appears so disastrous. Sanctions are going (in spite of a great victory on that issue at the general election last November), and now article 16 of the covenant will go too. That I fear will disrupt the League. For who will still rely on that broken reed, after the sanctions clause is gone? There were only two things that reconciled me to the disastrous peace—the disarmament of Germany and the covenant. Owing to our fads and delays Germany is again rearmed and Prussianism is worse than ever. And now the League is being sabotaged, through short-sightedness, wrong policy and (I fear) downright cowardice. Perhaps this is too bitter. But how could one feel differently when at the end your work is ruthlessly undone and your dearest hopes for our human future destroyed. I may be wrong, but I fear the next five years will realize much of this programme of despair. If Britain had stood firm and faced up to Mussolini, the world would have caught new hope and faith and would have rallied to the British standpoint. The world was waiting for a sign, for a lead. But what leadership has been here? To break the League in the hope of restarting it afresh on a new basis is a fond delusion. We shall not see the favourable conjuncture of 1919 for a new start again in our day.

[1] The first volume of *Smuts* was published in February 1936, the second volume in June.

If you are in despair for the Jews I am in a sort of desperation for humanity, which seems once more to be plunging into a night of misunderstanding, clashes and suffering. But we may not despair. The vision of the prophets was right. But God fulfils himself in many ways[1] and sometimes tarries in the execution of His plan. At present I am deeply perplexed. With kind regards, Ever yours,

J. C. Smuts

399   To L. S. Amery   Vol. 54, no. 173

Cape Town
29 June 1936

My dear Amery, Since my last letter to you, I have another letter from you in reference to the League and German colonies. I need not add anything on this latter point as I dealt with it last time. It would be a bad day both for Empire communications and for the future defence of British Africa if Tanganyika were ever surrendered by way of a mandate or otherwise to Germany. No support for that view will be found in South Africa, and I hope that such a development will not be entertained for a moment by British statesmen.

With regard to the League and its reform as you suggest, we have no doubt a first-class problem. British policy has now for half a generation been based on the League, and the dropping of the sanctions article would so transform it, that the League could no longer be a basis for foreign policy at all, and Great Britain and the British Commonwealth as a whole would have to re-think, and re-cast their foreign relations. With article 16 out of the covenant, I even doubt whether many countries would consider it worth while taking part in the expense of maintaining the League. It would of course serve a great number of quite useful minor purposes, but from the point of view of foreign policy and external relations, I fear most countries would consider it useless, or not worth while keeping up.

Then again, if we come to consider Commonwealth foreign policy, the question with us is going to be the new basis. There is no doubt that the League was a great support to the immense Commonwealth system by binding all of them for external purposes through the same machinery and the same treaty. Commonwealth countries would always be fighting on the same side, or all neutral together.

[1]   And God fulfils himself in many ways,
         Lest one good custom should corrupt the world.
              Tennyson, *The Idylls of the King, The Passing of Arthur*, l. 407.

Such was the immense value of the League to us. What is going to
be the situation if article 16 goes? Locarno has already separated the
Dominions from Great Britain in the case of a conflict on the Rhine.[1]
The Dominions are not much interested in the European situation,
and have in fact very much the mentality of America in this respect.
What is going to happen if Great Britain gets involved in a conflict
on the Continent, and the Dominions, either under Locarno treaty
or otherwise, stand aloof? May that not be the beginning of the end,
and do we not get on to very slippery paths if once we abandon the
League and the principle of collective action—for the Commonwealth also—which it brings with it? I must frankly confess that
I am very seriously perturbed over all these questions. If the League
goes, it may endanger in its *débâcle* the whole imperial system for
which at present it forms a very considerable support.

I want you to think these matters over carefully. We are without
a doubt in a great quandary, and up against very far-reaching
decisions for the future. To me the road appeared clear so long as
we were all bound by the League as the basis of our foreign policy,
but once that goes, I see only dangers ahead and no clear daylight.
I am afraid that isolation will be a most difficult policy to carry
through in actual practice. And if isolation is ruled out, and the
League is ruled out also, where are we?

You will therefore see why I am for extreme caution in dealing
with the present situation. If Mussolini had been told at Stresa that
an attack on Abyssinia would mean sanctions to the uttermost, I do
not think he would ever have embarked on the Abyssinian adventure. I am afraid the League was betrayed there perhaps more
through passivity and cowardice than malice aforethought. The
blame I think does not rest on the covenant so much as on the
disloyal members who did not act up to their duties. I am not even
sure whether there was not a secret understanding between Mussolini
and Laval at the time. It may be that the blame rests not on the
structure of the covenant, but on the principal members of the
League who did not do their duty. But why should the League be
decapitated for this crime?

I write to you this seriously because you are a very responsible
person with the deepest interest in the maintenance of our Commonwealth system and with a profound concern for the future of our
civilization. And I want you to think once and twice and again before
advising a step which may in the end have the most unforeseen and
lamentable consequences. I know you have been very much against
the application of sanctions, and that you have a very poor opinion

---

[1] *See* vol. v, p. 259, note 3.

of the present British government, and that you have been doubtful
all through the chapter about the League itself. But I do ask you
not to be deflected by these side-issues, and to concentrate your
mind on the real problems that are going to arise once we create
a vacuum at Geneva. With very kind regards, Yours ever sincerely,

s. J. C. Smuts

400   To M. C. Gillett   Vol. 54, no. 223

Tsalta
[Cape Town]
29 June 1936

Reid will be most welcome, and so will be the two-volume Locke.[1]
I have an old Locke but in a rather shabby edition. Their presence
in my library may even be a temptation to read them, which I have
not yet done. Indeed I have recently read very little philosophy.
One can find no time, what with internal politics and the international
chaos which one finds it practically impossible to understand, try
as one will. You will however be interested to hear that a letter from
a Dutch professor[2] tells me that holism is making rapid strides on
the Continent and is more and more becoming accepted as the key
position in science. If I had time now to follow up my earlier effort
of twelve years ago by another move on I could do some useful
work. But philosophy requires a very different atmosphere from
that which prevails all round.

I have today a clearer vision of what holism means than I had
twelve years ago, just as the effort of 1925 was an advance on that
of 1910. If I could retire to the Bush for six months at least I could
do some real thinking. The philosophical implications of the idea
have given me a good deal of trouble during the last few years.
I believe the key to religion is to be found along holistic lines, but
the subject is full of pitfalls, and one hesitates to write about it.

I have finished my Free State meetings and have returned from
those huge open air functions with a very bad cold. My reception
was everything that could be desired and I think I can notice a big
change for the better from my experience of last year. The wider
patriotism is beginning to make its appeal, and the difficult foreign
situation inclines people to take a more serious view of affairs.
Politics cannot be looked upon as a form of pure sport when people
think of Abyssinia and all it means. I was glad to be back, as the

---

[1] Second-hand copies of the works of Thomas Reid (1710–96), Scottish philosopher,
and of John Locke (1632–1704), English philosopher.   [2] Not identified.

physical call on one of these big tours is most severe, and after a few days of this heavy strain I feel pretty cheap. Today the Lamonts arrived at Cape Town and tomorrow afternoon they will be here. After a couple of days spent in looking at Pretoria and Johannesburg we shall move on on Friday to the National Park, where we shall be for six or seven days. I look forward to this contact with the wilds, but I am somewhat uncertain how this wild life will appeal to our somewhat sophisticated New Yorkers. I hope it will not prove too strange and upsetting or tiring to them. Their travels have always been of the most luxurious kind and you know how simply we take our pleasures in the veld. However we shall see, and my next letter will duly report. They must have had a good arrival, for Florence wires to me that they were overwhelmed by the strange beauty of the new scene.

The sight of Table mountain after an absence abroad always has a strange effect on me, and I can imagine that it must make a great appeal to first visitors. But give me the Bush, the silent scene, the mountains of the Transvaal with their eerieness and mystery!...

Your letter is full of the political situation and of what you heard at a lunch with the Murrays. Hardened old veteran of the political wars as I am I must confess that I am amazed beyond words at the doings of the British government. The fog is impenetrable and is only lighted by incredible indiscretions of ministers. If there is a policy (which I doubt) it seems to be one tending to the old pre-war Europe, with Great Britain closely bound up with France and Russia on the one side, and Germany with some minor satellites on the other. The League which but yesterday was the corner-stone of British foreign policy is today so poor a thing as none to do her reverence.[1] There is no explanation, no apology, nothing even to us far away watchers of the skies.[2] No wonder we can but stand pat, as we are literally too stumped to follow all these gyrations. You say that Baldwin is rapidly declining to the impossible role of Mac-Donald towards *his* end. One cannot say. Tonight the paper reports that he will not be in the house to reply to questions about [A.] Duff Cooper's speech in Paris.[3] To me it seems that both Neville

[1]   ....now lies he there,
And none so poor to do him reverence.
                              Shakespeare, *Julius Caesar*, III.ii.124.
[2]   Then felt I like some watcher of the skies
When a new planet swims into his ken.
                    John Keats, *On First Looking into Chapman's Homer*.
[3] This speech at a dinner of the Great Britain–France Society was interpreted by the British press as a threat to Germany and a proposed military alliance with France. *See* A. Duff Cooper, *Old Men Forget* (1954), pp. 202–4.

Chamberlain and Duff Cooper simply reveal what is in the mind of the government but what they dare not declare as their official policy. But what must be the position of people like me, far away, who have loyally tried to be loyal and friendly in the face of the heaviest odds, and who now find it quite impossible to defend British policy! What should one do when it becomes more and more a question whether we are not being led once more on the same road as that which led to 1914? Abyssinia seems to have upset the British apple-cart far more seriously than one could have imagined possible— with a people of such nerve and aplomb. (Is this correctly spelt?)

Tomorrow the League assembly meets, and I wonder whether in the general *débâcle* there will be anybody to stand by poor Te Water [C] when, like Casablanca, he refuses to desert the burning deck of the League. O if there was one with a tongue of fire[1] there to scorch them up; or some Elijah, to pray for fire to consume those Baal priests[2] of Europe's blind leadership. This would be the occasion to confront the dictators with all the majesty of simple sincerity and humanity. But we are all quailing. Machiavelli has won, O Nazarene! I suppose we are all in a fog and do not see the way through the war troubles overhanging Europe. But often in these cases the simple straight road is the only right one. Meanwhile one can but wait, in a humbling sense of impotence and inactivity when so much is at stake.

I wonder what is happening in France. One reads of fresh strikes breaking out in one place after the other.[3] Tonight there is the report of thousands of hotels etc. in the Riviera closed in the latest strike, with tourists adrift in all directions. I wonder whether [Léon] Blum is controlling the situation, or whether darker forces are gaining control. That has so often been my experience in our revolutionary strikes. It would be a bad business if, in addition to a Europe in turmoil, we are to have a France in the throes of revolution. Nothing appears more calculated to loosen the dogs of war[4] than such a development. There is no doubt that there must be deep divisions in France and that the Blum régime may not be able to keep control.

Your Philco is a great consolation. We can turn to one European station after the other and hear the news and the music. It was a noble gift. Now goodnight,

Jan

---

[1] 'And there appeared unto them cloven tongues like as of fire and it sat upon each of them.' *Acts* ii. 3.   [2] *See* 1 *Kings* xviii. 17–40.
[3] A series of stay-in strikes began among factory workers in France on 26 May 1936.
[4] 'Cry, "Havoc!" and let slip the dogs of war.' Shakespeare, *Julius Caesar*, iii.i.270.

401   To M. P. A. Hankey   Vol. 54, no. 174

Private and personal   17 July 1936

My dear Hankey, Thank you very much for your private and personal note of 3 July in reference to Pirow's work.[1] I am grateful for the trouble you took to be helpful to him in his mission, and to put him in touch with the various departments concerned. It is also a matter of great gratification to me that the arrangements come to are satisfactory.

I have been away from Pretoria since Pirow's return, and have not been able to see him, as I returned from Rhodesia only last night. I hope to discuss his work with him fully, and I am sure he is also most grateful to you for helping him in connection with his work. I am pleased that he has made a good impression all round. He appears to have been somewhat indiscreet in a personal statement he made to the press in reference to the ex-German colonies in Africa.[2] These matters have now become so delicate that one must speak with a great deal of reserve about them in public. Moreover we South Africans are in a very difficult position, as with regard to those colonies for which we have a special concern we have no intention whatever of returning them or seeing them returned to Germany, and expressions of generosity on our part therefore seem to be made at the expense of our friends, which is about the cheapest form of generosity going! Of course our private opinion is that some accommodation with Germany on this matter of some of her former colonies in Africa will be necessary, and from our point of view wise, if we want to establish friendly relations again with the most important power on the Continent. But at present no one knows the extent of the German demands, which seem to be expanding with the lapse of time, and one has therefore to exercise extreme caution in any public discussion of the matter. Judging from Hitler's private statement to Lothian and others, and his repeated public declarations, it seems a matter of sincere policy with him to come to an agreement with the British Empire, and it would be as well for us to speak with the enemy in the gate whilst he is in this mood. As you know, I have always taken the view that without the cordial co-operation of Germany no peace in western Europe is possible.

[1] *See* Smuts Collection, vol. 54, no. 90.

[2] In a press statement in Pretoria on 10 July 1936 Pirow said that South West Africa and Tanganyika would never be returned to Germany, that she should be given a foothold in Africa and that 'very influential quarters' in Great Britain supported this view. On 16 July the matter was raised in the house of commons. Baldwin then said that he regretted press interviews on 'matters that are of some considerable delicacy'. *See The Times*, 17 July 1936, p. 7.

The Abyssinian business has been a great sorrow to me, and the way it has developed has meant not only a most serious setback for the League,[1] but also a distinct loss of face to Great Britain. With the Empire, prestige is almost as vital as a good name to a woman, and I am afraid that events in the last twelve months have definitely damaged British prestige and influence.

Now I hear from my Jewish friends that another retreat is contemplated in Palestine, and that in deference to Arab activities, immigration is going to be suspended whilst the royal commission[2] is making inquiries. This looks like another retreat, and in a quarter and among people where firmness and the maintenance of British prestige count for more than almost anything. I am a good deal in the dark, and am sending a message to Ormsby-Gore[3] which may produce further enlightenment. If we alienate Jewish opinion all over the world in connection with the national home, we shall probably stir up more formidable trouble than could come from Arab quarters.

Here in South Africa things seem to be going normally well both politically and economically. Looking to the future, and the direction the world is moving now, I have had special concern about our defences of this important route in the world, and I am glad that this matter is now being attended to in a spirit of mutual co-operation and helpfulness between London and Pretoria. Very kind regards and good wishes, Yours sincerely,

s. J. C. Smuts

402   To L. S. Amery   Vol. 54, no. 177

23 July 1936

My dear Amery, Thank you very much for your letter of 22 June and especially for the trouble you have taken to put your views so fully and exhaustively before me. I need scarcely say that I feel very strongly the force of what you urge, and am perfectly sensible of the immense difficulties on the subject of collective security. At the same time I have a very strong feeling that in abandoning the Wilsonian system—for that is what your views amount to—we are opening the road to enormous possibilities of danger both for the world and our Commonwealth in future.

[1] On 6 July 1936 the League decided that sanctions should end on the 15th.
[2] The commission went to Palestine in November 1936 and reported in July 1937 (Cmd. 5497).
[3] *See* Smuts Collection, vol. 54, no. 179.

If the League system were abandoned as a measure of security, and if at the same time isolation is not a possible policy for Great Britain, we are faced with very grave prospects and with very far-reaching decisions as regards future policy. The only alternative seems to be a system of alliances in Europe, and it may be impossible for Great Britain to keep out of them. Western Europe cannot be isolated from central and eastern Europe, for the Great War has taught us that in the end peace is indivisible,[1] and that safety from one part of the world cannot be isolated from war conditions elsewhere. The whole situation is so difficult and obscure and so fraught with dangers that I cannot say that I see daylight through it, and I am not prepared to adopt any dogmatic decision. I am still thinking over the whole question, and exploring some possible way out. The difficulties in the way of a general agreement are so great that the end may well be that Geneva may go on as heretofore, with some quite minor adjustments in the covenant. But whether under those circumstances it will be of any real value as a security system is doubtful. For the policy of the League in the Abyssinian case has so destroyed confidence and so accentuated fears for the future, that the mere continuance of the League may be meaningless and valueless for the future. I am prepared to do more thinking, and I want you to do the same.

Now for another point. I am gravely perturbed over British policy in Palestine, especially the suspension of immigration which has been foreshadowed as a temporary step during the inquiry of the royal commission. Suspension in the circumstances of the present troubles will look like a retreat before Arab agitation, will inflame Jewish feeling against Great Britain, and set going a very serious agitation when this suspension has to be removed and immigration has to be re-started in terms of the mandate. To try and buy Arab good will at the expense of Jewish co-operation seems to me a most dangerous policy. Great Britain has given enormous assistance to the Arabs in founding Arab kingdoms both in Arabia and in Irak, and in the circumstances a vigorous promotion of the policy of the national home for the Jews seems to me essentially just and fair, and seems likely to conduce to the strengthening of our position in the Middle East.

Now that we have come to an agreement in Egypt[2] which seems

---

[1] This phrase was coined by M. Litvinov.

[2] By the Anglo-Egyptian treaty of 26 August 1936 (initialled on 24 July) the British protectorate over Egypt, in operation since 1914, came to an end and Egyptian sovereignty was recognized. Great Britain had, however, the right to keep a garrison and aircraft in the Suez canal area and to use Alexandria and Port Said as naval bases.

a very substantial surrender to the Egyptians, it becomes all the more important to strengthen our position in Palestine, and to me it appears a very grave matter to jeopardize the good will of the Jews in this connection. I am afraid that the Arabs will always be against us in Palestine, as they must continue to view the policy of the national home as a serious menace to themselves. Now we may have to add the Jews also to the list of the discontented. As you know, I have always taken a strong view of the support that Jewish influence can bring to our world-wide Commonwealth Empire system, and I should be very sorry to see us do this, and in the face of Arab agitation change a course which we deliberately decided on during the Great War.

I know how strong a supporter you have been all through of the policy of the national home, and I would urge you to use all the influence that you have, both with Ormsby-Gore and your other political friends, to see that no step is now taken which may have very far-reaching effects and still further lower British prestige in that dangerous quarter of the world. Actual suspension would be a most serious step. If the British government are driven to do something, why not rather curtail the numbers of immigrants very materially during the period of inquiry without going the whole length of total stoppage? The Jews in South Africa, who are very influential financially, are profoundly perturbed over the rumours which reach us, and if the same sort of feeling is growing up else-where among the Jews, I can only foresee a world-wide agitation and alienation of the Jews from our Empire policies.

I shall be very glad if you will give your attention to this grave matter. With all good wishes, Ever yours sincerely,

s. J. C. Smuts

403   To D. Lloyd George   Vol. 54, no. 180

23 July 1936

My dear L.G., You will remember that during the last Palestinian trouble you and Balfour and myself joined in a declaration urging on the British government the firm maintenance of the policy of the national home for the Jews.[1] That declaration was very successful, and achieved its object at the time. Now Balfour has gone, and you and I alone are left of the old members of the war cabinet who formulated that great policy. Rumours reaching us in South Africa

---

[1] This took the form of a joint letter to *The Times*. It appeared on 20 December 1929 (p. 15) and was the subject of a leading article in the same issue.

say that the British government are contemplating a total suspension of Jewish immigration into Palestine pending the inquiry of the royal commission which they propose to appoint.

I personally view that prospect with very grave misgiving. Not only would such a step appear as a retreat before Arab agitation, but it would also make the resumption of immigration thereafter very difficult, and subject once more to a renewal of Arab violence. What is worse, it would involve a departure from the spirit of the Balfour declaration.[1]

With the persecution of Jews in central Europe and especially in Germany, and the tightening of immigration laws all over the world, Palestine is and remains the principal outlet for the Jews. And for the British government, in the face of this situation and because of Arab agitation, now to suspend Jewish immigration, would seem to me a step calculated to inflame Jewish feeling all over the world, and turn them into critics if not enemies of the British Empire. The conduct of our foreign relations in the Mediterranean business has already affected British prestige very seriously, and I am afraid that a retreat before the Arabs in Palestine would still further lower our prestige. And this would be especially lamentable in view of the Egyptian agreement which now makes it more important than ever for us to strengthen our position in Palestine. I have written to Ormsby-Gore suggesting to him very strongly that there should be no total suspension, but merely a material reduction of the number of immigrants during the period of inquiry. That would be a much less far-reaching step, and not invite so much Jewish opposition, or make it very difficult thereafter to retrace steps in favour of the renewed flow of immigrants. May I suggest that you add your enormous influence in support of some such representations? Whatever view one may take of the present government, and of their foreign policy, one cannot sit still and see a step being taken which is bound to have very far-reaching consequences in the future. The weakening of the Balfour declaration, the lying down before Arab agitation, the certain hostility of the Jews all over the world, would add very much to the difficulties of our future path, and one feels bound to exert whatever influence is necessary in order to prevent a step which may have most regrettable consequences. Please see what you can do in the matter. I am sure your influence will be most potent especially as you have taken no line against the government in this matter.

May I add with what extreme pleasure I read your speech in the house of commons on the retreat from sanctions? I have never in all

---

[1] *See* vol. v, p. 19, note 1.

my life read a more effective and scathing indictment than that speech, and I am sure its effects must have been most far and deep-reaching. This calls for no answer. With very kind regards and all good wishes, Ever yours sincerely,

s. J. C. Smuts

404   To M. C. Gillett   **Vol. 54, no. 228**

Pretoria
27 July 1936

Once more I write to you from my office where a vacant moment has occurred. I am anxious to catch the next air mail, as I shall be away at Lichtenburg[1] later for some meetings and thus unable to write by the week-end mail. I do not like to miss a week, even if there is no particular news to chronicle. If there is no news, there are always views! We have been watching all the last week or two the news from Spain which points to sad happenings in that suffering country.[2] It looks like an out and out struggle between Communism and Fascism. I must frankly admit that in this case my sympathies are with the government[3] against the Fascists. It would be a double calamity if the rebels win, firstly because in that case yet another country would have to be added to the Fascist dictatorships, and secondly because the Roman Church which is at the root of this business has been a centuries old curse to Spain. I would like to see a clean up, even if it has to be bloody. Spain has been on a wrong tack ever since Inquisition[4] days. Perhaps the heavy penalty has now to be paid. There may however be international repercussions —for I fear Mussolini and perhaps Germany would like to give secret help to the cause which is also their own. France and Russia again would like to keep a socialist government going. It is curious how new trouble is all the time starting up unexpectedly, now in this and now in that quarter of the world. The world is evidently in a revolutionary phase, and nobody can say whether the upshot may not be what we all so much dread. The League has lost, perhaps has never had, a stabilizing position in this dangerous world, and now

[1] In the western Transvaal.
[2] On 18 July 1936 the civil war in Spain began with a revolt of the chief army officers in Spanish Morocco.
[3] The government, after the elections of February 1936, was supported by the *Frente Popular*, a coalition of Liberals, Socialists, Communists and Anarcho-Syndicalists.
[4] The Spanish Inquisition was set up in 1478 by the joint monarchs Ferdinand and Isabella and was controlled by the Spanish kings. Its chief function was to find and punish all suspected of acts or views inimical to church and state. It was abolished in Spain in 1820.

we are dependent on the wisdom and good sense of some great powers for seeing us through this explosive era. I cannot yet fathom Germany, and that is my great uncertainty in all this grave business in the world. *Can* anything good come out of a country whose deliberate policy it is to persecute Jews and Protestants? Is there not a fundamental vitiation there, which poisons everything else? Perhaps she has been more sinned against than sinning. But even so, can one count on her to help, and not rather to upset the apple-cart as soon as she sees a good opportunity? France is hopelessly unwise, but fundamentally stands for human freedom and conscience like Great Britain.

Is it wise for us to lean too much towards the Germans in this grand tug of politics which is going on in the world? I sometimes think we are again moving to a supreme religious struggle just as happened in the sixteenth and seventeenth centuries, with this difference, that the issues are no longer theological, but much wider human issues. But it is the same battle of the human spirit against tyranny and bondage. The battle for freedom is never won but always going on from the beginning, and shall continue to the end. The 'Free Sons of God' is the ultimate human ideal.

I have been reading again these last days in Stawell and Dickinson's *Faust*,[1] and in that connection have once more dipt into the glorious lyrical poetry of Goethe. What a treasury of poetry you have there! I must say I get somewhat tired of all the love episodes of Goethe and find them less interesting as I get older! But into what glorious poetry they flowered! He seemed to have wanted that sort of stimulus to set him going as a poet. And what life-wisdom there is in him! I have been struck too by the fact that he was through and through a holist. What a difference it would have meant to my future if I had written on him rather than on Walt Whitman in my first effort![2] I might have had a completely different career and never have become immersed (and submerged) in the world of action.

Doornkloof is now very empty, the children all gone to school after the holidays... Isie and I slept alone in the big house last night, with the exception of Annie the girl.[3] It felt strange, after all the wild life of the last weeks. The Lamonts thought Doornkloof one of the most live places they had ever been to. Certainly you could there hear discussions on every conceivable topic under the

---

[1] F. M. Stawell and G. Lowes Dickinson, *Goethe and Faust* (1928).

[2] *See* vol. I, 18–21.

[3] A devoted African servant of the Smutses. M. C. Gillett recalled that she had heard Mrs Smuts say that if she ever got to Heaven it would be on the shoulders of Annie.

sun. The Lamonts were a good deal given to reading, especially poetry, and in that respect resemble 102. Hence I suppose my renewed interest in Goethe!...

405 To M. C. Gillett   Vol. 54, no. 231

Doornkloof
[Transvaal]
6 August 1936

This morning (Friday) my secretary phoned from the office that there was no special engagement for me, so I could stay at home, read through the London *Times*, and write some letters...First many thanks for the recent books especially the Locke and two books by Boodin (*God* and *Three Interpretations*).[1] Locke is good for the library and Boodin I want to read. The dear professor writes on the outskirts of holism (he honours me with a footnote!)[2] and the reviews had made me think of writing to you to send his books. But you have done so of your own accord. I see he makes out that Aristotle is the father of holism and that his holistic conception of the world is his greatest contribution to subsequent thought. I have never read Aristotle's *Metaphysics* and will have to do so now. Ask Joachim [H. H.] what is a good translation and work on the subject. I am much intrigued to find that my little discovery is 2,500 years belated and that Aristotle had completely anticipated me! A local Greek professor has pointed out to me a passage in Plato's *Sophists* which puts holism in a sentence as in a nutshell. I have now quoted it in the coming third edition.[3] The curious thing is that Plato does not get beyond that sentence, which is dropped as a pearl of great price and has never been picked up—not even by Aristotle, for I don't really believe the concept of holism was seriously considered in its far-reaching range and importance until I drew attention to it in a long and tedious book. I am continuing to dip into Boodin for more hints and sidelights...

Of affairs it is very difficult to write. I get continual calls to come to Geneva for the September assembly. But my mind is clouded over with many a doubt. Will my coming mean any difference that

---

[1] This was one book, namely, J. E. Boodin, *God and Creation: Three Interpretations of the Universe* (1934).   [2] On p. 352.

[3] The third edition was published in 1936, the second in 1927 and a paperback edition by the Viking Press in the United States in 1968. The quotation from *Sophist* 245d is translated as follows: 'That which comes to be always does so as a whole; so that if a man does not count the whole among realities he ought not to speak of substance or coming-to-be as real.'

is worth while? Shall I be the simple clergyman among the company of horse-thieves of the old joke? Te Water, I hear, has been treated not merely coldly but almost hostilely in British government circles because he was carrying out our instructions for Geneva. Shall I not find that not only France and Italy etc., but even Great Britain [are] entirely hostile to my ideas of world welfare? And why venture into a business which is foredoomed to failure? Has the League not been so irretrievably damaged that it can now only continue as 'a handkerchief to blind people's eyes'—I use Arthur's expression in his last letter. If it is now merely dope and make-believe in its present form, is it wise to lend my support to its continuance? Is it not preferable to make a new start, and what can that new start be in the present temper of furious rearmament and rival balances of power? Some friends think my place is at Geneva next September, and others say I can only burn my fingers and damage future chances of good by going. My mind is not clear at all, and I do not wish to act unless I see a clear lead and light in front of me. There is also the view that nothing will be done at Geneva, which is simply used as a blind, and that the real business will be done later at the Locarno conference when the contending parties will be brought face to face. With Germany absent from Geneva no real business is possible or contemplated. I may be going on a fool's errand to Geneva, just as I did in 1933 to that silly, abortive economic conference in London.[1] I have none here to advise me and I don't quite trust the judgment of those abroad. This is where prayer is so useful. But [my] form of it is sleeping over it and revolving the matter in my mind in the early morning. But no daylight has yet appeared!

But how small our little local politics appear when the fate of our kind and perhaps of our civilization is in the balance far away! We read every day the horrible news of what is happening in Spain, and the question arises whether that is not merely a symptom of the general disease which is preying on the body of our civilization. What is the proper treatment? Is it a new religion which will bring healing to men's souls, or is it mere economic and intellectual maladjustments from which we are suffering? Do we see the wild plunging into chaos or the stirrings of a new life bursting the old framework? Who can tell? And in this blankness and confusion what is our duty, besides just carrying on in our own little circles. Dear love to you all,

Jan

[1] See vol. v, p. 558, note 1.

Doornkloof
[Transvaal]
29 August 1936

I fear I have missed a mail. But I have been in bed for a week with an attack of influenza and only got up yesterday afternoon, and this morning (Saturday) I find I am too late for the mail. There has been a great change from the summery weather of the preceding weeks, and for the last week we have had frosty nights and cold south winds during the day. The result is a great prevalence of influenza. I myself went down in consequence of an evening function at Nylstroom just a week ago. It was what is here called a *braaivlei-saand*—an evening function of a social nature—with a political object—where all sexes and ages congregate and roast meat on the veld fires and amuse themselves socially, and finally some make speeches. The evening was on the cold side, and although I found it very pleasant I felt that I was caught in a cold. I had to make a speech to a large assemblage, the wind was moving, and the air chilly. On leaving we encountered clouds of dust from other cars, and that must have completed my undoing. Sunday I went to bed and only today I begin to feel my old self again. The influenza has left my throat, but the cold continues in my head. I hope soon to be well again. It was a not unpleasant week in bed in my own little room near the study. I could read and got through some queer stuff, including a book on the Nazi ideology, called *Hans Schemm Spricht*, being his speeches while he acted as Hitler's chief man in his part of Bavaria. It is a queer compound of holism, romanticism, racialism, ethics and religion. On the whole—apart from the racial nonsense—by no means so bad. The impact of Communism on the German mind, and the destruction of the German values (family, religion, patriotism, poetry and general dreaming) seem to have been too much for the German mind; hence this devastating reaction. The Communist influence was purely destructive and left a vacant house for all the devils to enter. But the real motive seems to be to get back to the old German values and to eliminate all alien influences of race and thought. The *Ganzheit-Theorie* is everywhere in evidence, the smashed German wholes must be reconstituted, and family, race, fatherland, religion, God, art and moral wholesomeness must be once more the ideals of private and national life. From this brief summary you can see how much that is inherently sound underlies this vast national reaction. The moral break-up of the war, the defeat, and the Communism which arose among the workers and lower middle classes with all its destructive impact on German ideology proved too much. Hence this turning back to the past, and the ruthless extirpation of the new influences of which the Jews—*via* Karl Marx—were looked upon as the spearhead. Hence Nazi-ism started, not as a political but a national religious movement, and in Hans Schemm you find little politics but much of the various aspects of the German *Weltanschauung*. What a pity that this movement so soon degenerated into a wild persecution and a ruthless scrapping of ideas and methods which we consider part of the moral and political heritage of the human race. It becomes a case of Germany against humanity, a battle against the universal aspect of the Christian view which is so fundamental to it. Indeed, a purely national or racial view of the world is the direct negative of the universal human message of Jesus and takes one back to the Old Testament and the Judaic Jehovah. Hence Nazi-ism and Judaism are at bottom identical in principle. What an irony, after all their anti-Semitic persecution! When you read Nazi writers you always hear the echo of that 'come out of the house of the stranger'[1] of the Old Testament Judaism. We Dutch in South Africa have the same narrow strain in us, hence the racial struggle and the anti-Native outlook which the churches have not overcome or even tried to overcome. Of course I read much besides. Boodin's *Interpretations*, volume 2 of Hutch's families,[2] and I don't know what else.

How pleased I was to get your long interesting Carnac letter, with its description of French ways, of dolmens, of the Gilletts gathered there...I am sure Carnac is a good place and the beach a blessing to the bathers. I hope you will stay there till you have had your fill of good things. How I would love to loiter over that old world where the persecuted Celts found refuge from their pursuers. What memories those stones of the past carry; what glimpses we have of the upward stroke of the human soul in its long pull from the deeps of the past! Is God with us in this voyage—this exploration of the soul? In my reading this week I also did Dr Kolbe's *Up the Slopes of Mount Zion* which tells the story of his conversion from Protestantism to Roman Catholicism as a student in London. It was all about the Real Presence. It dawned or rather suddenly flashed on his mind that there was the Real Presence and no mere symbolism. God in actual reality is with us, and in Communion it is Him we eat and Him we drink. Is God really with us? Does our experience

---

[1] 'Lest strangers be filled with thy wealth; and thy labours be in the house of a stranger...' *Proverbs* v. 10.

[2] J. Hutchinson, *The Families of Flowering Plants*: vol. i Dicotyledons (1926); vol. ii Monocotyledons (1934).

bring us into contact with the Real, and not merely the symbolic, the representation, the image instead of the real thing? You see I am once more at my problem of perception, which I feel sure gives us reality, brings us face to face with the Other, and does not merely leave us in the air, with images and pale reflections. Friendship surely gives us the Friend, and not merely the appearance of the Friend. And does religion not give us something Real, however impossible for us to express in concept or word? And this brings me back to Carnac. Did those Celts sense something Real in the night of their struggles and strivings—some thing from which they drew strength and courage in the grim events of their times? Or are we and were they pursuing shadows of the mind?

I do not write about affairs as my space is exhausted. But something remains inexhaustible, and it fills the air between Doornkloof and Carnac Plage. It is love to love.

Jan

407   To A. B. Gillett   Vol. 54, no. 236

Doornkloof
[Transvaal]
7 September 1936

Last week brought very interesting letters from you and Margaret. Yours was written sixteen days earlier but arrived almost the same time. This shows what time in transmission is lost by using ship instead of air mail. I was sorry to see that you had cut your Brittany holiday so short. You may be sure that to you holidays are as essential as business, and are indeed business. You gave an interesting account of the origin and earlier phase of the Spanish revolution. Of course all that is long out of date. Judging from today's news the government have lost Irun, stand on the point of losing St Sebastian and their only land bridge with France, while in Majorca their days appear numbered. The Moroccan mercenaries are more than a match for the irregular levies that the Spanish government have had to arm. It now looks as if the Fascist revolutionaries will gain the upper hand and add another to the list of Fascist countries. The British position in the Mediterranean may then become an uneasy one. The dictators cannot rest on past achievements, considerable as these appear. That fire requires continual additions of fuel. Both Hitler and Mussolini must keep moving on, to prevent unrest at home, and the question is where the next moves will be. You are quite right that in grave emergencies the dictators are better

equipped for action than the democracies. That is how Sparta beat
Athens.[1] For a crisis the machinery of democracy is too slow and
too vacillating, unless the democracy is superbly led—which is not
the case today in either England or France. I think the old Roman
system was probably wise—that in a real crisis a dictator takes
charge, but his authority is severely limited in point of time. In
a crisis the civil authority should yield to a military régime, which
can act with speed and decision. But as soon as the crisis is past the
civil authority resumes control. The history of the civil war in
Cromwell's time is most illuminating on this point. The Long
Parliament only continued as long as it gave a fairly free hand to the
major-generals. So it must always be. In England a further question
arises whether, as things are now going, they can for long continue to
dispense with conscription. Why should people go and join the army,
as long as they are housed and fed under the unemployment relief
scheme? Young men mostly go into the army because of food etc.
It seems to me that under the social provisions of today it may be
impossible to maintain adequate military force without compulsion.
In Germany or Italy the young unemployed are sent to the labour
camps and the military machine. May England not be forced to do
the same, if the world continues to move on Fascist lines?

I agree with you that French policy has led to hopeless political
bankruptcy and to the dangers now looming up in the world. But
I do not see us supporting Germany in her present phase of racialism
and intolerance. And how could we support the unspeakable
Mussolini? We must now continue with France, but only on one
condition—and that is that British policy assumes the leadership
instead of submissively following in the wake of France. British
leadership now becomes essential. But is real British leadership
anywhere in sight? There is a weakness, a vacillation, a lack of
policy and even of clear-sightedness which is very saddening. Lloyd
George, I see, has now in despair gone to interview Hitler! What
are we coming to? I think the house of commons will be complacent
enough, once it feels the grip of a really strong hand. It was so in the
Great War. Baldwin is tired, and some of his colleagues are stupid.
And so nothing is done that is worth while. France cannot hold out
much longer financially, and I suppose Blum must crash in the near
future. And what then? How long do you think the franc can hold out?

I have not taken much interest in the coming Geneva meeting.
It looks to me as if nothing will be done. The difference between
those who want a stronger and those who want a weaker covenant
are too great for bridging in these dangerous times. It is like holding

---

[1] In the Peloponnesian War, 431–404 B.C.

a war council in the midst of a great battle. The League has now got into the fatal position of appearing futile and of not mattering. Nothing could be worse than to be of no account in these fateful days. Hence I have advised that we leave the League alone in these days and concentrate on the hammering out of sound policies which the democracies could hang on to. It is not documents but man who matters at the moment. I fear I am in disfavour with the present authorities in England. We have clashed on a number of points. I have had to cable very strongly on the Palestine position which seemed to me to be shaping to a second Abyssinia, with the Jews in the position of the Negus. These things are unpopular and make you disliked. So I had better keep away, and in the background, where I have been ever since the Abyssinian surrender. Leave the League alone for the moment, and try and concentrate on the preservation of the peace of Europe, which is quite a different matter. Both Germany and Italy are bluffing, and very successfully. Once they know their bluff will be called you will see an immediate improvement. But there; this is enough. Yours,

Jan

408   To L. S. Amery   Vol. 55, no. 132

Cape Town
4 January 1937

My dear Amery, I shall indeed be glad to show whatever attention I can to your Courtauld friends as soon as they appear. It is always a pleasure to meet your friends and have exchanges with them.

I suppose your reading of the international situation is right. What is happening is just the sort of combination which I have always feared, as it not only means mischief in the end but also forces our hands and makes the British Empire come in on the other side. That has been (and I suppose still remains) the great argument in favour of a League of Nations, which makes it unnecessary for us to take sides and also makes international co-operation for us as a Commonwealth group more easy. But alas! the League is of no account now, as you say.

My difficulty about a *real* German *rapprochement* is twofold—the undefined claim for colonies which is bound to create immense difficulties, as you know, and the racialism (anti-Jew, anti-Russia, anti-Liberals, etc.) which goes against the grain. It almost seems that fate is deciding the issue, as we are inevitably being drawn into the old groupings. I suppose if the League really goes we shall be back in the old friendships and the old enmities. Which is a thousand pities. Besides, there is the danger that in such a case we shall not see that Empire co-operation which existed so fully in 1914–18. The road before us is both dark and difficult. All the same I wish you and Mrs Amery a happy and prosperous New Year. Ever yours sincerely,

s. J. C. Smuts

409   To M. C. Gillett   Vol. 55, no. 167

Tsalta
[Cape Town]
27 February 1937

No letter from you this week, so I suppose the next mail will bring two! I shall however be fairly busy next week, so I shall write you without waiting for any letter to answer. This (Saturday) morning I have kept at home to deal with a lot of stuff which has to be read and some correspondence to be worked off. Much of the morning has been spent over a MS on *The Price of Peace* which the publishers have sent me for my opinion. It is written round a plan for European peace, which involves incidentally a revision of frontiers, a re-writing of the peace treaty and a renunciation of their sovereignty by the great powers! It reminds me of Plato writing his ideal *Republic* in the decline and fall of Athens. I am afraid my opinion has been somewhat discouraging, but I have no doubt the book (which is most highly commended by Lord Allen) will appear in spite of my criticism. Revision of frontiers! What the world most urgently needs today is a revision of tariffs; and that would be a practicable programme, and not a hopeless quest such as a re-writing of the peace treaty would involve. I do not mind academic discussion of great public issues, but one does get impatient with men who know nothing, or very little, of practical affairs and pose as would-be saviours of the world. Their views may win through in the long run but cannot affect current events. My practical pro-gramme today would be a reform of our tariff policies, a halt to armament policies, an amendment of the League which will bring in all the great powers (except the U.S.A.) on a basis of dealing with the more urgent discontents. I cannot think of anything that will work if the covenant (with an improved article 16) cannot be worked by the nations. Collaboration is possible, not a renunciation of our say over our own fate. Besides, is it safe today, with the ideologies running amuck in Europe, to place our destiny in the hands of Germany and Italy and Russia? I think the democracies should be specially careful in view of the general trend against our fundamental human rights. Co-operation is the furthest one could fairly go at this moment. [H. G.] Wells and a number of others urge the abolition of sovereignty. That is both impracticable and dangerous at present. I would adopt a much more limited programme in order to meet the Have Nots and to set the wheels of trade and free intercourse going again. With Hitler, Mussolini and Stalin in charge on the Continent I would be careful not to go farther than is necessary. You see the harm these rascals have already done in Spain. Now the non-intervention machinery has at last been set to work. I hope it is not already too late to save Spain from utter wreck.[1] It is surprising to me that the dictators are prepared to give up [General Francisco] Franco—if they do not already feel satisfied that he will now win. Of course it is possible that Blum has made some threat of active public intervention which has brought them to heel, but I have no information.

We have had some difficulty in parliament and in the cabinet over some colour bills introduced by private members of our party.[2] First it was some bill against mixed marriages which however has for the moment been side-tracked. Then it was two bills against Asiatics employing white girls etc. Hofmeyr [J. H.] took a strong line against the bills, while I have temporized, as not only public opinion even among our reform social workers is much against such employment and the social evils to which they lead or may lead. A select committee is now inquiring into them.[3] I think there is a good deal to be said for control of such employment, and am prepared to consider a fair compromise. But Hofmeyr continues very stiff. These colour questions are more and more a trouble, and are partly no doubt exploited by our opponents in order to foment differences of view in the United party. You will probably see references in the press to these troubles, hence my reason for writing about them to you. If Hofmeyr were to leave the government it will be a great loss and a distinct blow to me, as he is one of my most promising young men and the reactionaries don't like him. He is a good liberal with a fine human outlook. Unfortunately he is also somewhat academic and exaggerates things and aspects of no real

[1] On the initiative of Léon Blum the chief European powers, including Italy, Germany and the Soviet Union, signed a non-intervention agreement at the end of August 1936 and an international committee was set up to implement it. Italy, Germany and Russia infringed the agreement and negotiations for stopping intervention continued until mid-February 1937 when the flow of foreign forces into Spain began to decrease.

[2] The bills were introduced by General J. J. Pienaar, leader of the United party in the Transvaal and J. H. Grobler, member for Brits.

[3] For an account of the outcome *see* A. Paton, *Hofmeyr*, pp. 259–61.

importance. And his mother[1] is no help to him in these difficulties as she wants him to go out of politics—which would be a bad thing for the country and for him. I am doing my best to keep him with us, and to some extent sympathize with his standpoint, without thinking the actual points of difference as important as he does. Politics is the art of the possible and the practicable, and one has to give in in small things in order to carry the bigger things. But it is just in this comparative valuation that the snag lies...Love to you all,

Jan

410   To M. C. Gillett   Vol. 55, no. 173

Tsalta
[Cape Town]
3 April 1937

I wrote to you about our last heavenly week-end Sunday at Rooi Els,[2] amid the sights and sounds and scents of nature. A dull tiresome week in parliament has followed. A fussy week will follow, when the new governor-general and his wife[3] will be received ceremonially, with much official to-do and all the excitement connected with these occasions. But in reality I feel far away from all these things. And I was carried still further away by your letter which told of your happy walk with Jan [Gillett] over the Derbyshire hills, and communings with him over plants and human affairs. How blessed these oases of the spirit are, in all the arid spaces which surround our march! I love to dwell on these good things, which, although remote from the current of affairs and apparently insignificant, yet hold the most precious values of life...

How mysterious life is and how very little of it we really understand. In all our wanderings there seems to be some strange guidance which gives ground for the belief in Providence. Last night I was again glancing through the early chapters of Whitehead's *Adventures of Ideas* which have a strange fascination for me. He there talks of the Greco-Roman civilization with its belief in reason and culture and the way it was smashed by the irrational irruptions of barbarism and Christianity, and how in our own day the new culture has been smashed by the twin forces of steam and democracy which have

---

[1] *See* vol. IV, p. 337.   [2] On the False bay coast.

[3] Sir Patrick Duncan and his wife, born Alice Dora Amanda Dold, whom he married in 1916. He was the first South African citizen to be appointed governor-general of the Union.

taken the place of the former barbarians and Christians. We develop some beautiful habitation for the human spirit and then it is rudely demolished by senseless circumstances beyond our control. We mourn a vanished world. And yet out of the ruins, irruptions and smashings a new and better world of the spirit arises. So may it be again. When I look at the dictators and ideologies of our time making havoc of the fair world now left for ever behind us I have the faith that something bigger will be born out of the decay which is at present upon us. There is something which our culture ignored and which has come to the front and insists on our consideration. This must surely be the case with Russia and Italy and Germany and in fact with half the world. Our civilization has been partial; there have been neglected factors, sections, classes. There have been defective world views; and now the flaws are disclosing themselves, and a greater synthesis has become necessary. These ideologies (Communism, Fascism etc.) will pass away in their definite crude forms, but what was vitally urgent in them will be incorporated with the old culture into a new structure of belief and action, perhaps a new world view and religion. The neglected factor or interest avenges itself by wrecking the whole system which ignored it. Of course that is the trouble which faces South Africa in the future. Today our Native population do an economic service in the development of this country which receives inadequate consideration, and if this continues too long the inevitable result must take place. I see however a slight stirring among the dead bones, and awakening of a deeper sense of social justice. Justice comes, either in good time with good sense, or else ultimately as the avenger and wrecker. In any case it comes. That is the nature of the Universe. And that is what makes the Universe divine for me. It carries its own guarantee, though much time may be called for before it comes into action. Then it acts devastatingly in many cases.

I must now halt this talk which is scarcely stuff for a chatty letter. In a few minutes we shall go to Groote Schuur in order to present our good wishes to Hertzog whose birthday it is today. It will be an informal party function at which I shall have to speak. This afternoon I am pall-bearer at a funeral. Tonight I attend an informal dinner to talk over important business. It is these small things which eat into one's time and in their accumulation leave nothing for proper thought and meditation over the things that really interest one. But I suppose this is fate and has to be endured. This divine world is full of misfits and inopportunities in its time-table. This too I suppose has to be philosophically accepted.

So far I came on Saturday. It is now Sunday night and all are busy with their correspondence or other avocations. I shall complete my letter which has to be posted tomorrow. We have had a delightful Sunday; in the morning we visited Blaauwberg[1] beach, and in the afternoon we motored to Stellenbosch to visit Isie's relatives. They were not at home, but we enjoyed the drive in fine weather, and I walked down the oak woods on the Libertas farm[2] where Isie and I used to walk in the eighties of last century. What memories this walk brought back! Like all youth I had heaps of visions, but none like what has actually come about during the last forty to fifty years. It was interesting to walk the identical footpaths and to see some of the very trees which had attracted my attention at that time.

I have recently taken to reading the New Testament again in Greek, partly to recover some of my half-forgotten Greek but especially to see whether I can now get some fresh light on the Gospel story, which remains to me one of the most interesting and intriguing but also mysterious human documents I have ever come across. We have put such a thick varnish of glosses and interpretations on the original account that a special effort has to be made to get back to the simple intention of the original authors. So I am once more re-reading the wonderful story and have now done most of *Matthew*. I can only do a small bit each night, going to sleep. When I have done all four Gospels I shall try to clarify my mind and see whether any fresh conclusions are possible. When last I read the Greek Testament it was with very orthodox eyes, which I have no longer. And yet I am probably today more deeply interested to get at its meaning than I was in my orthodox youth. I believe you once told me that a parson taught you Greek or read the New Testament with you in Greek. Is that so? Whatever one's line of interpretation and whatever one's view point, the story of Jesus remains the most mysterious and amazing of all in the human record. I don't believe there is any other which even distantly approaches it. An appropriate interpretation for our age might render a first-class service. For in the message of Jesus lies embedded what is most precious in our human insights.

There is no doubt that the ideologies of today form a direct challenge to the spirit of Jesus, with its exaltation of the human soul and its emphasis on the divine Fatherhood and on human brotherhood. There may have been under-emphasis of the economic motifs of human society, but the spiritual foundations were well and truly laid. And the materialism of Stalin, the state worship of Fascism, and the race idolatry of the Nazis are all in direct conflict

---

[1] On the Table bay coast.   [2] Libertas Parva.

with the world view of Jesus as adumbrated in the Gospels. With unorthodox eyes, but with a broader view of what is essential in our human situation in all its complexity I should like to go once more through that Galilean vision of God and man. As a romance, as a Utopia, it would be the most wonderful in the world. But the remarkable thing is that it is not meant as either, but as a sober unvarnished account of the plain practical truth. We cannot now lay it aside but must once more reckon with it and come to grips with it. I have no time or opportunity for a searching analysis, but for my own personal satisfaction I should like to reconsider the whole story in the light of such experience as I have gathered in the years that have elapsed since my last reading of the original account. . . .

Now I must conclude. I fear these outpourings are too long and do not read as proper stuff for a letter. But I have just written as my mind has been running along, without sifting or compressing. Love to you all, ever yours,

Jan

411   To Lord Lothian   Vol. 55, no. 143

Personal and confidential   Cape Town
7 April 1937

My dear Philip, I was very pleased to get your most interesting and informative letter, and also the enclosure, which interested me personally. I have been following pretty closely your public speeches, and articles in the *Round Table* in which I could detect your fine Roman hand.[1] I now write to give you my reactions to what I see happening in the world. I do so in no dogmatic spirit, as my mind cannot see a clear way through the tangle into which world affairs have drifted. But I have a deep sense of foreboding that the course on which the nations are now moving must lead to disaster at a not distant date, and that a cataclysm can only be avoided by a change of course. In this crisis a very great responsibility rests on Great Britain as still the greatest reserve force in the world, and on her wise initiative the future largely depends. In view of past failures of our diplomacy it may be doubtful whether the present British government will feel inclined to make a new move, but a new move is imperatively necessary. The German attitude recently has been so discouraging that one might well feel inclined to doubt whether any fresh attempts will meet with success. Still I think they will

[1] 'I think we do not know the sweet Roman hand.' Shakespeare, *Twelfth Night*, III.iv.31.

have to be made—and the move should come from the British side, if there is to be any chance of success.

I leave for the moment the U.S.A. out of the picture, and think that the immediate future depends on Great Britain and Germany, and on a comprehensive accord between them which could thereafter be extended to other powers. The League of Nations as a means of collective security is for the present in cold storage and had better be left there until the air has become warm again. Likewise I see little use in the Locarno policy, which has been torpedoed by the Franco-Russian agreement.[1] It is little use providing for security against war in the West, when at any moment the East may set the West on fire. Neither Geneva nor Locarno is helpful in the present situation and Eden's policy in respect of both seems to me unfruitful. (Perhaps I speak in ignorance.) We must begin *de novo*.

We have certain favourable features to begin with. (*a*) There is the Anglo-German naval agreement[2] which I value very highly, whatever the foreign office may think of it. (*b*) Then there is Hitler's good will and sincere desire for Anglo-German co-operation. Before 1914 we had the menace of the German navy and the clear hostility of the Kaiser. Now just the opposite in both respects. My deep regret is that in the last three or four years we have left things too much to the French who have made every conceivable mistake and spurned Hitler's various offers, which today we and they would gladly accept with both hands. But it is now too late. We have a revived and armed Germany, capable of as much mischief as ever before 1914.

(*c*) At the same time Germany has also made terrible mistakes, and the worst of all is Hitler's obsession against Russia. Ten years ago an attack on a ruined down-and-out Russia could still be a possible policy. Today that has become mere midsummer madness. If Germany is now a powerfully armed power, Russia is no less so, with far greater material and mineral resources to sustain a prolonged war. And the emergence of Russia as a great power, and the cooling of her Communist ardour are bound to have a profound reaction on German policy, and call a halt to any military designs that Germany may have or have had. Italy is really only a diplomatic card for Germany, and the German military authorities have not forgotten Caporetto,[3] and have not essentially revised their opinion of the military value of an Italian alliance. Russian power thus makes for peace in Europe.

[1] *See supra*, p. 34, note 3.
[2] By this treaty of 18 June 1935 Germany might build a fleet up to 35 % of the strength of the British navy and, in submarines, up to 45 %.
[3] *See* vol. III, p. 565, note 2.

(*d*) Finally, Germany's four-year plan[1] has been a colossal mistake from an economic point of view and has so drained her of resources for carrying on a war that if she fails to deliver a knockout blow at the very start, she is hopelessly beaten. So bad has been this move of a four-year plan that today it constitutes a real danger to peace, as in desperation over its failure the German government may plunge into desperate courses; perhaps move against central Europe as a way of escape from an impossible internal position.

I think all these matters (and others I don't mention) create a situation in which a great peace move once more becomes possible. It must be made, as I say, from the British side, and we alone have the moral and material resources for such a move. We must at last make use of the good will of Hitler as a precious asset for negotiation and for peace. So far we have given him no chance or encouragement. He has had literally nothing from us to show to his people or to save his face as the ruler of the most powerful nation in the world. From a diplomatic point of view our behaviour has been grossly unwise, however suspicious we may justly have been of German policy. In his real good will we have a great card which we have never yet played. The time to do so has come or will come within the very near future.

We are in a strong position to make a move. We are the richest power in the world, after the U.S.A., and can make substantial concessions without really hurting ourselves. We are now arming heavily and cannot be accused of acting in a defeatist spirit. The world looks to us for a great gesture which might yet save Europe from the decay which aggressive militarism may bring upon her. The call now is for wise, far-sighted statesmanship on our part in the interests of the future of our civilization.

Our hands are full of bargaining counters.

(*a*) We do not mean to stick to *all* the ex-German colonies.

(*b*) We know that the Austrian *anschluss*[2] is only a matter of time, and could as well come soon (if Austria agreed) if thereby a stable European co-operation can be secured.

(*c*) We admit that the Danzig and Memel régimes[3] are mere passing makeshifts.

---

[1] In imitation of the Russian five-year plans, four-year plans for the economic development of Germany were announced by Hitler. The first four-year plan (1933–6) was ostensibly a programme of public works but became a programme of rearmament. The second four-year plan (1937–40), announced in September 1936, was intended to develop substitute industries to bring about economic self-sufficiency.

[2] The union of Germany and Austria.

[3] By the treaty of Versailles Danzig became a free city with its own government but under Polish suzerainty. The same treaty placed Memelland under Allied control but

(*d*) In making big economic and financial concessions to Germany for the sake of a real peace, we know we can also secure the cordial co-operation of the U.S.A. Roosevelt is burning to distinguish himself in that direction. I could go on, but the foregoing will serve as samples of the bargaining counters we can bring into play. But it must all be done for a lasting comprehensive European settlement which must include progressive disarmament, a resuscitated League with a revised covenant, and a revised economic and fiscal policy which will re-establish European commerce on a normal basis.

I do not think this an impossible programme if properly handled. France can thereby get all proper guarantees for the future. The menace of war now resting on central Europe will disappear. Russia can have perpetual peace on her west. The unnatural *entente* between Germany and Italy will disappear. The Mediterranean will become as safe as the North sea is already after the Anglo-German naval agreement. And in an era of peace and trade expansion the benefits accruing to all all round will soon obliterate the memory of past enmities and mistakes. Europe will enter on a new lease of a larger life. I think if we are prepared to give a really strong lead and are prepared for substantial concessions and take up the negotiations with Germany ourselves instead of leaving it to others, we can transform the present dangerous position into one of great hope and fair prospects for the future. The foreign office should drop the present lines of negotiation and start *de novo* with unofficial explorations and inquiries from Germany on the above lines. If Hitler is convinced of our real good will and that we have not in view a diplomatic defeat for Germany I think the outlines of a new comprehensive settlement will emerge on which our principal friends (including the U.S.A.) could be consulted and kept informed as talks go forward.

How and by whom such a move should be made is one for very careful consideration. Will Neville Chamberlain distinguish his term of leadership[1] with the biggest effort yet made for European peace—an effort which may very possibly succeed? Surely he will have at his service able and sincere men who can be used as unofficial intermediaries. This year or early next year the attempt will have to be made, as time is running short and the factor of desperation has to be reckoned with. Please think over the whole matter and let me know how you view it. Your plan about co-operation

it was annexed by Lithuania in 1923. Thereafter an international statute recognized the annexation but provided for local self-government.

[1] Neville Chamberlain became prime minister on 28 May 1937 but Baldwin's intention to resign and the probable succession of Chamberlain were known before then.

with the U.S.A. is quite sound, but though that may save *us*, it will not prevent the *débâcle* in Europe; and first and foremost I think a great effort should be made to prevent this *débâcle*, and to arrive at a settlement which Versailles failed to produce. I would not touch on any other territorial terms.

You may be sure that our South African representatives at the imperial conference will go all out for some way of arriving at a European settlement and will be extremely averse to South Africa or the British Commonwealth being involved in any European conflict. Whatever warnings can be given will be given. I think other Dominions will probably do the same.

I am not coming over now, as I have to act for Hertzog here. However, it may be that somewhat later I could be free for a short visit abroad, as I fear I am getting rather out of touch with things and personalities, and would like if possible to renew contacts. My movements will depend on developments abroad and party politics here.

Let me hear from you again. With kind regards and all good wishes, Ever yours sincerely,

s. J. C. Smuts

412   To M. C. Gillett   Vol. 55, no. 178

Tsalta
[Cape Town]
2 May 1937

Your last letter told of your happy homecoming from France and gave further details of the last phase of your very successful trip. It also contained the copy of Jan's [Gillett] letter about the mugs and the unfortunate Cheetham swan.[1] I was highly amused at this effort. Incidentally it shows great improvement in Jan's style. I was specially struck by the quality of his sardonic humour, which is a great advance on the past.

I am afraid the coronation[2] celebrations are being overdone on a scale which may cause a real reaction. It now looks like an enormous advertisement and political stunt—which is a great pity. Our own local celebrations will be on a modest scale and not likely to give offence either way. I shall have to speak at the Cape Town function and shall make use of the opportunity to draw attention to

[1] Jan Gillett's letter described the presentation of coronation mugs at his school and the efforts made at Cheetham to catch a swan thought to be a royal bird.
[2] Of George VI.

some of the things that matter. After all the British Commonwealth does stand for some of our major human ideals which are today in special danger. Mafficking does not suit our role at all. You appear to have enjoyed your French holiday immensely. It was a happy decision to visit that part,[1] which gave you the scientific interest in archaeology, in addition to the scenic beauty and historical interest in that part of France. Pity it was so short and that Arthur has to return to work so soon. The danger is that he may prematurely exhaust his strength by continuing to work at a rate beyond the power of incipient old age. I fear it is my mistake also. But I have far greater provocation than Arthur. Still, I do sometimes begin to feel physically tired, even here in South Africa. In England I am always on the point of physical exhaustion, owing to the strain people impose on one there...

Armstrong's *Grey Steel* has appeared and I have glanced through it rapidly. Isie is reading it now. It contains some details of my early years which are not found in Mrs Millin. Otherwise he seems to have been mostly dependent on her for his material, but to differ radically from her in interpretation and valuations. It is a most unlovely picture he draws of J.C.S. It is curious how my actions are really liable to misconstruction and how the ascription of evil motives makes the account a really good story, the interest of which will make it go down with many who do not like the apparently too favourable view of Mrs Millin. It is a good story. But it is not true, as I need scarcely say to you. However you will read the book for yourself, and no doubt enjoy it. The *advocatus diaboli* is usually a piquant and amusing fellow. My inner life of course is not touched on at all—so much the better. I should not like misrepresentation in that quarter.

We are now reaching the last stage of our parliamentary journey. This week ought to see us very near the end. I am trying to finish by 11 May, but we may be taken on to 15 May. The strain of sittings from 10.30 in the morning to 11 every night, with two intervals for meals, is a very severe one, and I shall be glad to salute the end.

This morning I took the family to Strandfontein in beautiful warm weather...Yesterday I saw the vast line of blue Winterhoek mountains stretched out before Klipfontein[2] with a beauty of colour and line and a majesty which made it even more to me than in the days of youthful romance in the far past. I could not think of anything more lovely in my long experience of scenery. And I blessed my good fortune in having been privileged to grow up in such

[1] Carnac, a village in Brittany, the site of famous megalithic monuments.
[2] *See* vol. I, p. 4, note I.

surroundings, and with home associations which remain an unforgettable memory. The beauty of home life was fully matched by
the beauty of the world around me. If anything has gone wrong
since I cannot blame it on my associations of home or nature...

413   From Lord Lothian   Vol. 55, no. 101

Seymour House
17 Waterloo Place, S.W.1
Confidential   14 May 1937

My dear General, You may have seen that I paid a visit to Germany
last week. I enclose notes of my interviews with Hitler, Schacht
[H. H. G.] and Goering [H. W.] and a covering memorandum of
my own which I think will interest you.[1] I have sent a copy to
Hertzog and also to Mackenzie King and Casey [R. G.], as well as
to H.M.G.

I was deeply interested in your last letter[2] and even more in your
suggestion that you might come home this summer. I greatly hope
you will. Unless we tackle the German position in the next six
months or year it will be too late, and I do not know anybody who
could have more effect than yourself. The difficulty in this country
is that you have got a combination between three forces, the traditional anti-Germans, the whole of the Left, which at the present
time is as mad about anti-Fascism as the Right used to be anti-Red,
and the foreign office which is pledged to the French view of
European politics. There is, therefore, no effective opposition
criticism of government policy, only a few voices crying in the
wilderness of apathy or prejudice.

Remember that during August and the first fortnight of September
practically everybody will be away on holiday. Please let me know
as soon as you can of any definite decisions about your movements
so that I may be certain of being here. Yours sincerely,

Lothian

P.S. I wonder if you could let P.D.[3] look at these memoirs. I have
no copies left.

[1] These notes are printed in full on pp. 330–51 of J. R. M. Butler, *Lord Lothian*
(London, 1960) and the memorandum is summarized on pp. 217–19.
[2] 411.
[3] Patrick Duncan.

414   To M. C. Gillett   Vol. 55, no. 180

Cape Town
15 May 1937

...We passed through the house yesterday the bill dealing with Natives in urban areas—the last of the Hertzog trio.[1] There has been much opposition to it in certain quarters, but on the whole the bill is better than appears. I voted for certain amendments which were carried. Hofmeyr voted against one important clause, but thought the bill on the whole good and voted for the third reading. The evils of the Native exodus from the reserves to the big centres of employment are becoming very serious and creating problems which may have revolutionary effects, for white and black alike. It is most difficult to know how to deal with them and one easily slips into measures which appear harsh and retrogressive. My view however is that some of the more severe clauses cannot be carried out as they are impracticable, and that the law will be administered in a milder and fairer form than many people think. The Native affairs department is on the whole wiser than the legislators of this country. And it is in this administration that the real crux lies. I write this because you may be unduly upset by what appears in the press that reaches you, or by Native views in South Africa. A fair administration of this bill when it becomes law might prove a boon rather than the opposite to Native development. But on most of these things the clash of opinion is pretty strong, as the Natives resent all differential measures.

...I have two interesting letters from Arthur, one already referred to, the other written after and about your French trip. It seems to have been an enormous success. Jannie [Smuts] will be deeply interested to hear from you about your Les Eyzies experiences in company with the Abbé.[2] He was very anxious that Jannie should come and study archaeology under him in Paris. But *dis aliter visum*,[3] and Jannie will pursue archaeology on his own lines. I have not yet heard whether his papers will be published by our Royal Society. I fear the pundits are a bit scared by his discovery (if correct) that ancient tool-making man goes well into the Pliocene of the Transvaal...

---

[1] The Native Laws Amendment Act (No. 36 of 1937). It provided for stricter control of the movement of Africans into the towns and for their expulsion in certain circumstances.

[2] The Abbé Henri Breuil (q.v.).

[3] The gods thought otherwise. Virgil, *Aeneid*, II.428.

Irene
[Transvaal]
20 May 1937

My dear Murray, For the last couple of weeks I have had it on
my mind to write to you and to say to you and Lady Mary how
deeply I sympathize with both of you on the passing away of Basil.
You have had great sorrows and have seen your dear loved ones
pass away one after the other in your own lifetime. Of all the pains
of life surely that must be the greatest to parents wrapped up in the
lives of their children. Agnes I knew best, and she was a creature
of delight, joying in the things of life and of this world. I can only
press your hand in deepest sympathy in this latest loss, of one who
must have been very near to you, a dear companion of old age. Your
consolation must be in your work for those causes which transcend
the ties of the family circle. There too you have had your disappointments. Frustration has been the badge of our post war age. But those
who believe in the imperishable things of the spirit will also have
the strength not to be unduly downcast by temporary set-backs to
the causes they espouse. That high faith smoothes out the ups and
downs of life and the world. And that faith is your consolation and
your strength. When as a young fellow of nineteen or twenty I first
read the *Oedipus Tyrannus*[1] I was carried away by that line which
has stuck to me as a treasure for life: μέγας ἐν τούτοις θεός, οὐδὲ
γηράσκει.[2] The divine things never go under. Tyrants may rage.
Propaganda may sweep a decade or more off their feet. Friends may
prove weak or false. But the divine seed is germinating all the time,
and in the end will sprout into glorious flowering. And so I am not
inclined to take the Mussolinis and the Hitlers and their tribe too
seriously. What is weak and faulty in our work will surely perish
in these set-backs; but what is sound and well-founded will survive
and appear in the better time.

Perhaps we have expected too much of human nature, too much
also of the League in the confusions of the post war period. Perhaps
the League was far from flawless in its mechanisms however sound
its fundamental ideas. Perhaps mankind had to pass through a longer
and harder schooling before it could work so ideal a system. But if
we slacken not in our faith and in our efforts this generation to come
will reap the fruit of our prayers and labours.

I do not believe that this is the end of the world, that an early war

[1] A tragedy by Sophocles.
[2] God is great in these things, and he does not grow old.

will follow the present manoeuvrings for position in Europe. Desperation is our gravest danger; the rope of the dictator is never a long one, and no one knows what he may do when he gets to the end of it. That is why I for one agree to the present British rearmament. It will give pause even to desperation planning its last throw. It will also assist the U.S.A. in realizing how dangerous things really are and how necessary for her to lend a hand more generously and unselfishly where so much is at stake for our human future. We shall have to mete out fair justice to Germany—even to an armed truculent Germany, where we missed the chance to settle with a helpless Germany. She will have to be led back into the League. Italy will of course follow. With a powerful Russia and a resurgent China Japan will also recoil before the dangers of isolation. I look upon a strong Russia and a prepared Great Britain as immense factors for peace. But the U.S.A. will have to come in, for moral support and collaboration and for economic restoration. She will not do more, but even helping to put Europe and the world on the road to trade and financial stability would be a very great contribution.

Such plans and possibilities console me for the future and make me feel that labour well spent will not be lost. And they may not be a sort of private fool's paradise, but may possibly be right. More one cannot say at present.

Our private sorrows merge in the greater sorrows of the world, and over both these spreads the great faith expressed in Sophocles' formula. With kindest and tenderest regards, Ever yours in spirit,

J. C. Smuts

416   From J. B. M. Hertzog   Vol. 55, no. 78

Hyde Park Hotel
Knightsbridge
London
24 Mei 1937

Amice, Môre is jou verjaarsdag en ik wil jou van harte 'n baie gelukkige lewe nog verder toewens. Daar is nog baie te doen vir jou, en ik hoop dat jij die krag en gesondheid daarvoor in ruime mate sal geniet. Sê vir Isie ik stuur ook vir haar mij innige gelukwens.

Laat mij jou bedank vir jou brief waarin jij mij meegedeel het aangaande die loop van die Parlement vir die eerste twee weke of so na mij vertrek, als ook vir jou kabel voor die verdaging. Ik het dit waardeer. Wat betref ons *mission of peace*, soos jij dit noem, wil ik jou meedeel dat ons eergister die buitelandse posisie onder discussie gehad het. Die besprekinge was interessant. Van Britse sij was dit ons voorgesteld dat die posisie dreigend was en steeds aan verergering, en dat dit toe te skrijwe was aan die gedrag van Duitsland en Italia. Dat hier in Regerings kring weinig sympathie vir Duitsland en Duitsers bestaan was duidelik te bespeur uit 'n paar woorde gevoegd deur die heer Baldwin bij die van Eden na die laaste klaar was met sij *general review of the situation*. Bij Eden was daar geen ander rede van afkeuring van Duitslands gedrag en vir vrees nie dan alleen Duitslands binnetree in die Rijngebied en haar bewapening gepaard met Hitlers diktatoriale mag. Bij Baldwin was dit alles omrede van Duitsland se onsedelike en onberekenbaar regeringstelsel in opposisie tot demokrasie as in Engeland. Waarom nou juis die wereld toestand moet beskou word as *a deterioration* gaande van erg tot erger ten gevolge van Duitsland, het nòg Baldwin nòg Eden opgegee. Ik glo dan ook nie dat daar enige rede voor te gee is behalwe dat daar in Regerings kring wel manne is—soos Chamberlain naar mij geloof—die in Duitsland niks anders dan 'n Britse vijand kan sien nie. Hoe dit ook sij, ik is blij om jou te kan sê dat die ander regerings—Canada, Australia, New Zealand en ons—soos hier verteenwoordigd, dit almal eens is dat ons geen rede kan vind vir 'n Europese oorlog omrede van Duitsland, as Engeland net die skaal gelijk wil hou tussen Frankrijk en Duitsland en haar wil inspan om vriendskappelik met beide saam te werk, terwijl sij sig onthou van verpligtinge en inmenging in sake Oost en Sentraal Europa. Ik sluit vir jou in 'n kopie van mij toespraak Vrijdag. Daaruit kan jij sien die rigting deur mij ingeslaan. Ik het gepraat na die ander Dominions. Jij sal sien aan die end het ik nog oor 'n paar onderwerpe verder opmerkings gemaak. Die gevolg was dat bij die discussies wat toe gevolg het al drie die ander geweste mij siensswijse ondersteun het; en die hoop uit gespreek het dat die Britse Regering gevolg sal gee aan mij siensswijse, voornamelik in verband met onthouding uit Oostelike en Sentraal Europeese aangeleenthede. Ik het alle rede om te sê dat ons discussies groot invloed sal uitoefen bij die Britse Regering en op meer dan een punt sal lei tot 'n meer besliste houding en beleid in die regte rigting van vrede en die bewaring daarvan.

Ook wat die Lega van Nasies betref het die Dominions daarin geslaag om die Britse Regering te oortuig dat daar nie langer moet gespeel word met die ware betekenis van die houding van die Lega in sake sanksies en tans weer in verband met erkenning van die Italiaanse posisie in Abyssinia; en dat ronduit moet erken word dat die Lega seksies 10 en 16 van die Verdrag beskou as geabrogeerd, en elke lid nou maar erken of nie na mate dit goed dink. Beide Chamberlain—die Voorsitter was van die vergadering—en Eden het mij toegegee dat dit die enigste gesonde houding was om te volg. Eden sal dan ook sien om, indien die saak van erkenning van Italia's posisie in Abyssinia sou opkom, dit in genoemde rigting tot 'n oplossing te doen kom, nou of later. Dit was die algemene gevoel dat 'n oplossing langs hierdie weg—wat eigenlik net 'n erkenning van feite sou wees—dadelik die weg van toenadering vir Amerika sowel as Duitsland naar die Lega sou bevorder.

Ons sal hede middag, terwijl Eden oor is naar Geneva, met andere sake b.v. verdediging, voortgaan. Intussen het ik besluit om op 11 Junie van hier mij terug reis te aanvaar. Mij ander kollegas sal nog 'n rukkie vertoef. Met beste wense

J. B. M. Hertzog

TRANSLATION

Hyde Park Hotel
Knightsbridge
London
24 May 1937

Amice, Tomorrow is your birthday and I want sincerely to wish you a very happy life in the future. There is still much for you to do and I hope that you will enjoy health and strength for it in full measure. Tell Isie that I send her my heartfelt wishes.

Let me thank you for your letter in which you told me how parliament has gone on during the first two weeks or so after my departure—also for your cable before the adjournment. I appreciated this. As regards our 'mission of peace', as you call it, I must tell you that the foreign situation was under discussion the day before yesterday. The discussions were interesting. From the British side it was represented to us that the position was threatening and getting worse, and that this was due to the behaviour of Germany and Italy. That there is little sympathy for Germany and Germans in government circles here was clearly to be seen from a few words added by Mr Baldwin to those of Eden after the latter had finished his 'general review of the situation.' For Eden there was no reason for disapproval of Germany's behaviour and for fear other than Germany's move into the Rhineland and her rearmament, together with Hitler's dictatorial power. For Baldwin it was all because of Germany's immoral and incalculable form of government, in opposition to English democracy. Why exactly the world situation should be regarded as a 'deterioration' going from bad to worse because of Germany, neither Eden nor Baldwin explained. Nor do I think any reason can be adduced, except that there are men in government circles—like Chamberlain in my opinion—who see nothing else in Germany than an enemy of Britain. However this may be, I am glad to be able to tell you that the other governments— Canada, Australia, New Zealand and we—represented here, all agree that we can find no reason for a European war because of Germany, if only England will hold the scales evenly between France and Germany and exert herself to work amicably with both while abstaining from obligations and intervention in respect of eastern and central Europe.

I enclose a copy of my speech on Friday from which you will see the line I took. I spoke after the other Dominions. You will see towards the end that I made further remarks on a few other subjects. The result was that at the discussions that ensued all three the other countries supported my view and expressed the hope that the British government would give effect to my view, particularly in connection with abstention from eastern and central European affairs. I have every reason to say that our discussions will have a great influence on the British government and will lead, in more than one respect, to a more decided attitude and policy in the right direction of peace and its preservation.

In the case of the League of Nations also the Dominions succeeded in convincing the British government that there must be no more playing about with the true meaning of the League in the matter of sanctions, and now again with regard to recognition of the Italian position in Abyssinia; and that it must be admitted outright that the League regards sections 10 and 16 of the covenant as abrogated, and each member must now recognize or not as it thinks fit. Both Chamberlain—who was chairman of the meeting—and Eden agreed with me that this was the only sound course to follow. Eden will accordingly try, should the matter of recognition of Italy's position come up, to bring about a solution in this direction—now or later. It was the general feeling that a solution on these lines—which would really be only a recognition of the facts—would immediately open the way for an approach to the League by America as well as Germany.

This afternoon we shall, while Eden goes to Geneva, proceed with other matters, e.g. defence. In the meantime I have decided to start my return journey from here on 11 June. My other colleagues will remain a little longer. With best wishes,

J. B. M. Hertzog

417 From N. C. Havenga Vol. 55, no. 75

Hyde Park Hotel
Knightsbridge
Londen
31 Mei 1937

Seer geagte Generaal, Ek glo die Eerste Minister het aan u geskrywe omtrent ons bevindings en besprekings hier in verband met die buitelandse posiesie. Ek wil graag korteliks hiermee vir u laat weet wat die ontwikkelings is met betrekking tot ekonomiese aangeleenthede. Die buitelandse posiesie het hier belangrike reaksies geskep ook in ekonomiese sake. Dit word deur die Britse Regering as allerbelangriks beskou dat nadere aaneensluiting en samewerking met die Verenigde State van Amerika verkry word, met die oog op die invloed wat dit mag hê op die handhawing van vrede en herstel van internasionale handel. Hulle wil reageer op die beroep wat reeds vir lange tyd op hierdie gebied gemaak word deur Cordell Hull om hinderpale op die weg van internasionale handel in die vorm van hoë tariefmure en handelsrestriksies te verwyder. Besprekings hieroor tussen die twee Regerings is reeds geruime tyd aan die gang, en het tamelik ver gevorder. Vernaamste gevolg is 'n sterk aanval op die hele voorkeurstelsel tussen Engeland en die Dominiums, en Engeland beskou die saak van so veel en groot belang dat ons gevra word om belangrike opofferings te maak van voorregte wat ons geniet onder die Ottawa ooreenkomste.

Die vernaamste artiekels van ons wat getref word is 'canned fruits and products', gedroogde vrugte en grape fruit. Dit is belangrik vir ons maar ander Dominiums sal nog swaarder getref word. Een ding is duidelik vir my, n.l. dat op die lange duur die hele stelsel van voorkeurregte gedoem is, en dat Engeland die behoud en ontwikkeling van haar handel met die buiteland, en die verwydering van diskriminasie en handels-hindernisse van so groot belang beskou, dat sy nie die belange van haar eie produsente en van die Dominiums in die weg sal laat staan nie. Die skyn van die handhawing van die beleid sal behou word, maar die opening in die muur sal so belangrik wees, en die hele tendens is so duidelik, dat dit nie langer verstandig sal wees vir ons produsente om in die toekoms staat te maak op hierdie soort van hulp vir die ontwikkeling van enige tak van hul nywerheid.

Indien die saak beklink word sal ons natuurlik moet aandring op afstand van 'n groot gedeelte van die belangrike voorkeure wat ons aan Engeland verleen, en wat ons reeds gemaak het tot haar beste klant in die hele wereld vir fabrieksgoedere, so dat ons ook in staat gestel mag word om beter ons eie posiesie te kan handhaaf teen ander lande waar ons vergoeding sal moet soek vir die verlies van 'n gedeelte van die afsetgebied wat ons nou hier het.

Dit is 'n baje belangrike en interessante ontwikkeling, en is 'n bewys van die oorwegende belang wat Engeland heg aan hierdie Amerikaanse oriëntering in belang van wereld-vrede en 'n beter internasionale gesindheid in die ekonomiese sfeer.

Ek het die goud-kwessie en stabilisasie op die konferensie geopper en het ook ander belangrike besprekings met Chamberlain en ander belange gehad. Chamberlain is sympatiek teenoor ons standpunt en belange, en het baje sterk beklemtoon sy voortdurende geloof in goud as die enigste basis van vertroue, maar hy sê dit is 'n kwessie waarby ander groot lande ook betrokke is, en alhoewel ons vandag nader is aan die doel wat ons moet nastreef is die oomblik nog nie daar om iets definitiefs tot stand te bring.

Ons verwag dat die konferensie teen 15 of 16 Junie sal klaar wees en Generaal is nou van plan om op 18 Junie te vertrek. Ek sal nog moet 'n week of so agterbly om verder besprekings te voer, maar ek verwag nie dat ons nou ons handels-ooreenkoms sal kan voltooi nie—met die oog op die Amerikaanse ontwikkelinge hierbo gemeld —en Te Water en sommige van ons amptenare sal waarskynlik besprekings later hieroor verder moet voortset. Met vriendelike groete, ook aan al die kollegas, *t.t.*

N. C. Havenga

TRANSLATION

Hyde Park Hotel
Knightsbridge
London
31 May 1937

Dear General, I believe the prime minister has written to you about our conclusions and discussions here in connection with the foreign situation. I want to let you know briefly what the developments are in regard to economic affairs. The foreign situation has had important reactions here upon economic matters. The British government regards it as all-important that there should be closer linkage and co-operation with the United States of America, with a view to the influence which this may have on the maintenance of peace and the recovery of international trade. They want to respond to the call which Cordell Hull has long been making in this regard to remove obstructions in the way of international trade such as high tariff walls and trade restrictions. Discussions about this between the two governments have already been going on for a good while and have progressed fairly far. The most important result is a strong attack on the whole preference system between England and the Dominions, and England regards the matter as of such great importance that we are asked to make important sacrifices of privileges which we enjoy under the Ottawa agreements.

The main articles affected in our case are canned fruits and products, dried fruit and grapefruit. This is important for us but other Dominions will be harder hit. One thing is clear to me, namely, that in the long run the whole system of preferences is doomed and that England regards the retention and development of her foreign trade and the removal of discrimination and trade obstacles as of such great importance that she will not let the interest of her own producers and of the Dominions stand in the way. The appearance of maintaining the policy will be kept up, but the opening in the wall will be so important, and the whole tendency is so clear that it would no longer be wise for our producers to rely in future on this kind of help in developing any branch of their industry.

If the matter is settled we shall, of course, have to insist on the surrender of a large part of the important preferences which we grant to England and which have already made us her best customer in the whole world for manufactured goods, so that we also may be in a better position to maintain our own position against other countries where we shall have to seek compensation for the loss of part of the market which we now have here.

It is a very important and interesting development and is proof of the overriding importance which England attaches to this American orientation in the interests of world peace and a better international disposition in the economic field.

I raised the gold question and stabilization at the conference and also had other important discussions with Chamberlain and other interests. Chamberlain is sympathetic to our standpoint and our interests, and very strongly emphasized his continued belief in gold as the only basis of confidence, but he says it is a matter which concerns other big countries also, and although we are today nearer to the goal that we must strive for, the moment has not yet come to effect anything definite.

We expect that the conference will be over on 15 or 16 June and the General now intends to leave on 18 June. I shall have to stay another week or so to hold further discussions—with a view to the American developments mentioned above—and Te Water and some of our officials will probably have to continue discussions on the matter later.

With friendly greetings, also to all colleagues, *totus tuus*,

N. C. Havenga

418   From L. S. Amery   Vol. 55, no. 5

112 Eaton Square
S.W.1
14 July 1937

My dear Smuts, My friend G. T. Hutchinson, who for many years has taken a fatherly interest in the Rhodes family, tells me that Miss Georgie Rhodes is going out to visit South Africa at the beginning of August on the *Athlone Castle* and that he is giving her a letter of introduction to you. He tells me that she is much the most interesting and attractive of the younger generation of the Rhodes family, and as he may not have put that in his letter of introduction I pass it on to you for your guidance, and to encourage you to be nice to the young woman if you come across her. I have not met her myself but was very fond of Rhodes's younger sister, Edith, who was a great character and the only one of the family who could really compare with him.

I am a little sorry that Hertzog should have given vent to his not altogether unnatural impatience about the Protectorates question, and I dare say the reporter gave the interview a rather more unqualified note than was intended.[1] I entirely agree that the transfer should not be too long delayed and that we ought to make a real effort to educate the Natives in the Protectorates in the right direction. But it isn't altogether an easy task, and you will remember that at the mere thought of financial assistance from the Union they stampeded a year ago. While I think we could perhaps do more than we have in the past, I think it is no less important that, on the Union side, there should be the effort to make it clear that the Natives are not to be simply assimilated to the ordinary status of Natives in the provinces but that they would remain with their special guaranteed position and under the officials whom they are accustomed to look to. Also I am not sure whether it isn't a mistake on both sides to discuss the Protectorates at large instead of concentrating on the particular question of Swaziland. The case for transfer there is

---

[1] Hertzog, in an interview with *The Times* correspondent at Bloemfontein on 6 July, deprecated the 'dilatory tactics' of the British government in transferring the Protectorates to the Union. *See The Times*, 7 July 1937, p. 15.

obviously stronger than in the other two territories, and the success of transfer would render subsequent approach in the other cases much easier. Meanwhile we are sure to have a debate in the house in the next week or two and Malcolm MacDonald[1] will be hard put to it to avoid promising the explicit consent of the Natives as apart from consultation followed by the conclusion that they are reasonably likely to acquiesce.

The Palestine report[2] is a remarkably able document and I think on the whole the government have been right in endorsing it. Personally I always believed that, given firmness in our attitude throughout, and not only at the colonial office, but right through the ranks of the administration, the policy of carrying the mandate into effect on the basis of creating a common Palestinian nationality with equal rights to both communities might have succeeded. But the last few years, and particularly [Sir Arthur] Wauchope's weakness, have so let down the situation and so exacerbated Arab nationalism that partition is now perhaps the only solution.

Weizmann and the more far-seeing of the Jews are ready to accept it, though they protest vehemently against the inadequacy of the area allotted to them and more particularly would like the Jewish suburbs of Jerusalem to be included in the Jewish state. They feel that 'Zionism without Zion' will not have much chance of acceptance by the Zionist congress in August. I see no reason why, on that point, the government should not meet them, and at any rate allow all the Jews in the mandatory enclave (and the Arabs for that matter) to opt for citizenship of their national state, so that they could take part in its public life even if their local administration remained under the imperial control.

I see no reason why the Jews, following the example not so much of their Hebrew ancestors as of their Phoenician cousins, should not, even on an area no larger than an English county, build up quite a considerable state based on intensive agriculture, industry, shipping, aviation, etc.

The European situation is desperately muddled but I think on the whole drifting towards peace rather than towards war. Yours ever,

L. S. Amery

[1] He was at this time secretary of state for the Dominions.
[2] *See supra*, p. 53, note 2.

419   To S. G. Millin   Vol. 102, no. 74

Irene
[Transvaal]
6 September 1937

My dear Sarah, Thank you for your note re Phil's appointment.[1] Phil thoroughly deserved it, and there is no special merit of mine. Why should a good man be kept back in South Africa merely because of his race? Last December when the Aliens Bill[2] was on, the situation was somewhat different, as I did not want the bench to be discussed in connection with the bill.

I read Weizmann's great speech[3] with the deepest interest and admiration. I approve his sentiments but doubt the wisdom of partition. I fear Weizmann has been driven to it by the weakness of British policy and his growing distrust that the Balfour declaration will be carried out in future. He knows more from the inside than we do, and we must be cautious in judging him in the line he has taken. But I feel (1) that the Jewish state [so] administrated will not last and is much too small and too closely linked up with the rest of Palestine to be a viable independent unit; (2) that Arab hostility will continue and be more formidable from the absence of all restraint, and may in the end prove fatal to the one Jewish state; (3) that self-governing institutions should be given to the Jewish and Arab nations of Palestine (including free rights of immigration) but that both should continue under British mandate, so that the Jews could look to Great Britain for support against Arab inter-ference or attack. The danger is that the Jews in Palestine may have to face alone and single-handed the hostile Arab world. Many of the detailed arrangements recommended seem to me absurd, but I don't go into them now. I would agree to a large measure of self-govern-ment but the mandate to remain intact.

You write most interestingly but also very pessimistically about the British and European situation. I hope your pessimism and that of your informants is not justified. But one feels uneasy. The worst sign is that Hitler should, *so soon* after his Austrian victory, have moved on to the Czechoslovakian situation. That is a most sinister sign, as if his time is short and his time-table arranged. If this is so we may very likely have trouble in the summer or the autumn. But

[1] Philip Millin was appointed to the supreme court bench when Smuts was minister of justice.

[2] The Aliens Act (No. 1 of 1937) regulated the entry of certain immigrants, in particular German Jews, into South Africa, and imposed various restrictions on them.

[3] On the Peel Report at the twentieth Zionist congress at Zürich, 3–17 August 1937. See C. Sykes, *Cross Roads to Israel* (Mentor edition 1967), pp. 184–5.

I really don't see how Germany could be prepared for a general war. She is bankrupt and destitute of the vital raw materials for a great war. If she loses the first moves she is lost absolutely. And that is why I still think we shall possibly have a further respite from what will undoubtedly be the most deadly disaster possible to the civilization which has been so laboriously built up in the West these last 3,000 years. Much of that civilization is of course already lost. Hence your Intellectual Protest.[1] But this lost ground could be recovered if war is averted and the forces of sanity get a chance. Once war breaks out the West will capitulate to the East in the coming era—as sure as fate.

Thank you for two nice letters. I had a similar most welcome one from Phil. Now I am on the point of going for a week to the wilds of the Zoutpansberg to recover physical and intellectual balance.

My best wishes to you for a most useful and worthwhile visit abroad. Ever yours,

J. C. Smuts

420   To A. B. Gillett   Vol. 55, no. 186

Irene
[Transvaal]
18 September 1937

...You write full of the coming war, and indeed you alarm me. I have consistently taken the view that Hitler is driven mostly by fear and Mussolini by bluff and that neither of them desires war, just as neither is in a position to make war—with Great Britain supreme on the high seas and France's army far the strongest on the Continent. Our mistake, as I take it, has been that we have allowed ourselves to be bluffed, and have in that way lost valuable ground and filled the smaller fry and the world generally with the impression that democracy is decadent if not moribund. We have been so slow and ineffective, so apologetic and timid in right doing, that people thought we had lost heart and power. Hence the movement of the smaller fry on the Continent towards the Berlin–Rome axis. There seems to be a change since N. Chamberlain became prime minister and I hope rearmament will stiffen our backs and our diplomacy. But really I don't think that war is waiting for us round the next corner. If we are alive and active in a peace diplomacy while

---

[1] This may be an article, written for 'the Argus papers', which S. G. Millin enclosed in a letter of 28 March 1937 but which is not attached to the document in the Smuts Collection.

strengthening our armaments at the same time we shall not have war in the near future. Of course I assume that France is going to put her house in order financially. Her economic confusion invites trouble—politically for her internally, and militarily from the outside. Today finance is bed-rock, and that is the great weakness of the dictatorships and our strength. But France *must* reform her finance, or she may be seriously handicapped and weakened.

I suppose the British government take my view that war is not imminent and therefore do not take unnecessary precautions for internal air defence so far as England is concerned. I don't know. You ask about anti-aircraft defences. Of course these need not be in evidence and in position. Such guns are very light and mobile, and may be kept in stock in large quantities for the right time and place.

I assume the government have made the guns and are keeping them in stock. Again I don't know. They should undoubtedly be there—ready to be moved out at a moment's notice.

It is a difficult time for the world. I believe behind the spirit of mischief there is also a great deal of mere fear, and a willingness and anxiety to conclude a real peace. Surely that is Germany's interest in her present economic weakness. I should like to see a greater peace push with her. But I don't know what is being done. Yours ever,

Jan

421   To M. C. Gillett   Vol. 55, no. 188

Doornkloof
[Transvaal]
25 September 1937

I believe you and Hilda [Clark] land today. I hope all has gone well and happily for you both on the high seas . . . I think I told you about my motor trip to Lourenço Marques and back in order to inspect some property for Andries [Weyers] and his Cullinan friends. On the way back I saw some wonderful country coming up from Swaziland to Carolina, which we should see together on some future occasion. From Bremersdorp by Mbalane and onwards the road rises almost 3,000 ft. up the Usutu valley and gives what in clear light would be most wonderful views of a marvellous country—only I came up in thick mist and therefore could only guess at the beauty of the scene. This week I have been mostly in Pretoria (with the exception of a visit yesterday to Krugersdorp to attend their jubilee celebration there). It was all very enjoyable among these happy folks, and I was glad to be away from office and political worries. Of these the week has been full. Last Sunday a small body of police made what is called a liquor raid on the location at Vereeniging. Suddenly, and apparently without provocation, the police were attacked and two white and one Native policeman killed.[1] I suppose the Natives must by Sunday afternoon have been so sodden with *skokiaan*[2] that they did not know what they were doing. You can imagine the wild irrational reactions all over the country. Meetings everywhere calling for vengeful punishment. Curses on the police, and more so on the poor negrophilist minister.[3] My case had been made blacker by my releasing four hundred Natives who had been caught in the round-up on Monday for being without passes or tax receipts. Politicians are exploiting this excitement all over the country for their miserable little ends. My colleagues are naturally very apprehensive of political repercussions in the country. To make matters worse Natives in a distant reserve in Natal seem to have attacked some police tax-collectors, again apparently without provocation, and to have beaten some of them to within an inch of their lives.[4] There is nothing that makes the European in this country so panicky as incidents of this kind, where Natives attack Europeans. My bad luck is that there is a sort of wave of this lawless behaviour—which is not confined to Natives. At Johannesburg a minor crime wave has led to a big mass outcry. So you can see that things have not been pleasant for me this week. My only consolation is that Jannie [Smuts] has just arrived from Springs, free till Sunday night, so that we two can go to Rooikop and I can forget my woes. I hope to do so just now, and write this note to post before I leave. Jannie was to have come only tomorrow afternoon but a throat affection has prevented his going down the mine and secured a short spell of sick leave. We shall enjoy the two days away in the bush among friendly surroundings. Next week I have a big municipal congress to discuss the application of the new (Native) Urban Areas Act,[5] and another big party congress, where no doubt I shall hear more about my pro-Native sins. A respite in the bush will therefore be very welcome. You remember Mrs Sauer's cook who retired to the bushes in her sorrows. I shall follow her example.

I write of all these small things and minor worries. But think of

[1] For an account of this incident see Edward Roux, *Time Longer than Rope* (1948), pp. 290–2.

[2] An intoxicating drink brewed by South African Natives, particularly in the towns.

[3] Smuts was at this time acting minister of Native affairs.

[4] At this time the government appointed a committee of inquiry into the methods of collecting taxes from Natives. *See* the *Natal Mercury*, 15 September 1937.

[5] *See supra*, p. 78, note 1.

Canton being bombed to extinction by the Japs![1] Think of similar
devilment all over that huge immobile population. And then the
British government declare their satisfaction with the Japanese note
that they have given strict instructions against bombing of civilians.

I really wonder what the world is coming to. For if this is permitted
in China, much worse will happen tomorrow in the West. I think
the troubles and manoeuvrings in Europe are trifling compared
to what is happening in Asia, where untold miseries are goading
hundreds of millions into madness on a colossal scale for which
mankind will have to pay. One cannot expect anything from the
session of the League now sitting, in the present weakness of the
League. But our consciences must be getting seared with this sight
of hopeless human misery which we do or can do nothing to allevi-
ate. These things cry to high heaven, but fail to reach this poor
helpless world in the west, which is impotent in its domestic
squabbles. And Hitler and Mussolini are prancing about in Munich
and Berlin. Only a Jewish prophet of old could do some sort of
justice to this bedlam of a world situation.

But you will think that I am raving. So perhaps I am, and that is
why I want to get away to Rooikop and have peace among the
cattle and the other wild things...

It is still dry here, although rain has fallen in many parts of the
country. But the $\frac{1}{4}$ inch we have had has started the grass and the
young leaves on the trees, and nature in its fresh young foliage is at
its loveliest. So let our hearts rejoice in the midst of deep sorrows and
tribulations. A bad letter, but it brings my dear love.

Jan

422   To A. B. Gillett   Vol. 55, no. 191

Doornkloof
[Transvaal]
2 October 1937

Just as I was finishing a letter to Margaret the mail came in with one
from you, and I reply at once to it. This is Saturday morning at
home, and a good time for a few words with you.

You write to elicit my views on the present situation. I shall tell
you in a word. Great Britain has in the last few years let herself and
the world down very badly. There has been incredible weakness and
slackness, and the dictators and others have taken advantage of their
unusual opportunity. I am glad that a marked change has set in.

[1] War had broken out between China and Japan in July 1937.

Rearmament is inevitable and right if Great Britain is once more to pull her weight. The time has come for firmness in the Mediterranean. That appears now to be the British policy. Nyon has been a great success, has called Italy's horrible bluff and suddenly put an end to piracy on the high seas.[1] This should be followed up by a joint demand by Great Britain and France for withdrawal of all volunteers from Spain—not in the distant future but *now*. And the demand should be stiff enough to make Italy realize that this time it is business. You will find the bluff will once more be called. Germany is not going to fight for Italy, and Italy will collapse, and perhaps the Italo-German *entente* also. Franco's position will become most difficult, and a compromise peace could then be arranged in Spain. Great Britain (jointly with the U.S.A.) should become *most outspoken* at least in regard to Japan's behaviour in China, and mobilize world opinion against the Japanese policy of aggression. I don't think she can do more at present, but at least the voicing of public opinion should take place. And Great Britain, who sinned greatly in 1931–2, should now take the lead in this effort to restore a healthy public opinion in world affairs. Japan has probably ventured beyond her depth, and a worldwide expression of horror and indignation, reinforced by boycotts and eventually by trade sanctions, might save the world from unimaginable dangers in Asia. This Chinese business is the gravest that has happened since the Great War. In comparison our European squabbles are petty family affairs. And world opinion should be mobilized in protest. The heroic resistance of the Chinese would thus be heartened and stiffened, and the turning of China into a bloody shambles and chaos might yet be prevented.

At the same time Great Britain should discuss the world position frankly and boldly with Germany, and explore with her a new peace on a basis of understanding and acceptance. I believe Germany's prospects are so bad, and her internal conditions so rickety, that she might turn a willing ear to such overtures for a fresh settlement and a fresh start.

I note what you say about Japanese trade and shall pass on the hint to my financial colleague. My love to you ever, dear Arthur,

Jan

---

[1] Following piratical attacks upon neutral and Spanish government ships in the Mediterranean, apparently by Italian submarines, a conference of the Mediterranean powers met at Nyon on 10 September 1937. Here arrangements were made for a patrol of the main routes, chiefly by the British and French fleets. On 30 September Italy, which had not attended at Nyon, was nevertheless made responsible for patrol duties in her neighbouring seas and the piratical attacks ceased.

423   To M. C. Gillett   **Vol. 55, no. 192**

Doornkloof
[Transvaal]
8 October 1937

Your Madeira letter duly arrived yesterday and was very welcome.
I note your readings, your companions on board etc. I am specially
glad that Hilda [Clark] has recovered lost ground on the voyage...
I am not surprised that a rereading of good old Matthew shocks you
in part. Jesus was very human and Jesus was a Jew. I never forget
that article in the *Friend* about his Jewishness which gave such
offence. You judge him not by these blots, but by his insight and
grandeur, his vision of a new God-filled world, his determination to
fulfil his mission at whatever cost. He still remains the high light
of the race. Comparing him with the good and the great I have
known in my experience the wonder of him continues to grow on
me. 'The kingdom of God *within* you' —was ever a greater revelation vouchsafed to this poor erring race of man?[1] If we could today
recapture that vision how different this sad world would be. I do
believe in Jesus and in a humble way I love him—though not in the
manner of my childhood sixty years ago. The mystery of the world
has since come home to me, and what was simple and plain then is
today very profound and mysterious.

I have been reading this week several interesting things. Joseph's
book of essays, mostly on Plato's *Republic*—college lectures at
Oxford.[2] Several interesting chapters in Seward's *Plant Life through
the Ages*.[3] Laird's *Recent Philosophy*,[4] which is not so good as I had
hoped. As I have no time to read the many works that appear,
I should like to read intelligible summarized accounts which could
show what is being done on what subjects. But Laird is far from
clear or illuminating. I have so little time left after doing my official
and political work that I must be careful in what I read. And the
tendency is to go back to the old books and writers. Thank you very
much for the new reading-light at Tsalta. It will be a great comfort,
for the old light swung above my head was a bit trying and only had
the good point of sooner making me close my eyes and going to
sleep!

I am glad you liked the spirit of Tsalta. It is a good place and has
given me great joy. I was so deeply sorry that my arrangements—

---

[1] 'The kingdom of God is within you.' *St Luke* xvii.21.
[2] H. W. B. Joseph, *Essays in Ancient and Modern Philosophy* (1935).
[3] A. C. Seward, *Plant Life through the Ages* (1931).
[4] J. Laird, *Recent Philosophy* (1935).

made in advance—prevented my being with you there this time. How good it would have been for us to have climbed the mountain together, and to have visited the places you now did not see. To me Table mountain is not just stocks and stones and things[1] but a deep living experience, wherein spirit holds converse with spirit, and time and space form no barriers but fresh means of contact. We enter through these visible means into the invisible world within them. *Alles Vergängliche ist nur ein Gleichnis.*[2]

...Last Monday I went to Rusthof[3] (General Botha's old home) to attend a memorial service and to make the inevitable speech. I was there last year also. Three hundred miles of motoring is no fun, but I am glad that I could do this small service to the memory of my friend. He is being forgotten in the rush of our day. But his work will live and his memory should be cherished. I do so most sincerely. Monday begins a very busy and trying week for me. I shall then lay a foundation stone at the Pretoria University,[4] and thereafter take train to the Cape where a long series of meetings awaits me for the rest of the week. I hope to be back here on Sunday or Monday, the 18th. You have no idea how tiring these long railway and motor journeys can be, with interminable meetings and tiresome functions sandwiched in at half a dozen different centres. On my return it takes me a full week to shake off the physical exhaustion of such an effort. Years ago I could keep this sort of thing up for weeks at a time, but age tells. And what troubles me is the thought that perhaps I am merely wasting time and strength, and that for the short spell still left me I could have done better and more useful work. I cannot make up my mind what my duty is. If I leave this show it may collapse, with far-reaching results. But the sands are running out elsewhere, and I seem to be selfishly sitting out while the call is there. I was so heartened yesterday to see Roosevelt's speech in which he appears to indicate that he will follow any lead that might save civilization from the new barbarism. Japan and Italy are as good as mentioned by name. The League has directly *named* Japan,[5] and a whole world approves. I still hope that some-

---

[1] *See* vol. IV, p. 60 note 1—a phrase in proverbial use among the Gilletts.

[2] All things transitory are but a symbol [of Love's diviner being]. Goethe, *Faust*, part II, act 5, Chorus mysticus.

[3] In the Standerton district, eastern Transvaal.

[4] Founded as the Transvaal University College in 1908; became an independent university 10 October 1930.

[5] Following an appeal by the Chinese government to the League of Nations in September 1937, a League committee reported that Japanese military operations in China were unjustified. The assembly adopted the report on 6 October together with a resolution asking members of the League to consider how they could individually assist China.

thing will come to stay this rot. If what is happening today does not galvanize the world into a sense of responsibility, I fear nothing will. If this happens to the green tree etc.[1] The Chinese are putting up a wonderful fight, and showing a spirit which may yet make them a menace to the world when Japan has thoroughly militarized them. Real sympathy now and a helping hand may create bonds between Europe and China which may save the future of our civilization...
My dear love to you all.

Jan

424   To T. W. Lamont   Vol. 55, no. 152

Palace of Justice
Pretoria
21 October 1937

My dear Tom, I owe you a letter for some time now. I find that I have a note from you on 8 September in regard to the invitation of the Medical Association, and another of 29 June in reference to the contemplated agreement between Great Britain and the U.S.A.[2] I find it of course impossible to accept the invitation of the Medical Association, as I am very much tied down at present to South Africa. Your previous letter remained unanswered because I saw nothing that could be usefully said or done in order to promote the cause which we both have at heart. Delay has not helped me to overcome my perplexities and I therefore write without waiting for further light.

As far as South Africa is concerned, we would most heartily welcome some accord in trade relations between the two great countries. We are most anxious to keep American good will. We know what your continued purchases of gold at thirty-five dollars per ounce means to us. Immense development is going forward in South Africa which is only possible by the continuance of American purchases of our principal product. Besides this strong argument from the point of view of South Africa, I personally look with you upon closer economic co-operation between the two great countries as possibly the best prospect we have at present for world security and peace in future. We in South Africa heartily approve of the policy, and the British government know that they have our strong support in whatever forward movement they may make in this

---

[1] 'For if they do these things in a green tree, what shall be done in the dry?' *St Luke* xxiii.31.

[2] Neither letter is in the Smuts Collection.

direction. As you know, the difficulty has rather been in other directions, with British interests and interests of other Dominions. I still hope however that these will be overcome without too much delay and that the good atmosphere which exists at present will not be spoilt by postponement of a settlement.

I had hoped to have an opportunity of discussing these and cognate problems with British statesmen personally. You know how little you do by correspondence and how much you get by personal suasion and pressure. I know that British statesmen are overwhelmed with European troubles and that it may be most helpful for them to come into contact with those who see world events from a wider angle, and for this reason I had wished to go to London after the session of our parliament concluded in June. However the absence of the prime minister and some other of my colleagues at the imperial conference and the necessity for me to remain at the helm in South Africa, made it impossible to leave the country, and even yet I see no prospect of getting into personal contact with the British leaders. This I deeply regret but I cannot help myself. My first duty is here, however deeply I may feel the importance of what is happening abroad. Perhaps in the not distant future some opportunity may occur for me to get to grips with our friends in London, and to endeavour to push some of the causes which I have at heart.

The atmosphere for better economic and other relations between the U.S.A. and Great Britain is very good at present, and I should think that this is the psychological moment for a move forward. Roosevelt's Chicago speech[1] has had and will continue to have a very good effect. Not that I expect that America will do anything spectacular, but the statement of her sympathies in the great controversy which is now dividing European civilization must have a very profound effect. What Roosevelt has in fact done is to warn the Fascist–Nazi powers that in the last resort American sympathies and affiliations will be with the democratic powers. I am sure that such a declaration must have a greatly stabilizing effect and must be a beneficial contribution to world peace. The British people in their world-wide anxieties at the present moment must be heartened to have heard that friendly voice. And I am sure that all over the world the brave words of Roosevelt have put fresh heart into people of good will.

While I am writing this, the European situation seems to be in a very bad way, but matters are in such a state of flux from day to day that it is useless to refer to them.

[1] For the gist of this speech on 5 October 1937 *see* J. M. Burns, *Roosevelt, the Lion and the Fox* (1956), p. 318.

At Doornkloof we are all getting along very well. You and Florence are a constant topic of conversation. We never visit a good place without thinking and talking of you, and we still cherish the hope that you will not look upon yourself as always quite indispensable to J. P. Morgan and Company, but will feel free to come and visit us and see some of the glorious places that we could not show you on your last very short trip. We are all getting older and when we are dead we shall not see the good things of this earth any more. Let us therefore make the best use of the little opportunity that is still left us.

Isie joins with me in sending love to you and Florence and our best wishes to the rest of the Lamont family. Ever yours sincerely,

J. C. Smuts

425 To M. C. Gillett

Vol. 55, no. 195

Doornkloof
[Transvaal]
23 October 1937

...Things have *apparently* taken a turn for the better in Europe. I say apparently because I don't feel convinced of the sincerity of the Italians. They may have given way on the question of the return of the volunteers,[1] either because they mean to spin that business out as long as possible, or because with the fall of Gijon they may consider Franco's victory is assured, and there is no call for further assistance on their part. Time will show whether the gesture was or was not genuine. Hitler and Mussolini have however to keep up the aggressive [*sic*], and now that tension is relaxed as regards Spain I ask myself what new trouble is in sight. Is it now to be colonies or Czechoslovakia? I do not think that we are going to have peace in the diplomatic world. I am all for considering the colonial question as part of a general settlement, but not as a separate issue. But it may be that this colonial issue is raised only to cover more dangerous moves in central Europe.

Here locally things are settling down. We have won the Klerksdorp election very easily and well.[2] The cabinet is settling down to its work, and Native troubles are also easing off. The whites are scared of Communism spreading among the Natives and look upon the Vereeniging incident as largely the effect of communist propaganda among the Natives. There is, however, nothing in this view, and the

[1] *See supra*, p. 61, note 7.
[2] J. J. N. Wilkins (United party) 2,449 votes; J. S. Smit (National party) 1,977 votes.

commission of inquiry[1] will report in that sense next week. I have been able to do a lot of good work during the four months that I have acted as minister of native affairs, and a number of necessary advances have been made—in health, lands, councils, improvement of reserves etc. etc. I could have wished to remain at this job for a few months longer, but my colleague Grobler [P. G. W.] will be back at his post next week. I have authorized municipal beer brewing at all the principal Rand centres, and I hope this step will prove beneficial, as the Natives will now be able to get clean good stuff cheaply, instead of buying expensive vile poisons. The temperance and some church people are opposed to my move, but public opinion on the whole is favourable, and I consider the experiment well worth trying. The Native must have some consolation, and beer has always been good company to him. At present it is no more than an experiment, and nothing could in any case be so bad as the highly doctored *skokiaan*[2] he now drinks.

You seem to be pretty active in your own sphere, and need not complain of retreating from politics. After all there is not much in politics at present to attract one. The government is very much at sea, the opposition is feeble beyond words. The world's tragedy is being enacted in China—and in that connection the League's downright resolution and the calling together of the Pacific conference[3] were the only immediate steps to take. I see no chance of sanctions in this case, and the unofficial boycotts now being organized by Labour and others are perhaps the only pressure to be applied. But how badly Russia comes out of this business! If ever she should have shown her teeth this is the occasion when her support of China would have won her world favour. Stalin's purges seem to have paralysed poor Russia beyond measure, and she is now apparently incapable of any effort worthwhile. What is happening to the old Bolshevists is the severest commentary possible to the Communism which has been so much vaunted. I think there must be some widespread economic breakdown there, in addition to plots and the like. I am not sure that Fascism and Nazism have not more to show than Communism. And that is about the severest condemnation one could express of the system. China I believe is a pivotal event in history, and no one can foresee the consequences even for the West. Love,

Jan

[1] Its report, entitled 'Vereeniging Location Riots' and listed as An. 53 of 1938, was apparently not published. *See also supra*, p. 92, note 1.

[2] *See supra*, p. 92, note 2.

[3] This ineffective conference took place in Brussels in November 1937. Japan did not attend.

426   To S. G. Millin   Vol. 102, no. 76

Pretoria
[Transvaal]
12 November 1937

Dear Sarah, Sorry to give you so much worry. I quite understand
and appreciate your comment on what I wrote. I was simply afraid
of what Blackwell might say as a result of your marginal note. We
quite understand each other.[1]

Frankly I don't like the look of things. The Axis has become
a triangle, as Hitler says,[2] and British policy becomes more difficult
than ever. If there had been wisdom in the handling of Germany
a few years ago all this would have been avoided. Now it is getting
very near to 'too late'.

South West Africa will *not* go to Germany. The thing does not
worry me. The consequences not only for South Africa but for the
British Empire would be too grave. So let that rest. This bit of
desert will not upset the apple-cart.

British statesmen have now to atone for grievous mistakes of the
past and although I don't approve of their methods I find it difficult
to condemn in view of the very grave world situation developing.

I am glad to see you still turn to the Bible in your troubles. Yours
ever,

J. C. Smuts

[1] Leslie Blackwell had submitted his book *African Occasions* to S. G. Millin and to
Smuts, who wrote the foreword. S. G. Millin had commented that Smuts agreed to
serve under Hertzog in 1933 to prevent bitterness among the Nationalists. Smuts had
commented that this was not the reason. When S. G. Millin asked him for an explanation he wrote to her: 'I objected to your note that I went into coalition because of the
"disturbance" which the Nats would cause if they were driven from power. This
might imply that I acted from fear, more than from the higher motives of bringing
peace and co-operation to our politics. This would have been misleading and, if
Blackwell had followed your suggestion, seriously prejudicial and damaging. Hence
my note of dissent. I did *not* act from fear, but from quite other motives, as you of
course quite understand.' (*See* Smuts Collection, vol. 55, no. 111; vol. 102, no. 75.)

[2] On 6 November 1937 Italy joined the Anti-Comintern Pact concluded a year
earlier between Germany and Japan and so converted the 'Berlin–Rome axis' into
a 'Berlin–Rome–Tokio triangle'. *See also infra*, p. 102, note 4.

427   From L. S. Amery   Vol. 55, no. 7

112 Eaton Square
S.W.1
22 November 1937

My dear Smuts, Hitler has not waited for Halifax even to leave Germany[1] before announcing that he means to shout for 'his' colonies till he gets them and that with a strong army behind him his voice will have to be listened to! I cannot see how anything can be done with Germany at the present moment, and in her present mood. If we could square Italy and bring things back to the Stresa position,[2] France could, I think, be persuaded to ease off on the Soviet Pact[3] and we could then offer Germany an outlet in that direction. At this moment we cannot do so without breaking with France and being left entirely friendless.

The question is whether it may not be too late to win back Mussolini.[4] We could have done it any time in the last year by recognizing the conquest of Abyssinia. But just now I hear he is in a very truculent mood and is piling up troops in Libya with the avowed idea of attacking Egypt and Palestine if the favourable moment should arrive. I don't know what help you or Australia or India could send in such an emergency, but it certainly would not be easy for us to get troops through the Mediterranean, at any rate in the first few weeks, if then.

I am still convinced that we made a profound mistake when we abandoned the conception of the League as a round table of the nations in 1935 and drifted into the idea that it could be used as an effective instrument of coercion over Abyssinia.

I think we are making a further mistake in imagining that a trade treaty with the United States, arrived at at the expense of Empire preference, will bring them in on our side in the event of a possible life and death struggle. Their action in such an eventuality will depend on many factors, but least of all on an agreement which will be as unpopular with the protectionist majority of American opinion as it succeeds in pleasing Cordell Hull. Meanwhile I should not be surprised if the attempt to interpret the treaty as calculated to bring America into our political orbit may not seriously injure its prospects with American public opinion.

---

[1] A meeting between Hitler and Halifax, then lord president of the council, took place at Berchtesgaden on 19 November 1937.

[2] *See supra,* p. 41, note 5.   [3] *See supra,* p. 34, note 3.

[4] The 'Berlin–Rome Axis' an agreement for close collaboration between Germany and Italy, was made public in November 1936 but had virtually existed since June when the relations of the two powers to Austria were settled to the satisfaction of Italy. *See also supra,* p. 101, note 2.

The trouble of the whole business is that both we here and the Dominions are being asked to give up definitely sheltered positions for possible reductions on a very high American tariff which will then also be available to the rest of the world and therefore may do us very little good. The whole situation would be different if one could get rid of the most favoured nation clause[1] and give to the United States second preference in the Empire over foreign goods, while the Empire received a definite preference over foreign goods in the American market. That would be a real practical move towards Commonwealth–American unity which naturally is an object aimed at by all of us. The present treaty, to my mind, is only likely to be a set-back to Commonwealth unity without having any real effect on our relations with America.

The most favoured nation clause indeed is the greatest obstacle to any progress in the world today. But for it, it would be possible for Germany and the Danubian countries on the one hand, Germany, Holland and Belgium and their colonies on the other, to enter into mutual preferential arrangements which might eventually cover the whole of continental Europe and its colonies and so provide an effective economic counterpart to the British Empire or to the United States. It would also provide a solvent to political problems and help to pave the way towards a European Commonwealth.

I am still much exercised in my mind about the protectorates question. Remember that you have to deal here with a combination of two elements, all the sentimentalists of the Left who mistrust the Union's Native policy on the one hand, and on the other hand the old Conservative imperialist who dislikes handing over any territory. Added to that there are pledges in parliament which ministers cannot well get out of. All this makes it the more essential to my mind that the question should be broken up and dealt with in respect of one territory, obviously Swaziland, first of all. The conditions are more favourable there and the experience of transfer would be a very strong argument both with the Natives in the other Protectorates and over here.

One real difficulty here is the complete inability to distinguish between Union Native administration in white areas and the kind of administration that would be set up or rather would be continued in the Protectorates. Nobody here knows anything about the Transkei or Ovamboland,[2] and I rather doubt whether even the

---

[1] Trade treaties have often included such a clause by which each signatory agrees to extend to the other any commercial favour, such as tariff reduction, that might be granted to any third country. It thus excludes preferences for any particular country.

[2] A territory in the north of South West Africa.

Protectorate Natives know much about them and are not convinced that transfer means absorption into the general Native policy of the Union. Wouldn't it be possible for you to do rather more propaganda than you have done on those points, both here and in the Protectorates and more particularly in Swaziland? Has it ever occurred to you, for instance, to invite a British parliamentary delegation to visit the Transkei? Or to ask a delegation of Swazi chiefs to do the same?

We have got a very difficult corner to get round and it will want a lot of skilful co-operation on both sides to turn it. Yours ever,

L. S. Amery

428   To M. C. Gillett   Vol. 55, no. 203

Irene
[Transvaal]
30 November 1937

This is Tuesday. Tomorrow Isie and I leave for the Bloemfontein congress of our party and from there I proceed to hold a meeting for Hertzog at Smithfield, so that I shall not be back at home till Sunday night at earliest. This is the reason for writing by an earlier mail.

I had three most welcome letters last mail and they show what a pleasure letters give in our otherwise drab world. The most welcome was of course from you... Then I had a very interesting letter from Florence Lamont who writes from their country home and from the midst of children and grandchildren rollicking round her. She is a capital letter-writer, being very much alive and making the most of even small happenings. Letters should not be leading articles, as I fear mine often are, but should catch the bloom on small personal domestic events as they pass. It is the personal that matters most to us, and in our intercourse and our correspondence we indulge the personal. In our interest in the larger and wider aspects of events we too often forget that truth and value reside in the particular and the personal. That is what is so valuable in the Gospels, that the emphasis is on the details. Science, philosophy and politics deal with the abstract or the general, with what concerns the world, the nation, the mass. But at the centre of them all stands the individual, the friend, the child or grandchild, and all the other dear relationships of life. (However here I am once more going off at a tangent into my leading article!) Florence is much preoccupied with what is happening in America. Roosevelt's Chicago speech, which I considered very good and opportune, even if he did not mean much by it.[1] But the U.S.A. has to be told that isolation is no gospel and no salvation, even for herself, let alone for the world. But Roosevelt has a curious habit of blundering into side issues which paralyse his larger more beneficent aim. In this he resembles Lloyd George whose intentions and sympathies were generally sound but who had no deep anchorage in principles and therefore continually got off the rails. Roosevelt's adventure against the supreme court and especially his appointment of that Ku Klux Klan Black[2] is one of the maddest escapades I have ever come across. I doubt whether he will ever really recover from the shock. It is a dreadful thing for a man in his position to outrage the sense of decency in ordinary decent people. He must have funny advisers. Florence says it is the dead albatross which he has hung round his neck.[3] He has such an immense position and power for good that one grieves over such disabling blunders.

While I am writing the conference between the British and French governments is going on in London. I think it is a good thing they are meeting. It was a good move to send Halifax to Hitler.[4] Halifax has on the whole the right human outlook, and is not a hard-boiled imperialist like so many of his colleagues. We have missed a thousand opportunities, and as a result Germany is once more going her way—the way of power politics, of relying on force and carrying things with a high hand. It is perhaps just possible (only *just*) to influence a mystic like Hitler before it is too late, and to make him realize that there *is* good will in the world, and a genuine desire to explore and find a better way. I don't know whether Halifax has succeeded. But contact can only be to the good. And it is good for the French to learn our points of view. They are dominated by the fatal fear complex, far more than the English are. They have now not only Germany but Italy as a potential danger, and their whole north African Empire, and therefore their European

---

[1] *See supra*, p. 98, note 1.

[2] The supreme court of the United States had invalidated several acts of congress by which Roosevelt sought to implement his 'New Deal' policies. Roosevelt then tried to change the composition of the court by securing legislation for the compulsory retirement of its members. In August 1937, when he was able to make his first appointment to the supreme court, Roosevelt chose Hugo L. Black (q.v.) apparently not knowing that Black had been a member of the Ku Klux Klan, a secret society founded in 1915, which pursued its anti-Negro, anti-Catholic, anti-Semitic aims by methods which were often illegal and terrorist.

[3]
> Ah! well-a-day! what evil looks
> Had I from old and young!
> Instead of the cross, the Albatross
> About my neck was hung.
>
> S. T. Coleridge, *The Rime of the Ancient Mariner*, part II.

[4] *See supra*, p. 102, note 1.

defence system, are menaced. They have had a baleful influence on British policy which has been far too complacent to their fear obsession, and now both are in the danger that has resulted from these mistakes of past policy. I hope a heart-to-heart talk will do both good. I am not much impressed with our British statesmen as you know. But there is no doubt that their difficulties are enormous and are increasing. And after all England and France are today the democratic front in the world, and one's deepest sympathy goes out to them in the difficult part they have to play. Japan is more and more revealing herself as far more Prussian than the Prussians and as the greatest potential danger to the British Commonwealth and the world in general. What is wanted today is a concert of western civilization (including Russia) to call a halt to aggressive Japan. Japan is making use of European disharmony in order to sabotage the civilization which Europe has built up. Now Germany and Italy are in practical alliance with her, and the world position has become unspeakably serious. I hope these broader aspects of the world situation and the necessity for European *rapprochement* are well to the fore in the minds of our leaders in London.

On my return from Smithfield I open next Monday the first meeting of the Natives' representative council, the elected Native Union-wide body which will in future advise government and parliament on all major Native questions. I am to open it because Hertzog has had his teeth extracted and cannot speak in public, and the minister (Grobler) does not feel equal to the occasion. This council is, as you know, a very important departure. If it proves a success it may well open a new era in our racial relations. But of course these relationships are difficult and becoming more so. And one is not unduly optimistic about the success of the new venture. Still we can but do our best.

It has rained a little here but the real rains have not yet come and the country is thirsty, very thirsty. It is a sad state of affairs. With dear love,

Jan

429   From L. S. Amery   Vol. 55, no. 8

112 Eaton Square
S.W.1
2 December 1937

My dear Smuts, The outcome of the Halifax visit has been, as I foresaw, closer consultation with France and a decision which is hardly likely to lead to a settlement. We have persuaded the French to agree to some measure of concession in the colonial sphere, but it is coupled—and in my opinion rightly—with the proviso that this is not to be an isolated concession but to be dependent upon a general European settlement. As there is no general European settlement to which France and Germany are likely to agree that will probably leave us in a state of deadlock a few months hence. As I said to you in my last letter we cannot really approach Germany with any hope of success unless Russia can somehow be eliminated, and France will not agree to that now, though I think she might be persuaded to do so after Italy has been won over. Whether that is still possible is now a doubtful question.

Failing that we may have to sit down and face frankly the division of the world into two hostile camps and hope that the German–Italian–Japanese camp[1] will be restrained in its aggressive tendencies by the strength of the other side, by exhaustion over China and Abyssinia, and by internal economic and political difficulties.

In any case I do hope your government will stand firm on the question of Tanganyika which is vital to the whole security of Africa and of the Indian ocean. If there is to be any colonial concession it should be over the Cameroons, possibly enlarged by a little piece of Nigeria or of the Belgian Congo, and at the other end of the world in the New Hebrides and Solomon Islands. Yours ever,

L. S. Amery

430   To M. C. Gillett   Vol. 55, no. 204

Doornkloof
[Transvaal]
6 December 1937

This (Monday) morning I opened our new Natives' representative council—the elected Native body which is in future to advise government and parliament on all important matters of Native policy. I have always attached much importance to this body and now that it has been established I was glad to have the opportunity to open and address it. The prime minister, owing to teeth trouble, could not [attend, and so I could take his place. The body contains all the most prominent Native leaders[2] except David

[1] See supra, p. 101, note 2.

[2] The first Natives' representative council consisted of eleven elected members as follows: R. V. Selope Thema, A. M. Jabavu, B. B. Xiniwe, R. H. Godlo, Thomas Mapikela, Charles K. Sakwe, R. G. Baloyi, Rev. Dr John L. Dube, W. W. Ndhlovu,

Jabavu[1] who would or could not stand (his brother[2] is a member) but practically all the others of note are represented—big chiefs, educated plebeians, journalists, and even capitalists—like Baloyi who owns a big bus and cab service at Johannesburg. So, like Galileo's earth, the world is still moving, and I hope this movement will mean sound and wholesome progress.

Many of the new Native senators (like Welsh [W. T.] and Malcomess [C. H.] and Brookes [E. H.]) and M.P.s (like Mrs [M.] Ballinger and Rheinallt Jones and Hemming [G. K.] etc.) were present,[3] and Mrs Ballinger and I had a pleasant talk over matters, in which she referred to you and Arthur. When I look at the number of good people, both European and Native, whom our new Native act has brought into the parliamentary arena, I think we have on the whole not done so badly. Some of the M.P.s most friendly to the Natives tell me that the latter appear more and more satisfied with the new changes, which at first they resisted strongly as an invasion of old 'Cape' rights. They now begin to recognize that the new substance means more to them than the old pretentious forms which were but a hollow shell. Mrs Ballinger looked well and important.

I returned home from the Free State yesterday (Sunday) morning. The congress of our party lasted from Thursday to Friday, and Saturday I spent at Smithfield to hold a meeting which Hertzog had been unable to hold himself. I spent a pleasant and useful day there. I found Tante Alie[4] still there. Seventeen years ago, when I was last at Smithfield as prime minister, the dear old soul (who was a devoted, indeed fanatical, follower of Hertzog) openly bewailed the fact that my soiled feet should tread that holy ground![5] We were all much amused at this outburst then; but no less was our amusement now to find that she was still going strong, and now as a fanatical adherent of Dr Malan! The more we change, the more we remain the same! There was much kindness in my reception (this time!) which of course was deeply appreciated. But Smithfield remains

Elijah Quamata, Chief Jeremiah Moshesh and four nominated members as follows: Mshiyeni ka Dinizulu, George Makapan, Chief S. M. Mankuroane, Chief Victor Poto.

[1] This was Davidson Don Tengo Jabavu (q.v.).

[2] A. M. Jabavu was the editor of *Imvo*.

[3] The first elections under the Representation of Natives Act, No. 12 of 1936 (*see supra*, p. 18, note 3) were held in June 1937. The four white senators returned were E. H. Brookes, W. T. Welsh, J. D. Rheinallt Jones and C. H. Malcomess. The three white members of the house of assembly returned were Mrs M. Ballinger, D. B. Molteno and G. K. Hemming.

[4] Tant Alie van Transvaal was the pseudonym of A. M. Badenhorst. Her *Diary* (1880–1902), written in Dutch, was translated into English by E. Hobhouse (1923) and into Afrikaans by M. E. Rothmann (1939).

[5] Smithfield in the southern Orange Free State was Hertzog's constituency.

a sad little village, with nothing to attract. The magistrate's wife made a piteous appeal to me to transfer them from that deadly monotony, where strong party politics was the only variation on the uniform dullness. They had spent four years at Pilgrim's Rest[1] before going to Smithfield, and she kept singing the praises of this place. I must admit that Smithfield is poor indeed compared to the incomparable eastern Drakensberg of the Transvaal. I could provoke her still further by talking of the glories of Mariepskop, the upper Selati, and the haunts of birds and flowers where we camped in 'Far Away and Quite Forget'. Oh the unspeakable dullness of life in these small villages on the veld, where there is not even hard work in the households to keep people sound and sweet. It says much for the good Dutch stock that it has not utterly deteriorated under these deadening surroundings.

Isie accompanied me to Bloemfontein but not to Smithfield, which would have been too much for her. She is once more getting deeply drawn into politics and has been elected to the head committee of the party both in the Transvaal and the Union. I feel sorry for her, as I think she has faithfully done her bit and should not carry on these heavy drudgeries in old age. I could so wish to slip out of it all, if only a suitable opportunity would offer itself. I saw in this morning's paper that Gandhi was retiring from politics and going to live among the wild fakir-ridden tribesmen of the north-west where, like the Boers of old, they are still fighting the British army. Is there no far away north-west for me as an honourable escape from politics?

No dear, I don't agree with you about Halifax. He is really a good man, instinctively good, and I am sure his goodness must have made a strong appeal to Hitler and so have helped to break the present spell in Europe. He was minister of education in very hard times,[2] and you must not judge a minister by his retrenchments under such circumstances. I shall never forget my talks with Halifax at the Indian conference in 1931 (was it?) when I formed a decided opinion in his favour. He probably was the best man to exchange ideas with Hitler. Of course I admit that he is probably more pacific and more honestly well-meaning than many of his colleagues. But surely that is good diplomacy to send a pacific man on a mission of peace! I think Chamberlain and the rest are scared by the Japanese menace in Asia, and perhaps the Germans are nervous about the carryings on of Mussolini and the dangers they are exposing themselves to as Mussolini's friend. So peace may have a chance, and some understanding between England and Germany

[1] In the eastern Transvaal.   [2] In Bonar Law's cabinet, October 1922–May 1923.

may yet come. The Lord has used worse instruments than Halifax before now!

...Something that Jan wrote me in his letter has sent me back to genetics, and in my few brief intervals of leisure I have been polishing up my small store of genetics. Hurst (*Mechanism of Evolution*)[1] is being read with much interest. There is nothing more mysterious than the cell nucleus with it stock of chromosomes and genes, which seem to hold the secret of life and mind. The Lord has certainly put the biggest things into the smallest, and it is these minimal things we have to study in our pursuit of the big things. And through it all the mystery deepens. And the greatest of all is love.[2] Ever yours,

Jan

431   To L. S. Amery   Vol. 55, no. 155

Palace of Justice
Pretoria
9 December 1937

My dear Amery, Thank you very much for your long and interesting letter of 22 November. I always find your letters very informative and interesting, and they are correspondingly welcome to me.

I am inclined to think that the British government did right in approaching Hitler in the first instance rather than Mussolini. Hitler is personally friendly towards the British Empire and has repeatedly declared himself for a *rapprochement* with us. Publicly and privately he has expressed his view that the cardinal mistake of imperial Germany was to menace the British Empire and he is not going to repeat that mistake. With Mussolini the position is just the opposite. He is unfriendly, he is mischievous, he has done his best to humiliate the British government successfully for the last four years, and his menace to our Empire communications and to those of France across the Mediterranean is probably the most serious danger that we have to face at the moment. The Mediterranean is taking the place of the North sea and is the prospective scene of vital trouble for us. On these grounds I think the approach in the first instance to Hitler was probably quite right. There is this to be said in addition, that if an understanding with Hitler is possible, Mussolini could not stand out, and the same cannot be said for the reverse situation.

[1] C. C. Hurst, *The Mechanism of Creative Evolution* (1933).
[2] 'And now abideth faith, hope, charity, these three; but the greatest of these is charity.' 1 *Corinthians* xiii.13.

I do not suppose that the Halifax talks have amounted to much, but still it is in every way desirable to bring the leaders together again and to make them discuss their various points of view. That is essential if our European system is to continue. Whilst the League was functioning properly, its council was a round table for the great powers, but as most of the great powers are absent now from that table, conversations have to take place in a different way. But it is clear that they are necessary in order to dissipate the atmosphere of suspicion which is now poisoning European relations. I myself am somewhat doubtful whether the German propaganda in favour of restoration of colonies should be taken very seriously. No doubt Hitler wants to save his face. He is a dictator who must constantly be able to deliver the goods. And in view of the widespread German propaganda for colonies to which Schacht has consistently lent his powerful support, Hitler is probably forced to do something and we may have to meet him a little way in order to save his face. I cannot believe that the Germans will make a point of it to get back South West Africa or Tanganyika. They know how keen we are to keep both and I do not think that they will attempt to force the pace as far as these territories are concerned. I may be wrong but that is my feeling.

The real policy of Germany appears to be economic expansion in central and eastern Europe. That is the doctrine of Hitler's book, and there are only too many indications to show that that is the real objective of German foreign policy. How far we should be prepared to fall in line with or acquiesce in such a policy is naturally a most important matter in which there are many considerations both ways. I have inferred that your view is rather to give Germany an outlet to the east and in that way to divert her from the west and from her colonial ambitions. I find it very difficult to come to any balanced conclusions on this matter. My main view is to take all steps to prevent forced measures which might easily precipitate a general war and rather to gain time and let the situation develop normally and let the natural forces which govern the European situation find their way to the future. The disappearance of the Austro-Hungarian Empire, and the precarious situation in which some of its remnants have been left have given Germany a very great opportunity for aggrandizement. How the situation will really develop, nobody can see; I think the chances are in favour of Germany. But whatever the evolution of the future may be, we should take every precaution that it develops peacefully, and that Germany is kept in check and prevented from embarking on policies that must inevitably lead to a general war. Our game is to play for time and for peaceful developments, and I think that if we are on good terms with the German government, we are more likely to succeed in this policy and in maintaining the peace of Europe, than we would be by dealing with her at arm's length.

Looking still further into the future, I see only one way for us to go, and that is in as close association with the United States as possible. We must get to the point ultimately where the United States would look upon the British Empire as in a very special sense her own concern. The position of Great Britain in the New Europe is becoming more and more precarious. The British Empire as a whole is a difficult problem from the defence point of view as you know. And it would be a wise precaution for our future to prepare the way for closer co-operation with the United States. The only way in which that could be done for the present is by improving economic relations. And that is why I wholeheartedly welcome the efforts now being made for a trade treaty with the United States. I appreciate the force of your arguments, and I know that the Americans have been very tiresome with their high tariff policy. But I do think it should be possible, without departing from imperial preference, to make such concessions to America on that and other matters, and with the consent of the Dominions, as to leave our vital interests intact and yet to secure American good will. A real gesture is becoming necessary, and that gesture should be economic, and indeed can only be economic with the present feeling in America. The present moment seems to me opportune. Everyone from America tells me that Roosevelt is really at heart pro-British, and his Chicago speech was a declaration of faith such as no American leader has ever made yet. I think the opportunity should not be missed for us to make it possible for him and for the United States to draw closer to us. The future is too full of dangers for us to miss this chance.

The main difficulty no doubt will be with Australia and New Zealand whose agriculture is so dependent on the British market. But these two Dominions are in such a weak position from a defence point of view, especially with the new dangers arising in Asia, that they must surely realize that some concession must be made to secure American good will and support in the future. Nobody knows what may happen in the next thirty or fifty years, but looking at the situation as it is developing now in Asia, I would, if I were an Australian, go a long way to meet the economic wishes of America now.

The most important development in the world today is the victory of Japan over China, and the most amazing thing is the paralysis of Russia who does not or cannot move a finger to stop the march of

Japan on the Asiatic continent. If anybody had told me years ago that Russia would or could stay still whilst Japan was securing the mastery of China, I would have believed it impossible. I find it very difficult to understand that complex situation. But whatever it means, the ultimate effect must be to make the British position in Asia and in the Far East far more precarious than it has been. Italy and Germany, by giving friendly countenance to Japan in her present adventure, may be sabotaging the West far more seriously than they imagine. It almost looks like a betrayal of Europe, and the effects of the betrayal no one can foresee today. We have made mistakes and France has blundered in the post-war period, but I do not see why Europe should be punished, and the position imperilled by the present attitude of Germany and Italy in the Far East. Perhaps I am talking foolishly, but that is how my mind works at the present moment.

To come now to the smaller matter, I agree with much of what you say about the territories. It is probably the path of least resistance to begin with Swaziland where there is everything to be said for immediate action. The prime minister and MacDonald have been corresponding with each other over the whole question, and I am hopeful that progress will be made and that a solution will be found. There is no doubt that something must be done. South Africa must not get the impression that she is considered in Great Britain to be unfit or unable to govern these Native territories. Such an impression will poison all our future relations and lead to desperate remedies. Relations between us and Great Britain are very good, but there is this small fly in the ointment, and the sooner it is got rid of the better. As a wholehearted supporter of what is called the British connection, I take a very grave view of this matter, which, however trifling in itself, may yet become an occasion and the cause of very far-reaching misunderstandings. If I were a British statesman, I would bend all my energies to remedy it as soon as possible. I hope you will continue your very powerful influence with the Dominions office to make them realize that this apparently small issue may very soon become one of first-class importance.

I am sorry to have inflicted this long letter on you. But then it is an answer to another long letter which I found very good. Let me conclude with wishing you and Mrs Amery a very happy New Year, success for the causes we have at heart and a way out of our present troubles for the poor old world. Yours ever sincerely,

s. J. C. Smuts

432   To M. C. Gillett

Vol. 57, no. 218

Tsalta
[Cape Town]
25 February 1938

I had pleasant letters from both you and Arthur...

Meanwhile serious things have happened in London. I don't know whether it was to you or to some other correspondent that I wrote last week that I had a foreboding of trouble between Chamberlain and Eden, and I had this simply from the general trend of affairs. And the ink was barely dry on what I wrote when the news came that Eden had gone.[1] It is a great blow, perhaps greatest to the government. Old man Baldwin had a wonderful appeal to the liberal, idealistic public to whom Eden also appealed. Chamberlain has ruthlessly shattered this dream and the government will in future lose the support of that large nebulous section of the public. But, apart from the party aspect, there is probably grave loss in this surrender to Mussolini, who would probably have failed in the inevitable course of events but will now exact a heavy price from the British government even if an agreement were come to. Of course Chamberlain may be moved by fear that Mussolini in his desperation would start a war in which Germany would back him up, and might therefore become a general conflagration. I don't however think that Germany would have gone that length, and the risk of war was even less than in the sanctions period. It is this impression of continual climb down and retreat before the dictators which is so disheartening. Time will show, but I fear this is even a worse action than the surrender of Hoare before Laval[2] and the paralysing blow struck at the League at that time. Once more the dictators have won, and the ranks of liberty are dismayed right over the world. I have no great opinion of Chamberlain and I fear he will be manoeuvred by cleverer men into a very damaging position. These are sad times.

Here we have had a regular storm—and not in the political tea-cup. It came about thus. At the opening of parliament the 'Stem van Suid-Afrika' was played along with 'God Save the King' as a concession to Afrikaner sentiment. That was quite right and generally accepted. Some mischievous member[3] then asked Hertzog in the house whether that meant that 'Die Stem' had now become a national anthem. The simple answer was no, but Hertzog, who

[1] Eden resigned as foreign secretary on 20 February 1938 in opposition to Chamberlain's policy of continuing to negotiate with Mussolini in spite of the Italian failure to withdraw from Spain.

[2] *See supra*, p. 31, note 1.   [3] Colonel C. F. Stallard (q.v.).

can never give a simple answer, went into a long disquisition to prove that 'God Save the King' was not legally our anthem, and that it was a mere invocation to God, and that 'Die Stem' had much more of the character of a national anthem and might in time take the place as such of 'God Save the King'. All perfectly unnecessary, but of course thereafter the fat was in the fire. The English resent this heresy and are fuming with rage. I won't say this will cost us the general election but it will lose us tens of thousands of votes and immensely help the Dominion party in the voting. It is said that the gods dement those whom they wish to destroy,[1] but here they have thus afflicted even those whom, I presume, they wish to save. What can you do with such leadership? And the fun of the thing is that, as my mouth is shut, the English say I am letting them down and am just as bad, and suspicion turns from Hertzog to me. Of course I have to sit tight and save the work in national up-building for which I have been mainly responsible these five years. I could not possibly, because of Hertzog's *gaucherie*, destroy the United party and my own laborious and successful achievement. One can but fume with rage internally but to the world present a bold and cheerful front. But it is more than hard. The general election would have been the easiest thing for us. Now I shall have to fight hard, and in any case a secret and undeserved suspicion has attached itself to me, which is damaging to the party.

Our parliamentary work is progressing rapidly and I shall not be surprised if by the middle of March we shall be free to go home. I may have to stay on for some meetings now to restore our shattered position. The election may then take place on 18 May and the new parliament meet in July. We shall then go on till September. If therefore you arrive here at the beginning of August we shall have time for some glorious week-ends in the Cape spring and we shall be able to visit Cedarberg,[2] perhaps Vanrhynsdorp, as well as the other great places nearer the Cape...

I have been reading this week Karen Blixen's *Out of Africa*[3] with much enjoyment. She has the atmosphere and the inner sympathy. There is also some mystery about her which intrigues one all along in the reading. I am very glad to have the book even though it keeps me awake too late at night. I know the country she describes and, of course, a good deal of the conditions. I have heard her private story but have for the moment forgotten it.

[1] 'Whom God would destroy He first makes mad'—from the Latin version of one of the *Fragments* of Euripedes (*Quos Deus vult perdere prius dementat*).
[2] Mountain range about 150 miles north of Cape Town.
[3] Published in 1937.

I have also been reading *A Study in Plato*,[1] parts of which I have found good and helpful. I suppose Joachim has put you on its track. It is curious how Plato, in a quite different environment of thought, was wrestling with the same problems which agitate us today. He was a mathematician turned philosopher like Whitehead, and Whitehead has even adopted his strange 'forms' as pre-existent moulds of experience. The similarity of Plato to the latest philosophy shows how continuous the European tradition in thought has been, and, incidentally, how futile the break which the Nazis now want to effect with that perennial tradition. Forms and externals change, but the inner substance of thought and aspiration has remained very much the same. It is in philosophy as it is in religion. And in many ways we are nearer to Plato today than we are to the Gospels. Although I read Plato at college I never realized this so clearly as I do now with my wider intellectual experience. In that higher world all the ages meet as in some common home. Some great Personality was needed to give force and vitality to the world of thought. Socrates played that role for ancient philosophy, and Jesus has embodied the religious, spiritual ideals. I wonder how we shall do without some supreme personal embodiment of all that is best in our age. Religion and personality remain the heart of the business, for us no less than it was for that ancient world.

Rufus Jones landed yesterday but I have so far failed to track him down. I suppose he will now appear to look for me, and shall await his approaches. His wife is with him and I am anxious to meet them. Time is up. This is a poor letter I am afraid. Ever yours,

Jan

433   To F. Lamont

Vol. 57, no. 107

Cape Town

13 March 1938

My dear Florence, And so you and Tom are on the Mediterranean coast not so far from Africa. It almost makes me sigh to think of you so near and yet so far. And then Kant says that space is not real, that time and space are but spectacles of our experience. To me it is very real, when I think of you at the end of Africa and me at the other, and that it is spring with you and autumn with me. And everywhere over the world a sort of winter of the spirit. But let us not be downcast too much. 'If Winter comes, can Spring be far behind?' as Shelley asks.[2] Surely, surely, some springtide of the spirit will come to us yet.

[1] W. F. R. Hardie, *A Study in Plato* (1936).   [2] *Ode to the West Wind*, l. 57.

I have your last two letters before me—both undated. On the one I have put 'Autumn 1937', all crimson and gold. On the other 'Spring 1938'. Both lovely letters full of deep interest. During these months you and Tom have often been in my mind. I have read his Chicago and Franklin addresses, both with deep appreciation. Tom is really a brick, and I love to count such a man among my inner friendships. And as for Florence—so far from 'forgetting' her, the very thought of her brings vividness and vivacity to me in my dullest moments. No, you two dear ones are very dear to us and never far from our thoughts. With recession and oncoming depression in the States and Roosevelt fumbling about it and about[1] I can sympathize with Tom in his deep anxieties and his desire to get away to Ese, to the Sierras, to anywhere away from it all. Surely we have souls of our own and must have something of ourselves and our own lives. As for me, you know the haunts I retire to for refreshment. I wish I had you there once more with us. In the next few months I shall, however, have no opportunity to go there. This is the end of a short session of parliament, and in a couple of days we go back to the Transvaal for an election campaign which will take up all my time until 18 May when the elections for a new parliament will be held. Thereafter I shall seek refuge in the Bush and recover from my political wounds. A general election is a horrid time when human nature is seen at its worst, and I look forward with anything but pleasure to this ordeal. We shall win, but the struggle will be bitter and the physical and mental exertions called for very great.

But why talk of our petty troubles when one looks at the woes of the great world? Think of China, with its peaceful innocent millions being slaughtered or hungered to death. Think of that mass human suffering. It positively baffles the imagination. I cannot blame you for being in a boycott league.[2] There *must* be some emotional outlet, even if it is otherwise futile. The world today is truly a League of sorrows, and that is the alternative to a League of nations. Unable to hang together we are being hung separately as the saying goes.[3] And now Austria is being jack-booted into the German Reich.[4]

---

[1]   Myself when young did eagerly frequent
            Doctor and Saint, and heard great argument
            About it and about.
                    Edward Fitzgerald, *Omar Khayyám*, edition 1, xxvii.

[2] Florence Lamont had joined the consumers' boycott of Japanese goods. *See* Smuts Collection, vol. 56, no. 167.

[3] 'We must indeed all hang together, or, most assuredly, we shall hang separately.' Benjamin Franklin's remark to John Hancock at the signing of the Declaration of Independence, 4 July 1776.

[4] On 11 March 1938 Hitler demanded and obtained the postponement of a plebiscite on Austrian independence or *anschluss*. On the same day he forced the resignation of

Of course the thing has been inevitable ever since Austria was destroyed and left derelict at the end of the Great War. But the manner in which it is now being brought about! The Germans are once more calling up universal fear and loathing of their mentality and their methods. *Anschluss* would have come all right, but the Nazis seem to be lacking in all consideration for others and for the opinion of mankind. Of course I very much blame France and Great Britain for their lack of foresight and statesmanship in not agreeing in advance with Germany and in blocking a step which sooner or later was bound to come. Now it has come—in spite of them and their futile protests—in a way which is most harmful to the peace of the world. The dictators are on the march, and brigandage is the public law of the world. This sounds like a public speech. Please forgive me. There is Spain, with all the horrors of destroying an ancient culture on which South America also lives. There has been Abyssinia, now a corpse and a curse, as Winston Churchill has called it. There is the exhaustion of armaments, and there is coming depression. In the decay of the Roman Empire and the barbarian invasions many Christians retired to the deserts and the caves from the wrath to come. One sometimes feels the pull of this defeatist spirit in face of the troubles now overwhelming our world and our proud civilization. Oh to be an anchorite or a troglodyte! One has of course to fight this urge to flee from the wrath to come. We are soldiers of the spirit and must see the fight through. You remember Blake's brave lines: 'I shall not cease from mortal strife etc.'[1] Beyond all these wild surgings of our storm lies the New Jerusalem of the spirit which we have to help to build for the future. The League of Nations is in eclipse and collective security has for the time being collapsed. But that is not the end of the business. Let us have faith, and let us play our part. The wild experiments in human government now being tried out will pass. They will shatter on the rock of human personality which they seek to submerge and destroy. The human soul will win in the end. To me it is not Hitler but Pastor [M.] Niemöller who is the hero of the struggle now going on in Germany.

It is curious how we are once more back in the wars of religion.

Schuschnigg in favour of Seyss-Inquart and that night German troops crossed the frontier into Austria. Next day they occupied Vienna and on 13 March Austria became a *land* of the German Reich.

[1]   I will not cease from Mental Fight,
         Nor shall my Sword sleep in my hand,
         Till we have built Jerusalem
         In England's green and pleasant land.
                                        William Blake, *Milton*, preface.

The struggle of the new ideologies is fundamentally a vast religious war. Is human personality inviolate? Is the human soul divine and free? Has conscience to prevail at whatever cost? These are the fundamental issues once again being fought out in the world. And from this elemental struggle will issue the religion of the future. We shall get back to the old vital truths once more. But they will have a new form and be instinct with a new significance and meaning born of the great sacrifices and sufferings once more endured for their sake. Our fires have burnt low in the materialism of the nineteenth century. They must be rekindled. They are being rekindled by Hitler, Mussolini, Stalin, and whoever is their opposite number in Japan. You quoted Walt Whitman in your last letter. Let me quote another line from him: 'The soul for ever and ever'.[1] *There* is the great message, the eternal gospel. This world is Spirit. Men are souls. Truth is eternal and indestructible. Once this conviction has come home to us once more there will be a new dawn. We shall feel like being drunk with the joy of it. We shall ascend a new curve of high living, out of the present depths.

As I write this on a Sunday morning I hear the church bells in the distance. They bring to me a message, which words could not express, out of the far-off past of our struggling race. Could God forsake his children? Could the lights which have been kindled in our hearts really be quenched? These are the thoughts and the questions that come to me at this moment. And I feel that, though our path is still downward, in due course it will rise again, and that final defeat will not be our lot.

I do not know when I shall be able to come to England, and as for America, I am doubtful whether I shall ever again see that dear land of hope for our future. I continue a member of a government and see no present opportunity of release from it. Nor does Europe attract me in these days. If I were to say what is really on my mind I might do more harm than good. And then, have I the right to find fault with others? Have I not my own small share of responsibility for what is today happening? Why cast stones on others, perhaps really more innocent? As a result of past mistakes we see the current now flowing strongly against us, and for the moment there is no stemming it. You ask about persons. Eden was right in resigning. Chamberlain was right in making a last desperate move to come to terms with the dictators. But he may fail, as Eden was certain he would fail. Still the attempt had to be made, and one prays it may not yet be too late. But this Austrian business may prove a very serious set-back, and will justify Eden's fears. We are passing

---

[1] *See* vol. v, p. 511, note 2.

through an awfully dangerous period when war may break out in sheer confusion and misunderstanding. If this could be prevented now we may thereafter find our way to calmer waters. Even armaments may help to prevent desperate measures and warn off the aggressor. Our principal business should be to prevent war in the immediate or near future. I suppose Chamberlain feels this too, and does not like diplomatic finesse to stand in the way. But he who sups with the devil must have a long spoon. Is Chamberlain's spoon long enough? My love to you and Tom. Ever yours affectionately,

J. C. Smuts

434 From L. S. Amery

Vol. 56, no. 10

112 Eaton Square
S.W.1
18 March 1938

My dear Smuts, Things have been moving with terrible speed in the last few weeks. The swallowing up of Austria in defiance of every pledge given by Hitler in order to forestall a referendum which would have given Schuschnigg a seventy per cent majority,[1] is both a tragedy and a portent. The tragedy lies not so much in the annexation of a people against its will, for that will was not strong enough to be prepared to fight. It lies rather in the crushing of a conception of Austria's unifying mission in central Europe, and of her saving the true spirit of German and Christian humanism, which Dolfuss and Schuschnigg had preached and to which they had won the great majority of Austrians. Tragic too is the immediate brutality and terror of the new régime, the sudden merciless degradation and plunder of the unhappy Jews, the letting loose of political vendetta against old adversaries in every direction. I believe there has been wholesale murder of which we are not likely to hear anything and still less shall we hear anything of more sordid robbery and ill treatment. We have to have our restrictions on alien immigration. All the same it makes one's heart sink to think of an Austrian political refugee taking poison when told by the customs officials that he could not land.

As for the portent it is clear that both the spirit and method of German aggression will continue. The method, of course, is amazing. Within a few hours Germany had taken over not only military control but police control with the help of some 10,000 special police and had staffed every post of any importance in muni-

[1] *See supra*, p. 117, note 4.

cipal or government services with its own men, whether Austrian Nazis or officials imported from Germany. What is to happen if the same tactics are repeated in Czechoslovakia or even in Switzerland?

The government will have to make up its mind very quickly as to whether it is prepared to join France in guaranteeing Czechoslovakia[1] or else wash its hands of central Europe. If it likes to call the former policy an effective implementing of the covenant of the League it is fully entitled to do so, and might perhaps get more support under that cover from the Dominions and from a wide section of public opinion at home. But it must be on the basis that the principles of the League are defended by a small group of nations directly concerned and acting on their own without bringing the League as a whole into the picture. For the League as a whole and for universal purposes is dead. No one has even dreamed of convening it over Austria.

As to which of these two policies is right I am not yet completely clear in my own mind. On the whole I believe the policy of saying 'Halt' to Germany now is the one more likely to avert war. But I should greatly hesitate before committing myself to a policy disapproved of by the other governments in the Empire.

One thing at any rate is clear, that Germany is certainly not going to be bought off by any colonial cession to behave better in Europe. The only effect of any concession would be to encourage her to make mischief at any point where she is admitted. I trust our government will now refuse to have any further discussion of the subject, and I only hope that you and Hertzog will be adamant over South West Africa and make it clear that Germany has nothing to say in the matter and that your only answer to any request is a flat negative.

As regards the Italian negotiations I was certainly in agreement with the prime minister, as against Eden, that it was worth while trying these, though the attempt should have been made much earlier and might then have saved Austria. The real difference between the two situations is that Germany has very fixed designs which she means to accomplish at all hazards unless restrained by force, and has nothing particular to fear from us, while Italy—in spite of vague ambitions in the direction of Egypt and Palestine—is relatively satiated and is in a much weaker position strategically *vis-à-vis* ourselves. If things drift to a war between two armed camps, Italy is likely to get the worst of it whichever side wins. Consequently, unless Mussolini has entirely lost his head, it must be to his interest to try and secure a position of neutrality similar to that which Italy

[1] The Franco-Czechoslovakian treaty of alliance was concluded on 25 January 1924.

used to occupy when she was a member of the Triple Alliance but not committed in any conflict which affected England.[1]

Of course such a settlement would have been much easier a year ago and possibly now, with Hitler on the Brenner, Mussolini may be too completely in his grasp to detach himself.

All of this of course goes back, to my mind at least, to the fatal blunder of letting Eden loose at Geneva in the summer of 1935. Just before that we had at Stresa[2] arrived at a more satisfactory state of affairs in Europe than has prevailed since the war, or is likely to prevail again in our lifetime. All of this was thrown away in order to make a show, for domestic purposes, of our adherence to the covenant of the League, in direct contradiction to that limited Locarno policy which we had maintained for ten years before. Of course if we had been prepared then not merely to play about at Geneva trying to secure unanimity, but had taken the lead by closing the Suez canal or sinking the Italian fleet and then asked for Geneva endorsement, something might have been done. But no one was prepared for that!

However, all that is past history. Yours ever,

L. S. Amery

435   To S. G. Millin   Vol. 102, no. 79

Irene
[Transvaal]
22 March 1938

My dear Sarah, I am very pleased to hear that your new book[3] is going well and the critics pleased. You will be in the limelight on your arrival in London. We shall miss you but the visit will do you spiritually and financially good. I am sorry I see so little of you but dual capitals and general elections are awkward facts to overcome. Bring good news from the old world and I shall be greatly pleased.

No, I can be of no use to you in your African anti-German propaganda. Partly for reasons of official etiquette, but also because for the sake of world peace there may have to be some compromise eventually over the mandates. We don't want *all* the mandates in Africa, nor I assume do the French. Some are essential, others are not, or less so. Some face-saving arrangement may in the end prove

---

[1] The first treaty of the Triple Alliance between Germany, Austria and Italy was signed on 20 May 1882. Italy insisted on an accompanying declaration, not incorporated in the treaty, that the alliance could not 'be regarded as directed against England'.

[2] *See supra*, p. 41, note 5.   [3] *What Hath a Man?*, published in 1938.

necessary. German policy is a grave danger, but even more so will be another world war, and the British sit with enough of the good things of this world to make them able to afford a generous policy so long as essentials are not touched. I assume you will find London opinion hard set *against* surrender of African mandates and your paper will need no introduction or assistance from me, which in any case I could not give. Please excuse me.

It is difficult to know what the next development will be. Austria is a real mouthful, and there may be a pause for the present. But again there may be ominous developments in Spain which France for one could not tolerate and thus once again the rough and tumble in the diplomatic world may restart. I don't suppose much will come of the Italian negotiations. What can Mussolini do, now that he is firmly caught in the German trap at the Brenner pass?[1] But he must hate to be thus trapped.

On the whole things may ease off in Europe. Asia remains—the dominant problem. You will learn a lot in Europe while we are working the parish pump in these elections. One feels pretty sick of it all, but has no choice.

Give my best regards to Weizmann. He also is trapped. I can't imagine any scheme of partition emerging which could be acceptable to Jewry, and that is the trouble ahead for him on his pro-partition policy.

I write as if I don't feel these things. But I feel them most profoundly and bitterly. Success is only for the dictators, and the tents of democracy are filled with confusion and despair. But let us not lose heart prematurely. We see our own but not the other fellow's troubles. They must be enormous and, in the end, ruinous. As in the Great War Germany may win all the battles and lose the war. The main business is to gain time, to prevent a premature clash, and to let the natural reaction come into play.

What is passing in men's souls? That after all is the great question. For we are spirits, we are souls and not machines. What is happening to the soul of Europe? Please find out for me. I am interested. There may be a new spiritual wind blowing, which will blow the new ideologies sky high. Watch for the inner signs.

I hope you will have a good time—a happy time would be too much to ask of the gods. Come back in good health, with eyes in order, and in good heart. If I don't see you before 7 April, then good-bye and good luck. Ever yours,

J. C. Smuts

---

[1] The Brenner pass frontier between Italy and Austria conceded by the treaty of Versailles had brought Germans under Italian rule. When the *anschluss* took Hitler's forces up to the Brenner Mussolini had cause to be alarmed.

436 To L. S. Amery

Vol. 57, no. 118

Palace of Justice
Pretoria
28 March 1938

My dear Amery, Many thanks for your interesting letter of 18 March. (Incidentally I may mention that I was reading it on 26 March, which shows how communications are improving. At an early date, I shall be reading your letters in six days after writing.)

I can understand your feelings in regard to this terrible Austrian business. I have always thought that the *anschluss* was coming, but never imagined that it would be accomplished in the way it was done, in violation of solemn treaties and undertakings, and with a display of brute force which amounted simply to the rape of Austria. What is passing there at present seems to be largely veiled in mystery, but it must in any case be a horrible business for Jews and independents and intellectuals generally.

Germany seems now to be in a fair way to accomplishing all she ever dreamt of doing. Russia, which was the only real check on her, is paralysed and out of action. People seem to forget this all-important fact when they try to size up the position in central Europe, and distribute blame freely on the West. It has always been a cardinal matter of European policy that Russia was to pull her weight, and to form a real check on German ambitions in eastern and south-eastern Europe. With the present impotence of Russia, Germany has a clear field, and she is deliberately marching on at a great pace. Today it is Austria. Tomorrow there will be internal trouble in Czechoslovakia between Sudeten Germans and Czechs, and once more Germany will step in 'for law and order', and I doubt whether anybody will raise a finger, and so she will march on through Hungary, through Rumania, and then through Yugoslavia, and realize her dream of mastery of the European continent. It will indeed be a Napoleonic empire once more but, as in the case of Napoleon, with sea power still intact in British hands. When Russia will revive to pull her weight, who knows? Italy is trapped; with one army cut off in Abyssinia, and another locked up in Spain, and the German army sitting at the Brenner pass looking down on the Tyrol, what can poor Italy do? Mussolini's house of cards has indeed tumbled and much sooner than I had expected. He will not be able to stand up to Germany in south-eastern Europe, and he will be compelled to remain in the Rome–Berlin axis, and play a quite minor role in the game of world politics, a useful satellite to Germany, a nuisance to Great Britain, deeply suspected by friend and foe alike.

As regards the Dominions, they will fight for Great Britain if attacked; they will not fight in the battles of central or south-eastern Europe. I even have my doubts whether they will fight again for France and Belgium. They are now out of that business under the Locarno treaty, and I think they will remain out unless the world situation changes very much from what it is today. Frankly I do not see what else there is for them to do after all the mistakes and *lâchetés* of the past. We are not a Continental power, and we shall have our hands full in maintaining our sea power, in building up our air power, and in defending a straggling Empire and Commonwealth in all quarters of the globe. For some time to come, and until the next break-up, Germany may become master of the Continent. What the effect of that position will be on America, time only can show, indeed the whole position both in Europe and the Far East is so obscure and so fraught with all sorts of alternative possibilities, that one is chary of forming any judgment at all about the future. I have, however, the idea that the United States may be drawn closer to the Commonwealth of nations in the situation that will develop in the world both in the West and in the East, and I hope that in that way some more or less stable equilibrium will be evolved which will prevent any world war with its threat to our civilization. We live in very fateful times. Not since the long slow fall of the Roman Empire has mankind passed through such a crisis, much bigger than most of our statesmen of today seem to realize.

It is of course possible that with such vast forces and means of destruction ultimately ranged against each other, mankind may at heart become pacifist, may recognize that there is no solution by way of war, that in the end, the winners may be even worse off than the losers, if any winners and losers are left. We may thus see a pacifism not born of defeatism, but of inner conviction, humanity and wisdom. *We* shall not see these developments if they are to come about, as they may lie fairly far off in the future. Today conditions and tempers give the League no chance. But it is a great vision, an ideal which always has its value even in the practical affairs of men, and even in the most untoward circumstances. After all, the League was only following the ideal which was incorporated into the practice of the British Commonwealth. But I admit circumstances have been too hard for it, and we shall have to go slow with any form of idealism amid the dangerous forces of the world today.

I do not think you will agree with much of what I have said above, but at any rate it puts the point of view of a far-off spectator and may interest you as such.

It is pleasant to hear from you now and then, and to hear your reactions to the world-shaking events through which we are passing. Please drop me a line from time to time. With kind regards and all good wishes, ever yours sincerely,

s. J. C. Smuts

437   To H. Minkowski   Vol. 57, no. 131

In 1931 Dr Adolf Adler of Vienna suggested that *Holism and Evolution* should be translated into German by either Dr Erwin O. Krausz or Dr Oppenheim. By the end of that year Krausz had completed a translation but its publication could not be financed. Some years later Professor A. Meyer-Abich of Hamburg initiated a second attempt to publish the book in German. A new translation was made by Dr Helmut Minkowski and the consul-general of the Union of South Africa in Hamburg, Fritz Brehmer, arranged for its publication. This was made possible by a contribution of £150 by Dr Hans Merensky (q.v.), and the book appeared in November 1938 under the title *Die holistische Welt*. Smuts wrote a special preface for it and also eight notes which are not included in the third English edition (*see* Smuts Collection, vol. 57, no. 131, enclosures). It also has an introduction by Professor Meyer-Abich which begins by saying that Smuts had 'inaugurated a new epoch in the philosophical and scientific thought of our time'. When war broke out in September 1939 the Nazis forced the publishers to withdraw the book from circulation and during the war the remaining stock was destroyed by bombing. Copies of this edition must be rare. The only copy seen by the editor is in the Johannesburg Public Library. In June 1945 Professor Meyer-Abich suggested to Smuts that *Die holistische Welt* should be reprinted and sent him a copy of his article *Der Holismus unter dem Nazi Regime* (*see* Smuts Collection, vol. 77, no. 6). But no second printing has been traced.

8 April 1938

Dear Dr Minkowski, I have your letter of 30 March with your imploring appeal for a preface[1] however short. I understand and appreciate the difficult position in which you are placed after the delays in publication which have already occurred. And I have been very anxious to meet you in this matter which is also important for the sale of the book in Germany.

Fortunately I have had a few free moments which have enabled me to write a short preface which I trust you will find suitable and helpful. In general terms it tries to link up the concept of Holism with what is happening in the world today and with the great change which is coming over human affairs generally. I have tried to give no offence to prevalent views in Germany, and I trust that no offence

---

[1] Omitted by the editor.

can be taken. As you know, Holism with me is not a mere abstract philosophical concept, but an insight that goes to the foundations, and I have the faith that it may yet prove of value in the re-shaping of our world-view in its practical aspects.

The preface goes herewith, and for safety's sake, I shall send another copy by next airmail.

Just one point more. You will see that in my preface I draw attention to the passage from Plato's *Sophist*, which is to be found on the front page of the third English edition.[1] This edition I hope you will have received from the publishers. This passage can either be prefaced also to the German edition, or, if that has not been done or cannot be done, I wish you to put it as a footnote to my preface at the passage where the word *Sophist* is referred to. In that case, you will have also to strike out from the preface the words 'which I have placed at the beginning of the book'. I should, however, prefer the passage to be quoted at the head of the book, as it is the most remarkable anticipation of Holism that I have found in all earlier philosophy.

I wish once more to thank you for the trouble you have taken with this book, and hope that the response from the German public will be a satisfaction to you also. Yours sincerely,

s. J. C. Smuts

438   To Lord Lothian   Vol. 57, no. 144

20 May 1938

My dear Philip, I have your note of 11 April to introduce the new Indian agent Mr Rama Rau. You may be sure that I shall show him and his wife such attention as I can. The job of an Indian agent in South Africa is not exactly a bed of roses, but on the whole we manage to get along without stirring up too much feeling in India. I hope that the new man will be a success.

We have finished our general election in which the United party has scored a great triumph. Of the 150 seats in the house of assembly, we have taken 111, with another result still to come in.[2] The feeling, especially in the English-speaking centres, has been exceptionally fine and I almost feel as if we are at last through our racial troubles. The last five years of close political co-operation in one party by English and Dutch has been a wonderful heartening experience.

[1] *See* **405**.
[2] The results of the 1938 general election were as follows: United party 111; National party 27; Dominion party 8; Labour party 3; Independent Socialist 1.

This election has now cemented the close racial alliance and I am very hopeful that as years roll on, we shall see real national fusion and the new South African nation slowly taking shape. I should say that on the whole South Africa is probably the best co-operating member in the Commonwealth today except Great Britain herself. Here things are improving all the time, whereas elsewhere I have the feeling that all is not well. I do not for instance know what New Zealand is heading for, and in Canada the internal situation seems to me to be fraught with great peril. It would almost look as if Canada is too big a unit for the very feeble forces of cohesion between the different provinces. Astronomers say that a sun coming too close to another bigger one runs the risk of breaking up, and Canada seems somewhat in this position in her close proximity to the U.S.A. A good word for South Africa in the *Round Table*[1] from time to time might be a very useful thing. Knowing what a past we have, and what a commotion we have made in the big world, I am glad that there is at last this process of internal settling down and what we call Fusion.

I have had a long talk with D. Malcolm without really getting much enlightenment on your foreign situation. I suppose that Neville Chamberlain was wisely guided in trying to smooth out Mediterranean troubles with Italy.[2] The question however remains how far Italy can be trusted to carry out her undertakings, and how far she is a free agent. Mussolini made an awful mistake in dissipating his resources in Abyssinia and thus making it impossible for himself to protect his Austrian flank against Germany. The result now is that with Germany as his next-door neighbour, and a skeleton in the cupboard like the Tyrol, he may not be a free agent at all, and may have to cling desperately to his axis whether he likes it or not. It may even be that he was acting under Hitler's instructions when he made his outrageous Genoa speech,[3] and made agreement with the French almost impossible.

I read your paper on the European situation in the last number of the *Journal of the Institute of International Affairs*, and was very much struck by your survey of the whole situation. To me it seems as if, with Austria in his possession, Hitler has unlocked the door to south-eastern Europe, and that there is nothing to resist his domination in one form or another finally extending right to the Bosphorus. The only real counterpoise to German domination on the Continent was the Russian power, and at present I cannot see Russia anywhere,

[1] *See* vol. III, p. 518, note 2.
[2] A comprehensive Anglo-Italian agreement had been signed in Rome on 16 April 1938.   [3] Delivered on 14 May 1938.

neither in the East nor in the West; whether she has gone underground for a number of years and will become a factor again thereafter one does not know, but certainly for the present she is scarcely visible anywhere except at Geneva. This of course gives Germany her great chance, and there must be a sort of inevitability now about her politically and commercially overrunning the whole of southeastern Europe. It may even be a pacific process to which Italy can make no response, and France unable to intervene effectively.

On Great Britain is imposed the duty of a very cautious policy. She is not directly interested, and she knows all the Dominions are averse to European complications. Apart from occasional diplomatic efforts, she therefore may have to confine herself to the position of a spectator while Germany becomes the master of the Continent. With Russia out of the picture, I do not see what else can happen. The power of Germany makes her a possible master of the Continent and in the end her march on to the south-east is inevitable, and Great Britain will have to be merely an interested spectator and no more. All this I think need not, and probably will not, lead to war. Why should Germany fight if she can achieve her ends by peaceful penetration and the spread of Nazism?

It is an ugly picture from the point of view of democracy, and it looks like defeatism to sit still under it all. But at present it seems to me that this is the way things are developing by a sort of inevitability.

Of course sea power remains. Napoleon was master of the Continent, and yet sea power finished him in the end. If Great Britain could be secure in the air, and have the mastery of the seas in European waters, we may in the long run see a situation very much like that of Napoleonic times. There is this further consideration that the U.S.A. will more and more develop an approach to the western democracies. The U.S.A. is at present a very uncertain and incalculable factor, but in a real first-class European crisis between dictatorship and democracy, it will probably again be found by the side of the democracies as in 1917.

How far off we are already from the halcyon times when we were thinking of making the world safe for democracy, and Peace and Disarmament were our slogans! But in fact the whole basis of our world outlook is altering. The after-reactions of the Great War are far greater and more far-reaching than we ever dreamt of, and the rosy view of the post-war period which we took at one time missed the real inwardness of the dark forces that were shaping the new world. One feels very humble in face of such a situation which has developed in our day, and one can but believe in the ultimate triumph of the well-tested old human ideals, without seeing much light in the immediate situation. It may be that still deeper forces are at work in the direction of more fundamental reforms in the world. It may be that religion will once more come to the rescue as it saved the European world with the fall of the Roman Empire. But it is clear that this new outburst of religious feeling will have to be very different from what is passing current for religion today.

Meanwhile let us keep the peace as long as we can. Let us promote human good will and international understanding by every means open to us. And let us not lose faith in the spiritual forces which in the end prove stronger than any other in men's affairs.

I just jot down these few points to show you what line of thought is running through my mind in these days. It may be very helpful to me if you just occasionally disclose your inner mind to me, and let me see how you view the passing scene. With kind regards and all good wishes, Yours ever sincerely,

s. J. C. Smuts

439   To E. F. C. Lane   Vol. 57, no. 148

Library of Parliament
Cape Town
11 July 1938

My dear Lane, Your letter of 4 June has had to wait a long time for an answer. That was due to frequent and sometimes pleasant absences from home. Our Cato [Clark] with her husband and son were staying with us and I took them to the wilds as much and as often as possible so that they should run no risk of forgetting this country. Now they are gone home and I am at Cape Town for a short session, and I can write you a short account of the news. Meanwhile I have heard from May Hobbs how you were getting on. She sang the praises of Poxwell[1] in no uncertain terms and was charmed with all she saw. But she was certain that Jessie [Lane] was the best! And that showed her shrewd insight.

Yes, it was a phenomenal election, with a wonderful result. I never worked harder—as if this was my last election. Perhaps it will be—who knows? But in this curious country of ups and downs much of the splendid effect of the victory has been spoiled by a *gaucherie* of the defence department on Union Day in reference to 'God Save the King'.[2] These mistakes are heart-breaking, and I sit

---

[1] Lane's family estate.

[2] On Union Day (31 May 1938) 'Die Stem van Suid-Afrika' was played at the military parades in the larger towns and, since the governor-general was not present,

with the broken crockery, even if not with a broken heart! We must endeavour to carry on, but frankly I find it often most trying to work with my old Nat friends. They are more influenced by fear of Dr Malan than of God. Some people do believe more in the devil than in God!

I am glad to hear the news about your dear old people. Please give them my affectionate greetings when you see them. They are a wonderful couple, both in mind and body. And dear old George Heys[1] is still travelling! I never knew that port-contracting could so permanently affect a man's ways. I hope he is well, even in Germany.

I agree with what you say about Northern Rhodesia etc. The British government will do as little as possible. In regard to the Protectorates they are doing nothing at all, in spite of their own South Africa Act,[2] and I fear when they are prepared to act it will be too late for South Africa to feel any gratitude. Their own assimilation in Africa and in Jamaica and elsewhere leaves much to be desired; but they *will* continue to feel how superior they are to these colonials! The amalgamation commission[3] I shall see when they return from their inquiries.

The European situation remains obscure but dangerous. I suppose Czechoslovakia will keep the pot boiling for some time yet. Hitler must have had a check there, and is not likely to forget or forgive. The policy of the British government remains to me obscure. I can understand them moving heaven and earth to patch up arrangements and keep peace as long as possible. But why this continued farce of 'non-intervention' which is converting Spain into a German–Italian province?[4] Why should only Franco get assistance—for which he is bound to tie up the future if he wins? A really independent Spain is as vital to our communications as to those of France, and I don't see how our policy is helpful in that respect.

By the way, have you read *China at the Crossroads* by Madame Chiang Kai Shek?[5] It is a most remarkable book. If that is the spirit

not 'God Save the King'. R. Stuttaford, minister of the interior, resigned but withdrew his resignation when the government announced that in future both anthems would be played on state occasions.

[1] Father-in-law of E. F. C. Lane.

[2] Article 151 of the South Africa Act envisaged the transfer of the British Protectorates to the Union.

[3] A royal commission with Lord Bledisloe as chairman had, since March 1938, been investigating the possibility of amalgamation between Southern and Northern Rhodesia and Nyasaland.

[4] The latest resolution of the non-intervention committee (*see supra*, p. 67, note 1) had been taken on 5 July 1938 when a costly and elaborate scheme to control the numbers of foreign troops in Spain had been accepted by all the powers concerned.

[5] General Chiang Kai-Shek and his wife were co-authors of this book published in London in 1937.

of China, Japan will never succeed, however many victories she may win. It is always the sane that wins in the long run.

It is a difficult world, and I suppose there are great lessons for us to learn. Germany is once more trying Prussianism, paganism as against Christianity. I cannot believe that paganism will win. We cannot return to the dead past. The human spirit will never submit to the old routine and the old chains. But we may have to pass through seas of suffering before this issue is once more settled. Love to you both and all good wishes, Truly yours,

s. J. C. Smuts

440   To M. C. Gillett   Vol. 57, no. 243

Tsalta
[Cape Town]
28 July 1938

...You will be pleased to hear that in parliament we have successfully weathered the storm over the anthem.[1] This is all to the good. We have also found a way to avoid the playing of 'God Save the King' at the Voortrekker monument next 16 December at Pretoria. The governor-general was to put in an appearance at the laying of the foundation and would naturally be received with the usual honours. Hence the tears that such a holy ceremony should be spoiled by the anthem of the Voortrekker's oppressors! The Nats were working up a fine storm of indignation over this sacrilege, and it was quite possible that the solemn occasion would have been a scene of brawling. However the government will now renounce its part in the ceremonies, the governor-general will not appear; and the shades of the Voortrekkers will not be offended by 'God Save the King'. So all is well that ends well. But that is not the end of our troubles. As I wrote you last week we may get into deep waters over Mr [A. P. J.] Fourie who was defeated at the elections and thus fell out of the government, and whom it is proposed to bring back into the fold by his appointment to the senate—as a Native senator![2] This is rather too much for some of us to stomach and there may be a serious row. If one of these days you find me out of the government you may have less respect for me, but you should not be surprised. It is a queer world. Fourie was not a success *in* the cabinet,[3] but out of it he may have the unusual success of my also leaving it.

[1] *See supra*, p. 130, note 2.
[2] *See* vol. v, p. 377, note 1.
[3] He had been minister of labour.

Of course I still hope to settle this little trouble, but it will be no easy matter.

...I have not read anything very interesting recently but have browsed through some of the heavier books, such as Einstein's *Evolution of Physics*[1] and other scientific works. With all this heavy office and parliamentary work I fall asleep at night shortly after going to bed, and perhaps this is better than imbibing fresh knowledge for which my appetite continues.

And so Runciman is going to Prague as a 'private' mediator or negotiator.[2] It shows the gravity of the situation when the British government goes as far as this unprecedented step. But I wonder whether a man like Runciman could do much good in unravelling that tangle. I should not have thought so, but the Lord sometimes uses indifferent instruments to show His power. May this be so here. Either the Nazis are playing a gigantic game of bluff, or matters are reaching a desperate stage. I hope peace will be maintained. Surely Hitler cannot be quite ready yet for the great conflict. But he may think that later France and Britain may also be in a stronger position as regards armaments.

In Spain the usual see-saw: one day a fine Nationalist advance, the next day the Republicans have scored elsewhere. I must admit my sympathies are with the latter. Franco seems to me a mere instrument of reaction and Fascism and his victory will bode no good to us or France.

I am afraid I am getting very prosy, and all this stale stuff must be boring you. However, there is little else to write about at the moment. You may however be interested to hear that Pole-Evans has gone up to Kenya and Uganda to advise their governments about grasses and to collect plants for himself. He proposes to return, not via Tanganyika, but the Congo, and visit Ruwenzori and the Kivu volcanoes and lake. In this way some valuable evidence may be secured about routes for our use later, if ever we get as far as those parts. Even if we don't it is pleasant to harbour these thoughts and to imagine good things! I should dearly love to get to those parts and if I could manage in some decent way to get out of office I may have the leisure, and even Arthur could perhaps be persuaded to prolong his African cure. Now this letter has to be posted for the mail. With dear love to you both and all, ever yours,

Jan

[1] A. Einstein and L. Infeld, *The Evolution of Physics* (1938).
[2] The object of the negotiations was a solution of the demands of the Sudeten-German minority in Czechoslovakia for cession of the Sudetenland to Germany. Runciman's proposals were accepted by the Czech president but not by the Sudeten-Germans.

441   From L. S. Amery   Vol. 56, no. 12

112 Eaton Square
S.W.1
2 August 1938

My dear Smuts, The session has ended on a note of optimism about the European situation. I hope this may be justified, but am by no means altogether sure. The very emphasis of Hitler's professions in favour of peace may quite possibly be either a deliberate blind, or a salve to his own conscience in case he should decide to take sudden and violent action this summer. Any real compromise between the views of the Sudeten Germans and of the Czechs is out of the question. Both may profess willingness to make concessions, but both mean entirely different things. It is a situation that you may remember in the summer months of 1899, only much more intractable. The Czechs are prepared to go any lengths in racial equality for Germans as such, and in local government, but not to break up their state. The Germans want to be a state within the state, able as a single unit to enforce Nazi discipline on all their members, taking their orders from Berlin, and in fact making any nominal unity in defence and foreign policy only possible on the condition that Czechoslovakia drops her present affiliations and comes within the German orbit.

That indeed will very probably be the result in any case, if the Germans accept the Czech concessions and then work them out in their own fashion and by their own effective measures of agitation and intimidation. I don't see that we either can or ought to go to war to prevent that. On the other hand we cannot well tolerate a deliberate aggression at the moment especially as France would be bound to take part in it whatever happened. On the other hand the knowledge that we are not prepared to tolerate aggression now, coupled with the knowledge that the same end can be attained by patience for a few years is probably the best guarantee for peace today. From that point of view the royal visit to Paris may have done much to preserve peace this summer.

The appointment of Runciman may be a stroke of genius. He is lazy, knows nothing about the situation, and is, I think, quite incapable of understanding the motives that influence either side. But that very fact, and his bland imperturbability may serve to lower the temperature, and that is always something. Nor is he likely to commit himself to any constructive suggestion, which, however excellent in itself, might commit us and the government more deeply than we wished.[1]

---

[1] *See supra*, p. 133, note 2.

I think the Italian agreement[1] undoubtedly served to preserve peace at the end of May. Now it is again somewhat endangered by the continuance of the war in Spain which Germany is doing her best to keep going. She is also making all the mischief she can in Palestine, where Italy is now behaving all right.

The Palestine situation has got steadily worse and worse through sheer indecision in handling it, and the infection has spread more and more into neighbouring Arab countries. To my mind the only solution now is a quick decision on partition, and prompt action to enable the new Jewish area to take at any rate some of the victims of Nazi cruelty in Germany and Austria. As to the brutality and cruelties there inflicted, it is incredible that these things should happen in the world today. To my mind also it is an outrage that Germany, not content with ill-treating and pushing out her own Jews, should first rob them and so make it doubly difficult for other countries to receive them. If those other countries only had the courage to act in concert they might impose a collective clearing arrangement on Germany, and deduct a few hundred pounds from Germany's trade balance in respect of the cost of settling each refugee in their own country. All these things make one glad that, in the British Commonwealth at any rate, the torch of freedom and human reasonableness is still held aloft.

You may think this letter rather pessimistic, so I will add in conclusion that I am off to Switzerland in a few days for five or six weeks' holiday and to that extent at any rate am not assuming war as the more likely outcome during the next few weeks! Yours ever,

L. S. Amery

442   To C. van Riet Lowe   Vol. 57, no. 157

3 August 1938

My dear van Riet Lowe, I have your note of 30 July in reference to an archaeological bureau in Kenya. I am writing as you suggest to Lord Francis Scott, and enclose you copy of the note I am sending.

I noticed your presence in Cape Town last week and was wishful to get into touch with you and talk over various matters, but unfortunately you had left before I could get hold of you. However we can confer later at our leisure.

Gregory [J. W.] has given a great fillip to [R.] Broom's work, and South Africa will in consequence be even more in the picture from a prehistoric point of view than ever before. I wish that Broom

---

[1] See *supra*, p. 128, note 2.

could be got to place his Sterkfontein fossils in the correct geological horizon. I understand from the papers that he is talking of two million years ago, while his fossils do not even go back to the beginnings of the Pleistocene. Perhaps you could be helpful to co-ordinate his work with that of your approximate geological time-table.

I am sorry that your building has to stand over, but by this time you have learned patience in such matters. With kind regards, Yours sincerely,

s. J. C. Smuts

443   To L. Blackwell   Vol. 57, no. 159

4 August 1938

My dear Blackwell, Yours of yesterday.

I am afraid I cannot comply with your request to convene a meeting of all the English-speaking members of the party in order to go once more into the matter you raise in your letter.[1] We have had a full caucus of the party which came to a definite vote after a debate in which you took part. It would under the circumstances be quite irregular and improper for me to hold a meeting such as you propose.

The only matter really in debate is the word *official* as applied to the national anthem. I think you attach an exaggerated importance to that aspect of the matter, and your earlier view as to the relative importance of the preamble and the operative substantive part of the prime minister's resolution was quite correct. To my mind there is nothing in this resolution which is in conflict with what I actually did say during the elections. 'God Save the King' will be played as a national anthem for ever. Of course this does not preclude the two sections of our people from ultimately coming to an agreed solution on the matter. The articles in the press you refer to were just a little attempt at mischief-making and should not be taken too seriously.

I trust you will think over the whole matter very seriously before taking any action, and that your earlier, wiser view will prevail. Ever yours sincerely.

s. J. C. Smuts

[1] The matter was the cabinet decision of 2 June 1938 that 'God Save the King' and 'Die Stem van Suid-Afrika' should both be played on all official occasions until a single national anthem had been agreed upon. *See* Smuts Collection, vol. 57, no. 159.

444   From P. Duncan   **Vol. 56, no. 69**

Private   Government House
                                          Cape Town
                                     11 September 1938

My dear Smuts, I am very glad that you have not allowed Hofmeyr's resignation[1] to break the government. You had a hard decision to make and his going has made the position of those who remain more difficult for the immediate future. But looking beyond that I have no doubt that you are right in thinking that the principle involved, such as it was, was not of such importance as to justify a break, with all that it would have meant in our present circumstances.

I once shocked Mrs Barnett by saying that 'principles' are good servants but bad masters. That, of course, is much too widely expressed, but things happen sometimes which confirm me in the belief that there is a grain of truth in it. We can make idols of 'principles'.

What has happened will not make your already difficult task any easier but events will justify you. Yours sincerely,

                                          Patrick Duncan

445   To S. G. Millin   **Vol. 102, no. 84**

                                          Cape Town
                                     14 September 1938

My dear Sarah, I am very sorry that I have not answered your letter of 29 August earlier, and even now I can only dictate a brief reply which I hope you will not mind. You will understand from what has happened recently that I have been in pretty rough weather, and I have had to give all my time and attention to the job or jobs in hand. Nor can I claim to have emerged successfully with Hofmeyr and Sturrock [F. C.] gone out of the cabinet, and a feeling of unrest and unsettlement remaining which is most regrettable. Meanwhile I must carry on.

I do not believe in resignations, especially in times such as those we are passing through. However much I have sympathized with Hofmeyr, I have not looked upon his resignation as justified, and mine would be entirely out of the question. I wonder what

---

[1] J. H. Hofmeyr, then minister of education, labour and mines, resigned on 9 September 1938 on the grounds that the appointment of A. P. J. Fourie as a 'Native' senator was 'a prostitution of the constitution'. F. C. Sturrock, minister without portfolio, resigned on 12 September. *See also* vol. v, p. 377, note 1.

people would say to me if I ran away at a moment when many are especially relying on me to keep things moving on a straight course. What a luxury resignation would be, but no such luck for me.

You write about the European situation. It has got much worse since you wrote, and in fact the issue is trembling in the balance at this moment. I myself do not yet think the position is absolutely desperate, but it is certainly very bad. There is just the possibility that the certain prospect of a general war may at the last moment frighten Hitler from his course. That in fact is the only hope one can have as things are today. His Nuremberg speech[1] read to me as having been prepared to justify the invasion of Czechoslovakia, but the fatal sentences have at the last moment been deleted in view of twelfth-hour news from London. What remains in the speech is bad enough, and leaves me in no doubt as to what he is driving at. But the prospect of France and Great Britain becoming involved almost immediately and of a world war not far off have most surely given him pause. That pause may yet save the situation. The next eight days will show. Bishop Butler[2] was once found meditating in his garden as to whether nations can go mad like individuals. The dear old Bishop would have had no doubt as to the answer if he had lived in our times. One has little faith left and can only hope. It is almost inconceivable that the world would be launched once more into a general war. I have spoken out as I have done in the speech you referred to[3] because I think it is best for South Africans to begin to realize their position and the position they may be almost certainly in if the world is once more to face Armageddon.

There will no doubt be a great deal of hubbub over what I have said, but at any rate the warning has been given, and I hope will be taken to heart.

We are speeding up the work of the session, and it now appears possible that we may finish by the end of the week. In that case soon thereafter I hope to be back in the old haunts, where I hope to see you and talk things over at greater leisure. Now I must end with kind regards to you and Phil, Ever yours,

s. J. C. Smuts

[1] Made on 12 September 1938. *See* N. H. Baynes, *The Speeches of Adolf Hitler 1922–39*, vol. II, pp. 1487–99.

[2] Joseph Butler, Bishop of Durham (1692–1752).

[3] In a speech in the house of assembly on 25 August 1938 Smuts repeated his personal view that the Union of South Africa would go to the assistance of Great Britain in the event of war. But he said emphatically that there was no question of the Union's automatic participation in any war; parliament would decide what course would be in the interests of the country. (*See* the *Cape Times*, 26 August 1938, p. 11).

Written 15 September

Since this was dictated yesterday the news of Chamberlain going to see Hitler has been made public.[1] Let us hope that this unprecedented step will have the desired effect.

446   To J. Power   **Vol. 57, no. 180**

Cape Town
15 September 1938

My dear Power, Just a line to thank you for your last couple of letters which I have read with deep interest and instruction. But the march of events has outpaced your information, and we have had to face almost daily new and menacing situations developing with frightful rapidity in the old world. Last night the news arrived of Chamberlain's move to meet Hitler personally. Time alone can show whether it was a wise and fruitful one. But beyond all doubt it showed great courage on the part of the prime minister. If by this extraordinary step he succeeds in bringing off some sort of settlement of the Sudeten question, he will have the praise of the whole world, with the exception perhaps of Czechoslovakia itself. My expectation is that he will succeed, as no great power today wishes to get involved in a general war. The operation may however be a most painful one to Czechoslovakia, and one feels deeply sorry for that small state in the difficulties in which it has become involved with its powerful neighbour.

I suppose after the Sudeten trouble we shall have the colonial question raised, and there the two protagonists, the German and British Empires, will be directly facing each other. What will the issue be? The British people have a genius for compromise, and if the Germans were normal, a fair and reasonable compromise could be reached. But with the Nazi mentality, it is difficult to know whether there will be a spirit of give and take on the other side. Of course the establishment of personal talks between Hitler and Chamberlain on the Sudeten business may prove especially helpful in this coming trouble and I hope Chamberlain will have success with both of them.

What wonderful times we are living in! For the old kings we have now substituted the new ideologies, which are probably far more troublesome and dangerous to the world than the old kings ever were. The war of ideologies may prove even more devastating than

---

[1] Following this meeting at Berchtesgaden the British and French governments advised the Czech government to cede to Germany, without plebiscites, all districts with more than fifty per cent of Germans.

the wars of religion proved to Germany in the sixteenth and seventeenth centuries. I hope the world will be saved from this disaster. If the co-operation of the United States can be enlisted, how much easier it would be to solve all these difficult questions. But I see that in his last declaration, Roosevelt affirms in the most uncompromising terms the isolation policy from which he had appeared to be departing in his previous declarations. Somehow it ought to be possible to consolidate the great mass of sane democratic opinion in the world into an effective working system. But somehow we have hitherto failed to achieve this object. The failure of Geneva and of the whole League system has exposed democracy to very grave dangers. Meanwhile we can but do our best to get peace and to prevent some sudden outburst and clash which may destroy most of the fine heritage we have derived from the past. At the moment our human lot appears to be a pitiable one, with intolerance and persecution the order of the day, and the things of the spirit derided in high places. This one hopes will be a passing phase, and it behoves us during this phase to prevent irreparable mischief happening from some sudden outbreak which is perhaps our greatest danger in these times. Bishop Butler was found meditating in his garden whether nations could go mad like individuals! We are living in times when nations appear to have gone mad, and when one must do one's best to see that this menace does not ruin the future of our civilization. Patience, forbearance, compromise—these are the weapons with which we can most successfully fight the disasters from which mankind is suffering at present.

However I am sure I am boring you with these reflections, and shall not pursue the matter. With kind regards, Ever yours sincerely,

s. J. C. Smuts

447   From L. S. Amery   Vol. 56, no. 14

112 Eaton Square
S.W.1
20 October 1938

My dear Smuts, Looking at a review of Lloyd George's book just published on the Versailles treaty[1] I noticed a quotation (enclosed herewith) from Emil Zimmermann's memorandum to the German imperial cabinet in 1918[2] which is very appropriate to the present situation as regards Tanganyika. The real difficulty about the

[1] D. Lloyd George, *The Truth about the Peace Treaties*, 2 vols. (1938).
[2] For the quotation *see* vol. I, pp. 126–7.

Germans is that they regard every position as a strategical jumping-off ground for a further advance, and Tanganyika in their hands would not only enable them to work, say with Italy, against our position in Kenya, Uganda and Egypt, but equally against the Union and against Australia. Whatever the technical position as to Tanganyika being within the jurisdiction of the United Kingdom, I should have thought that the interests of all the Dominions in the southern seas were so closely bound up with its remaining British that they could all agree upon making the strongest representations, individually or collectively, against its retrocession.

Whatever the German economic case might have been worth, and that was precious little, it has surely been entirely superseded by the absorption in Germany, not only of Czechoslovakia but of the whole Danubian region, which has been taking place with amazing rapidity within the last few weeks.

Our external policy, political and strategic, seems to me to have been enormously simplified by recent events. The League as an instrument of policy, apart from a meeting-place, is dead. The post-war French system for controlling Europe has just had its throat cut. France and ourselves are now in a very simple defensive position behind the Maginot line and the North sea covering our interests and territories and associates overseas. As long as we continue to control the seas, including so far as possible the Mediterranean, and the vital bridge, for air and other purposes, of Egypt and Palestine, we can look with less apprehension to the Germanization of central Europe.

Talking of that bridge I am afraid we have let Palestine get into a woeful mess. But a real effort is now being made to repress the rebellion[1] and it may be that some sort of tolerable policy will emerge afterwards. I fancy that the Woodhead report[2] is likely to throw considerable doubt on the feasibility of partition, but we shall know that in another two or three weeks. In case it may interest you I enclose a copy of my speech in the house on the Munich settlement[3] and a recent article to the *Sunday Times* pleading for unity in policy. Yours ever,

L. S. Amery

[1] Renewed Arab revolt followed the publication of the Peel report in July 1937. The Jews also rejected its partition scheme and from November began taking reprisals for Arab attacks. The rebellion continued until May 1939.

[2] This commission, appointed to work out the technical details of partition, was in Palestine from 27 April to August and reported, in October 1938, against partition.

[3] On 28 September 1938 Chamberlain, Daladier, Hitler and Mussolini met at Munich. Next day an agreement was signed providing for the immediate cession of the Sudetenland to Germany. No representative of the Czech government was present. The few limitations on the cession were brushed aside after German forces marched into the Sudetenland on 1 October.

448   To D. W. F. Ballot   **Vol. 57, no. 196**

15 November 1938

My dear Ballot, I have your letter of 5th inst.[1] in regard to the South West Africa League,[2] and the message which you say Steer [G. L.] sent, conveying my blessing. I am afraid that that does not convey my attitude. Steer saw me for a moment whilst a function was on at Kimberley, and told me he had been to South West and that this movement was on. I cannot remember that I expressed any attitude towards it except one of 'wait and see'. I have repeatedly felt that people in South Africa and even more so in South West Africa were inclined to be somewhat jumpy on the mandate issue, and that premature and excited agitation would cause reactions that might be harmful to us. What real force there is behind the League I do not know except the few remarks that you make in your letter. The movement will certainly have the effect of stimulating the Germans in South West Africa to renew agitation, and make the League their excuse.

Our attitude as regards South West Africa is well known, remains unchanged and is subject to no doubt whatever. The Labour party and other nondescript people in the Union have now started a movement against giving Germany *any* of her colonies back, and I notice that they have some speakers also from South West Africa. I doubt very much whether procedure of this kind is going to be helpful in any way. The government does not want to be associated with public agitation of this kind, and its silence in the face of this movement may create the impression that it is weakening on the mandate issue. You see therefore that the movement may create misunderstanding and prejudice.

Your League move may have one good effect and that is in keeping our Union population in South West Africa together, and giving them a feeling of reassurance. In that sense and in that respect it may do good. But the attempt to create a Union-wide agitation is both unnecessary and of doubtful value.

We have little information from London and less from Berlin. We do not even know if this colonial question is an urgent one or not. It may be with Pirow's return by the end of the year we may know more than is appearing so far on paper. When you are on dangerous ground, you walk warily and do not shout too loudly, and that seems to me to be the proper attitude for us at present.

[1] Smuts Collection, vol. 56, no. 23.

[2] Founded in October 1938 to oppose the return of South West Africa to Germany and to support Tanganyika in its opposition to return. The chairman of the League was J. D. Lardner Burke, M.L.A. Its first meeting took place on 4 November.

When Conradie [D. G.] was here last week I happened to be away on political business at the Cape, and therefore did not see him, otherwise I might have heard more about your League and similar business. With kind regards, Yours sincerely,

s. J. C. Smuts

449   From F. Lamont   Vol. 56, no. 169

107 East 70th Street
[New York]
[November 1938]

My dear Jannie, A merry Christmas to you and all sorts of blessings for the New Year. I do hope I shall be one of them!

Although I wrote a short time ago, I just *have* to wish you a happy Christmas and send you my love. So much has happened since I last wrote. I was so frightened by the crisis. I thought, 'There is going to be war, and I shall never see my lovely English friends again.' So when it was over, I jumped on a fast steamer, was twelve days in England, and the whole trip was twenty-two days, three weeks and a day. How's that for speed? I saw the Masefields and the Murrays and the Cecils and the [Laurence] Binyons, and dear old Henry Nevinson and all the people I care most about in England. It did me worlds of good and I wish South Africa had been next door, for during those September days, I thought I might never see you again.

I found England split from top to bottom. Of course the anti-Chamberlains are in a minority, but, ye Gods, what a passionate minority! I have never before seen such depths of feeling openly expressed in England. I hate to tell you that I had no character, no convictions, no principles; I agreed with the last person I talked to, every time. It was utterly bewildering. At least I am honest, that's something.

I went to luncheon at the Cecils and after talking with Lord Robert, I felt that Chamberlain and his foreign policy were *dreadful*. I then hurried home, changed my dress and had tea with the Astors, just about an hour after I had left Lord Robert. You would think my convictions would last more than an hour! But not a bit of it. Waldorf Astor said, 'Now, Florence, you know Bob Cecil has been living in dreamland for seven years. Tell me everything he said to you and I will answer it.' He then proceeded to answer it, point by point, sanely and quietly. And at the end of an hour I thought Chamberlain was the greatest man on earth!

Now that I am home, I am still bewildered. But it boils down to this. Probably at the last minute, Chamberlain did the best that could be done. But his foreign policy has been bad, and it is inexcusable that he did not tell Benes [E.] six months ago that they could expect nothing from England. Of course you have heard all the tales about the French, particularly the perfidy of Bonnet [G.]. No one knows if it's true. But most people here think so. England has lost prestige in America, no doubt of that. Of course all the League people in England are furious. And what a chance the government did have to try a little collective security. There was a risk, yes, but don't we have to take risks, don't statesmen have to? Tom is a good deal more pro-Chamberlain than I am.

And now this last horror of the Jewish terrorism. It is unbelievable. Would it have happened if England had been firmer? I said to a young foreign correspondent, who had been in the Sudeten areas when the Germans came in, 'But I can't believe what you tell me you saw. Human beings could not act like that!' He said, 'They are not human beings, they are rats.' He meant the present ruling party. I do not think public opinion in America has been so profoundly stirred since the sinking of the *Lusitania* as it is over this latest Jewish persecution.

I meant to write you just a word of Christmas greeting and affection, and here it has grown into this long scribble. I have only *touched* on things very superficially. There is so much more to say.

Hurrah for our grand Republican victory—three cheers for the death of the New Deal[1] (But it isn't dead yet.) That is the one heartening thing in a sad world. America may climb out of her depression. Business *may* find jobs for our 13,000,000 unemployed if only F.D.R. can have the fear of God put in him. Good-bye, dear Jannie, Blessings from

Florence

450   To Lord Robert Cecil   Vol. 57, no. 203

6 December 1938

My dear Cecil, I am very much obliged to you for your letter of 7 November,[2] and for the views which you express in regard to my

---

[1] In the congressional elections of November 1938 the Republicans had doubled their numbers in the house of representatives (170) and gained eight seats in the senate. Nevertheless the Democrats still held large majorities in both houses.

[2] Smuts Collection, vol. 56, no. 44.

recent armistice broadcast.[1] Let me say at once to you how much I appreciate the important work which you are carrying on on behalf of the League in spite of the years and of the other burdens weighing on you. I follow very closely what you say in the house of lords or on the platform.

It is our duty as believers in the League to continue to stand up for it, and in that way to counteract the general impression of the League as dead and as a matter of no account whatever. There has of course been a most lamentable change in the fortunes of the League in the last five or six years, but one hopes and prays that this may be a temporary phase, and that a favourable settlement in Europe and the absence of all other machinery for international purposes may make the League come into its own again. Meanwhile I am against all drastic amendments of the covenant so far as its main principles are concerned. It is of course quite impossible to work the sanctions provisions while so many important countries are outside the League, but I would simply regard those provisions as in a state of temporary suspense and destined to be revived again when the League has regained lost ground. The few suggestions which I indicated raised matters of machinery and of procedure more than of principle. In its working arrangements I am sure we shall have to be guided by experience and by our efforts to conciliate those who are now outside the League or who are very luke-warm about it, and make such changes as might meet their case or their views. At one time I feared that revision of the League might mean the scrapping of the fundamental principles of the covenant, but now I am glad to see that the general view at Geneva has been to make as little change as possible on fundamentals. I agree with you that the totalitarian states object to the League *in toto*, and not merely to this or that provision of the covenant. It may therefore be a hopeless course at present to try and secure their acquiescence and return to the League. But even so, I think we should not be weary in well doing,[2] and a conciliatory attitude on our part becomes the great institution whose welfare we have at heart. It remains my firm belief that the work we did at Paris will substantially stand, but we shall have to be very wary and practise a great deal of worldly wisdom to guide it through the extraordinary times through which mankind is passing today.

I agree with you that everything should be done to induce the U.S.A. to co-operate actively with the League on some basis or

---

[1] Smuts Collection, Box I, no. 112. The speech is entitled 'Twenty Years After —World Peace and the League of Nations'.
[2] 'Be not weary in well doing.' 2 *Thessalonians* iii.13.

other which requires careful exploration. It is really the defection of the U.S.A. that hamstrung the League and has made it practically impossible for it to discharge its duties satisfactorily. It will be no easy task to induce them to co-operate actively with the League in their present isolationist mood. This outlook of theirs will have to be modified, and this is more likely to be brought about by world events now transpiring in the East than by any arguments from our side. One of the unfortunate effects of our naval agreement with the Germans (an agreement I thoroughly approve of)[1] is just this, that the Americans have come to look upon the Atlantic as sufficiently commanded by the British navy and as there being no danger to North America from that quarter. Fascist designs on Brazil,[2] of which there has recently been so much evidence, is however rousing the U.S.A. government to a realization of the dangers that threaten the Monroe Doctrine[3] in South America, and that, combined with the dangerous situation in the Pacific, is already having its effect, and may in the end change the outlook of people generally in the U.S.A. Time is therefore likely to prove a very important factor in the U.S.A. attitude to the League. But I agree with you that other steps will have to be taken to help the U.S.A. over what must be a very difficult stile for them.

You are probably right that action from the British side may not prove helpful. I have often considered the matter of what could be done, but so far have seen no clear daylight in the matter. One wants to avoid all appearance of propaganda on behalf of the British Commonwealth of nations and to put the whole matter on its basis of universal human interests and not least those of North America. My American correspondents are somewhat dubious as to the line that should be taken with the present administration and congress. I had looked forward to more freedom in order that I might go myself to America and try to explore the position confidentially. But the longer these troubles last in Europe, the more difficult it is for me to extricate myself from South African politics, and set myself free for work of this kind. I remain however in close touch with responsible American friends, and it may be that some daylight may yet appear in a situation which at present is very obscure.

You in particular are looked upon as a leader of very impartial and large human outlook, and I have the feeling that you can do very much indeed and can carry a message to the leaders in the

---

[1] *See supra*, p. 72, note 2.
[2] In November 1937 Dr Getulio Vargas, president of Brazil, seized power, set up a new constitution which gave him dictatorial powers, and collaborated with Italy and Germany. But in 1938 he crushed the Brazilian Fascists and sought the friendship of the United States.   [3] *See* vol. III, p. 639, note 2.

United States such as no other British politician could take. I hope
you will not leave this aspect of your duty out of consideration.
I notice that Eden is going to the United States, and I have no doubt
that incidentally he will do his best to further the cause of the League
and of American co-operation. I hope that his work will bear fruit,
and that some progress will ensue. But even so, he is an active
British politician, and moreover has played a part in regard to Italy
and Spain which may not appeal to many Americans. I therefore
still hope that it will be possible for you to have a heart-to-heart
talk with Roosevelt, Cordell Hull and other men of good will in
America, and strengthen them in their good resolves.

I hope you will forgive this long screed, which is written simply
in order to help in the cause which we both have so closely at heart.
With very kind regards, and all good wishes, Ever yours sincerely,

s. J. C. Smuts

451   From M. P. A. Hankey   Vol. 56, no. 140

Highstead
Pain's Hill
Limpsfield
[England]
29 December 1938

My dear Smuts, It was nice to see your fist again. But Egeland and
I are not destined to meet. He has already left for Norway and
I leave next week on a business visit to the Suez canal. Before my
return he will have gone back to Natal. I am sorry. Your friends are
my friends and I would have invited him here.

I seem rather busy in spite of my retirement. All sorts of interesting odd jobs come my way and some take a lot of time, e.g. a broadcast I did last week on the Dominions and rearmament.

I am less troubled than most of my friends about the international
situation. It may be my incurable optimism. On paper and on the
surface it looks bad I must admit. I am sure we shall have 'wars and
rumours of wars'.[1] But my instinct is that we shall not be in them,
unless there is some unexpected change of government here. I feel
also that, while the superficial outlook seems to indicate war, the
fundamentals are against it. All my news from Germany and Italy
is that the mass of the people don't want war. The very thought
gives them the 'jitters'. I can hardly believe that the dictators are
such fools as to go into a war without a much stronger popular

---

[1] St Matthew xxiv.6.

opinion than they have for war. They may be able to whip up their people for the start of a war, but, if it is a long war, they can't hope to maintain enthusiasm. In fact the dictators will have to gamble on a short war. But all the evidence is against the short war. People can stand a lot of bombing when their blood is up, and they soon learn to scatter and go to ground. The defence here is getting very strong. I fancy that anyone who attacks will get some nasty shocks, and every week the position will improve. Of course we should sustain frightful losses, but in the end we should win through. I fancy that even to-day the deterrent is sufficient to discourage an attempt at a knock-out blow.

Hitler can pick up some easy things in eastern Europe. He has been fairly true to *Mein Kampf* and I fancy he will avoid war with us if he can. After all, he has his own difficulties, but he does not allow them to be shouted from the house tops. I reserve my opinion on the Franco-Italian affair until after Chamberlain and Halifax have visited Rome.[1] It looks bad, but a major war! I doubt. Very best wishes for 1939. Yours ever,

M. P. A. Hankey

452   To T. W. Lamont
Vol. 60, no. 38

Irene
[Transvaal]
10 January 1939

My dear Tom, I had a most welcome and interesting letter from you with the New Year. Thanks for it and for your good wishes which we most heartily reciprocate. Your trip to the High Sierras must have been a wonderful affair, and I can quite understand that your interest in central Africa has waned somewhat! I may however say at once that I share your doubts about Nyasaland. In the present international situation neither of us could afford to be far from home for long. And so (as I have written to Florence) I think we had better for the present make no plans for that trip, and keep it in reserve in case the political weather should clear up in the next couple of months. This I confess I hardly expect. Everything seems to point to trouble coming to a head in south-eastern Europe next spring or summer. Russia is weak and Germany has apparently

---

[1] Towards the end of 1938 there were violent anti-French demonstrations in Rome and demands for 'Corsica, Tunis, Savoy, Jibuti'. On 17 December Mussolini denounced the Franco-Italian agreement of 1935. Chamberlain and Halifax visited Rome early in January 1939 and were satisfied that Mussolini would stand by the Anglo-Italian agreement. *See supra*, p. 128, note 2.

a clear field to move towards the Black sea, and constitute a new Manchukuo in the Ukraine. This may possibly lead to other developments and before we know where we are we may be in another great war. I do not see why Germany should make such supreme efforts for air and general rearmament unless she wants to try conclusions with Russia while the going is good. Besides there is a nemesis behind these dictators and they have to keep moving on.

I agree with you that Chamberlain did good work in preventing a war last September. But I doubt whether he will deflect Hitler from his set policy as regards south-eastern Europe. The pity is that Chamberlain's policy has divided the English so deeply. All my correspondence goes in that direction. Even large numbers of good old Conservatives cannot stand this apparent knuckling under to the dictators. This is a time when the democratic countries should build up a spirit of national unity and co-operation, as grave dangers lie ahead. I have blamed Roosevelt sometimes for not keeping Americans together in such a period and for creating such a bitter spirit of party in the nation. His last congress address[1] has to me the true ring and he seems to realize to the full the dangers ahead. All the more reason therefore for a home policy of conciliation and co-operation.

We have had an interesting time here, with our centenary celebrations of the Great Trek of the Dutch pioneers into the wilds a hundred years ago.[2] They carved out three states[3] in the interior which now form the major part of the Union. So we often build better than we know. Now the festivities are over and we are back in the humdrum politics again. Next week I go down to Cape Town for the session of parliament which will keep me going the next five months.

The children and grandchildren (ten of them) are all well. Isie sends you her love. So do I. Ever yours,

J. C. Smuts

[1] For the substance of this speech on 4 January 1939 *see* J. M. Burns, *Roosevelt, the Lion and the Fox* (1956), p. 389.

[2] The central events of these celebrations, which lasted 130 days, were symbolic ox-waggon treks from the principal towns of the Union to the site of the projected Voortrekker monument near Pretoria and also to Blood river. At these places, on 16 December (the Day of the Covenant), the culminating ceremonies were held. (*See* vol. III, p. 147, note 1.)

[3] These were the republics of Winburg, Natal and Potchefstroom founded between 1837 and 1838.

453 To M. C. Gillett

Vol. 60, no. 185

Tsalta
[Cape Town]
29 January 1939

...Since my last letter Barcelona has fallen[1] and the republican cause has suffered an irreparable setback. I think something must have gone wrong at some vital points for this to have happened. As I said I feared that the collapse of the republican cause in Spain would prove the beginning of great troubles for Europe. Shortly after writing this the cables began to warn us of coming trouble in Europe. And now there are very disturbing signs from more than one source that fear is gripping Europe just as last September. Ministers are making speeches which presuppose inside information of new dangers. A number of English notables have addressed a radio message to Germany couched in the most grave terms.[2] Chamberlain has spoken with greater firmness than he has done hitherto. Hitler is expected to explode a new bombshell tomorrow, etc. etc. And the foreign press seems also dominated by the expectation of grave things to come. It would almost seem as if your return to England will synchronize with a new wave of the deepest pessimism about the world situation.

Without any inside information my nose tells me that the situation is becoming very grave indeed and that we may be on the eve of a new crisis worse than that of last September. For after all last September was a Czech crisis in which the British Commonwealth did not feel itself very directly concerned. But the Mediterranean communications of France and Great Britain are a different matter. The U.S.A. would also feel the proximity of trouble to the Atlantic which is their English Channel so to say. And the danger of a general conflagration is therefore much greater and more serious than last September. Is Hitler determined to force the issue, and does he think that the military position is more favourable for Germany and Italy at this juncture than it would be at a later stage? It looks like madness. But there has been madness before and we are not immune now, even with our warning experience of 1914–19. But is it conceivable that the German people or the more responsible men among them will allow themselves to be drawn into this unprovoked catastrophe? And can Italy afford to march with Germany into this

---

[1] It was occupied by Franco's forces on 26 January 1939.

[2] On 27 January 1939 eighteen prominent Englishmen issued a signed declaration addressed primarily to Germany and appealing for co-operation in building a better future and preserving peace and Western civilization. It was included in the B.B.C. broadcast in the German language.

madness? To me it is all something of a mystery. Whether this will be the end of the present order of things, it is bound to be the end incidentally of Hitler and Mussolini, and surely they must be aware of the vast dangers of this gamble with human fate. It is enough to make one despair of the world and of the divine order which we believe prevails in the world. I cannot believe that we are fated with our own hands and with open eyes to destroy this civilization of ours. Perhaps I am unduly pessimistic. Perhaps this is only another great bluff which is being launched, intended to strike terror into the hearts of responsible opponents and thus unnerve them and make them give way again as was done at Munich. This bluff, if it is such, will however not come off, and is more likely to create a situation from which honourable retreat will be impossible. And that is where my fear comes in—that the manoeuvre of bluff may this time fail and carry the world into the abyss. God forbid that an even greater blunder than that of 1914 should once more endanger all that has been done by human effort and sacrifice to improve our human lot. I think of London with its twelve million people under the devastation of air raids. And I feel like Jonah when he was sent to preach destruction and rather preferred to run away into the wilderness from this thought of horror.[1] But God took pity on Nineveh, and so He may take pity on these poor innocent people over whom the doom of destruction hovers. It is really an incredible situation. And yet the incredible has happened before. But let me end this lamentation. I wish I could believe in a simple way in an all-wise Providence which would never permit such things. But I think of China where millions are being destroyed, and my faith falters. We live in times unlike any known for centuries. But we pray to be spared the horrors of this Golgotha for our race. With deep love, ever yours,

Jan

454   To S. G. Millin   Vol. 102, no. 84

Cape Town
13 February 1939

My dear Sarah, I was very pleased to hear your ringing voice on the phone which indicated health and force at the other end of the line.

---

[1] Jonah, called by God to preach in Nineveh because of its wickedness, took ship to Tarshish (Spain?). Commanded a second time, he obeyed, Nineveh repented and was spared. It is clear that Jonah, so far from recoiling in horror at the threatened destruction of Nineveh, was most reluctant to save it, for Assyria was a threat to his own country. *See Jonah* iv.1–3.

In default of a chat I have had your long letter giving your English impressions. To me most interesting and informative.

A curious situation appears to exist in regard to Chamberlain. Intellectually [those] I meet and those you met seem to be almost unanimous against his policy. On the other hand all the business men I meet here on tour from England support him with one degree of warmth or another. There seems to be a very marked cleavage of opinion, and I suppose the British people must be very much divided. One can understand this. Chamberlain's policy is partly due to many years of neglect and their aftermath. And the question is what can be done now at almost a moment's notice. So people differ or hesitate.

The march of events is, however, rapidly forcing the pace of policy. The end of the Spanish trouble will mark the beginning of European trouble. I notice everywhere a tone of the deepest anxiety. Even Roosevelt is evidently becoming thoroughly alarmed. Whether the dictators are merely intending an immense game of bluff to shake the nerves and will of their opponents or whether they mean serious business this coming summer, the position is in either case most grave, and Chamberlain's appeasement policy looks like failing. But he will, at the worst, be in a position to say to his country and the world that he *did* try his hardest to save the world from war, and that the war guilt is clearly with the dictators. This will be a great card to play and I suppose he is clearly envisaging some such situation. Again, he has gained time for rearmament and our greater prepared-ness and the ripening of American opinion may yet call a halt to the dictators. I am not so sure that Chamberlain is wrong. The Spanish policy has been a tragedy, but for that Eden etc. were just as much responsible. My usual optimism is at a very low ebb, and I much fear that the chances are in favour of trouble next summer. Germany is pushing Italy into it, in order that Italy may be unable to retreat. It is like Germany and Austria in 1914.

Of course I write as an outsider with no real inside knowledge. The real secrets are necessarily kept on both sides and our inform-ation is very poor. We can but speculate as to the motives and reasons of statesmen. Churchill has great qualities as you say but I doubt his insight and wisdom. He is as often wrong as right in his appreciations. What one resents and loathes is that the dictators should be setting the time and the pace, and that everything seems to depend on their decisions. Everyone waits for their speeches etc. etc. But we shall have to swallow our pride in our concern for the world and civilization.

Here things continue as usual. The little things continually spoil the big issues. Some Puck-like devil seems to make South Africa his playground. Still we must bear our cross and carry on—for fear worse may happen. The centenary[1] has been a godsend to the political racialists, and everybody scans the ground over which he is moving very closely. Three bye-elections[2] are on which may show how the wind blows.

But how small our affairs and troubles really are—measured by the scale of world dangers. Think of the Jewish martyrdom, the coming of this new barbaric paganism, the intellectual Dark Age with which we are threatened. And in the Far East a new world situation is forming. These are terrible times—unbearable in their dangers and horrors if one did not believe in God, and did not hold on in firm faith in the Right and in the other spiritual ideals of our civilization. Kind regards. Ever yours,

J. C. Smuts

455   To A. B. Gillett   Vol. 60, no. 191

Tsalta
[Cape Town]
10 March 1939

Many thanks for a very interesting letter from you, mostly about the international situation. I was intrigued to see that you were quietly reverting to a pacifist attitude. Well, I admit the present is a most difficult situation. Where there has been so much blundering in the immediate past, and blundering is probably still continuing, it does take the heart out of one who views present world conditions seriously, and makes one inclined to return to one's shell, so to say. But on the other hand, that is exactly the attitude which has brought Germany and German conditions to their present dangerous pass. If the middle classes in Germany had done their bit for the republic and for wholesome government Hitler never would have gained his ascendancy. On the contrary his star was on the wane just before he came into power. If *we* do not go all out, by political action and if need be by fighting for our democratic principles, the totalitarians are certain to win and reduce our civilization to a confirmed servitude. We cannot face that. I would rather die fighting than become passive (pacifist) and thus contribute to the downfall. The Christians started pacifist and the New Testament is pacifist as I read it. But in the long run they were obliged to change their attitude. Pacifism may be possible for a small group but not for a state or a civilization.

[1] The centenary of the Great Trek. *See supra*, p. 149, note 2.
[2] In Bethal, Pretoria City and Lichtenburg, all in the Transvaal. The United party won all three seats with majorities of 546, 190 and 333 respectively.

I admire the Chinese for the grand stand they are making against Japan. They may thereby save the soul of China yet, whatever happens in the immediate future. Did you ever read Mrs Chiang Kai Shek's *China at the Cross Roads*? That book seems to me to set out what should be our Christian reaction to the new threat to human ideals, and it is different from that of Jesus or the early Christians. If fighting is at all justified for self-defence, indeed if self-defence is under any circumstances justified, we should be prepared to fight for our ultimate principles. These principles I think are at stake in the present conflict of the ideologies. Nazism is a form of what is called Anti-Christ. I am prepared to fight against that. There the old Adam and the new join hands in me! Of course you will not be called on to fight, no more than you were in 1914. But I see you in A.R.P.[1] and why not? Between A.R.P. and actual fighting I see no difference in principle.

I see a more optimistic tone in the cables. But I remain deeply concerned over things. Munich was only a truce—and a very poor one. Ever since Munich the tempo of war preparations has been steadily rising on the Continent. What does it mean if not business, or a bluff which may very likely lead to business? It will be purely by God's mercy if war is prevented this year. Mussolini is being pushed into it just as Austria was in 1914 so that there may be no defection when the hour comes. Let us pray that the unexpected will once more happen. All well and happy here. Ever yours,

Jan

456   To M. C. Gillett

Vol. 60, no. 193

Tsalta
[Cape Town]
17 March 1939

So events have moved even faster in Europe than even I in my pessimistic mood had expected. While the papers were announcing improving conditions and both Chamberlain and Hertzog talked of the prospects of a long era of peace—based on preparedness— Hitler has made another of his stunning blows, and another sovereign state lies prostrate before Germany.[2] Hitler sits today in the old castle at Prague where I found Masaryk in April 1919— revising his Czech or Russian dictionary![3] Freedom shrieked as

[1] Air Raid Precautions—a civil defence organization begun in Great Britain in 1935 which recruited volunteer workers.
[2] German troops invaded Czechoslovakia on 15 March 1939 and were not resisted.
[3] *See* vol. IV, no. 934.

Kosciusko fell.[1] But today freedom does not even get time to shriek, but is suffocated out of existence without warning. Nor do I believe this is the end of the process. We are probably coming very near now to the crisis which is to follow the Spanish victory.[2] I imagine Italy will not be satisfied to be a mere onlooker while Germany swallows all the feast in central Europe. Something must be preparing in the Mediterranean which may put this latest Hitler push in the shade. I hope my foreboding is incorrect.

The last week I have been reading De Burgh's *Legacy of the Ancient World*[3] which you sent me some weeks ago. I liked his work on religion so much that I wanted to see what this book of his (written after the Great War) was like. It is very interesting and informative. It deals with the immense contribution of Greece, Jerusalem and Italy to our spiritual assets. It is really a wonderful story—that uplift of the human spirit and human society which has come from the Mediterranean countries. And then there were the centuries during which the repeated German attacks were smashing that Mediterranean world to pieces and finally sent the world into the Dark Age. It all reads very curiously in our times when once more the German menace overhangs the world, perhaps in even more dangerous form than twenty years ago. But there was something rotten in that Mediterranean world, which even the infant Christianity could not cure, and in the same way this German scourge may once more help to cure deep-seated evils in our society. But what a scourge! And what destruction and suffering may lie under it! The way out for that old world was the message of Christianity. Neither Roman genius for administration nor Greek philosophy availed it in that crisis of its fate. Are we (beneath all the surface movements of the world today) approaching some similar fundamental recasting of our world view? Is religion once more the way out? It is difficult to see daylight in this darkness. I have always built great hopes on science and its civilizing message. But in spite of all our unprecedented progress in science we see a recrudescence of barbarism, of ruthlessness and intolerance which calls halt to all scientific optimism. We still are seekers and have not found, may never find, the solution to this mystery which is life. Meanwhile we can do our best to practise the gentle code of Jesus, and so soften the

[1]   Hope, for a season, bade the world farewell,
            And Freedom shrieked—as Kosciusko fell!
                        Thomas Campbell, *Pleasures of Hope*, Part I, l. 381.
Thaddeus Koskiusko (1746–1817) was a Polish patriot and hero who led an unsuccessful rebellion against Russian and Prussian rule in 1794.
[2] The Nationalist victory in the Spanish Civil War had been won by 13 March 1939.
[3] W. G. de Burgh, *Legacy of the Ancient World* (1924).

harshness of the world with the inner graces of the Spirit. And yet, and still we must fight on, and not fold our hands in the face of evil. 'Resist not evil'?[1] Yes, resist to the uttermost. But how? Shall we fight evil with its own weapons? Can we allow force to submerge everything without marshalling greater force to stop it? *That* in the end is the fundamental question—what weapons to use in the fight. Reason is so slow in action—takes centuries sometimes before its effect is felt. And meanwhile everything we value may have been wiped out. But never quite. There always remains some fragment which starts the new era or epoch thereafter. The new light is never quite quenched. The story of the Middle Ages is in many ways one of the most instructive in all history, as it shows how a smashed world revives after centuries. Of course I do not assume that there will be such another eclipse in our day, but our civilization may receive a stunning shock if this era of violence continues.

I read Chamberlain's speech in the commons after the German *coup*. What a feeble performance! Did British prime ministers ever before make such a feeble show? One cannot help feeling pity for him. His whole effort for peace has simply been set aside without further ado, and the naked reality stares him in the face. I have no doubt that his intention was good and the first results (in securing peace last September) all to the good. But how can one deal with these people if one genuinely wishes to avoid war? Must force be the last word, on our side also? So I come back to my previous question.

I am so glad to hear that Arthur's health keeps improving. Bancroft [Clark] thinks that Arthur should come and live at Street. In that case he would have to give up his beloved Oxford and Oxford bank first, and you would be farther away from your sons and daughter. It is difficult to make any decision about the future in these days. Perhaps events will decide for us! All well here. I am very busy and full of trouble as usual. Ever lovingly,

Jan

457 To M. C. Gillett   Vol. 60, no. 194

Tsalta
[Cape Town]
24 March 1939

Your last letter tells of happy visits to the boys and their families up north. There seems to have been no jarring note anywhere. It

---

[1] 'But I say unto you, that ye resist not evil: but whosoever shall smite thee on thy right cheek, turn to him the other also.' *St Matthew* v.39.

was all very good and welcome news. Yes, I have agreed to be referred to by dear Tona [Gillett] if he wishes to apply anywhere. It would be a pleasure to me to do him any small good turn of that kind—small enough. Your daily *Manchester Guardians* are still arriving. I have no time to read more than the weekly; so please stop the daily. Newspaper reading is one of the trials of my life. Several local dailies (English and Afrikaans) have to be read, in addition to your principal weeklies and *The Times* daily. And the time for reading is limited—what is given to the press has to be deducted from what could so much more profitably be spent on books.

We have here an Oxford pundit—Sir S. Radhakrishnan, professor of religion at Oxford—lecturing on religion at our universities. I have met him at lunch and will meet him again at other functions. He is interesting, without being profound. Religion is rapidly coming to the front in a world where everything else seems to be failing and the cry for help or comfort rises once more to heaven. He is an idealist in philosophy and his religious ideas are etherial and sublimated to a degree—as you would expect from an Oriental idealist. Incidentally he is collecting a book of papers on Gandhi who next September will be seventy. He has talked me round to half-promise to make a contribution to this volume.[1] Perhaps I could say some things about Gandhi which others would miss, but I have little time for this sort of extra. Gandhi's technique of reform consists largely in using suffering and the spirit of sacrifice and suffering as a motive power. Thus his appeal is to suffering, and he himself has once again won a spectacular victory by threatening to starve to death.[2] This use (or abuse?) of suffering as a dynamic of reform deserves attention, and I might usefully draw attention to it. It was to some extent the early Christian technique, when martyrdom was courted, and 'the blood of the martyrs was the seed of the church'.[3] It is a curious element in human nature that the appeal to suffering is often far more potent than the appeal to profit. Not happiness (as some philosophers have held) but suffering becomes the urge or the lure. Isaiah's portrait of the Suffering Servant seems

[1] The book, entitled *Mahatma Gandhi. Essays and Reflections on his Life and Work presented to him on his 70th birthday*, was published in London in 1939. Smuts's contribution, 'Gandhi's Political Method', is on pp. 276–81.

[2] On 3 March 1939 Gandhi started a fast because of a dispute with the Thakor Saheb about the personnel of a committee appointed to recommend constitutional reforms in the state of Rajkot. When, on 7 March, the viceroy of India intervened with an offer to refer the dispute to the chief justice, Gandhi accepted and ended his fast.

[3] *Plures efficimur quoties metimur a vobis, semen est sanguis Christianorum.* The more you mow us down, the more we grow; the seed is the blood of Christians. Tertullian (*c.* 150 – *c.* 230), *Apologia*.

to have made a deeper impression on Jesus than anything else in the old records and to have led him to the Cross.[1] But perhaps I am just wandering at this point and perhaps uttering rank heresies.

So friend Hitler has once more gobbled up a province—Memelland this time.[2] 'An apple a day'—a province per week. I can understand the perturbation all over Europe. But I am waiting to see what will be the next move by friend Musso. Surely he cannot remain naked and hungry while his partner has this Gargantuan feast. Perhaps when you get this letter Musso will have launched his demands on France. Franco has dutifully sent his congratulations to Hitler. I am waiting for the next moves, with my eyes still on Spain. Surely we shall have to pay dearly yet for the folly of so-called non-intervention. Did you ever hear the joke of Talleyrand, who in a somewhat similar situation in his day was asked by some innocent what non-intervention really was, and who answered that it was a mysterious, indeed mystic thing most difficult to define, but when defined turned out to be really very much like intervention! Democratic non-intervention = totalitarian intervention. This fraud will yet come home to us, and I am looking forward to see this ugly nemesis...

458   To M. C. Gillett   Vol. 60, no. 196

Tsalta
[Cape Town]
6 April 1939

Friday afternoon when I posted my last letter to you parliament adjourned for a longish Easter holiday and I went home like a schoolboy with a light heart. On Thursday I had put through its third reading in the house my important Companies Bill[3]—a very difficult piece of work, only piloted through parliament in a short time because very few understand the intricacies of the company laws. I could breathe freely again. The only thing on my mind was Chamberlain's pledge to Poland[4]—a complete departure from previous British policy—and its possible reactions on German policy and the future of our Commonwealth. But I was determined on banishing all thought and care from my mind, and so I prepared

---

[1] See *Isaiah* lii.13–15 and liii.1–12.

[2] No sooner was Prague occupied than an ultimatum was sent to the Lithuanian government for the return of Memelland to Germany. It was followed, on 23 March 1939, by Hitler's arrival in Memel.

[3] Companies Amendment Act, No. 23 of 1939.

[4] On 31 March Chamberlain said in the house of commons that if Poland's independence were threatened the British government would give the Polish government 'all support in their power'.

myself for the coming holiday. It began on Sunday with a visit to
Langebaan[1] of all places...What a curious place it is, with its
Coloured decadent population, its general air of decay, the mighty
tide rushing like a gigantic river at furious pace into that enormous
lagoon—birds everywhere, and the few Europeans making a very
poor impression on us. We motored as far as we could down along
the lagoon, but the rising tide made the seashore unsafe and we did
not reach the old governor's house at Oostewal.[2] Funny stories
I heard—of the band of English pirates who in the earlies scuttled
their ship near the present whaling station, and then settled far up
the end of the lagoon (at *Church* Haven!) and there married
Hottentot wives and founded a Coloured colony by itself. Today
they survive as a decent well-behaved little community now wanting
road connection with the rest of the world...

Chamberlain's Polish guarantee has simply made us gasp—from
the Commonwealth point of view. I cannot see the Dominions
following Great Britain in this sort of imperial policy the dangers of
which to the Commonwealth are obvious. We still remember Lloyd
George's Chanak escapade[3] when a merciful providence had unexpectedly carried me to Kosi bay! But of course there is another
aspect of this new policy. The British government may argue that
such a guarantee is necessary for the new policy of collective security
against Hitler, and that it will mean peace and not war and therefore
not involve Dominion obligations to assist Great Britain in war. For
this argument there is much to be said. But what if there *is* war—and
that over this sort of guarantee in eastern Europe? And in any case
what a commentary on Chamberlain's previous disregard for collective security, and his calling League sanctions 'midsummer
madness'[4] in the case of Abyssinia? The real midsummer madness
was letting the League down and rendering it useless for future co-
operation in case of dire need. Chamberlain's League policy and
flirting with Mussolini may yet produce other more dangerous
consequences. Time alone can show.

...I have been reading a great deal recently about the beginnings
of Christianity and the ostracism and persecution which accompanied it. And yet it was one of the most beautiful movements in

[1] A harbour on Saldanha bay, about 110 miles north of Cape Town.
[2] The house of Lord Charles Somerset, governor of the Cape of Good Hope
(1814–27). *See also* W. J. de Kock, *Joernaal van Paravicini di Capelli*, p. 205, note 789.
[3] To aid the Greeks in their war with Turkey and to safeguard imperial communications Lloyd George, in September 1922, ordered British forces to hold Chanak on
the Dardanelles against a Turkish advance and called on the Dominions for support.
All but New Zealand hedged or refused.
[4] *See supra*, p. 41, note 4.

this world. I don't rank Communism with Christianity but in the minds of converts there is the same impulse to human service and the same revolt against the comfortable attitudes. There was, however, the essential difference that Christ's message was one concerning the human soul and personality, its saving from sin and evil and its companionship with God. Out of this grandness of the soul sprang the social doctrine of service, not *vice versa*. Communism inverts this relation, and in that way gets out of focus. The love of man springs out of the love of God. This seems to me something quite different from historical materialism. Man is primary, not society...

459   From L. S. Amery   Vol. 58, no. 8

112 Eaton Square
S.W.1
11 April 1939

My dear Smuts, You may have considered some of my letters in the last six months rather pessimistic, but I doubt whether you will feel that now. Ever since Munich the dictators have become more and more swollen-headed and determined to keep us on the run the whole time. Even now that we have undertaken to defend Poland they do not really believe it. Anyhow I imagine they will, as the next move, deal with Rumania, possibly hounding Hungary and Bulgaria onto her and only helping 'non-intervention' lines [*sic*] while keeping Yugoslavia quiet by the threat of invasion. In that case the onus of declaring war might be forced upon us and Poland would be freed from any obligation to help unless indeed she had meanwhile pledged herself to Rumania. So the war may well come nearer to you than some of your South African isolationists seem to think. If the Germans should once re-establish themselves in Tanganyika they could, with the help of overwhelming air forces, attack both the Rand and the Northern Rhodesian mines and could indeed send air reinforcements and machine-guns to help a rising in South West Africa. So the fate of Egypt may concern you very closely and your help to prevent it being conquered may be of vital consequence.

I am afraid the government have through feebleness and indecision made an awful mess of Palestine. It would have been far better if they had had the courage of their convictions and stuck to the scheme of partition. By now the Jewish state would have been well on its way to standing on its feet, and might already be organizing military help of really serious value. What I fear has happened is that they have been intimidated by attaching a much too great importance to the Arab as a factor in the international situation, and much too little importance to the Jews. By that I mean both in the military and in the political sense. When the White Paper[1] comes out, as I believe it will soon after Easter, it will gravely shake American opinion. On the other hand, I am sure if we had taken a strong line with the Arabs and made it clear that we would stick to our pledges to the Jews we could easily have developed really important military help from the Jews both in America and in Palestine itself. If it does come to war then I fancy we shall find the Arabs not much help, and indeed, if the other side gain initial successes, openly up against us. In that case we should be driven to arming the Jews, and no doubt they will then have some right to decide the future of Palestine.

Yours ever,

L. S. Amery

460   To M. C. Gillett   Vol. 60, no. 199

Tsalta
[Cape Town]
23 April 1939

This is Sunday night; there is cheerful company talking and listening to music in the sitting-room, while I sit and write in the snug little study. An electric fire is keeping me warm, while outside it is cold and raining, has been raining all day. I have not been out all day. In the morning I read philosophy and this afternoon I have spent with the New Testament—quite agreeably in both cases. As the storms gather in the world and the prospect darkens I look for consolation to philosophy and religion—as becomes old age!

Yesterday was a heavenly day, so off we set for Rooi Els[2]—Jannie and Daphne[3] and myself. And what a day we had, there and at Hangklip[4]....It was a day of days, sent from beyond the skies,[5] and I felt much refreshed after a week of strenuous toil in parliament. We have got drawn into this war business, and as a precaution

---

[1] *Statement of Policy*, 17 May 1939, Cmd. 6019. The British government declared that Palestine should not become a Jewish state and envisaged the establishment within ten years of an independent Palestine in the government of which both Jews and Arabs would share.

[2] On the False bay coast about fifty miles from Cape Town.

[3] J. C. Smuts married Daphne Webster in 1938.

[4] Cape Hangklip.

[5]   It seemed as if the hour were one
                   Sent from beyond the skies...
                       Shelley, 'To Jane: The Recollection', iii.

against a *putsch* I sent some three hundred armed police to Windhoek to keep the peace, and at the same time introduced a bill to take over the policing of South West Africa[1] which hitherto has been left to an inefficient local administration. Of course I am accused of creating war atmosphere, of siding with Great Britain, of dragging South Africa into war etc. But I am quite right and shall not be deterred...

I do not wish to trouble you about the war. Things are pretty bad. Our new efforts to build up a united front are not very successful, and Russia will, I fear, exact a very heavy price for joining that front. It is a terrible thought, that we let down the League, destroyed collective security, and now have to rebuild it at a cost which we never could have contemplated as possible. And at best we shall have poor unreliable friends to lean on in eastern Europe. But now we have no choice, and must pay whatever price is exacted. The colossal preparations and manoeuvrings continue and one shudders to think of the end. At best we can have little faith in the British government, after a record of blunders probably unparalleled in British history. But the Lord may once more be merciful, and save us from our blunders and ourselves. It is not only in the West that a climax is approaching. I keep my eyes on the East and see Japan creeping south from week to week. She is not making much headway in China, but threatens Great Britain and France and Holland ever more and more. Hainan island has been occupied opposite Indo-China, and now the Sprackley islands much further south. I hope Roosevelt's transfer of his Pacific fleet back to that ocean means that he is awake to the vast dangers in that quarter.

I mentioned my reading philosophy this morning. I was looking through the latest number of *Philosophy*, and read a very interesting paper by Broad [C. D.] on present relations between science and religion. He confesses himself not a Christian and is very pessimistic about the future of Christianity. He thinks its world view obsolete, and the miraculous element on which it is based a growing handicap. This may be true, and yet I feel that he fails to get down to rock bottom. Christianity is based on first-class ethical and spiritual insights and discoveries which, however, need restatement in modern terms and in harmony with our enlarged scientific world view of today. Jesus may not have been all that is claimed for him by the orthodox, but he remains our highest light and did speak as no man of our race has ever spoken before or since. But this kernel of eternal truth must be freed from its ancient Jewish husks. It may be that some first-class religious genius may have to launch a new appeal to our moral and spiritual consciousness in order to lead in

[1] Police (South West Africa) Act, No. 19 of 1939.

this religious revival. At present, however, the oracles are dumb,[1] and we must struggle on in darkness and silence and confusion. Science has disclosed the universal harmony in the physical world; biology has disclosed the progressive evolutionary character of all life. Ethics and spirituality have yet to be shown as springing from the nature of things, and not to be foreign elements but incarnate with our humanity. Knowledge must cease to be purely intellectual, and love must be recognized as our deepest and surest form of perception and knowledge and as the real motive power in the world. That is a programme which could be realized *within* the framework of our fundamental Christianity. Lovingly yours,

Jan

461   To M. C. Gillett   **Vol. 60, no. 201**

Tsalta
[Cape Town]
7 May 1939

...I [am] reading once more my beloved New Testament. It fascinates me more and more. What did Jesus think of power politics? How invincible his faith that the things he stood for will redeem this world! And still, 2,000 years after, we are groping in the darkness of the principalities and powers of evil. Did he view the world in too simple a light, or have we failed in the vision and the faith which sustained him? Is the way of suffering, of the Cross, the way out? How can we justify the ways of God to man[2]—to his children, according to Jesus? How can we plant freedom in this world of fixed natural law? Milton does not seem to have succeeded in his great *Paradise Lost* attempt. If suffering is the way how does that affect the principle of holism, which I have assumed to be the way of healing, of purification and synthesis between the divine and the human? These are some of the questions which keep surging up in one's mind in contemplating the contemporary confusions and dangers. Deep down one has the feeling that suffering is the way to meet evil and to beat it on its own chosen field of battle. Evil means suffering, and suffering is the way which leads upward to God. The Cross stands as the real symbol of the Way. To one trained in the ways of science and reason this is a hard doctrine. And yet one feels that there is a profound element of truth in it all

---

[1] *See supra*, p. 17, note 5.
[2]   That...I may assert eternal Providence,
              And justify the ways of God to Men.
                            Milton, *Paradise Lost*, book 1, l. 22.

which somehow has to be cleared up and integrated with our other insights given by science and reason. The New Testament is full of pure gold, even for an unattached Christian like myself. And Jesus fascinates me more and more. What a Figure among men!

...A word about my Transvaal visit over the week-end. I flew away on Thursday and back again on Monday—both most enjoyable flights. Friday I congratulated Potchefstroom on her centenary and met large numbers of my old Boer War veterans. Potchefstroom was for some six months of the Boer War under my command and I have a very soft spot in my heart for those dear people. They did not know what had become of their original *Vierkleur*[1] which had been first hoisted at Potchefstroom. I could not only tell them that I was the proud possessor of that flag but that it was going to be restored to the town as their most treasured relic of the past. You can imagine with what feelings they heard this most unexpected news...

European news remains bad. I can't make out this Danzig business;[2] but Hitler remains enigmatic and the intervention of the Pope shows that there are serious fears in well-informed circles. But it is no use speculating in the dark and we shall know pretty soon. Then [M. M.] Litvinov's dismissal raises another riddle. Is Russia turning to Germany? Is Hitler playing Russia as his trump card towards world domination? Or is there some other explanation which nobody can understand? Perhaps Hitler is reinsuring himself as Bismarck did.[3] And Communism and Nazism are really close together...Ever lovingly,

Jan

462   To S. G. Millin   Vol. 102, no. 86

Tsalta
[Cape Town]
12 May 1939

My dear Sarah, Your welcome letter arrived yesterday and I now answer at once. It was a pleasure hearing from you.

When the time comes I shall consult with you as to your particular job. You can do what perhaps nobody else can, but it is no use

[1] The four-colour flag of the South African Republic.

[2] Exchanges between the German and Polish governments about Danzig had been going on since October 1938. Poland rejected Germany's repeated demands for the return of Danzig to the Reich and the building of a German extra-territorial road and railway across the Corridor.

[3] On 18 June 1887 Bismarck concluded the 'reinsurance' treaty between Germany and Russia mainly in order to prevent Russia from making an alliance with France.

anticipating. I think full use can be made of your exceptional powers.

I am interested to hear that your Testament[1] is nearing its end. It will not be your last testament. People who have much to bequeath continue to add to their list of testaments. How many did Rhodes write? Don't trouble about the Press Bill.[2] For the moment that is out of the way. Perhaps it will turn up later again. But I am thankful enough to achieve even the most temporary success. Who knows about the future, or even whether there will be a future?

Do not let us rehearse Chamberlain's errors. Their name is Legion. It is enough to make one savage, but what is the use? Think of all these futile efforts now to reconstitute collective security, on the part of the man who deliberately destroyed it in the League and called sanctions 'midsummer madness'.[3] But at any rate he is now doing his best according to his lights. With Russia he wishes to avoid a *formal* treaty, so as to avoid the taint of *redness*, and also the appearance of encirclement. He has therefore to fall back on *uni-lateral* declarations of support by Great Britain and Russia for the border states. I hope he will succeed. Without Russia Germany cannot be held in check in the east—that seems clear. The Turkish move has been a good one.[4]

I am deeply grieved over what is happening about Palestine. It seems that the Arabs have to be appeased at almost any cost and the Jews have to be cast to the wolves. It is a miserable story which touches my work and myself to the quick. I have warned, but without avail. Kisch [F. H.] saw me yesterday. Weizmann has appealed to me in his desperation. But I cannot continue futile arguments and courting snubs without doing any good. I have asked Kisch to convey to Weizmann that I consider the present setback, though very serious, not necessarily fatal, and that Great Britain should continue to be looked upon as a friend and not an enemy. Great Britain is in a terribly tight corner and thinks Arab support necessary for her position in the Mediterranean. Her view of the Arabs may prove hopelessly wrong. But there it is. I only trust that when they prove a broken reed, the position may be such that Great Britain will once more turn to Jewry, and that the national home will then finally come into its own. A Jewish declaration of war against the British

---

[1] *The Night is Long*, begun in August 1938, published in 1941.

[2] The object of the bill was to set up a controlling body with disciplinary powers exercisable over both newspapers and individual journalists and a status and functions similar to those of the medical and law councils. Press criticism led General Hertzog to drop the bill and ask editors to draw up a plan of their own.

[3] *See supra*, p. 41, note 4.

[4] An Anglo-French guarantee against aggression was given to Turkey in May 1939.

Commonwealth—whatever the provocation at the moment—will be a disastrous step.

Here in this country the position calls for close and anxious watching. Much is going on under the surface. It may all end in smoke, or it may once more develop on 1914 lines. It is my sense of all this that makes me see things through. Much is happening which goes against the grain, but first things first. And any moment we may be up against first things.

This does not mean that I necessarily expect war. Hitler knows his bloodless victories are at an end and that the next move means a world war. And this may give him pause. But of course he is an abnormal mind and his belief in his stars may make him face even a world war. But that is still uncertain. With kind regards and good wishes. Ever yours,

J. C. Smuts

463   To L. S. Amery   Vol. 60, no. 85

Telegram

From: Smuts

To: Amery

Dated: 15 May 1939

Please co-operate with other friends in last minute effort to prevent abandonment of Jews and Balfour policy. If real trouble comes Jews in Palestine and elsewhere will prove reliable friends. I favour temporizing with Palestine settlement while European situation remains uncertain.

464   To M. C. Gillett   Vol. 60, no. 206

Tsalta
[Cape Town]
27 May 1939

Your letter bringing birthday wishes written just before your visit to Street has just arrived this (Saturday) morning and I write in reply at once. Thank you very much for good wishes spoken and unspoken. The spoken part of us is so inadequate, the unspoken seems to go to the depths and to link us on to divinity—or the devil, whichever is your choice...

You write of the coming of spring, of leaves and colours coming, and of sky and cloud and air. How near we are to all this call of nature, and how ready our response! Here too, with winter on and lots of rain followed by warm almost summer weather the conditions are already springlike and an air of expectancy, of coming life, of twittering birds, and of joy is all around. 'He is made one with nature' as Shelley writes of the dead,[1] and as we feel in ourselves, alive, on such occasions. I wish I could go for a long walk or for a Kirstenbosch ramble among the proteas this morning. But I have to attend a university function at eleven,[2] and two other functions in the afternoon and evening. So I shall console myself at home with talking to my friends far away. My thoughts are often, very often, with you and Arthur, and I hate to be so far away from you. Spiritual sympathy is not enough to make up for this physical distance, and the sense of separation remains in the background all the time. I hope you two will enjoy the coming holiday to Talloires very much, and that it will refresh and refurnish both of you for what lies before. I shall be with you in spirit.

We are now in the final month of the session and the strain of parliament is heavy on us. I long for the end. So much of the work is just unutterable drudgery, a weariness to the flesh and the soul. And yet this is the way of human affairs. I could do all this far better by myself in a tenth of the time. But the pace of our human army is that of its slowest unit, and we cannot get away from this grievous dispensation. We have additional trouble of a very tiresome nature. Hofmeyr [J. H.] and Blackwell have behaved in a rather childish way in parliament and Hertzog, who is autocratic and intolerant in such matters, has taken their action as a challenge. Result—they have resigned from our caucus, and will now pose as martyrs, as champions for free speech and free conscience, and the party will suffer, especially in the towns.[3] Hofmeyr with all his great gifts has no sense and often behaves like a grown-up boy and not a sensible grown up with a due sense of proportion. All this is most distressing to me, as I have to oppose the prime minister and support friends who *will* be foolish. The trouble is worse because it is all over an Indian Bill which is likely to raise a storm both in India and here. And I think it could have been avoided with tact and restraint.

The international situation looks slightly easier, with the prospect

[1] *Adonais*, xlii.

[2] Smuts became chancellor of the University of Cape Town in 1936 on the accession of Edward VIII to the throne.

[3] Hofmeyr and Blackwell opposed the Transvaal Land and Trading Bill, introduced by the minister of the interior, R. B. Stuttaford. It imposed restrictions on the purchase of land by Indians and required them to possess trading licences. Hertzog asked the United party caucus, as an alternative to his own resignation, to censure Hofmeyr and Blackwell who declared that, if accused, they would resign from the caucus. On 24 May the caucus voted for censure.

of an agreement with Russia.[1] I have never liked entanglements with Russia which is to me an inscrutable country. But if that is the way to peace then for peace's sake let us have it. If a military agreement with Russia is concluded I believe the situation in Europe will be one of military stalemate, the opposing forces will be fairly balanced, and war may become unlikely. What is more, the continuance of the present intolerable situation of strained preparation will become senseless; consultations for a general settlement may ensue which may be the way out of the present dangers. Roosevelt's offer of an economic conference will then become a valuable suggestion and may pave the way to a new settlement in Europe. I hope there will be no flare up over Danzig in the meantime. This is just a wish-thought.

We have the young Duke of Devonshire here, I suppose to look over the Protectorates situation. We gave him a parliamentary dinner last night at which I spoke. He made a very good impression. He told me how his father and grandfather hated the very name of Conservative and adjured him never to join the Carlton Club under any circumstances! It is curious how this intense liberalism got foundered in the Irish bog. Think of your own grandfather's similar trouble.[2] Tonight we entertain him at our club and I shall have to speak again. Why did the Lord not create us dumb?

The birthday has once more overwhelmed me with messages, and it will take some time to extricate myself from this mass of correspondence. Some nice books have arrived which I hope to read—two from your Chinese source. Thank you. An Arabic one from the dear Boli[3] etc. etc. Is sixty-nine not frightfully old? What is left after it, and could I expect to do anything still worth while in this dotage? The prospect alarms me. I wish I could still write a book! Love,

Jan

465 To L. S. Amery

Vol. 60, no. 98

House of Assembly
Cape Town
8 June 1939

My dear Amery, I have your letter of 24 May in regard to the Palestine decision, and have been very deeply interested both in the

[1] On 27 May the British and French ambassadors in Moscow began discussions with the Soviet government for a pact of mutual assistance and a military convention.

[2] John Bright, Margaret Gillett's maternal grandfather, although a Liberal, was opposed to Gladstone's Irish policy.

[3] Frank and Harriet (Lulu) Bolus (qq.v.).

details you write and in the parliamentary debate enclosed, outstanding in which I found your own speech.

I have been doing my best to keep our Jewish friends in South Africa on the right track and prevent them from flying into a rage with the British government and the British people. There is no doubt that they have been very badly let down, and by no sort of ingenuity can the present decision be reconciled with the Balfour declaration or the provisions of the mandate, or with repeated declarations of the British government in former years. Naturally one understands that the British government must have acted as they have done for very grave reasons, but I cannot help thinking with you that they have been stampeded by the present very grave international crisis into the surrender they have been forced to accept. My only consolation is that this latest solution may prove a mere paper solution, and will be swept away hereafter by the force of circumstances.

I do not believe in the Arabs, and doubt very much whether in a first-class Mediterranean crisis their loyalty could be depended on. The Jews on the contrary are thoroughly loyal and reliable, and I am sure will prove so again if the need arises, and will, I hope, come into their own in due time. I have not been a partitionist as you know, but I have said that if partition is the way out of the difficulty, I am prepared to accept it. It may be that a loose cantonment system with the free right to the Jews to allow immigration into their cantons may prove the way out. It may also be that future developments may be such that the British government is compelled to take a much stronger line with the Arabs than they have ever done before, and in that case the possibility of a Jewish state in Palestine must not be excluded. We all deeply deplore the recent error, but must not lose heart on that account.

The recent surprises of the international situation have been the most astonishing I have seen in British policy. Not many months ago the course was almost pro-German, now we are getting pledged to guarantee all and everyone in eastern Europe; something which had never been contemplated before in British foreign policy is now to be our future course. I wonder what the after-effects of such a change of front are likely to be! The whole position into which we have been forced by recent developments will require very cool and calm consideration. It is one thing to have collective security under the League by which an organized effort is made to maintain world peace. It is quite a different thing to give these specific guarantees to the most unstable peoples in the most distant parts of Europe. If these guarantees are to be carried out by Great Britain, what is the future of the British Commonwealth going to be? Frankly, the prospect frightens me.

We have already abandoned the League, and this new development in British policy may involve the future of the Commonwealth too. The only ray of hope that I see in the present situation is that, with Russia allied to the western powers, and American benevolent sympathy in the background, the forces of both sides will be so evenly balanced that a military stalemate will be produced, and the warlike dictators may heed the warning. In that case however, it will be wise and indeed necessary policy at once to proceed further and try to come to some general pacific settlement in Europe. The present armament race cannot be continued without general bankruptcy and revolution. And if a settlement by way of a world war is excluded, then the only alternative will be a settlement by way of peaceful conference and accommodation. Roosevelt has already pledged himself to American support of an economic settlement. In the course of this summer there will either be war or it will become clear that the new alignment of forces may make war impossible. The British government should be prepared for either contingency, so that the opportunity for a peaceful general settlement may not be allowed to let slip again. I am frightened by the prospect of two huge masses of forces kept glaring at each other and keeping up a state of suspense and run of expenditure which must prove fatal at an early date.

If there is to be no war, let there be peace, and let America and the Commonwealth take the lead in this great movement. It may mean the United States at least being firmly drawn into co-operation with us in a great peaceful world movement.

I am just dictating a few of my reactions to the present situation, without intending to be dogmatic. I find the position most difficult and obscure, and have a feeling of dread at the courses into which we have been forced by the post-Munich policy of Hitler. With kind regards and all good wishes, Yours ever sincerely,

s. J. C. Smuts

466   From M. K. Gandhi   Vol. 58, no. 143

Telegram

From: Gandhi, Abbottabad
To: General Smuts, Pretoria
Dated 16 July 1939

Why is agreement of 1914 being violated with you as witness? Is there no help for Indians except to pass through fire?[1]

467   To L. S. Amery   Vol. 60, no. 111

Pretoria
2 August 1939

My dear Amery, Just a short line in reply to your most interesting note of 19 June. I do most fully agree with you that there is grave danger in the eastern Mediterranean, including Egypt, Palestine and Greece. If these countries are overrun we shall be at a very grave disadvantage—the navy without decent harbours, and the storm spreading over Africa, with the line of vital communications. Germany and Italy are not going to attack impregnable fronts, but the weakest, which appear to be in the eastern Mediterranean. I am glad to see our forces are being strengthened there, but hardly enough yet. Unless the navy is strong enough to hold the control of the Mediterranean the first fortnight of the war might see a terrible *débâcle* in Africa. Italy must go all out there, or lose all her African possessions. I trust our high command will not once more keep their eyes glued on the impregnable European fronts. Peace seems to hang on the Russian alliance, and that is going distressingly slow.

Note the date on this letter. Twenty-five years after we are once more facing the gravest situation in this poor old world. If war comes we shall eventually pull through once more, but I fear the initial go-off. Ever yours,

s. J. C. Smuts

[1] *See* vol. III, p. 135, note 1; p. 180, note 1; no. 581; and *supra*, p. 167, note 3.

468 To J. Martin

Vol. 60, no. 115

Irene
[Transvaal]
3 August 1939

My dear Martin, Your *Times*es have been arriving regularly and I have the news of the Thunderer[1] within six days of its appearance in London. This is of course a great convenience for which I am very grateful. I have also received Rauschning's *Revolution of Destruction*[2] which you have kindly sent me. I hope to read it as soon as possible. It is difficult to size up the Hitler revolution, and I am so prejudiced against its main principles that I am but a poor judge. At present it is nothing but a dire menace to peace. Here in South Africa a violent subversive propaganda is being maintained, I suppose to keep us engaged locally. The commissioner of police[3] who has just paid South West Africa a visit comes back with a very disquieting report about conditions there. It is clear that my sending the police there in April just forestalled a *coup* which had been planned. They say next time there will be no leakage and no forestalling! Our Nats have done the country a terrible disservice by announcing that if the Germans insist on having South West Africa back they can have it. I find they are very well supported financially. In the [Orange] Free State the *Ossewa-Brandwag* movement[4] is going on pretty strong. This is probably only a secret military organization masquerading as a 'culture' movement. I am keeping a close watch on it, remembering our experiences in 1914.

I have just returned from a most delightful flight to Lake Kivu in the Belgian Congo in company with Ernest Oppenheimer and Deneys Reitz. It is pleasant to have rich friends! We saw the great volcano in action, sending a river of redhot lava into the lake, greater than any river I have ever seen. It is a sight that rivals the Victoria Falls. You should see it some time when you can be spared from running the finances of half the world! I feel inspired, refreshed and keen after this experience. Why should we give so much thought to your dictator spouters, when there is such a real and

---

[1] This facetious name was first applied to *The Times* after the assistant editor, Edward Sterling (d. 1847) began an article as follows: 'We thundered forth the other day an article on the subject of social and political reform.'

[2] H. Rauschning, *Germany's Revolution of Destruction* (1939).

[3] Colonel I. P. de Villiers (q.v.).

[4] Founded in October 1938 to emphasize and preserve the national tradition of the Afrikaners and to advance their culture, the 'O.B.' soon became a semi-military political organization. For an account of its origin and growth *see* M. Roberts and A. E. G. Trollip, *The South African Opposition, 1939–1945* (1947).

natural spouter in the world? Kindest regards and remembrances. Ever yours,

J. C. Smuts

469   To M. C. Gillett   **Vol. 60, no. 215**

Doornkloof
[Transvaal]
3 August 1939

It is curious how unreal time appears sometimes. It is just a week since I arrived back from central Africa. I have been deeply immersed in affairs and the troubles of the world ever since; and it seems like ages since I was on that pleasure flight. It all happened long, long ago, and is now only a memory of the past. I suppose this sense of rapid transition comes because we have no time nowadays to pause and digest our experience, to savour it, and make it sink into us. It is just one sharp experience after another, and displacing it in the mind. Even so, however, a memory remains, however far off it may appear. And Kivu and the volcanoes will long stand out among the experiences of life. I promised to send you my fuller report.[1] I do not know why but my office typing girl has not yet finished the job. I suppose she has much else to do and finds my scrawl difficult to decypher. I shall forward it as soon as she returns it to me. Meanwhile I have been busy with the price of maize, the secret movements of a subversive character in some parts of the country—reminiscent of 1914[2]—the propaganda and fomenting of strife carried on by foreign agents with foreign capital, the doings in South West Africa, and all the other forms of mischief to which nationalistic South Africa is such an easy prey. I have been reading in Klausner's *Jesus of Nazareth*[3] of all the many false Messiahs who appeared among the Jews in the age in which Jesus lived, and one is at a loss to understand that so much high hope could have been abused by so much fraud. Something like that is going on in contemporary South Africa. Propaganda, falsehood, delusion are rampant among the people, and one has one's hands full in preventing mischief from taking a fatal turn. These are the local repercussions of the war rumours from Europe and German propaganda. It is all very human I suppose, but it is not pleasant to be brought down

[1] A manuscript and typescript of 'Notes of Trip to Lakes Kivu and Edward' is in the Smuts Collection (Box D—Writings).
[2] *See supra*, p. 172, note 4.
[3] J. G. Klausner, *Jesus of Nazareth—his life, times and teaching* (1925).

from the heights of my African flight with such a bump! But of such stuff is life made up.

You have now twice asked me what direction you should give about my letters and papers in your possession, and also what I propose doing about my own papers. I had not given the subject much attention until you asked your embarrassing questions. And I do not yet see the answer. I suppose the end is not so near, and that a little delay may bring light into this situation. I have never even thought of a literary executor! I doubt whether my humble position as an author justifies so extravagant a step. But of course there is a certain amount of stuff that might be of public interest hereafter—e.g. the hundred volumes or so of Isie's scrapbooks! I shall begin to think over the matter and write you or discuss it with you when next we meet again. I have never been careful about MSS and I do not even know what I have. The other day the University of Cape Town asked me for the MS of *Holism* as being the first original work in philosophy by a South African—and now their chancellor. Neither Isie nor I know where this MS is or even whether it exists![1] This may be very negligent but it shows how little attention has been given to these matters. Where is the MS of the *League of Nations* which was mostly written in illness in your prophet's chamber?[2] And what a sorry prophet I have been! Where is that vision of the Messianic Age now? Klausner ends his *Jesus* by calling the Christian message a '*Zukunfts Musik*'[3]—something for the unrealizable future and not for this dull practical world. Was the *League of Nations* also a foretaste of what never will be? Is Holism a similar vain hope in philosophy, in a world where we are doomed to grub in details and particulars and never shall rise to the whole? There is a sense of great failure over it all, and in these days when the foundations are shaking and nought abides in this transient world, this sense of human—and personal—futility comes home with special force. And still we must strive forward in the night, even when no clear light shines within or beyond.

You will perhaps think that my letters recently have been becoming subjective and introspective. But you must remember that my writing to you and Arthur is just a self-communing. Hopes and fears and speculations flit across the page and indicate the sort of

[1] Manuscripts and typescripts of the original draft chapters of *Holism and Evolution* are in the Smuts Collection (Box B).

[2] Smuts wrote *A League of Nations* during an attack of influenza in his bedroom at 102 Banbury Road, Oxford. It was first printed as a British war cabinet paper (P. 44 dated 16 December 1918). In January 1919 it was published as a pamphlet. There is no manuscript in the Smuts Collection.

[3] Music of the future.

trend in my thoughts. It is all light, airy stuff and should not be taken as fixed and deliberate conclusions. One just meanders in thought as one meanders across the downs. Not to be taken too seriously or tragically. With it all I remain cheerful in outlook, believing in goodness, and the overcoming of evil by good, but not always very certain of even that! Public affairs are more confused and difficult than I have known them for a lifetime. Leaders are under grave suspicion and their motives are questioned when perhaps their insight is to blame. Chamberlain I think has been guilty mostly of lack of comprehension and insight rather than of good intentions. At present the most puzzling matter to me is what Russia is thinking and up to. Is it simply a case of distrust of the British government that makes them decline to come to the point, or are there deeper plannings and cogitations? To me all the indications still point to trouble coming this summer, and if the Russian treaty is not carried through I imagine a European war is a certainty. I do not see Hitler retreating after the length he has gone. It is doubtful whether he could even afford to retreat. And so we are just waiting on events beyond our control. This is a very humiliating position to be in—to know that the initiative is not ours, and that our course is to be determined by others. But that is the position, and there is no getting out of it that I can see at present. The east Asian situation is also becoming most interesting. It may seem silly of Japan to go on girding at Britain when she has already so much on her hands. But I daresay that is done on German dictation. Germany is moving heaven and earth to get Britain deeply committed in Asia, and persuading Japan that she may safely flout Britain as the latter will not allow herself to be drawn into war in that quarter. Nor can Britain face a war on that front at this stage, unless America goes all out in support—which she won't. And so the darkness thickens. My dear love to you all,

Jan

470   To A. B. Gillett   Vol. 60, no. 217

Pretoria
17 August 1939

I had a very interesting letter from you this week, and as I have an open moment I write to you in my office.

I note the view you report that in your circle war is *not* expected. There is a good deal of evidence in that direction. I understand that Hitler in his talk with Burckhardt [C.] disclaimed all idea of forcing a settlement on Danzig or Poland. And it would also appear that Mussolini has been treading the soft pedal, as he knows his number will be up if things go wrong. And there is a good deal of peace talk. So things may be shaping towards peace *at present*, if not in our day; on the other hand you have the vast campaign of propaganda and the immense armies that have been mobilized, for what? Perhaps for intimidation and moral defeat of the enemy. One cannot say definitely, and so I suppose we shall continue in a state of suspense for some time longer. What has to be feared is that this suspense must have a disastrous effect on trade and industry (apart from war industries) and lead to depressed conditions which again become an excuse for war. And so the vicious circle continues.

What is happening at Moscow? Why this inordinate delay in fixing up an agreement? One feels all through that there are vital factors in the international situation which are hidden or unknown. And that makes one all the more uneasy, and unwilling to form definite opinions.

It is a great pity that there is this widespread distrust of Chamberlain. It is a grave handicap to the British cause. The enemy secretly thinks he will yet give in. The friend is not quite certain that he will not be sold. It is a lamentable position for any government to be in.

Here we have cold rainy weather and snow on the higher mountains. But all are well at home and look forward to spring. Love from

Jan

471   To M. C. Gillett   Vol. 60, no. 219

Civil Service Club
Cape Town
20 August 1939

So here I am, having arrived yesterday at 4.15 p.m. instead of at 12.30, as the schedule would have had it. We had a leak in our oil tank which was fortunately discovered when we came down for petrol at Beaufort West. But for the accident of our descent at Beaufort West we might have had to come down elsewhere in a dangerous forced landing on the Karoo. I spent the evening on my political business and thereafter had a perfect sleep. This morning when I got up the weather looked somewhat uncertain, but there were indications that it might clear up—the glass was rising and the sun fitfully piercing through clouds which had rained most of the night. At 8.30 a.m. I phoned Louis [McIldowie] that I was going up the mountain and she was to meet me at Kirstenbosch at 3 p.m. She said that it was raining heavily at Wynberg and she thought I was doing the wrong thing. Still, other club men agreed—perhaps politely—with me, and up I went—by way of Platteklip gorge. I had not been up that route for fourteen years, and Cape Town has developed enormously in that direction, so that the old familiar foot-paths had disappeared and I wandered about for more than an hour before I found the real ascent. By that time it was drizzling and I should have turned back. The drizzle became a steady rain, and long before I was halfway up the mountain I was sopping wet. But now there could be no turning back for the mountaineer. After three hours I reached the tea-room, without a dry shred on me. Nobody at the tea-room, of course, not even a fire. The wife of the engineer at the cableway gave me some clothes of her husband to put on while mine were being dried—far from successfully. Still raining, really pouring, with a biting cold wind in addition. I plodded towards Skeleton gorge via Maclear. The foot-paths were running streams, but I preferred walking in the water to slipping on the rocks with my rubber soles. I had many falls, one of which I feared had done me in, but after lying sometime on the rock, I quietly rose and found my thigh had after all not collapsed. The mountain was a network of streams and waterfalls—a sight I had never seen before. Finally Skeleton [gorge] was reached and welcomed. Little did I know what was in store for me. Some considerable distance down, as you know, the route follows the watercourse in the gorge. But when this point was reached I realized that it would be suicide to plunge into that mad river careering along at so many miles per hour. So I had to turn out of the gorge, climb the shoulder of the mountain and come down between Skeleton and Nursery—the most uncomfortable route possible in the continuous downpour. I was more than thankful when at 4.45 p.m. I reached Kirstenbosch. Louis was on the point of notifying the police. Think of the disgrace if I had been advertised tonight on the radio as lost on Table mountain! I have literally been continuously wet to the skin all day, but a hot bath and a little rest in bed have restored me wonderfully, and I have now no fear of chill or rheumatism. I shall be stiff to-morrow at the farewell functions to the Portuguese notabilities,[1] but they will be sufficiently astonished to hear that on *such* a day I had done the whole circuit of Table mountain. Tonight to bed early and I trust another night of perfect sleep. Tomorrow we have a lunch at Muizenberg, and a farewell procession to the boat, and then I take the train at night for Bloemfontein and the Free State tour. By the way my Abraham and Isaac story at the Jewish banquet on Wednes-

---

[1] The president of Portugal was making an official visit to South Africa.

day brought in £15,000 *on the spot* for their refugee children fund. All are overwhelmed at this result—magnificent, but *Fear and Trembling* has done it.[1]

Later, 25 August   Doornkloof

I complete this long letter at Doornkloof, after having finished the farewells to the Portuguese party as well as my trip to the Free State. Both the farewell and the trip were great successes. On my return to the north by train I found the country under water from heavy rains. I don't remember ever having seen the Karoo so under water—and this in August which is generally a specially dry month. It had rained heavily all the way from the Cape to the Free State. My visits to Thaba'nchu, Clocolan and Ladybrand[2] had to be done by motor over sodden roads. Still, all my engagements were successfully carried out and fine meetings held. Last night I returned by train and this morning was spent over very serious business at my office. For on my return I learnt of the most recent developments in Europe.[3] As you know I have been pessimistic for months about the European situation, and at last the great blow seems to be *about* to fall. I say *about* because *something* may still happen at the end. Hitler is to speak on Sunday and thereafter comes Nürnberg.[4] It is just possible that war may still be prevented. But at present it looks like a moral certainty. You can imagine how one must feel over this prospect. I can appreciate your feelings. For South Africa it is a terrible choice—all the harder as the apparent trouble is over Danzig, which nobody really bothers about one way or the other. But of course Danzig is only the pretext, and behind it lies the real issue of world domination and victory for the new ideology and the new Paganism. To think that the world has learnt so little from the last war, and that the next one may set the clock ages back. Surely, bad as we are we have not deserved thus to perish! The Pope, Roosevelt and others are still moving for peace, and one hopes against hope for the best. The behaviour of Russia has been parti-

[1] Shortly after reading Kierkegaard's *Fear and Trembling* about the temptation and faith of Abraham, Smuts spoke at a meeting in Johannesburg to raise funds to support the immigration of young Jews into Palestine and compared the sacrifice of Isaac to the sacrificial effort now demanded of the Jews to save their young people. *See* Smuts Collection, vol. 60, no. 218.

[2] Towns in the south-eastern Orange Free State.

[3] On 23 August the mutual non-aggression pact between Russia and Germany, which provided secretly for the partition of Poland, was signed. Next day a local Nazi was declared head of the state of Danzig. On 25 August an Anglo-Polish defence alliance, which reaffirmed the agreement of 6 April, was signed.

[4] That is, the annual rally of the Nazi party in September in Nuremberg.

cularly shocking—carrying on confidential negotiations with A and B and all the time secretly negotiating with C against them. But I feared all along that Stalin would let democracy down just as he has let China down. Perhaps he realizes that his real affinity is with Hitler and Nazism. And in fact there is little to choose between his brand of Communism and Fascism...

I found your letter here, telling of George's[1] passing away. It was really a mercy, much as one feels for the bereaved. I liked him very much, as a man in whom there was no guile, but only real human goodness. My deepest sympathy with Arthur who I know was so deeply attached to him.

And so the losses come and the clouds gather. It will once more be a mortal duel between 'Faith' on the one hand and 'Fear and Trembling' on the other. May faith in good, in God, in the ultimate ideals triumph. Lovingly yours,

Jan

472   To S. G. Millin   Vol. 102, no. 88

Pretoria
26 August 1939

My dear Sarah, I have just read your note, and with much interest.

The view I take of this Russian business—of course without knowledge of the real facts—is that Russia never wanted the negotiations for an alliance to succeed. They dismissed their previous foreign minister—the last real European among them—because he was keen on such an arrangement with the democracies. With Japan on their hands in the East they were determined to keep out of war in the West. Finally they have been tempted by Germany (bribe still unknown) to enter into this non-aggression pact. At least they can now deal with Japan if they so choose. And perhaps they may divide the spoils in the West, in addition.

Russia means and *meant* to sit out in this devil's dance in the West. Hence Litvinov had to go. She awaits her day as the overlord of a ruined Europe.

Things look pretty black. But of course something may come out of Mussolini's blue funk at this juncture, and out of Roosevelt's proposal to Hitler.[2] Next week will show.

---

[1] Sir George Masterman Gillett (q.v.), eldest brother of Arthur Gillett.

[2] Roosevelt had appealed to both Hitler and Mussolini for an assurance not to attack thirty-one named nations. In a speech on 28 August 1939 Hitler made a telling and scornful reply.

Our position here is awkward. It is a thousand pities that Danzig —a German city—has become the ostensible cause or occasion of the conflagration. Of course it is only *ostensible*—with much more behind it. That was an interesting evening over the Youth Aliyah! Ever yours,

J. C. Smuts

473 To M. C. Gillett Vol. 60, no. 220

Doornkloof
[Transvaal]
28 August 1939

This is Monday, and this morning I had your letter telling of the burial of George [Gillett], and of your quiet sojourn at Aston, with Jan and Nico and their families. It must be a searching time for all of you, what with this private loss, and impending doom for the world. But it is pleasant to think of you and Arthur at Aston with your dear ones, enjoying quiet and peace amid the gathering storm.

I have spent a quiet week-end at home, after my busy time with Portugal and the Free State functions. The fact is that I have not yet quite recovered from that strenuous day on Table mountain, a day I shall not soon forget, and perhaps the last of my mountain escapades. I have felt stiff in the joints and a strained muscle in one of the legs has further damped my ardour for walking...Saturday was a busy time in office, as Friday had been; and added to the office work a new tangle had turned up which has made us call precipitately for a meeting of parliament. The senate is due to expire next 5 September, but the elections for a fresh senate cannot be held till about the end of October. And this at a time when the world is in wild uproar. Of course we cannot leave this country without a full parliament at a time when very grave decisions may have to be taken; and so a meeting of parliament for next Saturday (2 September) to prolong the life of the senate had to be arranged. Saturday last was spent in making these sudden arrangements, and in preparing the necessary legislation and other steps. I hope to leave for the Cape in a couple of days and shall be a lonely grass widower at the Civil Service Club. We hope the affair will not take more than a week, and it is therefore unnecessary to reopen 'Tsalta'.

This is all a bad upset, involving the cancellation of plans and programmes for political work—tours, congresses in Transvaal and Natal, etc. It is curious that we should have overlooked this hiatus in our parliamentary machinery. But the fact is that nobody (except

myself) has taken the European crisis very seriously. It was looked
upon as the usual Hitler bluff; and not calling for any parliamentary
action. Now of course the aspect of affairs has suddenly become
most sinister—hence this belated action to keep the senate in being.

This week and the next will be the critical time of the crisis.
Hitler insists on the immediate return to Germany of Danzig and
the Corridor. I do not see Poland agreeing to this without war. And
so the Fates have woven new tangles for the world. There is a bare
possibility that the situation may improve, but I fear it has gone too
far, and the world is not in a mood for another Munich.

Hitler may have made a good stroke of business in his anti-
aggression pact from a purely military point of view, but it must
surely be bad political business for him. What becomes of his whole
gospel if Bolshevism ceases to be his Devil? His whole standpoint
is discredited as futile. Here our local Communists have already
started an infernal row over this somersault of Stalin, who is taken
to be a traitor to Communism. From my point of view, however,
Stalin has done very well. He lets the others fight it out while he
awaits the result with equanimity and probably with profit. (For
he must have exacted a very big price for his pact.)[1] But Hitler
is now—from an ideological point of view—in a very difficult
position.

With us there is no enthusiasm for Poland, and less for Danzig
and the Corridor. Moreover, neutrality is even more firmly held as
a faith than in the Middle West of the United States. And on the
other side (which happens to be my own) there is the difficulty to
understand how in the long run we could possibly keep out of the
fight, and how we could do so now consistently with our honour and
vital interests. A great storm is therefore brewing here too. I had
to face it twenty-five years ago and never thought of having it all
over again. But such are the choices before us. The Germans,
knowing my attitude at Paris, have published my notes to Lloyd
George and Wilson, protesting against the undue enlargement of
Poland as a sure cause of future war.[2] And now that my prophecy
may come true I have to tell the people that it would be wrong for
them to stand aside! And so wisdom is turned into the appearance
of folly, and my conduct convicted of inconsistency! It is a queer
world. I wish I were thirty-five years younger! Love and best
wishes,

Jan

---

[1] Germany had recognized the Soviet claim to control of Finland, Estonia and
Latvia and her interest in the Rumanian province of Bessarabia as well as agreeing to
the partition of Poland.   [2] See vol. IV, nos. 967, 986, 1011.

474   To Lord Brand   Vol. 60, no. 117

Pretoria
29 August 1939

My dear Brand, I had your cable about Tereshchenko [M. I.] and shall be glad to have an exchange of ideas with him on his coming to Cape Town. I myself shall be there in a few days time for a special session of our parliament in connection with the present emergency.

I note your pessimistic view of the situation. The next few days will prove decisive, one way or the other. We all agree that a recurrence of Munich is unthinkable, and the pity is that Hitler thinks only in terms of Munich. So the stage is set for tragedy.

The Russo-German pact may have been a military score, but I cannot but think that in the end it must weaken and undermine Hitler's political position. He seems to have surrendered the basis of his political faith—with what repercussions time will show.

I trust our friend Lothian will prove a great success at Washington, which is now more important than ever in world affairs. But the Middle West attitude with which Roosevelt has to contend is very much like a similar outlook in South Africa which makes our position difficult and obscure. We enter on a very dark era from now on. With all good wishes and kind remembrances, Ever yours sincerely,

J. C. Smuts

475   From L. S. Amery   Vol. 58, no. 12

112 Eaton Square
S.W.1
2 September 1939

My dear Smuts, My pessimism throughout all these months has, I am sorry to say, been justified, and here we are face to face with a clear and simple moral issue, on which I think nobody can doubt where the right lies.[1] It is in essence a war of defence on behalf of all that Greece and Rome, Christianity and chivalry, have built up for us over three thousand years, against crude barbaric tribalism equipped with modern weapons.

On the other hand, if the moral problem is simple, the military one is anything but. How Germany is to be brought to her knees in order to make her restore Poland and Czechoslovakia is going to be a difficult task, though it may be helped before long by internal

[1] On 1 September the Germans had invaded Poland.

crumbling of the structure of Nazi tyranny. Meanwhile, for the moment, and possibly for good, Italy stands out.[1] That disposes, even if only temporarily, of the danger to Egypt, and indeed to all Africa, which lay behind the Axis conspiracy. We cannot afford to let Italy remain a menacing neutral until such moment as, Poland being crushed, she can join Germany in presenting new demands to France and ourselves. On the other hand, she will have to be handled with a certain amount of diplomatic consideration and a few days at any rate given her before we can insist upon successive stipulations ensuring a genuine neutrality on her part.

Neville [Chamberlain] is, I believe, at last creating a war cabinet, as I have urged upon him again and again over the last two years. He is also doing a certain amount of reconstruction and has, I understand, already invited Churchill to join. Whether he will want to make use of me I don't know.[2] Yours ever,

L. S. Amery

[1] On 25 August Mussolini had informed Hitler that Italy could not, because of the depletion of her war material, join in military operations if a German attack on Poland should lead to a general war.

[2] Amery was not included in the war cabinet formed by Chamberlain on 3 September. Churchill became first lord of the admiralty.

PART XVII

THE SECOND WORLD WAR

5 SEPTEMBER 1939–16 AUGUST 1945

THE SECOND WORLD WAR

Smuts became prime minister for the second time on 5 September 1939 after his motion to put the Union of South Africa into the war against Germany was passed in the house of assembly by a small majority and Hertzog, who had insisted on neutrality, resigned. Smuts now entered upon one of the most active periods of his strenuous life. Although this is mainly documented in a great flow of official telegrams, many of them to Churchill, his private letters of the war years are important records and among the best in the Smuts Collection. They are thoughtful, spirited, deeply felt and show him summoning up and pouring out all his powers in a crucial struggle. Only a token selection out of many hundreds appear below.

The documents chosen are given in chronological order but fall into four groups dealing with Smuts's activities (a) as minister of defence; (b) as prime minister; (c) as Commonwealth statesman and soldier; (d) his personal life.

As minister of defence he is seen building up the South African forces for service in Kenya, Abyssinia, North Africa, Italy (**479, 480, 485, 494, 517, 540, 568, 611**); organizing war supplies (**482, 485**); taking moderate security measures (**491, 528, 533, 535, 536, 555, 560**); building national roads (**483**). As prime minister he faced fierce parliamentary encounters with a resourceful opposition which he tended to underestimate (**485, 489, 490, 492, 528, 564**); made a last approach to Hertzog for political truce (**501, 504, 505**); survived Nationalist pressure for a separate peace after the defeat of France (**505, 507, 511**); won a 'famous victory' which he thought would be lasting in the 1943 election (**608, 609, 611–13, 616**). He also took account of the effects of economic and social change on African life and labour and proposed to replace Hertzog's policies with what he called 'trusteeship' (**556, 589, 591**). And once again he tried, and failed, to assuage the dissensions of whites and Indians in Natal (**519, 534, 600–2, 604, 632, 646, 648, 654, 663**).

As Commonwealth statesman and soldier he was chiefly concerned with the war in Africa and the Middle East for the Mediterranean region was from first to last the core of his strategy (**519, 537, 538, 545, 573**). But the whole course of the war was acutely analysed in frequent letters to the Gilletts and to L. S. Amery, secretary for India in Churchill's cabinet. Repeated visits to north Africa and London kept him closely in contact with the Allied leaders (**516, 529, 567, 574, 582, 586, 619, 628, 634, 662**). He did not go to the United States but was in touch with Roosevelt (**567**).

From the start he was confident that the Allies would win the war (**517, 522**) which he looked upon as a 'crusade of the spirit' in defence of Christian civilization. But as it went on he became more and more pessimistic about 'the peace to come'. The rise of Russian power in particular alarmed him. How was it to be contained and world peace secured, the Commonwealth protected? He did a good deal of thinking about this (**561, 565, 583, 584, 598, 612**) and expressed some of his ideas in an 'explosive' speech in London in November 1943 (**624**). As the war drew to a close he began to despair of a statesmanlike settlement. He deplored the decisions at Yalta and Potsdam and British policy in Greece (**610, 653–6, 658**) and the part he took in setting up the new league of nations at San Francisco was dutiful but lacked conviction (**664–7, 670, 672, 674**).

Of Smuts's personal life during these years his papers record the making of new friends in Henry and Daphne Moore and the crown prince and princess of Greece (**565, 574**), continued absorption in New Testament study whenever he could find time to read, and the physical cost of the enormous load of work he carried (**483, 522, 559**).

476   To S. M. Smuts

Vol. 60, no. 118

Marks Gebou
[Kaapstad]
5 September 1939

Liefste Mamma, Jy sal natuurlik die jongste ontwikkelinge in die koerante gesien het. Waar ek met my koms hierheen gedenk het dat ek nou gou uit die regeering sal wees, is ek nou, of sal ek môre wees, Eerste Minister. Hertzog en Co. het vreeslike flaters gemaak— met daardie gevolg vir hul en vir my.

Ek hoop my regeering sal môre (6 Sep.) ingesweer word, en in daardie geval hoop ek op Donderdag 7 Sep. weer terug te vlie na die Transvaal. Sover gaan alles goed. Maar wat wag nie vir my nie?

Sondag oggend was Louis en ek te Kirstenbosch tussen al die fraaie blomme en had 'n heerlike tyd. In die namiddag is toe die Kabinet stryd voortgeset—met die bekende uitslag. Van toe af was alles in rep en roer.

Ek hoop die gaan jul baie goed en dat ons mekaar gou in welstand sal ontmoet.

Dit reent van telegramme. Met 'n soentjie,

Pappa

TRANSLATION

Marks Building
[Cape Town]
5 September 1939

Dearest Mamma, You will, of course, have seen the latest developments in the newspapers.[1] Whereas I thought when I came here that I would soon be out of the government, I am now, or shall be tomorrow, prime minister. Hertzog and company made terrible blunders—with these results for them and for me.

I hope my government will be sworn in tomorrow (6 September) and in that case I hope to fly back to the Transvaal on Thursday, 7 September. So far all goes well. But what does not await me?

On Sunday Louis [McIldowie] and I were at Kirstenbosch among all the lovely flowers and had a delightful time. In the afternoon the cabinet conflict was continued—with the result that you know. Since then everything has been in a state of commotion.

I hope all goes very well with you and that we shall soon meet in good health.

It is raining telegrams. With a kiss,

Pappa

477   To T. W. Lamont   Vol. 60, no. 119

Cape Town
6 September 1939

My dear Tom, I had a most welcome parcel of books from Florence from England. I thank her very much, but write this letter to you as the more important partner in the business! I do not know what future opportunities for writing there may be in the next few months. We have been passing through strange days—for the world and ourselves personally. A few days ago I left Pretoria thinking that I might be out of the government soon, and planning for the future when I should be free from public duties. Suddenly the whole situation changed. The prime minister declared for neutrality and I for severing relations with Germany.† Parliament supported me, with the result that I am once more prime minister of this country. Isie, back at Doornkloof, knew nothing of all this except from the newspapers. You could imagine her anxieties and feelings.

[1] On 4 September Hertzog's neutrality motion (*see infra*, pp. 190–1) was defeated and Smuts's amendment to sever relations with Germany was accepted in the house of assembly by eighty votes to sixty-seven. Since the governor-general refused his request for a dissolution of parliament, Hertzog resigned next day and Smuts was called upon to form a government.

It is a curious circumstance that just twenty-five years ago—to the month and the week—I had to be responsible for a resolution in parliament declaring war on Germany. I never dreamt that I would have to face the same situation in my lifetime; but here it is.

It is beautiful spring weather here. The veld is in flower. The birds sing. Sunday morning I spent with Louis [McIldowie] wandering through the flower beds at our National Botanic Gardens, Kirstenbosch. That is the benign aspect of nature. And on the debit side of the account we have this human tangle, this tragedy, the reach of which no man can foresee.

Shall we never learn our lesson? There is no solution through war. This war, whatever the ultimate issue, will be followed by another peace which may be no peace, for after a devastating conflict there is no mood for a real and wise peace, as you and I found at Paris in 1919. Meanwhile civilization is falling back, and the light of the spirit is being dimmed.

The outcome no man can foresee. I hope for the best and pray that Human Personality may triumph against the overwhelming forces threatening to submerge it.

Much will in the end depend on the attitude and action of the U.S.A. The last reserves of our human causes are in your great country, whose fine inner impulses are known to me.

And so the caravan passes once more into the night. May God be with us and take the hands of His erring children. With love to you both, Ever yours,

J. C. Smuts

† Rejection of neutrality by Smuts and other ministers who had been members of his cabinet was regarded by Hertzog as an act of disloyalty and a breach of a cabinet agreement. He made these charges, which later gained considerable credence, during a debate in the house of assembly in 1940. On that occasion he read out in the house a document (referred to as A–B) which had been drawn up by him in both Afrikaans and English. It was dated 1 September 1938 and ran as follows:

'Statement of the attitude to be adopted by the Union of South Africa in the event of war in Europe with England as one of the belligerents: The existing relations between the Union of South Africa and the various belligerent parties shall, so far as the Union is concerned, remain unchanged and continue as if no war were being waged, with the understanding, however, that the existing relationships and obligations between the Union and Great Britain and any other of the members of the British Commonwealth of Nations in so far as those relationships and obligations are the result of contractual obligations concerning the naval base at Simonstown; or of its membership of the League of Nations; or in so far as the relationships etc. must be regarded *impliciter* as flowing from the free association of the Union with other members of the Commonwealth shall remain unaltered and shall be maintained by the Union; and that nobody shall be permitted to make use of Union territory for any purpose calculated to infringe the said relationships and obligations.'

Hertzog said that, shortly after he had drawn up this document, he had read it to

478   From W. S. Churchill   Vol. 58, no. 81

Telegram

To: General Smuts
From: First Lord of the Admiralty
Dated [7 September 1939]

I rejoice to feel that we are once again on commando together.

Smuts and had also discussed it with Havenga, Pirow and Smuts and that all had approved it. He went on to read to the house a memorandum which he wrote immediately after a cabinet meeting on 28 September 1938. This was as follows:

'At a full meeting of the cabinet held this morning in the Union Buildings, Pretoria, I communicated to my colleagues that, in my opinion, in case war should break out in Europe in consequence of the dispute between Germany and Czechoslovakia, and England should be involved in it, then the attitude of the Union would be as is more fully set out in the accompanying documents A–B signed by me. The view submitted by me was briefly set out by me and, after some remarks, evidently agreed to by all.' Hertzog added: 'They all gave their approval to it after I had read out my view as set out in documents A–B.'

In Hertzog's opinion these documents showed that the full cabinet had in 1938 agreed that in a war in Europe in which Great Britain was a belligerent the attitude of the Union would be one of neutrality subject to the provisos of A–B.

On 1 April 1940 Smuts replied in the house to Hertzog's charges. He said that he had never, until Hertzog read it out in the house, seen or heard of the phrase with which A–B opens and which refers to *any* case of war in Europe in which England is a belligerent. His discussions with Hertzog on neutrality referred only to the case of a war which might ensue from the conflict between Germany and Czechoslovakia which was going on at that time, and so did the discussion in the cabinet on 28 September. He denied that any general policy of neutrality had ever been laid down for the future and went on to show the difference for the safety of the Union between the crisis of September 1938 and that of September 1939—a difference 'as wide as the heavens'.

In the course of the debate R. Stuttaford, D. Reitz and H. G. Lawrence, who were members of the cabinet both in September 1938 and in 1940, declared that neither A–B nor the memorandum had ever been put before the cabinet and that the cabinet had never taken any decision on neutrality either as a general policy or in reference to the German–Czech conflict. No decision of any kind had been taken at the meeting on 28 September where only 'a short and rambling discussion' (Lawrence) took place on the Czech crisis and the attitude of the Union if Great Britain should go to war. Nor had the question of neutrality come up at subsequent cabinet meetings because on 28 September Chamberlain went to Munich and the war crisis passed.

Hertzog admitted, in reply, that A–B had not been shown or read to the cabinet on 28 September but contended that, as prime minister, he had 'notified' the ministers of his views on neutrality should a war break out as a result of the Czech crisis and England be involved. These views were 'after a few remarks apparently accepted by all'. If ministers had not agreed it was their duty to say so but they had been silent. He insisted that the situation created by the German conflict with Poland was, as regards the Union, in no way different from that which existed at the time of the Czech crisis and held that he was justified in taking the 'tacit approval' of his policy by the cabinet on 28 September 1938 as applicable also to the neutrality issue which arose on 2 September 1939. (*See House of Assembly Debates*, vol. 37, cols. 1220–2; vol. 38, cols. 4063–137.)

479   To W. H. Clark   Vol. 60, no. 121

13 September 1939

My dear Clark, It is a joy to me to hear from your last note that you will continue with us till the end of November. Your presence and co-operation will be most helpful in these fateful months.

I am glad the coast defence questions are being rapidly settled. I think you will find everything going smoothly in future.

I enclose several personal messages which I shall be very glad if you will forward to the Dominions secretary.[1] The one in regard to war material is naturally secret and very important. I hope you will also as from yourself impress on the Dominions secretary how urgent and important it is that our requirements should be promptly met if we are to be prepared to make our contribution to defence in due course. If once I know the attitude of the war departments I could take up the matter officially thereafter. Yours sincerely,

s. J. C. Smuts

480   To M. C. Gillett   Vol. 60, no. 223

Doornkloof
[Transvaal]
21 September 1939

It is just fifteen days since South Africa declared war against Germany; what has not happened in that time! Abroad Poland has gone under,[2] Russia has joined in the war as a looter,[3] and the position for the democracies has grown much darker. Here in South Africa I have my hands more than full—in coping with all the new problems of organization for war, in reorganizing our defence department, and not least in fighting with our political opponents who are moving heaven and earth to strengthen their position and weaken mine. My stand has of course the unanimous approval of the English and of a large section of Afrikanders. But mere approval is nothing as against strong organization; so my opponents are organizing while I am governing the country and tackling its problems. It is a long time since I have been so fully and continuously occupied—morning, noon, and night. But my health continues good, and I look forward to some easing off when I am through the

[1] Anthony Eden, later Earl of Avon.

[2] The Polish army had virtually ceased to exist within two weeks of the German invasion on 1 September.

[3] On 17 September Russian forces began to move into the Polish territory assigned to them by agreement with Germany. *See supra*, p. 181, note 1.

first overwhelming rush of work. Last week-end I could evade my police guards and in company of Lennie Impey, Jannie [Smuts], and Joan [Boardman] I could take three long walks on Friday and Saturday afternoons and Sunday morning—about six and a half hours in all, up and down the hills of Doornkloof. I hope to do some solid walking each week-end and so keep up my physical form. The police guard are of course annoying, but say that they act on strict instructions based on information from confidential sources. I heard on the radio tonight that the prime minister of Rumania[1] has just been assassinated; so I ought not to be too confident about my own safety! Still, sixty-nine years is a long time to have lived, and in any case the end must come.

The spectacular and very early collapse of Poland is going to make our position much more difficult. It will be said: why fight for a state which had so little in it, and why sacrifice millions of lives and endanger civilization in the attempt to revive Poland? This argument will not impress Britain who has set her teeth; but what of the French who I don't think were ever very keen in this affair? Hitler may try to concoct some very specious peace offer in order to sow dissension, and this he can do with impunity as it will not be accepted. Danzig was a bad start, and Poland has proved a severe knock. Even so there is no turning back. This war may go on until Britain and France are utterly exhausted and Germany also is utterly exhausted—and Russia, the looter, strides on to the desolate scene to collar the spoils. I hate to think of a Hitler Europe, but no less to think of a Stalin Europe: it is a choice between the Devil and Beelzebub. Our hope is that there will be an early internal collapse of Germany and that this devastating struggle will not continue till Europe sinks down in utter exhaustion and despair. What an end to this glorious mother continent of Western civilization—the proudest achievement of the human spirit up to date. And into this war I have carried my country.

One of the funniest minor features of German propaganda is a nightly Afrikaans tirade against me from Zeesen.[2] It is the most awful filth imaginable. Night by night South Africa listens to my infamies—some distortions of the facts but mostly pure inventions.

---

[1] Armaud Calinescu, appointed prime minister in March 1939, was shot in Bucharest by members of the Iron Guard—a party formed on the Nazi model by Cornelius Zelea-Codreanu who had been arrested and 'shot while trying to escape' in 1938.

[2] A broadcasting station in Germany. Its chief propagandists against the South African government were Ernst Wilhelm Bohle, son of a professor at the University of Cape Town, and Sidney Erich Holm, a South African. Bohle (1905–60) was sentenced to five years imprisonment in Germany as a war criminal in 1945. Holm, charged with high treason and sentenced in South Africa to ten years imprisonment in 1947, was released in 1948.

I have not a shred of character left, and the question at the end often is why such a criminal is still allowed to live!!

My cabinet is a happy family, consisting almost entirely of old comrades who trust to my leadership.[1] Of course I have also old opponents in Madeley and Stallard. But with patience and experience of the difficulties of team-work in the government of a country like South Africa we may yet see them also mellow into real fellow-workers. But I expect some fun and even some trouble as we move along. I have the advantage of having inspired confidence through long years of patience and at last serving the country's interests in a supreme crisis. And this reputation may stand me in good stead in the very difficult days ahead. The Nats of course make out that all this was dark plotting on my part which in the end caught them napping.[2] The image of *Grey Steel*[3] is continually before their minds. I don't know whether you have read the book. I have not, but I gather that it sets out the record of the deep political schemer who manages somehow—often by unorthodox means—to get the better of his opponents. Sarah Millin is furious with the author—says he stole his facts from her and then proceeded to twist them so as to paint a sinister picture which has nothing to do with reality. Far be it from me to take part in this quarrel. My point is that the Nats have a popular biography to support their view of me. And now Goebbels [P. J.] comes forward to paint a picture infinitely blacker. At any rate I am not yet forgotten! This may all sound very egotistical, but it is part, and an important part, of the case and of the troubled politics of this dear land.

...Somebody was telling me today of a pleasing picture of me a friend from Cape Town had just written him: how on that Sunday (3 September), when everybody was in suspense about the cabinet crisis, and neutrality was the one topic discussed, he saw me with my daughter at Kirstenbosch kneeling down to examine flowers with my lens! I spent a blessed hour there with Louis [McIldowie], and the aroma of that hour remained with me till the final duel was fought next day. Good-bye.

Jan

[1] W. R. Collins (agriculture); R. Stuttaford (commerce and industries); J. H. Hofmeyr (education and finance); H. G. Lawrence (interior and public health); C. F. Steyn (justice); W. B. Madeley (labour and social welfare); D. Reitz (Native affairs); C. F. Clarkson (posts and telegraphs, and public works); F. C. Sturrock (railways and harbours); P. V. G. van der Byl (minister without portfolio); C. F. Stallard (mines). Smuts was minister of defence and of external affairs.

[2] On this allegation *see* O. Pirow, *James Barry Munnik Hertzog*, p. 245; F. S. Crafford, *Jan Smuts: A Biography*, p. 282; W. K. Hancock, *Smuts—The Fields of Force*, pp. 315–17.

[3] A biography of Smuts by H. C. Armstrong (q.v.) published in 1938.

481   To L. S. Amery   Vol. 60, no. 137

Pretoria
11 October 1939

My dear Amery, I have several very interesting letters from you to reply to. Thank you for them all, especially the last one in which you approve my action in regard to the war. I claim no merit for what I have done as I saw a clear straight course before me which I have tried to follow since 1902. I am very sorry that the prime minister has not yet seen fit to utilize your energy and ability in his new war machine. I hope that is still coming, as it would be a great pity not to use your experience and influence in this crisis.

I am preparing on a fairly big scale. If these forces are required for African defence they will be available; if not, there will be a fine reserve for contingencies.

The war itself begins in a deep fog. Hitler has placed the future of his country at the mercy of Russia and compounded with a power he has always held up as the Devil. He thus enters the war as a morally defeated person, and no man can foresee the ultimate results. But he will fight and rage like a wild beast, and we shall have to go all out. But what about Italy, Turkey, the U.S.A. and other factors? We can but do our duty, whatever the outlook.

In this country I shall have to go warily as the political front is most important. Reitz [D.] will soon be over with you and I have asked him to raise the Protectorates question. If this could be solved now my hands will be greatly strengthened. Please assist him as far as you can. Good wishes, Yours ever,

s. J. C. Smuts

482   To R. Stuttaford   Vol. 60, no. 141

Pretoria
14 October 1939

My dear Stuttaford,[1] It is probably a wise precaution to make a preliminary and cursory survey of the Union's agricultural and industrial requirements in the course of a long war, and to consider in advance what steps should be taken or initiated by us in order to secure their supply from our local resources. Nothing elaborate should be done at this stage, but we should be able to form some general idea of what may be our requirements and how they might be met locally, and what changes in our agriculture or industry may be involved.

[1] At this time minister of commerce and industries.

Perhaps your department might take the initiative in calling together the heads concerned for the purpose of discussing this matter. I suggest the secretaries of agriculture, commerce and industries, and mines, with their technical advisers. They may add others if so advised.

A summary of their provisional views may be useful.

I attach a memorandum from Professor John Phillips,[1] Witwatersrand University. Yours sincerely,

J. C. Smuts

483   To M. C. Gillett   Vol. 60, no. 229

Doornkloof
[Transvaal]
30 October 1939

This is how my days are spent at present: work in office all day except Saturday afternoon, and at home every evening. Saturday afternoon and Sunday morning I walk with some of the family and some friends, if any appear, accompanied by the inevitable police officer. Sunday afternoon I receive company. This is after lunch on Sunday, and so I write a line before visitors appear. Not a very inviting picture of the happy life. But not a bad one, compared with the millions who now spend their days and nights in mud and rain on the war fronts.

This week there will be a variation in this routine, as I have to go to Bloemfontein for a final meeting of the head committee of the United party.[2] It will not be a happy occasion—the final break after five-and-a-half years of co-operation. But the sting has been taken out of the bitterness by what has happened since the government broke up at Cape Town on 4 September. Still, for thousands the bitterness remains, and for me the poignancy of one more great failure in the many attempts to bring people together in a co-operative effort. Not all will be lost, and I feel that some of the good work of the last five years will remain and bear fruit in the future years. In these great human efforts we must take the long view, and not become impatient and disappointed at failure. The goal is 'man's vast future' as Lincoln phrased it, and that future will reap fruits of our work not visible today.

[1] Not attached to the document in the Smuts Collection.

[2] The United party had to be reorganized when, after the breach between Hertzog and Smuts on 4 September, Hertzog and thirty-six other United party members of the house of assembly joined the National party opposition.

Japie and Jannie [Smuts] are both here with their families, Japie's including the latest small arrival Marguerite, now just a month old. They are thinking of joining the forces, but I have advised them to wait a while as time is taken up with the preliminaries of preparation and organization. Sylma [Coaton] is also here with hers. It is a happy lot, and in their play and continual clashes a most amusing company. I love to watch them. This morning most of their time was spent in little bathing costumes which are suitable for this very warm day and also for their long play in the pond at Santa's [Weyers] house. In fact a good deal of the time of these youngsters is spent down at the farm—in the water, on the sand heap, and on the beautiful grass lawn now looking its best. Late this afternoon there will be a general break-up of the happy band as each goes to his particular home on the Rand, Santa's group alone remaining. We have had two very good walks this week-end, and I feel as if I have had enough. Andries [Weyers] joined us on both occasions, as he had just returned from harvesting at Rooikop. The thrashing will start this week and for that he will spend the time also at Rooikop. We ought to have a fair crop in spite of some rust and damage done by unseasonable rain. And soon we shall be eating our own home-grown Rooikop bread. For the harvesting Andries has had to use large numbers of Native women from Witlaagte, some days as many as ninety men and women being at the work in order to accelerate the harvesting before the next rain comes. They are daily fetched and taken home in lorries, paid 1s. 0d. a day with their food, and allowed to do the gleaning as soon as the sheaves are removed from the lands. In this way each family collects at least two bags of wheat, which at our price of 21s. 0d. a bag, is a good bonus for a week's work, and makes the employment very popular. My Natives on the farm have had a very big mealie crop this year owing to the good rainy season. They had the lands at Rooikop between the road and the river not used by us for lucerne, and also the fertile lands to the right of the road on the Droogegrond boundary. Even with mealies at 7s. 0d. a bag they must have done very well. This is in addition to their full pay daily. We are never troubled by want of labour, and it is worth while treating these people well as we do. Owing to great demands for mines and public works there is a dearth of Native labour on the farms, and this will force farmers to give better pay and conditions to their labourers if they don't wish to be left without labour. One item now consuming much labour is the national roads. I have given orders that the national roads from Pretoria to Messina, Komatipoort and Durban have all to be completed within twelve months, although the tarring may take a longer time. This speeding up of construction means a very large labour contingent on each of these roads. When you come here again you will find motoring to your distant beloved haunts in the mountains very much more comfortable. I hope you feel tempted! This morning after returning from our walk I took up Shelley before lunch. How good he is—what wonderful imagery and language, what elevation of thought and spirit! Comparing his lyrics with the feeble, blundering efforts of today, I cannot help thinking that the art of poetry is for the moment dead. There is no great vision, no inspiration, no outpouring in incomparable expression. In art it is as in religion and all the higher idealism: we are passing through a barren patch. But this cannot last. The light will shine again and kindle the fire in our hearts and brains. And what an outburst of beauty and what a revelation of truth there will then be! We shall not live to see that day, but may our dear children and theirs live to see it. Our machine age has produced its Frankenstein monsters in the shape of Hitler, Musso, Stalin and all the dreadful rest. But surely, surely, this is a passing phase. Did you note that the expression was officially used in the house of commons a week ago—the 'United States of Europe'.[1] It is a sudden flash in the dark, but it shows that something is happening in all this age which may bear fruit at the right time.

I had a very welcome letter from Arthur last week written from his club and giving useful public and financial and family news. He assures me that he is very well and very careful and I take his word for it! I shall not write to him as this weekly scribble is meant for you both, and for such friends as are interested in my speculations and vagaries. Ever lovingly yours,

Jan

[1] In a debate on 12 October on a post-war settlement L. S. Amery envisaged 'a European Commonwealth'. On 25 October G. le M. Mander asked the prime minister if a special committee could be formed to consider the problems of establishing such a Commonwealth. R. A. Butler replied that the government was not prepared at that stage to do this. (*House of Commons Debates*, vol. 352, cols. 592–3, 1371.)

484   To Lord Brand   Vol. 60, no. 162

Prime Minister's Office
Pretoria
13 November 1939

My dear Brand, Your writing in your letter of 7 October brought back long memories, very dear to me. What a time that was when we were settling the fate of South Africa![1]

You refer to the importance of my decisions on this occasion. How could I have done otherwise? It was a straight road ahead, as it has been a straight road behind from the time of our happy collaboration for a united country and a united people. I sympathize deeply with the errant portion of my people. South Africa has a divided soul, but if we are faithful to the vision of forty years ago that soul will be one yet. Time is a causal factor, and there has not yet been enough time. But in time it will come all right although we may not see it in our day.

And now the Devil is let loose among mankind. Hitler is a scourge of God, like Attila the Hun.[2] We shall stand the scourge and emerge a stricken, but not a beaten, world. Civilization will undergo vast changes but it cannot go under, and the world cannot revert to the brutality and bestiality that have disgraced Nazi Germany. There are certain fundamental ideals of life which have emerged and cannot go under again. So forward with a good heart!

I never saw your Tereschenko friend; at least he never appeared. I am sorry.

How I wish we could roam over this world in conversation once more. But I sometimes begin to doubt whether I shall ever see England again. The sands are running out and the work is not easing off. My kind regards, I may say my affection to you, dear Brand, Ever yours,

J. C. Smuts

[1] R. H. Brand had been one of the secretaries to the Transvaal delegation to the National convention (1908–9) which drew up the draft constitution of the Union of South Africa.

[2] Attila, king of the Huns (d. 453), was called during his invasion of western Europe 'The Scourge of God'.

485   To J. Martin   Vol. 60, no. 169

Irene
[Transvaal]
30 November 1939

My dear Martin, Last mail brought several good things from you—Rutherford's *Life*,[1] and the two white papers on [Sir Nevile] Henderson's last days in Berlin and on German atrocities. Thank you for all three. Henderson's paper is brilliantly written and will become a classic on Hitler after that gentleman has ceased to disturb the peace of the world. The *Rutherford* is specially welcome.

Politics is running its usual course in this country. The two oppositions under Hertzog and Malan have done their best to combine into an Afrikander bloc. The only result so far has been further fissures among them.[2] Have you ever heard in history of Afrikanders combining into a bloc? No people—except the Irish—are more prone to continual division. Their only real link is their hatred of me—and I admit that is a pretty strong link. It may yet succeed in bringing them together. Feeling in my party is good and the prospects on the whole are improving. I now hope to hold on till the end of the war, and I may even win a general election thereafter! You see I am still an optimist!

Your local mining friends are making a continuous chorus against the new mining taxation, although we have assured them that we hope to take increased costs into account, and to avoid crippling new development. Politically the repeal of the 150s. tax will hit us hard and perhaps bring about our downfall, which no reasonable person desires. I hope they will now revert to the soft pedal. We miss you here, but I admit you are greatly needed elsewhere. I wonder how the British government is getting on. One gets the impression that Chamberlain is losing ground and that his departments are not doing well. And on top comes this new German frightfulness and the heavy losses at sea. Of course this rot will be stopped but for the moment our stock in the world suffers.

I sometimes wonder why we have not made more resolute efforts to keep Russia really neutral. The danger is that Russia and Germany may next spring join hands in a Balkan campaign in which both are interested, and draw Italy in also with a promise of sharing in the

[1] Arthur S. Eve, *Rutherford* (1939).

[2] On 8 September 1939 thousands of Afrikanders had assembled at the site of the still unbuilt Voortrekker monument to support the reunion of the Hertzog and Malan groups and on 23 November leaders of these groups conferred at Pretoria. But the discussions broke down on the issue of republicanism. *See* M. Roberts and A. E. G. Trollip, *The South African Opposition 1939–1945* (1947), pp. 20–8.

spoils. There is stalemate in the West, and there will be stalemate on the seas also. And the danger is a move to south-east Europe in which all three powers may join, and which will carry the war across the Mediterranean into Asia and Africa. Russia seems to be the crux, and she should be rendered neutral. The Far Eastern situation might be used for this larger diplomatic strategy. I have urged my views in the right quarters, with what result who can say?

Most of my time has been taken up with the recasting of the defence department and the recruiting and training of our new defence forces. It has been heavier work than I had expected. I had first to break down what I found and then to rebuild from the foundations. My old experience of defence has come to my assistance, otherwise I could not have succeeded so soon. I have made Dr [H. J.] van der Byl with some fine Iscor[1] men a directorate of supplies, and I expect that innovation will be a great success. I have the men, but munitions and the like have still to be found. It is a case like the ministry of munitions in the last war.

I trust you are not overdoing it at the Bank. What a colossal task that must be, compared with the puny work we have to do here! Give my kind regards to [M.] Norman and [Sir H.] Clay. Norman is now among the supermen of Europe and we all speak of him with awe! Then remember me kindly to Frank Phillips, Reggie Holland, and Dougal Malcolm too if you ever see him. My love to you and Nora,[2] with best wishes for your health and safe return to this happy land. Ever yours,

J. C. Smuts

486   From L. S. Amery   Vol. 58, no. 15

112 Eaton Square
S.W.1
13 December 1939

My dear Smuts, Just a line to wish you all good things for Christmas which I hope will be a season of peace for you at home even if it is not in the world outside. As for next year, it may well be the great year of your life, and that a life not without its chain of high summits.

Reitz [D.] will have told you all about our affairs here and, inci-

[1] Under the Iron and Steel Industry Act, No. 11 of 1928, the South African Iron and Steel Industrial Corporation (ISCOR) came into existence. It was controlled and substantially financed by the government.
[2] Born Elinore Mary Scott-Waring Green; married John Martin in 1911.

dentally, conveyed to you my Christmas card in the shape of a book of wandering reminiscences[1] which may divert an idle hour, if you have any.

I am still not altogether happy about the intensity of our effort here. It is, of course, far above anything we did in the first year or more of the last war, but I don't know that it is yet up to the level of the attack we may have to meet or of the problems it is going to set us.

Whether Germany means to renew the invasion of Holland which all but took place last month,[2] is one unknown factor. She may well be planning that in conjunction with a break-through into northern Belgium in the hope that she may crush Belgian opposition before we can come up and consolidate it, and so catch us on the move as well. On the other hand there is a good deal of information to suggest that her real objective is south-eastern Europe. Benes, whose information is pretty good and recent, says that Hitler has definitely decided on a complete reconstruction of south-eastern Europe, re-taking Transylvania for the Magyars, giving Macedonia to the Bulgarians, and breaking up Yugoslavia into small bits, Slovenia to be incorporated in Germany, Croatia to be set up as a puppet state like Slovakia, and Dalmatia to go to Italy. He is convinced that Italy is still working in complete agreement with Germany. Whether she means to content herself with a small share of the loot such as Dalmatia, which may be got without fighting, or goes in at her selected moment some time next year, is another question. If she does the latter, the whole question of Africa will be opened up and you may have to play a big part in saving the continent. A very unpleasant broadcast by Gayda [V.] yesterday would tend to confirm the worse interpretation of Italy's motives.

As for Russia, Benes understands that Stalin has so far refused to join with Germany in a definite plan but is likely to co-operate independently to the extent of occupying Bessarabia. The Germans have offered him Constantinople, Iran and India, but I should think he realizes the inadequacy of his resources for such a task.

If Benes's prediction comes true and Yugoslavia and Rumania are to be attacked, the only way of preventing Bulgaria going wrong and the whole situation in that part of the world collapsing, is to make sure of the safety of our communications in the Mediterranean and that means forcing Italy to come out one way or the other, a very difficult decision to take.

[1] L. S. Amery, *Days of Fresh Air: Reminiscences of outdoor Life* (1939).
[2] In opposition to the German generals Hitler had announced that the attack on the Netherlands and Belgium would begin on 12 November, but he postponed this plan.

I think the Finnish business has shocked public opinion here and elsewhere in the world more profoundly than almost anything else.[1] One can only hope and pray that this gallant little people may hold out till something happens to save them. I don't know what conclusion your friend Malan [D. F.] draws from it all, or how he would envisage the prospects of South Africa with large German air forces and black armies in Tanganyika and South West Africa. If he liked to study the further consequences of such a situation he might care to inquire further into what is happening today in Czechoslovakia and Poland. I hear you are keeping fit and that these great issues have taken years off your age. Yours ever,

L. S. Amery

487   To M. C. Gillett   Vol. 60, no. 236

Doornkloof
[Transvaal]
19 December 1939

This is only Tuesday night and the mail does not leave till Saturday morning. But a very busy time awaits me and I must push on with necessary correspondence as far as I can. Tomorrow morning I leave for my constituency for the day. It promises to be a very big and hectic affair and from all surrounding parts people are gathering for the occasion. Both, or rather all, parties are going to be well represented, and with political and war passions running high you may imagine what sort of meeting or rather demonstration it is going to be. Isie always likes the tumult of battle and is going with me for the fun. I hope to return alive tomorrow night, but the following two days will be equally full, though I hope not so exacting or exciting.

The war the last week has been most exciting and interesting. First there was the drama of the *Graf Spee*.[2] I did like the nippiness of those small cruisers which so gallantly outfought the battleship. I can't say the same of the battleship. I feel that it should have gone down with flying colours and not with suicide. The difference between the *Rawalpindi*[3] and the *Spee* is too glaring. I admit it was

---

[1] The Russian invasion of Finland began on 30 November 1939.

[2] The *Admiral Graf Spee*, one of the three German 'pocket' battleships, was engaged and crippled by three British cruisers, *Exeter*, *Ajax* and *Achilles* off the river Plate on 13 December. She put into Montevideo and on the 17th blew herself up. A few days later her captain, Langsdorff, shot himself.

[3] On 23 November the armed merchant cruiser *Rawalpindi* (Captain Kennedy), on patrol between Iceland and the Faroe Islands, was attacked by the German battle-cruiser *Scharnhorst*. She fought back until all her guns were out of action and sank with the loss of her captain and 270 of the crew.

a difficult choice, but if the ship was to be lost it should have been with honour. The German stock is down. Then we have the gallant English submarines—the one which spared the *Bremen* only to torpedo a cruiser and battleship shortly after,[1] and the *Ursula* that entered the Elbe and sank the Kiln type cruiser.[2] This latter was as magnificent a feat as that of the submarine which sank the *Royal Oak*.[3] Our own first performance was also at sea, when one of our reconnaissance aircraft caught the *Watussi*.[4] The Germans are now bombing indiscriminately all merchantmen at sea, whether armed or not. This is a very beastly business, and may lead them into trouble in time. It is illegal and inhuman and hits friend and foe alike.

I have just done something of which I am rather proud. Twenty-eight fighter machines which I had secured from the British government were surrendered by me to Finland. Thus the League, which has at last behaved gallantly[5] has bound together the far north and the far south. Not that these machines will prevent the fate which is in store for poor gallant Finland, but they are symbols of human solidarity in defence of ideals which are much needed in these days of international decay. Only last week I had a personal message of appreciation from the League council for what I had done for the League from the beginning, and I was glad to be able to inform them today that I had given material assistance to Finland on their appeal.

Two days later. I had my meeting at Standerton yesterday, or rather demonstration, for it is improper to call a concourse of many thousands a meeting. It was a great success and I had my full say. It dealt mostly with the question: What guarantees the independence of small states? In America it is the United States with her Monroe doctrine,[6] and in Europe it is the fear of counter-attack from

---

[1] The German liner *Bremen* on her way to Germany from Murmansk, encountered the British submarine *Salmon* (Lieutenant-Commander E. O. B. Bickford) but was allowed to go on. On 13 December *Salmon*, on patrol in Heligoland Bight, damaged the cruiser *Leipzig* and the *Nürnberg*.

[2] On 15 December the British submarine *Ursula* unsuccessfully attacked the damaged *Leipzig* and sank one of the escorting destroyers.

[3] In the early morning of 14 October the British battleship *Royal Oak*, while lying at anchor in Scapa Flow, was torpedoed by the German submarine *U 47* (Lieutenant Prien). She sank within a few minutes with the loss of 786 officers and men, including Rear-Admiral H. E. C. Blagrove.

[4] The *Watussi*, a German passenger ship, was sighted on 2 December. Captain Stamer refused to obey instructions to put into Simonstown and scuttled his ship off Cape Point. The passengers and crew all reached Cape Town in life-boats.

[5] On 14 December the League declared Russia the aggressor and expelled her from League membership.   [6] *See* vol. III, p. 639, note 2.

the other great powers to whom the independence of one or other of those small states is important. It is always the big powers behind the small ones that safeguards them. South Africa, seceded from the British Commonwealth, would have no such great power to guarantee her independence, unless she enters into a reciprocal defence treaty, and in that case she is even more definitely bound to fight than she is now in the loose Empire system. And the only safe power with whom to enter into such obligations would be Great Britain. Secession therefore would not improve but worsen our position as an independent state. Quite good as an argument if people are still open to argument. The small body of opposition answered me by vociferous singing of the old Transvaal *Volkslied*![1] Why argue?

    ... Tomorrow (Friday 22nd) is Isie's birthday and the following day we leave for a few days seclusion at Rooikop—Jannie and Daphne [Smuts], Mr Police and I, with perhaps one or two more—unsettled yet. I shall rejoice to be away and only hope it will not be too hot and mosquity at Rooikop. I have a MS to read and write a foreword,[2] a broadcast to write for 31 December and several other similar tiresome things which cost as much trouble as a hard defence problem. It is these little rabbits that spoil the grapes—if my quotation is right.[3] But people cannot understand this. Reitz [D.] arrives back tomorrow[4] and will give me the latest news. Now I end, with love and good wishes to you all,

                                                                         Jan

488   To F. Lamont   Vol. 60, no. 179

                                                                      Irene
                                                             [Transvaal]
                                                      22 December 1939

Dear Florence, Needless to say your last letter, just arrived, gave the greatest pleasure. But it was dated 6 November and this shows that not only the seas divide us but large gaps of time in these war days.

    I was deeply interested in all you had to say about war and

---

    [1] The national anthem of the South African Republic *Kent gij dat volk vol helden-moed* composed by Catherine Félicie van Rees.
    [2] For *Emily Solomon* by J. J. G. Carson published in 1941.
    [3] 'The little foxes that spoil the vines.' *Song of Solomon* ii.15.
    [4] He had, with other delegates from the Dominions, attended a conference in London to discuss plans for the joint conduct of the war and had negotiated for the purchase of arms and aircraft in the United States and the United Kingdom.

politics and the American brand of neutrality. Thank God even for cash and carry[1] in these evil times. It will serve for a time anyhow. Tom knows better than I do how far our present 'cash' will 'carry' us in this awful expenditure of war. The day may not be so far off when the U.S.A. will have to go further in saving the rights of man. I am very happy to know that your and Tom's efforts have been so helpful in securing the repeal of the old law. It was worth while in every way, and in good time you will be helpful in carrying neutral America another stage forward. In the end you will be unable to keep out of this awful business. For the war will extend until it is a real world war. It has scarcely begun except at sea. Next year it will cover much of Europe, and thereafter what remains of the world. I take a very grave view of this menace to our present civilization—based on human personality and Christian ethics. The combination of Germany and Russia, which will probably become closer before it is dissolved, will play the devil yet with the present order of things. Germany will bring the brains and organization into the pool, Russia the endless docile man-power and very large resources. It will be Anti-Christ against what we conceive to be a more or less Christian outlook and order of things. While Germany holds the West, Russia is overrunning the flanks. Scandinavia may follow the Baltic states; Holland and Belgium are not yet out of danger. Next year the Balkans and Near East will be in flames, which may spread to north Africa. If Anti-Christ has great success, Italy will join them for the loot. And so on. Nobody knows what is brewing in the Far East. I do not see how America can finally keep out of the awful business.

I have had and still have pretty hard work out here. Large parts of South Africa are even more neutrality minded than your Middle West. The same factors here lead to very much the same situation, with this difference—that our connection with the British Commonwealth raises questions of honour and interest that cannot be evaded. And so I have succeeded in persuading my countrymen, or the majority of them, that they must fight. But a very large minority—headed by my predecessor—is fighting me every inch of the way. So the political struggle is very severe, while every nerve has to be strained to play our part worthily in the war. I know I have your sympathy one hundred per cent.

Of course for me the issue is at bottom a large human and

[1] Early in November 1939 congress repealed those provisions of the Neutrality Act of 1935 which required the president, in the event of war abroad, to put an embargo on the export of arms to all belligerents. But belligerents were now required to pay cash and to carry goods away in their own ships.

spiritual one. I believe in the Spirit which has led humanity on, and blossomed in all the great ideas which underlie our Western culture. The things Hitlerism stands for are the negation of all this, and if Nazism is a crusade, no less is that greater Crusade of the Spirit on which we have set out. Victory is not guaranteed us; the Right oftener than not is defeated. But still the Spirit beckons and leads us on, and we cannot but follow as the moth follows its candle light. It is the Divine in us which shapes our course through the world. Bacon has said that the human mind moves upon the poles of truth.[1] And equally truly it may be said that man follows the best and highest, even when it appears most hard to attain.

Now something quite different—and primarily for Tom. I find it most difficult to have my aircraft requirements met in England—for very understandable reasons. I have told our minister in Washington, Mr [R.] Close, to make discreet inquiries from American aircraft manufacturers. If there appears to be an opening there, and time of delivery appears an important consideration, I am going to appeal to Tom to use his personal influence on my behalf, and feel sure that he will help me in a good cause. I may therefore cable him through Close at a later stage, and this is just a first warning. He need not take any actual steps just yet.

And now, a happy New Year to you both, and the children and the $11\frac{7}{8}$ grandchildren. May blessings be on you, and on us, and on the erring race of men. Ever yours,

J. C. Smuts

489   To L. S. Amery   Vol. 63, no. 2

Groote Schuur
[Cape Town]
16 January 1940

My dear Amery, Some weeks ago I received a most interesting letter from you at Pretoria, and at the moment I cannot remember whether I answered that letter or not. Meanwhile Reitz has brought me your holiday book which I have begun to read with much pleasure. This is to thank you very much for this most acceptable gift, and also for the letter (if I have not already done so).[2] Both most welcome.

Your letter has been most informative and helpful to me. The situation in Europe is so strange and fickle that no one can confidently

---

[1] 'Certainly, it is heaven upon earth, to have a man's mind...turn upon the poles of truth.' Francis Bacon, *Essays, 1. Of Truth.*   [2] *See* **486.**

predict what may happen this year. The Russian development was quite unexpected; then the way Finland made a laughing stock of the Russian Colossus was another surprise. What is going to happen in Scandinavia and the Low Countries before surrender? What to the air? All these are questions; and yet I feel inclined to share your view that the Balkans may be *the* theatre of operations, Russia having a deep intent of her own to join with Germany there. Italy may stay out, or she may be bribed with more of the Balkans, and so the war may pass on to the Mediterranean, Near East, Egypt and Suez, Sudan and further south. This now may look far-fetched but cannot be ruled out as a possibility, and it is for this possibility that we in Africa have to prepare by land and air. I hope by next summer (your summer) to have a very considerable well-trained force for this and other contingencies, and if I can secure the money, airplanes and guns from London I am sure South Africa will be able to give a good account of herself. I myself feel there is probably a lot in the information you have from Benes on this development of the war. The material here is very good and with sound training ought to yield good results. The British government seem to have hopes of Italy going the other way—but who can tell?

I hope we shall not again make the mistake of the Great War and lock up all our forces on the western front, and have no big reserves for developments in other theatres. The lesson of that war was the necessity for holding big reserves for contingencies. It would be a great pity if the Maginot line absorbs too much of our British forces. Has Italy not been promised Egypt and north Africa to round off her Roman Empire? Is Abyssinia not a precarious affair until Suez is wrenched from the British Empire? What was all that talk of Mussolini about last spring and summer? But of course Mussolini may not be frightened by Germany's advances to Russia and be in a different mood. We should in any case be prepared for all eventualities.

The political situation was very uncertain when I took over at the beginning of last September, but since then there has been a marked improvement. The well-disposed people have found their voices and their feet, and I should say that the position today is much easier. In a military sense I have no fear of trouble, but Hertzog and Malan command powerful political forces, and my majority is both small and heterogeneous; so I shall have to be on the watch all this session which is on the point of beginning.

I don't feel quite easy about the British cabinet. There are so many men in it who appear to be passengers. Why did Stanley [O.] take the place of [Lord] Hore-Belisha? Surely there were abler and more experienced men in the Conservative ranks? Then what was all this Hore-Belisha rumpus about?[1] We shall now soon know, but what we like to hear above all is that the best men will be called upon and given their chance. This war is going to be an awful test and one likes to be satisfied that the supreme direction is quite satisfactory.

I wonder what is going to happen in the U.S.A.; whether Roosevelt will stand again and get in.[2] I keep looking in that direction in case we get bogged in Europe. I have the feeling that Roosevelt is really with us and will not see us go under. If Germany really gets control of Russia and organizes that vast man-power and those resources, we shall have the grimmest struggle possible to win through. Not that I am pessimistic, but we should not underrate the desperate forces arrayed against us.

All my good wishes to you and my kindest regards to Mrs Amery. Ever yours,

s. J. C. Smuts

490   To M. C. Gillett   Vol. 63, no. 77

Groote Schuur
[Cape Town]
24 January 1940

Your last came a few days ago, telling of Lucy's relapse, of Esther getting married notwithstanding,[3] of Helen [Gordon][4] off to Loughborough, of skating at Woodstock, and of thoughts about the war, which never cease to trouble our minds. Let me say at once that I have Hailey's portentous volumes,[5] three of them, and find them full of matter, in a very indigestible form. I cannot stand that dull official language as of a blue-book. It is so different from the live language of ordinary speech that it is almost another language. I commended Hailey for his work, but I could wish it was not so portentous and dull. It is an encyclopaedia of information, and valuable as such works are. But little guidance or illumination. So sorry to hear of Lucy's set back, but as no cable has come I suppose she has pulled round again. I cannot think of such a light going out

---

[1] Hore-Belisha, as secretary of state for war, was dismissed from that post by Chamberlain in January following differences between him and the military chiefs about the defences raised by the British Expeditionary Force on the Franco-Belgian frontier.

[2] Roosevelt stood for a third term as president in 1940 and defeated the Republican candidate, Wendell Willkie.

[3] Wife and daughter of Henry T. Gillett.

[4] *See* vol. IV, p. 471, note 1.   [5] Lord Hailey, *African Survey* (1938).

before its time. Poor Henry must feel it all very much. For the rest your letter calls up pleasant pictures of wholesome activities and goings on. The young fall in love, or are getting married, or look forward to increase in their little families. But what cold there must be! Cato [Clark] writes of skating, so do you. The papers tell of awful cold in France, of more awful cold in Finland. What suffering there must be among the poor soldiers! I remember bitter cold nights on the high veld in the Boer War, when I lay shivering most of the night and at dawn found my moustache a solid lump of ice. And the European cold must be infinitely greater. Tonight the cables tell of four hundred Russian soldiers frozen to death in their dug-outs on the Karelian front or somewhere. The horrors of nature added to the senseless cruelties of man. And think of the wrecked seamen in the North sea from mined or torpedoed ships struggling in the icy water for hours.

You ask what I think of a future settlement. I have thought and thought, and always come to a standstill. Will there be a temper for a decent peace at the end of this horrible business? Will there be the moral resources for a fair peace after the exhaustion and collapse of victor and victim alike? I fear for the worst. People talk of universal federation—a Utopian ideal which is really nothing more than a sort of escapism. If federation has proved impossible in the British Empire, how can it be a practical issue for the world? You mention the League. What a heart-breaking disappointment that has been! It was thought that that was the utmost that was practicable, but it has remained an idea, a light on the horizon which has not been reached.

Can there be any institutional change where there is no change of the spirit? Can we build effectively except from the depths of the human spirit? Is Jesus not right, and is it not at bottom a spiritual issue, just as it is a spiritual disease from which we are suffering? And yet, some constitutional form or mechanism must accompany the inner change of spirit. I have not yet got beyond the League, with some amendments which will fit it more closely to the realism of this world. But I have no longer the ardent faith in it which moved me in December of 1918 when I wrote that pamphlet in your upper chamber.[1] I am myself a sadder, not a wiser man. I have no faith in mere economic reform, as I believe both the disease and the cure to be of a spiritual nature. I am not a Marxist, but fundamentally Liberal with a pull towards spiritual and religious values. But now Liberalism also has failed! The fact is we have passed through that glorious Liberal era and now sit among its ruins, with no real vision

[1] See supra, p. 174, note 2.

of a new world emerging. Marxism does not appear attractive or
sound; Nazism appears brutal and horrid—a sort of devil worship.
But that fairer world of heart's desire has not yet assumed definite
shape. When some years ago I read *China at the Crossroads*—you
remember the Siam affair as set out by the Chiang Kai Sheks[1]—I saw
dim glimmerings of light, but no more. I am so afraid of false
visions. My recent studies of the times of Jesus have shown me how
dangerous it is to cherish vain hopes and illusions as an escape from
great disasters and sufferings. The Messianic idea which emerged
from the Dispersion and the Maccabean success proved the undoing
of Israel in the end. They were always looking for the Messiah,
missed the real one, and followed false ones until they were finally
crushed and finished. It is a curious story, in which Jesus forms
a link and was by his own people mistaken for one of the false ones.
Some false Messianic hope may emerge from the present world
despair which may once more prove a snare and delusion. The
Roman Empire, again, went because, or rather while decent, cultured
people accepted their fate and cultivated their little gardens of
culture while the weeds spread around them until their gardens
were also invaded and submerged. Both acquiescence and vain
expectation are dangerous. But what practicable middle course is
there? Perhaps we shall have to proceed step by step, guided by
practical experience, in the English way, and so grope forward to
the light and the truth. But it will be a pretty mad world after this
war, and goodness only knows what mistakes will yet be made. Some
Lear or Oedipus Tyrannus in his mad ravings and doings. Which
all comes to this, that I don't see any clear line at present, and must
continue my cogitations.

Here in parliament we are busy with a wild debate on a motion
by Hertzog for a separate peace! Think of it—a separate peace! It
is all very wild and crazy, but so is the world, so why blame poor
South Africa in particular? Meanwhile, with a small parliamentary
majority, I have to steer through these troubled waters. This whole
week will be thus taken up, and next week we shall come to my bill
for emergency war powers and indemnity for the last five months.[2]
You can imagine the debates, the charges, the heat and rage in
which all this has to be done. I pray for patience and strength to
stand and survive all this. One advantage I have: I know I am right
and have no personal ends to serve, and only hate this cursed spite

[1] *See supra*, p. 131, note 5.
[2] The purpose of the bill was to indemnify the government for action taken by
proclamation since September 1939 and to give it statutory authority to act during
the emergency. It was enacted as War Measures Act, No. 13 of 1940.

which at this time of life has saddled me with this task. But we are all soldiers at our post of life, and at the call can only go forward or go under. How much pleasanter it would have been to attend to my garden of culture, to have botanized and roamed the world in thought, and perhaps to have done some planning for the future! No such luck now. Long hours in office and in parliament; sometimes late hours at night; and all the time being told what a rascal and scoundrel I am!

I sympathize with all those in power and responsibility—except Hitler. Poor Chamberlain—what a burden he must bear, and not a demi-god either! Hore-Belisha must have got on people's nerves, with his reforms, his noisy self-advertisement, and general forwardness. He will be squared. Meanwhile a dreadful mediocrity takes his place who will give no offence.[1]

Everything round here reminds me of the past, of the wonderful times we spent here together in years gone by. It is a sadder world. There is absence, and the prospect is darker. But the Light is still there—somewhere. With dear love from us to you all,

Jan

491   To M. C. Gillett   Vol. 63, no. 85

Groote Schuur
[Cape Town]
3 March 1940

Sunday morning after breakfast. It is a perfect morning; wind, cold, and heat gone, the doves sing in the oaks, the little squirrels dart about like arrows. This morning I awoke with pleasant thoughts of my friends as from a dream, and so I turned once more to Paul's great Hymn to Love with its high poetry and higher spirituality. At breakfast I said I had been reading 1 *Corinthians* 13 in Greek, and then (to my envy) Isie started repeating the chapter in Greek, saying that this was the only chapter in the New Testament she could say in that tongue. There is something indefinable in the New Testament that often carries me clean off my feet, and this chapter is outstanding even in that book of the soul. It is not so much religion as something deeper that touches all the secret springs of life. The whole theory of perception is transformed by that wonderful line: 'Now we see in a mirror—in an *aenigma* (enigma!); then we shall see face to face.' This is the higher Realism. 'Now we know the parts; then we shall know the whole.' 'When the perfect

[1] *See* 489

comes the imperfect (the way of the partial) goes.' πίστις, ἐλπίς, ἀγάπη[1]—these three. Has anybody ever summed up the depths of the human soul in simpler and more effective terms? I look upon the New Testament as the spiritual highlight of the human race. No insight since, no expression since of the human soul in its highest and noblest phases, has equalled the vision and the expression of it given in the New Testament. And so, with all our science, all our wider world view of today, we still say 'Thank God for Jesus and his Testament of Love.' I can sit and think of those incomparable passages with my body literally in a quiver. The great poets do not affect me like that, except when now and then (as in Blake or Whitman) they but re-echo the music of the New Testament. To me the spiritual inspiration of that age remains a great mystery. How is it that at that time of all times there was such a flowering out of the human soul in noblest vision and expression? And how we have fallen from that vision since! But, whatever the relapse, the vision itself remains the abiding possession of the race. It is but a vision. That wonderful Transfiguration on the Mountain which came to Jesus and his three disciples was but a vision revealed in a supreme exhaltation of the spirit. But is it not as true and real as the most solid things that we see with our eyes or touch with our hands? Does the Soul-Vision not take us face to face with Reality? We look for facts, but in the world of Spirit are there not higher realities than so-called facts? Facts are precious, but they are still of the parts, the details (ἐз μέρους) whereas the Vision is the Whole, face to face with the Real, so far as one can ever know the real.

. . . This week will be a severe and trying one for me, as all of it will be spent over the War Measures Bill—our local Dora,[2] and my opponents will not spare me as I shall not spare them. But with the good assistance of guillotine, passed last week, I shall not be drowned in endless floods of talk. How good it is for democracy to have some of these weapons captured from the armoury of autocracy! Democracy plus the guillotine is good for erring politicians.

Friday morning (8 March). It is almost time for office and I must hurry to finish this and keep my appointment. We finished the War Bill last night with the help of the guillotine, Isie being in at the death to see the kill. Four days and nights this week I have sat glued to my seat in parliament in this endless spate of talk, varied only

---

[1] Faith, hope, love.
[2] *See supra*, p. 211, note 2. The Defence of the Realm Acts passed in Great Britain in 1914 were colloquially called DORA.

by bitter scenes and harsh condemnations. I have been talked and blamed to death; only inside I live. How precious it is, when the storm rages outside, to retire to the sanctuary of your own soul, your own integrity, and to feel at rest, even with your vituperative fellow men!

Finland has again been very heavy on my mind this week and I have sent some very strong messages to London. I wonder what the outcome will be. There is a lack of grip and decision, apart from the great difficulties of a most troublesome situation. I hope the Allies will be wisely guided in a situation full of great possibilities both of good and evil...

492   To M. C. Gillett   Vol. 63, no. 89

Groote Schuur
[Cape Town]
4 April 1940

Such nice letters from you and Arthur this week, telling of your motoring through beloved country to Abbotsbury, your restful time there, your neolithic surroundings, your meanderings and your reading of poet Barnes.[1] What an escape it must be for you and Arthur, not only from sickness and hard work, but also from the cares and sorrows of this world. Isn't it blessed to be far away and quite forget[2] the aches and problems and routines? And the blessedness is all the greater to one who knows these joys from experience but now seems for good deprived of them. But I shall have them yet, on the principle that every dog has his day. I agree with you that the *New Statesman* is very futile these days as most of the work of our left intelligentsia is. But the *Manchester Guardian* continues particularly good, so also the *Economist*. *The Times* is almost unreadable, and certainly not worth the air postage which brings it here in shortened form. The cables told this week of the passing away of John Hobson—there was a good man for you. I would write to his wife but am almost certain that she too is no more. Our circle is rapidly contracting, and soon the rest will be gone too. *Warte nur, balde ruhest du auch.*[3] You say you are silly about the war. Who is not? Is there any reason why as things are there should be a war at all? Both sides are afraid to make a start and are getting stronger and

[1] William Barnes (1801–1886) whose poems were written in the Dorsetshire dialect.
[2] 'Fade far away, dissolve, and quite forget...' John Keats, *Ode to a Nightingale.*
[3] Only wait; soon you too will rest. Goethe, *Wanderers Nachtlied.*

stronger in defence. Could they not continue to glare indefinitely at each other from behind their lines until the absurdity of the position automatically ends the glare or stare? It is an absurd thought but none the less intriguing. It would indeed be peace without victory, but in a better way than dear old Woodrow Wilson ever had in view.[1] I don't know whether you have ever seen two cocks standing fiercely up to each other, but both thinking better of it, till they quietly edge away from each other without coming to blows. I am sure Chamberlain is far from anxious to fight, and perhaps Hitler is equally so. A stage may thus be reached when some wise man or humorist might suggest to them that it is about time to stop this pose and come together again and settle up differences. You might suggest the idea to dear Gilbert Murray who might be able to make something of it. I am sure Aristophanes would have made good use of the idea, and Gilbert must have picked up some useful things from him.

Meanwhile my frail barque is ploughing its uneasy way through a stormy parliament. Last Monday I got my third reading of the War Measures Bill through the house of assembly and for the last two days I have been listening to all the sins of my political life from the wise men of the senate. So it will continue for days more though I should be done with that job by next week. Then my estimates as prime minister and minister of defence will come on in the house, and for another week I shall have to struggle with my wild beasts[2] over war policies and all the rest. The trouble is that one gets so little chance to sleep. The mornings are fully taken up with government work, and the rest of the day is futilely spent in parliament. And all the time an army has to be prepared for possibly grim business ahead. Who knows? If the war *does* come off at last, I fear it will go against us in the earlier phases, just as in the last war, when the Germans had it much their own way the first month and only by a miracle missed taking Paris. I much fear the first go-off of this business. Of course we are now much better prepared than a year ago, but so are the Germans—and so the vicious circle completes itself. But let us escape from all this dismal talk, and retreat at any rate in thought to more pleasant topics. My reading is now much neglected. Even my favourite little Testament is seldom read. I looked the other night into *Antiquity* which you kindly sent me and read the Mapungubwe article by Miss C. Thompson. *Mind* and

---

[1] 'It must be peace without victory.' Woodrow Wilson in an address to the United States senate on 22 January 1917.

[2] 'If after the manner of men I have fought with beasts at Ephesus.' 1 *Corinthians* XV.32.

the *Round Table* have been read, but not much else. I glance into Hutchinson and Marloth occasionally to look up forgotten plants. But these wanderings are rare in this pilgrimage of political troubles on which I am unfortunately set out. Last week-end I found time for Devil's Peak,[1] and on Saturday afternoon we gave a tea-party to the juniors of the party from the surrounding districts—about 400 to 500 of them. It was a good and useful function, but it took a heavy toll of such energy as I had left after a heavy week. Next Saturday I shall have another political function at Sea Point. I cannot imagine why people have no mercy on me, knowing as they must do that I am working to the full stretch of my physical endurance. I suppose it is just thoughtlessness and in my case sheer weakness in saying 'no'. Isie is also beginning to look tired. Sometimes she looks dreadfully tired, and then my heart is smitten for her. But it is very difficult to restrain her from good deeds, just as it is difficult to keep me from the opposite! The end of this month we shall have been married forty-three years, so not so far from the golden anniversary. It has been a most successful venture—with such a wife!...It is now nearing 11 p.m. and I must go to bed. So good-bye. Love from

Jan

493   To M. C. Gillett   Vol. 63, no. 90

Groote Schuur
[Cape Town]
7 April 1940

Sunday morning again. The sun is breaking through the clouds after several days of rainy and cold weather and the day may be a good one for going out. I have much work to get through for this week, but if the day is fine I may feel tempted to say good-bye to all that and enjoy myself. Besides there are the children and grand-children to tempt me out...

Yesterday (Saturday) was taken up with various duties, work and company in the morning, a party function at Sea Point in the afternoon and an official dinner to diplomats at night. You will call this dissipation but really it is all work and in many ways as tiring as real hard work. I work best when I am alone and can concentrate on the job in hand and can go on for hours in this way without getting tired. But interruptions, attending to others, and all the rigmarole of public life wear me out very soon...

[1] Mountain (3,287 ft.) to the north-east of Table mountain to which it is connected by a saddle.

I was much interested in what you wrote in your last of Nelson's Hardy and his Possum.[1] If I remember rightly he was with Nelson at the end and when Nelson fell he called on Hardy to support him. He must have been very close to Nelson. I suppose you are still at Abbotsbury and listening to Dorset language and eating good Dorset food. And resting—resting—resting. How blessed it is to rest from our labours. Will the world to come be such a rest or a more strenuous stage in the journey of life? I am only very mildly interested in this sort of question. If you go all out in this life you are not so much concerned what happens to yourself individually thereafter. I am always somewhat puzzled by the old world idea of being 'saved'. The Jews wanted to be saved from punishment for breaches of the Law, and the pagans wanted to have personal salvation from the evils incident to morbid ideas and practices. But surely all that belongs to an outlook that is dead and gone. What appeared to them impossible in this world was looked for and hoped for in the next. Jesus himself appears to have had another point of view—the new order and the new society in the Kingdom of God on this earth. It was a thoroughly social idea, and immortality was linked up with the new immortal order of God which was to come soon, very soon— perhaps before that generation had passed. It was something like Shelley's vision of the new earth in *Prometheus Unbound*, only more deeply spiritual. If the Gospel story as we have it is to be taken at its face value Jesus had a spiritual vision of this reign of God on earth, and his sacrifice might be the event to precipitate events and bring about this great change. It is only his words on the Cross (Why hast Thou forsaken me?) that makes me suspect that he hoped or expected the sacrifice would not be actually completed and that God would appear before the crisis. It is difficult to say; but in any case it is more the coming of the Kingdom than the question of immortality that interested Him in his Great Vision. It is difficult to conceive of all life being conserved in its *individual* form for all eternity. For if the souls of men, why not the souls of every living creature; and is matter itself not a lower form of life? This universal conservation not only appals me but is contrary to the most recent developments in science, which have done away with the conservation both of energy and matter. There is a suspense account labelled 'Mystery' in all our human knowledge, and personal immortality may be an item in that account. I am attracted by George Eliot's idea in her lines: 'O may I join the choir invisible'—the company of all who have in life contributed to the better and higher order of the future,

[1] Hardy's childhood home was at Portsham, near Abbotsbury. He called it 'Possum'.

and leave it at that. I can conceive my dear friends going and my living on and cherishing their sweet memory until I too go.

11 April. After writing thus far we had a pleasant morning's drive to Cape Point and showed David [Gillett] and our other friends the beauty of that place on a clear autumn morning. Sunday afternoon was spent in work. So have been the intervening days during which I have been occupied in parliament with the prime minister's estimates and in office with the tangles of this new invasion of Denmark and Norway.[1] I do not want to criticize but it appears as if we have once more been caught napping. While we were busy with some tin-pot job of mine-laying, the German navy was preparing to transport an army for the invasion of those countries. How different from the Nelson touch—when for many weary months he watched the French and Spanish navies until he could destroy them at Trafalgar. How could this invasion have been carried out if the British navy had been on the spot to prevent it as they could have done? I may be speaking in ignorance, but these questions trouble many minds, and may have serious repercussions, politically and otherwise.

Yesterday your letter to Isie arrived with an enclosed note for me. What you write about the good the change has done you and Arthur is most welcome as is also the news of your visit to Street and what you saw there. We are charmed with the new granddaughter with the grand name.[2] There are now twelve grandchildren and I feel truly patriarchal. On the threshold of seventy, with twelve grandchildren already, and up to the eyes in work and responsibility. That is an enviable lot, though I could wish for less years! You have three grandchildren and are thus well behind in this respect...

494   To M. C. Gillett   Vol. 63, no. 94

[Cape Town]
9 May 1940

A dreary night debate is proceeding in the house, so I shall use the flying moments to drop you a line. Your letter—written after a pleasant week-end at Aston—duly arrived a couple of days ago; another from Arthur, also most welcome. Your news on the whole

[1] The Germans successfully invaded Norway and Denmark on 9 April in spite of attacks by inadequate British naval forces sent to mine Norwegian waters.

[2] Petronella, daughter of Cato and Bancroft Clark. She was named after Smuts's mother.

good, so unlike the public news, with the retreat from south Norway[1]
and the repercussions that were bound to follow. At this moment
the debate on the government's conduct of the war is still proceedings in the commons. I shall express no opinion, but the Lord can
hear my inward groanings. We are undoubtedly at a most critical
stage of the war. Not only is Germany stronger than was thought,
stronger than in the last war, but Hitler's political and military
strategy has been uniformly successful up to now. It may not be
long-range successes, but for the moment the world is dazzled and
an impression of invincibility is created. The world tremblingly
takes note as one country after the other is swallowed—with the
Allies standing aside or retreating all the time. Musso may take
courage and think his moment has come; Holland thinks her turn
has come. And every Balkan state quakes and shudders. Nobody
knows when the hour of fate will strike which may determine the
future of Europe. One can understand the unspeakably deep concern
which people must feel. I hope the matter will not end with fine
speeches in the commons.

Our session has dragged on longer than we thought it would. It
looks like lasting another week. Next week (18 May) I have to be at
Pretoria for a big party demonstration which it is now too late to
postpone; and on 22 May there is a big civic welcome to me at
Pretoria, and another at Johannesburg on the 24th; the following
day at Heidelberg; and four days after our Cape congress meets at
Port Elizabeth, with more demonstrations. Four days after that
again another series of functions at Durban. After the fatigue of
a very trying session I shall therefore have to plunge into a whirl of
politics in the country. Meanwhile the defence preparations have
reached an important stage and much of my time and attention has
to be given to that side of my duties. I mention all this to show you
that my seventieth milestone is reached in heavy labours and not in
that calm which befits so solemn an occasion. How much pleasanter
it would have been if I could have retired for a few days to Rooikop
from the hurly-burly and enjoyed myself among the game and the
cattle! But perhaps fate has some kindness in store for me. Just at
present she is most exacting.

There is no doubt that a deep wave of feeling is moving over the
country over the line I took last September, and my undertaking the
heaviest burdens in the government to see the country through this
war crisis. It is not a case of popularity for, as you know, I shall
never be really popular. I make no such appeal to people's hearts.

[1] British forces which landed at Namsos and Andalsnes between 14 and 17 April
withdrew on 2–3 May.

But something in what I have done has gone pretty deep, and a wave of feeling has been set going which has surprised me. That accounts for these functions which nobody has engineered and which have arisen quite spontaneously. I dislike all this fuss and fever of public excitement. But there is real devotion behind it all.

Yesterday the members of parliament in the coalition (United party, Dominionites and Labour) gave me a most welcome birthday present, anticipating the 24th when I shall be away in the north. It is a beautiful ciné instrument, with telefoto lens, to take coloured films with. Abe Bailey has (also as a birthday gift) added the projector and other mechanisms necessary to complete the set; so that I am now provided with a complete ciné outfit, chosen by Pole-Evans for the purpose. I wonder whether I shall ever have time to make use of this wonderful photographic equipment. I should love to master the technique and to have time to take scenes and scenery as Pole-Evans is doing. Japie [Smuts] and Andries [Weyers] are already successfully operating with cheap sets of their own. Am I not getting too old to learn, and shall I not remain a public slave to the end?

The book on S. Alexander[1] has duly arrived and I have been spending some free night hours in reading a good deal of it. He was a queer old boy, combining a whimsical simplicity with much worldly wisdom and profound metaphysics. Like many other thinkers of the day he approached holism without seeing that landmark in human thought. He believed in deity, but not in one already existing but towards which the universe was tending. I saw him once in company with Leonard Hobhouse, a venerable patriarch with long, flowing beard, like Moses or Jehovah in the old pictures. Towards the end he was depressed, partly because he saw the greater star of Whitehead arising in philosophy. He need not have been. All metaphysics of today is but a phase, passing like all the effort of our time of rapid transition. 'Not in these noises'[2] will the new philosophy be written. We do but see in a glass darkly[3] the shapes of things to come.[4] We must transcend the Hebraic deity. We must view things in the wide setting which modern science has created. We must fuse the conceptions of the divine and the human. What was dimly foreseen in the Christian Incarnation must be expressed in a more adequate form, and shorn of its ancient imagery. The universe must be seen as the organic structure that it is, instinct

[1] S. Alexander, *Philosophical and Literary Pieces* (1939). It includes a memoir by his literary executor.

[2] *See* vol. IV, p. 241, note 1.   [3] 1 *Corinthians* xiii.12.

[4] *The Shape of Things to Come* by H. G. Wells was first published in 1933.

with divinity, big with the inner spirit which is shaping and creating it, and of which it is but the progressive expression. 'The Divine Vision still was seen—and Jesus still the Form was thine'—as old Blake put it in the language of our childhood.[1] I sometimes feel my own conception trembling on the brink of this vision. It is the holism which is at once the indwelling spirit and the outward expression of this mysterious universe. But there is something warm and near and intimate about it, which can only be expressed in the category of personality which it is so difficult to harmonize with the complexity of the physical universe. It is so difficult to realize and formulate in thought the truth that that vast *Other*, not myself, is yet not really alien or different, but the other *of myself*. The universal is incarnate in the particular. The universe and the soul are like body and soul in the human individual. The Infinite is the unit. I suppose we shall yet succeed in getting harmony among our intuitions and concepts, but at present there are still deep gulfs dividing them. The reconciliation will come. It is getting late and I must go back to the house. Good-night.

Jan

495   To M. C. Gillett   Vol. 63, no. 95

Groote Schuur
[Cape Town]
12 May 1940

This is Sunday morning before breakfast—a beautiful day, such as only South Africa can show on a May morning. The birds sing, the air is keen without being cold, fleecy clouds lie quietly far up, and the mountains beckon. It is, however, my last Sunday in Cape Town; on Wednesday I shall fly up to Pretoria after finishing what remains of our parliamentary session...

How fast things have moved! The Norway business has at last blown Chamberlain out of office, and Winston rules in his place. Norway is almost forgotten in the rush of events, and Holland and Belgium have suddenly rushed into the centre of the picture.[2] The cup is being filled and there is nothing which Hitler will not do to justify his title as the scourge of God[3] not only for his own but also for every other country. One feels bitterly sorry for these small innocent victims of aggression. Their behaviour in the past has

[1] William Blake, *Jerusalem*, f. 27.
[2] The German invasion of the Netherlands, Belgium and Luxemburg, began on 10 May.   [3] *See supra*, p. 199, note 2.

been exemplary. They have been excellent neighbours of Germany and have sympathized deeply with her grievances under the Versailles order of things. This is their reward. The world is thus being imbued with bitter hatred of the Nazi creed, and this may be the best cure for the ills of the world. The alternative to Christian civilization is now being seen in all its utter nakedness, and the revulsion of the world cannot but have a salutary effect. Devil worship will be decisively repudiated. Let us hope that the evil temper bred of war will not throw us into some new disastrous outlook. The Pope is taking a very courageous line[1]—in fact I prefer his pronouncements to those of Roosevelt. The Pope at least is braving the anger of Hitler and Mussolini and doing so at grave risk to himself. The Protestant churches seem to be voiceless in this grave crisis of our civilization. It is a very severe comment on their cause, and their helplessness even to protest (which is their business) is a condemnation which they have brought on themselves.

Here in South Africa the invasion of Holland and Belgium has had a stunning effect. The neutrality of Holland and Belgium has been repeatedly thrown at me by our Nats to show how a small country should protect its own interests in this storm. They never would believe that Holland would go the way of the rest. Not even Denmark and Norway's fate would move them out of their ostrich attitude. And now they are dumbfounded. Politically it will help me, for rightminded people will be more and more filled with disgust and repudiate Nazism with all it implies. Here, too, the cure is being effected, and people who have been violently against me are beginning to ask whether I was not after all right on 4 September.

I have deeply regretted it that I have had to rely so much on the argument of self interest: on the threat to South West Africa, on the gold mines as a bait for Germany. The real argument of course is the moral argument. We are in the war because the vital issues of our Christian civilization are at stake and for us to dissociate ourselves from Great Britain and the rest of the Commonwealth in such a matter would be cowardice and betrayal of the causes which are basic to our own existence. This argument will in future become more possible—now that German methods and aims are being more openly revealed and clearly realized. I feel that, whatever may have been the case in other great wars, we have now what is really a war of religion, a war of fundamentals of our human outlook and future. If Nazism were to triumph and Hitler's system spread over the world the calamity would be far worse than the Moslem con-

---

[1] Pius XII (q.v.) had sent telegrams to the rulers of the three invaded states on 11 May praying for the restoration of their countries to freedom and independence.

quest of the Christian world in the seventh century and thereafter. Mohammedanism at least retained the principles of equality and brotherhood among the faithful; while Nazism, following the creed of Nietzsche and others, exalts the minority over the rest of the people, and race over race, and destroys the very soul of our civilization. It may sound self-righteous for us to adopt this attitude, but it is the true attitude for us to take and to make plain to the world. On the Nazi foundations neither what we mean by religion nor what we have learnt to be ethical conduct could endure. Nazism is a plain contradiction of all that. I have not taken the same grave view of Bolshevism, for it never was clear to me that Bolshevism, in spite of its brutalities and cruelties, really threatened the essentials of our ethical civilization. And after all it was a revolution of a semi-barbarous people against a rotten government and an effete church. But Naziism in highly cultured Germany is a very different affair. Evil is enthroned and worshipped, and what we have considered good is spurned and suppressed. I wish some of our intelligentsia could put this viewpoint in plain and terse terms before the public, supported by relevant and indisputable facts. Such an exposition of the real meaning of this war may have far more propaganda value than most of the stuff which is now palmed off on the public. State what is the essence of our Western creed and show how German Nazism is the direct negative of all that—and many eyes will be opened and many hearts will be nerved for whatever struggle may lie ahead.

As I said I intend to fly up north next Wednesday. Much work awaits me there. For one thing defence preparations have somewhat suffered because of my heavy parliamentary preoccupations, and all that delay has to be made good. Then a very heavy political programme awaits me as I told you last week. I am dismayed at the prospect before me, but must grapple with it as soon as possible. No little holiday after the session this time!

This morning I learnt of the composition of your new government, with all three parties in it. I am afraid that after all that had happened, not so much in Norway as during a much longer period, Chamberlain had to go. His stock was exhausted, and it never was very great. Churchill will have a very heavy task, but at least he starts with a large measure of good will; he is dynamic, and his wiser colleagues must keep him out of mischief. He is capable of much mischief, as the past has shown. I wonder why Lloyd George is left out of the war cabinet. He is a friend of Churchill, and I am told he had much to do with the fall of Chamberlain in that devastating debate. I suppose the Conservatives do not like him, and Churchill had to bow to their prejudice. In a dynamic war Lloyd George would have been a great asset, owing to his courage and drive. It may be that if Churchill fails George will be there as the last reserve, as Clemenceau proved in France in the last war. I write of course without any knowledge of what is really happening behind the scenes.

I have done no reading this last week and am only too happy to sink into my bed when the long day's task is done. What a blessed thing sleep is! To the real hard worker it is a foretaste of that eternal bliss that is held out to us as a reward for our labours. Love from,

Jan

496   From W. S. Churchill   Vol. 61, no. 92

Telegram

From: Mr Winston Churchill, London

To: General Smuts, Cape Town

Dated 13 May 1940

To you, my friend of so many years, and faithful comrade of the last war, I send my heartfelt greetings. It is a comfort to me to feel that we shall be together in this hard and long trek; for I know you and the government and peoples of the Union will not weary under the heat of the day and that we shall make a strong laager for all beside the waters at the end.

497   From L. S. Amery   Vol. 61, no. 9

India Office
Whitehall
Private   18 May 1940

My dear Smuts, I have just given a line of introduction to you to Major [F. J.] Ney, of the National Council of Education of Canada, who is going out to South Africa at the invitation, I gather, of some of your education authorities both to promote cultural contacts between South Africa and Canada and to give them the benefit of his experience in working up cultural movements in Canada itself. Ney is a man of remarkable energy, who for the last twenty years or so has, through his National Council in Canada, promoted lectures, conferences, etc., securing good lecturers, both local and from outside, and has also done a great deal in the way of organizing tours for Canadian teachers and students in this country and on the

Continent. He is a live wire—almost too live and pertinacious for some people—but I think you may find his activities helpful to you at this moment, even if they do not bear directly on any political problem.

I need not say much to you about the details of the political crisis here. Dissatisfaction with the slowness and hesitation of the Chamberlain government had been growing stronger and stronger under the surface for months in every quarter, and only the tremendous discipline of the party system, as developed in recent years, had kept it under on our side. But Norway, which undoubtedly was a sorry example of indecision and defective organization, brought things to a head with a rush. With some hesitation, considering my old personal associations with Chamberlain, I went all out against the government in the first day's debate and, quoting Cromwell, suggested that they had better go.[1] Somewhat to my surprise the speech had a very big effect and not only encouraged the opposition to put the matter to a direct vote next day, but decided more than forty of the government supporters to vote with me, not to speak of considerable numbers who abstained.[2]

My motive, of course, and that of those who voted with me, was not merely to upset the government, but to make possible a national government, including all parties. I have pleaded for this ever since Munich, as well as for a small war cabinet free of departmental duties. The trouble with Chamberlain has been that nothing would make him accept the idea of a small war cabinet, while on the other hand nothing would induce the Labour men to come in under him. Rightly or wrongly, they have always thoroughly distrusted and disliked him and made his ceasing to be prime minister an absolute condition of their joining in. It was indeed as much as they were prepared to accept that he should remain in the government in any capacity.[3]

Anyhow, now we have got a national government, out of which we ought to get the fullest effort of the nation, and a reasonable structure of government. For many reasons I might perhaps have preferred to be in one of the departments directly connected with the war effort, or in the treasury, where I might have broken down some of the resistances that have strangled the development of our resources. On the other hand, Winston feels that India may become

[1] The debate began on 7 May. Cromwell's words were spoken to the Rump Parliament in 1653: 'You have sat too long here for any good you have been doing. Depart, I say, and let us have done with you. In the name of God, go.'

[2] Forty-one supporters of the government voted with the opposition and about 60 abstained. The government's majority of about 240 fell to 81.

[3] Chamberlain was lord president of the council in Churchill's cabinet of May 1940.

of increasing importance to the common effort of the war, especially if Italy should come in, and also that my past experience may help in solving the very difficult constitutional problems we are up against. Certainly the work promises to be of the greatest interest and I am glad to have the opportunity of trying my hand at it. I should not be surprised if before many weeks are out you and I may be finding ourselves co-operating actively in Kenya, or even in Abyssinia. You will remember my anxieties about the Italian danger last summer. They may well be realized now, for Mussolini is only waiting from day to day to see how the German thrust progresses before he thinks it safe to join in. Well, if that happens, the whole of civilization as we know it will be at issue, both in Europe and east and south of Suez. Do let us keep in touch as much as we can through all these troubles. Yours ever,

L. S. Amery

498   From L. S. Amery   Vol. 61, no. 10

India Office
Whitehall

Private   24 May 1940

My dear Smuts, I see in this morning's paper that you have reached the age of seventy. I know you are fit and in good trim and everyone tells me that the great issues of the day in South Africa and in the world have rejuvenated you out of all recognition. Well, more power to your elbow, or perhaps I should say your keen brain and strong will, for we shall need all the help we can get if civilization is to survive; at any rate in the old world, which includes Africa.

At the moment of writing, the situation of our army is still very uncertain. We have by no means abandoned hope that the French counter-attack may still be in time to close the gap through which the Germans have encircled us. If so, then the advance German units will be destroyed and the whole German attack will at best have got as far as it did in the last war, at much heavier cost, and with less of resources behind. On the other hand, before you get this, the Germans may have secured the whole of the Channel ports and the French line be back to the Somme, holding on defensively, while the remnants of our army are being reformed for the defence of England. That, I fear, would mean collapse in the Balkans and Italy joining in to attack Egypt. Well, I believe we can handle that problem, but it means a long and uphill business, as I said in my last letter. Only I would qualify the last sentence by my belief that Germany's internal staying power is much less than it was last time and that she may well crack before two years are out.

India is a curious complex. Wholeheartedly with us over the main issue, your old friend Gandhi is trying to stampede the political situation on the basis that Congress is India and that a numerical majority in British India is entitled to frame any constitution it wants for the future. We have whole-heartedly accepted the idea of complete Dominion self-government for India if only they can find among themselves a settlement which does not mean civil war the day after tomorrow and a government maintained only by British bayonets. As you know, no one is a more sincere believer in self-government than I am; but at the moment I can see no other course than trying to make Congress, Muslims, and princes realize that it is up to them to arrive at some measure of agreement before we can hand over. Meanwhile, the gravity of the fighting situation is, I think, steadying Indian opinion, as I imagine it has been steadying opinion in the Union.

Well, I seem to have rambled on dictating. After all, I only began this letter to wish you, my old friend, health and strength and a confident spirit through the time ahead. Yours ever,

L. S. Amery

499   To M. C. Gillett   Vol. 63, no. 97

Doornkloof
[Transvaal]
28 May 1940

Last night the Belgian army surrendered. I have just finished a broadcast to South Africa to steady public opinion. Your letter (written at Aston on Whitsunday amid the glories of the English spring) sorrowed over the invasion of Holland and Belgium. Holland has gone and now Belgium has once more gone— but in a very different way from last time. Albert the father, my friend, was a great man; Leopold his son thought himself a great man, overreached himself, and gave away his country, and his people's honour. I suppose by now all the Channel coast is in German hands, and the B.E.F.[1] and French divisions are trapped. It is a choice between surrender or fighting through against enormous odds and at a frightful cost. What will happen the next few days will show and it is idle to speculate. One's blood runs cold to

[1] British Expeditionary Force.

think of that situation and the responsibility of the commanders. From the Channel the German hordes will turn south and perhaps take Paris. I was speaking a couple of days ago at Heidelberg[1] to an enormous demonstration (5–6,000 people) and called this the most fateful hour of history. I pointed out what was at stake, and then compared the world situation today with that under the Roman Empire, when the highest and largest civilization which man had arrived at was smashed by the Germanic hordes, and a thousand years of Dark Ages settled over Europe. I asked whether history was repeating itself. Who can say? We only know that all we have lived for and hold dear in spiritual values is at stake once more.

Heidelberg was the third big function in one week. First there was the Pretoria City reception at Fountains, attended by a vast concourse whom I had to address; then followed the Johannesburg City reception—a very brilliant affair in the form of a dinner at night in the city hall, where I had also to speak; then Heidelberg. These three had been preceded the week before by the great party reception at Pretoria of which I think I must have written you. I am at last popular (for how long?) and receiving the honours of a king. My seventieth birthday is the pretext for all this fuss. I am human enough to enjoy all this—after it is over! But I am glad to think there will not be another seventieth birthday. Over 1,600 telegrams and letters of congratulation arrived; also some very nice presents. From the party in parliament a beautiful ciné camera; from A. Bailey the projector to put the pictures on the screen; from Johannesburg city council a beautiful portable wireless; and so on, and so on—too many to enumerate. Among others I received from Oxford a botanical Thesaurus as big as an old Dutch Bible, dated 1640—really the botanical encyclopedia of that time. I don't know whom to thank— inside is a list of donors, with [Sir Alfred] Zimmern's and [C. K.] Allen's (of Rhodes House) and A. D. Lindsay's names among many others. Headed by 'To Oom Jannie' etc. So it may be young Patrick Duncan or some other South African who started the business.[2] Will you ask Allen whom I have to write to to convey my

---

[1] In the southern Transvaal.

[2] Patrick Duncan, son of the governor-general of the Union, and other South African undergraduates at Oxford collected money to buy a Parkinson's *Herbal* as a present to Smuts on his seventieth birthday. One of the contributors, Sir Dougal Malcolm, composed the following inscription:

Ad I.C.S.

Arboreum omne genus, camporum gramina, tellus
　Daedala quo niteat quove colore nemus,
Iam bene novisti, doctrinae cultor agrestis;
　Hoc tamen accipias munus amicitiae.

thanks? And all this time while these hectic doings were taking place round me I had to concentrate on what was happening in France, and sometimes had to sit up till two in the morning in order to deal with urgent cables. So light and foolish things jostle the gravest things in the world. For I *do* believe that what is now happening in Europe is of decisive importance for our fate for a long time. If Hitler wins the currents of the future will be turned into strange new channels which will carry us far away from the civilization we have known. If he is beaten—as God give he will be—some new reconstruction on the spiritual foundations of the past could be attempted and the continuity of our civilization could be secured in some form or other. At the moment Hitler is winning all along the line; seven countries have already fallen into his power, and really only France and England are still holding out. But the end may be far off and quite different from this brilliant beginning for him. Napoleon conquered Europe and died at St Helena. The present situation is, however, not quite a parallel to that of Napoleon, and the peril today is much greater. Air power seems today to be the decisive power, as the navy was a hundred years ago and more; and in the air the Germans are still supreme. I mention only one of the great differences between then and now. I keep believing in God, but I don't forget that He favoured the English more than the Boers, although then too we thought He would stand by our righteous cause. I hope He won't favour Hitler this time; indeed I cannot believe it.

I have now only been fourteen days at home but already—with all these hectic events and doings—it looks like an age since I left Cape Town. I have never lived through such times, and the pace is almost more than one can bear.

Your letter from Aston told of the family reunion at Aston under such happy spring conditions. I can imagine all that—the bluebells, the sprouting leaves and bursting buds, and the feel of the air for which language has no words. I suppose it must be exactly the same in France where all this mortal fighting is going on under the most heavenly conditions of nature. Surely human nature must be shamed

> Arma inter sileant leges: non Flora silebit;
> Ver vel nunc aevi spem melioris habet.

> Yours are the trees, the grasses of the field,
> The varied beauties earth and forest yield.
> This gift of friends, master of rural lore,
> Take, though it tell you what you knew before.
> War stifles Justice, yet shall Flora say
> How Spring holds promise of a happier day.
>   (*See* Smuts Collection, vol. 63, nos. 23, 28.)

by its besmirching God's world in this foul way. We, who should be
the spiritual crown and glory, are really the darkest blot on this fair
world. I am reminded of Baldwin's words to the Canadian Pilgrims
in Westminster Hall some years ago: 'If through our bitter experiences of the last war mankind has not yet learnt its lesson, it *deserves*
to die.' It almost seems as if that curse is coming home to us in these
days of endless carnage and destruction. One is numbed. One cannot die, but does not know how to see daylight in this utter darkness.
No philosophy or religion comes to your assistance, and you simply
drift on mechanically, doing the daily task as it comes to hand in the
absence of any alternative. If your vitality is low you can sink into
a sort of torpor of dull brain, as some do; but if your vitality is high,
as yours and mine, you can only drug yourself with all sorts of
activities of more or less importance. Life becomes a cry into
vacancy, where nobody hears or answers, and the universe seems to
lose all meaning. I think this sense of emptiness and meaninglessness
must be coming home to millions of thoughtful people in these days.
And that is the real horror of our times. Can we bring back the sense
of home, of intimacy, of a family world once more, as Jesus did for
his little Galilean circle? There's the rub. Love to you all,

Jan

500   From L. S. Amery   Vol. 61, no. 12

This letter is annotated by Smuts as follows: 'C.G.S. This letter from Mr
Amery, especially the barred passage, may interest you. I have taken no
action on it yet.' The chief of the general staff was General Sir Pierre van
Ryneveld.

India Office
Whitehall
5 June 1940

My dear Smuts, I really forget whether I sent you any part, in proof
or in typescript, of my last *Round Table* article on 'The Strategy of
the War'.[1] Anyhow, I am sending you a copy of the *Round Table*
with the article itself. In case you should ever have time for so
purely retrospective an amusement as reading the account of what
actually happened in Finland and Norway.

The first phase of the western front battle is over[2] and I shall not

[1] Three articles by Amery were published in the *Round Table* in December 1939
and March and June 1940.
[2] Operation Dynamo, the evacuation of the trapped British forces from Dunkirk,
was completed on 2 June.

attempt to repeat what Winston said so magnificently yesterday. I think the Germans mean now to renew the attack upon the French army with the very minimum of delay.[1] If they should succeed in pushing through then Paris may well be lost and France put to a test of her spirit which I believe, but am not perfectly certain, she will stand up to. As for Italy, it looks as if she meant to come in some time next week. At the same time the whole thing may be bluff.

If Italy does come in then it is going to be largely a question of the Empire east and south of Alexandria holding its own by its own resources. I am particularly anxious to develop Indian resources to the utmost for that purpose. If you will be sending troops up to Kenya or Abyssinia will you be wanting any supplies for them that India can provide? If so, will it be most convenient for you to instruct Waterson [S.] to get in touch with me or are you in convenient direct touch with the government of India? My impression is that so much has been centralized here that it may be easier to find out at this end exactly what can or cannot be done. In haste, Yours ever,

L. S. Amery

501   To J. B. M. Hertzog   Vol. 63, no. 26

Pretoria
13 Junie 1940

Waarde Hertzog, Vriende beide van u en my het in die laaste tyd met my geraadpleeg oor die wenslikheid van 'n politieke wapenstilstand tussen die partye in hierdie ernstige tyd, en my is meegedeel dat sommige van hul ook u geraadpleeg het.

In antwoord het ek hul gesê dat ek in grote mate met hul saamstem en so'n stap sou verwelkom indien dit prakties uitvoerbaar sou blyk. In nader bespreking met hul is dit geblyk dat so'n party wapenstilstand veral oor twee punte sou loop, nl.:

1. dat alle politieke vergaderings wat bedoel of bereken is party propaganda te maak of party bitterheid te verwek vermy sal word; en

2. dat die leiers hul sal beywer dat die nuusblaaie aan weerskante en in beide landstale kritiek of aanvalle op ander partye sal vermy wat party gevoel en bitterheid sal verskerp en gevoelens van die een teen die anderkant sal opsweep. Dit sou natuurlik nie kritiek oor publieke kwessies in 'n matige of besadigde gees geuit of op die meriete gebaseer uitsluit nie.

[1] The Germans began the Battle of France on 5 June 1940.

So'n wapenstilstand sou nie die uitvoering van die regering se oorlogsbeleid of maatreëls vir handhawing van rus en orde affekteer nie. Die bedoeling is meer bepaald om die uiterste partygees in die politieke stryd en die daaruitspruitende bitterheid en verwydering onder die volk uit te skakel. Dit word gevoel dat die stryd vorme kan aanneem wat rusverstorend mag word en die volkseenheid in die toekoms blywend kan benadeel.

Op u en my as leiers van die vernaamste politieke partye rus daar 'n sware verantwoordelikheid vir die vrede en welvaart van die volk, en waar dit binne ons vermoë is, veral in hierdie onstuimige tyd, om die euwels en gevare van politieke ekstremisme te voorkom, sal ons albei bereid wees al ons invloed in daardie rigting uit te oefen.

Ek voel oortuig dat dit in u bedoeling lê, veral na die oproep van Senator Brebner in dieselfde rigting wat ek met groot belangstelling gelees het. Ek het dus die vrymoedigheid u in oorweging te gee dat ons so'n poging maak om die politieke vrede te bevorder, en so moontlik trag tot 'n wapenstilstand te geraak op die bovermelde basis.

Ek kan natuurlik begryp dat die saak nie sonder moeilikhede gepaard is nie, maar ek voel ook dat 'n baie groot deel van ons ondersteuners aan beide kante so'n wapenstilstand vir die oorlogs-tydperk sal toejuig. Ek wil dus hoop dat u u ernstige aandag aan die saak sal wil skenk. Steeds die uwe,

get. J. C. Smuts

TRANSLATION

Pretoria

13 June 1940

Dear Hertzog, Friends of yours and mine have recently consulted me about the desirability of a political truce between the parties in these grave times and I am informed that some of them have also consulted you.

In reply I have told them that I agree with them in great measure and would welcome such a step if it should prove to be practicable. In further discussion with them it has appeared that such a party truce would in the first place cover two points, namely:

1. that all political meetings which are intended or calculated to make party propaganda or to arouse party bitterness shall be avoided; and

2. that the leaders will do their best to see that the newspapers on either side and in both languages avoid criticism of or attacks on other parties which might sharpen party feeling or bitter-

ness and arouse feeling against each other. This would, of course, not exclude criticism on public questions expressed in a moderate and calm spirit or considered on its merits.

Such a truce would not affect the carrying out of the war policy of the government or the measures for the maintenance of peace and order. The intention is rather to do away with the extremes of party feeling in the political conflict and the bitterness and estrangement among the people of the country that flow from this. It is felt that the conflict may assume forms that would be disquieting and permanently injure national unity in future.

On you and me as the leaders of the most important political parties there rests a heavy responsibility for the peace and prosperity of the people; and where it is within our power, especially in these agitated times, to prevent the evils and dangers of political extremism, we shall both be ready to use all our influence in this direction.

I am convinced that this is your intention, especially since the appeal of Senator [W. J. C.] Brebner[1] in the same sense which I have read with great interest.[2] I thus take the liberty of suggesting to you that we make such an attempt to advance political peace and possibly try to achieve a truce on the above-mentioned basis.

I understand, of course, that the matter is attended with difficulties, but I feel that a very large part of our supporters on both sides would applaud such a truce for the duration of the war. I therefore hope that you will give serious attention to this matter. Ever sincerely yours,

s. J. C. Smuts

502   To M. C. Gillett   Vol. 63, no. 101

Doornkloof
[Transvaal]
14 June 1940

My recent letters to you have been punctuated by our set-backs and disasters on the western front—so rapid has been the march of events. Today Paris was occupied by the enemy—in many ways much the most disastrous event of all. One can understand what must be going on in the hearts of Frenchmen and Frenchwomen. One sees the endless stream of fugitives along all roads south of Paris. Hitler has once more won a resounding and far-reaching

---

[1] *See* vol. IV, p. 303.
[2] For this speech made by Brebner, then chairman of the Hertzog group in the Orange Free State, on 31 May in Bloemfontein *see* the *Cape Times*, 1 June 1940, p. 16.

victory. I sent today, on receipt of the news, a message to the prime
minister of France from the government and people of the Union,
and tonight it was broadcast over the land. When the radio finished
the message it struck up the deathless 'Marseillaise', and Isie rose
at the table and stood to attention while it lasted. The idea of the
broadcast was freedom—deathless freedom for which we shall
continue to strive to the end. This war, which began as Hitler's war,
may end as God's war, the war for the greatest cause of the human
race. The message of the British government to France yesterday—
also broadcast today—was a magnificent one, and it was spoken
from the heart. I know Britain will fight on till the end, even if she
has to stand alone. I would rather lose in this fight than win in
Hitler's. As Shelley said in the preface to *Prometheus Unbound*—
I would rather go to hell with Plato than to heaven with Paley.[1]
I have been occupied the whole of today with our plans for the future.
It is all very curious that for the third time in my life all my mind
and energy should be given to war. It is certainly not from love of
it, but from love of those things which are to me the very soul of life.

Short accounts appear also in the news of our air attacks in
Abyssinia by a portion of our air force defending Kenya. That is
another strange echo from the past, when east Africa was with me
night and day for eleven months. Now, once more, I have to study its
map and the doings of our men up there. I myself would be there but
for age and responsibilities down here. Andries [Weyers] and Jannie
[Smuts] will soon be going, so I shall be represented in the family.

This letter will have to go by sea, the air mail having suddenly
come to an end since 10 June when Italy entered the war. I fear my
last letter to you, telling of my visit to Durban, will be floating
somewhere in Africa, and may perhaps never reach you. We are
trying to have an air mail along another more western route, but
with the vicissitudes of war one does not know whether this effort
will succeed, and for how long. So our correspondence may not have
as smooth a course in future as it has had in the past. Still, we have
had a good innings, and must not mind if misfortune hits us there
too. After all we have very little to complain of in this good world.
And if we had nothing else there would still be the grand fund of
wonderful memories from which to draw inexhaustible delight.

Your last letter which arrived a few days ago (and two from dear
Arthur) told of your visit to the Cotswolds, where the young Windrush frolics among the hills. Windrush and Evenlode[2]—what poetry

[1] 'For my part I would rather be damned with Plato and Lord Bacon, than go to
Heaven with Paley and Malthus.'

[2] Two small rivers.

they convey! The very sounds act like magic. It must be charming country, judging from your description. I hope there will be great peace and refreshment of mind and body for you both. How blessed the great rhythms of nature are to the soul! For according to atomic physics the great enduring masses of the earth—mountains and all solid things—are essentially nothing but continuous rhythmical repetitions of the wave mechanics which is matter. An atom is just a continuous repetition of a particular set of electronic waves or pulsations. And Cotswold hills but a grand symphony of such rhythmical waves. Looking at the earth, its hills and mountains, is in essence the same as listening to a continuous musical symphony, only with a more monotonous soothing series of notes. Matter is really the frozen music of the universe. And what a peace, a consolation, an appeasement to mind and eye there is in that solemn frozen music, whose winding rhythms are constituted by the pleasing outlines and contours of hill and dale. As the ear hears one kind of music, so the eye is enchanted by this more massive music of the earth. God to whom there is no distinction of ear and eye, enjoys it all in his infinite bliss. Perhaps when we have shoved off this mortal coil[1] with its differentiated senses we shall also hear that universal music which we now see as matter.

Thank you very much for some recent books. Schweitzer on Paul[2] has duly arrived, but is not yet read. I am now looking through at night Bradley's *Ideals of Religion*, Gifford lectures delivered in 1907![3] Much of it sounds old-worldly, almost prehistoric. It is curious how the climate of thought has altered in thirty years. But there is a good deal of fine stuff in him. He was a literary thinker—the philosophic mind with a keen spiritual power and aesthetic perception. I must read his *Shakesperian Tragedy*[4] which I am told is very good stuff. I am still looking for the God within us—'The kingdom of heaven among you'.[5] I believe if we could see rightly and think clearly, we could see that in us which represents the common root of God and Man, the point of incarnation, so to say, in our personality. Great souls sense that divine within, but of course transpose it to something objective without—and so the immanent becomes the transcendent. But this immanent is really not ourselves; it is something more than the individual asset. It is also the point where the individual and the universal meet—in some other form of incarnation. The God which is my soul is really not myself, but something far

---

[1] 'When we have shuffled off this mortal coil...' Shakespeare, *Hamlet*, III.i.67.

[2] Albert Schweitzer, *Die Mystik des Apostels Paulus* (1930).

[3] A. C. Bradley, *Ideals of Religion*, transcribed from the MS of the Gifford lectures 1907 and published in 1940.

[4] Published in 1904.   [5] *See supra*, p. 95, note 1.

235

more universal, whose dwelling is the light of setting suns,[1] and not merely my poor body. I wonder whether you and Arthur follow this simple line of thought—simple and yet going to the very roots of religion and philosophy and much besides which is great in us. This is the Source, in us, and yet more than us, just as love is in us, and yet fills the universe. But this is scarcely fit matter for a chatty letter. I fear my letters with their divagations into side issues, must be boring to you. But they just flow from an uncontrolled pen as I write.

Arthur's letters—more concerned with war issues than yours—are naturally very interesting to me. I hope he will continue to write, even if I don't answer. My letters to you are meant for him equally, and both of you are before me as I write. With love from me and all in our small circle,

Jan

503 To L. S. Amery Vol. 63, no. 29

Pretoria
19 June 1940

My dear Amery, I owe you an answer to two most welcome letters, and I have not yet written to congratulate you on your come-back. Nothing in the new cabinet has pleased me more than to see some measure of justice at last done to you. You had lost Baldwin's favour, and Chamberlain also passed you by for men far inferior in ability and service to you. I am glad you have fought your way back, and so valiantly too. Your great speech in the commons at the final inquest made me literally sit up.[2] India is a good post, indeed a key post in these days—very close to the war and to high politics. I think you have a great service to render after the years in the wilderness.

We have struck a bad patch, how bad time only can show. If we win this war it will be by God's grace. But why should we not see it in a case like this? If ever there is devil's work in this world, Hitler is doing it. He will smash our civilization in addition to the political organization of Europe. And a mere barbarian! If he had been

[1]
         ...a sense sublime
         Of something far more deeply interfused,
         Whose dwelling is the light of setting suns,
         And the round ocean and the living air,
         And the blue sky, and in the mind of man.
  William Wordsworth, *Lines Composed a Few Miles above Tintern Abbey*, ll. 95–9.
[2] *See supra*, p. 225, note 1.

a Napoleon one might have had doubts, but Hitler is a mere barbarian of the spirit for whom I have no time. My views are from time to time passed on to Waterman[1] and [Lord] Caldecote and sometimes direct to Churchill, so I shall not trouble you.

I am most dubious about that Anglo-French union,[2] except as a tonic to a very sick patient. But no more about politics.

I am getting on fairly well and making real headway. It was 50–50 at the beginning; now more like 60–40. I shall hold on grimly to my job and my policy. I only wish I were twenty years younger.

My very kind regards to you and Mrs Amery. Ever yours,

s. J. C. Smuts

504   To J. B. M. Hertzog   Vol. 63, no. 31

Pretoria
20 June 1940

Dear Hertzog, Your letter of 17 instant[3] has been received. In it you ask 'that the Union shall immediately adopt all measures and take all steps to withdraw from the war and to secure peace'.

This dishonourable proposal was already submitted by you yourself to the house of assembly in its last session and was decisively rejected by it.[4] There is therefore no sense that the same request contained in it should now be submitted to me, only with more rhetoric. Not only was this request expressly rejected by the house of assembly, but it is also in conflict with the policy adopted by the house of assembly on 4 September last year in all seriousness and after full consideration. I have no doubt that if a similar proposal were again submitted it would once more receive the same fate at the hands of the highest authority in the land. Under these circumstances you surely cannot as a democrat expect from me that I shall solely on your personal pressure violate the decision of parliament.

The reason which you urge for this singular request is 'that the war has already been hopelessly lost by the Allies'. This may be your opinion, but it is not a fact on the basis of which I should be called on to act contrary to the decision of parliament. The war has not been hopelessly lost by the Allies, just as little as it was hopelessly lost by the Allies in the first four years of the World War,

[1] Probably a typist's error for Waterson, then high commissioner for the Union in London.
[2] On 16 June the British government suggested to the French government the political union of their two countries. The offer was rejected.
[3] Hertzog's letter was given to the press and appeared in *Die Vaderland* on 19 June 1940.   [4] *See supra*, p. 211.

from August 1914 to July 1918, although its progress and the victories were uniformly in favour of Germany. Within a couple of months after that 'triumphant' progress, Germany was beaten and her power had hopelessly collapsed. Just as now, the supporters of Germany had then hoped and expected that the war would be hopelessly lost by the Allies. They were disappointed. Now once more the friends and advocates of Hitler, who look expectantly for a Nazi victory, will most probably meet with the same disappointment.

The groundless and false supposition on which your entire argument is based, is that the Union could have kept out of danger if we had remained neutral towards Germany. Has Germany not herself exposed the falsity of this argument? What has the neutrality of Denmark, Norway, Holland and Belgium profited them? Why should the Union, which incidentally holds a mandate over a former German colony, and against whom she has shown her malice by continuous hostile propaganda and the formation of a fifth column, have been able to save herself if she also had remained neutral? Your argument has been refuted by the action of Germany itself.

You then point to the folly of our declaration of war against Italy. You omit to mention that Italy had first declared war against our friends—Britain, and her colonies—Kenya, Northern and Southern Rhodesia—which form our best line of defence. These three colonies are not in a position to defend themselves against the preponderance of power of Italy in Abyssinia and north Africa. Is it your view that we must just allow Italy to conquer these countries and march on to the borders of the Union with her powerful air force? And should Italy's ally Germany also be allowed to do the same? What would in that case happen to the independence of the Union? Surely nobody who takes the independence of the Union seriously can honestly use such an argument as yours. I do not believe that even your own followers will swallow such nonsense.

Finally you fall back on threats. You refer to the pressure which your supporters exercise on the party leaders, and anticipate 'mass protests' which may perhaps follow. Even 'far-reaching disorders among the people' are mentioned.

We live in grave times, which remind us of other grave times in our history. It is to be hoped that the party leaders whom you refer to will realize their responsibility towards the people, and will avoid situations whereby the people may be involved in calamity through party political propaganda and mass protests, for which the main responsibility will rest on the leaders.

As far as concerns the government, to whom lawful authority

has been constitutionally entrusted, all measures will be adopted and all steps taken to maintain law and order, and to carry out the policy which parliament has approved.

I do not consider it necessary to discuss your allegations of 'self-deceit and deceit of the people', of 'compulsory measures', of 'invasion of liberties, scorn, threats and force'. In the absence of any facts I have to look upon those expressions as just rhetorical exaggerations.

The people of South Africa has laid down its war policy in a constitutional manner. That policy is designed to maintain the independence and vital interests of the Union. The government will carry out that policy on the mandate of parliament, and will not allow the execution of that policy to be nullified by political propaganda or threats of violence. Yours faithfully,

s. J. C. Smuts

P.S. Copy of this letter is also given to the press.

505   To M. C. Gillett   Vol. 63, no. 102

Doornkloof
[Transvaal]
24 June 1940

I do not remember when I last wrote to you. Life is so overcrowded with events, time passes so rapidly that the things of last week appear to have happened ages ago. The rush seems to destroy our time-sense. I returned to Pretoria from Cape Town about five weeks ago, and that was just after Holland and Belgium had been invaded. Now a Fascist government of France has signed a dis-honourable armistice for France,[1] and made the future position of France as a great power all but impossible. Between these events lies a series almost without parallel in modern history. If this pace is continued I wonder where we shall be in a few months or by the end of this year.

I received your wire last week asking me to urge Cato [Clark] to bring her children to South Africa. I immediately cabled her, including also the other youngsters in the wider family circle. The answer was unfavourable. This morning I received another cable, from Bancroft [Clark] once more asking us to urge Cato. A stronger

---

[1] The armistice with Germany was signed on 22 June by a French government of which Marshal Pétain was prime minister. An armistice with Italy was signed on 24 June. The greater part of France was to be occupied by Germany and the French navy demobilized.

cable pressing her to come has gone today. I hope she will come, as I don't think small children should remain in England at this time if they have a chance of going to healthier countries. Of course Street is not a particularly dangerous place and may escape bombing. But it must be an anxiety to parents to think continually of what *may* happen. I hope she will come.

We are also making provision to receive refugee and evacuee children here, and even to adopt them with their parents' consent. There is a very strong feeling in South Africa to do so, and I believe many hundreds of well-to-do households have already offered to give asylum to such children. A well-organized scheme under our welfare department will soon be in operation and bring many thousands of children to this country. It is a curious sidelight on our party politics that Dr [D. F.] Malan has uttered a public warning against the scheme. Jewish children or even English children might (I suppose) contaminate the pure breed of Afrikander! What an outlook! I only hope that many of these children will stay permanently and eventually bring their parents after them, and so help to strengthen the European basis of our population. In that case we shall profit beyond measure from this act of humanity and hospitality.

This only shows what a bad spirit is about. But it is not the only indication. A week ago Hertzog wrote me a poisonous letter to protest against our declaring war on Italy at a time when the 'Allied cause was hopelessly lost'. I replied with less than my usual Christian charity.[1] But I felt that his letter was only the first shot in a bitter campaign to come. The second shot was fired last Saturday, when a vast procession of Nationalist women, mostly in Voortrekker dress, marched from old Pretoria to the Union Buildings to present a petition to me to make immediate peace. I had declined to receive the deputation and was not in Pretoria, but Hofmeyr [J. H.] received the dear old ladies, and offered them morning tea which was curtly declined. Now the third shot has been fired—in the form of a flaming manifesto by Hertzog and Dr Malan[2] indicting me for involving the country in war, etc. etc. and demanding the instant meeting of parliament (which by the way, had in two sessions approved of my action). They threaten that if this is not done, a series of meetings of protest will be held culminating in a vast demonstration 'such as South Africa has not yet seen'; and finally vigilance committees will be formed all over the country to form (I suppose) the nuclei of a revolution. Meanwhile I have to strain every nerve to meet the other enemy on the borders of

[1] *See* **504**.   [2] *See* the *Cape Times*, 25 June 1940, p. 15.

Abyssinia and prevent Kenya and other British colonies from being overrun in the north. The Italians have a very big army well provided with planes and mechanical transport in Abyssinia and Eritrea, and the northern British colonies are almost unprotected. If they are overwhelmed the march down Africa will follow until South Africa is reached, and our cities are destroyed from the air. Now that the war in France is over and Hitler's army is without occupation they will very likely join the Italians in this joy ride through Africa. This menace I have to deal with at the same time that I am plotted against and attacked within the gates. South Africans are curious people. If we were wise and could sink differences we could now secure such a measure of defence co-operation among all our neighbours, including the Belgian Congo, that after this war we could be a great United States of Africa right up to the equator. This prospect of future expansion and security is before us, but instead of firmly grasping it we have to submit to what passes for politics in this country, but elsewhere is looked upon as national sabotage and betrayal. I shall not be deflected from my course, but you can imagine what a rough road I am treading. It has lasted so long already that I should not mind the continuance for the remaining few years! And there have been pleasant intervals between, such as, e.g. the seventieth birthday celebrations a month ago.

Maybe when this reaches you by sea the great attack on England will have begun. This will be Hitler's real effort, and it will probably come soon, before American planes have arrived in large numbers. I should be more than surprised if this attack is not beaten off and Hitler finds his Moscow[1] in England. The English fighter machine has done so well against the German bomber, as notably at Dunkirk, that I confidently back your defence. In fact I think Britain will prove an impregnable fortress against which the fury of Hitler will lash in vain. The war has so far gone so consistently against the Allies that many people are becoming pessimistic. Not I, however. I think we shall once more win the last round—and the war. I have been giving rather cheerful broadcasts the last few weeks which have made people see the other—not so obvious—point of view, and now the British government have asked me to give an Empire and American broadcast. I shall do so if I can find time, but I have never been harder worked in my life than in these strenuous days. How could Hitler win this war, and win the world, and sabotage the civilization which has been so laboriously built up? And yet Attila and his brood torpedoed the Roman Empire. I suppose if we win it will be by the grace of God...

[1] A reference to Napoleon's retreat from Moscow in 1812.

506   From L. S. Amery   Vol. 61, no 13

India Office
Whitehall
Personal   29 June 1940

My dear Smuts, I haven't attempted to write to you for some weeks and things have moved so fast that anything I might have told you about the situation here would have reached you as ancient history. Anyhow, we are now up against the position in which we may anticipate a formidable attack on Egypt and on the whole position in Africa as soon as the Germans have finished with their attack on us here. That may take them some time before they give it up and meanwhile possibly things in the Balkans or in connection with Spain and north-western Africa may hold them up for a bit longer. All of which makes it to my mind essential that we should take the initiative in north-east Africa while we can and if possible eliminate the Italians from Abyssinia during the next two or three months.

In all this, as I think I have said to you before in my letters, it looks to me as if India and the southern Dominions have got to co-operate in order to hold the situation by their own resources. I have got great ideas as to the immense possibilities of expansion from the point of view of munitions, supply and equipment which India might be capable of with sufficient stimulus and with some balancing up of her existing resources with machine tools, etc. from outside. I am hoping to send a strong mission out there to see what can be done to enlarge the whole field of output. Meanwhile, the viceroy[1] himself has been getting busy in the most praiseworthy fashion and has already got quite a move on. He has, I know, telegraphed to you as well as to Menzies [R. G.] to ask if you could let him have a good liaison officer in connection with supply matters. I am sure that that would be very useful to you in enabling you both to draw upon India for supplies, especially for your forces in east Africa, and also for the converse purpose of letting India know what materials or supplies she might be able to draw from you, so I hope you have been able to accede to his request.

The constitutional position in India is still difficult. But, apart from the Congress, there is a general desire to co-operate and I hope somehow or other to see progress made in that direction. I should like to fly out myself if I could, but it may not be easy to get away from here. If I did, I suppose it is just possible that I might have to come by steamer as far as Cape Town first, which would give us a chance of meeting and talking over things. Yours ever,

L. S. Amery

[1] Lord Linlithgow (q.v.).

507   To M. C. Gillett   Vol. 63, no. 105

Doornkloof
[Transvaal]
10 July 1940

Another week passed, and another most amazing stage reached—
Britain and France fighting each other![1] Could anyone in his senses
have predicted such a development before the end of the war? The
democratic front is shattered, and Britain now faces the all but
omnipotent enemy alone. Any day or night now the storm may
burst over her. Every week almost there has been some surprising
development in the last couple of months. What surprise will next
week bring? Will it be Spain in the Axis, with Gibraltar evacuated
and Portugal in danger? Or will it be somewhere else in the Mediterranean lands? Whatever happens Africa is certain to be affected
and the war to come nearer to us. I notice in the cables tonight that
the French parliament is voting a new Fascist constitution. And so
the torch is quenched in that land of the revolution. The black-out
is settling down on Europe. As Sir Edward Grey said in August 1914:
the lights are going out over Europe one after the other.[2] Will
England save the world, as Athens saved the future of civilization at
Salamis?[3]

Here too my difficulties are increasing. The German victories are
putting great heart into my opposition. They are holding meetings
all over the country in favour of a separate peace. The Allies are
finished, they say, and Smuts will be finished in a couple of months,
and thereafter they will seize power and proclaim secession and the
republic. There will be a new constitution modelled on that of Italy
or Portugal, and with an alliance with Nazi Germany. We have been
sitting quietly looking on at this campaign. But inaction does not
mean surrender. At the right time and in the proper form we shall
take up the challenge. Meanwhile it looks like parliament having to
meet soon. There has been very heavy war expenditure, and the
money voted by parliament for the purpose will soon be exhausted.
Towards the end of August we shall be in the parliamentary treadmill again. You can imagine the difficulties of running a war from
Pretoria and sitting in parliament a thousand miles away, talking

[1] On 3 July three French battleships were put out of action by British attacks at
Oran in north Africa. On 5 July the newly-established French government at Vichy
broke off relations with Great Britain.

[2] 'The lamps are going out all over Europe; we shall not see them lit again in our
lifetime'. Viscount Grey, *Twenty-Five Years*, vol. II, chapter 18.

[3] At the naval battle of Salamis (480 B.C.) the Greeks destroyed a large part of the
Persian fleet, a victory which made the Persians abandon their plans for conquering
Greece.

day and night. Such are my difficulties. They have to be faced, and I shall face them with as much cheerfulness as my impatient nature will permit. But the Lord hears my inward groanings.[1] Isie is very much upset at the prospect of an early change to Groote Schuur from her beloved Doornkloof. But we are public slaves and must obey the whip of our democracy...

508   Speech (1940)   Box J. no. 126

This speech by Smuts was broadcast on 21 July 1940.

I speak to you today as the representative of South Africa, the representative of one small free people, to the two greatest free peoples in the world—the peoples of the United Kingdom and of the United States of America. From this distance I speak to you about the war, a war of freedom if ever there was one, a war in which the fundamental question is whether freedom shall prevail or perish from the face of the earth before the most gigantic and diabolic onslaught that has ever been made against it.

Speaking thus as it were in the household of freedom on the subject which touches us all most deeply, I wish briefly to discuss two questions which, I am sure, are uppermost in the minds of millions of people in our free countries. These are the questions: First, what are our prospects at this stage of the war as I view them? And, secondly, what is the sort of peace we are striving to reach as the result of this mortal struggle?

The views I shall express are my own personal views, based on my individual experience of war and peace. They must not be taken to have any official character.

First, then, as to our prospects.

The Germans have so far had an uninterrupted series of most spectacular successes. Poland, Norway, Holland and Belgium, and, finally, the most colossal of all—the most stunning of all—the sudden and unexpected collapse of France. Everywhere the Germans have won not only by superior numbers but also by superior equipment, technique and strategy. Everywhere their opponents were fore-stalled, outwitted and surprised and they appeared to have no chance.

These successes have created an air of invincibility which has been most effectively exploited by German propaganda. They say the war is already won and that only the final *coup de grâce* to

[1] 'Lord, all my desire is before Thee; and my groaning is not hid from thee.' *Psalms* xxxviii.9.

Britain is awaited. Many people who are either defeatist by temperament or who do not look below the surface of events have reluctantly come to accept the German view and look upon the war as already lost. They regard the chances of Britain in the light of what has happened to France and the other unfortunate countries I have mentioned.

It is just here, I think, that they make a profound mistake. The case of Britain is very different from that of the other countries referred to. I do not wish to minimize the danger of a German invasion of Britain, and I do not say a word in the least likely to tend to the relaxation of the preparations now being taken for the defence of Britain. But to the faint-hearted I wish to point out two considerations which should be carefully borne in mind in this connection.

In the first place, an army is not defeated by mopping up its minor outlying units separated from the main force. The capture of these minor units is a mere incident of no special importance to the main issue of battle; and if anyone regards these minor set-backs as pointing to the defeat of the main army he makes a mistake at variance with all military history. The overrunning of the small neutral countries I have mentioned is in the nature of such a minor military incident. Of course, the downfall of France is no minor incident; it is indeed one of the most serious catastrophes of modern times. But it may be fairly completely accounted for by the incredible mistakes of the French high command, the deep internal fissures of French politics and the hopeless weakness of its political leadership at the most critical moment. France was a divided, sick soul *before* the end came and her case deserves our deepest sympathy.

The British people on the contrary are today united as never before in their history, under a leadership of unrivalled brilliance and courage and the competence of their military command is not questioned among those who know. Here, then, is the crux of the war situation. Britain is and remains the inner core of the Allied cause—the main bastion of the Allied defence—the force with which the Germans have to deal before a real decision is reached. Until that force is disposed of it is futile to talk of defeat. There is no defeat until this main force is defeated—until a mortal blow has been struck at this heart of the Allied defence. The affairs of outposts do not affect this main battle-front. And the Germans have not won the war by any means until they have overcome the main Allied force, entrenched as it is in the island fortress of Britain. Nothing that has happened so far in the war justifies the inference that the fate of Britain will follow that of the other countries that have been overrun. The correct inference is just the opposite.

245

How different, indeed how unique the case of Britain is, is forcibly illustrated by the most astounding incident of the whole war. I refer to the escape of the British Expeditionary Force at Dunkirk. The significance of this most memorable event for the real inwardness of the war has not been sufficiently noted. Consider it for a moment. If ever a force was trapped and doomed it was the British Expeditionary Force at Dunkirk. The German government announced that it was trapped and their high command concentrated the bulk of their vast bombing air force in the effort to achieve this crowning victory. They realized that on the fate of the British Expeditionary Force might depend the fate of Britain itself. But the combined action of the royal navy and the royal air force succeeded in saving the entire British Expeditionary Force and the major part of the associated French army as well. If the German army and air force together could not succeed in a supreme effort in their attack at a single point like Dunkirk, how can they fairly hope to succeed in an attack on such a huge area as Britain where, moreover, every physical and moral factor would be vastly in favour of the defence? Sea power and air power combined are the real keys to the problem of Britain's defence and Dunkirk was a test case which showed how effective that defence is likely to be in the more favourable case of Britain itself.

No, the cause of the Allies is very far from being already lost and it will not be lost until Britain itself is taken. If Dunkirk has any message for us, it is the heartening one that Britain will prove an impregnable fortress against which Germany's might will be launched in vain. If that attack fails, Hitler is lost, and all Europe, aye, the whole world, is saved.

And if Hitler does not venture to attack Britain he is equally lost. For the same combination of sea power and air power which baulked him at Dunkirk and which would have saved Britain from invasion would then be turned in a victorious offensive against Hitler—an offensive which in the end would throttle and strangle and bring down in ruins his vast land empire in Europe. For in a war of endurance the time factor must prove fatal to Hitler's plans. Under an ever-tightening blockade his essential war supplies must rapidly dwindle until he can no longer hold down the vast populations whom he has overrun and oppressed and starved and sought to enslave.

This brings me to my second point—the kind of peace we envisage and hope to establish at the end of this titanic struggle. Our vision still is freedom, the liberation of Europe from the deadly Nazi thrall and its organization in a new creative freedom. Perhaps the position could best be indicated by contrasting it with the sort of world order which Hitler is aiming at and which he will probably yet proclaim in a great peace offensive.

Hitler is today in a very strong position. He is master of most of Europe and will probably succeed in putting the rest of it also in his power or in his pocket. It is the whole Continent, with Russia reduced to a subservient, acquiescent role. This Continent he will mould to his will. He will pose as the regenerator of the old Europe. The old effete European order, with its chequer-board of sovereign states, he will sweep away. A new United States of Europe will be erected on an elastic Nazi model. Being master of Europe, he can afford to restore the semblance of freedom to his victims and establish a system of so-called free states, which will, however, all be held together in the bonds of the Nazi order. Internal tariff walls and economic barriers will disappear and a large, closed, Continental market will be established, with Germany as its centre and regulator, on the economic lines which have already become manifest during the Nazi regime. It will be a new mechanized Europe, with some of the forms but none of the substance of freedom—a Europe in which the units will be held together by the central controls of the Nazi ideology and the Nazi economics, with the mailed fist in the background. Real freedom, personal or national, will have perished. The principles of freedom of speech, freedom of thought, freedom of religion and freedom of the press, which have been the guiding ideals of the West, will have been effectively suppressed. The name of a Monroe Doctrine for this Europe will be invoked, but it will be a mere mockery and travesty of that Monroe Doctrine of America which is the bulwark of free national self-development for a whole continent.

This in essence will be the Hitler plan. It will, no doubt, be dressed up in attractive forms and make its appeal to a certain order of minds everywhere. A tired, war-sick Europe, racked with suffering and appalled by the spectre of coming starvation, may even accept it as an escape from greater miseries. But it will be the negation of what the human spirit, the free human soul has stood for through the long ages and looked forward to as its inspiring ideal. The vision which has guided our long, slow advance will have perished in utter darkness and defeat.

As against this spectre of a Nazi-dominated Europe we oppose the vision of a truly free Europe. Freedom still remains our sovereign remedy for the ills from which human society is suffering We envisage a free Europe, free for the individual and for the nation, free in the sense of giving full scope for personal and national self-development and self-perfection, each according to his own individual lines. In

247

that fundamental sense we continue on the historic trail of human progress.

But we have also learned that discipline and organization must go hand in hand with freedom. The failure of the League of Nations was largely due to the absence of a central control which could harmonize the freedom of each with the proper functioning of the whole of human society. We therefore aim at a society of nations which will supply this defect and which will possess a central organization equipped with the necessary authority and powers to supervise the common concerns of mankind. Intercourse between the nations will be free, and commerce, economics and finance will be freed of all hampering restrictions and obstructions. As between man and man there shall be social justice; as between nation and nation there shall be the rule of law, the absence of force and violence, and the maintenance of peace. In such an international society there will be no place for self-appointed leaders and *führers*. He who will be master shall be servant.[1] Our aim and motto will be:

> A nation of free men and women:
> An international society of free nations.

This will be our reply to the challenge of the dictators. And we shall back up that reply with all the strength that God has given us.

509   From W. S. Churchill   Vol. 61, no. 93
Telegram

From: Winston Churchill

To: Smuts

Dated 22 July 1940

We are all deeply grateful for your splendid and inspiring broadcast.

510   To W. S. Churchill   Vol. 61, no. 93 A
Telegram

From: Smuts

To: Winston Churchill

Dated [23 July 1940]

Thank you. Anything I can do to support your magnificent leadership will always be gladly done.

---

[1] 'He that is a master must serve.' George Herbert, *Jacula Prudentum*.

511   To M. C. Gillett   **Vol. 63, no. 115**

Groote Schuur
[Cape Town]
8 September 1940

...We listened to the 6 p.m. Daventry report which is always attended to. It told of the last terrific air raid on the London docks, and the serious damage and loss of life there. We always rejoice to hear of the large numbers of airplanes brought down by the R.A.F. because that is the most significant fact from a military point of view. The damage to the civilian population is inevitable and will go on increasing until it assumes horrible dimensions. That will however not end the war or bring victory to the enemy. It is only the blows struck against his air and other military resources that will affect the issue. Our loss of twenty-two machines compares most favourably with theirs of eighty-two, and that is the really significant fact. I suppose in the end everything will be done to wipe out the cities indiscriminately and thus break the morale of the people. It will not succeed—did not even succeed in Spain, still less with a people like the English.

The New Testament speaks of the horror of destruction in the last days (more expressively rendered in Dutch as the *gruwel der verwoesting*), and we shall experience this form of warfare to the full before the final shot is fired in this war. Both the attack and the defence will be pressed to the physical limits with little respect for moral considerations. And so the war will become worse and worse, and we are up against the gravest dangers and most grievous losses. But in the end high spirit, moral qualities and that faith that a good cause inspires will surely see us through. So one hopes and prays.

Last week was a very heavy one for me. Daily occupied in the house and with all sorts of important issues. I had to speak at an important party function on Friday night. Our supporters had circulated a 'Peace Through Victory' petition in reply to the Nat women's petition to the house for an immediate separate peace. *They* secured 148,000 signatures of women, *we* 634,000 signatures of both sexes in less than three weeks. The function at the city hall was extremely well done and a brilliant affair, and I did my best— tired as I was—to trounce the enemy for his senseless and dangerous propaganda in the country and his dishonourable separate peace policy. Saturday I was all day in the house over war finance and war measures; and I was glad when Saturday evening came, even though we had to spend it at the Mount Nelson Hotel at a diplomats' dinner. What made things worse all last week was the most trying weather—most unseasonable and as cold as the coldest winter here.

This week will again be a most full and trying one, but it will break the back of our task, and the following week will see the end. I shall be happy to see the end of this bitter session. The Nats expect and, I fear, pray for an early German victory, not for love of the Germans, but in their hatred for me and lust for power. Since the fall of France they have been buoyed with the most extravagant hopes, but latterly the stubborn British air defence and the attitude of the United States have made them less sure. But even this seems only to embitter them the more. The spirit is very much like that of 1915 after we had finished the rebellion. One wonders when these wounds and divisions among our people will be healed. One can but practise patience and restraint, while resolutely pushing forward with the prosecution of the war. In great difficulties I like to act up to high standards, as trimming and expediency generally fail in a big crisis, such as the world is now passing through. How much more honourable and satisfactory is the course followed by Norway and Holland than that followed by Belgium and France, and what a fate these two latter countries have brought upon themselves by a lack of moral fibre and resolution. Great causes are apt to win of their own force if we only remain staunch and loyal to them. The gods are behind them, though divine power unbacked by human loyalty is often not adequate. I don't know whether these wide statements are quite sound, but that broadly is my feeling and conviction. I believe in the moral government of the world, but that is inseparable from *our* moral backing. The divine ideal must be incarnated in human effort and loyalty in order to be effective in this world of ours. The driving force is founded in Divine Grace, but human activity is a necessary condition for its realization. That is how Grace and Works conspire to achieve moral progress. Hitler is busy with the Devil's work, and however much he may achieve he cannot in the long run succeed if the democratic powers remain true to the light of their cause.

I have done practically no reading in the last couple of weeks. Too tired at night for bedside dipping into books, and as a rule I have no other time available for reading except when I go to bed. The books you send are read by the members of the family and are very welcome. I can only look forward to better days so far as I myself am concerned.

Later. 12 September... The battle for London is on, and we hang on to the Daventry radio to hear all that is going on. You can

imagine our feelings. We have no doubt of the issue. The ordeal is
terrible and it will grow worse, but the English champions will not
fail our cause. But the sufferings of those who do not know their
right hand from their left are simply terrible. I liked Churchill's
description of Hitler as a product of the wrongs and shames of the
past. That is exactly what he is—the offspring of our and his people's
sins. What a horrid monstrous brood!

Here we are hurrying to the closing stages of our session. The
principal War Measures Bill[1] passed its third reading last night and
now awaits the senate. The additional war vote will be finished this
week in the house. Some think we will finish on Saturday but it
looks more like Monday. In either case this is better than we have
reckoned for I thought we would go on till at least Wednesday
(18 September). My plans are however fixed, and even if parliament
is adjourned earlier I shall stay here and only leave on Wednesday
or Thursday next week for Pretoria. I shall be glad to have a couple
of days free after this strenuous short session—and perhaps there may
even be an opportunity to go up Table mountain. My health keeps
good, but a few days' break will make it even better. Isie also, as
head of Gifts and Comforts for the troops and in other numerous
activities, is kept going at full stretch all the time. I wonder how she
does it all, without showing signs of fatigue. . .

512   To P. Duncan   Vol. 63, no. 45

Personal   Groote Schuur
                                                    [Cape Town]
                                                    16 September 1940

My dear Duncan, Your remarks attached to your letter of 14 September[2] in reference to possible peace negotiations are very pertinent and
important. First, of course, there is the question whether we should
be prepared to make peace before a military decision—that is,
a negotiated peace. Such a peace, as you in effect point out, will
leave the continent of Europe under German economic control, and
that in the end also means political control. This also is the essence
of the German overture just made in Sweden. I do not think such
a peace should be faced by us, and the British government have
already declined it.[3] A Nazi-dominated Empire is a black prospect,

---

[1] Enacted as the War Measures (Amendment) Act, No. 32 of 1940.

[2] Smuts Collection, vol. 61, no. 136.

[3] In an address to the reichstag on 19 July Hitler made a peace overture to Great
Britain which was dismissed by the British foreign secretary in a broadcast. Following
German diplomatic steps the king of Sweden approached the British government on

and if we agreed to it, we would be accused of betraying Europe and indeed Western civilization itself.

Whether it is within our power to achieve a military victory time alone can show, but it is up to us to do all in our power to achieve it.

Even if we achieve such a victory, the making of peace will be a desperate affair. To all the inherent difficulties is now added the problem of France. I do not think the Germans will force peace terms on her at present; that peace may once more send France into war. The Germans can afford to wait, knowing that if they win they can do with France as they like. The reconstitution of France and the colonial empire appear to me to be necessary, even for the safety of the British Empire in future. But with her catastrophic collapse, will such a restoration ever be possible?

Then again, will disarmament be a wise policy? Was not our own self-disarmament after the last war the cause of our present plight and danger? A great power, especially one like Germany, can always secretly arm, as she did. We cannot, under our democratic conditions of publicity. And what about the danger of an armed Russia and Japan? Should disarmament not follow, instead of preceding, the re-establishment of normal and orderly conditions in the world? I was strongly for disarmament in 1919; I am seriously hesitating at present. There remains the central problem of a society of nations, held together in an association which will have authority to maintain peace and also to provide for peaceful necessary change. We failed to solve it in 1919. It *must* be solved next time.

And behind this problem lie others, which arise from the scientific, economic, psychological, and ethical conditions of the world situation today. What, for example, about propaganda, national and international; about nationalistic and fascistic education, which is today poisoning the young mind from the start; about tariffs which are a protection to young and undeveloped countries against the economic penetration of advanced countries? The spiritual human problems, back of the political and legal problems, were not solved by us in 1919, and today they are almost insoluble.

Of course the real solution is a spiritual one, which is called a change of heart. But that is a long-range solution, and today time is pressing—the human need is urgent, and we cannot adopt far-reaching solutions which will take a long time to mature. Even Christianity—with its spiritual message for the ills of the Roman times—contemplated an early coming of the Kingdom of Heaven.

In 1918 when I turned my attention to the problem of peace

the matter on 3 August. The British official reply stated that the war would go on until Hitlerism was finally broken.

organization the solution seemed to me, at least in principle, fairly simple, however difficult it might prove to make it work in practice. Today, after the failure of the League, and with the far more difficult situation likely to face us at the end of this war, I look into a glass darkly,[1] and I do so with the deepest doubts and hesitations.

Please give your mind to a problem which we shall have to solve or fail miserably in maintaining the spiritual heritage of the past. I am sure your training and experience can prove most helpful in dealing with this grave problem of the peace which will face us, rather sooner than later. Ever yours,

s. J. C. Smuts

513   To J. Martin   Vol. 63, no. 46

Pretoria
21 September 1940

My dear Martin, Many thanks for your note and for Wavell's *Allenby*,[2] which I am specially glad to have.

I wired Norman through Waterson in fairly strong terms, and trust you will now be left us—at any rate for some time to come. I understand the fomenters of strife had built great hopes on this strike, which fortunately seems to be still-born.[3] But knowing what forces of evil are on the move in this country, and remembering our past of industrial troubles, I am naturally most anxious to have and keep you here with me.

The session ended sadly for the opposition. They were so openly overdoing it, and we were so transparently reasonable and moderate that the man in the street saw through them. But there is a bitter spirit abroad with which we shall have to reckon.

Is London not grand? And the R.A.F. is doing what the fleet used to do in Britain's past. Hitler will not pass there. Will he then come to Africa? It looks like it. With kind regards to you and Nora, Ever yours,

s. J. C. Smuts

[1] *See supra*, p. 212.
[2] A. P. Wavell, *Allenby: A Study in Greatness* (1940).
[3] On 17 September there was a minor strike on the East Rand Proprietory Mines but it did not spread to other mines.

514   From L. S. Amery   Vol. 61, no. 18

[London]
2 October 1940

My dear Smuts, I enclose a copy of my last remarks on India[1] in case you might care to glance at them and see the general perspective of the Indian situation. Since then your old friend Gandhi's negotiations with the viceroy have broken down. Gandhi himself, I think, would have been content with some comparatively innocuous compromise, but he is above all things concerned to keep Congress together and there are too many elements in it spoiling for a fight with the authorities who would have flown off at a tangent if he had been prepared to accept the kind of freedom of speech in favour of non-co-operation which is enjoyed by conscientious objectors, etc., here. What he wanted instead was the kind of liberty that Malan and Co. have been exercising in South Africa without realizing the great difference in conditions or in the extent of mischief that Congress might create if it were allowed to indulge in a general campaign of propaganda against the war.

I am afraid it all means trouble. I expect it was bound to come in any case and I am at any rate glad to have anticipated it with a declaration of policy, both as to the present and the future, which should appeal, not only to moderate opinion in India, but also to opinion in America and elsewhere. It has at any rate fairly placed on Indian shoulders the responsibility of trying to find some adjustment between the claims of different elements. At present the position is that Congress won't take part in the expanded executive largely because we have ventured to say that the Moslems must have their voice in the settlement of the future constitution, while the Moslems refuse to join in unless they have as large a representation as all the Hindu elements together! I hope Linlithgow will be able to go on and form at any rate some expanded executive of men who are not afraid of responsibility and who are thinking of India first.

We lead a queer sort of life here in London retiring to our homes by dark and staying there quietly, and sleeping in the basement while the nightly hate rages from eight to five or six. Those who have no comfortable basements like ourselves have to spend the night in shelters, which is not so pleasant. However, the public are keeping wonderfully cheerful. Meanwhile the German preparations for invasion seem to be going on steadily, but the season is getting less and less favourable and I should not be surprised if Hitler gave it up

[1] This speech, entitled 'India and the War', was made to the Overseas League on 25 September. Omitted by the editor.

and concentrated everything now on Egypt. There, as I have always thought, is the danger point, and I only trust that the substantial forces which have been going round there latterly will give Wavell the necessary strength to keep his end up until further reinforcements arrive once we know that the invasion business is off. I think Wavell is a stout-hearted fellow and is not going to be frightened and will, if necessary, play a delaying game till he is stronger. Yours ever,

L. S. Amery

515   From L. S. Amery   Vol. 61, no. 19

Private and personal   India Office
                                                            Whitehall
                                                        16 October 1940

My dear Smuts, I can't tell you how heartily I agree with your telegram of October 12 about the Middle Eastern situation. I have no doubt that Germany is planning for the methodical swallowing first of Greece and Bulgaria, then of Turkey, even if the Turks resist, with a view to getting down to Iraq and Syria, and so with the help of the Italians finally pushing us out of the whole of the Middle East and northern and eastern Africa. The operation is not going to be an easy one or a speedy one, if only Greece and Turkey are prepared to fight for their freedom. That they would both do so I have no doubt if only we were in a position to promise them something more by way of reinforcements than naval help. But no one can understand better than you the dilemma with which we are faced here. We are doing wonderfully well with a much inferior air force against the continuing German attack. Our whole defensive arrangements have now reached a point at which the invasion of this country might seem a pretty desperate venture, though preparations for it are going on all the time. One might say that in those conditions we could afford to transfer some of the troops and air forces to the Middle East and that a comparatively small deduction of air forces from here would be a substantial addition at the other end. On the other hand, one cannot leave out of sight the fact that the whole future of the war depends on our being able to get the mastery of the air and that most of our aircraft production is in this island. Our aircraft factories have escaped very luckily so far, but you can understand Beaverbrook's desperate anxiety lest any weakening of our air force here should lead to the destruction of several vital factories.

Meanwhile, the importance of your point of view is being increasingly appreciated by Winston and the cabinet as a whole.[1] Such air force as we have in the Middle East is being modernized and expanded, and considerable reinforcements of ground troops are going out shortly. India is increasing her forces, but I am afraid that the actual results of the Delhi conference from the point of view of the equipment of troops can hardly show themselves till late next year. They may be of immense importance then, but the danger is that the enemy push will come very soon and reach its maximum by the spring.

All the same, there are a good many hopeful factors. The Italian forces east of Egypt and the Sudan are, after all, marooned from the point of view of supplies and ought to be getting to the end of their oil before long. Once we can inflict a defeat on them we ought to be able to begin raising the Abyssinians in their rear. Nor am I without hope that Wavell may be able to give the main Italian army a nasty knock in the Western Desert. Further, there is always the chance that we may catch the elusive Italian navy some day and inflict a really important defeat on it. Lastly, all the news that gets through does suggest that the Italians are desperately weary of the war already.

So much for Italy. The Germans are weary too, but that won't have practical results for a good while to come. Nor do I build too great hopes on Russia swinging our way sooner than see the Germans at the Dardanelles. It may well be that they have been squared by the hope of cheaper successes in Iran and Afghanistan. On the other hand, their problem, like Napoleon's, becomes inherently more difficult both technically by the absorption of troops and Gestapo, and psychologically, with every further advance. Only, unlike Napoleon, they are all the time vulnerable at the heart to the attack of our air force. Allowing every sort of discount, I do believe we have inflicted far greater damage upon their power of production than they have on ours. We have smashed a lot of their oil refineries; their railway transport seems to be badly hung up; the invasion itself must have been crippled a good deal by our continuous attacks on the ports.

Have you met [Lord] Cranborne? He is a charming fellow, and though he knows little yet of Dominion problems he is both intelligent and sympathetic.

I hope you are keeping fit. So much of the world's fate depends on you today. Yours ever,

L. S. Amery

---

[1] See Winston Churchill, The Second World War, vol. II (1949), p. 431.

516   To M. C. Gillett   Vol. 63, no. 123

Doornkloof
[Transvaal]
5 November 1940

Since last I wrote to you I have had three letters from you and two
from Arthur. That must be a record. I must be content to write one
in answer. That one will, however, tell of an adventure. As you will
have heard through the cables I spent last week in the far north to
visit my troops. I flew off on Saturday 26 October and returned on
Saturday 2 November, reaching as far as Khartoum and covering
little less than 8,000 miles in cross flights to the troops in addition
to the main flight and return—I mean 8,000 in all. I saw Eden in
Khartoum and Jannie [Smuts] on the border of Abyssinia. Jannie
was quite happy in one of the hottest, most forbidding parts of this
continent. He was only one of the thousands of 'happy warriors'
whom I visited. I need not go into details as I send by the same post
a press account and a broadcast by me on my return. What *will* however interest you is that I flew twice over the great craterland of east
Africa and looked down on all that collection of vast mountains and
extinct volcanoes. From south to north—first Hanang (14,000 feet)
and west of it the salt lake Eyassi; then the vast Oldeani, and next
Ngorongoro, with the small lake in the bottom of its vast area; then
several other high craters, and finally, and in some ways most
striking of all, the Mountain of God of the Massai (Oldenjo and
Engai) rising like a steep cone about 12,000 feet high, white bare
lava rock all the way—the lava still too fresh and undisintegrated to
allow of vegetable growth. Then followed the soda lakes, Natron
and Magadi, pink of all shades—the African counterpart of the
Asiatic city—the 'rose red city half as old as time'.[1] By Natron
another giant, Gelai; and two others by Magadi. And so on to
Nairobi. I also flew by the Kenya lakes, Naivasha Elmenteita and
Nakuru. At the last I flew over the huge crater of Menengai, with
dark, almost black, sinister cedar forests growing in the crater. The
Natives avoid it and nobody ever dares to venture into it—like the
woods of Westermain.[2] I suppose there are poisonous exhalations.
I saw Kenya mountain uncovered like some old hag's tooth, also
Kilimanjaro—cloudless, immense, brooding over the great Massai
plain, with the white cap on it like some old grannie of forgotten
time. I flew over the great desert stretching between Kenya and
Abyssinia in which Marsabit lies like paradise. Jannie had been
stationed there before he moved on to the Abyssinia–Somali border

---

[1] John William Burgon, *Petra*, l. 132.   [2] *See* vol. IV, p. 265, note 2.

where I found him. As I saw all that immense land with all its grandeur of scenery I wondered whether we would ever be lucky enough to visit it in the years after the war. Roads are good now and motoring is possible in all directions. Tell Hitler to wind up this sorry business of his and to give us the opportunity to enjoy this good earth of God. I could wander about in suitable company for months, collecting plants, taking ciné pictures and watching big game. And there are birds enough to satisfy Arthur [Gillett]. In addition to seeing the country and meeting my beloved South Africans I had many conferences and talks with soldiers over the coming campaign in the Middle East, north and east Africa. It was pleasant hearing all the inside news from Eden. On the whole my impression was favourable and I still remain the chastened optimist. The trip was refreshing to me, although it was most strenuous and left me little sleep all that week. A big change like that is always useful.

And now to come to the five letters. I am so glad that Arthur has gone down at least one floor at his club. Also that he can once more enjoy long walks. This is good news indeed to his old wayfaring companion. But it *was* bad news to hear that you are going to give up Crossways and live in that congested 102. Judging from your account of the number of evacuees and refugees it must be rapidly becoming a slum area. Is that a proper place for an ex-mayor of Oxford?[1] I fear you are sadly overdoing your hospitality and that both you and Arthur will break down under the human pressure of 102. Neither of you is really sociable enough to stand that strain. It would certainly kill me, morally if not physically. So do restrain your excessive hospitality and let 102 be more of a home to you.

I can imagine what the state of affairs in London must be, and the stolid if not angry endurance of its population is one of the bright lights of this dark time. It will be worse yet. People in time to come will speak with awe of the martyrdom of London. But it is standing in the breach for man, the rights of man, civilization. Very few soldiers are killed nowadays. The agony is concentrated on the civilian population, and this more than anything else will help to make war impossible in future...

I do not write of the war or of politics. What is the use? I hope Roosevelt has won in today's election in spite of Florence Lamont's impassioned plea for Willkie. The untried man with an untried team will take another couple of years to get into his job, and in the meantime what may happen in the world? There is a general feeling that Roosevelt will win, even if by a narrow majority, so I shall wait

[1] Arthur Gillett was never mayor. Smuts confused him with Dr H. T. Gillett who was mayor in 1938-9.

and see.[1] Tomorrow I fly to Barberton for an inspection of troops and at the end of this week I go to Potchefstroom for another inspection and for a political function. Time is very full and I sometimes feel as if I am doing more than my share of the job. But I cannot afford to spend all my time at the office table and must get about in order to help people along. 'Spend and be spent' is the order of the day, and like a soldier I must obey.

Good night now, dear children. I often think of you especially in these dark barbarous times. Lovingly,

Jan

517   To T. W. Lamont   **Vol. 63, no. 56**

Prime Minister's Office
Pretoria
8 November 1940

My dear Tom, Many thanks for your note of 11 September and for the kind help you have given Mr [G. H.] Swingler. Our American requirements are now being well attended to, and our air force is getting well armed and active against the Italians. I have just returned from a visit to Kenya and the Sudan and saw many of the great sights to which I had planned to take you and Florence, if my and your circumstances had permitted. But now we have the war, which may last a long time, and at the end of it we may no longer have any desire for the wild places.

Roosevelt has won as I have expected all along. From our (British) point of view it was the best ending to the contest. The problems already in hand can be dealt with without a break by the same people and not by a new team, beginning some time next year. And as time is most important in this war, a change, an interregnum, might have had very regrettable results.

The Axis is on the move all the time and we have to strain every nerve to keep abreast of their moves and manoeuvres. I trust nothing will come of these Pétain–Hitler negotiations,[2] and I know your government have done good service in keeping Vichy from giving way to very great pressure. The final result of it all is not known yet. Meanwhile Italy has moved into Greece, just as Germany has

---

[1] Roosevelt won a decisive victory over Willkie. The popular vote was, roughly, 27 million to 22 million and the electoral vote 449 to 82.

[2] On 24 October Hitler and Pétain met at Montaire. Pétain agreed that France would support the Axis powers in bringing about the defeat of Great Britain and Hitler agreed that the French colonial position would not be diminished.

moved into Rumania,[1] and both moves are evidently part of a plan which includes the Middle East and Egypt. Here again it is a question of time whether we can be ahead of the Axis. The war will next spring and summer have gone to the Middle East as one of its decisive theatres. Developments may also take place in the Far East which will require action on the part of the U.S.A. Everything is rapidly getting into the melting pot. We must do all we can to see that the brew is not against us. So much is at stake for the whole world and the future of our civilization. I do not mean capitalism or any other temporary form of our economy. I refer to the spiritual values which are the gains and goods of our western civilization. Freedom for the individual to hold up his head against the omnipotent state, the responsibility of the individual to his own conscience in all the deepest concerns of life and thought, self-government as we have evolved it in our Western democracy—all these are at stake. Seriously, the Nazi or Fascist system as it has been working these last years is the quintessence of evil—Gestapo, spying, oppression by the state, and the reduction of the human to the insect level. Some people say that these are but temporary phases and Nazism and Fascism will discard them. I don't know. I only know that these systems in their actual working have proved hostile to all our highest cultural and spiritual values and I will have nothing to do with them.

The problem that faces us in the West is how to make peace after this war and prevent other wars from breaking out in the following generation. I think we shall win the war all right. I fear about the peace to come. Perhaps there America could yet render her greatest service in the days to come.

After having written so far I received Florence's last letter which was, as usual, most interesting and most welcome. Both of you must have worked very hard in recent months and be worn out. But she writes with all her old vivacity and vividness, as if she is just back from a holiday. Our love to both of you and your dear ones. Here all well, one boy is at the very front in Kenya, the other is a mine manager and therefore in a key position here. The son-in-law, Andries Weyers, is also at the front. The adopted girl, Kathleen de Villiers, is a sergeant in our Women's Air [Corps] and also going to Kenya. Only the old crocks like me are left.

Good-bye and the best of luck. I hope you can read my scrawl. Ever yours,   J. C. Smuts

[1] In September General Antonescu set up a dictatorship in Rumania and asked for German troops to secure its defence against Russia. Considerable German forces moved in on 7 October. The Italian attack on Greece from Albania began on 28 October.

518   To M. C. Gillett   **Vol. 63, no. 128**

Doornkloof
[Transvaal]
8 December 1940

This is Sunday evening, and I write to you at the beginning of what promises to be a very busy week. The day has been occupied to the full—the morning with a three-and-a-quarter hours' walk in a hot sun which has made me look like the proverbial turkey cock, and the afternoon with visitors. Now in the cool of the evening, with a much longed for rain storm coming on, I shall give you my quiet hour, before I start reading official documents again...

I have sent a column of motorized troops through the Union, partly to show people what we have been doing in war production, partly to show the flag as they say—and let the disaffected see that they can have no chance in mechanical war, and that rebellion is out of the question. This Steel Commando as I have called it has gone right through the Union and will be back at Johannesburg Tuesday afternoon (day after tomorrow) after a march of 4,000 miles. They have had the most tumultuous reception ever given to a trek in South Africa, and even in small villages people have come up in their thousands to see the show. Even the centenary trek in 1938[1] did not create such a furore in the countryside. People were really deeply interested and amazed to see what a mechanized war unit of today is, and it has been an eye-opener to all. Everything made in our workshops except the parts of the aeroplanes. Well, I have to attend the end of the trek on Tuesday afternoon at Johannesburg when you will again have a great demonstration, and much of the day will be taken up. The following morning I fly to Winburg to speak and take part in our fight against Swart [C. R.] who is the Nat candidate *vice* Nico van der Merwe deceased. It will be a great fight, with the odds heavily against us, but that will not prevent us from doing our best. And I have to open the campaign with heavy attack which will set the keynote to the struggle. So another day will be gone. And so it goes on endlessly and remorselessly. And meanwhile the administration has to go on, the many war problems attended to, numerous wires from London answered, and cabinet here to prepare for the arduous coming session.

There is one comforting result for you from all this heavy preoccupation, and that is that there is no time to trouble you with my boring philosophical and religious reflections. For this relief much thanks[2]—you will no doubt say. I am afraid my letters to you and

---

[1] *See supra*, p. 149, note 2.   [2] Shakespeare, *Hamlet*, i.i.8.

Arthur often look as if they were notes for a dissertation of sorts instead of a chatty note as between dear friends. But even that you will bear from me. Now however there is happily no time for such diversions.

The war news is mixed but on the whole good. Italy seems to be going to pieces, and that is all to the good. Hitler is bad enough, but that bounder brigand in Rome whose whole policy has been based on deceit and treachery—in Abyssinia, in Albania,[1] in Greece and in his entry into this war at the moment when France was down and out[2]—and one feels comforted to see his bluff called, and by Greece of all people whom he has thoroughly despised. The Greeks are indeed doing very well, even allowing for much exaggeration in the reports, and one is thankful that here at last a real bit of luck has come our way. The resignations of Mussolini's high officers[3] one after the other are proof that this campaign was entirely his doing and that the responsibility is now rightly placed on his shoulders. They rumour that he has degenerated and is far from the brilliant improvisator which once he was. May he go to the father of all lies as soon and thoroughly as possible, and a great blow thus be given to the Axis for which he was largely responsible. I hope that 1941 will see Italy out of the war, and our efforts concentrated against the other member of the Axis. If France had not failed us and died at the core, so to say, the prospect of an early end would have been much brighter. But with us single-handed against the enormous German war machine it may prove a long road to victory. All accounts seem to agree that poor France was politically corrupt and rotten and that hers was a moral rather than a military collapse. How she is ever to rise again to great estate is a very difficult question to answer, and I shall not vex you with my reflections on that sad point. She has sinned greatly against the European order since 1920, but her punishment may involve a terrible burden on others besides herself.

Isie continues her amazing activities and figures more in the press than I myself. This is of course a source of pride to all of us, but does not prevent us from pulling her dear leg as much as possible. You know how she hates publicity and loves the work. And Gifts and Comforts in all their ramifications give her ample scope for her motherly soul on behalf of our soldiers and their dependants. I fear she is overdoing it and may break down from overwork. I sleep at

[1] In April 1939 Italy attacked Albania, drove out King Zog and annexed the country.

[2] Italy declared war on the Allies on 10 June 1940.

[3] Marshal Pietro Badoglio, chief of the general staff, and count Cesare de Vecchi, 'Governor of the Aegean'.

night—she seldom. Her sleep as you know is by day over her work, and is the sleep of exhaustion—which is very bad...

I am still reading Dickinson's *Faust and Goethe*. Poor Goethe seems to have got lost in a bog of classical mystery in the second part, and it is a weariness to try to discover his secret meaning through it all. But here and there one comes across pearls of poetry and wisdom. But the impression of a vast poetic failure remains as my final impression. I am very sorry to say this. There is so much in him and he is so great a European. Hitler and Goethe! Ever yours,

Jan

519   To L. S. Amery   Vol. 63, no. 66

Pretoria
9 December 1940

My dear Amery, This letter will bring you my best wishes for the New Year, best wishes not only for you and Mrs Amery personally, but also for your work and for our cause.

I have several letters from you to which answers have been delayed. If an answer does not come immediately to your correspondence you may be sure that the reason generally is that I am in agreement, as usual, with your views.

In your letter of 22 October, you approve the appointment of a high commissioner for India[1] and raise the point of a high commissioner to India. I do not think there is any urgency at present for such an appointment. Very few South Africans are to be found in India, and our business relations are not excessive. Naturally as these relations increase, as we hope they will, the question of reciprocating with the appointment of a high commissioner to India will come up for consideration. I have been repeatedly pressed by Japan to reciprocate with an appointment of a minister to that country. I have pleaded war-time preoccupations as an excuse for delay, and am glad I have done so. I fear Australia has made a blunder by the appointment of [Sir John] Latham to Tokio just at the time when Japan entered the Axis. Several South American states are also pressing for reciprocal appointment of ministers, but I have in all cases asked for delay because of the war.

Our Indian troubles are for the present easing off. The wide opportunity for war service in the north which I have given Indians

[1] The first agent-general for India in the Union of South Africa was S. Sastri, appointed in November 1927. In 1941 the then agent-general, Sir Rama Rau, became the first high commissioner.

have produced a good atmosphere. And other steps are also being taken to relieve avoidable tension—for instance, permission to India's commercial travellers to enter in limited numbers. The Japanese have similar privileges which Indians now also claim, with some justice.

But these are small matters compared with your gigantic Indian problem. I have wondered whether it is necessary for you to take such drastic steps to combat civil disobedience. After all the bulk of the Indian people join in the war effort, without much heed to the counter agitation. The imprisonment of leading Indians is liable to provoke an entirely exaggerated and distorted impression of such trouble as really exists. This is merely my personal impression, and no criticism of your policy. I have here a most virulent opposition to my war effort, but I do not take undue notice of it, for the simple reason that it does not seriously interfere with that effort. A blind eye is often a real political asset. India's troubles are now limited almost entirely to internal feuds and clashes, and it may be wise policy for the paramount power not to become too deeply involved, and so to deflect criticism to itself instead of to the warring factors and their relations. Masterly inactivity is also an active policy!

As regards the war I think we have turned a very bad corner. For Great Britain to have successfully survived the French collapse is indeed a great feat, and the wonderful defence of the air force and the indomitable spirit of the people have had a world-wide effect. The Germans will continue to batter at Britain, but they cannot now succeed beyond damage and destruction. And at that game the air force will soon do better than the *Luftwaffe*.

The tide of war is now flowing south-east as some of us have always expected. Here too we have had unexpected luck in the splendid defence of Greece in which our air force and the navy have had no mean share. What an intense pleasure it has been to see Mussolini's bluff called, and by Greece of all countries. The resignations of leading generals[1] are a symptom of a very rotten state of affairs. Mussolini personally will never survive these wounds. But no doubt Hitler will soon come to his aid. He cannot afford to let the Axis go to pieces like that. It may start a movement which he dreads, and these tyrants live in an atmosphere of dread, which they camouflage with immense bluff and bravado. German divisions will soon filter through farther, and next spring we may see the Middle East in flames.

I rejoice at the great effort the British cabinet is making to counter this coming move. Armageddon may again, as so often, lie in that

[1] *See supra*, p. 262, note 3.

Middle East. Wavell was in good spirit when I saw him at Khartoum. 1941 ought to see the end of Italy in Africa, except perhaps the extreme west. And if we can successfully withstand the German drive the beginning of the end may be in sight. May this be so.

But I have already written too long, and now conclude with best wishes and prayers for our cause in the difficult days ahead. Ever yours sincerely,

J. C. Smuts

520   To A. P. Wavell   Vol. 63, no. 68

Telegram

From: Smuts

To: Sir Archibald Wavell

Dated 12 December 1940

Hearty congratulations on your brilliant success in the Western Desert.[1] An acceptable Christmas-box and a fine augury for the future of the Middle East campaigns.

521   To J. B. M. Hertzog   Vol. 63, no. 70

Pretoria
13 December 1940

Waarde Hertzog, Dit is met gemengde gevoelens dat ek hedenoggend die brief van u en Havenga aan u kiesers in die pers gelees het. Oor die politieke aspekte van wat gebeur het wil ek hier niks sê nie. Maar daar is die menselike situasie, die tragedie wat inherent is in die jongste party gebeurtenisse, die persoonlike aspekte wat my diep tref. Wat met u gebeur het doen selfs u teenstanders pynlik aan—nie in die mins my wat vir so vele jare in dieselfde stryd voor en teen u gewikkel gewees is. In een opsig kan ek u beny—dat ten langer laas die strydtuig afgehaal en weggesit kan word. Wie weet wat die toekoms verberg!

Omstandighede het my tot hiertoe nie toegelaat om met u oor 'n seker saak te praat nie—die kwessie van 'n pensioen vir u. Die saak kon natuurlik nie aangeraak word solang u nog 'n hoofrol in die politieke stryd gespeel het. Maar as u nou die stryd verlaat, dink ek

---

[1] On 6 December the British forces began an offensive against the Italians in Libya. By 12 December they were in possession of the coastal region round Sidi Barrani and had taken a large number of prisoners.

dat dit alleen reg en billik is dat u na u lange publieke diens en die
hoë posisie wat u vir so lang beklee het op u ou dag 'n gepaste
pensioen van staatsweë sal kry. My kollegas deel my sienswyse en
meen met my dat die dankbare erkenning van die land u ten minste
langs hierdie weg sal toegebreng word.

Indien u geen beswaar hierteen het nie sal ek bly wees om die
nodige stappe te neem en die goedkeuring van die Parlement daarvoor te vra. Met beste wense, Steeds die uwe,

J. C. Smuts

TRANSLATION

Pretoria
13 December 1940

Dear Hertzog,

I read the letter from you and Havenga in the press this morning[1]
with mixed feelings. I do not wish to say anything here about the
political aspects of what has happened. But there is the human
situation, the tragedy inherent in the latest party developments, the
personal aspects, which affect me deeply. What has happened to you
is painful even to your opponents—not least to me who have for so
many years been involved in the same conflict, both with and against
you. In one respect I may envy you—that at long last your fighting
harness has been taken off and can be put away. Who knows what
the future hides?

Circumstances have until now not allowed me to discuss a certain
matter with you—the question of a pension for you. The matter
could, of course, not be raised as long as you still played a chief part
in the political conflict. But if you are now leaving that conflict,
I think that it is only right and fair that you, after your long public
service and the high position which you held for so long, should in
your old age receive a suitable pension from the state. My colleagues
share my view and agree with me that the gratitude of the country
should at least be shown to you in this way.

If you have no objection to this, I shall be glad to take the
necessary steps and to ask parliament for its approval. With best
wishes, Yours ever,

J. C. Smuts

[1] Following differences in the Herenigde Nasionale party on the republican issue
and on equality of rights as between Afrikanders and English-speaking South Africans,
and a growing opposition to Hertzog's leadership, Hertzog resigned his membership
of the party on 6 November 1940 and resigned his seat in parliament on 12 December.
N. C. Havenga did the same. *See* M. Roberts and A. E. G. Trollip, *The South African
Opposition 1939–1945*, pp. 37–61.

522   To M. C. Gillett   Vol. 63, no. 133

Doornkloof
[Transvaal]
30 December 1940

My last letter, about the flight to South West Africa, must have
missed the mail as it was written on Christmas day and that and the
following day were both closed against posting. But if you do not
receive letters regularly console yourself with the thought that I have
the same disappointment! Ships do not go regularly, and there are
no set post days. My last week-end was spent in putting together
two broadcasts—one for the English world[1] and the other for South
Africa. These broadcasts are a great trouble to me, and I have never
been able to know just what to say and how to say it. They are
finished now, and one has gone to England while the other will be
broadcast from Doornkloof at 11.45 tomorrow night. I have now
done this last year, and I suppose once a move like this is made it
becomes a precedent for the future. And this is a sort of frill added
to a programme of official work which I find it impossible to get
through. Papers pile up and special correspondence is set aside for
answer in the future—and perhaps that future never comes. I have
letters from several of your cabinet ministers to answer and can find
no time. And so on *ad infinitum*. I suppose in Heaven they write no
letters; what a glorious place!

One of the ladies in my constituency is raising funds for a Spitfire
and has asked me to send an autographed book of mine to auction
for the purpose. I was looking at my St Andrews address[2] last night
to see whether it would do. I was really much interested to see what
a prophetic document it was, and although I did not then expect
a war in the near future the entire address might have been delivered
during the *last* few months. I generally never look at my old stuff
and was therefore specially interested in this reminiscence of happier
days. I told you that a fortnight ago Isie and I attended a Spitfire
function at Settlers[3] (Springbok Flats) where a cheque for more than
£3,600 was given me—and that by a poor community. The Natives
made their contribution—most welcome of all.

In many ways it is a quiet time here now and most of my colleagues are away on short holiday. Not so I. The minister of defence
has no respite and I shall continue at the job until I go to the purga-

---

[1] **523.**
[2] Delivered on 17 October 1934 when Smuts was installed as rector of St Andrew's
University and entitled 'The Challenge to Freedom'. See *Greater South Africa, the
Speeches of General J. C. Smuts* (1940), pp. 57–68.
[3] A small farming centre about seventy miles north of Pretoria.

tory of parliament. Sometimes I feel tired enough to know how it must feel to drop dead from fatigue. But after a good night's rest I rise fresh and fit for another bout. New Year this time will be spent quietly at home, but I hope to get off for a day or perhaps two at the week-end if it is not too wet to go so far as Rooikop. It is raining a lot here nowadays. We have had a week of almost continuous rain, and the river below the house is running in flood as in olden times. I have not been able to get any walks in all this wet, and *long* for some exercise. I suppose too much rain will be followed soon by too much dry in this land of extremes.

The war news continues good—all except the alarming tale of our U-boat losses at sea. It sometimes sounds like the bad months in the summer of 1917. The convoy system does not seem to have the same success now as before. New methods and devices are called for. Roosevelt's broadcast last night was very strong and good stuff. I expect he will now come out more fearlessly, as he is now firmly in the saddle for another term. His whole action is of course unneutral—if there still is such a thing as neutrality—and the U.S.A. is being used as a great base of supply for Britain, and the government of the country openly takes the lead in this business. In former times this was looked upon as an act of war, and one of these days Germany will go mad with rage and America will be really in the war. I think it will be a good thing. Not that America will be able to do much more than she is doing at present, but the moral effect of becoming an Ally would be enormous and put heart into all the forces on our side. Everybody will then know and feel confident that we *cannot* lose the war. That in itself would be a tremendous moral reinforcement for us. I should like to see the long faces of the Nats here the moment America comes in, and their bubble of a Nazi victory is finally pricked.

You know that Hertzog and Havenga have resigned their seats in protest at the scurvy treatment meted out to Hertzog by the reunited Nat party.[1] They are the limit in baseness and ingratitude. But Hertzog's going is a major event in our politics. He has been the troubler of Israel[2] for more than a generation, and at last he is booted out by his own party who think he does not go far enough! I suppose the young men are getting sick of the old men hanging on and barring their way to advancement. I shouldn't mind myself if I had to go, but I should like to choose the time and manner of my going, and not be booted out as Hertzog has been. I found him most

[1] See *supra*, p. 266, note 1.
[2] 'Achar, the troubler of Israel, who transgressed in the thing accursed.' 1 *Chronicles* ii.7.

difficult the six years I worked with him, and I am a patient man, with no ambition for place or office. These young Turks found the position under his endless leadership intolerable. But they did behave disgracefully over it. I am going to propose a good pension for him, as I know he is a poor man.[1] To the honour of South Africa her political leaders generally retire poor men. And that in a land where there is endless opportunity for graft. I wish this honourable tradition could be maintained for ever. We may be wrong headed but we are not thieves.

Pole-Evans's films of the Kalahari, the Okavango swamps, the Ovambo country, and the Kaokoveld have come out exceptionally well. Japie's [Smuts] are fairly good. Mine have not yet returned from the Kodak office, but I fear that in comparison they will be much inferior. I am far less expert than these two old hands, and really I was so interested in watching the landscape all the time that I mostly forgot to snap the good things which the connoisseur does not miss. Thus I even forgot to film the Ruakana falls on the Kunene, which are in many ways second only to the Victoria falls. I shall, however, soon know how far I have succeeded.

I sit and write to an accompaniment of a great noise from the river coming down in flood. Yesterday morning we motored up to the Rietvlei dam where an immense flood was pouring over the spillway. These noises of water are pleasant to the ear of Africa. One always feels the better for them. It is difficult to motor about the farm in this wet as even the roads are sodden; but I went up by the hard road via the station. And now I end. I wish you all a very happy New Year, at least a happier one than last year, which was one of the blackest in history. I feel you will beat back the Nazi invasion, and thereafter Germany will break. The sooner the better. Ever lovingly,

Jan

523   Speech (1940)   Box J, no. 129

This speech was broadcast to Great Britain on 31 December 1940.

In a short while the old year will have passed. Surely it has established a record, an unenviable record, in history. A great historian has said that on those whom the gods love they lavish infinite joys and infinite sorrows.[2] Such truly has been our lot in this eventful year. It has been a tale of disasters and sufferings immeasurable. But

[1] See 521.
[2] See Theodor Mommsen, The History of Rome, translated by W. P. Dickson (1901), vol. II, p. 379. The reference is to Hannibal.

through all there have been flashes of hope, and in the latter part of the year these flashes have broadened into a continuous light. Let me rapidly run through this record.

We began the year with the Maginot line and its fancied security. Then suddenly, unexpectedly, followed the lightning break-out of Hitler in the West. In a couple of months the small states of Europe in the West—all of them among the highest types of our civilization —were submerged in the Nazi flood. Denmark and Norway succumbed to treachery.[1] In spite of the most solemn assurances Holland and Belgium were unexpectedly attacked. Belgium had a repetition of many of her worst sufferings in the last war. Rotterdam suffered a fate worse than that of any city in the barbarities of the Eighty Years War.[2] France, the torch-bearer of the European advance, fell and her fall seemed to herald the doom of the West. The British Expeditionary Force had to flee from the Continent. From the North Cape to the Pyrenees Hitler dominated Europe. Then at this darkest hour Mussolini struck at prostrate France in the hope of sharing in the immense loot in prospect. All seemed lost. So many people thought or feared. The dictators seemed on top of the world. Then the gods laughed—the tide began to turn.

Britain, standing practically alone in her island home, faced the great onslaught of Hitler which was to end the war. In vain the mighty German air force continued the attack for months.[3] In vain the German army of invasion waited on the beaches and in their barges. The royal air force, the royal navy, the half-armed island forces, the men and women proudly enduring havoc and slaughter in their homes, proved too much for the vast, soulless German war-machine. The tide *had* turned.

Baffled in his main war effort Hitler once more resorted to the diplomatic weapon which he had used to such effect on previous occasions. The comings and goings between the chancellories became a veritable general post. Hitler visited Franco and Pétain, and was visited by Molotov, Mussolini, and many of the smaller fry from the Balkans. The threats and promises, the bullyings and cajolings at these conferences can be imagined. All in vain. Rumania alone fell in this diplomatic war, and her fall, accompanied as it was by large-scale massacres, general chaos, and large loss of territory, has been an added warning to the rest to keep away from the Pied Piper

---

[1] Vidkun Quisling, leader of the Norwegian Nazi party, was to carry out a *coup d'état* with German support but, in fact, his role in the German occupation of Norway was a minor one.

[2] The war between the Northern Netherlands and Spain by which the Netherlands gained independence—1572–1648.

[3] The Battle of Britain lasted from 10 July to the end of October 1940.

of Munich. The diplomatic defeat of Hitler in this vast diplomatic campaign has been second in importance only to the failure of his attack on Britain.

And so the turn of the other star in the Axis had now come. Mussolini singled out Greece for the attack, which was once more made in violation of recent assurances to the contrary. But she was weak and an attack on her promised large strategic results. The gods of ancient Greece, who had watched over Thermopylae, Marathon and Salamis,[1] laughed once more. Even weak forces fighting for home and country can prove more than a match for the proud armies of men who have no heart in their cause. And so the Greeks have once again made their signal contribution to the cause of freedom—'the glory that is Greece'.[2]

The time had now come for Britain to take the offensive. And how she has struck in north Africa! Wavell's victory has been devastating. Mussolini's bluff has been effectively called, just as the vain boasting of another tyrant predecessor of his was answered by the desert sands of Libya:

> I am Ozymandias, king of kings,
> Look at my works, ye Mighty, and despair![3]

And so for us the year, in spite of its black beginning, ends on a cheerful note, and so far as Mussolini is concerned, even on a comic note. One of the two partners in the Axis is a very sick man,[4] and the Axis is in a bad way. Britain, with her own gathering strength, and that of the Empire and Commonwealth behind her, is much stronger than she was at the beginning of the year. Hitler's position has definitely deteriorated. He is rapidly exhausting his own resources and those of the countries he has overrun, and the final upshot of his victories earlier in the year will simply be to surround Germany with a wall of implacable hate from all the neighbouring countries which before had been good and friendly neighbours to her—a blockade of hate established by herself, far worse than the blockade by the British fleet. The final harvest which she will reap from her criminal victories over innocent neighbours may, and

---

[1] Battles in which the ancient Greeks defeated the Persian invaders in 490 and 480 B.C.

[2]   The glory that was Greece
            And the grandeur that was Rome.
                              Edgar Allen Poe, *To Helen.*

[3]   My name is Ozymandias, king of kings,
            Look on my works, ye Mighty, and despair!
                              Percy Bysshe Shelley, *Ozymandias.*

[4] 'We have on our hands a sick man—a very sick man.' Nicholas I of Russia's description of Turkey quoted in a letter from Sir G. H. Seymour to Lord John Russell, 11 January 1853. Hence the phrase 'the sick man of Europe, the Turk'.

probably will, be a deep fear and fierce hatred of her, which may make the conclusion of a real peace in Europe almost impossible.

So much for the interim balance-sheet of the war so far as 1940 is concerned. What about 1941?

I am no prophet nor am I going to don the prophet's garb and pretend to forecast the future. But some things are certainties and others are highly probable, and it may serve a useful purpose briefly to put these things in their proper connection and perspective, as I see them.

Among the certainties I reckon the fact that the Allied victories and the enemy set-backs during the second half of 1940 will continue to have a profound effect in 1941. World opinion no longer regards a German victory as certain or even probable. The attitude of neutrals will become stiffer. The glamour of a German connection has disappeared. The possible alternatives before Hitler have thus become definitely more limited. If, for instance, he tries his fortunes in the Balkans and Middle East he will be up against serious difficulties in the Balkans and in the end will have to face in the Middle East a far more formidable force than the defunct army of the West of Weygand.[1] The defeat of Italy has greatly contributed to that situation, and Italy's fate will dog the footsteps of Hitler also. He will have to attack a formidable force in a very distant theatre, at the end of long lines of communication through hostile or inhospitable lands, while his opponent will have the advantage of rapid and safe sea communications. There will also be the Turkish army to consider. Nor can Russia be ignored—that enigma looking ardently to the exhaustion of both combatants, but no less ardently dreading a German victory. With such considerations before him Hitler will surely hesitate before he embarks on a Balkan and Middle East campaign.

There remains Spain as a possibility, but its occupation will be at least an unprofitable business, with twenty million more mouths to feed from the depleted larder. And its use as a base for an attack on north Africa might rouse the sleeping spirit of France and lead to dangerous repercussions both in France and in French north Africa. Gibraltar in any case will prove another Verdun.

From whatever way we look at it Hitler's initial failure against Britain and Italy's disaster in north Africa have seriously changed the situation and have narrowed the choices before Hitler. This fact and his own pride and instinct will in all probability lead him to adhere to his original desperate plan of winning the war in Britain

[1] General Maxime Weygand had been the supreme commander of the Allied forces that were defeated in May–June 1940.

itself. While other moves will have to be carefully prepared against, the defeat of Hitler in an invasion of Britain must therefore be and remain the pivot of British war policy. The probabilities all point that way.

If that is so, another point emerges. Hitler will probably seek a decision in 1941. If he is going to stake his fortune on a successful invasion of Britain, there would be no object in delaying the attempt. I presume that Hitler is fully prepared. The British war effort is growing rapidly; and behind that expansion is the immense effort of the United States of America to provide Britain with war supplies. The longer the invasion is delayed the stronger relatively the defence will become. A decision to be favourable for Hitler must therefore be sought as soon as possible. It may come very soon in the New Year, and in any case is not likely to be delayed beyond 1941. While Britain does well in envisaging the possible continuance of the war till 1942 to secure final victory, it would be wise to be as fully prepared next year as is humanly possible. The speeding up of war supplies for 1941 is thus a matter of cardinal importance.

Of course Hitler may have his special reasons for delaying the invasion. He may wish to continue the present air attacks on an intensified scale in order to destroy British industrial and transport resources and to sap the people's morale. Or he may plan to intensify his campaign against British shipping with more U-boats. Or he may intend to give time to his third Axis partner to develop her aggressive policies in the Far East and so deflect American attention and resources in that direction. I doubt whether he will succeed in any of these objects, but they may at least cause him to postpone his moment of striking. However, with Italy in mortal difficulties and the internal situation in Germany and her occupied territories deteriorating all the time, it is questionable whether he can afford to wait beyond 1941.

When the attack *does* come off Hitler will put all the vast strength of his incomparable war machine into it. For him and his Nazi order it will be a mortal issue, a question of life and death. But so it will also be for Britain, her Empire, and the whole British Commonwealth group. And so it will be for the cause of freedom throughout the world. It will be Armageddon, from which will issue either a new birth of human liberation, or an eclipse of the human spirit and a fall back to another dark age. Next year may therefore be the most fateful year in modern history—for the New World as much as for the Old.

The consciousness of the immensity of the issues at stake and their world-wide reach has been rapidly growing in America. The recent elections have proved that. The Nazi menace is felt to be world-wide. So much is this the case that I feel convinced that in the last resort America will not, as indeed she cannot afford to, stand out. Under the great and inspiring leadership of President Roosevelt she will once more, freely and of her own choice, dedicate herself to the greatest of human causes. In the spirit of Abraham Lincoln she will take her rightful place among the champions of a free world as against a slave world. Deeply as Americans desire to keep out of the war they will find necessity laid on them,[1] and in the last resort they will *not* let freedom perish from the face of the earth.[2] Their stake in this grave issue transcends all other political or national considerations. Their way of life is menaced as truly as ours. None of the forces of democracy can be spared if a final and lasting victory has to be won. Of that victory I feel assured, but American intervention is necessary for the victory and the peace which has to be shaped thereafter. The old order is passing away. The general plan for the world community of the future will have to be laid down in the new peace. Together that new peace has to be won and planned. Together we must pass through the night in order *together* to salute the new day for mankind. Let us all cheerfully and resolutely face our duty. And let us welcome the New Year, the year of destiny, with a cheer.

524   To Lord Cranborne   Vol. 66, no. 87

Pretoria
2 January 1941

My dear Cranborne, Your letter of 2 November has had to wait too long for an answer. But it only reached me a couple of weeks ago, owing no doubt to the perils of the Atlantic, and since then the scene has changed so continually that an answer had necessarily to be delayed. All you say has been most interesting and cheering to me, especially the extent to which our views coincide. Previous to my meeting with Eden I had feared that my views might be singular and that I might be a voice crying in the wilderness. But his conversations and now your letter have dispelled that impression. Whenever I have urged definite points of view the intention has always simply been to be helpful and not critical. We are moving in such a tangled world that one always feels the other man may be right.

My broadcast on Old Year's day you have probably seen and it

---

[1] *See* vol. v, p. 50, note 2.
[2] Abraham Lincoln at the Gettysburg National Cemetery, 19 November 1863.

succinctly put the view of the war to which I am leaning at present. Italy's double defeat in Greece[1] and Libya has vitally affected the situation confronting Hitler also. The position in and across the Mediterranean has materially worsened for him too, and he is now probably once more thrown back on his original plan of staking it all on a British invasion. I now view this possibility much more seriously than I did some months ago, but the change of view is due to the change that has come about the Mediterranean scene. If now we could by next spring clear up the situation in Abyssinia, we could release larger forces for any future developments in other parts of the Middle East, and perhaps knock Italy out of the war.

I agree with you that the fall of France must have come as a great blow to Russia, who knows what awaits her at the hands of a victorious Germany. It is possible that Russia may now at heart become more favourable to us, and certain indications both at Sofia and Ankara support that view.

Roosevelt's Old Year broadcast was very good, especially his stiff warning to Japan, and he will no doubt follow up his speeches with appropriate action. I have, however, cautiously gone the whole hog and advised intervention as the right course even in American interest. To me it is clear that our propaganda in America should become more daring, and Americans should be habituated to the outlook of intervention. The moral effect of intervention on world opinion would be enormous, as the doubters will at last become convinced that Germany cannot win against a British–American combination. Public opinion in the world and in the occupied countries and in Germany itself is one of our most potent weapons. It was not so much the German army that broke in 1918 as the home front; and unsettled and disturbed conditions in the occupied countries would not only necessitate large forces of occupation, but also start a rot that will spread far into Germany itself.

We feel very proud of Britain these days, with a pride which is itself a strong reinforcement in war. With the ruthless German bully on the one side, and a Britain rising to the loftiest heights of heroic defence on the other, sympathy becomes overpowering and overflows into strong action. Churchill has been very good. It is not only the Fascists and Nazis who can produce leaders. And our leader has the immense background of the liberal European outlook which the Nazi upstarts entirely lack. It is the great imponderable in our cause.

Halifax will do very well at Washington, and I am glad to think of Eden once more at the foreign office—if only because of the transports of rage which it must cause in Hitler and Mussolini! After

---

[1] In December the Italian forces in Albania were in retreat.

your sacrifice in the appeasement days[1] you have also come proudly into your own, and will, I am sure, be a great source of strength to Eden and the government.

On the whole the recovery in our prospects since the black June days of last year is almost unbelievable, and I look forward with hope towards the future. This year may now see the end—at least I pray it may.

With kind regards and remembrances to Lady Cranborne, Ever yours sincerely,

s. J. C. Smuts

525 To R. G. Menzies

Vol. 66, no. 89

Telegram

To: Prime Minister, Canberra, Australia
From: Smuts
Dated 6 January 1941

Heartiest congratulations on magnificent Australian share in Bardia victory.[2] Aussies have once more justified highest expectations. All good wishes for continued further success up to final victory.

526 To M. C. Gillett

Vol. 66, no. 206

Irene
[Transvaal]
6 January 1941

I had a very amusing letter today from Arthur (none from you) and I was just sitting down to reply, when I remembered that in your last letter you hinted that you had first to decypher my letters by yourself and only thereafter could read them to the rest of the family. I therefore write to you to save Arthur the trouble of decypherment. I do not know why my writing should become so bad, for my hand is not at all shaky yet, and I don't write too fast. It must be the paper, or the ink, or the pen!...

Jannie [Smuts] has been in his first fight, when a South African unit in Kenya attacked and captured an Italian force at El Wak on

[1] When Eden resigned as secretary for foreign affairs in 1938 (*see supra*, p. 114, note 1) Cranborne, then the under-secretary, also resigned.

[2] Continuing their advance along the coast of Libya British forces, including the Sixth Australian Division, captured Bardia on 3–4 January, taking 45,000 prisoners and 462 guns.

the border of Somaliland. He makes a joke of the whole business but evidently some others were more deeply impressed. He has written amusing accounts of these wild doings and described how the Italians simply ran at the end, leaving much booty behind—including 'their black concubines'! I trust this particular item of loot was not appropriated by the South Africans. Daphne [Smuts] reads these titbits with great relish. Isie has asked her to type out proper and appropriate passages from Jannie's letters for your information. I trust she will do so for he is a very capable letter-writer. You will be interested to hear that in that waterless desert, where now people are entirely dependent on deep wells for water, Jannie has found many Fauresmith implements, thus showing that in the long ago there must have been a climate of normal or heavy rainfall. Jannie is now returning to Kenya—whether for a short leave or a transfer to another area I don't know...

Well, history has been made these last couple of weeks—if by history is meant events that matter. Greece and Wavell between them have pricked the bubble of Mussolini. You refer to our war aims. Well, here is a war aim being achieved. For remember that the defeat of evil is just as essential as the envisagement of the good. I look upon Sidi Barani and Bardia, on Koritza and Santi Quaranta as essential war aims.[1] And I hope more, much more of the same sort is coming. I love these war aims. The defeat of the devil is almost as much as the triumph of the Lord—though not quite the same. I wish that Hitler could also be thus unmasked. But he is a tougher devil, and is determined not only to reduce Arthur to a windowless club but our whole civilization to a hideous darkness. To beat Hitler much more effort and force will be necessary. Hence my delight to see brother Yankee at last beginning to sit up and take note. I have felt, and now more than ever, that Roosevelt's victory was essential to the triumph of our cause. Our dear Lamonts who pinned their faith on Willkie were sadly mistaken. Roosevelt's heart is in this business, and he will carry America as far into the war as is humanly possible. I *do* want America to come in. All the forces of democracy will have to be mobilized for this Armageddon. Munitions and aeroplanes are not enough. People must back this cause with their lives and their all. And you can imagine what the moral effect will be on the world if America ranges herself unreservedly and wholly behind our cause. All the defeatism will go, and a new

[1] Between 9 December 1940 and 5 January 1941 Allied forces under General Wavell advanced into Cyrenaica, captured Sidi Barrani and Bardia and took large numbers of prisoners and guns. The Italian invasion of Greece from Albania was repulsed and advancing Greek forces took Koritza and Santi Quaranta by the end of November 1940.

inspiration will be infused into all of us. Let America come in. That should be our propaganda over there. I do not think we shall win without her. We could prevent Hitler winning. But that is not enough. A stalemate would be a disaster. A stalemate might mean Germany winning within a generation, and imprisoning the human spirit in a blackout of barbarism. The resurgence of Germany in one generation since 1918 has taught me a lesson.

There is something barbaric in her, and this accounts for such awful abortions as Nazism and Hitler. The German people contain large numbers of good people, but there is too much of the devil in the nation as a whole. I know Arthur will like this language although you won't. But we must save the world from another such ordeal in another generation. They are not civilized in spirit. They are barbarians of the spirit, and must become tamed and moralized before leadership can be entrusted to them. Having said this I now feel easier.

You will be surprised to hear that in odd moments I have been reading the life of Edgar Wallace of all men. He was a hopeless fellow, untrustworthy, selfish, unscrupulous, faithless even to his nearest and dearest. But he had an elemental power which showed itself not only in his journalism and short stories, but in many other ways. Power devoid of morality is a dreadful evil, and he was a type of that sort of thing. It is the Greek ὕβρις,[1] which the Greek genius showed up as the challenge to the Gods which they always punished most severely. Power must be restrained, moderated, moralized to be tolerable in this world. That is why science—that greatest of powers—can be so destructive if it is not allied to great social ends. Although I can't stand this fellow I have read his *Life* (by Margaret Lane) with much interest and benefit. In the end not power but spirit, soul, is everything.

For the rest my story for this week is very simple. A hard slogging week, followed by a short week-end at Rooikop, where I picked up many ticks and a severe tummy complaint due to eating watermelon! I should have remembered and known better. Since I was there last a month ago eight-and-a-half inches of rain had fallen and the scene had been transformed as if by magic. I have never seen Rooikop in greater glory. And the air was cool after much rain. This will be my last visit there till next June. In a fortnight I shall be gone to my purgatory at Cape Town, or rather to my amphitheatre where I shall be fighting with the wild beasts.[2] But the memory of this day at Rooikop will remain a pleasant savour in all that bitterness.

[1] *hubris.*   [2] *See supra*, p. 215, note 2.

Forgive this long ramble over nothing. But I suppose letter writing means meandering through pleasant nothings. Ever yours,

Jan

527   To C. van Riet Lowe   Vol. 66, no. 97

Telegram

To: Prof. van Riet Lowe, Witwatersrand University

From: Smuts

Dated 22 January 1941

Your letter. I have wired Abbé Breuil through minister offering him employment at £50 (pounds) a month under you.[1] University can arrange suitable appointment.

528   To L. S. Amery   Vol. 66, no. 104

Prime Minister's Office
Cape Town
18 February 1941

My dear Amery, Many thanks for your last two interesting and welcome letters, one about Indian policy, and the last one of New Year greetings and reflections on the war and other matters. In return I can but wish you and us all the greatest possible measure of success in the most threatening situation that has faced us since the days when the Muslim forces menaced the very heart of Europe.[2] Grey spoke at the outbreak of the last war of the lights going out over Europe,[3] but if Hitler wins the light will go out over our civilization as it has been moulded by two thousand years of human effort.

I believe a very heavy ordeal awaits us. The great battle front will be ablaze from the British Isles to western Asia. Japan may even extend it to eastern Asia, but then we hope to see America at last in the line of battle. At present the French and Italian failures cancel each other out and the two principal antagonists face each other grimly for the final round. Hitler is trying to bring the French fleet and ports into the picture, and Mussolini is being used to secure Franco's acquiescence in an attack on Gibraltar. Hitler means to

---

[1] The Abbé Breuil was at this time a refugee in Lisbon.

[2] By A.D. 732 the Muslim world extended from the valley of the Indus river over the whole Mediterranean region to southern France.

[3] *See supra*, p. 243, note 2.

attack the western Mediterranean if he can pull in Franco and Pétain or Pétain's successor. And in the Balkans there are all the preparations for a vast drive south-east. We shall be tested indeed. Luckily Wavell's army has had a brilliant preliminary canter over the ground,[1] and will give a great account of itself. I should like to see Abyssinia wound up and finished as soon as possible in order that some four or five divisions may go north to reinforce the army of the Middle East.[2] They will be needed. Anyhow this year will be the year of Armageddon, as never before in history.

In South Africa the retirement of Hertzog has brought a good deal of confusion in the Nationalist ranks, and a minor split in that camp has occurred.[3] In that way my party has been somewhat benefited. The Hertzog or Afrikaner party (as they call themselves) continues to condemn my war policy, but in other respects will probably prove, or be forced to prove, more favourable to me. The situation is intriguing and I await developments with equanimity. The Nationalists are in a bad way as a party, but a semi-military organization, the *Ossewa-Brandwag*, formed on somewhat Hitler lines, is pushing ahead in their ranks, and may finally take their place as a sort of militant political party. I am watching the position carefully, and for the present consider it no real danger, though our security regulations have been tightened up.

Philip Kerr's death is a grievous loss, but the right thing has been done in sending Halifax to Washington, and restoring Eden to his old post.

You know the Bible line 'in quietness and confidence shall be thy strength'.[4] I am reminded of this great line by the present quiet firmness of Britain. It is truly a magnificent spectacle, and an inspiration to all the forces of good in this troubled world.

Good luck to her and to all of us. Ever yours,

s. J. C. Smuts

[1] The capture of Benghazi on 6–7 February completed the conquest of Cyrenaica by the British forces.

[2] British and South African forces were at this time engaged in attacking Italian Somaliland where Kismayu had been taken on 14 February.

[3] On 30 January 1941 ten members of parliament who adhered to Hertzog's policies formed the Afrikaner party. Of these, two later joined the United party. Twenty-seven members, formerly followers of Hertzog, remained in the Herenigde Nasionale party which reverted to its earlier name—the National party.

[4] *Isaiah* xxx.15.

529   To M. C. Gillett   Vol. 66, no. 215

Government House
Nairobi
4 March 1941

Here I am once more, and now on my journey to Cairo, which will
be resumed tomorrow morning.[1] My party left Irene on Sunday
morning, two days ago. It consisted of some military staff, Lady
Moore, the governor's wife,[2] and Jannie's Daphne [Smuts] who is
coming up to help her with welfare or 'Gifts and Comforts' work.
Daphne will remain here as long as she can usefully work here, and
she hopes to see Jannie some time or other. He is up north, Lake
Rudolph way. I am spending my time here reviewing the situation
with my officers. The campaign is entering on a new phase which
calls for reconsideration of many matters. Kenya is clear of the
enemy. Somaliland has been occupied by our forces, and the advance
into Abyssinia is only slowed down by the rain. Meanwhile plans
have to be made for the prosecution of the campaign to Addis
Ababa, and up in the Middle East a bigger campaign may soon
develop. All this and matters connected with the change-over of war
plans have to be discussed, and the visit of Eden and [General Sir
John] Dill to the Middle East gives a convenient opportunity for
these discussions which will take place this week. I hope to be back
in Cape Town at the beginning of next week (this is Tuesday). The
weather may of course affect my speed of movement. Sunday we
were to have reached Nairobi from Pretoria. As a matter of fact,
when near Nairobi, we were wirelessed that owing to rain, low
clouds, and ground mist we could not land, and we had to go back
to Dodoma to land and spend the night. I slept in the same old
German fort where I had slept in September 1916 in the height of
the last campaign, and was reminded of many things which had
almost slipped out of my memory. Then on Monday morning
(yesterday) we started off in fine weather, and passed over that great
volcano country once more, and from a great distance could see the
white crown of Kilimanjaro aloft above the clouds. As we approached
nearer the clouds diminished and we decided to fly towards the
mountain as near as possible. By this time it was practically free of
clouds, except a few scattered bits of drifting fleece. So we circled
round, higher and higher; on the second round we passed over the
plateau between the two high peaks, and on the third we flew over
the top, at about 300 or less feet above the top, and looked down

---

[1] This was the second war-time visit of Smuts to Egypt.
[2] Daphne Moore, wife of Sir Henry Moore (qq.v.).

into the inner central crater which looked like a big circular black pipe going down into the mass of the mountain. We were just over 20,000 feet high and all felt a little dizzy. I kept using my ciné Kodak all the time and must have taken about a hundred or 150 feet of film. Of course, the result could not be so good in a machine moving at 200 miles an hour and through panes not quite clear, and with the light changing from moment to moment. But I hope in the lot there will be parts which will give a good representation of the grand mountain at and near the top, with the glaciers gleaming in the morning sun. Colonel [P.] Nel, our pilot, who has flown this route some fifty times, says he had never before seen the peak to such advantage. I used my exposure meter as often as possible, but the changes in the light were so rapid that I could not possibly keep pace with them. We passed the forest belt, then the scrub zone, and then the low mossy flora, and finally came on the bare scree on which nothing could be seen, although we were only about a hundred feet away from the stony surface. I can now say that I have been on Kilimanjaro, and the only effect on me was a certain dizziness. The rest of the travel party suffered more and felt pain in the head or ears or throat, in addition to that strange sensation of extreme light-headedness at very high altitudes. Sir Pierre van Ryneveld, our C.G.S.,[1] who was a distinguished flier of the Great War, says that this effect on the human organism is the greatest trouble of all in the very high flying now carried on in this war. The strain of flying at 30,000 feet for an hour or more is practically unbearable, and I can quite appreciate that now. Besides, your mind and organism seem to be slowed down; you think with less speed and alertness, and all your movements are slow and almost lethargic. The rest of the party were interested to see how alive I remained, and the energy with which I changed films, filtered the air, and did my filming job. As a fact I only felt somewhat giddy in the head. It was a grand sight, but one of the greatest features was on looking down and sailing down from 20,000 feet into the Masai steppe below, which looked infinitely far away in the haze of distance. It felt like falling into infinite space. I don't think I shall ever have this experience again, and it was worth having, whatever the value of the film which was taken. For a real expert it would have been chance of a lifetime. Good-bye to greatness! This is the state of man.[2] All that is left at the end is the experience, and that remains an unforgettable memory.

[1] Chief of the general staff.

[2]
  Farewell! a long farewell, to all my greatness!
  This is the state of man.
  Shakespeare, *Henry VIII*, iii.ii.352.

The campaign here has passed very quickly. The Italians made
the great military mistake of massing their force into their front
defences. When that was pierced and crushed nothing remained to
stop our advance, and in a few days we had moved from the Juba
to Mogadishu, a distance of hundreds of miles, with no real opposition. The enemy who had fled into the bush could not live there and
are still coming in to surrender in small or large parties. It has been
a shattering blow, and shortened the campaign by many months.
Our losses were ridiculously small. May our luck continue to the
end.

Cairo. 7 March 1941. My job here is finished and in a couple of
hours we shall be flying south once more. It has been most interesting to review the whole position in the Middle East with Eden and
the army, air and navy chiefs, but I am sure it has been as useful as
it was interesting. The situation after the invasion of Bulgaria[1] and
the threat to Greece is very grave and it has been no easy task to
weigh up all the pros and cons and decide on a course of action
which may have far-reaching results for the future. But the work
has been done, and as far as I am concerned my message to the
British prime minister has gone forward. Now I hurry south.
Tonight at Khartoum again, tomorrow at Nairobi and the following
day at Irene; and on Monday morning again at Cape Town. The
whole trip, with much hard work thrown in, will have occupied just
a week, with the two week-ends added. It is really amazing what one
can do nowadays with rapid air travel to save time. So far the trip,
from a purely travel point of view, has gone very smoothly and well,
and I trust our luck will hold to the end. I saw a couple of days ago
that our dear old Rendell Harris had departed this life, but at the
age of eighty-nine that is to be expected. He was a good man, and
a grand scholar. He will now not stay under your staircase.[2] 'Come
up higher, friend!'[3]
    I sit in the embassy, in a room looking out on the Nile. I rather
think it is the same which I occupied in February 1918.[4] How much
has happened since! Then the campaign in Palestine against the
Turks was being worked out. Now Turkey is the friend, and no one
knows what groupings will be made yet before the end...

[1] As part of his plan to control the whole Balkan region Hitler, having already
reduced Hungary and Rumania to satellite states, sent German forces into Bulgaria on
28 February.
[2] His house in Birmingham had been bombed and there was a plan to house him
with the Gilletts. (Note by M. C. Gillett.)
[3] 'Friend, go up higher.' *St Luke* xiv.10.
[4] *See* vol. III, **816**.

530   From L. S. Amery   Vol. 64, no. 5

India Office
Whitehall
3 April 1941

My dear Smuts, What a wonderful turn in the tide we have seen in the last fortnight. What with your boys sweeping up through Somaliland and now approaching Addis Ababa, with Wavell's troops triumphantly entering Keren,[1] the naval victory[2] and the self-recovery of the Yugoslavs,[3] we seem at last to have got the initiative in our hands, not only as against Mussolini but also against Hitler.

The really big thing is throwing Hitler's plans out of gear both psychologically and actually. Being what they are I imagine the Germans will require a fortnight or more before they try to attack Yugoslavia and that will give the Yugoslavs time to mobilize and us time to work in together with the Greeks for our defence plans in Macedonia. If it were not for the anxiety of the Serbs to make sure of the Croats,[4] by not being the first to provoke war, the right thing technically would be for the Yugoslav army, or part of it, to push into north Albania at once. I believe the whole Italian position there could be mopped up in a week leaving the Greek army free to concentrate, beyond Salonika, while also giving us the Albanian aerodromes, a clear run up the straits of Otranto and the use of the Yugoslav harbours and inlets further up the coast.

All this may very well force Hitler, on grounds of prestige, to concentrate all the more on his attack on our shipping and even, perhaps, try actual invasion. Well, we shall see.

Here things are going remarkably well, though there is a certain amount of parliamentary criticism of Bevin [E.] for timidity in handling both the question of fixing wages and enforcing compulsion for necessary work. I suppose in this, as always, we have to move by stages and in response to pressure from below rather than by vigorous leadership from above. However, that is not my concern

[1] After a stubborn resistance by the Italians this stronghold in Eritrea fell on 27 March.

[2] The British victory over the Italian fleet in the Ionian sea off Cape Matapan on 28 March.

[3] On 21 March the Yugoslav government, threatened by Hitler, adhered to the Axis powers. But on 27 March a *coup d'état* under General Simović overthrew the government headed by the regent Prince Paul and took power in the name of the young king, Peter II.

[4] The Croat nationalists opposed the government and aimed at the separation of Croatia from Yugoslavia.

as under the present war cabinet system[1] I am really almost entirely limited to my Indian work.

There I think things go reasonably well. The stage demonstration of martyrdom which your old friend Gandhi has been organizing has somehow created very little interest or excitement in India.[2] Except for leaders, magistrates seem to be giving very light sentences and, in many cases, simply sending the accused home after the rising of the court. Meanwhile the development of the Indian munitions programme and the increase of the Indian army are going on well, and the army itself has won undoubted credit for its performances in Eritrea.

I imagine some of those at your end of the world who have been banking on a German victory are beginning to look down their noses and that the Nazi creed is beginning to look to them as in a somewhat less rosy light. I trust that the progressive disintegration is advancing merrily and that you are keeping fit and give yourself reasonable relaxation from time to time. The war is not over yet and there will be a lot of tidying up to do when it is. Yours ever,

L. S. Amery

P.S. Since dictating this I have had your welcome letter of 18 February with its happy final quotation 'in quietness and confidence shall be thy strength'.[3] That is, I think, indeed, true of the nation here. Whatever its other failings its moral outlook has never been wrong.

Talking about the future, it is bound to be shaped in the main by our relations with the United States. I am not one of those who believes in Streit's federal union schemes,[4] even if confined to the British Commonwealth and the United States. We have never been able, and no doubt with good reason, to find a federal constitution for the Commonwealth, and joining in such a constitution with the United States would mean an even greater degree of swamping for the Dominions than a narrower federation of Empire. Nor would the Americans themselves look at it. Finally, I don't believe that federation is the last word in international co-operation and I am much more inclined to believe in the extension of the Commonwealth principle, both to our relations with America and among nation groups in Europe and elsewhere. What is, of course, one of the main

---

[1] Churchill's government contained twenty-seven ministers of cabinet rank but only five of these formed the war cabinet which was responsible for war policy.

[2] After the outbreak of war Gandhi and the Congress took exception to the action of the British government in declaring India a belligerent country and withdrew Congress members from the assembly. Gandhi organized a campaign of non-co-operation.

[3] **528**.

[4] Clarence K. Streit advocated a federation of democracies in his book *Union Now* (1939).

sources of strength in our Commonwealth, over and above common ideals and traditions and economic interests, is our common and interchangeable citizenship. I see no inherent reason why that bond of union should not be established as between the United States and ourselves. What I mean is that there should be a mutual agreement by which American citizens in the Empire and British subjects in the States should be entitled, after a certain limited period of residence, to enjoy full citizenship rights, including voting power, without abandoning their original allegiance. So many of the best Americans who come over here would wish to take part in public life if it were not for the sacrifice of their citizenship, and the same applies to the best type of Britishers who go to the United States. Such an arrangement would raise no constitutional questions and would entangle nobody. But its influence, like that of the Rhodes scholarships, would increase year by year. In other words Anglo-American unity should come not from the top, but from the bottom upwards. The Greeks had something of the same sort between some of their states, and the idea has been at the back of my mind for many years. I wonder what you think of it and whether you feel that you might on some occasion ventilate it with advantage.

Another simple bond of union that might be usefully developed would be the celebration throughout the Empire and in the States of 15 June, Magna Carta Day, as the symbol of our common free institutions.

531   To A. G. Cunningham   Vol. 66, no. 118
Telegram

From: Smuts

To: General Cunningham

Dated 7 April 1941

Most cordial congratulations on your occupation of enemy's capital[1] which reflects equal credit on your brilliant leadership and the valour and endurance of your troops. South Africa feels specially proud of an achievement in which her sons have so great a share.

[1] The British forces entered Addis Ababa on 5 April.

532   To M. C. Gillett   Vol. 66, no. 220

Doornkloof
[Transvaal]
14 April 1941

...I refer to the things which I know will interest you. But all the
time war and defence matters, for which I had specially come up,
were being attended to. Conferences on Thursday and Friday and
today. There is much to do, with the switch-over from Abyssinia to
Egypt, whither our forces are now beginning to move. Our work in
east Africa is over, in record time, long before I had anticipated the
end would come. In fact I had thought that all this summer (yours)
we would be kept busy there. But it is all over, except the final
clearing up which can be left to the black African troops and the
Abyssinian patriots. Grimmer work awaits us in the north, where
the German forces have retaken all that Wavell took from the
Italians in December to February.[1] Egypt is now once more in the
danger zone, and as our British troops in the Middle East are mostly
wanted for the Middle East and the Balkans etc.,[2] the brunt of the
defence in Egypt may now have to be borne by our South African
divisions. It will be a heavy task in face of a formidable enemy. But
the South Africans look forward to the job.

The Germans have started their spring campaign quite well.
Libya retaken, Yugoslavia in a bad way, Greece invaded, a revolution in Iraq,[3] and mischief preparing in France, Spain and the Far
East.[4] But the attack on England is not coming off, at any rate not
for the present, the U.S.A. are getting deeper into the business, and
are now even sending their ships to Suez. Russia seems however to
be freeing her hands by the agreement for neutrality with Japan.[5]
She may be getting concerned about the Ukraine and the Caucasus.
Japan may equally want to free her hands in order to come to grips
with Britain and possibly the U.S.A. in the Far East. Evidently the
whole war scene is on the move and we may expect very big developments this summer over the whole world. This may be the year of

---

[1] The German counter-offensive in Cyrenaica, with General Erwin Rommel in
command, began on 31 March. By 12–13 April they had reached Bardia near the
Egyptian border.
[2] British forces were defending Greece against a German invasion of that country
and also of Yugoslavia which had begun on 6 April.
[3] On 13 April the Germans entered Belgrade. On 3 April Rashid Ali, who supported
the Axis powers, became prime minister of Iraq with which Great Britain had a treaty
giving her the right to maintain air bases in, and move troops through, the country.
[4] Germany was at this time putting pressure upon both Japan and Spain to enter
the war and it was feared that French warships would become available for German use.
[5] The Japanese–Soviet neutrality pact was signed on 13 April.

destiny, as I said in one of my broadcasts.[1] Everything points that way. South Africa is working to her full strength—perhaps even beyond it. I have just had a warning from high officers that we may be overstraining ourselves. Still, there is no other course. I believe everything is at stake, everything dear to us in the values of our civilization—not only for the world in general but particularly for South Africa on which Hitler's baleful and covetous eyes have been turned for some time. It is neck or nothing.

I brought with me up here the Groote Schuur copy of Renan's *Life of Jesus*[2] in order to finish reading it. I find it more interesting than when I read it a lifetime ago. He is a wonderful master of language, and carries you over the rough places in the narrative with immense power. He is specially severe on Jesus for his crude economic views, his exaltation of the poor and illiterate, his depreciation of property and his lack of understanding of the vast apparatus of an advanced civilization. Of course this is all very true, but Jesus shows the power of the neglected factors, the importance of the unknown or forgotten man, and the strength there is in the economically lower levels of human society. I am reminded of Goethe's distinction when he pointed out in *Wilhelm Meister* that the pagan civilizations worshipped what was above us (the gods), the philosophers emphasized what was on a level with us; and Christianity what was below us— the common man, the common human virtues, the pain and sorrow which train the soul for higher things. One always has the feeling that the deepest aspects of the inner life escape Renan, and that his insight is not equal to his literary and other gifts. And beyond everything else you come to that deepest insight which Jesus unfolded to man— that 'God so loved the world'. It is such an overwhelming insight— that the power of this universe is no other than love, and that it is directed not to the glories, but to the humble creatures of God...

533   From J. F. van Rensburg   Vol. 66, no. 281

Bloemfontein
Posbus 668
17 April 1941

Seer geagte Generaal, By twee vorige geleenthede het ek getrag om u in Kaapstad op u kantoor te spreek in verband met sekere beperkings wat die Noodregulasies aan die Ossewa-Brandwag opgelê het. Veral die verbod op driloefeninge sonder verlof. Dit raak die dissiplinêre gehalte van ons Beweging en ek het derhalwe gehoop om

---

[1] *See* 523.   [2] Published in 1863.

van u sekere driloefeninge veroorloof te kry. Dit sou heeltemal binne die raam van u voorskrifte moet geskied en kon beperk bly tot 'n paar elementêre bevele wat die ordelikheid van 'n vergadering en 'n optog kan vergemaklik.

Ongelukkig kon Mnr. Pohl weens u menigvuldige werksaamhede g'n oudiensie reël nie.

Ek neem derhalwe by hierdie geleentheid my toevlug na papier oor 'n ander en dalk meer ernstige vraage.

Die Randse Onluste Kommissie het verslag gedoen en onder ander heelwat oor die Ossewa-Brandwag te sê gehad. Mynsinsiens by wyse van *obiter dicta*, want wat die onluste betref was ons, as Beweging, bloot negatief betrokke. Elke bevel en elke georganiseerde optrede van die Beweging tydens die onluste was streng onthoudend. Maar ek wil nie argumentatief word oor 'n bevinding wat in elk geval nie u bevinding was nie.

Veelmeer gaan my besorgdheid oor 'n gerug dat die Regering nou die wenslikheid oorweeg om die hele organisasie in die ban te doen.

Ek neem aan dat dit bloot 'n gerug is en dat ek u in u moeilike pligte nie moet lastig val nie oor elk en ieder ongegronde gerug wat die rondte doen.

Ek neem dit aan, maar my verantwoordelikheid is sodanig en die moontlik gevolge so verreikend dat ek, om beide u en myself reg te doen, my genoodsaak voel om u te nader en die vertroue uit te spreek dat u ons nie onverhoord voor so'n wanhoopstoestand sal plaas nie. Met wanhopiges is sleg te redeneer.

Ek meen met 'n goeie gewete te kan sê dat die georganiseerde optrede, die sentrale wil, van die Beweging sedert 1 Januarie 1941, steeds gemik was op die vermyding en demping van uitspattings en rusverstorings; op die saamsnoering van die aktiwistiese neigings onder een verantwoordingsbewuste beheer en op die voorkoming (in belang van die land) van die losbarsting van die chaos in wye landskringe waar die gevaar daarvan definitief nie uitgeslote was nie, en selfs vandag ewe definitief nog nie uitgeslote is nie. Ek hoop dat u met my saamstem, Generaal, en ek kan u in elk geval die versekering gee dat hierdie mening deur my tergoedertrou gekoester word.

Waar ons nie ten volle geslaag het nie was dit te wyte aan inherente moeilikhede en die menslike 'imponderabilia'. Sulke dinge het ook in die gedissiplineerde geledere van die militêr plaasgevind, nie omdat hul militêr was nie, dog tenspyte daarvan. By ons insgelyk.

Dit is in die vertroue, Generaal, dat wat ook al die neigings van sommige van u kollegas mag wees, u versiendheid nie sal toelaat dat die gros van die Afrikaanssprekendes onverhoord op die *obiter dicta*

van 'n amptenaarskommissie in hul grootste volksorganisasie on-
wettig verklaar sal word nie.

Ek besef u moeilikhede, maar tegelyk ook—in alle beskeidenheid
—my eie verantwoordelikhede; om hierdie rede het ek nie geskroom
om hierdie skrywe aan u persoonlik te rig nie. Respekvol, Die uwe,

J. F. van Rensburg

TRANSLATION

P.O. Box 668
Bloemfontein
17 April 1941

Dear General, I have tried, on two earlier occasions, to see you at
your office in connection with certain restrictions which the emergency regulations have imposed on the *Ossewa-Brandwag*—
especially the prohibition of drill exercises without permission.[1] This
affects the disciplinary level of our movement and I had therefore
hoped to have certain drill exercises allowed by you. These would
have to be entirely within the bounds of your directions and could
be limited to a few elementary commands which would assist the
orderliness of a meeting or a procession. Unfortunately Mr [J. D.]
Pohl could not, because of your many activities, arrange an audience.
On this occasion, therefore, and in connection with another and
perhaps graver matter, I have recourse to paper.

The Rand Disturbances commission[2] has reported and has had
much to say, among other things, about the *Ossewa-Brandwag*, in
my opinion by way of *obiter dicta*[3] for, as to the disturbances, we as
a movement were merely negatively involved. Every order and every
organized action of the movement during the disturbances was
strictly abstinent. But I do not wish to become argumentative about
a finding which was, in any case, not yours. I am much more
troubled about a rumour that the government is now considering
the desirability of banning the whole organization. I suppose that
this is a mere rumour and that I should not bother you in the middle

[1] War Measure 4 of 1941 proclaims that the government may declare illegal associations regarded as a danger to the state and prohibits all persons from taking part in
military exercises or drills except on the authority of the minister of defence. Proclamation No. 44 of 1941 states that the *Ossewa-Brandwag* is an association to which
War Measure 4 applies. (*See* Government Gazettes Extraordinary, 4 February 1941
and 1 March 1941.)

[2] The commission was appointed to inquire into a serious riot (in which some
hundred people were injured) following a meeting of the *Ossewa-Brandwag* in
Johannesburg in February 1941. Its report, issued on 8 April, contained severe
strictures on the *Ossewa-Brandwag* for its part in the affair.

[3] Expressions of opinion without authority.

of your difficult duties about every unfounded report that circulates. I suppose this, but my responsibility is such and the possible consequences so far-reaching that, in fairness both to you and myself, I feel compelled to approach you and to express the hope that you will not put us, unheard, into such a desperate situation. One cannot easily reason with people in despair.

I believe I can with a good conscience say that the organized action, the central will, of the movement since 1 January 1941[1] has always aimed at avoiding and subduing excesses and breaches of the peace; at drawing together activist tendencies under one responsibility-conscious control and at preventing (in the interests of the country) the explosion of chaos in large regions where the danger of this could definitely not be excluded and even today can equally definitely not be ruled out. I hope you agree with me, General, and I can in any case assure you that I hold this view in all good faith. In so far as we did not entirely succeed, this was due to inherent difficulties and human imponderabilia. Such things have also happened in the disciplined ranks of the military forces, not because they were military but in spite of it. So also with us.

I trust, General, that whatever may be the inclinations of some of your colleagues, your far-sightedness will not allow the majority of the Afrikaans-speaking people in their largest national organization to be declared illegal on the *obiter dicta* of a commission of officials and unheard.

I recognize your difficulties, but at the same time—with all deference—my own responsibilities; for this reason I have not hesitated to address this letter to you personally. With respect, Yours sincerely,

J. F. van Rensburg

534   From Lord Linlithgow   Vol. 65, no. 86

The Viceroy's House
New Delhi
21 April 1941

My dear General, Through our high commissioner in the Union, Sir Rama Rau, I have been kept informed of your constant solicitude, in spite of your many preoccupations, for improving the lot of the Indian community in South Africa and for better relations between India and the Union. The most important steps, in this respect,

---

[1] J. F. van Rensburg became commandant-general of the *Ossewa-Brandwag* on 10 December 1940.

taken recently by your government are the passage through the Union parliament of the so-called Feetham resolutions[1] and the appointment of Mr Douglas Buchanan as liaison officer at Cape Town to make arrangements for Indian troops and other Indian visitors. May I utilize the opportunity that these afford for an expression of our gratitude to write to you personally to say how deeply I appreciate what has been done? To those of us who know what the British Commonwealth owes to your far-seeing and generous statesmanship, this will be only another example of your political vision and courage. Yours sincerely,

Linlithgow

535 To J. F. van Rensburg   Vol. 66, no. 119

This letter bears an annotation showing that Smuts instructed his private secretary to send it to the police for their information.

Kaapstad
23 April 1941

Waarde van Rensburg, Insake u brief van 17 April.

Dit spyt my dat ek u nie kon sien met u jongste besoek aan Kaapstad nie. Die enige rede kon alleen druk van ander werksaamhede gewees het, daar ek altyd 'n gedagtewisseling met u sou verwelkom.

Wat die kwessie van driloefeninge betref sou ek graag dat u dit met die polisie outoriteite bespreek daar dit meer by hul tuis behoort.

Op die oomblik bestaan daar sover ek weet geen voornemens om die Ossewabrandwag in die ban te lê nie. Die houding van die Regering sal grotendeels afhang van die rigting en gedrag van die organisasie en sy lede. Daar is sake hangende en getuienis kom voor die dag wat 'n onaangename lig op lede van die organisasie werp. Ook is ek bewus dat binne die organisasie daar stromings bestaan wat baie verder gaan as wat die res van die lede sou goedkeur. In hoever die hoofde daardie rigtings in toom kan hou sal die tyd alleen leer. Daarom neem ek 'n afwagtende houding in, in die hoop dat uiterste stappe nie nodig mag blyk nie.

---

[1] The Transvaal Asiatic Land Tenure commission, under the chairmanship of R. Feetham (q.v. vol. IV), was first appointed in 1932. Some of its recommendations were embodied in the Transvaal Asiatic Land Tenure Amendment Act, No. 30 of 1936. The commission continued its investigations and in April 1941 a motion giving effect to further recommendations was passed through the Union parliament. *See House of Assembly Debates*, vol. 42, cols. 6150 *et seq.*

By ons laaste gesprek in Pretoria het ek u meegedeel dat ek dit afkeur dat siviele amptenare lede van die Ossewabrandwag sou wees, omdat met die reël van gehoorsaamheid in die organisasie daar 'n botsing kan ontstaan tussen plig teenoor die Staat en plig teenoor die Organisasie. Daar die Organisasie nie hierin self handelend opgetree het nie, was die Regering verplig 'n stop aan hierdie dubbele pligsgevoel te sit.

Ek wil nou weer 'n woord van waarskuwing tot u rig, en hierdie keer met betrekking tot jong skoolgaande kinders wat nou in 'n onderdeel van die Ossewabrandwag opgeneem word. Van die oogpunt van die Staat beskou ek dit nog minder gesond als die lidmaatskap in die Ossewabrandwag van volwasse staatsamptenare. Ek wil u dus in oorweging gee om 'n einde te maak aan die opname van skoolkinders in 'n ondertak van die Ossewabrandwag. Op die wyse sal dit onnodig wees vir die Regering om ook hierin stappe te neem. Ek wil hoop dat hierdie saak u ernstige aandag sal geniet, veral daar die Voortrekker-beweging genoegsaam voorsiening vir die behoeftes van die jeug maak. Steeds die uwe,

get. J. C. Smuts

TRANSLATION

Cape Town
23 April 1941

Dear van Rensburg, With reference to your letter of 17 April.[1]

I am sorry that I was unable to see you during your last visit to Cape Town. The reason could only have been pressure of other activities for I should always welcome an exchange of views with you.

As to the question of drill exercises I should like you to discuss that with the police authorities since it is more appropriate to them.

At the moment there is, as far as I know, no intention to ban the *Ossewa-Brandwag*. The attitude of the government will largely depend on the course and the behaviour of the organization and its members. There are cases pending and evidence is appearing which cast an unpleasant light on members of the organization. I am also aware that there are currents within the organization which go much further than the rest of the members would approve. To what extent the leaders can keep those tendencies in check time alone will show. For that reason I am taking up a waiting attitude in the hope that extreme steps may not be necessary.

At our last discussion in Pretoria I informed you that I disapprove

[1] 533.

of civil servants being members of the *Ossewa-Brandwag* because the rule of obedience in the organization may cause a conflict between duty to the state and duty to the organization. Since the organization did not itself take action in this matter the government was compelled to end this double sense of duty.[1]

I wish now once more to address a word of warning to you and this time with regard to young schoolgoing children who are now being taken into a sub-division of the *Ossewa-Brandwag*. From the point of view of the state I regard this as even less healthy than membership of the *Ossewa-Brandwag* by adult civil servants. I would therefore suggest to you to put an end to the inclusion of school children in a sub-division of the *Ossewa-Brandwag*. In this way it will become unnecessary for the government to take steps in this respect also. I hope that the matter will receive your serious attention, especially as the *Voortrekker* movement[2] makes sufficient provision for the needs of the young. Yours ever,

s. J. C. Smuts

536   To J. C. Opperman   Vol. 66, no. 9

This telegram was sent in reply to a letter to Smuts from J. C. Opperman of Heilbron, Orange Free State, asking him to restrain the *Ossewa-Brandwag* from holding provocative meetings in the Heilbron district where members of the United party are in the minority and without protection. (*See* Smuts Collection, vol. 66, no. 9.)

Telegram

Van: Privaat Sekretaris

Aan: Kolonel J. C. Opperman

Gedateer 23 April 1941

U brief van 18 deser verwys. Eerste Minister sien geen rede om sodanige vergadering te belet tensy daar vrees bestaan vir gebeurlikhede. Die hele beweging word goed dopgehou.

[1] As early as 28 February 1939 officers of the Union Defence Force were forbidden to join the *Ossewa-Brandwag*. After war was declared in September the government not only prohibited civil servants from becoming members but also called in all rifles in private ownership.

[2] The *Voortrekker* movement is the Afrikander equivalent of the Boy Scouts and Girl Guides.

TRANSLATION

From: private secretary
To: Colonel J. C. Opperman
Dated 23 April 1941
With reference to your letter of the 18th. prime minister sees no
reason to prohibit such a meeting unless fear of contingencies exists.
The whole movement is being carefully watched.

537   To M. C. Gillett   Vol. 66, no. 225

Doornkloof
[Transvaal]
18 May 1941

Sunday morning after breakfast—a blessed time. No callers yet,
time to loll about and enjoy the warming sun and listen to birds in
the trees. All the more welcome after a week of heavy labour, so
heavy that I can scarcely remember all the matters that had to be
dealt with. Yesterday afternoon (after a morning spent in office and
at a head committee of our party) I thought I should enjoy a good
walk, and so with my two guards I set off and had a real go at it for
three full hours. It was a real pleasure and I would have had more of
it if I didn't have to hurry back to keep a tiresome appointment in
the late afternoon. The evening Isie and I spent at a war function to
collect funds for the governor-general's fund and returned home
very late. The high light of the week was the arrival of letters from
Arthur and you. You wrote while alone at Aston and told of other
days. I would have enjoyed your brew of coffee and other good things
if I could have been there. But we are toiling onward through the
night and may never see dawn again on those hills divine. Arthur
wrote quite cheerfully of the war. Of course a good deal has happened
since to take the edge off our cheerfulness. The Balkans gone,
Greece overrun, and German and English planes engaging each
other at Habbanyiah.[1] The pace is very hot, and it is still all the time
in the wrong direction. The Germans are advancing everywhere and
we are hard pressed to hold our own, except in Abyssinia where the
end is now very near. Vichy is apparently entering the New Order[2]
and opening all the doors of the French Empire for the advance of
this New Order. What a fate for proud France! What a humiliation,

[1] At Habbanyiah, the royal air force training base in Iraq, fighting had been going
on since 2 May, the Iraquis being supported by German aircraft based on Mosul.

[2] In a speech on 30 January 1941 Hitler had said, 'I am convinced that 1941 will be
the crucial year of a great New Order in Europe'.

and how great the bitterness will yet be against *Britain* when she has ultimately to rescue France and restore her to her place in Europe. The humiliation of that rescue after all that will have happened would be almost worse than being overthrown by her historic enemy. Such is human nature.

I feel deeply concerned over the whole Mediterranean position. Germany is evidently going to put all her enormous strength into the effort to drive us out of the Mediterranean basin. Syria may prove our Achilles heel. The French and, I daresay, the Spaniards also, will give free passage to Morocco from which the straits of Gibraltar can be rendered useless to us. Our people both in Egypt and London continue confident that they can hold that position, but it will be one of mortal struggle and danger. All our South African eggs are going into that basket. So I too have taken my fate in both hands. What a rejoicing there will be in certain quarters if disaster overtakes us in the north! But not even that will make me give in. Not that I expect the worst, but one studies all possibilities in war. We are conscious of our troubles but do not know what are the other fellow's. Hess is a sign of what is passing in that amiable family.[1] And so much more may be brewing there than we are imagining. In the summer of 1918 nobody dreamt that Germany was at her last gasp, and yet in a few months she had to apply for that fatal armistice. So may it be again this time. Apparently she is still very strong. Of course the one bright spot for us is the rapidity with which public opinion in America is coming round to us. Vichy's adherence to the New Order may possibly be the last straw. And so good may come out of evil. I believe the leaders in the United States have all made up their minds finally but are holding their hand for public opinion to swing round completely. It is not right to leave Britain and the Dominions alone to carry this burden of the world —new as well as old. And I fear it may prove beyond our strength unless America comes in. That is the view I have openly expressed. It is now all a question of time. *Too late* are the most awful words in all language. It *could* have been done; it *could* have been prevented; but the effort, the help etc. came too late. On those words hangs the history of the world. With our power of endurance I trust however that formula will not apply in this case. We shall hang on grimly to the end—be it victory or defeat. My concern at present is not so much over the Atlantic battle as over the Mediterranean, the importance of which cannot be over-estimated. But I should not say

[1] On 11 May Rudolf Hess, the Nazi deputy Führer, flew secretly and alone to Scotland on an unauthorized peace mission and was imprisoned by the British government.

more on this head. I have said and written a good deal in the proper quarters.

This week will again be one of very full activity, ending up next Saturday with my birthday amid a great war and political demonstration at Pietersburg. I hear all the northern Transvaal will be there. We shall fly up—Isie and I and other members of the family, and we hope to enjoy it all. But what sort of enjoyment is this at our age and with all the burdens resting on us!

I note that, according to your reckoning, two of my letters have gone down. I have not made a similar reckoning of dates for your and Arthur's letters, but since as much as four or five weeks have passed without any letter arriving I fear that I have suffered similar losses. But never mind, we shall make up for it when next you come to this land and friendship's circle! After all, what are letters! How poor compared to the Real Presence!—with the free flow of the currents of the spirit. You and Arthur must however keep in good health and not let the infirmities of the body create new obstacles for that free flow. I mean to survive it all and enjoy a glorious sunset at the end! By the way, yesterday (17 May) was secretly reported to me from several European capitals as a day of grave personal danger for myself. But it passed off without a hitch; I only had to work harder than ever and expose myself as recklessly as ever. The old bold mate of Henry Morgan will yet be found drinking at that inn![1]

We come across curious incidents to cheer us up on the rough passage of life and affairs. At the end of last session Deneys Reitz took ill and so I took charge of the Native estimates in the senate, where I was plied with questions and complaints from the Native senators.[2] I replied simply and sympathetically, expressing my views on Native health and economic conditions, life on the farms, wages and other matters of interest to the Natives. I was so pleased to get a letter last week signed by all the Native senators thanking me for my sympathy and understanding and helpful remarks and for the cheer they would carry to heavy hearts all over the country. I had simply expressed views which I have long held and am trying to act up to in our handling of Native affairs. But from the highest official quarters that message evidently meant more than I had thought it would. I am sure simple humanity and decency are the way out of much of our difficulties. We are so grudging of our sympathy and the poor Native is so disheartened by apparent apathy or even unfriendliness, that even simple words of helpfulness shine like lamps in the dark. [D.] Smit, the secretary of Native affairs, wrote me that even he was much moved and that my outlook as publicly stated would

[1] See vol. IV, p. 53, note 1.   [2] See supra, p. 108, note 3.

have a far-reaching effect. The Natives are so helpful to us, we often so grudging in our thanks and help to them. More than 30,000 are now serving in non-combatant capacities in my army, and as many more will soon be coming on. I pay them well, give them very good treatment and am thus establishing a standard which will more and more permeate our practice in farming and industry. This is the only thing humanly to do. But it is also sound policy, unless we wish to drive our Natives to the influence of the Communists or the Nazis whose activities among them are already pretty all too clear. Isie and her friends have set the Native women working for their men folk's 'Gifts and Comforts', and it is a pleasure to see how they take to this activity. But the most pathetic instance of all came to my notice last week. Two leper women in the Native territories had started on their own to work up articles for sale among their fellow lepers, and had thus collected £16 which they sent up to the 'Gifts and Comforts' fund. Sylma [Coaton] wrote them a nice letter of acknowledgement, saying that the money would go to their own people in the army. (Visitors are now coming in, and I must stop, and leave space for some further items which may emerge before mail day. Good-bye.)

Later. 20 May. No, there is nothing to record before the mail goes. Everything here goes well. I have had some good walks and keep well. For the rest it is just work, work, work. Your three philosophical books have arrived, also Gilbert's *Antigone*.[1] I browse into them at night. The war news is not so bad at the moment. The great Italian surrender at Amba Alagi[2] is good news, and I hope the finale is not far off. In other theatres things are developing, but some time will pass before we can say it is forward or backward. Now I must close, with all good wishes to you both. Ever yours,

Jan

538 To A. P. Wavell   Vol. 66, no. 125

Prime Minister's Office
Pretoria
19 May 1941

My dear Wavell, Many thanks for your letter of 8 May and its interesting enclosure[3] which threw much light for me on recent

[1] Gilbert Murray's translation of the play by Euripides.

[2] The Italian forces which were under the command of the Duke of Aosta at Amba Alagi in northern Abyssinia surrendered to South African troops on 16 May.

[3] *See* Smuts Collection, vol. 66, no. 289. The enclosure is entitled 'Note for General Smuts on the situation in the Middle East, May 1941'.

developments. I have also had the benefit of talks with Butler [S. S.] who could enlighten me on other points.

With Butler I have also discussed my views of the Mediterranean position generally and he will no doubt convey to you the gist of what I said to him.

In short, I think the main effort of the enemy this summer may be concentrated against the countries of the Mediterranean basin, and you may feel the brunt of all his fury. Vichy is already co-operating with the Axis, and I fear Franco will follow the same course. From Morocco the Germans will make the straits of Gibraltar unusable to us, while the French ports and resources in north Africa will be available to the enemy. Syria will be occupied by them unless we forestall them, and Turkey, quite cut off from us, will then become neutral and even afford passage to them. And thus the main attack against Egypt may come from the north and the east. I do not minimize the danger of an attack from Libya, but it could never be a very formidable one in that desert, and with your forces strongly equipped with aircraft and tanks, the Lord may deliver them into your hand as He did the Italians. I can even conceive a big German force being cut off from its base in the west and compelled to a spectacular surrender.

Of course the loss of Egypt and the Mediterranean would be an awful blow to us, though not necessarily fatal. We have, however, the utmost confidence in you and do not anticipate any such result.

I have urged the home government to get aircraft, tanks, and material equipment for you from the United States of America via Suez, carried in United States ships. It ought to be possible for the Americans to support you on such a scale that victory is assured. But no time should be lost.

No invasion of England is likely to take place before next autumn, and by then the fate of the Mediterranean should have been decided one way or the other. In the meantime you should have your full share of American production.

Some people think Russia is the next objective, and there is a good deal of evidence pointing that way. But I still believe it is Egypt, first and foremost, and this Syrian–Iraqi move[1] is most sinister.

The fall of Amba Alagi is most welcome. Cunningham has indeed done brilliantly, and both he and [General Sir William] Platt have deserved well of us. I hope they will have their reward.

[1] The Vichy government had agreed to give the Germans military and air-base facilities in Syria, a French colony, from which the Iraqui revolt could be supported and attacks on Egypt launched. *See supra*, p. 287, note 3.

In our small way we are helping you as much as we can, and where we cannot we shall tell you so. With [O. J.] Hansen, our technical liaison officer, we have discussed the question of using our steel works as repair shops for your maintenance as far as possible, and I think we shall be helpful in that way.

If you require horses or mules in Palestine, we have plenty, and you must let us know.

The Second Division is now ready to leave and I am saying good-bye to them next week. You will find them an excellent body. The two South African divisions are likely to serve you well in the coming struggle. My best wishes for your health and success, Ever yours sincerely,

s. J. C. Smuts

539   To King George VI   Vol. 66, no. 127

Telegram

From: Smuts

To: George VI

Dated 24 May 1941

I thank your Majesty most sincerely for your gracious congratulations and good wishes on my birthday, and for the honour of my appointment as field marshal in the British army. I accept this high distinction not only for myself but more especially as a compliment to the people and army of South Africa from our Sovereign.

540   To M. C. Gillett   Vol. 66, no. 227

Doornkloof
[Transvaal]
2 June 1941

We have entered upon a new month, and beautiful May is behind us. It was the most wonderful May we have had for years; only a few quite cold days and nights. And now it will soon be midwinter —your midsummer; and one longs for summer to pass, for it will be the time of severest fighting. Crete has come and gone.[1] What next? This summer it will be the Mediterranean countries, and in autumn

[1] When Greece was occupied by the Germans the Allies decided to hold Crete (16 April). The German conquest of Crete took place between 20 May and 1 June, the evacuation by the British forces having begun on 27 May.

there may be the attempt to invade England. If the Germans fail in both they may be afraid to go into another winter of war. But that may be too much to hope for in these days when towards the end of the second year of war we are still retreating before the enemy. That is still due to our inferior armament. Whatever shall we do in future? The nation that does not arm continuously is lost—as France has been lost, as Britain will be lost but for the grace of God. In this mechanistic era mere bravery and improvised organization at the last moment will not help. The only alternative is a league of the nations or of some nations strong enough to withstand aggression, and they too will have to be armed all the time. It is very difficult to see how one can ever feel safe again without full armaments quite up to date. After our experience in our lifetime we are inclined not to be too optimistic about disarmament. It almost seems now that in disarming after the last war we ran a risk which may be as nearly fatal to our civilization and all we prize as anything we could conceive. As things are today disarmament is *not* the way to peace as we had imagined, indeed just the opposite. It could only be the way to peace if there is such a coercive union of the nations that it becomes impossible for any of them to arm without being at once dealt with. And so close and coercive a union may be also destructive of liberty and national self-determination. It is a problem which requires more thinking out than I have been able to give it. You will remember that in my Sheffield lecture in 1929 or 1930 I uttered a warning about too rapid and drastic disarmament,[1] and many of my Liberal or League friends were puzzled at my attitude. But it was a sense of danger that even then moved me in that lecture ('The Disarmed Peace'). Another thing that has puzzled me is that the *Bismarck* could blow the *Hood* up like that and our battleships after a series of dreadful salvoes at close range against the *Bismarck* could not sink her and she had finally to be sunk with torpedoes.[2] It would almost seem as if the German armour or shells or both were better than ours. I should like very much to know how all this is explained, but I don't suppose anybody has the answer at present.

But enough about the war. I spend much of my time with problems of war and strategy, and it is a shame to trouble your pacific soul with my difficulties...

[1] The Basil Hicks lecture, delivered on 8 October 1931 at the University of Sheffield and entitled 'The Disarmed Peace' (Smuts Collection, Box I, no. 74A).

[2] On 24 May, in a naval engagement south-west of Iceland, the battle-cruiser *Hood*, after being hit five times by the new battleship *Bismarck*, blew up and sank in a few minutes. The *Bismarck* eluded the British ships but was found on 26 May about 500 miles north-west of Brest. She was put out of action by heavy gunfire on the 27th but did not sink until she had been repeatedly torpedoed.

I may just add in passing that two days of last week had been spent in inspecting my troops. Another division is going north to take part in the war in the Mediterranean basin. The First Division that has done so brilliantly in Abyssinia is already there or partly on the way. This Second Division will join them there. You can therefore see what an enormous stake we have in this battle of Egypt. This Second Division is also a magnificent body of men and I was proud to review such a body of South Africans. Part of them were in Natal, at Maritzburg,[1] and I had to fly to Durban and motor to Maritzburg in order to review them at 11.30 a.m.! At 4 p.m. that afternoon I was once more back at Doornkloof! Such is speed of travel in these days. Isie is going to Durban this week for some functions, but she will travel more quietly by train. She will take three days for what took me less than a day.

I had some very good letters from Arthur travelling over the same ground as yours received earlier—that is, the period of your quiet stay at Aston. He describes how he passed through a night of heavy air raid in London and he and the other old club fogies could do no better than spend the night reading in their library or whatever was the most suitable place. You remember the night in 1917 when a heavy raid was on and the Savoy was stricken and Cleopatra's Needle splintered and John Bull's offices were wrecked, and you and Alice and I sat quietly watching the hullabaloo. There is really nothing very terrifying in these things, once one makes up one's mind to take them quietly. The only time gunfire ever frightened me was the first time I was in the thick of it in the battle of Ladysmith in October 1899.[2] After that initial experience heavy gunfire never gave me any real trouble. This is how I explain the quietness with which London takes her severe bombings. One is so made as to adjust oneself to such strange experiences. Of course if you can't you just suffer from shell-shock or worse. I have however never been under a dive-bomber attack and wonder whether I could stand that without squirming. It must be a terrible experience—such experience as has been the lot of our men at Crete. In my travels to visit my troops I may yet have it and so sample this experience of war also.

By the way I see a new book has appeared by Croce, translated into English under the name of *History as the Story of Liberty* (Sprigge).[3] Please get it for me. It was most favourably reviewed in the *Manchester Guardian* and of course the *subject* is always with me. I wonder how he was allowed to publish such a book in Italy,

[1] Pietermaritzburg.   [2] *See* vol. 1, no. 131.
[3] Sylvia Sprigge was the translator.

where Musso is still 'stamping on the putrid corpse of liberty'. Poor Musso.

Will you please tell Mrs Burtt-Davy that I have arranged with the agricultural department to finish her husband's *Flora of the Transvaal*.[1] The national herbarium at Pretoria will complete the last two parts and the whole will be reprinted. The agricultural department will communicate with her and ask for such MSS and notes as Burtt-Davy left of the two remaining parts. Miss [I. C.] Verdoorn and Dyer [R. A.] are very willing to undertake the task of completing what has been done. Please tell Hutchinson also as he is sure to be interested. With love, ever yours,

Jan

541   To Lord Linlithgow   Vol. 66, no. 135

Pretoria

4 June 1941

My dear Viceroy, It was a great pleasure to receive your personal note of thanks[1] for what little service I have been able to render in making relations between India and the Union more normal. I am in hopes that with patience this process can be continued in future, and that the trouble may dwindle in importance in the whole perspective of our relations. But our European public are inclined to be very critical and restive, and that is why I use the word patience. Knowing what your difficulties are and the way small things are magnified in the Indian press, I have done what I could to ease the strain and shall continue to do so.

Rama Rau has been very useful in this connection. His wide training as a civil servant and his fairness and moderation of outlook have made it possible to use his services in smoothing away difficulties, and I was very sorry he was going. I hope we shall have another man of his outlook and calibre as your next high commissioner.

I am watching your internal situation as much as that is possible from the official reports and memoranda. I am afraid the trouble of India is not merely constitutional but much more fundamental, and the prolonged controversies and the singular unwisdom of the Congress party have at last brought India face to face with these deeper racial and religious difficulties. Dominion status in its full implica-

---

[1] J. Burtt-Davey was chief botanist of the Union department of agriculture until 1913 and died in 1940 (*see* vol. IV, p. 305). The book referred to is *A Manual of the Flowering Plants and Ferns of the Transvaal with Swaziland, South Africa*. Parts I and II were published in 1926 and 1932. The unpublished MS of part III is in the national herbarium in Pretoria.   [2] 534.

tions should not be denied them, but rather given freely and graciously, as it is in any case inevitable. But how the Muslim–Hindu chasm is to be bridged is quite another and a far more serious matter. Constitutionally India is to me very much in the position in which Egypt was a generation ago, and if we could let her set up house under another [Lord] Cromer as guide, philosopher and friend we should not hesitate to do so. But we are warned about a house divided against itself, and that in truth is the case of India. Still we must be helpful and generous to the limit. It will be a dangerous world in which this new vast venture will be launched.

Indian troops in Libya, Eritrea and Abyssinia have done extremely well, and if possible increased the claim which India has on British statemanship. What a magnificent service to humanity it would be if England could guide her faltering footsteps at the beginning of her new career!

The war has reached a critical phase for us. This summer will be a trial of our very souls. But with the high spirit of the whole Commonwealth and the weight of America behind us, we have no reason for despondency or doubt. With all good wishes, Yours sincerely,

s. J. C. Smuts

542   To A. P. Wavell

Vol. 66, no. 137

Prime Minister's Office
Pretoria
9 June 1941

My dear General, I have to thank you for two very interesting letters[1]—one in which you gave a luminous account of what happened in Crete and led to the evacuation of our forces,[2] the other in regard to desert patrols from [Major-General G.] Brink's division.

I was much interested in this latter proposal and should think that South Africans would be naturally predisposed to this class of work. Their experience in the deserts of northern Kenya and Italian Somaliland would have accentuated this aptitude. I therefore look forward to good results from this move.

I had the opportunity to inspect the Second Division a week or two ago and was most favourably impressed by their form. They are

---

[1] Smuts Collection, vol. 66, nos. 289 and 290.

[2] The German invasion of Crete began on 20 May. On 27 May Wavell authorized the evacuation of the Allied forces which was completed on 31 May.

going to be a real acquisition to your fine army, on which so much depends for our success this summer.

I fully appreciate all you say about Crete. The result has of course been a bitter disappointment to us as to you. But I was appalled by the naval losses,[1] and as soon as I heard of them I saw the danger of our hanging on to a disastrous position. The result has shown that in the absence of adequate preparation in advance against air attack a place like Crete, with the enemy in Greece and the neighbouring islands, is a hopeless proposition. Malta is the opposite case.

Of course Crete is going to be a nasty thorn in our side. But on that I need not dilate. The pacification of Iraq[2] has been a measure of compensation for its loss. If now we can hold Syria firmly, as I trust you will do, the enemy will depend on the Western Desert for the attack on Egypt and Suez. And there I have no doubt you will beat the Germans, as you have beaten the Italians. If we can hold the Mediterranean position this summer and the attempt at invasion of England fails thereafter, we shall be nearing the end of this war.

I am afraid the Vichy people will now come out in their real colours and put their Mediterranean resources at the command of the enemy. Weygand is probably a broken reed to lean on, and we shall have to defend our position against a virtual tripartite alliance of Germany, Italy and France. That will be a difficult, indeed critical, position, and you and Cunningham will be tested to the uttermost. But you have stout people behind you. And besides we shall not be quite alone. America will, I am sure, be there when things come to the worst. If America can provide your supplies via the Red sea and Suez so as to make you independent of the straits of Gibraltar, you may defy all the elements.

You know how anxious I am to support your efforts to the utmost extent of our limited resources. You need therefore never scruple to appeal to me, and whenever I can I shall do my best to help you in a situation which will continue one of extreme tension and danger all this summer. With all good wishes, Ever yours sincerely,

s. J. C. Smuts

[1] On 22 and 23 May two British cruisers and three destroyers had been sunk, one battleship put out of action and several other ships badly damaged.

[2] On 31 May the pro-Axis movement led by Rashid Ali collapsed, a new government was set up and the country passed into British occupation.

543   To M. C. Gillett   Vol. 66, no. 230

Doornkloof
[Transvaal]
25 June 1941

. . .What a kaleidoscope this war is—what a rush of events! Yesterday it was Greece and Crete and Libya and Syria. Now it is Russia.[1]
I must confess this latest move of Hitler did surprise me. I could not
think that he would take on this war job in addition to what he had
already on hand. It looked so much like a wild mad gamble that
I would not believe it until it actually came off. Either Hitler thought
he could bluff Stalin into a great surrender or, if Stalin stood firm,
then he thought he could beat Stalin in a short space of time. But
what if this Russian venture takes all this summer, and Hitler
reaches winter with two western and eastern fronts still going
strong? One prays that he may have miscalculated this time and
overreached himself. That would be the end of him. But the Germans have been so often correct in their planning, that one hesitates
to pronounce judgment in advance. One can only hope and pray.
I have seen accounts which make out that Hitler can be in possession
of the Ukraine and astride the northern Caucasus in two months.
I hope these armchair strategists are wrong, but one cannot say.
Our Nationalist friends have already started saying here that I am
now in alliance with Bolshevism which Germany had done her best
in restraining from overrunning the world. They forget that Stalin
and Hitler have been bedfellows for two years, and what bedfellows!
The trouble is that I have so little faith in Stalin that I am not
certain that we shall not once more be sold a pup by him. His
double-dealing and treachery in 1939 remains an unforgettable
memory. But for that double dealing Hitler might have hesitated
before attacking Poland. But having squared Stalin with a share in
the loot he thought he could take a legitimate risk with the forces of
appeasement. And so war came. Is Stalin not going to accept another
seductive arrangement with Hitler? We shall see. But I am on my
guard. These unspeakable rascals one can never trust again.
    . . .I am still kept very busy, partly with war work, partly with
general political work and problems which should really fall to my
colleagues but with which the prime minister has finally to deal.
I am glad when evening comes and I can return home. And there
it is usually a case of having to dispose of a batch of correspondence
for which there was no time during office hours. Callers are also
another time-robbing affair. Of course, mostly Union people,

[1] The German invasion of Russia began on 22 June.

political friends etc., but often distinguished visitors. South Africa is now full of them. They come from Yugoslavia, Greece, and other parts of southern Europe. The English from the north, right up to Egypt and Palestine are coming here from the storm of war. We are a real place of refuge from the storms raging in the north, and I have never seen South Africa so full of distinguished strangers. This morning I had the ex-governor of Athens[1] among my callers. And Royalties in plenty. You can imagine what a happy impression South Africa must make on these visitors—no black-outs, plenty of food, beautiful warm days, crisp cold nights, and a general air of being out of the war and out of the world! They all hold their breath when they speak of this happy land. They note the beauty of our larger towns, the distinction of our domestic architecture, and the great friendliness of the people. (They of course do not come into touch with our politics and our party rancours!) Anyhow it is pleasant to hear such good reports of our country.

Your little book on the *Flowers of the Spirit*[2] has duly arrived. Thank you for it. I was glancing through some passages last night and thought of you two sending me such a good gift. I am also reading a book you sent me years ago by Professor Burkitt: *Church and Gnosis*.[3] It deals with the curious gnostic developments in the early church of which I have been blissfully ignorant. I wish I had more time for this sort of stuff. Love to you all ever,

Jan

544   From L. S. Amery   Vol. 64, no. 7

India Office
Whitehall
26 June 1941

My dear Smuts, Events have indeed moved apace since I last wrote to you. The attack upon Russia opens up a tremendous new field of possibilities both ways, though on balance I have little doubt that the Germans have miscalculated and have let themselves in for a much bigger undertaking than their plans have provided for.

In part I suppose the attack on Russia has been due simply to the desire to clear Germany's eastern front for a whole-hearted concentration against us. In part it may be due to a genuine belief that

---

[1] M. Kotzias.
[2] By Edward Grubb, a member of the Society of Friends.
[3] F. C. Burkitt, *Church and Gnosis. A study of Christian thought and speculation in the 2nd century* (1932).

Hitler can not only rally Europe on the anti-Bolshevist ticket, but even weaken our unity here and in America. All the same, I am not sure that the main motive is not the fear of the exhaustion of his oil stocks by next year unless he can get hold of new supplies. We are so prone to magnify our detailed reverses that we are apt to overlook the fact that the enemy's detailed successes may yet have meant a failure of his major strategy. I believe Hitler genuinely hoped, a few months ago, that he could get to Suez via Libya and, having occupied the Balkans without fighting, sweep through Asia Minor or Syria to join hands with a friendly government in Iraq, and have no difficulty, once the British navy was expelled from the eastern Mediterranean, in shipping his Iraq oil to Italy and Germany. The plan has miscarried and the alternative now is to make a German lake of the Black sea by conquering southern Russia, to 'liberate' Trans-Caucasia and so secure a free hand in expanding and exploiting Baku oil. Incidentally success in that direction may enable him to threaten not only Iraq but India itself. Well, we shall see.

Before this reaches you you will have heard that Wavell is being succeeded in command of the Middle East, for the time being at any rate, by [General Sir Claude] Auchinleck, the present commander-in-chief in India. There is no doubt that Wavell has had a very gruelling time and is a pretty tired man. Auchinleck, whom I spent months in trying to secure for India, is quite first-rate and, much as I deplore his loss in India, may well do big things in north Africa. I don't know when you will have a chance of flying up to confer with him but I am sure you will be greatly taken with him when you do.

Turning to a very different field, I am increasingly concerned about the economic reconstruction after the war, and about our own attitude, for propaganda purposes, towards that reconstruction. I think we make a great mistake if we underrate the attractiveness of Hitler's 'New Order'[1] for most of Europe. The conception of Europe as a single economic system based, if not on customs union, at any rate on mutual preference and a common currency, and providing a substantial and stable market for the products of its various units, does offer a great deal, even if these advantages have to be paid for by a measure of economic as well as political servitude to Germany. Our natural answer is to hold up the banner of a better New Order to Europe, based, not on the dictatorship of one favoured nation, but on mutual economic co-operation freely agreed to on a basis of equality. In other words we can hold up before Europe the ideal of a free commonwealth with its internal preferential system. That I know would make a great appeal. On the other

_____

[1] *See supra*, p. 295, note 2.

hand, if all we have to offer is a return to the pre-war anarchy in which every European nation has to fight its way in the world as a unit and is forbidden by the most favoured nation clause[1] to make any arrangements for freer trade with its neighbours without letting in the rest of the world, then I think many of them would sooner prefer economic stability under Hitler.

Now, most unfortunately, Cordell Hull, to whom in other ways we are deeply indebted, is a complete crank and fanatic on the subject of the most favoured nation clause. He really believes that it is an instrument for spreading freer trade through the world, as indeed it may have been eighty years ago, instead of being the most serious obstacle to it under present conditions. In his passion for the restoration of the nineteenth century he will try and do everything to get us to abandon inter-imperial preference[2] as well as to prevent Europe coming together as an economic commonwealth. In that way he is a real danger, not only to the cohesion and economic development of our own Commonwealth, but to the prospects of world recovery. He seems incapable of realizing that a mutually preferential system covering a wide area is actually a contribution to freer trade in the world, not only in so far as there is freer trade among its members, who might otherwise not be able to afford to reduce their tariffs, but also because the assurance of wider markets within the group makes rigid protectionism against the outer world less necessary. I am sure for instance that if it had not been for the preferences established at Ottawa in 1932,[3] both England and the different Dominions would have been forced to adopt a higher tariff policy towards the outside world as well as towards each other. This is what actually did happen to Europe in the great depression, because it had no way of escape from the most favoured nation clause except by all kind of quotas, licences, exchange controls, etc.

The real future for bringing economic development and peace to the world seems to me to rest, not in going back to the nineteenth century and disregarding the far more complex structure of national life which is developing today, but in mitigating the autarkic tendencies which that complex structure encourages by the formation of mutually co-operative economic and political groups. In that way one would be building up by stages a sounder foundation for world peace and world economic co-operation than by a general fragmentation, economic and political, with certain enormous units like the United States completely upsetting the balance of the others.

Now it is very difficult for our people at this moment, engrossed

[1] *See supra*, p. 103, note 1.   [2] *See* vol. v, p. 193, note 1.
[3] *See* vol. v, p. 519, note 1.

as they are with negotiations for American help, and naturally anxious to avoid even the shadow of a difference of opinion with Cordell Hull, to bring out the right conception or to avoid creating in Hull's mind the impression that we are preparing whole-heartedly to accept his views after the war. You are in a much stronger position to do so, and it may well be that you might find some opportunity in your speeches of indicating the dangers of a too facile assumption that the world can be restored after this war to nineteenth century conditions. Possibly you might also be able to put in a warning word with my own colleagues here. However, that is a matter which only you can judge about. What I was anxious to do was to put my own misgivings before you and to discover how far you share them. Yours ever,

L. S. Amery

I wish you were free to come over here, but I quite realize the political difficulties, insuperable I fear.

545   To A. P. Wavell   Vol. 66, no. 143

This letter is annotated as follows: 'Not sent'. On 21 June Wavell had been relieved of the command of the British forces in the Middle East.

Prime Minister's Office
Pretoria
30 June 1941

My dear Wavell, I use the opportunity of [Major-General F. H.] Theron's return to Cairo to send you this note. Stallard has not yet returned from the north and I do not therefore know what impressions his visit has made on him and what views he will lay before me. I therefore record only some of my own thoughts for your information.

Germany's attack on Russia shows that she does not intend to attempt an English invasion till later in the year, perhaps not till much later. She means to clean up the situation in the east first. This may mean a respite for you too in the Middle East, but perhaps you are next on the list for attack on a grand scale.

I would suggest that this respite be utilized by you to the utmost extent possible and as speedily as possible. Your force is still much too small for what may be coming against you. This is forcibly illustrated by the recent set-back in the Western Desert which proved that the enemy there is already a match for you.[1] What will

[1] An operation designed to drive the Germans west of Tobruk, which was held by a British garrison, was launched on 15 June when enemy strongpoints at Halfaya and Capuzzo were attacked. The operation failed. By 17 June the British forces had withdrawn to their original positions.

be the position when he is continually being reinforced for the coming months? In the autumn when Russia has collapsed Egypt may be in grave danger.

The following steps seem called for:

1. A very early liquidation of the Syrian affair,[1] and the concentration thereafter of your force for the relief of Tobruk. The fall of Tobruk would be a disaster which I hesitate to contemplate in its possible effects. But if the enemy is given enough time to increase his Libyan forces, this risk may become a serious one. No time should therefore be lost in regard to Syria and Tobruk.

2. A continuous stream of reinforcements for Middle East in material and personnel should be kept up. Unless this is done I doubt whether we could successfully withstand the shock of a first-class German attack from the west. The collapse of Turkey under German threats, and the recrudescence of trouble in Iraq are also possibilities, especially if Germany has great success in the Russian war. Every consideration points to the gravity of the coming situation in the Middle East if the present respite is not exploited by us to the utmost. And the loss of Egypt cannot be contemplated. I trust you will keep on asking for more reinforcements, as I feel certain you are going to be attacked on a very large scale. The Germans know what a counter the conquest of Egypt and Suez will be for them in any possible peace negotiations. The reinforcement of the Middle East must be carried out now while there is still time. Any pressure you may wish me to exert from here I shall gladly exercise, if you keep me informed.

3. India should reinforce Iraq on a large scale. This will not only secure your Syrian flank and keep Iraq quiet, but may be a check to Germany if she should plan to push through to the Persian gulf. If Hitler gets to the Caucasus the position farther south-east will be in danger, and India might take time by the forelock in this connection.

Take these suggestions as coming from an armchair strategist, and attach to them such importance as you deem fit.

Theron is discussing a number of smaller issues with the defence department, and in regard to them you will hear from the chief of the general staff[2] and Theron. With kind regards and all good wishes,

Ever yours sincerely,

J. C. Smuts

[1] The British campaign to gain control of Syria was fought against the forces of the French government at Vichy. It began on 8 June and was successfully concluded on 12 July.   [2] General Sir Pierre van Ryneveld.

546 To C. E. Raven

Vol. 66, no. 145

Prime Minister's Office
Pretoria
2 July 1941

My dear Master, Your letter of congratulation,[1] like the cable of Rackham [H.] before it, has given me the deepest pleasure. How good it is to feel that in all the vicissitudes of experience I have the good will and love of my old friends.

But your offer to place me in the Hall with Milton and Darwin almost knocked me clean over. No less surprising was the suggestion that I might be substituted for Paley![2] And this from a divine of the church!

Your offer to make me one of the trio brought back to my mind a joke I heard long ago. Some fool who fancied himself great said that three great men and three only had adorned the pages of human history. And then he went on to add: Jesus Christ suffered on the Cross. Julius Caesar went the way of all flesh. And then after a pause he added quietly: 'I do not feel very well myself!' I am afraid in that trio I would be this fool. However, after the war, when we have all recovered our mental balance, we may discuss the subject in the common-room at Christ's, if by that time it has not yet been forgotten.

It is pleasant to hear from you how Christ's is getting on. What dear memories bind me to those cloistered halls! How far off from this world in its present phase of violent transition to a new order. And yet not so far off; think of the times of John Milton!

My kind regards and best wishes to all my old friends. I value their sympathy and good will more than I can say, and look forward to the times when we shall once more sit together in the common-room. Yours ever sincerely,

J. C. Smuts F.M.

547 From Lord Linlithgow

Vol. 65, no. 87

Private

Viceregal Lodge
Simla
13 July 1941

My dear Prime Minister, Your welcome letter of 4 June[3] has reached me today. I well appreciate the very difficult political issues raised

---

[1] On becoming a field-marshal.

[2] William Paley (1743–1805) was senior wrangler at Christ's College in 1763, later Archdeacon of Carlisle and author of a famous theological work, *A View of the Evidences of Christianity.*   [3] *See* **541**.

by the Indian problem in the Union. I was brought up in Australia, and so am able to understand the passionate conviction that lies behind the popular cry of 'White Australia'. I don't doubt, though the matter assumes a different guise with you, that the same deep chords are struck. In such circumstances argument is worse than useless. Time alone, that most effective of all healers, can bring about a measure of relief. Therefore I am in whole-hearted agreement with you in holding that patience is what is most required. Unfortunately, neither press nor politicians—out to capitalize race hatred and the inferiority complex—are disposed to display that admirable quality.

I am so glad you think well of Rama Rau. Between ourselves, I have tried to persuade him to take an extension in the Union, but family matters prevent his acceptance. I will do my utmost to secure an adequate successor to Rau. But one of the difficulties of steering public affairs here is the dearth of first-rate men and *cherchez l'homme* is (*pace* the French!) our daily preoccupation.

Your interest in Indian affairs is a thing very pleasing to me. I have often felt that with your broad outlook and sympathy and—if I may so put it—with your gift for imparting the qualities of high interest and persuasion to your public utterances, you might well make a unique contribution towards the right orientation of political feeling in the country.

Some day I should like to talk over the Indian situation with you at length. As a mere intellectual exercise, and proceeding upon premises whose validity is outside the region of controversy, the problem is difficult enough. Add the vagaries of Indian nature and the uncertainties of the future world environment in which India will find herself, and you have a dragon of difficulties worthy of any man's skill. Let me, in strict confidence, picture for your entertainment three scenes, all enacted in my office. In the first, Mr Gandhi is with me; the date is October 1940. 'I shall never cease to regret, Mr Gandhi, that Congress has made the profound error of abetting the Muslims and the princes in their policy of seeking to destroy the act of 1935.[1] For in the fashioning of the scheme of that act, Hindus, Muslims and Indian rulers had each a share, and so His Majesty's Government, and I speaking for them, could at least hope to hold all parties together in implementing it.' Mr Gandhi: 'I never myself read acts of parliament, but I have recently had converse with one who does, and I now understand that, had we agreed to work it, we

[1] The Government of India Act which provided for responsible government in the provinces and for a federal legislature and council of ministers to advise the viceroy.

could have got out of it all we want as early as we could hope to carry the load.' Myself: 'Mr Gandhi, that's the saddest thing I have ever heard you utter.' Mr G: 'Well, that may be, but after all, every party makes mistakes, and Congress has made one over that act!'

The second scene finds me with Mr [M. A.] Jinnah, leader of the Muslim League. Mr J. is saying: 'We Muslims are a separate nation. At one time (he was an active member of the Congress party in earlier days) I used to believe that we Muslims might work together with the Hindus for a self-governing India. But experience has taught me that this cannot be: Congress is out for a Hindu raj. Our culture and all we as Muslims care most about is in jeopardy. You British must stay in India and hold the scales between the two principal communities. Your presence in India is necessary to us Muslims, and—whatever your inclinations to the contrary—we mean to keep you here!!'

This very day, the prime minister of the Punjab has been in to see me in connection with a very mild expansion of my executive council that Amery and I have devised as earnest of H.M.G.'s desire further to associate non-official Indians with the war effort. A rumour (baseless in fact) has been put about that the defence portfolio is to go to a non-official Indian. Sir Sikander Hyat Khan, the premier, and all his colleagues have handed in their contingent resignation of office which is to take effect immediately if the defence portfolio goes outside the Punjab. He tells me that he and his friends are opposed to *any* change in the direction of expanding the central executive at this stage. By this post, comes a communication from the Hindu Mahasabha,† to the effect that the handing over of the defence portfolio to any Muslim would be something no Hindu could ever forgive!

I add nothing to these three examples of (1) Congress's folly and intransigence, (2) of communal prejudice and division, (3) of the intense provincialism with which one has to contend. Like you, I wish to Heaven it were otherwise, and that I might have been privileged to lead India in my time further and faster along the road of her destiny. I would, however, conclude this paragraph by saying that we have made some headway since 1936. We have established provincial autonomy which is working tolerably well in four provinces, and which—I do not doubt—will some day work again in the seven provinces in which Congress deserted their posts. Now, we are about to establish at the centre the principle of an Indian and non-official majority. If parties can agree after the war to a reasonable plan for the centre, which will include the Indian states, the machinery will be complete and workable. Whether India is going to show herself able to work a system of popular government without extraneous props and aids, remains to be seen, and upon that it is better to be agnostic. But neither Indianization nor home rule, nor a given status in the British Commonwealth, need necessarily presage any particular type of internal government—a fact often forgotten.

As for the war and our prospects for the rest of this year, I entirely agree with your presentation, and I write at the end of the third week of the Russo-German campaign when the general impression is that the Russians—all things considered—are not doing too badly. But I don't doubt that three months will see the Russians more or less knocked out and that we shall see the German armoured formations making their weight felt in the Middle East *via* the Caucasus and Caspian. The German communications will be difficult, but I don't myself doubt that they can do it, and will think it worth while. When people ask me what I feel about our prospects, I tell them that in my opinion we—the Empire—are in the position of a bull terrier which has dared to close its jaws on a tiger's back view, and that we shall be extremely lucky if, at any time over the next eight months, we manage to feel the ground with more than one of our feet at a time; but that (like the bull terrier!) the one thing we can not afford to do is to let go our grip, for if we do we shall be chawed up in a trice! My judgment is that we shall just about make it, but that margins are going to be uncomfortably narrow and the strain tremendous. I gather that that is about your own far more experienced opinion.

Wavell has arrived, and I am most glad to have him here. Auchinleck, as an officer of the Indian army, and the good leader he is, was doing A.1. and I was most sorry to lose him after only five months, particularly as I had a tremendous struggle to drag him out of Winston Churchill!

I see something of General [F. R. G.] Hoare, and Messrs Fahey [F. J.] and Anderson [P. M.] from time to time, and am glad to believe that they are happy here in India in their work on the Eastern Group Supply Council. I hear on all sides that they are most helpful and effective in the work of the council.

I deal with a personal matter on a separate sheet[1] in case you may wish to forward that part of my letter to some third party. With renewed thanks for your letter and your help to Indian interests. Yours sincerely,

Linlithgow

† The principal Hindu organization—Congress posing as an 'all-India' organization, and as speaking for all communities.

[1] Omitted by the editor. The writer wished to find a suitable holiday house in South Africa.

548   To G. R. Ellis   **Vol. 66, no. 149**

Pretoria
14 July 1941

My dear Ellis, I have just seen a copy of the letter[1] which M. [E. M.] de Simonin[2] wrote you on 12 July in reference to an article 'Vichy Fights for Germany'.[3] This article I had not seen before.

I wish to say that I am in full agreement with the spirit in which M. de Simonin writes to you. I do not believe that the attitude of the French towards Germany has changed. The nation is under brutal coercion, is hopelessly divided and distracted, but will (as before in history) recover their great spirit, and once more be our allies as they have continued to be our friends at heart. No purpose is therefore served by rubbing salt into their wounds, and adding to the bitterness and confusion which may exist. The speeches of Mr Churchill, and my own occasional references, have been continuously friendly to the French, and in some degree to Marshal Pétain. The French have their Quislings, but they are not representative of France, and long before the end will be turned down by France as soon as the opportunity comes.

Let us therefore be fair and generous, and avoid language and phrases and captions which only wound and embitter.

This is a word to the wise. Yours sincerely,

s. J. C. Smuts

549   To L. S. Amery   **Vol. 66, no. 167**

Pretoria
9 September 1941

My dear Amery, Thank you for another interesting and provocative letter.[4] You touch on very important points, and I can only refer to them in the briefest terms.

First the attack on Russia. Much calculation may possibly be behind this most surprising step. But we have also to bear in mind that Hitler is a fatalist, a somnambulist in outlook. Perhaps he has really reverted to his original outlook of intense hatred of Bolshevism and thinks his chance has come—now that he is really master of all Europe and only Bolshevist Russia still remains outside and a

---

[1] Smuts Collection, vol. 64, no. 110, enclosure.
[2] Arrived in South Africa 1932; was French consul-general in the Union 1934; *chargé de la légation* 1936; minister plenipotentiary 1937–40; left South Africa 1942.
[3] Published in the *Rand Daily Mail*, 10 July 1941.   [4] **544.**

menace. He may have such a contempt for the British effort that he simply ignores us and proceeds to eliminate Russia at this stage. If this is so, it is not very flattering to us. But looking at our past failures in Europe, at Libya, Greece, Crete, and North Africa, he may think that he is justified in showing his contempt for what Britain may still do. Having brought all Europe under his control, he may plan to say to us that he has no more concern about us, and is prepared to leave us alone, and carry on with his European empire. He may also plan a new peace offer, after having got Russia under his thumb. All this implies a very poor opinion of us, but he may have it, and not without some show of reason. Again, look at this picture from our point of view. Russia will probably be out of it within so many months, and we may have to face Germany alone—America still choosing to remain out. Is Hitler not justified in thinking we shall have an awful time? If Turkey falls to German threats, and Germany moves her immense forces through Anatolia against us, what have we to oppose her? What if a simultaneous move is made from Algiers and Tunis in the west, with French resources in north Africa pooled with German and Italian resources? He may have some such plan.

This is not a case for facile optimism, and we shall have to do some hard thinking and preparing while German land resources are still occupied in Russia. My suggestions are with Churchill.

Next, the most favoured nation clause. I largely agree with you. The economic weapon is part of our security scheme, and to open the door to German intrigue and fifth columns through that clause would be fatal. The democratic group will after this war have to keep this weapon in their own hands. I think this should and will be done. America will have to agree to limit the most favoured nation clause to this democratic group. The rest will be dealt with on their merits, not deprived of world markets, but neither treated on the most favoured basis. Don't you think this is the line to take? And it is well within the Atlantic Charter of eight points.[1]

Thirdly, Palestine. This is my addition to your list of points. We have got ourselves into a thorough mess over Palestine, and we must get out of it. The way we have dealt with Palestine and the Jews is no particular credit to British statesmanship. Isn't the way out now to deal with this question in conjunction with the new situation in the Arab world? We have promised independence to Syria and

---

[1] In August 1941 Churchill and Roosevelt met off the coast of Newfoundland and agreed upon a joint declaration of principles on which a democratic post-war settlement might be made 'after the final destruction of the Nazi tyranny'. Known as the Atlantic Charter, it contains eight articles. *See* A. J. P. Taylor, *English History 1914–1945*, pp. 534–5.

Lebanon;[1] we have guaranteed independence to Iraq. Eden has expressed his sympathy with Arab unity. Why not now put Palestine into this pot and brew something new and get out of impracticable White Papers and the like? Why not put Palestine into an Arab confederation on condition that it (the confederation) be open to Jewish immigration and equal rights in landholding and otherwise? The Arabs will surely be prepared to give a *quid pro quo* for a large Arab state or federation and the Jews would get a refuge from the persecutions of a mad Europe.

You have your preoccupations with Indian and imperial and war questions generally. But I know, like me, you are interested in the decent settlement of the age-long Jewish question, and I hope you will find some time to explore it with your colleagues in the F.O. and C.O.

I found Auchinleck a very live person and I hope he and Lyttelton [O.] will between them be able to move that huge administrative machine at Cairo. It will have to be done if we wish to save the Middle East from the wrath to come. I think it is within our power to give the Axis a fatal blow in that area. But we shall have to exert ourselves to the utmost.

I have the impression that Churchill, what with running parliament and government and the war and public opinion, is doing more than mortal man can do at his age. You may also use your great influence to great advantage in this direction. Hamlet without the Prince of Denmark[2] will be a poor affair.

But enough. This is already too long. All good wishes to you and kind remembrances to dear Mrs Amery. Ever yours,

s. J. C. Smuts

550 To A. A. Louw

Vol. 66, no. 166 A

Kantoor van die Eerste Minister
Pretoria
9 September 1941

Liewe Vriend Louw, U brief van 19 Augustus is onbeantwoord gebly omdat ek nog steeds gehoop het die vriendelike uitnodiging te kan aanneem. Nou op die laaste oomblik het dit onmoontlik geblyk en het ek 'n telegram gestuur om u dit mee te deel. Ek sou so graag

---

[1] The promise, in which the British government concurred, was made by General de Gaulle.

[2] Sir Walter Scott, in the introduction to *The Talisman*, refers to 'the play-bill, which is said to have announced the tragedy of Hamlet, the character of the Prince of Denmark being left out'.

persoonlik wil gekom het om die laaste eer te bewys aan die gedagtenis van Cinie—my liewe vriendin van lang verlore jare. Ek kan
nou nog nooit aan haar denk sonder 'n gevoel van liefdevolle smart,
as ek dit so mag uitdruk. Sy was 'n skone blanke siel en haar werk
volg haar na.

Die hospitaal sal nie alleen haar gedagtenis bewaar maar haar
werk voortset in die gees wat haar steeds besiel het—die gees van
opofferende liefde vir God en mens.

Ek sluit in 'n klein tjek as my persoonlike bydrae tot die hospitaal
en my klein steen in die gebou. Met baie hartelike groete en beste
wense, Steeds getrou die uwe,

                                                          J. C. Smuts

TRANSLATION

Prime Minister's Office
Pretoria
9 September 1941

Dear Friend Louw, Your letter of 19 August has remained
unanswered because I had hoped to be able to accept the kind
invitation.[1] Now, at the last moment, it has become impossible and
I have sent a telegram to tell you this. I should so much have liked
to come personally to show the last honour to the memory of
Cinie—my dear friend of long lost years.[2] Even now I can never
think of her without a feeling of loving grief, if I may express it so.
She was a beautiful white soul and her work goes on.

The hospital will not only preserve her memory but will continue
her work in the spirit which always animated her—the spirit of
self-sacrificing love for God and man.

I enclose a small cheque as my personal contribution to the
hospital and my small stone in the building. With very hearty
greetings and best wishes, Ever sincerely yours,

                                                          J. C. Smuts

   [1] To attend the opening of the Cinie Louw Hospital.
   [2] Francina Susanna (Cinie) Louw (q.v.). She and Smuts attended the same village
school at Riebeeck West.

551   To M. C. Gillett   **Vol. 66, no. 243**

Doornkloof
[Transvaal]
23 September 1941

I have just written the telegram of good wishes for Hugh and Helen.[1]
Looking at the date I saw it was the date on which I sailed in 1891
for Cambridge. What happiness in friendship and so much more
that voyage has brought me! I think of another voyage in 1905
which was another link in that chain, that growing chain of friendship.[2] And so may friendship's garland continue to weave itself till
the end—'till all the seas gang dry' as the Scots song has it.[3] Today
our thoughts and prayers are for the young couple who set out on
another great voyage. Fair seas and good luck for them.

Isie and I were watching two barbets enjoying themselves on the
garden in front of the house, now converted to a grass lawn on which
the small grand-children can play more suitably. It was a fine sight,
and we longed for Arthur to be here to witness the colour and joy of
the scene. Birds are surely among the happiest of God's creatures.
Even their search for food and their feeding seem to be occasions of
joy and happiness of which they make the most.

It remains dry here, so dry that the watering of gardens in Pretoria
has had to be curtailed and farmers sing a wail of woe. On the other
hand at the Cape it continues to pour deluges and the train services
in the far west have been seriously dislocated, even at places like
Paarl, Hermon, and Worcester. No wonder those parts are now
a real garden of Eden. People who have visited Namaqualand—and
they are many—say that the blaze of colours is indescribable and
that nothing like it has been seen in our lifetime. I remember passing
over that country in somewhat similar conditions when I went to the
German West campaign. But that was in April, not in September,
and the spring display must be so much more gorgeous than the
autumn show, though at that time (in 1915) I thought that nothing
could be more gorgeous and glorious. Surely it is all God. We call it
His works, but how distinguish between Him and His works. It is
all but the revelation of that mystery which lies behind and within
all—the mystery we are longing to identify and lose ourselves in, the
mystery of the Whole.

Since last I wrote to you I have done a little reading, as I have not

---

[1] Helen Bright Gillett married Arthur Hugh Gordon.
[2] *See* vol. II, p. 205.
[3]
> And I will luv thee still, my dear,
> Till a' the seas gang dry.

Robert Burns, *A Red, Red Rose.*

been sleeping so well (a small tummy trouble). Thus I got through a small book by Miss Verdoorn on the edible wild fruits of the Transvaal,[1] and *Kenya Chronicles* by Lord Cranworth[2] who was a settler there for thirty years. I also read Castle's Swarthmore booklet[3] and enjoyed reading it very much. It is full of good stuff and the tone and spirit are even better than the stuff. I think he makes too much of Protestant influence on the capitalistic system—in this following Tawney.[4] Capitalism is inherent in the rise and growth of our Western system, and would flourish under Catholicism and other forms of religion just as luxuriantly. It is largely due to the doctrine of the inner life and the neglect of social and economic factors in the New Testament—in conditions where the 'Coming' was expected almost daily and people did not care to bother over the things of this life. The saints in Jerusalem, after having eaten up their little in their communistic way of living, had to be kept going by Paul's collections from the Greek missions in the West. It is the neglect of the economic needs of society, inherent in the original message, which largely and, I think mostly, accounts for the free hand given to capital in the rise of modern Europe. One thing however Castle says towards the end of his booklet, which he has taken from Arnold Toynbee and which I think one-sided and dangerous. Toynbee says that in historic time human nature has not changed and is too permanent a factor to change, and all we can hope to do is to change and improve the conditions, the social and economic environment for others, so that they may have better opportunities for living the better life. I agree with the conclusion but not with the premise—that human nature is so fixed and unchangeable as all that. Nothing is more flexible and capable of change than human nature. All Christianity, all reform is ultimately based on that flexibility. 'Repent ye' as John the Baptist said, as Jesus said after him; μετάνοια, change of mind, change of heart *in the individual* is the basis of all real advance. And it was on this fulcrum that Jesus founded his Kingdom. I notice a strong tendency nowadays to ignore this basic truth—that the individual soul or personality is the point of departure in human regeneration—and that the reform of society and institutions is in comparison secondary and consequential. The pendulum has swung too far. We must begin with *ourselves* if we wish to start on the journey of reform; though of course we must proceed beyond ourselves to make the journey effective.

[1] Inez C. Verdoorn, *Edible Wild Fruits of the Transvaal* (1938).
[2] Published in 1939.
[3] Edgar Bradshaw Castle, *The Undivided Mind* (Swarthmore Lecture, 1941).
[4] R. H. Tawney, *Religion and the Rise of Capitalism* (1926).

I had a letter today from good Mrs Subbarayan in which she writes about Parvati calling at Cape Town and the sad vicissitudes of her family in the present troubles in India.[1] I have made such arrangements for Parvati as I can in our total ignorance of ships and dates. Somebody will keep a look out for her.

The Subbarayans are or have been mostly in prison in recent months—poor things. I don't approve the government policy, but neither can I approve the silly attitude of the Congress party which seems to lead nowhere and only to widen the breach between the various communities. It is a sad story, with mistakes on both sides. I do not like interfering, especially as I have already written my opinion pretty clearly to Amery. I may, however, write to Linlithgow now that I see his term has been extended to 1943.

Tomorrow I fly to Queenstown in the Eastern Province in order to open a congress of local public bodies and also to address the public. It will be a full day—half in office, and the other half flying to Queenstown, attending the two functions and spending the night there, flying back the following day. But people very much appreciate these appearances, and I do not often go to that part of the country. In fact I am now keeping an appointment made for September 1939 but which was suddenly made impossible by the outbreak of the war and the break up of the then government. What has not happened in those two years! Of course it is very difficult for me to move about the country and hold meetings as in bygone years. I am chained to my work as a chief of three departments,[2] one of which is war in all its ramifications. But something has to be done now and then to establish touch with the public.

You have had a breathing spell in England while Russia has had the full blast. But your turn is coming again. And ours in the north. Love and all good wishes,

Jan

[1] The Subbarayans became friends of the Gilletts during residence in Oxford. Their daughter, Parvati, had been a student in England and was returning to India. Dr Subbarayan was at one time premier of Madras and his wife a member of the round-table conference. He later became Indian ambassador to Indonesia.

[2] Smuts was prime minister, minister of defence and minister of external affairs. He was also commander-in-chief of the South African and Rhodesian forces.

552   From M. L. Ballinger   Vol. 64, no. 22

P.O. Rivonia
Johannesburg
13 October 1941

My dear General, I am making bold to send you a copy of a letter[1] I have just addressed, not too hopefully, to Colonel Stallard. I feel the principle involved in the question of a cost of living allowance for the Native mine worker is sufficiently important to justify my bringing my views on and my efforts in regard to it to your personal notice.

In my letter to Colonel Stallard, I have used strong terms in regard to the exclusion of the Native mine worker from the ordinary cost of living allowance. They are not really strong enough to express my sense of the injustice done to these fruitful and docile workers, and my own enormous sense of frustration that the government should, in the midst of a war for social justice, have yielded to the no doubt strong pressure of the mining industry to exclude these workers from the benefit of an obviously legitimate and highly necessary assistance. I know the sort of argument put forward by the industry in support of its claim that the Native mine worker does not need a share in the concessions so easily granted to other workers with political influence—that he is well fed, well housed and alto-gether well-off and does not need more money than he is getting since his family are provided with land on which they live; that the money he earns is 'found' money to his family, a mere subsidization of a comfortable and secure standard of living. And this argument goes down with quite respectable people ignorant of the true facts; while the Native affairs department contends increasingly desperately with the problems of overcrowding, malnutrition and general im-poverishment in the reserves where even the consumption crop, maize, has to be sold as soon as it is reaped to provide money to buy inadequate quantities of other foods and the clothing which the people cannot produce for themselves. And all these things have risen in price for the Natives as for the European, rises that come on top of prices which have always been higher for the man in a rural area far from the larger shopping centres than for his urban brother.

I feel particularly acutely what I cannot help regarding as the niggardliness of the mining industry to its best servants in view of the circumstance that since 1932, while literally millions of pounds have been given by the mines to their European workers as their share of post-gold-standard prosperity, nothing has been given to

---

[1] Omitted by the editor.

Native workers beyond about a half-penny increase in average wages and a few thousand pounds, often derived from the Natives' own money retained by the Deferred Pay Board, to social services which benefit the mines themselves as much as their Native employees. My husband has been engaged in a comparative analysis of the gains of the European and the Native mine worker in these recent years, copy of which I shall forward to you in a few days in the hope that you may find time to peruse it. I think it will convince you of the urgent necessity, if we are to be true to the cause that we have undertaken to support, of re-thinking our own problems and re-building some of our own house. My only hope that we shall see and meet this necessity is that of many other people in the necessities which they see with the same force as I see this one, namely your personal courage and strength, and your declared intention to see that we in South Africa live up to the spirit as well as the letter of the obligations we have taken on in the name of democracy.

Lest you should think me ungrateful for what is already being done in this regard, I feel I ought not to close this letter without acknowledging and expressing my deep appreciation of the generous and liberal attitude of Mr Sturrock in the matter of Native labour, expressed practically in quite substantial improvements in the wage rates and other conditions of service of the very considerable labour force employed by his department,[1] and of the adventurous lead that he gave last session, with your consent and support, in the matter of pensions; and let me say that I see these actions of Mr Sturrock's as only the most conspicuous reflections of a more generous spirit towards Natives which has been making itself felt increasingly since you took over the reins of government. I am only anxious lest our largest vested interest, which in the last resort dictates the pace of change in our labour field, should escape the mellowing influence of this new spirit; hence this appeal for your personal interest in the matter, made in the confident belief, I might say in the knowledge, that your attitude can and will decide that of the great majority of the people of this country. Yours sincerely,

Margaret Ballinger

[1] The department of railways and harbours.

553   To M. C. Gillett   Vol. 66, no. 248

Doornkloof
[Transvaal]
29 October 1941

No mail from you since my last letter, so I am thrown on my own resources in this letter. Ten days have passed since my last, which included a pleasant week-end with Santa [Weyers] at Rooikop and three busy days thereafter spent in entertaining their Excellencies the governor-general of Mozambique[1] and his wife and party. The entertaining was done at 'Libertas'[2] where we lived for the purpose. Tonight we are back to familiar and happy quarters in the Old Kentucky home. Our guests proved unusually attractive people— I hope they found us the same! Nothing could have been more cordial and indeed homelike and intimate than our living together those three days. In spite of their limited English—some members of the party were quite ignorant of the language of Shakespeare—we got on exceedingly well. I say 'in spite of', perhaps I should say 'because of'. For silence is often more helpful and soothing than conversation, especially when people are worked hard and enjoy just sitting together and occasionally smiling sweetly! Isie of course completely captured them. I could see the ladies of the party hanging on to her with evident affection and devotion. With regard to the field marshal their attitude was perhaps one more of respect and awe. They were dear people, as the good class of Portuguese usually are, and we enjoyed their visit as much as they themselves. Tonight they are in Johannesburg as guests of the government and will be sight-seeing for the next two or three days. I am sure the trip will do them good, and our official relations will be humanized on both sides. In welcoming them at the first official dinner I referred to the beautiful story of the wife of the Portuguese commander at Lourenço Marques who a hundred years ago nursed the dying wife of Louis Trichardt and other sufferers from malaria on their arrival from the distant Zoutpansberg.[3] It is a story the Boers will not lightly forget. But please tell me what will happen when next spring Spain and Portugal fall into the hands of Germany and Mozambique will be in the air? Perhaps Arthur could throw light on this subject.

The week-end at Rooikop was not as good as usual. It continues very dry there, and the poor animals wander about amid withered

[1] General José Tristão de Bettencourt, governor-general from 1940 to 1946.
[2] Official residence of the prime minister in Pretoria.
[3] Louis Trichardt, or Tregardt (q.v.), married Martha Elizabeth Bouwer, born in 1795, on 4 November 1810. She died on 1 May 1838. *See* T. H. le Roux, *Die Dagboek van Louis Trigardt* (1964) for an account of her last illness.

grass and ticks. I took no walk at all—which is most unusual, and shows how the general malaise affected me. The men are thrashing a very large wheat crop—the best I think and certainly much the largest we have yet had there. It was a sight to see the heaped-up sheaves over almost 500 acres of land. The thrashing will take many weeks, perhaps the whole of next month. And after that it has all to be taken by lorry to Pienaar's river station. Meanwhile all work has come to a stop at Doornkloof, as all the hands are engaged at Rooikop, and we suffer from great shortage of labour. At Rooikop I read through the *Acts of the Apostles* in English and the latter part of *Romans* in Greek. Paul sounds much better in Greek than in English, even though it is the Greek of Tarsus and not of Periclean Athens. It is very expressive and more easily understood. I find Paul's letters difficult to follow in English, easier in Moffat,[1] and easiest of all in the original. To me Paul remains something of an enigma—a hard-boiled Pharisee trained to all the Old Testament literalism of the pukka Jew; and yet a mystic of mystics, who not only saw deeper into the heart of religion than any other religious thinker, but also could express himself intelligibly in an alien language. I have read Schweitzer's book on Paul's mysticism,[2] without, however, finding answers to the questions I ask. I am sure to Paul it seemed all perfectly plain and natural, and as much axioms of religion as Euclid's of geometry. What seems to us figurative language was quite real to him. The 'indwelling Christ' was really dwelling in the believer's soul, and Jesus was the Son of God in quite a special and real sense. To me it is true and beautiful but in a figurative or rather transfigured sense: to Paul it was true literally. And yet he was no muddled thinker, but one of the clearest and deepest, even though one may not always exactly accept his logic. What in the truest sense did he mean by 'faith'? Love or charity which plays so great a part in his message I can understand; ἀγάπη is not what we usually mean by love, but some inner devotion which finds expression in service, benevolence, good will, brotherly and neighbourly feeling—something very intelligible and real in human relations. But his 'faith' seems to mean mere brute acceptance—against facts and against logic—the sort of thing which the old Schoolman put in the formula 'I believe because it is impossible.'[3] This of course is something very alien to our modern outlook, something most unsatisfying, but yet apparently descriptive of Paul's

---

[1] J. Moffat, *A New Translation of the Bible* (1934).

[2] *See supra*, p. 235, note 2.

[3] *Certum est quia impossibile est.* It is certain because it is impossible. Tertullian, *De Carne Christi*, ii.5.

outlook. 'The wisdom of the world is foolishness before God.'[1] If wisdom means what we call worldly wisdom or mere superficial science or clever sophistry I can understand and agree. But the wisdom which is real knowledge, science in the best sense, can surely never be foolishness in any real sense. But Paul's mysterious 'faith' seems to imply that this is so. Here I don't follow and rebel. But yet I feel that his spiritual insight pierced down to a very fundamental truth which my blindness cannot see.

The war is at a very critical phase. Russia is cracking, and although she continues the struggle it will no longer be the old Russia. Once more we have to face Hitler alone—unless the U.S.A. comes in at last and in time. I think next spring will be the moment of mortal struggle for us—with Germany all out against us, and America not yet in or ready. Is this the case for 'faith' in the Pauline sense—when every odd is against us and yet we cling to faith in our cause and final victory? 'Though He slay me, yet shall I trust in Him.'[2] Is this the Pauline faith? If so, I understand and agree. Ever lovingly and devotedly,

Jan

554   To M. C. Gillett   Vol. 66, no. 255

Doornkloof
[Transvaal]
13 December 1941

...During this eventful week great things have happened in the world. The treacherous attack of Japan on the United States fleet at Hawaii—with very serious loss to the latter.[3] The Japanese attack on the British in Malaya and Hong Kong.[4] The loss of our two big battleships on the coast of Malaya, and the loss among others of Admiral Tom Phillips in the *Prince of Wales*.[5] After the latter announcement a letter arrived from Phillips thanking me for the good time and talks I gave him at Pretoria some weeks ago. I don't know whether I told you that on Churchill's suggestion he had visited me on his way out to Singapore, and we had a night of very interesting talks at 'Libertas'. His letter came like a voice from the

---

[1] 'For the wisdom of this world is foolishness with God.' 1 *Corinthians* iii.19.
[2] *See* vol. v, p. 606, note 1.
[3] On 7 December Japanese aircraft made a surprise attack on the United States key naval base at Pearl Harbour.
[4] The Japanese invasion of Malaya and their first air raid on Hong Kong occurred on 8 December.
[5] The battleship *Prince of Wales* and the battle-cruiser *Repulse*, in an attempt to oppose the landings in Malaya, were attacked by Japanese torpedo-carrying aircraft and sunk on the morning of 10 December.

grave. I had formed a very high opinion of him. Again the same fatal mistake as at Crete where we lost four of our best cruisers in a fight with dive bombers against our fleet and our own aircraft were not there to protect them.[1] It is a sad business, and the results may be very serious. The Americans have not told us what their losses were at Hawaii,[2] and that in itself is a very bad sign. The Japs have scored heavily in their treachery and our remissness. I go into no further details which must form the subject of correspondence with Winston. But however bad this whole business is both for the United States and for us, it is more, much more than offset by the fact that at last the United States is in the war with us up to the neck and on to the end. This in itself is a guarantee of victory. At last we have a more or less united democratic front, and we can face the dictators with a totalitarian reply to their assault. Good news also comes from Libya, where the Axis is definitely on the run,[3] and from Russia where Germany has failed in her attack on Moscow and Leningrad, and must now retire to winter quarters, with the Bear on their heels.[4] I think it is this bitter Russian disappointment which made Hitler force Japan into the war,[5] although he must know what that must mean for him also in the long run. Russia has indeed been the greatest surprise of all. So far she has more than pulled her weight, and when we are ready to do the same, and the United States too, the end will not be far off. But we may have grievous losses and disappointments before that happens. We South Africans have suffered heavy losses in Libya, and so I am broadcasting on Monday night in connection with a renewed recruiting campaign to fill up the gaps in our ranks. Churchill sent me a wire today expressing his admiration for the brilliant part the South Africans have played in the Libyan battle. The higher command says their sacrifice has been the turning point in the prolonged battle. We have heard nothing from Jannie [Smuts], but his language is sure not to lack in force when we do hear from him! His division has borne the brunt of the hard fighting.

[1] *See supra*, p. 305, note 1.

[2] The main target of the Japanese bombers was the light battleships of the Pacific fleet. Of these four were sunk and three others badly damaged.

[3] On 18 November British forces under the command of Auchinleck began the attack designed to drive the Germans and Italians out of Libya. On 26 November they took Sidi Rezegh and relieved Tobruk but were again thrown back by Rommel. However, a renewed British attack had recovered the lost ground by 10 December and forced the Axis troops into retreat towards Gazala.

[4] On 6 December a Russian counter-attack under General Zhukov threw back the Germans from the environs of Moscow. By 10 December the Germans were in retreat from Leningrad as well.

[5] In fact, the attack on Pearl Harbour had been a surprise to Hitler.

Last night I gave an official dinner at 'Libertas' to the foreign ministers here. It was a pleasant and useful function. Most of the ministers are very good fellows, and their wives are certainly the better halves. The Greek lady[1] spent weeks or months in supplying the Greek troops with gifts and comforts in Albania—in all that atrocious weather. Last night we discussed Plato and Aristotle, and her complaint against them was that they had no real religious sense. That shows her measure. But this rambling must now end. Happy New Year to you all, and our affection in greater measure than ever.

Jan

555   To S. M. Smuts   Vol. 69, no. 115

Groote Schuur
14 Januarie 1942

Liefste Mamma, Net 'n reël met Jan, en ook 'n paar reëls vir Santa ingesluit.

Hier gaan alles biesonder goed—beide in die parlement en daar buite. Sylma is gelukkig en so ook die twee dogters. Klaas het dit hier by ons geniet en was 'n waardige figuur by die Opening. Sampie is ook heel gelukkig en geniet die verandering en die geselskap van Sylma en Daphne.

Ons was almal baie opgenome met jou groot ontvangs te Johburg laaste Vrydag en jou groot tjek. Ongelukkig het ons nie na die uitsaai geluister nie daar een of ander oponthoud tussenbei gekom het. Maar ons vreugde oor die eer, en die 'reflected glory' op die huisgesin was baie groot.

Die doctor sê my dat Innes nou op sy uiterste is en die einde kan in 'n paar dae verwag word. Lady Innes is ongelukkig ook siek in bed. Klaas het eers getwyfel of hy langer sou bly, om die begrafenis by te woon maar 'n saak neem hom van oggend terug na Bloemfontein.

Hier alles wel. Sondag was ons te Miller's Point vir 'n swem in die namiddag en te Kirstenbosch vir die oggend. Die kinders viral geniet sulke veranderings. Gister is ons groot debat in die Parlement begin, en het ek op Malan geantwoord. Die arme ou kêrel het maar baie gesukkel.

† Ons is nou reg op die spoor van die O.B. sameswering onder die polisie en eersdaags sal honderde vasgekeer word. Wat 'n land, en watter gevare al die tyd!

Gesondheid goed. Baie liefde.

Pappa

† Net vir jou en Santa.

[1] Princess Frederika (q.v.).

TRANSLATION

Groote Schuur
[Cape Town]
14 January 1942

Dearest Mamma, Just a line to send with Jan [Weyers]; and also, enclosed, a few lines for Santa [Weyers].

Here everything goes particularly well—both in parliament and outside. Sylma [Coaton] is happy and so are the two girls. Klaas[1] enjoyed staying here with us and was a dignified figure at the opening. Sampie[2] is also quite happy and enjoying the change and the company of Sylma and Daphne [Smuts].

We are all very pleased about your big reception in Johannesburg last Friday and your big cheque. Unfortunately we did not listen to the broadcast as some delay or other prevented it. But our joy at the honour and the reflected glory on the household were very great.

The doctor tells me that [Sir James Rose] Innes is now *in extremis* and the end can be expected in a few days. Lady Innes is unfortunately also ill in bed. Klaas was at first in doubt whether he would stay longer to attend the funeral but a case will take him back to Bloemfontein[3] this morning.

Here all is well. On Sunday we were at Miller's Point for a swim in the afternoon and at Kirstenbosch in the morning. The children in particular enjoy these changes. Yesterday our big debate in parliament[4] began and I answered Malan [D. F.]. The poor old fellow plodded along with difficulty.

† We are now right on the track of the *Ossewa-Brandwag* conspiracy among the police and hundreds will soon be trapped. What a country, and what dangers all the time!

My health is good. Much love.

Pappa

† For you and Santa only.

[1] N. J. de Wet, then chief justice of the Union. As acting governor-general he had to open parliament.

[2] Susanna, daughter of N. J. de Wet; born 27 July 1904; author of *An Hour of Breath* (1950)—an autobiography.

[3] Bloemfontein is the seat of the court of appeal.

[4] On the motion of Dr Malan that South Africa be converted into a 'Christian national' republic protected against 'the undermining influences of hostile and un-national elements'. *See House of Assembly Debates*, vol. 43, cols. 33 *et seq.*

556   Address (1942)   Box J, no. 147

This address was delivered by Smuts at a public meeting under the auspices
of the South African Institute of Race Relations on 21 January 1942 in Cape
Town. It was subsequently printed by the Institute as a New Africa Pamphlet
(No. 2) under the title 'The Basis of Trusteeship in African Native Policy'
(1942).

Mr Chairman, Mr Mayor, Your Lordship, ladies and gentlemen: I
am not going to address you in any of the capacities mentioned by
the chairman.[1] I thank him very much for the kind references to me,
but I am going to speak to you tonight as one of yourselves. I am glad
to be for one evening out of the political turmoil and I am not even
going to speak to you as a politician tonight. Don't expect any
message from me and don't expect any declaration of policy from
me. I am here tonight, like the rest of the members of the Institute
of Race Relations, as a student trying to explore one of the greatest
problems which face us on this continent. I am not here to make
a declaration or to lay down the law to you, but merely to exchange
ideas with you on a matter which I consider, of all, the most important to South Africa and to this continent of ours.

I have also another reason for being here tonight, and that is that
I want to show my appreciation for the good work, for the fine work,
which is being done by the South African Institute of Race Relations.[2]
Most of the workers in that Institute are people who lead busy lives
and have lots to do, but, notwithstanding this, they find time to
devote to this great subject which is, of all, the most important to us
in South Africa. They are giving their attention—their patient and
dispassionate attention—to this subject of race relations in South
Africa in order to discover the facts, to find out in a calm and
scientific way what the facts are. They have for the last ten years or
more been busy at this work. It is work I am sure, ladies and gentlemen, which is of the highest value for this country. It is work which
very few people are willing to undertake, but which must be undertaken. We shall have to take this subject of race relations—of the
relation between Europeans and Africans—out of the heated atmosphere of politics and controversy. We have to get down to the basis
of facts, the calm consideration of the facts, before we shall be able
to find a way out of the tangles in which we are. In the Institute, we
have a body of men and women who are doing this work and giving
their attention to this task, and I think we are deeply indebted to

---

[1] The chairman, Professor R. F. A. Hoernlé, referred to Smuts as 'a soldier,
a statesman, a thinker'.

[2] Founded in 1929 to study racial problems in Southern Africa and to work for good
will and practical co-operation between the various racial groups.

them for this work and for the amount of time and attention that they are devoting to it. It is, in my opinion, the only approach to, and the only way of arriving at, a solution. Years ago, when, as Rhodes Memorial Lecturer at Oxford University,[1] I was dealing with this Native question in South Africa, I pointed out that one of our main troubles is that we knew so little of the facts of this continent. Not only is it a 'dark continent' to others, but it is also a 'dark continent' to ourselves, as we know very little about the facts which concern us. I made the suggestion then that there should be a continent-wide survey of the position here in Africa; that we should try to find out through a calm, dispassionate and scientific inquiry what are the facts, so that we might have a sound basis for scientific judgment. That suggestion made many years ago was followed up. Funds were found for the purpose and you know that the result was the Hailey report. Lord Hailey was sent out with a mandate over the whole of this continent, to find out what are the facts about race relations as well as about other problems in this continent. His inquiry has resulted in his *African Survey*,[2] which is one of the most valuable documents which we have before us. If you want to know the facts about any part of Africa, facts which alone enable you to come to a conclusion, you will find them in that voluminous survey. But something on a more intensive and more intimate scale has to be done in South Africa, and the only body I am aware of that is doing this work is the Institute of Race Relations. Its officers and members are making inquiries in all directions into race relations, into conflicts that arise in this country, and into the rights and economic conditions of the under dog in this country. Ladies and gentlemen, they are doing that valuable work as a labour of love, as a labour in the cause of knowledge and science. I am sure that this work is necessary and essential in order to form a good judgment on race relations, and it will certainly bear good fruit. My presence here tonight is largely a tribute to the fine work which is being done by this body.

So much by way of introduction. I turn, now, to our great problem, the problem of the relation which should exist between Europeans and Africans if we are to have peace, if we are to have harmony, and if we are to have progress on this continent. This has been a problem for the last hundred years or more, and different answers have been given from time to time. It has been the great battle-field of public life in South Africa—to find the right answer to the question, 'What should be the relation between Europeans and Africans on this continent?' You have a school of thought which

---

[1] *See* **265**.   [2] Published in November 1938.

advocates equality; which says that the only proper relation is one of equality between Europeans and Africans, between white and black. There has been another school, based more on what might be called 'African realism'. It says there is a superior race, viz. the European race, and it bases its views, not on equality, but on the superiority of one race over the other. For a hundred years and more this controversy, this dispute, has gone on as to whether it should be equality or superiority; whether the one principle or the other is to be followed. Both principles have had their advocates. The whole subject has been fought out from end to end, but the debate has achieved very little result. It has produced very little good for this country of ours or for this continent.

More recently, another viewpoint has been urged and has come to the fore, viz. the viewpoint which is called 'trusteeship'. I am not sure who originated this idea in its application to South Africa, but I remember from my young days that Cecil Rhodes used repeatedly to say that the proper relation between whites and blacks in this country was the relation between guardian and ward. This is the basis of trusteeship. Whether Rhodes was the first to say so I do not know, but I remember that the principle was repeatedly urged by him. Much later, this principle of trusteeship was put into one of the great formal documents of the world, the covenant of the League of Nations. The celebrated article in the covenant of the League of Nations, the article which deals with the question of mandates, puts it this way: 'the lot, the advancement, the upliftment of the backward peoples is the sacred trust of civilization'.[1] There the word 'trust' was, for the first time so far as I am aware, put into a formal legal document of the world, and it may be that this is, if not the origin, then the first occasion where the word 'trust' was used in an international document, as affirming the relation between European and African to be a 'sacred trust of civilization'. That was in 1919. Since then the word 'trusteeship' has become usual both in Europe and in South Africa. You know how commonly people in this country talk of 'trusteeship' as the proper relation between the Europeans and Africans in this continent. Doing so renders one important service. It by-passes that barren controversy concerning who is higher and who is lower, that barren controversy between equality and superiority, which for a century and more produced nothing at all except ill-feeling and bitterness. The word 'trusteeship' brings in a new element: the language used by the covenant of the League of Nations is ethical, indeed is almost religious, when it talks of the 'sacred trust' which is imposed on the more

[1] Article 22.

advanced people to look after the more backward. I think that people do not realize what a notable advance it was to get to this idea of trusteeship.

But, although it was an advance, it still remains a very difficult subject. Ladies and gentlemen, we are here in the region of very great difficulties. Race relations are, most probably, the most contentious field in the whole range of human culture, and it has always been so since the dawn of history. There has always been a feeling between races, and here in South Africa you have this old primordial race-feeling accentuated under our conditions by another very great factor, and that is the factor of fear. The Europeans in this country, being in a decided minority—a small minority; having regard to the dimensions of this continent, I may say an almost insignificant minority—are victims of the motive of fear, which is a further complicating factor in the situation in this country.

Then you have this further difficulty, that whites and blacks are not equals in their levels of cultural advance. In our country, we have a more advanced and a less advanced race side by side, and although the beautiful word 'trusteeship' has been found to describe the situation, we have not yet found the right way of translating that word into better race relations in practice. But I say it is an advance and it does carry us some distance further.

However, there is another difficulty. I am trying to discuss round this subject in order to make you realize how intricate and how difficult the whole matter is for which we are trying to find a solution. In our day, in the twentieth century, the factor of race has very suddenly and very unexpectedly come to the fore in human thought and human relations. In the nineteenth century we were travelling a straight road in another direction. We were travelling away from narrow concepts of race and country towards something like international good feeling which was growing up between the peoples of the world. But, after the Great War, something very ugly arose in central Europe which has added to the difficulties of the problem that we are considering now. There was an upsurge of the idea of race. Race feeling became intensified: in fact, in National Socialism, or 'Nazism', you have the deification of race—the apotheosis of race. Race in central Europe has become not merely an idea, it has become a religion. Race in the Nazi ideology becomes something divine: your race is your God. You see, therefore, that the factor of race, which already had complicated our problem, now made that problem still more difficult to solve, in proportion as this German ideology has spread over the world. It has come to this country, too. Everywhere it has influenced thought and the trend of development on a very large scale, and we are feeling the effects of it here in South Africa, too. The immediate effect of this intensified, deifying form of race idolatry has led to the idea of a 'master people', the over-lordship of one people. It leads at once to that, and, therefore, you have in Germany, as an immediate by-product of this new ideology of race, the idea of a master people, the *Herrenvolk*—the chosen people who alone are fit to govern, and whom the rest have to obey. That is going back to the old discarded idea of slavery. But this intensified form of race doctrine that had its origin after the Great War in central Europe, has also had its effects here in South Africa. It has, once more, inclined people to accept and to consider favourably the old idea of superiority, of one people being superior to the other, which we have had in the past. Here in South Africa, as I have already reminded you, we have had as a complicating difficulty the motive of fear—the fear of the small minority that, if they do not assert themselves to the fullest and retain complete mastery, then their position will be in danger. That fear has been a profound motive, a profound influence on our views here in South Africa in the matter of race relations.

Attempts, as you know, have been made to get round this fear by the policy commonly called 'segregation'—the policy of keeping Europeans and Africans completely apart for their own self-preservation. We have tried to carry out this policy. Legislation giving effect to it has been placed on the statute book. But I am afraid, ladies and gentlemen, that there is very great disappointment at the result which has been achieved. Our fervent hope that fears would be allayed and that everybody would find his place—that whites and blacks would live happily in this country—has not been realized yet. The high expectation that we entertained of that policy has been sadly disappointed.

How can it be otherwise? The whole trend both in this country and throughout Africa has been in the opposite direction. The whole movement of development here on this continent has been for closer contacts to be established between the various races and the various sections of the community. Isolation has gone in South Africa and it has gone for good. Today, if you discuss a question like the Native question—the question which we are discussing tonight—you cannot look at it merely from the South African point of view. If you touch this question, you touch Africa, because in this generation this continent has made enormous strides—an enormous march forward towards contacts which we had never dreamt of. The continents have largely come together. There is no isolation today. We have opened up communications; we have interstate trade. We have movement from one part of Africa to the other and much of it to South Africa, with the result that a question such as we are considering tonight cannot be considered merely from the South African point of view. That simple viewpoint of long ago has gone, and if you consider this grave question which affects us here in South Africa, you have today to look much further afield. You have to see not only how our policy fits in with our conditions here, but how it fits in with the whole pattern of Africa.

There has been in recent years a migration of Africans to this country on a colossal scale. The attraction of South Africa for Africans in all the neighbouring countries almost up to the equator has been overpowering. There has been the lure of the diamond-mines ever since Kimberley was discovered, and the resulting migration of Africans was very much intensified by the discovery of the gold-mines on the Rand. I repeat, there has been this enormous attraction for Natives from all parts of the continent to South Africa. In the years before the war, when I had opportunities of travelling and often travelled in all directions over southern Africa, one of my most remarkable experiences was to see troops of young Native boys from all parts of South Africa on the roads leading to the Transvaal. The higher wages, the lure of this new world—it was an Eldorado to them—was attracting them, and, ladies and gentlemen, the result has been that there has been an inter-mixture of the various Native tribes and races, and of the population generally in South Africa which was never dreamt of before. Isolation has gone and segregation has fallen on evil days, too.

But there are other phenomena springing out of these conditions. You have what I may call the urbanization of the Natives. A revolutionary change is taking place among the Native peoples of Africa through the movement from the country to the towns—the movement from the old reserves in the Native areas to the big European centres of population. Segregation tried to stop it. It has, however, not stopped it in the least. The process has been accelerated. You might as well try to sweep the ocean back with a broom. It is going on all the time.

With this urbanization, we have had the phenomenon which we call 'detribalization'—the breaking-down of the old tribal traditions and culture and the authority of the chiefs. All these are breaking down far more rapidly than is desirable or good for the Natives of this country. It is the greatest revolution that has ever happened on this continent, and it is taking place right in our midst.

Lastly, we also have the industrialization of the Natives. They are forsaking their old rural culture, their old rural system of communal labour in their areas, and instead they are all flocking into industrial service in this country. The change is very far-reaching and no one even today sees the limits of it.

I mention all this, ladies and gentlemen, to make you realize the difficulties of the problem that we are dealing with. We have now in the face of all these facts, the detribalization of Natives, the movement of Natives into European areas and urban centres, and the movement of Africans into European industry—in view of all these complicated and novel facts, once more to answer the question: 'What is the proper relation between Europeans and Africans, between whites and blacks, and how does the idea of trusteeship fill the bill?'

How does trusteeship help us out of the difficulties of the problem we have to solve? There is a tendency amongst some of us once more to hark back to the old idea of superiority. You all know there is a dual aspect in this concept of trusteeship, because in a trusteeship you have a dominant person who is trustee for the other. You have the guardian, if I may say so, who has to look after his ward, and who has a superior position to his ward. The temptation, and a pretty strong temptation, too, still is to emphasize this idea of mastery, overlordship, and dominance on the part of the trustee. That is one aspect of the subject. But it is not the fundamental aspect.

The fundamental aspect is the responsibility which the trustee has towards his ward. The whole concept is meant, not for the benefit of the trustee, but for the benefit of the ward whom he has to look after. If the trustee exploits his ward, he breaks his trust, he denies his responsibility, he neglects the duty which rests upon him. But our position, in all the complexities I have mentioned and tried briefly to analyse to you tonight, ought to be quite clear. The whole idea of trusteeship is that there is a trust imposed on the European—as the covenant says, a 'sacred trust'. There is a trust on him and there is a responsibility placed on him. There is a duty placed on him to look after the interests of his ward—to look after the interests of the people who have been put in his trust—and I have no doubt in my own mind that this is the point of view, the underlying conception, of trusteeship which we have to put into practice. Difficult as it may be, that is the conception we have to make real if ever we are to have success and happiness in this country. There are helpless people on our doorstep and we are the trustees for them. We have to look after them, and if we do not do so we are breaking our trust.

It is an ethical question. At bottom one may say it is even a religious question. It is closely connected with our Christian ideals, and it even goes to the roots of human nature—decent, clean, good human nature. This sacred trust has been imposed upon us and we have to carry it out if we are to come to any good.

But, it is not merely an ethical or religious question. There is the question of interest too, because there is no doubt that, unless the guardian or trustee carries out his trust and advances the ward, whose interest he has to promote, he himself will in the course of time sink down to the level of his ward. There is, therefore, not merely the question of abstract ethics, but there is also self-interest in support of the ideal of trusteeship. I think our people—I am speaking now to the Europeans of this country—will have realized more clearly than they have done before that the old disputes about who is the boss and who is the under dog, who is superior and who is inferior, do not affect the question at all. They are just a tangle of barren words, and for a century we have made no advance with those ideas. We have to realize that, if any advance is to be made, it has to be made along the lines of this new concept which is embodied in the covenant of the League of Nations, which is in harmony with our religious and ethical ideas, and which is probably the only basis on which we shall see happy relationship established between Europeans and Africans.

But there is more. Ladies and gentlemen, I think we must take the long view in these matters. We must look ahead not merely for generations but for centuries. We have had in the past a fairly happy relation existing between Europeans and Africans on this continent. There have been misunderstandings and little wars, and no doubt, we have had several grievances which cried out for redress, but on the whole the European and the African have got on fairly well together. But the question is: if we do not fulfil our trusteeship—if we do not come up to the proper standard as trustees—whether in the end the Europeans will not have to pay a very heavy price on this continent for their neglect of duty. That is the question which we have got before us. I hope that the day will never come when there is alienation between whites and blacks in this country; when they will no longer look upon themselves as true South Africans standing by each other in the hour of danger—in the hour which may be much more dangerous than the one we are passing through now. It will be an evil time for us if ever the day comes when in the testing hour there is alienation, distrust and hatred between the two sections of mankind that Providence has placed on this continent. We shall have to work out honestly and sincerely the effects and implications of the idea of trusteeship. Leave alone the question of higher race and lower race. Simply look to your plain duty that lies ahead of you, and you will find that there is a lot we can do and should do to discharge our trusteeship.

Let us consider a few instances of what is plain duty in front of us. Take the question of education. We Europeans on the African continent have done something for Native education. Missionaries have made a point of it for generations now, and they have done a great deal. We recognize with gratitude the good work done by them. The government has slowly, tardily and haltingly followed and done its bit. But, if we honestly and sincerely ask ourselves the question, 'Are we doing our duty—are we fulfilling our duty as trustees—are we discharging our sacred trust?' I do not think we can lay our hands on our hearts and say we are doing it.

I have mentioned this matter of education for Natives, because in that line we are doing something, but we should do much more than we are doing. Let us take some other matters, such as health and housing. Now these are matters in regard to which we have done practically nothing. As a matter of fact, we are just beginning to make a start. So far, we have always looked the other way and given no thought to these helpless people. We cannot do that as trustees. The idea of trusteeship carries heavy implications and very serious duties. We shall as trustees have to look after the health and housing conditions, not only of our European, but also of our African, wards. We shall have to do it and we must do it.

I have stated it before, and I repeat it here tonight, that if there is one thing which we have to do in this continent, and do it soon, and do it thoroughly too, it is to look after the health of the Natives. There is a very heavy death-rate among Native children, and a serious incidence of sickness among adults which we cannot tolerate. If we want to see South Africa as a prosperous, contented and happy country, we shall have to tackle this problem without delay.

This continent is full of disease. I have seen it myself and I know it to be so. Years ago, when I was commanding the South African forces in east Africa, we required thousands and tens of thousands of Natives to do the transport of our army. In those days we did not have the motor transport or the mechanized units of today which have carried our forces like lightning through Abyssinia and Libya to swift victory. We had to have porters, and wherever I went through the length and breadth of that huge country, German east Africa, I had to comb the country for Native porters. They were difficult to find. The doctors usually informed me that, physically, they were not up to standard. Sickness, disease and general weakness were even then undermining the health of the

African race. The African is full of disease—much more so than the European—and, ladies and gentlemen, the Native forms a very large part of our population.

When people ask me what the population of South Africa is, I never say it is two millions. I think it is an outrage to say it is two millions. This country has a population of over ten millions, and that outlook which treats the African and Native as not counting, is making the ghastliest mistake possible. If he is not much more, he is the beast of burden; he is the worker and you need him. He is carrying this country on his back.

In connection with the health of the Native we shall have to do much more. It is, of course, difficult today when all our resources are locked up in the most deadly struggle that the world has ever seen. It is, therefore, difficult to make a move, but I do hope that with the years to come we shall provide health services in this country, not only for the Europeans, but also for the Africans, which will do justice to our duty as trustees.

We are beginning to make a move so far as houses for Natives are concerned. I think that the Native huts are very much better than some of the houses of Europeans. I think there is much to be said for the Native huts. I do like them very much more than the bricks and stones that we call houses. However, when you bring the Natives into the urban areas and when you plank them down in your centres of civilization, that is the time when all the insanitary conditions arise. We are only now beginning to attend to these matters, and I think the trustee will have to do very much more in the years to come than he is doing now.

There is also the question of feeding. I am not talking high politics—I am not talking of the franchise—I am merely talking of our plain, simple, Christian and civic duties as trustees. What are we doing about the feeding of the Natives? There is no doubt about it that conditions are arising today here in South Africa which cannot be tolerated for long, and if we connive at their continued existence, we shall have to pay a very heavy price for it in this country. We have made a start by giving milk to white and Coloured children, but I think it will have to be made much more of a public policy for both whites and blacks. Native children in urban areas have not yet had the benefit of this policy. In the old days the Natives had a more or less balanced ration, a balanced food supply. They had their mealies, but mealies alone are a bad thing. Incidentally, mealies were introduced from abroad. I was going to say they come from America, but now that we are all Allies, we had better not draw invidious distinctions! Together with milk, which the

Natives had, mealies supplied quite a good diet, but if you go to the locations today, you will find that milk is very scarce, and the Native children, when they are a couple of months old, are fed merely on mealie pap, which their mothers ram down their throats.

That is what is happening today, and the result is that nutrition conditions among our Natives, even in the rural areas, are steadily deteriorating. When you come to the towns the position is much worse. There you have the question of wages, poverty and, in addition, artificial feeding, which is not good, and the result thereof is the maladjustment which has now arisen. Ladies and gentlemen, unless we deal with the question very drastically, we shall have conditions in South Africa the results of which will be most lamentable.

Let us take the question of wages and living conditions of the Natives in South Africa. Leaving aside, tonight, the rural areas, the farms, and looking merely at the position in the big towns, all the evidence goes to show that, in general, the African cannot support his family in most places on the wage he is getting. Now what is going to be the result if those conditions continue? What services are given to them? Generally, our Natives for good and sufficient reasons, which I quite approve of, have been put apart in the urban areas; they have been segregated and given their own locations or townships to live in. But these areas are, generally, a good distance away from the town, and the Natives have to travel a long distance in order to get to their work, and they have to pay their own transport. In every way, conditions under which Natives live in our towns tend to be expensive and tend to make demands on them which their wages cannot carry. The result, ladies and gentlemen, is that conditions are arising which certainly cannot be tolerated. I think that we as a community and our municipalities ought to give far more attention to these matters; to extend a helping hand, to be sympathetic and to do far more than we are doing today. And even if we do not do it in the interest of the Natives, sooner or later we shall have to do it in our own interest. It will be to our good if we do it, because, if we do not, there will be something to pay.

Ladies and gentlemen, I have mentioned to you tonight some of the implications of this idea of trusteeship. We have accepted the idea. We have accepted it now as the basis of relationship between Europeans and Africans and we must now begin to carry out our obligations and do what we can. I have faith in this country. When I speak like this I am not merely blaming people. A certain amount of blame does rest on us as people and on the government as well. I admit that, but at the same time I am sure that deep down in the hearts of the people in this country there is a sense of justice and fairplay. Things have to be pointed out even if they sometimes involve politics. Even if they are unpleasant, they must be pointed out, because the pointing out will be helpful to people who mean to do the right thing if they see it. They will follow the light when they see it and I have the faith and the conviction that the people in this country—as in the past and even more so in the future—will rise to the occasion, and they will do their duty, so that conditions which are today lamentable, unwholesome and intolerable, will be removed and ameliorated in the days to come.

I think one of the factors that is going to be helpful is what is happening up north. There you have in northern Africa our people, white and black, European and African, together doing their duty to their country. I am told in all the accounts that reach me that there exists the happiest relation amongst them; that the South Africans are getting on very well, and there is the best of feeling between whites and blacks in that big army that we have up in the north. But, what has cheered me and what is very significant is the news I get that wherever our European South African boys come into contact, as they have repeatedly done on a very large scale, with black units and regiments from other parts of Africa, from central Africa, from east and west Africa and from Nigeria, they have liked each other and good relations have sprung up between them. The significant thing is that those Bantu and Africans from other parts of Africa who previously had looked upon us with suspicion, now say that they like the boys from South Africa. I hear this from many sources that come to me and, I repeat, it is significant. It shows that there is a good and sound basis to build on for the future of this country, if we will follow the light and if we will do our duty as trustees. I think what is happening up in north Africa, where the common task is shared by whites and blacks alike in the service of their country, is going to build up a happier relation—a more wholesome relation—and is going to be helpful in the building up of that South Africa to which we are all looking forward.

The European has a duty to this continent and we want that duty to be discharged. We want the European contact to mean for Africa, and South Africa in particular, a blessing and not a blight. We do not want ill feeling, hostility and alienation of races to arise from this great experiment which is being tried in our sub-continent. Let us, under conditions which I admit to be trying and difficult for a masterful people like the Europeans, try an experiment. They are very difficult conditions under which to try the experiment but I think it is possible. The great problem in the world today is to adjust race relations so that conditions of fairness, harmony and happiness will result. Our hope for South Africa, where we have both Europeans and Africans and where they will always be, is to build up a future pattern for Africa. Our hope and our faith is that both races will manage to live together in a spirit of helpful co-operation—in other words, that they will improve their relations so as to be helpful to each other, and on the basis of trusteeship see their future brighter as the years go by. I think that if we were to give a holiday to all the old ideas that have brought nothing else but division and strife to this country—if we were to by-pass this controversy under which there is no benefit any more, and if we were to come down to facts, and try out, to the best of our ability and with honest intention, this principle of trusteeship, we may build up that pattern of a new South Africa, variegated unlike the pattern of any other continent, but something worth having—a pattern which may be a lesson to the rest of the world.

557   To Abbé H. Breuil   Vol. 69, no. 117

Telegram

From: secretary for external affairs, Cape Town
To: South African legation, Lisbon
Dated 22 January 1942

Following from prime minister for Professor Abbé Breuil, address Service Géologique, Rica Academia da Ciencia, Lisbon, begins:

Your letter to van Riet Lowe. You are most welcome to our hospitality—you will work in archaeological bureau Witwatersrand University under van Riet Lowe. Salary £50 per month.   Ends.

Please be helpful to him in any arrangements for his transport to South Africa.

558   To M. C. Gillett   Vol. 69, no. 218

Cape Town
23 January 1942

While a debate is going on in the house in which I am not particularly interested I may as well occupy the time usefully in writing to you. I have been looking the last few nights before falling asleep into

Jan's Somali list[1] and have found it very interesting. It is curious how very close that flora is to our Transvaal flora—the genera almost all the same and often the species also. Jan collected at least fifty new species, which is quite a number for so brief a trip, and the total collection is a very large one and covers the widest range. It would have been an experience for him if he could have accompanied our forces in the Somali–Abyssinia campaign and could have made still further large additions. I was much attracted by what I saw on the trip when I visited our forces on the Somali border, as I told you at the time. Now I suppose neither he nor I are ever likely to visit those scenes again.

Pole-Evans writes me that he has been with Miss Verdoorn to the Krantzberg in the western Waterberg[2] 6841 ft. high and somewhat to the south-west of the Bokpoort gorge which we visited years ago. I am anxious to visit this mountain and collect on it and Pole-Evans was to make a preliminary survey. He found it very interesting, with miles and miles of *Pterocarpus* ('goldener than gold') on the way to it in full bloom. The mountain is not difficult to climb and from it rises the Matlabas river. They found a number of plants, some of which must be new. From it on the west there is the deep depression of the Limpopo river and the scenery is very striking although the flora is on the whole xerophytic. Maybe I could get away for a week-end after the session and climb it—somewhat higher than the Mauchsberg near Sabie where we made the great montane collection years ago. The mountain is 75 miles from Warmbaths—140 miles from Pretoria and is reached in less than five hours by motor. By the way, we are also now going on to petrol rationing, but we allow 400 miles per month, and so treat the public quite generously for the present. We may have to reduce later.

This week I opened the meeting of the Institute for Race Relations[3] in a large meeting in the City Hall here and could thus give the Institute a bit of a push. They are doing quite good work for our Africans and Coloureds as you know. My address was well received and much commented on in the press. I made an appeal for getting away from the old political battleground and the fight over equality or superiority, and in a true spirit of trusteeship to attack the practical problems before us, such as education, health, housing, feeding, wages and conditions which are now (with the urbanization and detribalization of the Natives) rapidly becoming acute. I could point to the barrenness of the old disputes, and the wider African horizons now opening out before us, the migration of the African

[1] Jan Gillett was sent by Kew herbarium in 1932–3 to collect plants in Somaliland.
[2] In the central Transvaal.　　　　　　　　　　[3] **556.**

which has the dimensions of a great revolution and which is giving rise to quite a new economic and social situation, full of perplexing and dangerous problems if allowed to drift. A new constructive out-look and the necessity of a more earnest and sincere facing of the situation were confronting us, and chaos if we failed to cope with our task. The factual scientific outlook which I had advocated at Oxford in 1929 and the dropping of the old political shibboleths had become necessary, and the time had come for positive action. This policy was well received and will I trust become the programme for the future. Hertzog's segregation policy has proved barren and has created more problems than it promised to solve. Of course, everybody in this country is agreed that European and African should live apart and preserve their own respective cultures. But much more than that is called for today in the new Africa.

The war in the Far East continues to develop with alarming rapidity. New Britain (at the end of New Guinea) has been occupied by the Japs and I suppose next they will take New Guinea, and so be near the northern door of Australia. Most of Malaya is already lost and the retreat continues unabated. Soon only Singapore will be left, and it may then not be much use to us unless we can re-master the straits of Malacca. Burma and the Burma road are not out of danger. We don't know much of what is happening in the Philippines or Dutch islands. It is not a bright situation, and I suppose will continue so for months yet. The Australians have good reason to be nervous. Wiser than they, we kept our men in Africa and can do all in our power to hold the home continent. I still believe that great danger threatens us in north Africa and the Middle East. In any case our South African forces are well placed to help to meet any coming danger in that quarter. What a fine, clean, nippy performance Bardia–Sollum–Halfaya has been! We are proud of that record. Jannie writes from Halfaya where I suppose he had to do his share in the dangerous work. For the moment we are stuck at Agheila.[1] But soon the South Africans will be there and things will begin to move. I only regret that I am held here and cannot visit my gallant men in the north.

Off and on during the last fortnight I have been reading Seeley's *Ecce Homo*,[2] and have enjoyed it very much. Even the bookmark of your mother (a Christmas card!) is still in the book, which she got in 1865. This makes the book doubly dear to me—I now reading it

[1] The British forces subdued German garrisons cut off at Sollum, Halfaya and Bardia in Rommel's retreat to Agheila where, however, the Germans stood fast.
[2] First published in 1886.

in 1942! I read it first at Cambridge and enjoyed it, even more now after fifty years. Seeley had a much deeper insight into the real meaning of that great movement than Renan, in spite of the latter's much greater scholarship and knowledge of biblical times. Seeley describes the drive behind the new religion as the 'enthusiasm of humanity' or the passion for humanity which characterized Jesus. Jesus had not only the insight of great genius into spiritual values but the spiritual energy which springs from passionate devotion, and which he could communicate to his followers and burnt like a flame in their hearts too. I describe it as the Vision of God, and the desire for God which he translated into terms of love. The New Testament is really the new Vision of God and the New Testament of love. It is curious how real the Gospels become to us now, with all the wracking experiences of our generation. Once more we are sounding the depths and reaching to the real foundations below the veneer of our modern outlook and culture. The social Gospel of Jesus still remains the standard and ideal for us to work up to, and like all ideal standards will never be reached, but will always exert its pull on our hearts and minds. And what authority: 'Follow thou Me!' Who ever spoke like that!

Isie and the family arrive on Monday and although she hopes to have a rest a heavy programme awaits her—poor dear. But we are well and happy. Love from

Jan

559   To M. C. Gillett   **Vol. 69, no. 219**

Groote Schuur
[Cape Town]
31 January 1942

...I find a family round me very healing and satisfying and often wonder just what the physical or psychological explanation of this phenomenon is. Somehow, in a mysterious way, the friction gets drawn out of the functioning of the machine, and normal conditions and peace reign once more. The noise of children is quite unlike any other noise, and if they happen to be your own, why, the noise becomes music!

On Saturday morning I wanted some exercise and asked Daphne [Smuts] whether she also felt so inclined. She is an excellent walker, and so we set off, going straight up to the contour path above the vegetable garden, and from there south along the path until we reached the bottom of the Saddle; then up the Saddle to the neck, and down the other side towards Cape Town until we once more struck the contour path, and so round the northern part of Devil's Peak until we once more reached the Groote Schuur gate under the nose, and on to the house once more. It was a good stiff going up, and down, and on the level for four full hours. Daphne later admitted that she inwardly prayed for journey's end, and the police also admitted that they had had enough. I felt fine and refreshed and was glad to think that I was still capable of such a sustained effort. All the week thereafter I have noticed no evil results.

This was on Saturday; and on Sunday [Sir Godfrey] Huggins the prime minister of Rhodesia arrived to stay with us and we were glad to have him. It seems as if we have now to carry all the smaller fry of Africa on our backs. In years gone by they looked to Europe for their supplies, but now that that prospect has failed they crowd in on us, and we have to do our best with the very limited supplies at our disposal. There is this season a great shortage of various articles of food owing to the strange freaks of the weather; and as a result there is dangerous shortage for which they look to us. I make a point of it to help as far as we can, and a little farther, mindful of the advice of Scripture to cast your bread upon the waters.[1] We are quite popular nowadays, and hope that something greater may be built on these foundations in the future. The Portuguese and British colonies, Congo and French Congo are all in this plight. They may yet be in the net. I am working on some such plan as that of the Pan-American Union[2] of our Yankee friends. After all, the day for these pygmy units are past, and Hitler has at least proved that. Perhaps he will also prove that there are some large dangerous units for which the world equally has no time!

Since beginning to write this letter I have had letters from Arthur and you—both most welcome. Arthur's as usual full of war. Yours on the other hand looks away from war. You are like the Pharisee who has no eye for this ugly thing on our roadside.[3] And so you tell the story of home affairs, of the dear small things which we sum up as 'life goes on'. I believe in 'life goes on'. It sounds so cheerful; it by-passes so much that is painful or insoluble. And after all why knock our heads against things beyond our control? Does wisdom not consist in accepting the inevitable? 102 is a more cheerful topic than the Far East. I agree, but still it is pleasant to hear Arthur on

[1] 'Cast thy bread upon the waters: for thou shalt find it after many days.' *Ecclesiastes* xi.1.

[2] Founded 14 April 1890 at the Pan-American conference at Washington to further the movement towards economic and political co-operation among the twenty-one republics of North, Central and South America.

[3] *See St Luke* x.30–6.

the war. The inevitable also has its attraction for us. To me now-adays it has the melancholy attraction of proving what I predicted. Practically everything happening now in the Far East was predicted by me, put on paper, passed on to the responsible quarters, who no doubt put the tiresome stuff in the patient pigeon-hole. But there the ugly thing once more is, out of its pigeon-hole! If the British fleet at Singapore and the American fleet at Pearl Harbour had been together somewhere in the Pacific Japan might never have ventured into this war, at least not now, and both we and America would still have had our big battleships, now at the bottom, and the prospect before Hitler would have been one of unrelieved gloom. First Japan has a great innings and Hitler need not only think of the second Moscow. In north Africa the same thing is happening. But why weary you with this subject? Rommel once more plays with us and drives us out of Benghazi[1] after having had to flee from it not so long ago without even venturing to fire a shot. It is difficult to make general staffs realize that we are once more in the Boer War, only more so. Movement, mobility, fight and run, stratagem and ruse are again the order of the day—with the aeroplane and tank added. But people will still live in the days of the Great War and follow the rules of that obsolete game. To me it is all intensely interesting as a revival of vivid old experiences of my youth, which the young people of today have now to relearn for themselves.

Churchill has done great work in America, interspersed with some fine speeches; and now he has had his debate in the commons and had his great motion of confidence. All interesting to read and to contemplate as a human drama. But to think of all his energy thus absorbed, and taken off the grim business of war which is his real job. Democracy does really involve a cruel waste. How can a man find time and proper concentration for some of the hardest and most fateful problems of all time, when he has continually to pause and prepare for and make speeches which surely involve an immense amount of physical and mental energy? I think not so much the war as his own people are consuming him, literally eating him up, and I fear he will not stand this cruel process for too long. The one in-dispensable man in the war used up in order to pacify the qualms and impatiences of his people. Surely there is something wrong in all this. He, being a great orator may not mind it, but *I* do, and I could dispense with many of these brilliant oratorical displays if I knew that the time thus saved would go into thinking and planning for the war and its aftermath. Sitting through a three days' debate and

[1] On 21 January Rommel began a counter-attack which, by the 29th, had forced the British Eighth Army to abandon Benghazi and withdraw eastwards.

having to make two big speeches in it is really not a fair deal either for the man or the nation![1]

I can find no time for reading nowadays. At the end of a long day one feels so exhausted that even if there are some vacant moments you let your mind just lie fallow. And so I do not trouble you with the things of the spirit. Do you know the 'Song of the Shirt'—where a woman goes on stitch—stitch—stitch—in hunger, poverty and dirt?[2] I feel my lot is much like that poor woman's, perhaps a little harder, as this poor patchwork on which I am engaged belongs to a more difficult realm than that woman's shirt. But I have found no way of so arranging my affairs and economizing time that this constant pressure and drain on one could be divided. So one just goes on mechanically, and in the end loses that joy of work which is the labourer's real reward.

This is Friday evening. Tomorrow I fly to Robben Island[3] to inspect defences and see that everything is in order. Isie wants to go with me, but I won't take her as we have now a non-stop south-easter,[4] and I fear she will be horribly sick if she goes, and perhaps also get one of her bad bilious attacks lasting some days...

560   To M. C. Gillett   **Vol. 69, no. 221**

Groote Schuur
[Cape Town]
11 February 1942

...We have had General Sir William Platt with us for a few days—he commanded in Eritrea and at the battle of Keren,[5] and now in Kenya and Abyssinia. He proved a favourite with the family, which pleased me, as I have a high opinion of him. We gave him a good interesting time here, short as it was, and I hope he has carried away good impressions from his first stay in South Africa. Next week Sir Philip Mitchell, former governor of Uganda and negotiator of the agreement with Haile Selassie, will be here to explain to me the details of the arrangements come to. It must have been a difficult affair, as the Negus put his claims very high, without having a correspondingly strong position in his country. In fact scarcely half the country follows him, and his position may be disputed by

---

[1] In a three-day debate in the house of commons (27–9 January) Churchill called for a vote of confidence which was given him by 464 votes to 1.

[2] A poem by Thomas Hood (1799–1825).   [3] In Table bay.

[4] The prevailing summer wind in the Cape Peninsula.

[5] At Keren, in Eritrea, stiff Italian resistance was encountered in early February 1941. It fell on 27 March.

others unless British bayonets keep him on his throne. But I shall hear more from Mitchell. This being my day for some exercise I absented myself from office and climbed with Japie [Smuts] the branch of Constantia berg which just overlooks Constantia Nek. It took us an hour to reach the top, and proved a most pleasant climb, amid flowers and a great variety of greenery. We were back after a most enjoyable two and a half hours...In the afternoon Pole-Evans and I had a good look at the grass pastures he has established in the upper reaches of Groote Schuur estate and I was much impressed by his work. We are clearing large patches of pine trees and putting in grasses as we both dislike the pine thickets which uselessly cover the estate and cut off the view of the lower reaches of the mountain which forms the chief glory of this place. Besides, much soil erosion is resulting from the bare areas beneath the pine trees which kill off the vegetation cover and cause a rapid run down of the rain on these steep slopes. I hope in time we shall once more have grassy slopes with sparse silver trees in place of these useless horrid pines the planting of which in the Peninsula has been a calamity. Nothing can be finer than our indigenous mountain vegetation, nothing more ugly than the monotonous imported flora of the pine tribe. The pine in particular has shallow spreading roots which kill everything underneath.

Sunday 15 February. This morning we went again to 'Christian' beach at Muizenberg for a bathe in most delicious water, and the rest of the Sunday has been spent quietly in my room, reading despatches and writing some for London and Washington. I have been looking through messages and reports of some months ago, and it is interesting to watch the rapid kaleidoscopic changes of the war scene. Just at the moment the aspect is pretty grim. But so it must be for the enemy when he surveys his prospects for the spring and summer. On the whole there is not much to choose between us, with the distant prospect distinctly in our favour.

The passage of the German warships from Brest through the Channel[1] has been an eye-opener to the British public, following as it does on the loss of our great ships in Malayan waters.[2] There is an element of luck in all this, but one cannot help thinking that there is more careful planning and preparation on the German side. Of course, that is their strong point, while we have ours in other

[1] On the night of 11 February the battle-cruisers *Scharnhorst* and *Gneisenau* and the cruiser *Prinz Eugen* left Brest and reached their home port by way of the English Channel on the 13th. They all suffered damage, mainly from mines, and were temporarily out of action.
[2] *See supra*, p. 327, note 5.

directions. But both air and naval authorities must feel pretty chastened after the German passage through the English Channel which they carefully avoided in the last war. It shows what an enormous difference the possession of French coast ports and aerodromes has made in their favour. I suppose the press will once more start a hue and cry for the reorganization of the war cabinet as the cure for these ills, and Churchill's position will be secretly challenged by his enemies. But whatever the organization we should face open-eyed the position in front of us, which is one of grave danger and very heavy responsibilities. The Russian advance has at the same time slowed down almost to a standstill, and in north Africa Rommel may resume his initiative while in the Far East Japan is knocking her way into Singapore and occupies most of the Dutch towns and bases of importance. But the tide will turn, and I imagine the next round may go in our favour, especially if we can get some of the big American warships into the Far East. I note that in the Far East both the land and sea commanders are Dutch[1]—of course under the supreme command of Wavell. That is a great tribute to our Dutch friends who so far come best out of the ordeal in the Far East.

Here our fifth columns are still busy, and a good deal of sporadic bombing and sabotage is still going on. There is good reason for thinking that this pro-German effort is stimulated and financed from Berlin. That also is our information from American sources. I have however no doubt that we shall keep the upper hand as we have it and that in the end most of these so-called patriots will be locked up and out of harm's way.[2] That is the most merciful way one could be with such misguided, and in some cases treacherous, folk. What a topsy-turvy world this is—when people who want an independent republic can be furthering the cause of Germany and Japan, who are the least likely of all to grant their claims. The furthest these powers go is to appoint Quislings and the like. However there is not much chance for them in South Africa. I hear the latest attempt is to bring together all the discordant opposition elements under Hertzog, who will, as a sort of Pétain, serve as a cover for the other leaders who have failed. Hertzog has already publicly declared for national socialism as the best régime for South Africa, and he may therefore be induced once more to enter the lists against me.[3] It is a tragic situation for the old man, whose failing powers have not diminished his vanity and his feel for a 'call' from

[1] Major-General H. Ter Poorten and Vice-Admiral C. E. Helfrich (qq.v.).
[2] For the number of persons interned and the nature of their activities *see* W. K. Hancock, *Smuts—The Fields of Force*, pp. 338–40.
[3] Hertzog did not return to public life.

the people to lead them out of the mess into which I have led them. Old age can be very pitiable and unlovely, and I shall have to keep a close watch on myself! The urge to rule seems to grow with age. But in my case the urge seems to be the other way.

I have been continuing to read Glover's *Disciple*[1] which you and Arthur so kindly sent me. It is a very pleasant book to read, and with his knowledge of the Graeco-Roman world he throws a good many sidelights on the New Testament story. To me the marvel is the intense *passion* and fire that there was in that movement, and remained in it for so long. Seeley (*Ecce Homo*) talks of the 'enthusiasm of humanity' as the keynote of the mission of Jesus. But 'enthusiasm' is a poor word for that intensity of spirit that moved people's souls. It was more like the burning bush, which never was consumed.[2] The love of God for man and all it implied and set going was certainly the most enormous force that has ever been released in human affairs. And in the centre of this fire stands the calm, quiet figure of Jesus in all his majestic authority. He seemed to set everybody round him on fire while himself remains at perfect peace—the centre of quiet in a raging tornado. Paul's letters prove how men were roused and moved and fired to their inmost depths.

Is that the real dynamic to which we must look for world reform? Must religion once more take the lead over economics and all the other urges in our world? The situation today is so much of a parallel to that of Rome in the Christian era that one stands amazed at the solution presented in the New Testament and asks what is its message for us too. I have never before so felt the significance of Jesus's message as in our times when a much greater civilization than that of Rome seems to be in the balance. Of course we could never go back to the primitive conditions and society of the New Testament. But have we not there the pointer to the way out of our sad plight? Has the Gospel not a vital message for us? And what of Jesus? Is the Gospel the answer to this war? But I must end. Love to you all.

Jan

[1] T. R. Glover, *The Disciple* (1941).   [2] *See Exodus* iii.

561   From L. S. Amery   Vol. 67, no. 7

India Office
Whitehall
13 February 1942

My dear Smuts, I think the Lease Lend[1] difficulty is now being happily solved on the understanding that article VII does not commit us in advance to the abandonment of preference, but only to the general discussion of the subject in the spirit of the Atlantic Charter. To that I have no objection. If, as the outcome of the war, there should emerge a free trade world, then clearly there would be no case for preferences of any kind. If it should be a really low tariff world, then likewise preference would naturally be limited in scope and character, say to special products which one or other part of the Empire wished to get on to a permanent footing, like South African wines. If, on the other hand, we find that we shall be after all entering upon an era of controlled economics, and the United States reversed the present trend in their economic policy, then we retain and may develop an instrument of great possibilities both for protection of our existing position and for economic development for all of us in the Commonwealth.

Singapore has been a tragic disappointment.[2] I am afraid it is simply a case that those who deliberately prepare for war, whose troops are intensively trained and as avid for battle as a swarm of wasps, have an immense advantage over those who have put war out of their minds, both in preparation and psychologically. It looks as if we were at the eve of very great changes in the relation of Asia to Europe. It will not be all roses for us if we finally defeat Japan, largely with the help of Chinese armies. Indeed the whole question arises whether in the future empires like our Asiatic empire, based on a very low degree of militarization and interference with the life of the people, can subsist. Is not the possible and not too pleasant alternative that these peoples should either militarize and industrialize themselves, as the Japanese have done, or be tyrannized and exploited in the fashion in which Japan is running 'Manchuria'.

However, sufficient for the day, and meanwhile, even if the area of trouble in the East extends, I think our gathering naval strength in the Indian ocean and that of the Americans in the Pacific ought

[1] The Lend–Lease Act (11 March 1941) empowered the president of the United States to take any necessary steps to ensure the shipment of vital materials to Great Britain. It was followed by a mutual lend–lease agreement between the two governments for the exchange of 'defence services' signed on 23 February 1942.

[2] The Japanese attack on the island of Singapore began on 8 February. On the 15th the British forces (85,000 men) surrendered.

presently to tilt the scale. But it will be a slow business if we should lose Burma and Ceylon and had no naval base to work from in the Indian ocean east of Durban. I trust this is much too pessimistic a speculation but we must be prepared for all possibilities. Yours ever,

L. S. Amery

562   To J. Martin
Vol. 69, no. 124

House of Assembly
Cape Town
26 February 1942

Dear Martin, Thank you for your note of 21 February re missing profits.[1] What you say is welcome. I showed your note to Hofmeyr who is also pleased. He happens to be discussing this very question with Stallard.

I do not propose to show your letter to Stallard unless you authorize me to do so.

All going well here. I wish I could say the same for the larger scene. The appointment of [Sir Stafford] Cripps is a daring move by Churchill.[2] Cripps has an indiscreet tongue and has more than once said outrageous things. I hope he has learnt discretion. I am told that a quite recent speech of his (in favour of Russia) created a wide commotion on the Continent.

But Churchill is hard pressed and probably has no choice. He could not possibly continue to carry the burden of leading the commons in addition to his other more pressing duties. I myself find parliament a sore trial in the midst of all the other far more urgent claims. It is my constant fear that Churchill will break down, and there is none to replace him. I do not know how Roosevelt does his work. I suppose he too is vulnerable, and probably has more fragile health than Churchill.

Men, men, men—that is our fundamental need in this crisis. Kind regards. Ever yours,

J. C. Smuts

[1] Smuts Collection, vol. 69, no. 124. Martin advised against curtailment of development in the gold-mining industry, which would mean higher immediate working results, on the grounds that it would be too difficult to put into practice and might create political difficulties.

[2] Churchill reduced the war cabinet from eight to seven members and included Sir Stafford Cripps (q.v.) as lord privy seal and leader of the house of commons.

563   From Lord Harlech   Vol. 68, no. 10

Personal   High Commissioner's Office
                                                        [Cape Town]
                                                       5 March 1942

Dear Prime Minister, The draft of the 'political' declaration to
India[1] such as you suggested a few weeks ago, and which, like you,
I have long thought to be necessary and inevitable is pretty sen-
sational in its phrasings. I refer, of course, to the explicit statement
that Dominion status involves the free right of secession from the
Commonwealth. Personally, I have always believed that such a right
was the inevitable consequence of the equally inevitable Statute of
Westminster, and have never shrunk from or feared it. Its formal
recognition by the United Kingdom government will be a bitter pill
for old Stallard and the Dominion party here, with whom I got into
a bit of trouble for saying something to this effect, thought necessary
then wrapped up, in a speech I made at Port Elizabeth last year.
Frankly I'm glad it has come to this, and 'circumlocution' will no
longer be necessary. Each partner in the Commonwealth has now its
own absolute destiny in its own hands without any legal or constitutional impediments.

After the Indian declaration it will be interesting to see whether
De Valera will equally formally declare his secession and proclaim
a republic.[2] His secession has already been *de facto* though not *de
jure*, but I fancy he will shrink from the ultimate step of declaring
a formal republic and so making all Irishmen *ipso facto* aliens in
Great Britain!

The other gain in the Indian declaration is that it throws upon
Indians and not on the United Kingdom parliament, the drafting
of their constitution. This move has clearly been overdue. I found
the long conferences and debates on the Hoare–Willingdon reforms
intolerable and unreal and am glad that chapter of errors has been
closed.

The doubt in my mind is that the declaration has come too late in
time, and has in truth only come about by our ghastly collapse in
British Malaya and Singapore.

I should like, if I may some time, to see a copy of your reply and
comment when you have sent it.[3]

---

[1] The British government undertook to create, as soon as possible after the war,
a self-governing Indian Union with Dominion status, a constitution of its own making,
and the right to secede from the Commonwealth.

[2] Eire formally became a republic in December 1948.

[3] On 6 March Smuts wrote as follows in a letter to M. C. Gillett: 'A declaration
about India's future is at last coming, but much too late, in spite of my strong earlier

I suppose Malan and Co. will raise the consequence of the declaration in parliament here.

Harlech

564   To M. C. Gillett

Vol. 69, no. 224

Groote Schuur
[Cape Town]
10 March 1942

Two letters from you both since last I wrote: thank you both. Arthur refers to the Russian successes and to British staunchness in the crisis. A caveat in regard to both. I think there may be a tendency to magnify the Russian recovery, welcome as it is. I do believe that the German high command has withdrawn very large forces from the front to rest them for the spring and summer offensive, and that the Russian successes are in part due to their having to deal with a weakened front. The risk is that the Russians are getting tired out by continual fighting under the most awful climatic conditions and that meanwhile their opponents are largely recuperating for the great effort ahead. I therefore feel some concern about what may happen when the Germans go all out against Russia in their next offensive. We must not build all our hopes on Russia—the disillusion may be very great. Russia has been a godsend to us so far, but in the end it may be we and America that will have to see the grim and terrible business to a conclusion. This is just a note of warning against too much Russian optimism.

As regards the firm temper of Britain I do accept that and hear this from all sides. But since you wrote the whole East has gone and only Australia remains. Churchill has had to make a reshuffle which is not much of an improvement. Public restiveness is on the increase. Cripps is very much of a dark horse and he is the only substantial change. I don't see faith-inspiring men coming forward, and the changes are still rung on the old tune. America, like the waves in Clough's poem, advances so slow, oh so slowly.[1] The Libyan business has again been disappointing and our men don't measure up well to Rommel. I don't think there is any crack in the national temper, but

advice. I wonder how the new statement will be received. I have sent severe comments which I fear will not be acted on. Why can't they act swiftly and with Campbell-Bannerman's courage?' (*See* Smuts Collection, vol. 69, no. 223.)

[1]   ...the tired waves, vainly breaking,
Seem here no painful inch to gain...

In front, the sun climbs slow, how slowly,
But westward, look, the land is bright.
        Arthur Hugh Clough, *Say not the Struggle Nought Availeth.*

I sense danger, and regret our complete dependence on one man, and he an old man, not much younger than myself! I think we shall be tested most severely this summer, and shall need all the courage and other good qualities which our peoples possess. America must really accelerate her pace and talk less of her coming effort and give us some small instalment on account. So far it is only [General D.] MacArthur that has done well, and he is defending one small peninsula in a vast lost Pacific ocean.[1] Perhaps when this reaches you two months hence we shall see more clearly. But at the moment the outlook is far from inspiring, and a real success anywhere will be more than welcome. Of course Hitler may have even greater troubles than we, but that is not much consolation to us, who mean to win and are still so far from victory. Rangoon just fallen.[2]

Margaret's letter is full of domestic news as well as of the great snowfall of ten inches and walks in it. All very interesting to me who have not seen the colour of snow now for many years. This must have been a very severe winter and I wonder how it was possible to carry on all that fighting in Russia where of course conditions are so much severer than in Britain. You write of seeing the Clement Joneses: give my kind regards to him when next you see him. He was one of the best in my day. Dover Wilson's *Hamlet*[3] has arrived and will be duly enjoyed; at the moment I have no time for intellectual puzzles outside of my job or jobs! I have usually only enough energy left to browse in a well-known botany book such as Marloth or Hutchinson. I think it is a shame to be reduced to such intellectual bankruptcy, but what can one do—with all day and often half the night in office and parliament, wrestling with problems to most of which there is no solution.

I am however fitfully dipping into Seeley's *Natural Religion*,[4] very old fashioned and yet full of interest from the nature of his problem and the wide culture he brought to bear on its discussion. To me the problem stated in my last letter remains: is natural religion enough or is some extraordinary element, such as a revelation or a supreme personality, necessary to supply the necessary dynamic to make it an effective force? In Christianity there were both the revelation and the personality, and Christianity derived its impetus from these two elements. Is Goodness enough to win through on its own merit with us frail humans? It almost seems doubtful. But I don't wish to dogmatize on so big an issue when, as I say, I am tired to mental bankruptcy.

[1] The Bataan peninsula in the Philippines.
[2] Rangoon, capital of Burma, fell on 8 March.
[3] J. Dover Wilson, *What Happens in Hamlet* (1935).   [4] Published in 1882.

I see in the cables that Hodder and Stoughton are publishing a selection of my speeches from 1917 to 1941. This comes as news to me as I cannot remember having given authority for such a collection. I fancy it is merely a republication in England of a volume already on the market in South Africa.[1] This was a fair collection, but omitted most of the stuff which I thought deserving of some record. However, I have had no time to give to these matters, and others, interested in making money for good causes, have had to do it without the benefit of my advice. I say this to explain to you, when you happen to see the new volume in England. My own feeling is against republication of ephemeral stuff never meant for preservation in book form. Somebody has just sent me four big volumes of Roosevelt's speeches. I don't think I shall read them again, having seen them at the proper time and in the proper perspective when they were reported in the press. Speeches are a nuisance, to the maker and the listener alike. Stale speeches are intolerable.

Later. Since I began this letter I have had three most gruelling days in parliament, fighting my departmental estimates as prime minister and minister of defence through the house, in the teeth of most violent opposition. But it is all over and the final phase was more peaceful and quiet. All the time the heavy war work goes on; all the time very serious internal problems arising from war conditions have to be attended to. And there is the usual paraphernalia of deputations and interviews galore. I sometimes sit back and think what it is that makes an old man like me, whose heart and head are in quite another world, continue untiringly and unrestingly in tasks like these. It is a question not so easy to answer. We are curious mixtures in which the high and the low curiously blend, and we deceive ourselves if we put it all to the credit of our virtue or other good qualities. There is a good deal of the devil also in it. There is an elemental drive which will not give in to opposition and which sometimes uses the same weapons with which the opponents fight. But I do flatter myself that behind it all is a deeper faith and loyalty to what is good and really worth fighting for. But oh, how tired one gets of this unending effort and toil! I can understand the case of those monarchs in history who as they passed their prime voluntarily retired to seclusion and meditation or enjoyments of the flesh. I could retire to the enjoyments of the spirit and the mind, if

[1] A volume of speeches made by Smuts between 1895 and 1940 was published in Johannesburg in 1940 under the title *Greater South Africa—plans for a better world* and sold in aid of war funds. The English publication, entitled *Plans for a Better World*, covers the period 1917–41.

I could honourably let go. But I can't. It is a case of bondage to the ideal, to the light one is compelled to follow, whatever the cost. Determinism and free will join hands here, and in being a slave one is really free. Such is our human lot, and so the temporal and the eternal join hands in shaping our course through this world which is yet so much more than this world.

Well, keep well and cheerful and after all life is not so bad or so hard. My love and loving thoughts with you both and you all. Ever yours,

Jan

565   To M. C. Gillett   Vol. 69, no. 229

Groote Schuur
[Cape Town]
12 April 1942

Nothing from you last week but an interesting letter from Arthur in which he gently vented his wrath on the fall of Singapore and the escape of the battleships from Brest. Coming several months after the event it sounds like Caesar's *Gallic War* or some other chapter from ancient history. Such is the pace of events, such the delays of mails. I fear my war comments must sound equally belated to you. But there are compensations in these afflictions, e.g. you have the new Bevis,[1] and Arthur shared a bottle of red wine with his wise friend Wright.[2] Yesterday recorded another misfire—the failure of the Cripps mission.[3] The Indians really have no practical sense and I am afraid are making for one of the greatest *débâcles* in their long story of national disasters. They cannot accept a practical scheme, the only practical scheme for the moment which guarantees them the fullest independence at the end of the war with the good will and assistance of their wise old schoolmaster. They *must* have everything *now*, and in the end will sit with a Britain withdrawn from India, with an India utterly disrupted by the communal struggle and perhaps involved in a civil war. They have no sense, and have probably missed the one great chance of united independence that has come to them however late, or that may ever come to them. I am glad that at any rate the Cripps mission has started no fresh quarrel and left no nasty feeling. In that sense it has not been a failure. And to India and the world it has been a proof of Britain's desire at long

---

[1] Second son of Nicholas and Ruth Gillett.   [2] Lord Wright (q.v.).

[3] On 11 April the British offer (*see supra*, p. 355, note 1) was rejected by Congress which demanded immediate self-government and control of war policy by an Indian minister of defence.

last to meet India's aspirations in a sincere and whole-hearted measure. Gandhi seems to have dropped completely out of the picture, ingeminating peace in a whole world at war. He has risen to the purely religious plane, far above these mundane struggles in which we are all involved. No such privilege is given us who have to do our best for a world which may be worth living in, even if it is no place for heroes or fighters. We shall fight the Lord's war to the end; that is at any rate one way of preventing it from becoming a devil's world. It must never be.

The failure in India and the fall of Bataan[1] are grievous blows. Although we have succeeded in keeping Ceylon from collapse in a great blitz we have suffered grievous losses, and the Japs seem now to be dominating the bay of Bengal.[2] If this success is not countered soon we shall find them dominating the Indian ocean and carrying the war to South Africa, Suez, and the Persian gulf. Not a pleasant prospect for us. But I feel confident that we shall be able to prevent this. But you can understand our anxieties and the heavy additional tasks imposed on us. I am, however, confident of our chances to prevent this disaster. I am far from equally confident that the Russian front will hold against the coming impact of the German armies. Evidently Hitler *must* conquer Russia or fail utterly. He cannot advance far to the east and south with a powerful Russia on his flank. And I know the Germans take the Russian menace to their left flank most seriously. If Russia is pushed beyond the Urals, we shall have a long and difficult road to go to victory, and much sorrow and loss may still be in store for us before the end. But even then I feel confident of victory. I have not reckoned on the Russian front holding as a *certainty*. It may be that we have yet to win without Russia, however hard a job that may be. I think it is a mistake to put all our faith in Russia; it is mistaken propaganda. We can win without Russia, though I admit it will be a most arduous business. If Russia holds, we shall have victory in Europe before it is reached in Asia. If Russia is beaten back to Siberia, we shall have victory in the Far East and the collapse of Japan before it is reached in Europe. This is how the future looks to me. Of course it is all surmise and speculation. But our defeat does not enter into my speculations! One would rather be dead than live as a slave in a Nazi world. It will not come to that. This is not wishful thinking; it is *purposeful* thinking.

This is Sunday morning. I think our last Sunday in Cape Town

---

[1] The peninsula fell in early April but the fortress island of Corregidor off Bataan was held until 6 May.

[2] Attacks by Japanese dive-bombers on Colombo and Trincomalee on 5–9 April were countered by British fighters but the British Eastern fleet having lost two cruisers and a destroyer, withdrew not only from the bay of Bengal, but from the Indian ocean.

before our return to Pretoria. We hope to fly back next Saturday, as the session is expected to close on Friday. This is therefore my last letter from here. It has been an arduous session, and often I have felt as if every drop of strength has been squeezed out of me. But new strength has welled from unseen reserves, and so I have gone on, and hope to reach the end in fairly good form. Isie has really improved during her stay here, which has not been as strenuous as her work in the Transvaal. People are much more alive and exacting there than here. But for me the addition of the work and especially the worries of parliament, added to the heavy burden of the war, creates an almost unbearable burden. However, I have survived, in however battered a form. Friends and well-wishers say I look re- markably fit and in form, perhaps in their desire to be sympathetic and cheer me on. 'On, Stanley, on' were the last words of Marmion![1] And so to the end, which I hope will not be that of the bold Marmion.

I was in office yesterday (Saturday) and in the afternoon had my usual long walk up to and by the contour path to Kirstenbosch, and fossicking round the gardens, altogether two-and-a-half hours of good exercise and sweat. In the evening we entertained Greek royalties[2] and other diplomats, and showed them films of east African volcanoes, while Princess Marie of Greece showed wonder- ful films of Westbrooke on fire, of Piraeus burning down when the British ammunition ship was blown up in the harbour, and of Greek soldiers wounded and with frozen feet coming back to Athens in hospital ships. These Greek war pictures were really terrible, and made one realize, more than any war accounts, what happened in Albania and in Greece. It was all like a nightmare. And still it goes on, horror piled on horror, as in some colossal *Macbeth* tragedy of world-wide dimensions. Think of what is happening to that surrendered Filipino army in Bataan! The stories coming to us from the Dutch in the Far East are quite unbelievable. The Jap navy is not so bad, but the army seems to consist of raving devils. This country is full of refugees from the overrun British and Dutch areas in the Far East, and we hear a lot of first-hand evidence of what happened.

[1]　　　　　　　　　　'Charge, Chester, charge! On, Stanley, on!'
　　　　　　　　　Were the last words of Marmion.
　　　　　　　　　　　　　　　　Sir Walter Scott, *Marmion*, canto VI.32.

[2] After the German conquest of Greece and Crete members of the Greek royal family fled to Egypt where they were unwelcome. They then asked for asylum in South Africa which they reached in the first week of July 1941. The Greek king, George II of the Hellenes, was accompanied by his brother, the crown prince Paul; the latter's wife, Princess Frederika; their two children, Constantine and Sophia; the younger sister of the king, Princess Katharine; his aunt and uncle, Princess Marie and Prince George, and their daughter Princess Radziwell.

And now to end on another note and not depress you unduly. A couple of nights ago when I could not sleep I read in the report of the conference of the British Association for the Advancement of Science a message from Dr Harlow Shapley, the great astronomer. It was about the blueprints for the new world structure we must be preparing. He referred to the vast changes that have come about in science and in our modern outlook, and added that it was not enough piously to repeat the ten commandments or to make grand pronouncements on ethics and so on, as these are the accepted axioms of almost all ethical systems. We have now to plan on a basis which recognizes the small size to which our world has shrunk and added: 'The blueprints should recognize the present small size of the planet, the futility of the presumption of racial superiorities, the futility of striving for the restoration of a previous social order, the recognition that possibly some good points can be obtained from the social philosophies of the totalitarian states. And they should recognize especially that if we strive to model the future on the Anglo-American present we are just setting up another great world sorrow' etc. All profoundly suggestive stuff, and fitly coming from an astronomer versed in the scales of the universal cosmos. But the task of adjusting our ethical and social viewpoints to the new scale which science and invention have brought home to us is almost too much for us. Nationalism, superiorities, and old racial prejudices still hold us in thrall, and we wander about on the dismal shores of that lake where Keats's knight at arms was palely loitering.[1] Science has opened the grand vision of a scientific democracy far greater than the political democracy we have been accustomed to. There is a grand equality as of the Kingdom of God. Distance in time and space has disappeared in the everlasting arms of truth which enfold us. But we do not yet realize what has happened, what science has done for us, and what opportunities of human advance lie open before us. Shall we realize them at the end of this war? Or shall we return to the weary old treadmill of the past? Good-bye, dears. Dear love to you both and you all.

Jan

[1]
Oh what can ail thee Knight at arms
Alone and palely loitering;
The sedge is withered from the lake,
And no birds sing.

John Keats, *La Belle Dame Sans Merci.*

566   From F. D. Roosevelt   Vol. 69, no. 56

The White House
Washington
7 May 1942

My dear General Smuts, Very often I rise up in protest against geography, because even with modern transportation it is almost impossible for me to see and chat with my old friends who live at a great distance. There are so many things that you and I should talk over—matters relating to the old days when we met in London in 1918 and the equally important threats of the present—that some day and in some way we must meet again.

I have been made very happy by your splendid fight against Nazism. As a Dutchman like yourself I find it difficult to understand how any Netherlander of the Union of South Africa or the United States, or any other place in the world, can fail to appreciate that all we have lived for through the generations might be blotted out in the future if Germany and Japan should win.

Your minister here has sent me the Union postage stamps of the new war issues and I am very happy to add them to my collection. With my very sincere regards, Faithfully yours,

s. Franklin D. Roosevelt

567   To F. D. Roosevelt   Vol. 69, no. 137

[Cairo]
19 May 1942

Dear Mr President, By accident I met your personal representative Colonel [L. A.] Johnson here at Cairo on his way back to the States and had an opportunity to discuss with him the present war situation as I see it. And it is partly on his urgence that I write you briefly on the same subject.

I have been visiting our front in the Middle East[1] and given much thought to the strategical problems confronting us, as well as discussed them with others who have done the same. While remaining confident about the outcome of this war I feel the gravity of the immediate situation which appears to me greater than is generally realized.

To me the all-important consideration is our time-table. It is 1942 that matters most. No doubt we can develop and deploy huge resources in 1943 and 1944, but we must first pull through 1942, during which the enemy is going to make his maximum effort to

---

[1] Smuts left South Africa for Cairo on 8 May and returned on 22 May.

obtain a decision. Already we have lost so much during the last two-and-a-half years of the war that further grave set-backs may put us in dire peril. We cannot afford mistakes in 1942.

To me it is not the Far Eastern situation that at present matters most, grievous as the losses have been there. That position can in time be recovered. Nor do I consider Australia in dire peril. It is really off the real line of the enemy advance, and the apparent move of Japan in that direction may only be a clever feint to induce us to divide our resources.

There is an area which we cannot afford to lose, without the greatest danger to our future victory. That is the Indian ocean and the lands bordering on it, from the Middle East through Iran and Iraq to India and Ceylon. Their loss would put us in such an unfavourable position for defence and eventual offensive and the enemy in such a powerful position for the future, that we dare not risk such a loss. In effect it is therefore this year 1942 and this area which seem to me to dominate the whole position of our war strategy. We must concentrate our forces to hold this area in 1942, just as it will be the enemy's plan to obtain control of it and so paralyse our future effort, whatever our resources may then be.

As regards the land position in this area, we must prepare for further Russian set-backs and the advance of Germany this summer to the Caucasus and its oil, and the virtual outflanking of the position we are now holding in Egypt, Syria and Iraq. The Japanese may at the same time advance into India, the position of which is grave, as Colonel Johnson will tell you. As regards the sea we have so divided our naval forces that we run a serious risk. While the British naval forces cannot separately face the Japanese navy in the Indian ocean, the American naval forces in the Pacific bordering on Australia may also be unable to defeat the Japanese navy. The British navy has already suffered grievous losses. The case seems to me imperative for the two navies joining hands in the Indian ocean and delivering a smashing blow at the Japanese navy at the earliest opportunity. Our naval dominance of the Indian ocean and the bay of Bengal would put an end to the Japanese advance westwards and keep open our communications with the Middle East round the Cape. In fact the Cape route appears to be the way to victory so far as this part of the world is concerned. If we could meet the German and Japanese menace in this area this summer, we may have a good base from which to start an offensive towards Italy, Greece and the Balkans, and our air attacks as far as Italy and the Rumanian oilfields would have a deadly effect. We would be in a strong offensive position for the decisive campaigns of 1943.

For these and other reasons I therefore urge as great a concentration of our forces, especially naval, in the Indian ocean as soon as
possible, and avoidance of their dispersal in the Pacific or Australian
areas.

As regards Germany in the West, I would urge concentrating our
land and air forces in the British Isles for the reconstruction of the
western front in 1943 and launching from there the maximum
Anglo-American attack by air and land in 1943. This great move
I assume is in course of preparation and vigorous prosecution. It
would enable us to strike at the heart of the German power. But the
Middle East and the Indian ocean should meanwhile be firmly held
and developed as a base for the offensive across the Mediterranean
against the weaker members and hangers-on of the Axis, and the
further advance of Japan westwards should be prevented. Japan
could then be dealt with at the proper time.

My point is that the further advance of Japan in 1942 and the
imperilling of the position in the Middle East must be prevented at
all costs. And we must not build our hopes too much on Russia
during this fateful year. We should then—but then only—be in
a favourable position for victory in 1943.

Pardon this insistence on what may appear to you to be the
obvious. But the obvious course is not always followed or the easiest
to follow in human affairs.

I cannot end without expressing my admiration for the immense
effort of your people and their total concentration on the job. That
spirit and your great leadership which match the spirit of the British
people under Churchill's leadership will make our victory a certainty if, meanwhile, unnecessary strategical risks are avoided.

With all good wishes for our course and for your health and
strength in a superhuman task, Yours faithfully,

s. J. C. Smuts

568   To M. C. Gillett   **Vol. 69, no. 237**

Doornkloof
[Transvaal]
7 June 1942

Again Sunday night, a time I love to write and exchange ideas and
news with you. Isie sits inside with Lady Delamere of Kenya,[1] who
has brought a young daughter to school in Johannesburg, and has

---

[1] Formerly Lady Gladys Markham, daughter of the Honourable Rupert Beckett;
married Lord Delamere in 1928.

been particularly kind to our troops in east Africa. She is the widow of the prominent east African about whom| Elspeth Huxley wrote her interesting book *White Man's Country*[1] which was really also a biography of Delamere. Isie is glad to be able to entertain her here for a day and two nights, and I find a good deal of real stuff in her. ... I think this war is bringing women into their own, and the world cannot be the same thereafter. Think of all these Boer girls in their tens of thousands coming from isolated, uninteresting farm life to camps and munition factories, getting fair wages, and imbibing all sorts of new ideas! This is a mobilization of women not only for war but for life—with far-reaching social consequences to follow.

Last week I was at Durban to inspect defences and confer with officers, and at night I had a great meeting in the city hall. I inspected thousands of imperial troops in addition to my own. Everywhere of course the usual tumultuous reception, and the night meeting was a grand success. As my old opponent the *Natal Mercury* said next morning, Natal or rather Durban was at last reconciled to me and no misunderstanding left. For how long? (This is *my* question, not theirs!) I announced the transformation of my infantry divisions in the north to armoured tank divisions, and also the creation of two additional divisions in the Union for interior and coastal defence, together with other important developments intended to meet the menace of Japan in the Indian ocean. That menace is very real, as I know from facts which I shall not write about. My proposals have received universal support, and I am going ahead with them. Of course it all means great additional calls and burdens on this country and its small population. But needs must when the devil in the form of Japan drives. I came back to heavy office toils, and then yesterday I attended, with Duncan and Alice [Duncan] and Isie, the non-European (Native) review at Johannesburg. It was a wonderful sight and a vast crowd watched the splendid performance of my Native recruits, of whom I have now at least 60,000 in the army. Here, too, war is going to be the potent agency of change. Think of these men getting good pay and treatment and a view of the larger life and experience of the world. They can never be the same again. The Nats are continually and bitterly accusing me of this mobilizing of Native life and thought and outlook. But it is all inevitable, and if wisely guided may become a powerful instrument of reforms and progress. Of course here too there are two sides to the question. I have heard of Natives saying: 'Why fight against Japan? We are oppressed by the whites and shall not fare worse under the Japanese.' But I am sure the

[1] Published in 1935.

great majority are still loyal in their conservative way. The poor behaviour of the people of Burma and Malaya is said to have been largely due to this same feeling that an exchange of the English masters for Japanese ditto might not after all be such a bad thing. They will find out their mistake when it is too late. For English dominion has on the whole been mild and human, while Japan in Korea, Manchuria, and everywhere else has behaved with exceptional brutality to the natives. Alien rule may be a bad thing, but I would rather be under the superior English than the slave-driving Jap if I had a choice. The populations of Further India remained passive and on the first approach of danger ran away *en masse* from their work, so that the moment of greatest need of their services resembled a general strike which paralysed all activity. I am told that the collapse was due more to this than any other cause. Of course all this has also its meaning and message for us in South Africa. But I do believe that our Natives have far more guts than these Orientals. The politics of India in this crisis seem to me to be largely an exhibition in defeatism and irresponsibility, and a refusal to face facts and dangers. All this, however, is more or less speculation, and you are quite entitled to differ from me to your heart's content.

...I was much interested in what you write of the problem of war as it concerns sincere Friends and of the difficulties of composing a Minute for Q.M.[1] I feel the tragedy of the situation as any Friend, and I do believe that under ideal conditions the Christian message is the only answer to our difficulties. But, of course, the situation for Jesus was much simplified by the existence of the omnipotent Roman Empire, and by his sound principle of leaving to Caesar what was Caesar's. *We* on the other hand are in the position of Caesar, responsible for peace and war, for the maintenance of social order against brute violence and aggression. Ours is therefore a much more complex situation than that which Jesus had to face. What would *he* have done if in Caesar's place and faced with a ruthless attack on the values which man's age long endeavour had laboriously accomplished? Is that not a very different position from that which the Gospel envisages? Is that not the position of old man Blake where he says: 'I shall not cease from mortal strife, nor shall my sword sleep in my hand' etc.[2] I do believe that this is not mere poetic imagery, but the true heroic attitude, and that it is in the ultimate spirit of Christ. The passive defeatist view of Jesus does him no justice. He did not spare himself in the cause of right, and would not have spared anybody if called to maintain the right.

[1] M. C. Gillett was chairman of the regional (Quarterly) Meetings of the Society of Friends.　　　　[2] *See supra*, p. 118, note 1.

The true Christians are those in all lands who by prayer and endurance where possible, and by heroic self-sacrifice and battling where that is possible, stand up for the right as they see it and refuse to knuckle under to wrong. The heroic Christ is to me the real Christ, and the passive acquiescence in omnipotent wrong is to me a negation of all that he stands for.

I shall look forward with much interest to your Minute, and you must not look upon the above as condemnation in advance! I only feel that the wars of the spirit may not and are not sufficient if evil has to be routed in this practical world. Carnal weapons must be used if necessary! Good-night,

Jan

569   To M. C. Gillett   Vol. 69, no. 239

[Doornkloof
Transvaal]
[23 June 1942]

I have another busy and hectic week behind me. Besides the usual routines of work and problems I had to deal with two conferences —one with governments to the north in regard to military command in southern and east Africa—the other with generals in regard to the Madagascar operations.[1] 'Libertas' was full of people and I resided there while Isie (for reasons of limited space) remained on the farm. Both conferences in excellent spirit and with good results. Southern Rhodesia wanted to come under my command in the Union—what a change from the old times when they would have nothing to do with us! But so times change—quite welcome in this case. Scarcely had these conferences ended when there was a thunderbolt from the north in the sudden capture of Tobruk.[2] As we had a division of South Africans in it you can imagine our concern and the possible reactions in this country. Such a loss of the very troops who months ago captured Bardia, Sollum, and Halfaya. Thank goodness the collapse was not due to them but they share in the immense misfortune and we all in the feeling of loss and set-back at a time when our cause cannot afford it. We do not yet know details but at any

[1] Japanese control of much of the Indian ocean made it necessary for the Allies to take Madagascar, a French possession. On 7 May British forces occupied Diego Suarez. Smuts urged Churchill to extend British control over the whole island.

[2] On 26 May the Germans attacked the Allied defensive position in Cyrenaica from Gazala to Bir Hacheim. Both sides suffered considerable losses in the ensuing battles. On 21 June Tobruk fell to the Germans who took 33,000 prisoners, among them most of the Second South African Division of 13,000 men.

rate we know that Jannie [Smuts] is not in this fatal haul. It is a bitter blow. But we shall overcome it and recover. Already I have offered to send very large reinforcements to take their place. My opponents will of course be jubilant and create as much trouble for me as they are capable of. But I shall see it through to the end which I do not doubt. Not for us the slave order miscalled the *New* Order —as if it were not as old as time itself! While these heavy doings were on, Churchill was conferencing with Roosevelt in Washington, and I sent a memorandum (by cable) in time to be considered before Churchill's return. The war theatre today is globe-wide and so much will depend on the correctness of our strategy. If our forces are disposed in the right areas and we have the offensive spirit we must of course win, but sitting behind defences or in the wrong places may prove fatal. The future of man is the stakes for which we are contending and one cannot give too much thought to the right lines for our world-wide strategy. Of course I cannot here discuss what my views are although I am sure you would both be interested. Unfortunately, with this large and distinguished company at 'Libertas' I had no free time, and had to dock my hours of sleep for drafting documents and thinking out plans. But even so I found some sleepless midnight moments to read Raleigh's little book on Shakespeare[1] which interested me very much—especially his point that those terrible tragedies, such as *Macbeth, Lear, Othello* etc. which one can scarcely bear to read in their concentrated horror, must have racked the very soul of Shakespeare in the process of composition, and brought his mind to the very verge of sanity. I had never thought of this aspect. But of course it must be so. You cannot in imagination work out those awful problems of human fate without being shaken to your own foundations. And another point he makes is that in the white heat of sacrifice even the worst of crimes are transmitted and become sublime and awe-inspiring in a way which makes you quite forget the crime. Thus Othello's murder of his wife because of his passionate love. Human nature in its peak moments passes beyond good and evil, and becomes almost godlike in spite of the breach of the moral law. I suppose that is why the ancients looked upon madness as divine. And how much more godlike must the high passion and sacrifice be when its object is itself the highest! Think of Jesus, conscious that he is the Messiah Elect, going up to Jerusalem to suffer those horrors and agonies which he so clearly forebodes! His is surely the greatest drama in all history. And what must have passed through that great soul in those last days, when his disciples did not understand him, his own people hated him to death,

---

[1] Sir Walter Alexander Raleigh, *Shakespeare* (1907).

and he was only upborne by his high resolve of sacrifice. And there came a moment at the end when he thought that even God has forsaken him. What a drama! And then a woman, a woman he had saved from shipwreck, in her blinding love, saw that vision of him which became the resurrection and the foundation of the Christian order. His sacrifice *did* force the Kingdom of God, but not in the way he had thought, but through that vision born of love and tears.[1] This surely is the high light of tragedy, surpassing anything that even the imagination of Shakespeare could encompass. Not the Virgin Mary but Mary the Magdalene is the mother of Christianity. But Jesus stands out even beyond that as the very God. I think that is the nearest to the Godlike we can ever and shall ever come and we do right in bowing down before him in worship and adoration. All this was borne in on me when I was reading Raleigh on Shakespeare's tragedies. And is not Mary a lovely character, lovely beyond anything in Shakespeare's wonderful women! I think she must have been the Mary who anointed him with fragrant oil and dried his feet with her dear hair. At least I hope so. These colourful ways of the East express what is lovely in life much better than our restraints and inhibitions. Did you send me Raleigh? How wonderful are these high moments of life! And they come in the most humble surroundings and commonplace circumstances. What could be more lowly and modest than that primitive Galilean society where these mighty wonders of human nature were wrought? How much greater and more wonderful than anything in the experience of the mighty contemporary Tiberius[2] or the philosophy of the contemporary Seneca.[3] (At least I think they were contemporaries of Jesus.)...

[1]   She sat and wept beside His feet; the weight
        Of sin oppressed her heart...
        I am a sinner, full of doubts and fears,
        Make me a humble thing of love and tears.
                                        Hartley Coleridge, *Multum Dilexit*.
   [2] The Roman emperor Tiberius was born 42 B.C. and died A.D. 37. He became emperor A.D. 14.
   [3] Lucius Annaeus Seneca, Roman Stoic philosopher, dramatist and statesman, was born *c.* 3 B.C. and died A.D. 65.

570   From Lord Harlech   Vol. 68, no. 15

Office of the High Commissioner for the United Kingdom
Pretoria
26 June 1942

My dear Prime Minister, The admiralty have been considering the
selection for Wingfield aerodrome[1] of a suitable 'ship' name such as
is customarily given to most royal naval establishments.

They have suggested that the Afrikaans name of a bird of prey
might be the most appropriate, for example, *Visarend Cape*, *Slikop
Giant*, *Hoenderjaer* or *Lammervanger*, or any similar name which you
might wish to suggest. Yours sincerely,

Harlech

571   To Lord Harlech   Vol. 68, no. 15 A

Pretoria
29 June 1942

Dear High Commissioner, What is wrong with 'Malagas'? This is
the guano bird, so useful on all our west coast islands. I would
suggest *H.M.S. Malagas*! Yours sincerely,

s. J. C. Smuts

572   To M. C. Gillett   Vol. 69, no. 241

Doornkloof
[Transvaal]
10 July 1942

Two such nice letters from you since my last to you. Also two very
welcome ones from Arthur. I can see from yours that you are at last
really smitten with the grandmother's disease. Your letters are full
of them and they are becoming real entities instead of merely names
to us. The snaps of three of them (Simon, Rachel and David) are
most welcome. I do believe in children—in the great promise, often
followed by such poor fulfilment. But the promise is the thing: it
seems the riches of the world, however much poverty may be the
actual lot. I have before quoted to you Schiller's line *Wie gross war
diese Welt gestaltet* etc.[2]

   ...'Tsalta' is again at a loose end...I have asked the good Burgess
[R. E.] of Barclay's to look for another tenant...I doubt myself
whether we shall ever occupy it again. When this war is over I shall

---

[1] Near Cape Town.   [2] *See* vol. v, p. 41, note 2.

retire from affairs and my place will know me no more.[1] There will be some years for botany and African travel and meditation and writing up some notes of experience. So I am afraid 'Tsalta' may not come into the picture again. But what a pleasure it has been! It has been worth it and much more to me in those years of disappointment but of comparative freedom. Please think over the matter and let me know.

Your *Disciples*[2] have already arrived and been read with deep interest. It is good stuff, well done. Isie is reading it now, and thereafter the rest of the family will enjoy it. A really good effort. Of course the mystery remains. How ever did Jesus put it across those simple folk, even that much that he did get across? Socrates had the advantage of the greatest literary craftsman of all time to paint his immortal picture. But these simple folk, with their primitive language like the story-telling of children. And yet the result is so immensely impressive. Not even a Shakespeare could have done that last phase of the Master better, and the heroic simplicity of it all becomes so telling that one can scarcely bear to read. The great Figure in all his sorrow and faith, the disciples milling round, the women standing afar, the priests in their hour, the governor in his defeat, the stranger from Africa who bears the cross, the darkness, the sorrowing sobbing women at the tomb, the vision of Magdalene through her tears, and her final cry: Rabboni; the joyful running back, the spreading of the Vision; the passing away in glory in the clouds. All in the simplest lisping language as of a child's fairy tale—and the tremendous effect on one's mind. How much *did* get across there, perhaps even more in some respects than there was; in other respects so much less. The whole thing looks like a miracle of human nature and experience. And yet always the impression remains that the truth is greater than the story, and there is something far greater in that tragedy than the pen has conveyed. There are indeed two mysteries: the one is the Master, the other is the disciples whose weakness could convey and accomplish so much. Surely there must be something godlike in man, and both the Master and his disciples are a proof of that fact. There is here a revelation of spirit which makes us see into the depths of the spirit which lies embedded in our mortal clay.

We have been passing through a week on heavy anxieties about the situation in the north. I am so glad that it was our First South African Division that stopped Rommel at El Alamein in two or three

---

[1] 'He shall return no more to his house, neither shall his place know him any more.' *Job* vii.10.

[2] *See supra*, p. 352, note 1.

days of heavy fighting.[1] It was touch and go there, and if El Alamein had gone and Rommel had got to Alexandria, the loss to us would have been far more serious than Singapore and all the rest that went in the Far East. The men of Abyssinia, of Amba Alagi, of Sidi Rezegh once more rose to the occasion and did what I expected them to do. At one moment, when the Indian Brigade on their left was overrun the situation looked black, but it was once more restored. Then the New Zealanders came as reinforcements; then the Australians; and since then there has been not only a check but a great change in the situation. I have good hopes of the future. But it is best to be patient and await developments. At any rate the sad and inexplicable surrender of Tobruk is not the last word. The First Division may yet avenge the Second, lost at Tobruk. Meanwhile I am doing all I can to replace the Second Division by a great recruiting drive which I hope will give me the men. But we have practically drained this country of its willing hands, and there is not much left on the bottom. The opponents who stand aside are many, many are wanted for home defence and for munitions, and for food production and the like. Still we shall raise what we can and not fail in this hour of adversity and misfortune. So much is at stake. It is as if we are once more called to fight the great fight for which martyrs went to the stake and men held life cheap and worthy only of being sacrificed for the cause. I wrote you that Jannie [Smuts] escaped, with only the clothes he stood in, in the retreat from Gazala—bombed continuously for four days in that unceasing retreat of the First Division which was to halt Rommel at El Alamein. He saved his clothes on his body and his ciné camera, but lost everything else. What an experience! I am so glad that he has had this fire baptism and this taste of retreat. It is so different from the victorious advance and bites so much deeper into the soul.

I suddenly find I must now stop. My pen wants to run on and beat even time. But it must not be. Love to you all.

Jan

573   To F. H. Theron   Vol. 69, no. 159

Secret and confidential   Pretoria
21 July 1942

My dear Theron, Your letter of 17 July[2] just to hand confirms the impression created by previous correspondence that a retreat from

---

[1] The Allied retreat in Egypt stopped on 1 July when a defensible position between the Qattara depression and the sea at El Alamein was reached. The first three German attempts to break through here were repulsed by the First South African Division.

[2] Smuts Collection, vol. 69, no. 277.

Egypt to Palestine is under consideration as a possibility and steps are being taken by the General Staff to plan for such a contingency. I am sending my C.G.S.[1] up to probe into this situation and to gather information for my guidance. Meanwhile I wish you to have for your guidance a general indication of my reaction to some such move in the near future.

1. I know absolutely nothing which justifies or even explains such a move. Our forces are at least equal to that of the enemy. Our air is superior, our tank position will also soon be superior. The commander-in-chief[2] appears confident and (at least to me) has never given the least hint that the position may become dangerous. I do not know whether this impression has been conveyed to the United Kingdom government, but certainly I have heard nothing from Mr Churchill to indicate or even hint such a development in the Middle East position. Of course Germany may attack and beat down Turkey, the Syrian front may collapse, and a double attack on Egypt from east and west may knock us out of Egypt. But then we would retire south, not eastward to Palestine. That however is a very different situation from the present, when we have only to face Rommel's move from the west. I know of nothing which should make us contemplate a knock-out by Rommel. What is the basis of this present outlook? I don't know. I should know. Certainly the British government should know.

2. For, let there be no mistake, the loss of Egypt may, probably will, lose us the war. That has been my outlook from the beginning and has largely determined my decision to defend the Union in Middle East. If the Axis get Egypt they pass into the Red sea, they will recover Eritrea and possibly Abyssinia, and once more threaten east and south Africa. They will pass on to Iraq and establish contact by land and perhaps by sea with India. They will join hands with Japan and, whatever happens to Britain, the British Empire will be looked upon as lost. There will be a political change in South Africa, which will cease to be a line of Empire communication. The end will have come, I fear. The Mediterranean route may become so precarious as to be useless to us. That need not be fatal. But retreat from Egypt will, I fear, bring us perilously near the edge.

3. These points will, I think, be conceded by those who have seriously considered the whole matter. The very idea of our retiring from Egypt is therefore a most serious matter, and if there is the least ground for it, it should be at once communicated to the governments concerned. And if there is no ground for it, I fear it is purely

---

[1] General Sir Pierre van Ryneveld.   [2] General Sir Claude Auchinleck.

a mischievous idea, likely to spread defeatism, and very soon to reach our enemies, to their great comfort and encouragement. In my previous wires I have warned against anything likely to spread panic. Nothing is more likely to do so than the rumour, even the guess, that the Allies are planning for a retirement from this vital strategic area of the whole war. It will dishearten all our friends and supporters; it will give fresh heart to all our enemies. The matter should be looked upon as one of high policy and strategy in its effect on the war. I would therefore press strongly for a frank confidential exposé to the governments concerned so that they may know what is in the minds of the staff. Let at least London and Pretoria know most confidentially. Let us not drift into an atmosphere of rumour which is bound to result from the present dangerous procedure.

4. Should the worst happen, and a retreat from Egypt become necessary under present circumstances (only Rommel's threat), what should be our line of retreat? Clearly in two directions: eastward into Palestine, clinging on to the Delta and the Canal as long as possible; and southward to Suez, Port Sudan, Eritrea and the Sudan. The reason for the eastward retreat is obvious and needs no further explanation. The reason for the southward retreat is really equally obvious. For an enemy in possession of Egypt must necessarily move up the Nile, and in this case, where Italy has to recover, with German help, her former colonies of Eritrea and Abyssinia, there will be an added inducement to move southward.

If there is no considerable force blocking the way, this move will continue until the Sudan and the Red sea ports are recovered, and will most probably proceed to the recovery of Abyssinia itself. At that point, in any case, large opposing forces will once more become necessary to hold east Africa, including Mombasa. And the movement, unless held by strong forces, may proceed all the way down Africa. In the meantime a revolution would probably have set in in South Africa, and the whole African position will be in danger of irretrievable collapse—with the route via the Cape to the Indian ocean also gone in the general *débâcle*.

5. The retreat from Egypt must therefore be covered on the south by a strong fighting force of all arms which will be able to hold Suez, and the upper Nile, and be able to hold the enemy, or to conduct an orderly fighting retreat to Port Sudan, to the Sudan and the Eritrean highlands, and to bar the enemy's further progress south.

The South African forces would, in case of such a retreat, be assigned this defensive role, and they would have to be well equipped in all arms and with much transport to hold a considerable enemy force pushing south. They would have to be a real going concern as an army, able to maintain itself and to move and fight like a first-class military force. It is from this point of view that the extrication of the South African forces in Middle East will have to be considered. They will have to leave Middle East as a real self-contained going concern in the military sense. Infantry, guns, aircraft, tanks, transport, field recovery units, and all the technical apparatus for such a force and such a retreat, based on long lines of communication to the far south—all this will be wanted. And the division of forces and resources in Egypt, when this retreat begins, should have regard to the requirements for such a force in its long retreat. Any staff plans for a retreat from Egypt should keep these requirements for the South African army moving south well in view.

6. The South African forces are so closely integrated with the whole Middle East forces that the separation into two will not be an easy matter. Many South African services are essential for the functioning of the army retiring eastward from Egypt, and the separation from it of these services may cripple it badly. Some give-and-take line will therefore have to be followed. The principle to be followed in such a segregation of the South African personnel and services from the rest of the Middle East army will therefore have to be somewhat as follows:

Whatever South African personnel or material is not clearly wanted by the South African forces for its proper functioning, and is on the contrary badly needed by the Middle East force, should be left with the latter. This would apply, e.g. to the women personnel functioning in the British units, signal and other technical South African units on which the Middle East army is dependent, certain workshops necessary for repair work, and other services for which the Middle East army has relied on South African personnel or equipment. On the other hand, again, the South African force will require large M.T. equipment from the Middle East force, as well as other apparatus to equip it for a possibly long retreat down Africa. Road units and equipment and similar engineering services will also be needed by the South African force on a generous scale. A joint staff committee may have to work out the division of personnel, services, and equipment on practical give-and-take lines on the above principle. The spirit in which the division will be effected will be that between close allies determined to be helpful to each other, and to see that neither force is crippled in the difficult task facing it. Both are comrades fighting for common victory against a dangerous enemy.

7. I do not say that the time has come for such an onerous, one

might also say odious, job. Indeed as at present advised I consider the whole matter premature and possibly dangerous. But if it is decided that the situation in Middle East justifies this sort of confidential preliminary planning then the above should be the general basis on which the apportionment between the two forces should be made. And in any case I think the two governments should first be confidentially informed and advised by the high command in the Middle East that the time has come to prepare such a scheme of possible retreat, with the consequential division of forces and resources between the two armies of retreat. No such information or advice has yet been given that I am aware of.

I therefore send my C.G.S. to Cairo to inquire confidentially into the whole matter for the information of the South African government, and for its eventual action, in case action would unfortunately become necessary, which God forbid! Yours sincerely,

s. J. C. Smuts

574   To M. C. Gillett   Vol. 69, no. 247

Doornkloof
[Transvaal]
10 August 1942

Since my last letter I have again been up to Egypt and spent a strenuous week there, returning yesterday in a two days' flight to here. I had an unexpected summons from Churchill on a Friday to meet him in Cairo on the Monday following, and on Monday morning[1] I was there in due course. We had a great time together, dealing with the military situation in the Middle East, discussing the war situation over the whole world, and finally winding up with war and post-war politics. Most of the matters under consideration cannot be written about, but the changes we made in the military command in the Middle East[2] you will know long before you receive this. We stayed at the embassy in adjoining rooms and spent most of the time together night and day. I had little sleep and was glad to get away on the Saturday morning, arriving here Sunday after-

---

[1] 3 August. Churchill reached Cairo on the 4th. Writing to Attlee on the 5th he said: 'I am discussing the whole situation with Smuts who is a fount of wisdom.' (Winston Churchill, *The Second World War*, vol. IV, p. 415.)

[2] General Sir Harold Alexander became commander-in-chief in the Middle East in succession to Auchinleck, and General Sir Bernard Montgomery became commander of the Eighth Army in succession to General Ritchie. An independent command for Iraq and Persia was created and offered to Auchinleck who declined it. Later General Sir H. Maitland Wilson accepted it.

noon. He pressed me to accompany him to Moscow whither he was also bound; but I had had enough of it and besides Moscow had no particular call on my presence. And my sudden departure to the north had left a number of loose ends which I was anxious to pick up as soon as possible. Truth to tell I am somewhat afraid of Moscow and its temper in these days of tremendous set-back in South Russia and retreat in the Caucasus. I only hope that there will be no falling out between Stalin and Churchill, as I don't think the two see eye to eye on what is happening. Anyway I am out of it and can attend to my own arid potato patch in this country.

You will be amused to hear that I took as a book companion with me the small *Ring and the Book*[1] which you gave me long ago, and that I read almost half of it in the air. I found it interesting and good reading. But of course the best stuff is in the later books which I have read many times. The best in the earlier parts are the lines I have sometimes heard you quote:

> O lyric love, half angel and half bird,
> And all the wonder and the wild desire etc.[2]

Those lines are an apostrophe to his dead wife and are among the best he ever wrote. I found Guido's defence of himself a very powerful piece of writing, and somehow had not read it before. It is a pity he is so deliberately and irritatingly obscure here and there, and thereby repels people; for essentially *The Ring and the Book* is a great poem, and would be greater if not so cryptic and elliptical in many places.

This is a trying pen and I fear my scrawl will be even more trying to you than usual. But I left my own pen in Cairo and am now using a harder one of Isie's. If you feel decypherment difficult just think of my trouble in reading the above book! I have now changed to a new pen which seems more promising and will prove more acceptable to both of us.

Churchill pressed me very strongly to pay London a visit before the winter. I told him that if the situation continues to be more or less normal for the immediate future I might feel free to absent myself. It depends on the extent to which the war and other situations may change, and I am not definitely committed. But at any rate there is now the possibility of my coming over within the next three months. It is of course possible that before you receive this there may be some public announcement bearing on this question,

[1] A long poem by Robert Browning.
[2]   O lyric Love, half angel and half bird
             And all a wonder and a wild desire.

(line 1391)

and in that case you will understand. To tell you the truth I had practically given up all idea of coming to England during this war, and as it might still last long that might mean practically for ever. But this bit of pessimism may turn out to have been overdone. Anyhow I cannot say that I shall leave South Africa with pleasure or even an easy mind. I never feel comfortable about the position here, especially in my absence. My opponents do really fear me when here, but whether fear will restrain them from unwise action in my absence is another matter. I do feel very sincerely that my place is here during the war, and that that should be the first consideration with me. However, I am beginning to appear churlish in my persistent refusal to come to London while all the other Dominion prime ministers have been there and are willing to go again. So my resolve is at last weakening, but whether this is wise is not at all clear to me. I also fear the physical strain and exhaustion of a visit which is certain to be strenuous for me and make great demands on such small resources as I still command. I am not what I was twenty-five years ago, and even then I felt my strength taxed to the utmost limit in London. And again, what time will there be to see my friends in all this pressure? Taking it all in all, I remain doubtful about this visit which scarcely accords with my own feelings and intuitions. Still there it is: team-work is essential in this struggle, and I don't wish to appear to hold aloof. Churchill was most insistent and kept repeatedly returning to the subject.

I fear our governor-general[1] is a very ill man, and this is another load on my mind. He has been a wonderful success and only a few months ago he was reappointed for five years. But since alarming symptoms of ill health have appeared which make me anxious even for the near future. And in South Africa governors-general do not grow like mushrooms.

The Greek royal family minus the king is now staying at 'Libertas' as our guests, while we continue to reside at Doornkloof. Isie and I usually lunch with them and like them very much indeed. She, the crown princess, is a granddaughter of the Kaiser[2] and a fine intelligent young woman with three children.[3] The king's sister Katherine is unmarried and also a high-class woman. We shall soon have the Portuguese colonial minister[4] and family as our guests at 'Libertas' and shall for those days send the Greeks on a tour of the

[1] Sir Patrick Duncan.

[2] Her parents were Ernst, Duke of Brunswick-Hanover and Victoria Louise, daughter of Wilhelm II of Germany.

[3] The third, Princess Irene, had been born in South Africa in May 1942 and Smuts was her godfather.

[4] Dr Francisco J. V. Machado (q.v.).

Kruger Park. I dislike these social activities which are distracting and time-robbing. But such things belong to my position and cannot be evaded. And poor Isie who hates all this!

...Now enough. This letter may possibly go by special service. Ever yours,

Jan

575   To T. W. Lamont   Vol. 69, no. 161

Pretoria
14 August 1942

My dear Tom, I have your last welcome note of 13 July[1] and received it on my return from a sudden flight to Egypt to meet Churchill and discuss war policies. He could inform me of the result of his contacts with Roosevelt, with whom I have also been in touch by wire. The war has now—in the summer of 1942—reached its most critical stage, as I had always felt it would, and the whole future issue is already at stake at this stage. Planning and action are therefore all important now. What I saw and heard in my exchanges with both these leaders has been on the whole encouraging. If we can hold this year what we have and build the groundwork for the great offensives of next year (when our American reserves will be fully mobilized) we can look forward with confidence to the issue.

You mention Luce [H. R.][2] and I enclose a little note for him, for you to forward kindly. It may be a useful contact.

Except in the realm of religion there is no resurrection of the dead and I agree with you that we shall not see again in its old form the dear friend (I had almost said child), the League of Nations. The new organization will be the United Nations—a good name too, corresponding to the United States.[3] There will be a nucleus, an outer circle, and a fringe round that, signifying varying grades of responsibility and power. No council of gate-crashers as in the League.

What troubles me more is the point of the spirit and outlook which will animate the new machine. All will depend on that. The spirit of the old League was fatal to its success.

[1] Smuts Collection, vol. 68, no. 93.
[2] H. R. Luce had sent Smuts, through Lamont, an autographed copy of *Fortune* containing an article on post-war relations with Great Britain.
[3] This name was first officially used on 1 January 1942 when twenty-six nations at war with the Axis countries joined in a declaration to continue their war activities and not to make peace separately. Roosevelt suggested the term which, so Churchill reminded him, appears in lines from Byron's *Childe Harold*. *See* Winston Churchill, *The Second World War*, vol. III, p. 605.

I value your and Florence's letters very much, and look rather wistfully to the times when we may meet again and perhaps see more of this great continent. But when will that be? And in the meantime some of us don't get younger! Isie keeps well and a wonderful war worker. Her popularity with all is simply wonderful and she is a great support to me in all good things—God bless her. You both are also deeply engaged and perhaps overdoing it. But we shall never have another such chance of service. So never mind.

Affectionate greetings and all best wishes from both of us, and all of us. Ever yours,

J. C. Smuts

576   To L. S. Amery   Vol. 69, no. 170

Telegram

From: Smuts

To: high commissioner, London

Dated 28 August 1942

Following message for Mr Amery from prime minister.

Thank you for interesting letter of 10th August.[1] Your position appears fairly strong, and while civil disobedience continues[2] I see no alternative but to keep leaders interned in India, but not to move them outside, which might cause new flare up. If, however, civil disobedience peters out, as appears likely, it would be impolitic to keep leaders interned without making another move towards settlement. In that case it is worth consideration whether they and leaders of other sections should not be approached with following proposal, viz., government to call fresh conference of leaders of all sections in order to come to agreement on future government of India, either as a single entity or partitioned into Pakistan states on agreed basis of co-operation or confederation for defined common purposes such as defence and foreign relations, such basis to be part of future constitution. If agreement is secured at conference British government to undertake to put it into force as soon as peace is made. During war government of India to continue on present lines of majority Indian representation on it. Such a proposal would remove uncertainty still existing as to when after the war India will receive free constitution and also compel emergence of real issue, viz. non-

[1] Smuts Collection, vol. 67, no. 12.
[2] After Congress rejected the Cripps proposals it set in train another passive disobedience (*satayagraha*) movement in accordance with Gandhi's policy of neutrality in the war.

agreement among Indians themselves as only obstacle to immediate grant of freedom after the war. Reference to Dominion status might usefully be avoided. I am afraid that it would be dangerous both from point of view of general world opinion and that of internal Indian peace to sit tight after civil disobedience has finally collapsed. Some new move will be necessary at that stage, and it should be calculated to show quite clearly that disagreement among Indians themselves and nothing else bars way to freedom at the end of the war. This is for your personal consideration. All my best wishes.

577   From A. W. Tedder   Vol. 69, no. 268

Cairo
1 September 1942

My dear Field Marshal, I do want to thank you most sincerely for the magnificent case which arrived a day or two ago while I was away. I hope it will not be long before we have events in the Western Desert worthy of such celebration.

As you will have heard, the party began yesterday.[1] We had been expecting it for some days but I think the delays and losses to his shipping made Rommel hold back a little longer. Of course every day extra has been a help from the army point of view. There is no doubt that Montgomery has brought the whole Eighth Army to life again. The effect has been almost electric, far more rapid than I had thought possible. It is going to be tough going but with a new spirit there should be no doubt about it. I feel that your presence and advice during those days of your visit may well prove to have been the turning point in the whole battle for the Mediterranean—and all that goes with it. All the same I did wish you had been here when we came back from Moscow.[2] I personally had a very difficult passage while the future command of Iraq and Persia was being settled[3] for a long time it looked as though Wavell, in addition to his eastern war and his internal problem in India was going to take over Iraq, Persia, and the Caucasus (including the air). I had to fight single-handed, but I felt strongly that such a solution would be wrong from every point of view. The separate army command for Iraq and Persia has now been formed—under 'Jumbo' Wilson.[4] The air

[1] On the night of 30 August the Germans launched an attack on the British positions defending Cairo. It was repulsed. Rommel withdrew on 3 September with heavy losses.

[2] From the meeting at Cairo in the first week of August Churchill and his service chiefs went to Moscow and returned to Cairo on 17 August.

[3] See supra, p. 377, note 2.   [4] General Sir H. Maitland Wilson.

remains with me. I hope this split between Middle East army and
Iraq and Persia will only be temporary.[1] I feel that strategically, as
well as from the supply point of view, it is all one theatre. It certainly is from the air point of view.

The Russian visit was intensely interesting and, I think, useful.
One felt that they were worried about their own situation and had
been counting a lot on the 'second front'.[2] They were honestly
bitterly disappointed. I don't think for a moment that we convinced
them of the soundness of our military reasons for not doing what
they expected, but I did feel that we did convince them of our
honesty and wish to help them—which is at least some achievement.
[Field Marshal K. Y.] Voroshilov told me, 'off the record', that he
thought we overestimated the efficiency and skill of the Hun on land.
One could not but sympathize with them as regards their attitude,
not least as to our 'offer' of air assistance. I was pressing them to
agree to collaborate with us on preparations and yet, when asked,
could give no firm indication as to what that assistance would be and
when it would come. My trouble of course is aircraft, especially
fighters, and the immediate prospects look no better.

May I offer my good wishes to yourself and your wife? Yours
sincerely,

A. W. Tedder

578 To R. Craigie   Vol. 69, no. 173

Pretoria
11 September 1942

Dear Sir Robert Craigie, Thank you very much for the great
pleasure you have given me in allowing me to read your draft report
and attached memorandum.[3] I have read both with enormous
interest, all the greater because as a fairly constant reader of your
despatches I have often not seen eye to eye with you. Nor am
I convinced even now by your most able apologia. Perhaps the
difference between us lies in those final evaluations in which people
constitutionally differ in the last resort.

The Japanese were determined to control and bestride the East
—by peaceful penetration if possible, by force if necessary, but

---

[1] It was. On 21 January 1943 the Middle East and Persia–Iraq commands were
again united under General Wilson.

[2] The Russian leaders wanted their Allies to open a major offensive against the
Germans in Western Europe in order to relieve the pressure on them. They had hoped
for a cross-Channel operation in 1942.

[3] Not in the Smuts Collection.

their resolve was inflexible, and that you admit. Your object was to gain some little more time for us in our state of unpreparedness. The risk your policy was running concerned America's entry into the war. The more we appeared to appease Japan the more we were delaying the entry of the United States of America into the war on our side. And here delay appeared to me likely to be fatal. Her entry into the last great war was almost too late. In 1918 France was breaking and I believe only the American reinforcements saved us then. And now? Is she not almost too late already—with France out, Russia in parlous plight and Germany in command of practically all Europe and its resources? Her mobilization is so slow, her movement to the war fronts takes so much time.

It is again touch and go. Japan's attack has been a grievous blow. But how much longer would it have taken the United States of America to make up her mind, and what would the effects on the final issue have been, even if she had come in, but at a time when we were much nearer to a state of exhaustion?

These considerations made me conclude that the risks of even offering to appease Japan were too great, and that it was a wise instinct which guided British statesmen in giving Washington a free hand to negotiate with Japan, and for us to keep step with the United States of America, even if her handling of the negotiations might leave much to be desired—as it did. Your policy struck me as too risky if we had to carry the United States of America with us without incurring dangerous delay.

What has happened on 10 December '41 might yet prove to have saved the world, terrible as the price of American disillusionment has been. The shock and the loss have been enormous, but not too great a price for the ultimate victory which has thus—and only thus—become possible.

Japan was the enemy in the long run, and the vast future very much dependent on Anglo-American co-operation. The pattern for victory is now in order, but it still remains a question whether the time-table is also in order. Your policy might have jeopardized that vital time-table, even though it may have given us a few more months of respite as far as Japan was concerned.

I fear you will not agree with me, but you may be interested in my view, as I am deeply interested in yours.

What we see today is probably the greatest happenings in human history, and it was right to get the right alignments before it was too late. Time only can show whether we have succeeded in doing so. With cordial greetings and all good wishes. Yours sincerely,

s. J. C. Smuts

579   From L. S. Amery   Vol. 67, no. 14

India Office
Whitehall
12 September 1942

My dear Smuts, I am not sure whether this will still reach you before you start on your journey over here. But in case it should I send it along as something to read in the aeroplane.

As I telegraphed you the other day, I think your suggestion of a small committee or conference of party leaders to discuss the future constitution of India while the government is carried on on its present basis, so as to enable Indian freedom to start at the earliest possible date after the war, is probably the only practical thing that can be done in the near future. The trouble is that the party leaders are not at present disposed to meet even for that purpose. They have been encouraged to do so ever since August 1940 and the main parties at any rate have made no attempt even to get into touch with each other. Even those who have talked about coming together (and have not been able to deliver the goods) have, so far, always coupled their proposal with the demand for the immediate transfer of all powers, without facing the difficulties of the situation that would ensue. For the moment also, and until the civil disobedience movement stops entirely and the Congress leaders show some change of heart, it is impossible to deal with them, and yet without them it is not easy to come to any sort of conclusion as to India's future.

Things may be a little different in six months' time when a new viceroy[1] takes over, and he might very possibly be in a position to take an initiative in calling a conference together which would meet with some response. Meanwhile I sent a copy of your telegram to the viceroy as soon as I received it and it will be reaching him in the next few days.

I am looking forward greatly to the opportunity of some good talks with you when you are over here, not only about India, but about the whole future, both in the British Commonwealth and in the world. Yours ever,

Leo Amery

[1] Field-Marshal Viscount Wavell became viceroy and governor-general of India on 19 June 1943.

580   To General C. de Gaulle   Vol. 69, no. 174

Pretoria
16 September 1942

My dear General, Colonel [Z.] Pechkoff is taking this letter to you, and I welcome this opportunity once more to come into touch with you.

From recent messages I have gathered the impression that matters were not going smoothly between you and the British authorities in Syria, Cairo and London. This I deeply regret, and all the more so in view of what you told me in Cairo, namely that Washington was not seeing eye to eye with you in regard to the full recognition of the National Committee.[1]

Without going into details let me say this word to you. From personal knowledge I feel completely satisfied of British good will to you, and I know that British leaders have repeatedly used their influence in Washington to be helpful to you.

About the difficulties of the Syrian situation I am not informed, but I do know and appreciate the British anxieties about Syria possibly becoming a major war front in certain eventualities which cannot be ignored. Their attitude in Syria is and can only be dictated by this governing consideration which I would beg you to keep constantly in mind when difficulties arise. They can have no *arrière pensée* in reference to French interests.

Most unfortunately what has happened in Syria is now having its repercussions about Madagascar and plans for its future administration have had to be postponed for the present. This is most regrettable, and the sooner an end is made of these small differences, which may lead to bigger differences, the better.

I venture to express the strong hope that you will without delay accept the invitation of Mr Churchill to return to London and discuss matters with him personally. I feel convinced of his good will; I also am confident that a personal talk between two big men like you will dissipate this atmosphere of misunderstanding which is unfortunately gathering round the problems we have to deal with in common. We are comrades together; we are comrades in the greatest cause and in the most dangerous phase of history. No human differences or weaknesses should be allowed to interfere with our utter devotion to our great task. Here the spirit of comradeship is the highest statesmanship and the best strategy. Between two such men as you and Mr Churchill there should in this crisis be

[1] In July–August 1940 a Free French National Committee headed by de Gaulle and with headquarters in London, came into existence. In opposition to the French government at Vichy, it directed the French forces which continued the war against the Axis powers. *See* A. Werth, *De Gaulle* (1965), pp. 110–11.

the utmost frankness and mutual confidence, and any little differences should be thrashed out in personal exchanges.

I write to you exactly as I have spoken to him, and I feel sure that
the sooner you meet and discuss the situation frankly and candidly
the better will be the understanding and co-operation between you.

I would have invited you to visit us in the Union on this occasion,
but I think the call of London on you must have priority, and therefore I will only wish you a safe journey to London, and a successful
solution of all pending questions. Whatever I can do to promote the
best feeling and the happiest solutions I shall most gladly do so.

Let me add that I have a very high opinion of Colonel Pechkoff,
and in him you have a very able and devoted officer to represent
you in South Africa. Yours sincerely.

s. J. C. Smuts

581   To M. C. Gillett
Vol. 69, no. 253

Doornkloof
[Transvaal]
24 September 1942

Today I received two good letters from you and Arthur written near
the end of July—yours when you were on the point of going north
to York, and his from London while you were away. The war items
sounded like an echo of far-off happenings, and condoled with me
on the loss of Tobruk, and referred to the Germans marching on
Rostov. Now my lost division at Tobruk has been replaced, and the
Germans are in Stalingrad, though not yet in full possession—I hope
they will not be for some weeks yet. Meanwhile we have had our
bit of luck in occupying most of Madagascar.[1] That has been 'O.K.'
as Winston wired to me. Here too on the home front there has been
success, though not always due to me. Thus the great party congress
of Dr Malan has turned out a hopeless flop, and all are laughing at
him. The united front which all the groups against me were to form
has not eventuated, and the feud between them is as great as ever.[2]

[1] See supra, p. 368, note 1. Between 10 and 23 September a joint British–South
African force commanded by General Platt had taken Majunga on the west coast and
Tamatave and Tananarivo on the east coast. The French governor retreated south-
wards with his troops but surrendered on 5 November.

[2] The Union-wide congress of the National party which met in Pretoria on 16 September 1942 was, in fact, a marked success. It was attended by over 1,100 members who
gave Dr Malan a vote of confidence and plenary powers. It is true that the various
Afrikaner bodies (the National party, the Afrikaner party, the New Order and the
Ossewa-Brandwag) failed to unite in spite of several attempts at this time to bring
them together. But this was not a defeat for Malan, for his party had insisted that the

I have taken no notice of them and have simply gone on with my own difficult job. That has been my simple tactics during this war —not to mind my political opponents too much, rather to ignore them, and to concentrate on my own war and governmental business. That is the positive way, and means least waste of time and energy. The negative way of contraverting your enemies and countering their knavish tricks[1] is exciting but essentially barren. Whenever you can afford it, ignore your opponents, don't answer back, but give the public instead something constructive and positive of your own. Put something of your own before the public instead of meeting the enemy on his own ground by endeavouring to answer him back. I have found this simple way of dealing with him both effective and time-saving. One very funny attempt of Dr Malan to get republican kudos was to be drawn by enthusiastic young students in the thirty years' old motor of General Beyers in which General De lay Rey was accidentally shot. Think of the silliness of the business—enough to make even lunatics laugh. Some fools of mine did Malan the service to remove two wheels of this old bus the night before this triumphal progress through Pretoria had to take place, and so unfortunately the plan did not actually come off. I should have preferred the procession and the ribald laughter. Even so, however, decent people must have felt disgusted at this resurrection of the dead for the little political profit of the present. Meanwhile Malan's opponents—Pirow, van Rensburg (the *Ossewa-Brandwag* chief) and Havenga[2] were trying to come to an arrangement with Malan and form a united front. This also failed. And all the time we simply ignored them, except to laugh at their folly and discomfiture. All this good fortune is welcome but may not last too long, alas!

...This letter is written late in the week, but that is because I have been over busy all the time with work and engagements. Thus yesterday was spent at Johannesburg in opening a great military hospital we have built for the British government at a cost of about £400,000. It is near the Orlando Native location and will after the war serve as a Native hospital, and much needed as such.[3] It will be

other Afrikaner organizations must accept its sole political leadership as a condition of union. Their continued division was therefore an indication of the strength of the National party.

[1]   Confound their politics,
      Frustrate their knavish tricks...
            Henry Carey, *God Save the King.*

[2] On 16 August 1941 O. Pirow and seventeen other Afrikaner members of parliament formed the New Order. Its national-socialist doctrines based, according to Pirow, on those of Salazar, had been set out by its leader in a pamphlet published in December 1940. N. C. Havenga was the leader of the Afrikaner party although he had resigned his seat in parliament.   [3] The present Baragwanath hospital.

the largest and best equipped hospital in South Africa. The usual speech had of course to be made and wards had to be visited and men spoken to. I arrived home pretty exhausted. This sort of thing goes on pretty well all the time that I am not occupied in office. And so time passes with little relaxation and no holiday, except Sundays when we are occasionally free from visitors. I lunch daily at 'Libertas' with the Greek princesses who are great fun and splendid company. They are clever, educated, well-informed women of the world. Princess Katherine a full nurse, and the crown princess Frederica a thoughtful, well-read woman, very young and good to look at, and as I told you before, a student of holism. They tell me of many curious incidents of recent years with which they have been associated, and the lunch time—which is barely an hour daily—passes smoothly and fast—a real relaxation for me. The Huddlestons brought me *Grey Eminence* by Aldous Huxley[1] which I am now reading. It is a curious story of the priest who was Richelieu's right hand man in his political work during the Thirty Years War,[2] and withal was also a religious mystic, given to all the perfervid religious devotions of that age. Huxley gives a strange description of the mystic cults then existing in France, and of the way these religious societies were intertwined with the politics and wars of that time. I am slowly reading through this book whenever I have a waking moment at night. This is a curious sort of book for Huxley, but he seems to have recovered from his Marxist or infidel phase. The work is very well written. It will interest Arthur if he has not already read it. The priest is the historical Grey Cardinal, whom I have often heard mentioned but have not till now made closer acquaintance with. 'Brother Joseph' he was called in the Franciscan Order.

Dear Frank Joubert, the Cape administrator, has just passed away and will be buried tomorrow. He was our South African party secretary for a lifetime and in the end turned out a capital administrator, whom it will be most difficult to replace. You know him and his little wife, Enid, who was half a Jewess by descent. I would have flown south for the funeral but am so dreadfully busy that I may not add this flight to my other burdens. Poor Hertzog is also in the General Hospital here and underwent an operation for internal trouble yesterday which was very serious, according to gossip which has come to me. Poor old fellow! According to his latest declaration[3] he has virtually become a Nazi

---

[1] Published in 1941.

[2] General European war fought between 1618 and 1648 mainly in Germany and ended by the treaty of Wesphalia. The war brought about significant territorial and political changes, particularly in furthering French dominance in western Europe.

[3] This declaration was made on 22 October 1941 in an address to the head committee of the Afrikaner party. Hertzog then said that the democratic system had

under Pirow's malign influence and had nothing but damnation for the parliamentary system and democracy in general. What an end to have come to! His friends have been moving heaven and earth to get him back into politics or at least to keep him in cold storage for the peace conference, where he was to get the restoration of the Nazi republic of South Africa from Hitler! Now I am afraid he will not last till the conference, and I don't think Hitler will either. But what a comedy is South African politics! If you wish to see wishful thinking at its worst come to South African politics. I sometimes think I am the only real realist here, and even I am generally mistaken for an optimist...

582   To J. H. Hofmeyr   Vol. 69, no. 187

Cairo
12 October 1942

My dear Jantjie, Just a line to you before I leave tonight for the rest of my trip.[1] We had a record flight of less than a day and a half from Pretoria, reaching Khartoum before sundown on the first day. Here I have had talks with all the authorities, and a very cheerful spirit prevails. I saw Admiral [W. H.] Standly last night on his way from Moscow to report to Roosevelt. He gives a cheering account of the Russian situation and says it looks quite firm,[2] whatever further successes the Germans might have.

I was so sorry to hear that Conroy [A. M.] is also on the sick list, and for the same reason as Deneys [Reitz]. I hope you will pull through even with this decimated team.[3] It is all bad luck with three ministers out of action, and so much to do. It only means that I shall have to do my best to return as soon as ever I can. How soon that will be time alone can show. I went pretty thoroughly into the military situation here, and on the whole it looks satisfactory. The front was too electric for a visit, but Dan Pienaar, who came to see me, said that the spirit among our men was very good, and for the moment nobody talks of leave!

Japie [Smuts] and Louis [MacIldowie] both accompanied me.

disappointed Afrikanders and that national socialism was in accordance with their moral and religious outlook. *See* C. M. van den Heever, *General J. B. M. Hertzog* (1946), pp. 753–5.

[1] Smuts was en route to London. Here he attended meetings of the war cabinet and on 21 October addressed members of both houses of parliament in the Royal Gallery. *See* J. C. Smuts, *Jan Christian Smuts*, pp. 423–6.

[2] The Russians were at this time making their great stand at Stalingrad.

[3] J. H. Hofmeyr was acting prime minister.

There is a call for the services of both up here,[1] and they may have to return here soon.

Good-bye. My love to you and Borrie,[2] and my best wishes to you in your heavy burdens. Ever yours,

s. J. C. Smuts

583   To Lord Cecil   Vol. 69, no. 192

[Hyde Park Hotel
London]
10 November 1942

Dear Cecil, It was a great pleasure to meet you and Noel Baker once more and to exchange thoughts over the post-war future, and to thank both of you once again for the devoted service you and the League of Nations Union have rendered to the cause of peace.

Whatever the future may hold in store for us the international humanitarian work which the League initiated and still carries on will surely stand as one of the great historic human advances. That aspect of its activities will remain an abiding possession of our future civilization.

For reasons you have so ably set forth in your *Great Experiment* its work for world peace was in the end unsuccessful, and the failure points to the imperative necessity for new, more effective machinery to provide against the periodic recurrence of war. Such machinery it is now possible to create under more favourable conditions in the new organization of the United Nations, and indeed *must* be created if the human race is to survive.

At the same time much more attention will also have to be given to the economic factors in international life which are more and more becoming of such fundamental importance for world co-operation and world peace. After the economic and trade disasters of the post-war time all this is now much more fully appreciated. And it should be possible after this war to rebuild an organization on the foundations laid twenty-two years ago, which will no longer be merely experimental but be an assured and reliable defence for world peace.

The brilliant League experiment and the bitter experience of the last twenty-five years place us in a strong position to build better next time. Let us not despair of the future, where the human material has proved so good and the cause so great. The Experiment will yet be a success. With all good wishes, Ever yours sincerely,

s. J. C. Smuts

---

[1] As liaison officer between the Union and the British military authorities, and medical officer in the Women's Auxiliary Army Service respectively.

[2] Deborah, mother of J. H. Hofmeyr.

584   To T. Lie   Vol. 69, no. 194

[Hyde Park Hotel
London]
12 November 1942

Dear Dr Lie, I have your letter of 6 November with the enclosed statement on Norway's foreign policy. I thank you for your kind inquiries about my health. I now feel much restored from the severe attack of cold which overtook me and unfortunately prevented me from attending His Majesty King Haakon's lunch.

Your statement of policy appears to me to be, generally speaking, a fair and balanced statement of the position of the small countries in western Europe. With a powerful and predatory power in the heart of the Continent their position round it remains precarious and dangerous, unless a really effective peace organization can be created. The lines on which such an organization is possible lie to hand and are fairly sketched by you. The League in its technical humanitarian work on universal lines may continue to function for mankind at large. But for effective disarmament and maintenance of peace in the difficult years ahead a new organization of and inside the United Nations is called for. The great powers among them will necessarily have to take the lead and assume a heavier responsibility than they were prepared to undertake after the last war. This is in effect foreshadowed in the Atlantic Charter. The smaller powers will no doubt welcome this development even if it may appear to affect their technical sovereign rights. The modern developments of war have brought about a far-reaching change in our old-time concepts of neutrality and sovereignty. And we have to shape our future course, not according to the old textbooks, but the hard and cruel lessons we have all learned in this era of world war.

I gather from your statement that the smaller powers in western Europe have indeed learnt this lesson and would willingly make some surrender in exchange for real security. The problem will be to work out such effective arrangements for future peace not only for western Europe but also for southern and eastern Europe and the Far East and the world generally. The task will be no easy one but certainly not beyond our capacity for future planning. Exploratory talks among the smaller powers and their consultations with the great powers of the United Nations in this connection will help to clear the ground and to facilitate the final decisions when the peace stage is reached. Unless some practical and effective *modus vivendi* is reached the position of small independent countries will in future be quite hopeless, and it is therefore right in their own vital interests that they should take the initiative in preliminary discussions of the whole question. I am sure they will find their quest by no means hopeless.

I was very glad to meet you at the foreign office and to have a brief talk with you. Yours sincerely,

s. J. C. Smuts

585   To F. D. Roosevelt   Vol. 69, no. 195

[Hyde Park Hotel
London]
15 November 1942

Dear Mr President, Mrs Roosevelt will kindly bring you this letter from me.

First let me say to you how much her visit to England has been appreciated by everybody. The people of this country have for more than three years been passing though deep waters, and have gallantly and stubbornly borne the heaviest burdens. They feel the strain, and one like me who has not been here for many years can see the strain and the difference. To them her visit has been a great refreshment, not only because she is the wife of the president of the U.S.A. and the emissary of its great people, but also because of herself, of her kindliness, her deep sympathy and evident interest in everyone and everything. She has not spared herself to see everything and everyone, and has done far more than could have been expected of her. The effect of all this profound interest and interestedness has been very great and very welcome, and her visit has, from the human point of view, been of the greatest possible service. She has unstintedly given herself and of herself, and people high and low are filled with gratitude. I wanted to tell you this as you might like to have the opinion of another visitor and spectator of this most human scene at this great moment.

Secondly, I want once more to thank you for your repeated invitation to me to visit the States. Mr [J. G.] Winant has passed your kind message on to me, and I have felt more than tempted to accept and thus have the opportunity of personal talks with you over the course before us both in war and after the war. Unfortunately it has finally proved impossible to come now, and when you receive this I shall probably be on my way back to South Africa. I need not trouble you with the details, but only wish you to believe that it has really not been possible. I shall look forward to a visit as soon as a convenient opportunity comes next year. With the efficient air service between South Africa and the States I may be able to come direct to Washington from there, and talk things over. And it is possible that a visit later at the proper moment may be more useful than one at present when the immediate course before us is so clear.

We have had great luck in the whole Mediterranean basin, greater than could have been expected, the first stroke of real luck we have had in the war.[1] The effect on public morale has been electric, and everybody feels delighted. As I have always been an advocate of this theatre I feel specially happy. We seem at last to have reached the right road and to be moving freely and rapidly forward. So may it continue—so *must* it continue. I have seen your messages to Churchill and his to you. I need not say how fully in accord and in personal agreement I am with both of you. I think our course is clearly set out before us, and the initial success is further proof how right you have been. The rest seems to be a logical development and following up of that course. The great thing now is to keep the initiative and to give the enemy no chance to recover it and himself. These plans involve the hardest blows we are at present capable of striking against Germany and Italy, the best way of helping Russia in her great task, and later of getting eastward to China and finally of striking devastatingly at Japan.

Finally I wish to say how very warmly I thank you for the help you have been giving South Africa in the war. Your sympathy and support with the service and production departments concerned have been invaluable, and my representatives, Close and John Martin, have continually reminded me how effective your sympathy has been in securing necessary supplies for South Africa. My political and other difficulties have been great, and your help has eased my position very considerably. And so I continue to look forward to paying you a visit and personally thanking you for all this assistance and exchanging thoughts with you 'as from one Dutchman to another'.[2] With all good wishes, Very sincerely yours,

s. J. C. Smuts

[1] On 23 October the Allied offensive in Egypt had begun. By 6 November the battle of El Alamein had been won and Rommel's forces were in retreat. On 8 November British and American landings took place in north Africa at Oran, at Algiers and in Morocco.

[2] *See* 566.

586   To M. C. Gillett **Vol. 69, no. 258**

Doornkloof
[Transvaal]
29 November 1942

This is my first letter after my return and I shall begin with a short itinerary. I left Friday (20 November) morning 2 a.m. from the aerodrome whither the prime minister had accompanied me, and arrived at Gibraltar for breakfast, occupying the rest of the day with conferences about military and political matters in north Africa.[1] Friday evening off to Cairo where I arrived Saturday (the 21st) morning early, and again spent the day in conferences and meetings over war matters. Sunday (the 22nd) morning I flew to Tobruk and visited our air units in that area. Montgomery's headquarters had moved too far for me to see him that day. I then flew back to the Canal area where I visited and addressed the South African Infantry Division and other railway and engineering and medical units which constitute the bulk of our forces in the north. A very full and useful Sunday, winding up with dinner at the embassy where I was staying. I valued these contacts with my gallant men and I am sure they were greatly pleased with all I could say to them. On Monday morning (the 23rd) I flew off to Nairobi; taking the Greek crown princess with me,[2] and after refuelling at Khartoum, we reached Nairobi at 10 p.m. and stayed the night with the good Moores at Government House. In Cairo I saw Louis [MacIldowie] who is now installed as doctor of our female units, and Andries [Weyers] who has been promoted to lieutenant-colonel. At Nairobi I had no time for dinner as military talks were necessary which kept us busy till 1 a.m. Then, at 7 a.m. on Tuesday (the 24th), off to Pretoria which was reached at 6 p.m. after refuelling and seeing the governor at Lusaka, and flying over the Victoria Falls which the crown princess was anxious to see. We had a great welcome on arrival...To you and Arthur I wish to say how deeply I appreciated your arrangements for being so much near me.[3] But for your arrangements I would have seen very little of you and nothing of the rest of the Gillett family, and that would have pained me very deeply. Now I have enjoyed your dear company to the full (though of course never enough) and I have seen and enjoyed the children and their little families...

I enjoyed my English visit very much and believe that others

---

[1] *See* W. S. Churchill, *The Second World War*, vol. IV, pp. 569–70.

[2] She had travelled with Smuts to Cairo to visit her husband.

[3] Margaret and Arthur Gillett took rooms at the Hyde Park Hotel where Smuts had a suite.

have done so too. The prime minister has been most profuse in his expressions of gratitude, and I know that he has meant all he has said to me on this. I find the war position has improved since my departure. Hitler has failed in his desperate attempt to obtain possession of the French fleet,[1] and this failure will have a significance far beyond its immediate occasion. If anything this final act of treachery ought to rouse the French from their stupor and deal a death blow to Pétain's policy of appeasement with the Germans. The French in other parts of the world will now be more solidly than ever with us. Stalin has struck hard and successful blows against the enemy,[2] and it almost looks as if the Germans will this winter have an even harder time than last winter in the bitter Russian weather. In Tunis the progress is slow but solid;[3] in the far Pacific the position is improving. The U-boat menace is going to be most seriously grappled with. All this shows how great a change has come over the scene since last month. May this progress be accelerated and see us next spring much farther on the road to victory.

Here the situation is also good. The opposition continues in a state of confusion and the elements that looked to Hertzog have had that support knocked down.[4] Poor man, what an exit after fifteen years of prime ministership in this country! And in the last three years his reputation has been badly eclipsed when he might have retired gracefully in 1939 and retained the halo of past glory. In spite of the plight of the opposition I shall have to be careful and watch developments closely and actively. One never knows, especially in this country where even small things often have such unexpected results. For the old slogan 'watch and pray'[5] I shall have to substitute 'watch and work', which is a much more arduous business. Prayer is often resorted to as a form of escape from hard endeavour. In that sense it is a source of weakness and not of strength and refreshment and illumination as prayer normally should be. Prayer is a very holistic function, and more than many other forms of activity establishes our contact with the whole—it is a nexus of the part of the whole, and a spiritual nexus of the deepest significance. I think the old religious slogan was *laborare est orare*[6]—and

---

[1] On 11 November the Germans invaded Vichy France but before they could occupy Toulon the French fleet based there (seventy-three ships) was scuttled. The order to scuttle was given by Admiral Darlan whom the Allies had placed at the head of a provisional government of French north and west Africa.

[2] The Russian counter-offensive at Stalingrad began on 19 November. Four days later the German Sixth Army under General Paulus was encircled.

[3] From 11–17 November several Tunisian positions had been occupied by British and American forces.   [4] Hertzog died on 21 November 1942.

[5] From the hymn 'Christian! seek not yet repose' by Charlotte Elliot (1789–1871).

[6] To work is to pray.

that expresses more accurately what I consider should be our attitude.

Isie is quite well again and has resumed her numerous activities. I hope she will not again overdo them. But I am most thankful that she looks fit and well again...

But enough. All good wishes and love from

Jan

587   To M. C. Gillett   Vol. 69, no. 260

Doornkloof
[Transvaal]
14 December 1942

I am sorry that I did not send my birthday congratulations to Arthur and Nico [Gillett] earlier but they will understand that, birthday or no birthday, they are never far from my mind. Years and blessings on both of them. We shall specially remember them this week. Isie follows next, dear thing.

It has been a busy week for me since last I wrote, culminating in a huge demonstration at Standerton of many thousands of my constituents. I there announced that South Africans will be asked, after this African warfare is over, to go anywhere in the world;[1] I myself was prepared to go even to the gates of hell! We were going to release our boys captured at Tobruk and bring them home. This was on Friday, and on Saturday I had to open a big fête for Red Cross funds at Pretoria where I said this war was more than a war, and would yet prove one of the pivotal points of history. This I believe will prove true. The world is being cleared for the new moves forward in our civilization, and dreadful as the process is, the far-off end may yet prove to have justified the means, although it is dreadful to think so. I do not see that the human spirit is dead. It will survive and rise above this awful suffering and destruction of the material apparatus of civilization. May it be given us to build a fairer world on more durable foundations. This week I have heavy work before me, winding up with two or three heavy tasks at Johannesburg. And so on to the end of the year. It has not been a dead year of defence, as 1940 and 1941, but one of movement towards victory. Only this morning the wireless announced that Rommel had been beaten out of El Ageila and was now being pursued towards Tripoli. And the Russian offensive continues. And the Japs have been halted in New Guinea and now only hold the narrow strip round Buna. And poor

[1] Recruits to the Union Defence Force were volunteers and might or might not undertake to serve 'anywhere in Africa'. Those who did so wore a red shoulder flash.

Italy is being subjected to the new phase of air bombing by night and day. No, it is no longer a case for our passive endurance and suffering but for bringing the war home to the enemy. And it will be brought right home to him in a way he never thought even possible, let alone actual.

Yesterday (Sunday) we had the pleasure of having Abbé Breuil and van Riet Lowe here. It was a good time, especially for Jannie [Smuts] who had taken leave for the day specially to meet the Abbé. Most of the day was spent over stones and things[1] in his little crowded prehistory museum. And you may be sure that the discussions were animated. In the end the Abbé thought that Jannie was right in concluding that Pliocene man in Africa is proved, but some of Jannie's *oldest* implements might prove to be natural and not human and he, Breuil, was doubtful about them. But Jannie's main point of the vast antiquity of man—far beyond the oldest Stellenbosch culture—is proved by Jannie's collections. So in the end there was agreement on the main point. I had long talks with the Abbé over his experiences in occupied and unoccupied France and Portugal—all both interesting and useful. He is very fierce in his anti-Nazi attitude and sees no possibility of future peace unless the nations round Germany who have suffered and are suffering hell are allowed a free hand to destroy Nazis at the end. He is full of the story of horrors by which the Jews and the *élite* among the other peoples are being eliminated by many devilish devices. I listened without expressing an opinion, which must have been a disappointment to him. I only remarked that I had heard strange doctrine from an Abbé of the Christian Church! He maintained that if the Nazis are allowed to escape there is no moral or legal basis for punishing criminals in human society. And so on, and so forth. So we returned to stones and paleolithic man. They will come again, but of course parliament is drawing near and meanwhile my hands and time are over-full.

...I am reading Fausset's *Life* of Walt Whitman[2] at night before sleep with great interest. Fausset has much more factual knowledge than I had fifty years ago, and can reconstruct Whitman more fully and adequately. I don't agree with him in all respects, especially in his speculations about Whitman's sexual character and behaviour. But in many respects his analysis both of Whitman and his work is very searching and instructive, and you and Arthur may find the book well worth reading. The deeper aspects of democracy are well in the picture, and this is of special importance in these times, when

---

[1] *See supra*, p. 96, note 1.
[2] Hugh l'Anson Fausset, *Walt Whitman: Poet of Democracy* (1942).

democracy is so often on our lips. Behind democracy and the City of God there is a human Vision which keeps floating before my mind's eye. Lovingly yours,

Jan

588   To M. C. Gillett   Vol. 69, no. 261

Doornkloof
[Transvaal]
26 December 1942

I am somewhat in doubt whether I wrote to you last week and only the receipt of my letters will eventually show whether there is a week missing. I am in doubt because I usually write on Sunday, and last week-end I had the prime minister[1] and some other members of Southern Rhodesia staying with me to discuss military matters which could not have left time for private correspondence. I may however have written earlier in that week. I don't like missing these pages of what is almost a diary! Last Sunday it was Rhodesia; this Sunday (tomorrow) it will be the burial of Dan Pienaar and his companions.[2] It will be a very big affair at Roberts Heights[3] and I shall have to do the principal speaking. I am not good at funeral orations. His loss is a very great one to me as he was our most distinguished 'fighting general'[4] up north. I am pleased that such world-wide recognition has at the end come to him for I have received telegrams of condolence from far and wide beyond South Africa and some from quite unexpected quarters...

I told you before that I was reading Fausset's *Walt Whitman*. I have now finished it and consider it a really valuable piece of work. If you had time you would enjoy reading it. Fausset has a great deal of fresh material about Whitman which I did not have in 1894 although I then read everything there was in the British Museum. Practically all the material has only been published since. It would now appear that Whitman was not quite normal in his sexual make-up. His *Children of Adam* is more imaginary than indicative of real experience. Besides he had slight homosexual leanings, which

[1] Sir Godfrey Huggins, later Viscount Malvern.
[2] General D. H. Pienaar with eleven other officers and men was killed on 19 December when the aircraft on which they were returning to the Union crashed in Kavirondo gulf in Lake Victoria.
[3] Headquarters of the Union Defence Force near Pretoria; renamed Voortrekkerhoogte in 1938.
[4] Literal translation of *vechtgeneraal*, originally a military rank in the Boer forces during the Anglo-Boer War.

I might have inferred from *Calamus* but did not infer in my simplicity and ignorance of such abnormalities. This is all valuable stuff, in a way, unknown to me when I wrote about him. Whitman did a great service to me in making me appreciate the Natural Man and freeing me from much theological or conventional preconceptions due to my very early pious upbringing. It was a sort of liberation, as St Paul was liberated from the Law and its damnations by his Damascus vision. Sin ceased to dominate my view of life, and this was a great release as I was inclined to be severely puritanical in all things. A great release and a useful service. But in after years and from deeper thought and experience of the realities, I have come to think that there was much more in the older views than Whitman ever understood or at least put into his poems. You do not reach your full human stature by reverting to the natural or biological man but by moving onward and making a higher synthesis of the old and the new in our experience, by appreciating the dreadful *reality* of evil and not shutting one's eyes to it, and by rising from the experience of our limitations, our weaknesses and flaws to a deeper conception of the real human. Experience is really the stepping-stones by which we rise to this higher self,[1] and only in that process is peace and harmony to be attained, and not by reverting to the earlier, purely natural phase. There is this much in the orthodox view, and it means a deeper reading of the problem of life. Good *and* evil are realities to be squarely faced, and we do not get at the real truth by ignoring or glossing over evil. In a very true sense the Human–Divine is based on this deeper experience and on the synthesis arising from such experience. Whitman, according to Fausset, made the same mistake by his view of democratic man, who also is not the last word, but has to learn to rise above the shortcomings of a crude democracy, and the evils of the competitive society, in order to form that society or brotherhood of man which is the next stage in our social and communal progress. In both cases we move from the natural to the spiritual level in our 'holistic' rise. (The word is of course not used by Fausset.) I had assumed that his move had been made by Whitman and understood him in that sense, and thought him an illustration of personal holism. But it is now clear from the fuller biographical material that I was wrong there. It is a curious but profoundly true fact that the higher integration is only reached through experience of the lower, that in a way almost blasphemous to say, the higher good incorporates the evil we have done and passed

[1]
> That men may rise on stepping-stones
> Of their dead selves to higher things.
>> Alfred Tennyson, *In Memoriam*, canto i.

400

through, and that the highest does not negate so much as absorb and incorporate the lower and the lowest. Evil becomes an ingredient in the final good which we attain on the higher synthesis or integration of life. Holism seems to imply this deeper spiritual view of the universe. Evil is not extrinsic to it, but, in some way difficult to comprehend, natural to it and a constituent element in it. The great lesson of experience is to absorb, transmute and sublimate evil and make it an element to enrich, rather than a dominant factor to dominate life.

You have some strange speculation in your last letter to me—about God and His changeable characters at different times and under different circumstances. Perhaps you were touching the same difficult issues which I here refer to. The problem of good and evil is not so very far from St Paul's problem of Law and Grace. True religion calls for very deep soundings of our human experience.

Good-bye dears. Good be with you during this coming year. Ever yours,

Jan

589   From Friends of Africa[1]   Vol. 70, no. 28

Cape Town
5 January 1943

Dear Sir, Disturbed by the recent happenings among African workers, we feel that as representative citizens concerned for the maintenance of peace in South Africa and in closer touch with the African population than most, it is our bounden duty to place our view of the situation before you.

For some time back, a sense of grievance has been growing among African workers. This has undoubtedly been directly due to increasing economic pressure, the mere difficulty of making ends meet on a traditional wage with a rising cost of living, and the frustration begotten of inability to rise out of the ranks of unskilled labour in spite of experience and ability. But it has equally undoubtedly been encouraged by the rising consciousness on the part of Europeans of the inhumanity of breeding disease and crime among a subject population through poverty, and of the danger to the labour supply and the accepted economic organization of the country of the

---

[1] This body originated in a committee formed in 1934 in London on the initiative of Winifred Holtby (1898–1935). It sought to promote the social, economic and political organization of Africans. Its South African branch was started by William and Margaret Ballinger.

progressive deterioration in the physical standard of the Africans, which poverty and disease is causing.

The war has served both to reveal the extent to which this sense of grievance and frustration has progressed among the Africans and to aggravate it, both through the increase in economic pressure and the talk of democratic obligations. We have been fully alive to the dangers of this situation and have from time to time, both through the office of this organization and through those members of our executive whose political position affords them independent access to the government,[1] done our best to warn the government of the need, if trouble were to be avoided, for its careful handling and for timely concession of the urgent and justified demands of the people both for relief of the economic pressure on them and for the provision of constitutional channels for the expression of their grievances. We were duly encouraged to feel that these warnings had been sympathetically and understandingly received by your promise to amend the Industrial Conciliation Act next session and place African employees on the same basis as other employees.[2] This promise was conveyed to the parliamentary representatives of the Africans through the minister of Native affairs[3] and by the secretary,[4] and was passed on to us. We have used it to stimulate new hope in the African people, even where the slowness of the work of the Wage Board[5] and the inadequate levels of wages established by the Board have been consistent counter irritants. The last two months, however, beginning with an announcement by the minister of labour[6] that the Industrial Conciliation Act would not be amended at present, has seen the progressive deterioration in the general position. This, we venture to submit, could only end as it has done in the unfortunate episodes at Pretoria,[7] which we all, too late, deplore. We have no doubt and no hesitation in saying that those episodes are the direct result—

[1] Mrs V. M. L. Ballinger and D. B. Molteno were representatives in the house of assembly of African electors in the Cape Eastern circle and the Cape Western circle respectively.

[2] The Industrial Conciliation Act of 1924 provided machinery for the discussion and settlement of industrial disputes but 'pass-bearing Natives' were excluded from its terms.

[3] Colonel D. Reitz.   [4] D. L. Smit.

[5] Set up by the Wage Act of 1925 to fix the wages of unskilled and unorganized workers, whether Europeans or Africans.

[6] W. B. Madeley.

[7] In December 1942 riots occurred at the Marabastad municipal compound in Pretoria. Fourteen Africans and one white man were killed and 111 wounded. The riots began at a meeting at which the superintendent of the compound was explaining delay in the payment to African municipal workers of increased wages awarded by the Wage Board.

(1) of the recession of the hope on the part of the Africans of their being given the same constitutional position as other workers in the field of industrial organization by amendment of the Industrial Conciliation Act;

(2) of the amazing concession of the minister of labour to the requests of Johannesburg, the richest municipality in the country, for a postponement of the application of the wage determinations which would impose on them the obligation to pay the still shamefully low wage of 25s. per week to workers who, on the evidence of the Inter-Departmental Committee on Social, Health and Economic Conditions of Africans,[1] cannot maintain their families on any level of efficiency and decency under £7 14s. 0d. per month;

(3) of the fact that even though the minister of labour withdrew this concession, he apparently did so too late to enable other municipalities like Pretoria to make arrangements to meet their obligations in time, as they could have done easily if they had not been led to expect exemption;

(4) and finally to the issuing of an emergency regulation of a purely racial and discriminatory character.[2]

We cannot too strongly deplore the publication of this regulation which singles out African workers—already excluded from the Industrial Conciliation Act—and imposes compulsory arbitration on them in all instances, not merely in those covered for all workers by Emergency Regulation 9, which applies only to occupations and industries designated by the minister as essential to our war effort, and we feel we must state openly our firm conviction that this measure, taken with the very unfortunate colour bar clause in the Factories Act,[3] will go far to persuade the African workers that this government has indeed sacrificed them to an alliance with the vested interests of white labour.

Again Sir, we urge upon you the danger of allowing the Africans' sense of grievance, which is today more acute than ever, to remain and to spread. The purely economic pressure on the people is enormous, as the report of the [D. L.] Smit committee[4] reveals in every line; and is not only unwise but unnecessary. Today Cape Town municipality is paying willingly a weekly wage of 45s. per week to its unskilled employees. Yet Johannesburg boggles at 25s. and when

[1] Department of Native Affairs: *Report of the Inter-Departmental Committee on the Social, Health and Economic Conditions of Urban Natives*, March 1942.
[2] Emergency Regulation No. 154.
[3] *See* vol. v, p. 243, note 2.   [4] *See* note 1 above.

pressed for an explanation, says the government does not itself pay even as good a wage as that. Industry in Cape Town pays a minimum of 40s. per week, while in Port Elizabeth and in Durban it pays 22s. per week; and the main centres of industrial trouble are the Transvaal and Natal, a fact which speaks for itself.

But apart from the purely financial pressure, the people are labouring under an increasingly acute grievance at the discriminatory treatment meted out to them whereby they are refused the ordinary constitutional means of airing their grievances. The long overdue concession of this right would undoubtedly have obviated many of the dangers of the purely economic position. Instead, once again, the Africans have been singled out for a special control and repression; instead of an extension of such rights as they have, they are faced with a further loss. Undoubtedly this is due to the alarm which the recent strikes[1] have inspired in many unthinking Europeans, but again, we repeat, these strikes need not have taken place; they were the result not only of legitimate grievances, but of unwise handling of a situation the outlines and essence of which should have been quite familiar to anyone with that industrial experience which we have the right to expect from a minister of labour.

Since the last thing we wish is to be unconstructively critical, we would respectfully submit for your urgent consideration the wisdom—

(1) of dealing immediately, and more effectively than the Wage Board has been able to do, with the wage position. Government service should set the standard of a living wage, and while private employers all over the country should be warned that within a limited time they will have to come into line with the best wage standards in the country, provision should be made now for the subsidization of the livelihood of all those workers who are well below, not the bread line since this is not within measurable distance of being reached by Africans generally in South Africa, but the level on which they could acquire the basic minimum necessities of life. The policy of subsidies has been widely used in South Africa as has the policy of price fixation, but neither of these with the only essential justification—that of providing the people lowest down with the means to survive efficiently.

We are aware that many people would say this is an impossible plan we are proposing, that it is too difficult. We are ourselves convinced that, with the will to meet the urgency

---

[1] Towards the close of 1942 there had been a wave of strikes by Africans, chiefly on the Witwatersrand but also in Natal. The strikers included workers in sweet factories, brickworks, and dairies; coal-miners, dockers, and railway workers.

of the very serious problems of Africans' ill-health and discontent, it is not impossible to work out plans along the lines we propose and we believe, Sir, that you are not afraid of difficulties;

(2) of withdrawing the racially discriminatory Emergency Regulation No. 154 and introducing the promised amending legislation to provide ordinary constitutional channels of communication between workers and employers through which reliable information can be passed and grievances aired. We may add here that, where the government feels it incumbent upon it to impose compulsory arbitration on other employees neither we nor the Africans for whom we speak will oppose the inclusion of African workers in the operation of such machinery. But we would make it clear here that we strongly support the proposition of the South African Trades and Labour Council that arbitration courts should be constituted of representatives of employers and workers under impartial chairmen selected by the parties themselves, in preference to the present arrangement whereby the arbitrator must be an official of the department of labour.

Should the government be prepared to follow the lines we have here proposed, we have no doubt that the unrest now so widespread among the African people will steadily give place to a new confidence in the government, and the adoption of such a policy as these proposals represent would of itself be some guarantee against the sort of handling of African affairs which has so largely contributed to the present unfortunate position.

We sincerely hope that you will receive this letter in the spirit in which it has been sent. We have no other interest than to see the present war brought speedily to a victorious conclusion by the combined efforts of all our people inspired with the conviction and armed with the spiritual might of unshakeable belief in the virtue of the democratic cause which we claim to serve and uphold. We know we cannot achieve this unless the African people are with us; and we know they cannot and will not be with us unless we take the adventurous road necessary to show them that the Atlantic Charter, with its aim of a world free from want, fear and oppression, is our objective for them as well as for ourselves. We are, Sir, Yours faithfully,

Members of Committee: Douglas M. Buchanan
Margaret Ballinger   *Chairman*
Donald B. Molteno
C. H. Stohr   W. G. Ballinger
W. G. A. Mears   *Organizing Secretary*

590   From L. S. Amery

Vol. 70, no. 6

India Office
Whitehall
7 January 1943

My dear Smuts, There is one point in your telegram about a possible declaration of colonial policy which is of real importance, apart from the rest with which I generally agree, and ought not to be overlooked. That is the question of strategic routes and bases. After all, we cannot ignore the possibility of danger recurring in the world and if it does it will come in forms conditioned by new methods of warfare, more particularly in the air. It was the failure to realize that in time that cost us Singapore. On the other hand it was a realization of some of those problems during the last war that has proved invaluable this time. During the last war there were two committees, of both of which I was secretary, one of the British war cabinet, and a subsequent one of the imperial war cabinet which you may remember, which looked into the whole question of post-war territorial arrangements and did so largely from the point of view of defence. I remember very well the difficulty I had in laying stress upon the importance of Tanganyika, Palestine and Iraq from the point of view of strategic air communications, and how old Admiral [Sir Arthur] Wilson at one moment threatened to resign from the committee unless my draft paragraph on that theme was omitted— 'fantastical nonsense' was, I think, his comment.

Anyhow, it seems to me that we ought to be beginning to consider that kind of problem now. As the French will presumably keep Bizerta it seems to me essential that we should insist on a long lease of either Benghazi or Tobruk from whatever Arab state we set up in liberated north Africa in order to give air support to Malta and Greece. Again, if by any chance the question of a cession of Cyprus to Greece were seriously contemplated it would be essential not only to keep an adequate air, seaplane and destroyer base inside Cyprus, but to insist that in exchange we should have an air and naval base at Suda bay.[1] In Malaya similarly we should insist that the little Malay states on the Kra isthmus, hitherto under Siamese protection, should join the other Malay states, thus giving us not only a really defensible land frontier, but also continuity of territory with Burma.

These are only a few instances that occur to me. The problem really wants working out with the help of the service technicians from the point of view of what is going to be the effective range both of fighter and bomber forces in the next thirty years. I have urged

[1] On the north coast of Crete.

the point upon Winston and I think he is receptive, but it might do no harm your contributing your own views on the matter at some time that you feel convenient. Yours ever,

Leo Amery

591   To M. C. Gillett   Vol. 72, no. 198

Groote Schuur
[Cape Town]
13 January 1943

...I have been busy and will continue busy till the opening of parliament next Saturday. From then on I shall be very busy with that body till we go home again in April or May. There will be a break for us on 20 March when Isie flies north to get the degree of LL.D. in the Witwatersrand University, of course accompanied by her husband who will share in her reflected glory. Isie will be the first woman to be thus honoured since Queen Wilhelmina received the same degree at Johannesburg last year. I would not miss that function for anything. And besides we shall have two nights at Doornkloof. These will be the pleasant variations of an otherwise very full and tiresome life.

I expect a stormy session, all the more unpleasant because it may be the last before the next general election. We had our last in May 1938, and so another is due in May–August this year, unless we prolong the life of parliament as you have done in Britain and others have done elsewhere. We have not yet decided what to do, and I am waiting to see how the war goes this next European summer before I decide. I want a good atmosphere for an election and must wait for the heavenly and the war omens! At present the situation looks favourable, but who knows what may happen in six months' time? And I want to run no risk where so much is at stake for this country and for the world. Much in this war depends on the attitude of South Africa which occupies a key position in our world-wide war strategy. I shall keep the opposition guessing and cursing, and go on with the work of parliament in pure innocence of spirit! How angry they will be at such tactics. But they deserve no better after the way they have served this country with their miserable tactics and squabbles. But of course at some point I shall have to show my hand, well before the end of the session. They will howl, let them howl!

We are having a very difficult time with the Natives who are getting infected with the virus of change and unrest, and have more-over fallen into the hands of our Communists. Strikes are once more becoming common, and some regrettable shooting incidents have taken place.[1] Of course the Natives are not without a case. They are dreadfully underpaid and feel the economic stress very severely in the towns. I have urged our Wage Board to accelerate the determination of higher minimum wages for unskilled workers, but the needs and the demands are outpacing these reforms. Hence the unrest, and the outbursts. This morning I saw a very influential deputation of the churches who urged me to hurry on the good work, and the necessary reforms in social and political conditions. This is easier urged than done, and the proximity of the election makes the situation still more awkward. I am going to do whatever is politically possible, and may even exceed the limits of political expediency. But I dare not do anything which will outpace public opinion too much just on the eve of an election which may be the most important ever held in this country. To their election repertory of republicanism, secession and neutrality the opposition will now add that of Communism, and this issue will be a veritable red rag to the bull. Such are the ways of politics and the trials and alarms of politicians. And in it all you are expected to act coolly and wisely, and do the right thing. Truly the lot of the politician is a hard one. I shall do as much of the right thing as possible, but always keep before me the paramount necessity of winning the election! Don't you agree that this is right? What will it profit this country if justice is done to the underdog, and the whole caboodle then, including that underdog, is handed over to the wreckers? To that question I see only one answer.

Isie collected for her Gifts and Comforts fund in connection with her 72nd birthday something like £160,000; is that not splendid? It is a wonderful performance—indeed a record.

What delicious fruit we are having here! None of it can be exported, so we shall have to consume it all or turn it into jam or canned fruits. The government are seeing to the disposal of the whole crop in any of these ways. Of course the prices are also guaranteed, but nothing like people abroad would have been delighted to give for the fruit. Still, our farmers have little to complain of, except that I take so many of their Native and Coloured servants into the army, at better pay and allowances than they could ever get from the farmers. These better conditions will of course create another serious problem at the end of the war, when these ex-soldiers will return to civil life and will not be satisfied either with the pay or the conditions which will be offered them. There is no doubt that the economic standard has been very much raised in the war

[1] *See* pp. 402–4 *supra*.

services, and that this will create a difficult situation when peace conditions are re-established. War may be bad, but it often is a great economic reformer. So it will be here...

592   From Friends of Africa   Vol. 70, no. 56

4 Wale Street
Cape Town
15 January 1943

Dear Sir, Our executive met this morning and requested me to thank you for your reply of 14 January. We noted that you, Sir, intend consulting the Africans' representatives in parliament in regard to the suggestions contained in our letter of 5 January and we request that you will notify us of the result.

We feel that the time factor, in the matters raised, is of extreme importance. We are, Sir, Yours faithfully,

Douglas M. Buchanan
Chairman

593   From L. S. Amery   Vol. 70, no. 7

India Office
Whitehall
18 January 1943

My dear Smuts, I have written and spoken to you more than once about the ever increasing importance of air transport from the strategical point of view. It seems to me to be growing every day and I doubt whether we can effect a landing in Sicily or Sardinia or regain the islands of the Pacific and Indian oceans until we are in a position to accompany, or rather precede, every sea landing by the landing of several airborne divisions.

However, what I want you to turn over in your mind is not so much the war aspect of air transport, as the possibilities of its immense development after the war. With the hundred to hundred and fifty ton flying boat of the near future and the much bigger craft of the coming generation, it seems to me that the command of the air in the economic sense is going to mean the command, not only of passenger traffic, but of an enormous volume of light or perishable traffic as well as of all pervading economic and political influence. The Americans have got the ball at their feet in this respect. They already had a large civil aircraft industry and they are building thousands of great carrier planes, while we are perforce condemned to continue devoting all our energies to the production of bombers. The most we can do at present is to work out designs and prototypes to which we can transfer immediately after the war. The Americans are convinced that they are going to dominate the air of the world and in companies like Pan-American Airways they have got most efficient instruments.

Roosevelt's view, as I understand it, is that after the war there should be a new air convention making air transit and air facilities equally available to all nations, much as shipping transit is, for international purposes, but with the right of each country to preserve its internal traffic. That would of course suit the Americans perfectly. No doubt it would also suit the Russians with their vast internal area. But it would clearly not suit any of the members of the British Commonwealth unless inter-Empire air traffic were treated as internal. Failing that the Americans would be able to compete with the immense advantage of their bigger organization in all the traffic between south and east Africa and the Middle East as well as in the traffic between the United Kingdom, west Africa and south Africa, and though we might each reserve our local internal traffic, that would not afford for any of us a market big enough to warrant the building up of a really effective industry.

On the other hand if, by common agreement within the Empire, we can insist on inter-Empire traffic being treated as internal, we should not only have the advantage each of us of flying across neutral territory but would be able to build up between us an aviation market of a character and size which would warrant the establishment of the very best services and the best machines in really substantial quantities. In the long run we might even catch up with the Americans. It need not of course follow from our insistence on the reservation of inter-Empire traffic that particular members of the Commonwealth should not reserve their own local internal traffic if worth while. I imagine, for instance, that India and Australia as well as Canada and I dare say you as well, may wish to develop local services by purely national companies. The important thing is that there should be an effective opportunity, in which all should share, for the development of a really powerful and efficient inter-Empire air system.

Such a system by sheer virtue of its efficiency ought to be able, like the Pan-American system in South America, to secure a great deal of traffic in countries outside the Empire, e.g. transit traffic across Europe, across the Belgian Congo and the Middle East.

I know a good many people are talking in terms of an internationally operated and controlled system of civil aviation. But it seems

to me that any such system is bound to break down and prove un-
workable. In any case I am sure the Americans will not look at it.
Yours ever,

Leo Amery

594   To M. C. Gillett   Vol. 72, no. 199

Groote Schuur
[Cape Town]
19 January 1943

It is now more than two months since I left you, but nothing so far
has been heard...But I keep in touch with war news and am glad
to read of Russia's victories and now of our renewed advance in
Tripoli. I suppose in a few weeks more we should be in possession
of Tripoli and follow up the enemy to Tunisia. It is a great pity that
owing to weather conditions and probably other causes also we have
had this long pause in Tunisia, and so much most valuable time has
been wasted. It must also make the worst impression on the Russians
to see us beaten by the weather while their far worse weather
conditions make no difference to their heroic effort. I wonder whether
they do not sometimes feel a contempt for us, in addition to being
generally suspicious and distrustful of our loyalty as Allies. It is all
very distressing. And meanwhile our silly press on both sides of the
Atlantic are conducting a caterwauling match over [General H. H.]
Giraud and de Gaulle. Poor Darlan is gone and no longer a bone to
chew at.[1] It is very disheartening—all this mischievous bickering
and sowing of dissension which people look upon as news but which
I regard as unconscious fifth column activity. Even my intervention
has been solemnly invoked to get us out of this foolish bickering, but
I am like Gallio[2] in these matters and look the other way—not
without soreness of heart. I suppose in so vast a combination as we
are these things will happen. But they make a laughing-stock of
democracy in wartime. All the time the seeds of dissension and
suspicion are being sown in fertile soil. The French themselves are
awfully tiresome with their bickerings, and I fear only a drastic

---

[1] When the Allies were about to launch operation 'Torch'—the landing in French
north Africa in November 1942—differences arose as to which French leaders should
exercise civil and military authority there. Neither the British nor the United States
government would entrust de Gaulle with that authority. The latter government at
first negotiated with General Giraud (q.v.) but later accepted Admiral Darlan (q.v.)
as the chief civil authority with Giraud as commander-in-chief. On 24 December
Darlan was assassinated at Algiers by a young Frenchman. Giraud succeeded him.
De Gaulle now made an approach to Giraud which was evaded.

[2] *See* vol. IV, p. 272, note 2.

cleansing, approaching a sort of minor civil war, will restore them to cleanness and integrity as a nation. I am sick of all of them, even of the patriots among them, who somehow cannot set self aside, but keep up the personal squabbles which have brought about the downfall of their country and their people. All of them dislike the English and show no gratitude for what we have done to save them and their Empire from their historic enemies. And yet they have such high qualities and could bring something so valuable into the pool of our future effort at recovery.

Here in South Africa people seem to think the victory has already been won, and they become preoccupied with post-war problems of social security and all the good things which the new times will have in store for us. This craze is doubly mischievous; it lames our military effort and produces war slackness, and it also produces differences and divisions of opinion which distract attention and destroy national unity. Everywhere people are pursuing the mirage of security in a world which will be more insecure than ever after the destruction of this war. There will be very little to divide and share, unless it is first created by hard work. Of course for statesmen the problem will be so to organize the work of production that there will be work and decent livelihood for all. But I fear many look to easy conditions to follow and to compensate them for their great war effort. I imagine we shall have to keep much of our war-time organization going to meet the new situation and the new needs. It will be a different world from the old liberal régime to which we were accustomed before this storm broke on us. The problem will be to keep the light of freedom alive in a world so dominated by controls and regimentation. It will be a great problem. People are quite prepared to have their rights, but do not realize that rights imply duties, that consumption presupposes production, and that only the true worker will be entitled to a share in the goods. We shall have some hard lessons to learn in that drab order of things which people call the new order. I am told that in recent years you did not see a happy face either in Germany or Russia, and this exaggeration no doubt points to some truth behind it.

You will notice from the above that I am now in a political-economic mood, and have little time for the shining speculations which I am so prone to pursue! I read nothing, except a little botany now and then, and just dabble in official stuff and the sort of thing which does not very much appeal to me. It is either war or politics. But this phase will pass, and happier times will come, when I shall once more see visions and dream dreams.[1] But first we must win

[1] ' . . . your old men shall dream dreams, your young men shall see visions.' *Joel* ii.28.

the war. And here I must win a general election and hand over a good strong going concern to my successor. And in the great world we must lay the basis of a human peace which will do justice to the spirit of man. Then we shall go on that long safari to distant places, and look for the plant which no other botanist has yet found! And there will be the stars at night, and the distant tomtom beating in the African village, and the blissful sleep under the open sky. That is the dream to which I still cling in the midst of all my present stresses and strains. Good-bye dears, Ever yours,

Jan

595   To W. S. Churchill   Vol. 72, no. 59

Telegram

To: Churchill

From: Smuts

Dated [23] January 1943

I have already sent my congratulations to Alexander and Montgomery on the occupation of Tripoli and Tripolitania and the virtual conclusion of the brilliant campaign for the conquest of Italian north Africa. But to you whose planning and ceaseless drive have sustained this campaign throughout I send my most hearty congratulations on a victory which is as much yours as theirs. This decisive feat together with the achievements of the Russian army[1] and our increasing air supremacy will carry us a long way towards the victorious end. I look forward to good news from French north Africa.

596   To L. S. Amery   Vol. 72, no. 69

House of Assembly
Cape Town
21 February 1943

My dear Amery, I have just received your letter about civil aviation after the war,[2] and appreciate the importance of the point you make.

I daresay you are creating a body to plan for the switching over of war production to civil production of aircraft, and that all the

---

[1] The Russians had, in December, thrown back a German attempt under General Manstein to relieve the encircled Sixth Army of General Paulus before Stalingrad.

[2] 593.

planning and other arrangements are being carried out, so that no time will be lost when peace comes. The Americans are undoubtedly far advanced in this respect.

When you come to the other point, of international air service, I find the position much more difficult and obscure. You wish to treat this Empire as an entity for these purposes. But will the United States accept this position? You know how they have been fighting against this idea all along. Here, too, they will invoke their sanctions against *discrimination*, now mentioned in the agreement with us.

Then again, the reservations of local air services with various Dominions will raise new difficulties between us. All these matters will call for careful consideration and exploration of the way out. Not that it cannot be found.

I much regret the delays in north Africa which have sadly upset our time-table as [I] had read it. Unless we can get pretty far this coming summer we may fail to reach the goal next summer (1944) and that would be most regrettable. Time is not altogether in our favour now.

Winston's illness[1] has caused deep concern here. Everybody feels he is our only man for this colossal crisis. I hope his friends will restrain him from doing more than he can and should at his age. A reserve of strength is essential in this terrible continuous strain.

Things here are not so bad. Indeed I should say that my position is improving all the time. I don't like all this preoccupation with the post-war paradise on earth which makes us concentrate less on the war and more on schemes which confuse and divide us. It is here very much as with you, where people talk Beveridge[2] instead of war and Hitler.

Well, enough. With kind regards and all good wishes. Ever yours,

s. J. C. Smuts

597 To M. C. Gillett

Vol. 72, no. 204

Groote Schuur
[Cape Town]
22 February 1943

I have just been reading letters from you and Arthur and Japie [Smuts]. Japie writes to congratulate on our Barberton bye-election victory which we won with a greater majority than that of Reitz

---

[1] He had pneumonia.

[2] Sir William Beveridge (q.v.) had, in 1942, as chairman of a government committee on social insurance, made a report proposing a comprehensive scheme of social security for all British citizens (Cmd. 6404).

in 1938, and with a poor candidate too.[1] That is a pointer of how the wind is blowing. Your and Arthur's letters were written at Christmas and therefore took two months to reach their destination. You must therefore not complain if mine take that time or longer to reach you. I have not yet missed a week, and that should reassure you. Arthur writes of the good effect of my short visit and of his liking my last broadcast which was meant to help Churchill in his troubles which I know are many, in spite of his hold on the public and the strength of his position. People tend to become critical even of their friends in time of great stress and strain; and this has been a long time which has still further frayed nerves. And now Churchill is ill, apparently a touch of pneumonia, and I pray no worse. May he have an early recovery, for frankly I am frightened by the prospect of his long illness or worse. How with his big body and lack of exercise and endless work he keeps going is a real puzzle to me, and I am in a special position to judge. I am always terrified that I shall hear suddenly and unexpectedly of his breakdown under the strain. Roosevelt is another man who carries impossible burdens, and in his case there is the further handicap of a sick body. These are days when we should pray for health and strength of body no less than of mind and soul. Poor Gandhi! Now he has run to suicide as the way out![2] I have just had a wire from his son Manilal in Durban to send him by plane to the Aga Khan's palace at Poona, or to let him talk on the telephone to his father or other relatives. I have agreed to the latter course, but I don't know whether this will pass the Indian censor. It is such a pitiable end—to try and change men's minds by a sort of moral blackmail. But there is always something peculiarly disagreeable in the Gandhi technique, much as I honour and respect him for great qualities. I suppose the Indian and the European minds work too far apart really to understand each other. The news about his condition today is very grave. I should be most sorry to see him die in this miserable way. And yet I have the feeling that Gandhi is the main stumbling block to a satisfactory settlement of the Indian question. His unique position and being a Hindu gives the Hindu majority too great a pull to leave much chance of a fair communal compromise.

Arthur's letter is occupied with the wonderful Russian news, now much more wonderful two months later. What a colossal effort the

[1] The result on 17 February 1943 was: L. J. Raubenheimer (United party) 2,390; H. S. Webb (Independent) 873. In 1938 D. Reitz had polled 2,574 votes and W. J. C. Brink (National party) 1,193.

[2] Gandhi, aged seventy-three, was detained in Poona following a dispute with the viceroy about the responsibility of Congress for recent acts of violence. On 10 February he began a twenty-one days' fast.

Russians are making, far beyond any we ever thought them capable of.[1] But there must be more in this big business. I am sure it is not Russian prowess. There must be a serious crack in the German machine, and Goebbels's astonishing broadcast speech lends colour to this idea. Something is snapping in Germany. Whether it is Hitler or the generals or the army or the people time only will show. If the Russians can keep up this terrific pace, the Germans may have to fall back on the Ukraine or the Odessa–Kiev area. And if this happens the Russians may hope to reach the border next winter. And then the end will not be far off. As against this magnificent success has to be set off our fumbling in north Africa and our retreat in southern Tunisia. Perhaps things will change now that Alexander takes fighting command. But in any case precious time—perhaps months of it—has been lost, and time is the greatest of all the factors in this war. Churchill did such fine work in Turkey[2] that one feels all the more this loss of face on our Tunisian front. The Americans must feel it worst of all. They have not yet had much success in the war theatres, although their munition and economic effort has been truly magnificent. I suppose they are learning the lessons it took us almost three years to learn. But time now has become more precious! I specially fear a great breakdown of China if we dally on the way to victory. Japan must be dealt with from the Asiatic continent and the Chinese air and sea bases. And if they recede from the prospect this war may last a long time.

This is Monday. Yesterday I was up the mountain to attend the annual memorial service. There was some breakdown of the cableway and so the parson did not appear, and as there was a large gathering which we could not send away empty I stepped into the breach and gave an address on the spur of the moment. I am told that it was very acceptable. Anyway I saved the situation, and thereafter my small party, which included the Greek royalties, marched down and we took lunch behind and in the shadow of a mighty rock, and then descended into the forbidden valley,[3] where in forbidden waters we bathed, men and women in separate pools, with police sentries on the outposts! You know the places in Disa Gorge...

[1] By 2 February the German army before Stalingrad had surrendered and 90,000 prisoners had been taken.

[2] Churchill and the military chiefs had met President Inönü and members of the government of Turkey on 30 January at Adana. The Allies were anxious to draw Turkey into the war on their side and ready to equip her with arms and aircraft. A military agreement was reached.

[3] Catchment areas for part of the water supply of Cape Town which are closed to the public.

Isie is making fine progress and is almost her old self again; takes her meals with us, and joins in all the jollities of life at Groote Schuur.[1] Simon Elwes has almost completed his portrait of me—said to be a very good one—and is now engaged on one of the crown princess. But his picture of Isie remains his masterpiece. It reproduces all her vivacity and suppressed fire, and brings out something which is not often seen in portraits.

Parliament is plodding its weary and tiresome way through public business. Day after tomorrow we start on our budget, and I hope we shall finish by the middle of April. There is so much to do that I grudge every moment devoted to mere talk and debate. How little there is in all these empty parliamentary triumphs! There is the great world whose future is being decided and we strut about our little talking stage as if it matters more than a tinker's curse! But such is life itself—twenty per cent good stuff, and eighty per cent nonsense. But I suppose the roughage is necessary for the feeding of the time machine.

But enough. Our best wishes and dear love with you both and all. I am so glad to hear that Jan's news is good.[2] Japie [Smuts] has just declined high promotion because he fears I shall be accused of favouritism! That is the stuff. Ever yours,

Jan

598   To M. C. Gillett   Vol. 72, no. 205

Groote Schuur
[Cape Town]
27 February 1943

Another couple of interesting letters from Arthur and you—thank you both. Arthur writes most interestingly about free exchanges. Though it is a difficult matter I confess I agree with Arthur and not with *The Economist*.[3] These blitzes of free money from one country on another have had, and may in future have, more and more the most devastating effects and will have to be under control. Exchange invasion may be just as bad as military or air attack. I shall read the *Economist* article with interest when it arrives.

You write of the Murrays giving up their house, of doings at 102, with Helen [Gordon] and her husband visiting you, of Lindsay's

[1] She had suffered a thrombosis in January.
[2] Jan Gillett was serving with the British forces in India.
[3] *See* Smuts Collection, vol. 70, no. 128. A. B. Gillett wrote on 6 January: 'I was surprised last night in reading an article in *The Economist* on Foreign Exchanges...as though "free exchanges" was the only goal to aim at sooner or later...'

account of things in America, and finally of my *Life* article.[1] All your news and views are very interesting. The article on the future Empire was written for *Life* as that has been the principal vehicle for Wendell Willkie's attack on the British Empire, and I wanted to dispel some of the possibly mischievous effects of his criticisms. Willkie seems to be in search for a programme for the next presidential election and may be thinking of 'imperialism' and the British Empire as an issue likely to appeal to Americans. I sketched the change that had come over the Empire scene since the Boer War—a revolutionary change—and then went on to talk of the future. My views are a development of the old mandate idea of which I was probably the original source.[2] But something far bigger is possible and called for, both in the Empire and in the colonial system of the world. And so in the article in *Life* I sketched in large and vague outline the thought of international consultation and collaboration in the development and control of policies in backward countries. In the British Empire the small colonial units should be suitably grouped into larger combinations, and both in regard to them and colonies of other powers a conference system of interested countries and certain great powers should be established to shape and guide policies. Sovereignties may be left intact but policies and development and resources should be shared. Thus even countries which have no colonies would come well into the picture and have their 'place in the sun' as the Kaiser used to say.[3] Americans should be pleased and not merely criticize. Strategic positions for future world security could thus be established, without resorting to the silly leasing system which the United States has forced on Britain in the West Indies.[4] The United Nations would have the necessary strong points on a world-wide scale for maintaining future security. What the British Empire did for its communications would be done on a world-wide scale by the United Nations in future. Colonies, instead of a source of envy and bone of contention, would in future become links in the peace system of civilization. And meanwhile their development will become an object of international interest. And so on and forth. I may say I had discussed these views with leading members of the British government on my recent visit and

[1] The article, entitled 'The British Colonial Empire', is dated 15 December 1942 (Smuts Collection, Box E, no. 10).

[2] These views had been put forward in Smuts's Paper on a League of Nations in 1918. *See supra*, p. 174, note 2.

[3] He used the phrase in a speech at Hamburg on 27 August 1911.

[4] On 3 September 1940 arrangements had been concluded to hand over fifty 'over age' United States destroyers to Great Britain in exchange for the lease or gift of British naval bases in Newfoundland, Bermuda and the West Indies.

found a sympathetic hearing. I hope some good seed has been sown, though old prejudices will no doubt continue and smaller powers with large colonial possessions will be suspicious, much as my mandate ideas were suspected at the last peace conference and finally cut down to a mere shadow. I don't think the short article was reprinted and have no copy for you. But above is the main idea of it.

I am somewhat doubtful about the policy of devoting too much public attention to these post-war matters. There is a real danger of people pushing the idea of the war and its early conclusion into the background, and of escaping into dreams of the better world to come—so much pleasanter a vision than this terrible task of fighting the war to a finish. A wrong perspective is thus created and concentration on the war effort undermined. Besides, people have all sorts of visions and hopes and views about the future, and then contentions and divisions arise which destroy the unity which alone will secure victory. You see how already your public divide over a simple matter like the Beveridge report.[1] We shall soon be fighting each other over future schemes rather than the enemy. Stalin is a fanatic for the war, and see what he is doing. We fight over the French situation in north Africa, and see what the results are! We cannot win without single-mindedness and unity, and must avoid undue preoccupation with the future. Here in South Africa I notice the same thing. The war may recede from our view, our efforts may thus slacken, and the result may be a prolongation of the war. I am of course not against planning for the future but against excessive propaganda on the future order as that may prove most distracting to our war effort.

5 March. Thus far I came almost a week ago and then I fell into a stormy patch and had to concentrate on work which made all thought of correspondence out of the question. And now I have reached the week-end and have only time to wind up this letter without finishing it. Just a few concluding items.

Isie is making good progress in her recovery, although not yet her old self. She still has to avoid all public occasions but the doctor thinks she will be quite well again with long rest for convalescence...

The war news remains good, with Russia still advancing in several sectors, the air victory of MacArthur in the south-west Pacific, and our intensified air activities in Europe. We now wait for the advance of the Eighth Army from Tripoli.

Parliament is getting along fairly well with its work and we hope

---

[1] *See supra*, p. 414, note 2.

to go home by Easter, 23 April. I shall be glad as so much requires attention at Pretoria.

Your news from home continues good and I hope will remain so. We all rejoice at Winston's recovery. He was saved by M. & B. It would have been a final calamity if he had died, as was quite possible. With love and good wishes, Ever yours,

Jan

599   To M. C. Gillett   Vol. 72, no. 207

Groote Schuur
[Cape Town]
14 March 1943

...I am at present going out at full stretch. In parliament the budget and my own departmental estimates have been under discussion and will continue such till I leave on Friday. You can imagine what a drain it must be on my time and energy to sit continuously in the house and deal with all the discussions and criticisms. I sometimes think of St Paul's statement of fighting with wild beasts at Ephesus.[1] Naturally I must be the main target for an opposition that knows no limit and shows no mercy for age or overwork. I try to remain patient and affable, but fear not always successfully. From the opposition's point of view and opinion of me they are perhaps justified in their bitter rancour. They look upon me as the main cause of their discomfiture, the misfortunes that have overtaken them, and as having deliberately laid the trap into which we walked in September 1939.[2] Of course there is nothing in all this, and I acted only on compelling conviction and as it were against the probabilities of the case, as there was good reason to expect that they would beat me at that critical vote. But to them my action was simply deep Machiavellian plotting. And so they feel justified in unlimited attack. But that is my burden 'which I have borne and yet must bear'—as Shelley has it.[3] And my health still remains good, and my conviction of rectitude bears me up under it all. The great thing is patience and serenity of spirit, in the conviction that I am serving a great and good cause, for which no sacrifice can be too great. It is a pity however that I am so very deeply immersed in heavy tasks which leave me practically no time

[1] *See supra*, p. 215, note 2.   [2] *See supra*, p. 194, note 2.
[3]   ...the life of care
            Which I have borne and yet must bear...
                    Stanzas Written in Dejection, near Naples.

420

for serious thought on the great issues ahead. The war has to be carried on, two vast departments administered,[1] parliament to be attended to, the party fight to be led, a general election to be prepared for. And this and much more leaves little or no time for the greater problems of the end and thereafter which are even more important and difficult. How is the war to end; what is to be done about the manner of that ending, to prevent a wild orgy of revenge which would be as bad as the war itself; how is the armistice to be arranged; and will there be a peace conference or not? For if there is a postponement of the peace till a quieter time, the armistice becomes one of paramount importance and must be such as to provide a tolerable interim period and create conditions for a successful peace thereafter. Then we have the problems of the peace and its maintenance, the new organization of the world and the leadership which is to guide and sustain that organization. We have, besides, the national problems of a better ordered national life and economy and healthier conditions in our several countries. The old democratic formulas—like the articles of our Protestant or Christian religions—do not suffice us here, and a new outlook towards a new ordered society is called for. All this requires detailed thought and planning, and I personally feel that neither I nor any of the other more responsible leaders have the time or opportunity for such fundamental pondering and planning in the difficulties which face us day to day. If we could give half our time to the jobs in hand and the other half to long-range thinking and planning we could look forward with more confidence to the future. But we are drowned in the present struggle and cannot see the distant shore. Perhaps this is exaggerated, but not much so far as the leaders are concerned, and the final solutions will depend on them and not on the pundits who are at present dealing with the problems of the future. At Paris most of our vast preparatory work was simply scrapped or ignored, and the Big Four[2], or who they were, made the decisions on such light as they had. It must not be so again, but I fear much a somewhat similar situation if this war is to be followed by a peace conference. How tired we shall be! How much we shall long for rest after these exhausting Herculean labours; and how unfair to expect us to have prepared minds and outlooks for the still heavier labours of the peace.

Arthur writes about money and exchange and similar financial and economic questions. There the experts could do much by

[1] *See supra*, p. 194, note 1.

[2] The Council of Four consisting of president Wilson, Clemenceau, Lloyd George and Orlando, prime minister of Italy.

adequate preliminary thinking and planning, and I hope this is being done. Lovingly, ever yours,

Jan

600   From J. H. Hofmeyr   Vol. 71, no. 50

House of Assembly
Cape Town
7 April 1943

My dear Prime Minister, As a result of the decision to proceed with legislation this session in regard to the Asiatic problem, I consider it necessary to place on record the position arrived at in the verbal discussions which have taken place.[1]

I regard the proposal to extend for a further period the provisions (other than section 1) of the Asiatics (Transvaal Land and Trading) Act of 1939 as one which cannot be justified by the available evidence.[2]

Personally I am unable to support that proposal, and cannot therefore as a member of the cabinet accept responsibility for it.

In view of this it would be in accord with constitutional practice that I should cease to be a member of the cabinet which is going forward with that proposal, and I have therefore tendered my resignation to you.

You have asked me however not to press my resignation, urging the importance in the present position of emergency of a united effort being maintained in furtherance of the war effort.

I have therefore agreed to remain a member of the cabinet, it being understood that I do not accept responsibility for the proposal referred to, and that I retain my freedom of action in regard thereto.

I propose to exercise that freedom by stating my position on the second reading of the bill, but shall thereafter abstain from any speaking or voting in connection therewith. Yours sincerely,

Jan H. Hofmeyr

[1] In the cabinet.

[2] See supra, p. 167, note 3. Following the findings of the second Broome commission (1942) on accelerated Indian purchases of land in European areas in Durban, the government decided to 'peg' the existing position there for three years. This was done by the passage of the Trading and Occupation of Land (Transvaal and Natal) Restriction Act of 1943 by which Indians could not buy land in predominantly white areas in Durban nor whites buy land in predominantly Indian areas there without a permit. The 'Pegging' Act did not introduce new restrictions in the Transvaal but merely renewed the provisions of the act of 1939 until 1946. It was these provisions that Hofmeyr would not accept because they were discriminatory. He did not oppose the provisions relating to Durban because those applied to whites as well as to Indians.

601   To J. H. Hofmeyr   Vol. 72, no. 78

Prime Minister's Office
Cape Town
[7 April 1943]

My dear Hofmeyr, Yours of 7 April. Your record of what transpired at our cabinet meeting yesterday is correct. You are therefore free to follow the course you propose to take.

While saying this I wish once more to point out the unhappy impression that such a course would create at the present time of grave national emergency. I would therefore suggest that you consider whether your disagreement with the views of all your colleagues would not be sufficiently expressed by your maintaining a discreet silence in the house and abstaining from its proceedings on the Asiatic bill. This would at least be a less extreme view of indicating your disagreement and cause less pain to your friends in the party. I must, of course, leave the final decision to you. Yours sincerely,

J. C. Smuts

602   From J. H. Hofmeyr   Vol. 71, no. 51

House of Assembly
Cape Town
8 April 1943

My dear Prime Minister, I thank you for your letter of 7 April in reply to mine, and would like to express my appreciation of the consideration which you have extended to me in this matter.

I have given careful consideration to what you say in the last part of your letter. I am, of course, very anxious not to raise avoidable difficulties at a time like the present, nor to cause pain to yourself and my other colleagues, but it seems to me to be quite impracticable to remain silent on the Asiatics bill. Quite apart from anything else, there is the fact that at present there is an impression that I am opposed to the bill as a whole, which is incorrect. Moreover, as it is known to the public that I am not in agreement with my colleagues on this matter, it is inevitable that I shall be asked at some time or other to explain my position, and my constituents at least would be entitled to demand a reply to such a question. It seems best that I should make such a statement before it is dragged out of me, and there is no place where I can more appropriately do so than in the house during the discussion of the bill. Yours sincerely,

Jan H. Hofmeyr

603   From D. M. Buchanan

Vol. 70, no. 57

Temple Chambers
4 Wale Street
Cape Town
9 April 1943

Dear General, Possibly Mr [H. G.] Lawrence and other members of the cabinet have not realized the strength of the opposition to the further segregation implicit in the Coloured Advisory Council.[1]

By separating the Coloured people and Malays from the main stream of national life, like the Natives, serious concern has been aroused in more than Communists and agitators.

I am taking the liberty of sending you, Sir, a copy of the letter I have sent to Mr Lawrence.[2] With kind regards, Yours sincerely,

Douglas M. Buchanan

604   To M. C. Gillett

Vol. 72, no. 211

Groote Schuur
[Cape Town]
15 April 1943

This is 3.30 a.m. and I have just awakened while the lions roar near by[3] and the frogs and crickets sing their song in between. This therefore is the time to remember friends in a tender spirit. Whenever I work hard and have difficult matters to occupy my mind I awake like that knight of old—in the middle of the night[4]—and keep awake for an hour or two. This is the time that I read or make notes or (as now) write letters. Then in due course towards morning I fall asleep again and awake with the coming of day. As one gets older the long uninterrupted sleep through the night becomes rarer, and in my case almost unknown now. But I don't mind, as this is nature's way. And I *am* working hard in these last weeks of the

---

[1] Appointed in 1943 to advise the government on Coloured affairs and consisting of Coloured members. The chairman was Dr H. Gow. Some Coloured leaders co-operated with it and others regarded it as a step towards the political separation of the Coloured people from the whites in the Cape Province.

[2] Omitted by the editor. Smuts made an annotation for his secretary as follows: 'Acknowledge and say I have read his letter to Lawrence, but don't agree with his conclusions. The intention and effect of the appointment of an advisory body like the Coloured Commission [*sic*] is simply to be helpful to our Coloured friends and not to create a colour bar.'

[3] In the neighbouring Groote Schuur zoo.

[4] Refers to a Gillett family riddle which Smuts found bewildering. (Note by M. C. Gillett.)

session, and have much to keep me on stretch night and day, as you can well understand...

Monday night I was at Johannesburg to preside at the diamond jubilee meeting of the Salvation Army in South Africa. It was a grand and most interesting meeting and I had to make the principal speech. I spoke of the social service of the Army, and of social work as of the essence of Christianity and religion, and of the transformation of our conception of the state which is now also largely becoming a grand organ of social service. I could thus work in a good deal of my ideas of social advance and could emphasize that the twentieth century is going to be the social century and to be distinguished for the social services and general levelling up of the standards of human society. My speech was well received, but I understand that its radio transmission has been very poor and practically a failure. So that is that. At any rate it was well heard all over South Africa and will, I hope, help to boost up the new ideas which I am keen on. Unfortunately the church makes little appeal in these days, and thus it is left to us great sinners to keep alive the ideas of the new Kingdom as well as the vision which has so often before brought fresh hope and heart to mankind. Think of Jesus in the villages of Galilee, of George Fox[1] in Puritan England, of Wesley[2] in the misery of the dawning industrialism of the eighteenth century, of Booth[3] in Darkest England, and now again of the Nazi night through which mankind is passing, with sufferings of the human race such as probably surpass the worst of all human history. But we still wait for the call, the Voice Divine which will point the new way in this agony of the race. Perhaps it will yet come, and perhaps not till the worst is over. But let me not continue on that theme, on which you know the run of my ideas.

Tuesday morning I left early, flew over the country in cloud and rain and was at 'Groote Schuur' again at 12 a.m. and in parliament at 2 p.m. There again hard and unpleasant work awaited me. For at the moment we are busy with a bill to stabilize the Indian situation in Durban[4] where there is wild excitement because rich Indians have been buying up properties on a large scale in the heart of Durban and panic has set in among the Europeans. You know the sort of situation and the fear which naturally possesses the whites on such occasions. There is nothing for it but to peg the position and forbid property transfers there for three years so that the whole

---

[1] Born 1625, died 1691. Founder of the Society of Friends.

[2] John Wesley (1703–91), English evangelical preacher and founder of Methodism.

[3] William Booth (1829–1912), founder with his wife, Catherine Mumford Booth, of the Salvation Army in 1878.

[4] *See supra*, p. 422, note 2.

position can be judicially inquired into. But this again has created commotion among the Indians here and in India and moved the Indian government to do its bit in the general hue and cry. What a commotion and noise there is all about me! What taunts flung at me, what charges of deserting the idealism which I preach. And so on and so forth. And all because some utterly selfish wealthy Indians choose to spend their ill-gotten gains, not by investing in war funds, but in buying up the properties of whites and thus raising the fears of the whites for the future of European civilization in South Africa. However, these are moments to be endured in patience. I can never get away from this Indian tangle and the troubles of East and West. Did the Twelve Labours of Hercules last all his life? I rather think so, and in the end he was found on a funeral pyre. Perhaps that may be my fate too! Not that I am a Hercules, but certainly there are again the twelve or more labours to be endured for a long lifetime. When we have finished with this great contention in the house we shall have to grapple with the problem of soldiers voting at the coming general election, and that again must lead to a violent clash of the parties in the house. And so on and so forth as they say. I wonder now whether we shall finish the session by Easter which is the end of next week. Perhaps not, and perhaps this purgatory of talk will continue longer, while my presence up north is most badly required.

The war has gone well since last I wrote and Rommel is now bottled up in the north of Tunisia. I hope that will not be a long story. The Germans are certain to have a final and desperate go at Russia this spring or early summer and no one knows what may happen there if we are not in a position to draw off large forces from that front and relieve the pressure against Russia. The sooner therefore that we can menace southern Europe the better for that front and for preventing this war continuing for years more. If the Russians can hold firmly this summer and we can soon transfer our activities to the European continent the end may not be so very far off. That is the problem before us. Let me however not continue about the war. That must be always with you as it is with us, and we do like to get away a little from the thought of it, even if it were only in our letters!

...I see it is now near 5 a.m. and I have spent a pleasant hour in bed with this talk to you. And now I must try to get some more sleep before 6 a.m. when I finally awake for the day's long pull.

Good-night, dears, and may the spirit of good be with you both and all. It really is never far from us, even in these dark days and nights. Good-bye.

Jan

605   To W. S. Churchill   Vol. 72, no. 62

Telegram

To: Churchill

From: Smuts

Dated [7 May] 1943

South Africa's heartiest congratulations on brilliant victory of First Army in capture of Tunis simultaneously with American capture of Bizerta. This is indeed the blitz in its Allied form. We have gone a long way from El Alamein last October when you modestly spoke of the end of the beginning. Tunis and Bizerta four [*sic*] months later mark the beginning of the end. I am proud that South Africa was also in this blitz, as it will continue to be to the end wherever it may finally come.

606   To F. D. Roosevelt   Vol. 72, no. 63

Telegram

To: President Roosevelt

From: Field-Marshal Smuts

Dated [7 May] 1943

My heartiest congratulations on magnificent victory of American forces in capture of Bizerta simultaneously with British capture of Tunis. Politically and strategically it is also a matter of great significance that owing to your wise action French troops effectively took part in this proud achievement. This feat of arms will prove historic. From now on the Allied tide of victory will roll on until it covers and refertilizes our fair world and saves it from the new barbarism.

607   To M. C. Gillett   Vol. 72, no. 215

Doornkloof
[Transvaal]
14 May 1943

It is very late in the week for a letter to you. I should have written last Sunday according to custom, and it is now Friday already and not a line written yet. It has been a crowded week, full of official troubles and full of events. When it is a question of a general election all sorts of snags and unforeseen difficulties emerge, and I have had to struggle with several of them, as a decision had become urgent.

And then you have had the crowded canvas of events. The end has with most unexpected suddenness come in Tunisia, and Churchill is once more in Washington—the one very good, and the other one hopes may be good too, though I don't much like these flittings of the prime minister over the oceans whether by sea or air. The secret of this visit has been well kept and even its exact purpose is only to be guessed at.[1] But one hopes for the best.

The spectacular end in north Africa is the real meat in the news —and it is very good. The tactics of Alexander have been brilliant, and [General S.] von Arnim has been both outplanned and out-fought. First the enemy fought our First Army to a standstill in the Medjez el Bab area. Then the Eighth Army tried the Zaghouan mountain block and could not find a way through. But the Medjez el Bab plan was evidently the best way, and so Alexander switched three picked divisions over from the Eighth to the First Army at night. All depended on secrecy, and the secret was well kept. The mountains at Medjez el Bab were pierced by a sudden blow which carried the First Army right on to Tunis, while the Americans could seize the less heavily defended Bizerta. And so the rear of von Arnim was cut off and taken, the Cape Bon peninsula occupied and the whole German army was left in the air, in the Zaghouan block, and in the end could only surrender.[2] It is the cleanest, neatest, most sudden and spectacular victory of the war, and in size is quite comparable to the German defeat before Stalingrad.[3] In Africa it is a crowning mercy as Cromwell would have said,[4] and for the whole war it may now have far reaching results. I made a broadcast last night which however dealt more specially with the South African effort in the war, which has not been much publicized. We have been somewhat out of the war picture, partly owing to the surrender of our Second Division at Tobruk and the withdrawal, after the El Alamein break-through, of our First Division in order to rest, refit and reform into a tank division. Our air and other very important services, however, continued with the Eighth Army and were in at the end and did splendid service, especially our air squadrons which were largely

[1] Churchill's third visit to Washington was undertaken in order to discuss with Roosevelt whether Italy was to be invaded and Turkey brought into the war and what action was to be taken in the Far East. (*See* Winston Churchill, *The Second World War*, vol. IV, chapter 43.)

[2] The German surrender took place on 12 May. The final capitulation at Cape Bon was made next day by the Italian commander, Marshal Giovanni Messe.

[3] Churchill wrote later of the Tunis victory: 'It held its own with Stalingrad. Nearly a quarter of a million prisoners were taken.' (*The Second World War*, vol. IV, p. 698).

[4] 'The dimensions of this mercy are above my thoughts. It is, for aught I know, a crowning mercy.' Letter to William Lenthall, 4 September 1651.

responsible for the defeat and wreck of the big Junkers carrier or transport planes, I believe thirty of them in one day alone. Our war effort as a whole was not much advertised and so I thought I should go into some details last night. Unfortunately a thunderstorm was raging here, so that it must have been heard badly here, and perhaps even worse overseas. You can never quite time or arrange these things! But this is minor. The great thing is the victory, and the consummation of the African strategy which I have steadily advocated until it was at last fully accepted, and now carried through with brilliant success. I am a happy man and deeply thankful for this great 'mercy'—once more Cromwell's language!

...I may have to go to England again and perhaps even to America after the elections in July, and then to parliament, and so on to world without end, amen! There is no rest and no time for self-collection and reflection. It is just all drive, drive, drive! And whither? The tempo of our time is destructive of all the silences and the repose of the inner life. I wonder whether the inner life will ever adjust itself to this everlasting preoccupation with the outer world. It must be wrong, and yet our whole tendency is to speed up and keep on the move without rest or pause. I have not looked into my Greek Testament for some months now, and that is a measure of my immersion in the stream of affairs, much of which can be of no great importance, most of which is forgotten as soon as they are past, but which yet fill up the picture of the present without leaving a vacant moment for more important abiding things. It is a sad lot for one who craves for quiet and reflection and release from the external pressure. But one has no choice, and just marches on like a soldier in a battalion on the march. The marching orders of our time are very severe, but one can but inwardly groan and obey.

This is not a satisfactory letter. But you must be satisfied, and will be forgiving. All our love and loving thoughts are ever with you and yours.

Jan

608   To M. C. Gillett   Vol. 72, no. 216

Doornkloof
[Transvaal]
17 May 1943

This is Monday night, and I write thus early for fear that I may not have an opportunity later this week. Tomorrow I am heavily engaged on the office front; on Wednesday I shall be at Bloemfontein to attend a function into which Colin Steyn has inveigled weak me; on Thursday I must be at Johannesburg to make a tiresome propaganda film for the elections; on Friday I attend another function which I don't now remember; and on Saturday I finish at Germiston with a big fête to collect money for the national war fund. Practically every week is similarly filled up with things which you perhaps think nothing of, but which I in my position cannot very well avoid, and which take up a lot of time. Last Saturday I made my announcement that we are to have a general election on 7 July and this of course has started the ball rolling. At first we had thought that it could be held somewhere in August. But owing to departmental speeding up we have gained about five weeks. The opposition profess to be furious as they say I am rushing into a khaki election. But I don't see why they should squeal so loudly as they have been challenging me for the last four years to go to the country and all that time they have—in the intervals of their quarrels—done nothing but make propaganda and prepare for an election. I think we are on a good wicket at present. The spectacular victory in north Africa has impressed the doubtful, who now wish to be on the winning side. None so keen as those who come up when the fight has been won! I shall be darting about all the time for the next seven weeks and if I survive physically and politically I shall be a happy man. Of course the trouble for me is that all this time while I am engrossed with election affairs the war machine has to be run, and at least half of one's time has to be given to that task. Still, the fight is worth it and I ought not to wait till the aftermath is on us and the air is full of post-war grievances and disappointments. I should like to have my hands reasonably free for peace-making, if and when that call comes. It will be far worse than war-making, and I should not be saddled with an election at that time. I do not like all this strain just after a heavy session of parliament, but it is a long time now since I have had a holiday, and I might just as well push on and through now, and hope to have a little respite after the elections. At any rate that is my hope. And after that what jobs will be awaiting attention?

The function at Bloemfontein next Wednesday is one which Colin is giving for the Greek princesses in connection with a fund they are raising for Greek relief after the war. I can give a fillip to that good cause, and at the same time I can plead for the little nations and a world order in which it would be possible for them to live and not be gobbled up by the aggressors and Hitlers of the future. Unless we can have an order which will stabilize and maintain peace I should not like to belong (as I do now) to a little nation. Unless Germany is made safe for the world, I should not wish to be a Belgian or

Hollander or Dane or any of the small folk on her borders. And this applies not to Germany alone. We must *now* do the great thing or face the extinction of freedom as we have known it for the modern age. The Boers went under and others may not have such a glorious resurrection in so short a time. I think in the capital of a small people like the Free Staters quite a telling appeal can be made for a decent right peace which would recognize human solidarity and the duties as well as the rights it involves. I wonder whether we shall cross the Rubicon this time and come to grips with isolationism which is the disease from which our civilization is suffering and from which it may die. Unless the bonds of the sovereign state can be burst and human society be linked up in a world-wide brotherhood there is little chance of survival in a world where science has perfected all the weapons of destruction. Even if one particular power were to be the great conqueror, as Napoleon and Hitler tried to be, that victor power would probably also succumb to the internal struggle for freedom, and the whole miserable process would start over again. It is by agreement and persuasion that the unity or whole of mankind will have to be accomplished, and not by the sword. But once accomplished, the force of the whole should be at the disposal of the whole for maintenance of peace. I often wonder whether mankind is ripe for this great change, this switch-over from national isolationism to the co-operative order. Time only will show whether there is not once more to be a sad and heartbreaking disillusion, such as one had after the last war. Will America fall into line? Will South Africa? 'The world is weary of the past, O may it die or rest at last!'[1]

The trouble of course lies far deeper than politics or political arrangements or constitutional concepts. At bottom it is a question of religion. Unless man comes to grips with the problems of his soul, with human nature itself, it seems almost vain to expect any real and lasting cure for our national and international troubles. To me it is sometimes an intriguing thought how much Jesus knew of the situation in the Roman Empire, and of the vast attempt then made to bind civilization into a peaceful order. It is perhaps doubtful whether he knew much; but in Galilee, which had a partly Roman culture, where Roman troops were stationed to keep the peace and Roman ideas might have been in the air, He may have heard of the great human experiment of organization. The Jews were in any case looking forward to a wordly kingdom for their resurrection and rise from thraldom. And Jesus spread the message that not along those lines would the salvation come. The soul, man's relation to God, the inner purification and the practice of the gentler

---

[1] Shelley, *Hellas* l. 1100.

virtues would herald the new dawn—the Kingdom of Heaven. Is this thought not basic in the truest sense? Has mankind not first to find its soul again before it finds the new Kingdom? 'Not in Jerusalem nor in this mountain but in spirit and in truth'—is the new hope, as the woman of Sychar was told.[1] But we cannot wait until the new religion, or the old in a newer more appealing form, arrives and takes possession of mankind. We must tackle the job according to our human lights and means, hoping that Heaven's blessing will follow in due course. But the fact remains that the ultimate abiding solution is religious even more than political. The tragedy of man is much profounder than his politics, his striving for power. There is a deeper longing which, unless satisfied, keeps us hungry still. And it is this hunger, this unrest in the body and especially the soul, which lies at the root of all that is best and also all that is worst in this world. But enough of this.

The world situation after the brilliant victory in north Africa, is a truly intriguing one. What is happening in Italy? Is she to be defended, or can the Germans no longer hold both that and the Russian front and at the same time hold down the tortured prostrate body of Europe under occupation? We are all deeply impressed by the extent of the German power. But is it really so colossal? And are the limits not being reached? The Russian victories were wonderful. In some ways the north African victory is equally wonderful, if not more so. It is certainly a more sudden and crushing defeat than was inflicted on Germany in the whole of the last war. And so one begins to wonder and ask questions. I think the air attacks are already producing a terrible effect. Germany remained untouched in the last war, but the devastation of German cities in this war must be something terrible, and terrible on human morale and endurance. This summer may see surprising developments, unless Germany is really still in a position to deliver crushing blows against Russia. Against *us* she can no longer deliver them, and that too is a fact being borne in upon her people which must seriously affect their morale.

Here all going well at home. I hear (as I write in my study) the gentle hum and occasional laughter in the dining-room. They are a very happy lot, Isie with her three daughters and many grand-daughters. God bless them; and bless you too, dear ones. Ever yours,

Jan

I regret this illegible scribble, but hope you can decypher it.

[1] Jesus saith unto her, Woman, believe me, the hour cometh, when ye shall neither in this mountain, nor yet at Jerusalem, worship the Father...But the hour cometh, and now is, when the true worshipper shall worship the Father in spirit and in truth...' *St John* iv.21–3.

609   To C. F. Stallard   Vol. 72, no. 98

[Pretoria]
17 May 1943

Dear Stallard, Your letter[1] with the enclosed cutting of Clarkson's remarks[2] only came into my hands this morning.

You will have noticed that at the meeting of the head committee of the United party at Pretoria last Saturday I asked members of the party to give their strong support to the Dominion and Labour party candidates, and to do so not only as against opposition candidates, but also against Independents. This appeal, I think, sufficiently covers the case of Point, and there is no particular reason for me to single out Shearer [V. L.] in a public declaration. I have personally put the case to him in clear and explicit terms, and I have followed it up with my general declaration against all Independents. I think that should be enough.

I am passing your letter on to Clarkson for his information. Yours sincerely,

J. C. Smuts

610   To George II of Greece   Vol. 72, no. 107

Pretoria
4 June 1943

Your Majesty, I take the liberty to send you, through General Theron, this letter by the same plane that carries the crown princess back to Cairo. I have not troubled you about this step, assuming that you would welcome her return to her husband. I have, however, ascertained that such a step would be welcome to the British authorities. It has been good for her to be with her small children for a good while, but I personally feel that the time has come for her to rejoin her husband, and also to be near Your Majesty, now that you have returned to Egypt—preparatory, as I sincerely hope, to a final return to Athens. From the point of view also of the future, and the close linking up of the royal house with Greece and the Greeks I think this move of hers to the Mediterranean

---

[1] Smuts Collection, vol. 72, no. 43, written on 12 May.

[2] The cutting, from the *Natal Mercury* of 8 May, reported Clarkson as saying that Dr Vernon Shearer who had, after resigning from the Dominion party, joined the United party, would now have to fight the election at Durban Point as an Independent because the Dominion party were demanding this seat for their party in terms of the election agreement between the parties supporting the government. Shearer was reported as saying that he, as an unreserved supporter of General Smuts, could not be classed with other Independents.

politic and timely. Her great charm with people, her very outstanding ability and striking character make her an asset of the greatest value to the royal house which it would be wise to exploit to the full. Here in South Africa she has become universally popular both with the general public and the Greeks, but South Africa is very far from Greece. She has launched her Greek fund for post-war relief, and it is certain to go well, even after her departure, and it will enable her to have a fund in hand to take back with her as the fruits of her labours in the Greek cause during her absence from Greece.

My interest in this matter is not merely personal but is partly due to my conviction that the royal house is essential to the stability of post-war Greece as well as to the vital Mediterranean interests of the British Commonwealth. Greek politics have been singularly unstable, instability which has not grown less in war time, and the royal house is the main hope for stability in future.

The royal house and its members have therefore the duty cast on them to secure the maximum popularity in the national interest. As Your Majesty knows, the members of the English royal house are worked to the limit to strengthen the monarchy in the loyal affections of the British people. The same would no doubt be no less necessary in the case of Greece. The crown prince and princess can be most usefully employed in this important task with the Greek people. And it is my hope that Your Majesty may prevail with Prince Paul and the princess to take as active a part as possible in the public, social and relief activities which will be so important a task when the royal house returns after the war. Their active interest and labours on behalf of the people in their sad plight will undoubtedly serve to secure strong support for the royal house against all subversive or republican elements and will contribute greatly to its popularity. The prince and princess could thus do much that would not be possible for Your Majesty in your high position, but which yet is necessary to secure the loyal devotion of the people to the throne.

I know from repeated talks with British statesmen how sincere is their support for Your Majesty and how conscious they are of the value to Britain of her loyal support for Your Majesty. They know that Greece must play an important part in Mediterranean policy after the war, and her friendship with Britain must be in no doubt. But their support for the Greek throne is not sufficient. Far better is it for the Greek people to stand unalterably behind their king. And it is just here that the prince and princess can be most helpful to you and render a great service to the good cause. I would therefore respectfully suggest that the fullest use be made of both of them for this important purpose, and that their active service in all social and relief measures be utilized to secure popularity for the Greek royal family. I suggest this because of the wise policy similarly pursued with regard to members of the English royal house.

I wish I had the opportunity to discuss these and other matters with Your Majesty in an unofficial way and in a spirit of friendship for the Greek cause. But I don't know how soon I shall be able to visit Egypt again, and therefore write to you along these lines. It may be that matters in the Mediterranean theatre may develop faster than has been expected, and Greece may soon be called upon to put her house in order. Let the royal house play an active part in this direction and so secure the enthusiastic support of the Greek people. With respectful good wishes, I remain Your Majesty's obedient servant,

s. J. C. Smuts

611   To M. C. Gillett

Vol. 72, no. 218

Doornkloof
[Transvaal]
9 June 1943

Although I write every week I have written recently on different days as an opening offered itself, and in the rush of events through which I have to make my way I forget whether I have already mentioned matters to you and whether I am not repeating. If so you will please excuse my forgetfulness. I resume the chronicle.

It is less than a week since I left the Cape where I had held a great military demonstration at Robertson, attended by many thousands, and the following day a big political meeting in the city hall at Cape Town. Both were great successes, especially the first. That was on Monday and Tuesday of last week. On Thursday I flew back in order to attend a big demonstration at Brakpan (East Rand), ostensibly to collect funds for the war fund, but really to give a helping hand to our candidates in the elections. It was a big and most successful affair, much appreciated by our political friends. That same night I attended a dinner in Johannesburg where the crown princess was to launch her appeal for her relief fund for Greece. I have told you that she is a remarkable woman, with great gifts of heart and head. She made a really wonderful speech in a voice which had a great emotional appeal, and I watched with much interest that hard-boiled crowd who listened to her with growing amazement until they seemed to melt before her appeal. Money has been coming in ever since. Today the Chamber of Mines gave £10,000. Women are much better at this sort of thing than men. Still, I found my name on the list and had to follow her, and did my best. But of course hers was the star turn. I rejoiced in her success. She was so obviously surprised and taken aback as she had never before done any public speaking. It was a huge success for her fund; and you can imagine her feelings of gratitude and satisfaction.

Saturday and Sunday following I spent at Rooikop with her and Santa [Weyers]. I had not been there for many months, nor had Santa. It was a joy to get away to that peace and solitude. The nights here are now bitterly cold and although there was frost at Rooikop also, it was nothing like the biting cold here. So we could enjoy ourselves at night by the big log fire and by day in wandering through beautiful wheat fields just an inch or two high, and in watching impala and kudu in the bush. We discussed the war, and the coming peace, and God's ways with man, and philosophy and Greece— indeed there was no end to these discussions except at night when we slept the deep sleep of the Bushveld. I returned Sunday night completely refreshed after a really heavenly time. She left this morning early for Egypt to join her husband, in my plane which also carried Lord Harlech on his way to London, and some officials to their destinations up north. Unless fate is unkind to her she will go far—by force of character, high principle, and a great measure of ability. You can imagine what she as a German must have passed through in this war, a persecuted refugee from her own race, and with high humanitarian views very much as we ourselves hold. She said it was like hell, but she passed through it, and now has found her peace. It must have been an experience for one so young, who had lived such a sheltered court life. But the real human stuff was there and in the end won through. It is a victory for that *Reine Menschlichkeit*[1] which Goethe says is in the end the solution and redemption of all our errors and wanderings. Her husband I know well. He is also a fine human, with a very likeable character. I am glad that they are together again. Their three small children remain at the Cape, and may later join us here.

In the intervals of all these activities spread over the country I have had to attend to a number of difficult war and administrative as well as electoral questions. But luckily I see daylight and am getting through heavy arrears. Practically every sort of question dealt with in London comes to the Dominions for information and consultation, and these are all heavy additions to our own local burdens. Today, for instance, I had to deal with American supply

[1] pure humanity.

questions which affect us vitally as we are now so dependent on America for essential supplies. An organization (Anglo-American-South African) has at last been created for the purpose. Then the whole knotty and risky question of post-war civil aviation had to be dealt with and a long despatch on our views as to the future of aviation had to go to London. I mention only two big problems from among a much longer list. This all adds to our work out here, which is heavy enough in all conscience. I don't write about the war. We live in suspense, in the great expectancy before the zero hour, for it is evident that the great summer storm must now burst soon. Churchill has indicated that much in his great speech in the commons after his return from America and north Africa. And indeed everyone sees that we are on the eve of the great events which will determine the outcome of the war. I am busy reorganizing our South African forces for the invasion,[1] and it means much work as we were organized on a voluntary basis for African service only. Our Coloured and Native people also give much trouble when they come to inhabited areas with all its drink and seduction. I am busy with this transformation of the fighting army which occupies much of my attention besides the political and electoral questions. Next week will be another heavy week, with numerous appointments. I hope I shall stand this strain, this continuing and increasing strain, to the end. Thank you both for nice letters received. Ever lovingly,

Jan

612   To M. C. Gillett   Vol. 72, no. 222

Doornkloof
[Transvaal]
4 July 1943

I am getting rather restless as the general election is only three days off and my thoughts have to be concentrated on the last steps and the finishing touches. This produces an unconscious inner strain which I had better work off in writing to you. This is Sunday night, my usual letter time, and so I shall kill two birds with one stone. This will be my last general election—tenth and last—as I am not likely to be in the running after five years of what is now awaiting me. I shall be seventy-eight five years hence, and that is too close to dotage to be called old age. If there is one thing I would hate it would be lingering on beyond my years of real usefulness. I have the sad example of Merriman and Hertzog to warn me off the

---

[1] Of Sicily.

course in time. I hope to be able to do this before it is too late. But another danger, and a much more serious one, stares me in the face. And that is some crowning disaster in the near future, when I have once more to tackle the problem of world peace. It is a baffling, an appalling prospect—that of making peace at the end of this war. I failed miserably twenty-four years ago, and fear another and more tragic failure next time. I doubt whether I could have done much at Paris where I was not in a prominent position and the real reins of power were held by other hands. But since then I have come to be looked upon as one of the elder statesmen and one to expect much from. I have heard quite responsible people say that they pin their faith on me and expect me to be one of the main hopes of a good peace. This is all so wild and exaggerated and I feel so humbled and discouraged by the thought of previous failure and the risk of still greater failure in the coming ordeal. Perhaps I shall be spared this bitter cup; perhaps I may have to drink it, and go under at the end. It is an awful thought. Peace-making at the end of *this* war will be the hardest task that could be set our poor human statesmanship. After what has happened it may even prove an impossible task. And I do so long to see no chance of human good missed, no precious opportunity of serving the great cause of man well and saving our race from a reign of hate leading up to another world disaster. It may in the end be a superhuman labour and one where one could only pray the Griqua prayer.[1] But it will be a dreadful confession to have to make and for me a devastating disaster. It would be like passing into black night after a day of glorious light and shade and colour.

These dismal thoughts and forebodings have been stirred in me partly by the reading of two books, one of which I have not finished yet. The one is *The German Home Front* by Schutz[2] which deals with the Germany which is under the Nazi heel and must feel very much as we do, the Germany of Goethe and Schiller and the millions of Germans of good will today suffering in body and soul. The popular view is that there is no such Germany, but we know better. This is the seed from which a noble harvest for man may yet be raised by wise and prudent statesmanship; but will this states-manship have a chance? It is not a very good book, but there is a lot of good stuff and reliable information in it. Evidently written by a religious Catholic. Perhaps you can get it to read. Mine is the copy in the parliamentary library. The second book, much abler and

[1] Refers to a favourite story of the old chief who prayed to God not merely to send His son to the aid of the Griqua people in their great trouble but to come himself.
[2] W. W. Schutz, *German Home Front* (1943).

better written, is *How to Win the Peace* by C. J. Hambro[1] who, I think, was the speaker in the Norwegian Storting and seems now to be a refugee in the United States. Written in beautiful English and full of first-rate thinking and material. You and Arthur may like to read it (Hodder and Stoughton). I am half way through it, and shall go right through it. Very informative and suggestive, but I fear scarcely practical in most of its suggestions. Evidently this Nazi revolution touches the bedrock of our human advance and something very deep and far-reaching will have to be attempted to deal with the evils now emerging on our path. The situation is at bottom a religious problem reaching down to our fundamental way of life. And the question is whether the ordinary methods of political action can be usefully applied in such a case, where really a religious reformation in the human spirit is called for. No voice divine is heard in our day; only the political pundits are left us, and what poor folks they are, with what poor instruments of reform for such a situation as Nazi Germany! Still we should not despair even here, and have faith in that good which in the end, the far off end perhaps, overcometh evil.[2]

Of course much may yet happen before the end which may simplify our problem. The better Germany may in the end get control and settle its own Nazi problems. That would be the best way out. Or Germany may break up and cease to be a menace and sink into the background to work out its own salvation in the coming generation. Either would be a perhaps too hopeful view, and we may be left with the main problem on our hands, with not only the United States and the British Commonwealth to deal with, but also Russia and France and all the outraged neighbouring peoples now under her awful harrow. I remain sorely troubled over it all. I wish I were twenty-four years younger!

This is Sunday night. Tomorrow night I close our campaign with a big rally at Johannesburg, which will be a vast demonstration. Then the following two days I shall spend in my constituency which I have not visited since 1942! On 7 July will be the poll here, although actual counting will be delayed till the soldiers' vote from abroad has arrived, which may not be for another two or three weeks. So there will be a period of suspense and wild guessing. I shall fill up that gap with cabinet meetings to deal with urgent current problems, and with some post-election functions in the country. I have also to visit Rhodesia as their commander-in-chief. There appears little chance for a holiday, but I may be able to get away for

---

[1] Published in 1943.
[2] 'Be not overcome of evil, but overcome evil with good.' *Romans* xii.21.

one or two week-ends. With it all I am thankful to say my health remains good, and as long as I don't overdo it and take my one or two long walks per week I may continue without a breakdown such as Isie has had. She is getting on very well, only more slowly than before and with more careful watching by us to keep her from overdoing it again. . . .

This is all. Our dear love to you and all best wishes. Please go slow and take your summer exercise before winter comes or before 'the autumn leaves fall' as Churchill puts it. Ever yours,

Jan

613   To Mervyn Ellis   Vol. 72, no. 125

Pretoria
13 July 1943

My dear Ellis, Thank you very much for your letter of 9 July[1] which I read with much interest and some concern.

But first let me express to you my very deep gratitude for your able and valuable assistance during the past election. I cannot tell you how much I enjoyed reading many of your forceful articles.[2] My wife told me that she was keeping quite a number of them—they were so good. Your whole-hearted support—even where it was against the grain—was as valuable as it is highly appreciated by me. Of course our press generally has been outstandingly good and effective in this fight, and the result will in no small measure be due to the wonderful support I have received from you and your confreres.

I think you take the cutting you enclosed[3] much too seriously. I have read it carefully in view of your complaint against Wilks [E. C.],[4] but I must confess that I cannot find in it any sign of disloyalty to the Standstill Agreement.[5] All he seems to be out to make clear is that—with the exception of the Nationalist candidates—*all* votes cast in Natal were for the war policy, and have therefore to be counted in favour of the referendum for the war which I had called for. I find no approval of the Independents, but only the plain and admitted fact that the vote for them is pro-war, and must not be counted on the other side.

[1] Smuts Collection, vol. 70, no. 103.
[2] Ellis was editor of the *Natal Mercury*, established in Durban in November 1852.
[3] The cutting is not attached to the document in the Smuts Collection.
[4] Wilks, organizing secretary of the United party in Natal, had, on 8 July, given an interview to the *Natal Daily News* (established as the *Natal Advertiser* in 1878, title changed in 1937).   [5] *See* **609**.

I do not think that the United Party in Natal could be accused of calculated disloyalty to the agreement. On the contrary I fear the small parties[1] might have suffered grievously if there had been no agreement and if it had not on the whole been carried out by the United party supporters. Of course Oakes [R. E.] proved too bitter a pill to swallow after the unsavoury revelations,[2] and I therefore feel all the more gratitude to you and the *Mercury* for not having succumbed to temptation. But I do not think anybody would be justified, after the support we did give the two small parties, to accuse us of not having played the game by them. I even did my best to secure a Standstill between them, but failed, and hence the trouble and confusion in the heat of the battle between them,[3] which unfortunately, but understandably, involved also a number of the United party supporters.

This election may have far-reaching reactions. Dr Malan and his principal colleagues made it repeatedly clear that the future of Afrikanderdom—as they conceive it—was at stake, and that defeat for them would be a mortal affair. When the result will prove a clear, and perhaps a spectacular, defeat for them, the result cannot but be a pointer to the future of the most important character. Things could not be again what they were, and the ding-dong fight could not in all conscience be resumed. I think this is a point which could well be made by you and others who labour in the cause of racial peace. Ever yours sincerely,

s. J. C. Smuts

614   From L. S. Amery   Vol. 70, no. 11

[London]
14 July 1943

My dear Smuts, I have just seen Harlech who confirms all the cheering reports about the prospects of your election. I trust by the time you get this you will have got in by a majority which will leave no doubt as to the true feelings of South Africa.

The Sicilian enterprise has begun well[4] and we are all very hopeful

---

[1] The Dominion and Labour parties.

[2] R. E. Oakes, who was the official Coalition (Dominion party) candidate at Durban Point, had appeared in court on a charge of underpaying an employee. The seat was won by V. L. Shearer, the sitting member, who stood as an Independent. *See supra*, p. 433, note 2.

[3] W. B. Madeley (Labour party) and C. F. Stallard (leader of the Dominion party) had crossed swords when Madeley, after accepting the candidature of Oakes, made public attacks on him.

[4] The invasion of Sicily by the Allied forces began on 10 July.

about it. All the same we are necessarily rather strung out with our backs to the sea and a really enterprising opponent might be able to strike pretty heavily at one or other flank of our front. We shall see.

I was greatly pleased by your clear telegram on the subject of the future of civil aviation. It has taken over a year for the cabinet committee here to realize that it is no good pushing theoretical schemes which no one will look at and that the practical question is how to find a policy which will commend itself to others, more particularly the Americans, and yet also protect the most vital interests of our own Commonwealth. I see no real difficulty about that, but fear that the line we took at the outset has frightened the Canadian government and made them foolishly sticky about any Empire consultation before entering an international conference. Meanwhile Campbell Stuart will, I think, have shown you a short memorandum in which I indicated what has seemed to me the most practical solution. It does not differ widely as a matter of fact from the policy which our government has laid before you. In practice I think we shall be pushed out of the somewhat lopsided definition of free air which we have put forward, and can then no doubt fall back upon the one which I have suggested, namely, the reservation of internal traffic, coupled with the right of any two or more nations to combine their internal traffic. That, as I have already suggested, would enable you not only to participate effectively in any Empire scheme, but also to rope in the Portuguese colonies and possibly the Belgian Congo in a South African scheme.

I enclose a pamphlet by a Canadian ex-Rhodes Scholar,[1] addressed mainly to American audiences, which I think is very much to the point and I think will interest you. Yours ever,

L. S. Amery

615   To M. C. Gillett   Vol. 72, no. 224

Doornkloof
[Transvaal]
21 July 1943

I missed last Sunday writing to you, and now it is Wednesday afternoon, and it is not safe to wait longer as much work lies ahead. This morning we had the funeral service for Patrick Duncan and I had of course to give the address. This afternoon he is being cremated at Johannesburg. I think most of our family are now deciding for this manner of exit. It saves space and looks cleaner.

---

[1] Not attached to the original document.

Little Katusha of Japie [Smuts] just now asked me how I was going to be buried. I voted for cremation and she for ordinary burial, and then she asked me why I preferred cremation. I replied that I did not want to be eaten by worms and to smell. She said 'then I want also to be cremated'. After a pause she added: 'But best of all is to be like Jesus and rise again the third day'! However that honour will not be reserved for the likes of us, and so we plump for cremation, Isie most strongly of all. My short address was liked by many. If it is published by the papers I shall include a cutting. I did a rather daring thing by referring to young Patrick[1] Duncan who disappeared in the cauldron in the disastrous Libyan battle of which Tobruk was a part. He was never found again, 'claimed by unknown Libyan sands' I said. And so on. I generally avoid emotional stuff on these occasions as one never knows whether there will not be a breakdown in the audience or by the speaker himself—in some emotional wave. But nothing happened this morning. I am told, however, that my young lady typist in the office who typed my notes shed tears over the MS, and another noticing this and reading the stuff did likewise! So you see how near the wind one sometimes sails. My information officer had written a speech for me which I thought very good. But the one I had roughly written overnight *he* thought so much better that he persuaded me to stick to my own version. These are the small byplays of great events which are often more interesting from a human point of view than the events themselves. But death always is a most poignant thing—except in battle when it almost means nothing. I have told you how for the first time in my life I saw heaps of English dead on the Dundee battlefield,[2] and to my surprise I remained completely unmoved. Usually, however, death and the ceremonies connected with it are among the most solemn and arresting events in life, and much of human thought and religion and emotion centre round that fact. It is the sadness of the last and greatest farewell and the rupture of the most abiding ties and there-fore the most poignant of misfortunes. Walt Whitman's song of praise to death[3] does not ring true, and Fausset may be right in thinking it an expression of a defeatist and unsound strain in his make-up. But death remains a mystery, however we view it—a mystery like birth, but oh, so different in its meaning for us. There is nothing quite like the longing for life in the face of death, especially of our loved ones.

Duncan leaves a great blank, not only for his family but in our

[1] A slip for Andrew.   [2] *See* vol. I, p. 561, note 2.
[3] *Memories of President Lincoln*, section 14. The song begins: 'Come lovely and soothing death...'

public life. He was just the right man for that job, and is quite irreplaceable from our own resources. [N. J.] de Wet, the chief justice, who now acts, resolutely declines to be governor-general although from all points of view he would be far the most suitable person. For several good reasons I am not anxious to appoint, or rather recommend, an English governor-general, but in South Africa it is difficult to find a suitable person for this post. Duncan on 4 September 1939 did an imperishable service to South Africa and the world in declining to accept his prime minister's advice, according to the usual practice. His judgment was superb, and no less his courage. The consequences for the world have been very far-reaching. And so there are times when the king or the person in his position is all-important, though these times may not be frequent. The people chose Roosevelt, but technically it was George VI who chose Churchill, although Churchill had been an Edward VIII man. But then it was again the people who chose the unspeakable Harding [W. G.] after Woodrow Wilson. Kings can make no greater mistakes than the sacred people sometimes makes in its sovereign wisdom. And the next choice in the United States next year deeply troubles me. But you see how far I have wandered from the funeral of Patrick Duncan!

I had a most interesting letter from Arthur this week, none from you. It is to me not only amusing but most interesting to see how much and how fast he is moving to the left. And the fun is that he has just—in spite of my qualms—become deputy chairman of Barclay D.C.O.[1] I wonder whether the pundits know how red he is becoming! For his health's sake I dislike his undertaking these new and partly onerous duties, but I must admit that my vanity feels flattered by the promotion of my friend. And it is so thoroughly well deserved. No, Barclay D.C.O. has decidedly risen in my favour. And yet, and yet, I don't like it. I hope Arthur will not in an excess of zeal go too far and spoil the wisdom of his colleagues by overdoing it in office. At sixty-seven one goes slow. That is in the Ten Commandments of nature which one disobeys at one's peril.

On the merits of Right and Left I am myself somewhat Laodicean. But my education was Right, and I cannot quite see how the structure of civilization and progress which we have built up on the concepts of property can be preserved on Leftist conceptions. In the end I suppose property will remain, and money will still be worshipped

---

[1] Arthur Gillett was deputy chairman of Barclays Bank D.C. and O. when the chairman, Sir John Caulcutt, died in April 1943, but did not, on grounds of health, accept the chairmanship for which he was to be recommended. (Note by M. C. Gillett.)

in a corner of the Temple, but no longer in the old way. The state
will take such a whack for general purposes that only the shell or
a fragment of the shell will remain for the individual owner and
financier. Of course, as long as the state can look after upbringing,
education, health, housing, and the higher life as well as, or better
than, the private owner or person, no harm is done and much can
be said for levelling away classes and vested interests. But I have
still to learn that the state, with human nature as it is, is equal to
this job. And what becomes of the family, perhaps the most sacred
and fundamental institution of civilization and means of progress?
The future of marriage and the family is not at all clear to me on
Leftish principles and tendencies. And what of religion which is
generally frowned upon by the Left? We have a whole framework
or pattern of concepts on which human progress has been founded,
and much of it embodied in the wonderful Roman law of which I have
always been an admirer. I don't see the outlines of the Left pattern
yet. Family, property, contract, privacy (which largely is religion
according to Whitehead) these are an intelligible proved code. What
is the comparable code of the Left?

Yes, I received Arthur's note on exchange and see that he defines
it as I do. I found his observations very informative. But now, what
about Bancor and Unitas?[1] What does he consider the salient points
of difference between the two proposals, and has he any preferences
as between them? It is what lies *behind* the two schemes, and what
remains unexpressed in their details that troubles me. How are they
likely to work out, in that struggle for power which I foresee coming
between Europe and America? Surely the men who have thought
out these contrasted plans have envisaged the future, and it is their
future consequences which I should like to grasp more clearly.

The war is going amazingly well, both in Russia and the Mediterranean. I think Sicily will go rather faster than most thought. What
next? And in Russia the German offensive has petered out[2] and been
replaced by a daring, large-scale Russian offensive. In the Far East
also things are moving in the right direction. I don't mean China,
on which we are very poorly informed, but in the south-east Pacific.
Rome has been a real bombshell. The Italians never thought Rome

---

[1] At this time British and American schemes to internationalize monetary and
exchange policy were being discussed. The British plan, proposed by Lord Keynes,
required a new international currency (Bancor) and the American plan, proposed by
Harry White, suggested a new unit of account (Unitas). For details of the two schemes
see R. F. Harrod, *The Life of John Maynard Keynes* (1951), chapter 13.

[2] On 5 July the Germans had begun an attempt to destroy the Russian salient into
the German front at Kursk. After a fortnight the Russians threw back this offensive.
Meanwhile they had launched an attack on the German salient around Orel on 12 July.

would be bombed, and the city had become a place for refugees and evacuees. Now they are disillusioned, and the spirit of pessimism may carry them far. How far, while Mussolini is still in control, and Hitler behind him?

I think the remainder of this year will be profoundly interesting and important. The whole Plan is beginning to work out as I foresaw. If only we can now avoid fundamental mistakes in our strategy! Then 1943 will carry us very far. Good-bye. Ever lovingly,

Jan

616   To M. C. Gillett   Vol. 72, no. 226

Doornkloof
[Transvaal]
31 July 1943

Saturday afternoon, after a long walk and a delicious warm bath. I am sitting in the sitting-room in front, with a fire in the hearth on my left, and through the windows on the right a gorgeous sun is setting behind the thin clouds. There is the hush of a late winter afternoon, the world is at peace, and I myself feel at rest and contented. A very busy week lies behind me. Saturday last I spent in Rhodesia inspecting troops, and yesterday I returned from a big war fund function at Port Elizabeth. The rest of the week was spent in office, with much that called for attention in times like these. I spent this morning in office, and now I feel at rest in a world at rest.

The results of the general election were finally known yesterday,[1] and our victory is far greater than any of us had expected. The United party under me is more than double the Nats, and in addition we have the Labour and Dominion and Native representatives, which give us in all a majority of sixty-seven in the house, compared with the thirteen with whom I went to war in September 1939. No such victory has ever been won in the political warfare of this country. And when I think of my years in the wilderness, of all I had to endure even when I was not in the wilderness, and at sunset I find such recognition of what I have stood for and suffered for, I feel that at last I have been repaid with more than compound interest. The Hertzog party[2] with Havenga their leader has completely dis-

[1] The results had been delayed because the soldiers' votes had to be counted first. The full results were: United party 89, National party 43, Labour party 9, Dominion party 7, Independents 2. The three Native representatives had been re-elected in the second such election in 1942.
[2] The Afrikaner party.

appeared, the Pirow New Orderites sunk themselves at the start and funked the election. The *Ossewa-Brandwag* people are in hiding. It is indeed 'a famous victory'![1] The political front is now secure, with a parliamentary majority which is an embarrassment. And we can go on with the job.

The job too has improved, though heavy tasks still lie ahead in spite of the catastrophic disappearance of Mussolini.[2] But I believe that Musso's fall will mean that of Italy also in the near future. I do not see [Marshal P.] Badoglio riding that storm where Musso has failed so miserably. The confusion in Italy must be such that the end can only be a total collapse. And so here also we are at last beginning to gather 'the far off interest of tears'.[3] When I think back to the years of endurance—what you people had to endure in silent agony and immeasurable effort in the years of threatening defeat and what we had to endure here with the foe right inside the camp like a Trojan horse and our not knowing from day to day what the end would be—when I think back to all this, and now find Musso gone as a first instalment, and the opposition here routed as an instalment for me I am filled with deep thankfulness. It has been a triumph of soul, of faith in the invisible, of holding on firmly to the unseen. I think of that moving passage on faith in Hebrews, where it is described as 'endurance as seeing the Unseen'.[4] That is the greatness of this world—that it is not mere matter or machines or brute force, but the spirit dominant in defeat as in victory. Hitler could not take London because he could not take Mansoul.[5] He could take Paris because the soul of France was paralysed, asleep, or worse. The meaning of this world is not so much in what is seen or known as in the unseen or unknown. And it is therefore intelligible how people came to locate an 'unseen world' as part of their geography of the universe. But the unseen is but the inner meaning and real heart of the seen, and not a world apart. All true philosophy tends to that view. And it is also the testimony of poetry and art, and of real religion itself. The secret is within and not beyond. Or one might say the beyond is the within. Omar Khayyam's 'Thou thyself

---

[1]
> 'But what good came of it at last?'
> Quoth little Peterin.
> 'Why that I cannot tell', said he,
> 'But 'twas a famous victory.'
> Robert Southey, *The Battle of Blenheim*.

[2] On 25 July Mussolini was superseded as president of the Grand Council by Marshal Badoglio and taken three days later as a prisoner to the island of Ponza.

[3] Not traced.

[4] *Hebrews* xi.27.

[5] The metropolis of the universe in Bunyan's *The Holy War* for which Diabolus and Emmanuel, the son of King Shaddai, contend.

art Heaven and Hell'.[1] (By the way, some people have taken Jesus's saying, 'The kingdom of God is *within* you', as meaning what I have just said. But I believe that Jesus really said, the kingdom of God is *among* you, is already come, although not yet clearly manifested. His message was that *He* was the bringer of the kingdom, which was not something far off in the future. I think Schweitzer has made this quite clear. But this is by the way.) The moral crisis of this war takes us to the very depths and a new appreciation of life and its values will arise from it...

617 From F. D. Roosevelt

Vol. 72, no. 11

The White House
Washington
15 August 1943

My dear General, May I send you my heartfelt congratulations on the result of your elections. They constitute not only an expression of common sense on the part of your people but they are a great tribute to your own leadership.

Mr Churchill has been here at Hyde Park for two or three days and he tells me he hopes you will soon be able to come to London. I need not tell you that I hope if you do this you will surely come to visit us in Washington.

You will have a wonderful reception here and it is my thought that you might appear before the congress for a short speech, and speak either in New York or Chicago to a large audience. I do not think, however, that it would be at all necessary for you to make an extensive tour of the country. I want especially to have a good chance to see you personally. With my warm regards, Always sincerely,

Franklin D. Roosevelt

618 To M. C. Gillett

Vol. 72, no. 230

Doornkloof
[Transvaal]
1 September 1943

...I listened to Churchill's Quebec broadcast last night. The most striking thing he said was apropos of the difference between interest

[1]   And by and by my Soul returned to me,
And answered, 'I Myself am Heaven and Hell.'
Edward Fitzgerald, *Omar Khayyám* vii.

and duty—the first too difficult for even the cleverest to know, the second known to simple folks the world over and followed by them as their rule in life. He could not of course give any information about the planning of the conference[1] and was evidently more at pains to mollify Stalin about his having not been invited to the conference. Our alliance with the United States is a difficult matter, but nothing compared to the awkwardness of the Russian alliance. They are suspicious of us and of everything, and are no doubt conscious of a deep-going difference in our respective outlooks on life. We shall have no easy time under this alliance, but better for us to be with them than with the Germans whose outlook has almost undone Europe—twice in our day. I do think that we are leaving too heavy a share of the military burden to Russia. It is no credit to us that the Anglo-American combine do not pull a heavier weight in this war. It is not good for us to appear inferior in our war effort.[2] And it would be a disaster if it afterwards appeared that Russia had won the war. It would make her the master of the world and this might go to her head. Nor do I think that Russia is qualified for world leadership. There is something still immature, almost barbaric, about her procedure and her outlook, and she has much to learn before she can set up as the teacher and guide of mankind. That terrible business with the 10,000 Polish officers at Katyn continues to haunt my thoughts, though the affair is still partly wrapped up in mystery.[3] I hear that the Germans have now taken from our Dominion prisoners of war a number of unwilling witnesses to the pits at Katyn, and no doubt we shall hear a lot about these and other unbelievable atrocities of this war. What the Germans have done to Jews, Poles and Czechs is quite unbelievable, but unfortunately they are not the only sinners. Concentration camps of the Boer War look like happy Elysian fields compared to these camps and tunnels and dungeons of horror. If one did not cling to faith beyond the evidence of one's senses, 'as seeing the unseen',[4] one would despair of this world, of man, and of God. But there is that in us which puts

[1] Churchill, Roosevelt, their Service chiefs and advisers met at Quebec on 19 August to decide upon future strategy and commands, particularly in south-east Asia.

[2] For an exchange of views between Smuts and Churchill on this point *see* Winston Churchill, *The Second World War*, vol. v, pp. 112–16.

[3] German occupation forces found a mass grave in a wood near the village of Katyn west of Smolensk in July 1941 and later accused the Russians of having massacred and buried in vast graves in the forests some 15,000 Polish officers and other prisoners of war who came into their hands in September 1939 and of whom all trace had been lost since April 1940. When the Russians reoccupied the Katyn region in September 1943 they held their own investigation and claimed that the Polish prisoners had been slaughtered by the Germans. A breach between the Polish and Soviet governments followed.

[4] *See supra*, p. 447, note 4.

us on our guard and warns us not to follow the evidence of sense merely, to realize that there is something deeper at the heart of things—something which will emerge after our long human march and the experience of our savage years. He who faced the Cross and despaired not has taught us a lesson of faith, enduring faith in the Divine, which remains our treasure of religion and true wisdom.

I have been writing the last few evenings a broadcast for this coming week-end on the four years of war behind us.[1] It is of course very vague and sketchy, as anything must be that purports to survey this vast panorama within a twenty minutes talk. I could only point to what appear to be the most salient features. Whether the broadcast will reach you I don't know. The air is not very favourable from here to England, and still less so between the United States and here. I could hear Churchill last night quite well and clearly speaking at Quebec, but I suppose very special arrangements had been made for the purpose. I get the usual treatment and am thankful for it.

I had a caucus of the United party in Pretoria this week. As parliament may not meet till January I thought it best, after the recent elections, to call members together and compare notes and ventilate their points of view with the government. It was a very successful gathering and served its purpose very well. We parted in a happy mood. At the very end I was told that, should the war situation call for my presence elsewhere out of South Africa, I could safely go and they would support the rest of the government satisfactorily. This is quite handsome, though I told them that some might interpret this as a wish to get me out of the way! The party is however quite loyally behind me, though not equally so behind some of my other ministers. In wartime it is impossible to please everybody. Things must almost inevitably go wrong where the whole situation is so abnormal, and the tendency is to blame the government even where they are not in the least to blame. As for going out of the country, I feel like waiting for a clear call and not going away unless there is a good case for so doing. So you must look upon a visit to London as still quite uncertain. I shall certainly have to go as the war moves to an end, but I see no sign yet that it is doing so. Things are definitely moving in our favour but Hitler still sits with much of Europe and I fear much very hard fighting will yet take place before the end. Especially is this so because we demand unconditional surrender and have announced our policy of punishing war criminals. The war lords now know what is in store for them and even neutral countries have been notified not to receive them.

I have done little worth-while reading this last week. There are

[1] Broadcast on 4 September. *See* Smuts Collection, Box K, no. 176.

too many odd functions additional to the hard regular office work and I look forward to some blessed sleep at night.

All well here and busy at their various tasks. All send love to you and to 102. Ever yours,

Jan

619   To S. M. Smuts   Vol. 72, no. 156

Tunis
3 Oktober 1943

Liefste Mamma, Ek skryf 'n paar reëls voor ons vertrek van Tunis in 'n half uur. Ons is gehuisves in 'n pragtige gebou op 'n koppie bokant die plein waarin die ou Carthago geleë was en sien oor die vlakte en die seefront daaronder. Dis 'n skoon uitkyk, een van die pragtigste in die wereld, en voor ons lê die kus en berge waar die finale slae in die veldtog gelewer is. Ons vertrek netnou na Sicilië en Malta waar ons die dag gaan deurbreng en vanaand is ons in Algiers om morre van daar te vertrek na Gibraltar en Engeland. Tot dusver was die tog baie aangenaam en interessant. Japie en Jannie het ons te Cairo ontmoet en ek het by die Caseys gebly vir my konferensies in Cairo. Toe na die 6de Divisie in de woestyn en van daar na Alexandria om die res van twee dae baie lief en aangenaam met Palo en Frederica in hul heerlik klein huis deur te breng. (Kleiner as Tsalta en £80 huur per maand). Japie en Jannie was in 'n hotel. Ek het ons klein skepies besoek en die Italiaanse vloot nou in die hawe bekyk. Jannie sou met my verder gaan maar ek het besluit om Japie saam te neem tot by Algiers, en so is ons Donderdag 1 Oktober weg en langs die kus al die ou vegplekke bekyk en laat die namiddag na 1,500 myl hier aangekom. Laatste twee dae op konferensies hier en vandag en morre verder konferensies te Algiers. Alles leersaam en nuttig. Gesondheid van almal uitstekend en niks sover om oor te kla. As daar tyd is skryf ek verder vanaand van Algiers want hierdie brief moet met Nel terug en sal miskien die laaste vir 'n lange tyd wees wat jy van my sal ontvang. Briewe neem so lang dat dit skaars die moeite werd sal wees om te skrywe voor my terugkoms. En ek kan altyd boodskappies per telegram deur die kantoor stuur. Totsiens—vanaand!

Later 4 Oktober. Ons is gister aand hier aangekom na 'n visite aan Sicilië en Malta wat ons baie geniet het. Ons het die heele Sicilië omgery en alles van belang gesien, die verwoeste hawens en stede, Etna en ook ons lugmag nog op die eiland. Te Malta het ons met die Gouverneur Lord Gort gelunch, en daarna terug op pad. 'n

451

Moeilikheid met die Lodestar het ons terugkeer vertraag en ons moes dus weer die nag te Tunis deurbreng in plaas van na Algiers te gaan. Ons sal met 'n ander machine vanoggend daarheen gaan en vannag voort na Gibraltar en Londen waar ons vir ontbyt morre weer sal wees. Ons hoop alles sal goed gaan. Japie draai van Algiers terug en sal briewe na jul neem. Jy sal verbaas wees te verneem dat hy kom nou op Eisenhower's staf as Staf offisier, viral met die oog op die feit dat gedeelte van ons vegmagte onder Eisenhower se bevel sorteer. Dit sal hom goed doen en kanse van ondervinding gee wat hy natuurlik nooit in 'n Afrikaanse [*sic*] eenheid kan kry nie. Dit is eers aan Jannie aangebied maar hy verkies om by ons engenieurs te bly. Vir Japie sal werkswinkels in Egipte van minder belang wees as 'n groot internasionale staf met alles en almal daarop.

Tot ons verbasing is Generaal Klopper hier aangekom, na 'n baie sware en gevaarlik ontsnapping uit sy kamp in Middel Italie. Baie ander is ook ontsnap maar ek vrees weer deur die Duitsers gevang. Die Italianers help ons mense, maar die Duitsers is ooral. Nu vaarwel, my liefste. Ek sal gedurig aan jul denk in my afwesigheid en bid jul almal veilig weer te sien.

Pappa

TRANSLATION

Tunis
3 October 1943

Dearest Mamma, I write a few lines before our departure from Tunis in half-an-hour. We are lodged in a lovely building on a koppie above the plain in which old Carthage was situated and look out over the flats and the sea-front below. It is a beautiful view, one of the loveliest in the world, and before us lie the coast and the mountains where the last battles in the campaign were fought. We are leaving soon for Sicily and Malta where we shall spend the day, and tonight we shall be in Algiers and leave there tomorrow for Gibraltar and England. So far the journey has been very pleasant and interesting. Japie and Jannie [Smuts] met us in Cairo and I stayed with the Caseys for my conferences in Cairo. Then I went to the Sixth Division in the desert and from there to Alexandria to spend the rest of two days very affectionately and pleasantly with Palo and Frederica[1] in their delightful little house (smaller than Tsalta and the rent £80 a month). Japie and Jannie were in an hotel. I visited our little ships and saw the Italian fleet now in the harbour. Jannie was to have accompanied me further but I decided

---

[1] Prince Paul of Greece and his wife (qq.v.).

to take Japie with me as far as Algiers and so we left on 1 October, saw all the old battle-fields along the coast and arrived here late in the afternoon after 1,500 miles. During the last two days there have been conferences here and today and tomorrow there will be more conferences at Algiers. All instructive and useful. Everybody's health excellent and nothing to complain of so far. If there is time I shall write further from Algiers because this letter must return with Nel [P.] and will perhaps be the last you will receive from me for a long time. Letters take so long that it will hardly be worth while to write before my return. And I can always send little messages by telegram through the office. Good-bye, until tonight!

Later, 4 October. We arrived here last night after a visit to Sicily and Malta which we enjoyed very much. We drove right round Sicily and saw everything of importance—the destroyed harbours and towns, Etna, and also our air squadrons still on the island. At Malta we lunched with the governor, Lord Gort, and then resumed the journey. Trouble with the Lodestar delayed our return and so we had again to spend the night in Tunis instead of going to Algiers. We shall leave by another aircraft this morning and go on this evening and tonight to Gibraltar and London where we shall arrive for breakfast tomorrow.[1] We hope all will go well. Japie turns back from Algiers and will take letters to you. You will be surprised to hear that he is now to go on to Eisenhower's staff as staff-officer, especially in view of the fact that part of our fighting forces fall under Eisenhower's command. It will do him good and give him opportunities of gaining experience which, of course, he could never get in a South African unit. It was first offered to Jannie but he prefers to stay with our engineers. For Japie workshops in Egypt will be of less interest than a big international staff with everything and everyone on it.

To our surprise General [H. B.] Klopper has arrived here, after a very difficult and dangerous escape from his camp in central Italy. Many others have also escaped but have, I fear, again been captured by the Germans. The Italians help our people but the Germans are everywhere. Now good-bye my dearest. I shall constantly think of you in my absence and pray to see you all in safety again.

Pappa

[1] This was the second war-time visit of Smuts to London.

620   To J. H. Hofmeyr   Vol. 72, no. 161

Telegram

To: secretary for external affairs, Pretoria
From: General Smuts
Dated 12 October 1943

Following for Mr Hofmeyr from General Smuts. I much appreciate your and [D. D.] Forsyth's messages. All going well here and I am hard busy [*sic*] studying up all the war fronts. Churchill most anxious I should continue to help for some time and American visit is in cold storage. On 19 October I speak at Guildhall as guest of City. Reitz [D.] looks much fitter than I had expected and is happy in his work.[1] Gie [S. F. N.] is here with valuable information. Please inform colleagues and de Wet [N. J.].

621   To J. H. Hofmeyr   Vol. 72, no. 165

Telegram

To: secretary for external affairs, Pretoria
From: General Smuts
Dated 18 October 1943

Following secret for Mr Hofmeyr and Mrs Smuts from General Smuts. I may be detained here till December for meeting of prime ministers now being arranged. Churchill declines to let me return earlier and this is provisional warning about my probable time-table. More definite information later. American visit still unsettled. All well here and very busy.

622   To J. H. Hofmeyr   Vol. 72, no. 172

Telegram

To: secretary for external affairs, Pretoria
From: Field Marshal Smuts
Dated 28 October 1943

Following for Mr Hofmeyr from General Smuts. I think I have found our future director of scientific research. It is Professor, now Brigadier [B.] Schonland who is in charge of all the scientific work

[1] He was then high commissioner of the Union in Great Britain.

at the war office. Both as administrator and scientist he is held in highest esteem here, and risk is that unless we appropriate him in time he may be offered post-war appointment by war office. Do you approve my approaching him for post-war appointment as our director? I suggest his pay should be at least that of a head of department.

623 To J. H. Hofmeyr Vol. 72, no. 181

Hyde Park Hotel
London
11 November 1943

My dear Jantjie, I send you this line by hand of Van Ryneveld who leaves in a couple of days. Everything has gone uncommonly well with my work and my reception has been very good indeed. I think I have been able to be helpful in regard to the larger questions of our future strategy which has been, and still continues to be, very difficult. We now work in harmony with two exacting allies!

As I wired you, I intend dropping the American trip for this visit, but have not yet announced this. I may thus be home by the middle of December.

I am very grateful that you have kept me so well informed and that our work in South Africa has prospered so well. The provincial elections have been very encouraging,[1] and will have to be followed up by action. I am grateful also that you have been able to persuade De Wet [N. J.] to remain on a little longer.[2] I wish he would make up his mind to remain his five years; otherwise we shall have great difficulty about his successor. The war accounts are well cleared up —thanks to my three assistants. But I can see John Anderson is much concerned over this gold question. They now have to pay India £1 million *per day* for war and other purposes! Very kind regards to all my colleagues. Ever yours affectionately,

J. C. Smuts

[1] The results were as follows: Coalition parties: 37 (Cape), 55 (Transvaal), 25 (Natal), 4 (Orange Free State); National party: 18 (Cape), 8 (Transvaal), 17 (Orange Free State).

[2] As acting governor-general.

624   Speech (1943)   Box K, no. 178

This speech, which became known as the 'explosive' speech, was made at
a private meeting of members of the United Kingdom branch of the Empire
Parliamentary Association at the houses of parliament, London, on 25 November 1943 and was published by the Association under the title *Thoughts on the
New World*.

Lord Cranborne, my Lords, ladies and gentlemen: I intend to have
a general informal talk with you this afternoon. I have no set
opinions; I have no dogmatic beliefs to place before you; I am going
to put before you certain lines of thought which are running through
my own mind. I think the times in which we live do not really
permit of very rigid fixed opinions, or of any dogmatic outlook on
life or on the problems before us. We are facing today probably the
most perplexing complicated human situation that has confronted
the world for many generations, and anybody who thinks he has
a panacea at his command to deal with these problems must either
be sub-human or super-human. I simply want to suggest certain
lines of thought, and you must not hold me responsible for them
hereafter.

There are two dangers that face us in a situation such as ours
today. One is the danger of over-simplification. In a world where
the problems are so complex we may feel tempted to over-simplify
and thus falsify the real character of the problems before us and
miss the real solutions. The other danger is what I may call the
danger of following slogans or catchwords, and so missing the real
inwardness of the problems before us.

Let us look at these two dangers, which are really the same,
though I wish to keep them separate for the moment. Let me refer
briefly to the first danger of over-simplification. Where you are
faced with a situation and problems such as we are faced with, you
dare not over-simplify. In such circumstances you can only proceed
towards a solution step by step in the old empirical British way, for
if you begin to theorize and rationalize and simplify you are lost.

I think particularly of several occasions when we have been confronted with such a situation. Take our situation at the time of the
last peace. Twenty-five years ago we had before us very grave
problems, but we proceeded to solve them in a few months. The
peace conference met in January 1919 and it dissolved in May.
Within that period, by a process of side-tracking real issues and
over-simplifying others, we produced the peace treaty, and I am
sure if we were to follow the same procedure in the situation before
us today in the world, or the situation which will be before us at the

end of this war, we shall move to even greater disasters than we have seen in the past. When I look at the sort of problems that we shall have to deal with at the end of this war, the problems of the New Europe and the New World, I doubt whether any peace conference will be able to settle those questions in a reasonable time unless it proceeds by a process of over-simplification and falsification. I am myself doubtful whether we shall ever come to a peace conference at all at the end of this war. It may be that we may be faced with questions so vast, so complicated, so difficult and intractable, that in the end we shall have to be satisfied with making a pretty comprehensive armistice dealing with the general military question of ending the war, and leave the rest of the problems to a long series of conferences, to a long process of working out solutions without coming to any general peace conference at all.

That is one sort of situation that I consider probable—that we may never come to a peace conference at all, and that we may have to be satisfied with a comprehensive armistice on a basis of unconditional surrender, an armistice which will open the door to a long series of investigations and researches, which may take a long number of years before finality is reached.

I am also thinking, when I talk of over-simplification, of the situation which exists in our own British Empire. I do not think that either today or in the near future you could have any more complicated situation than that in our own group, quite apart from the general world situation. Take one particular problem—the problem of race and of colour, which is a root problem in our Empire. There are no doubt people who have a patent solution for that sort of problem, they have a general formula, they have a simple standard procedure for its solution. But it will not be the right one. To my mind we have there in the Empire a problem which is going to test our wisdom, our farsightedness, our statesmanship, our humanity, probably for generations before any solution can ever be reached. You can have no simple standardized solution. You can have no simple straightforward approach to a problem such as the vast diversity of race and colour, culture, and levels of civilization existing in our Empire. That is the sort of problem with which we have dealt in the past, and which will face us even more in the future. It calls for continuous experiment, for variety of treatment, and for very prolonged practical experience before any satisfactory solution could be reached.

I mention this because I know it is one of the questions on which people are thinking deeply and with which they are very much concerned nowadays. Many well-meaning people think you can by short cuts arrive at a solution. But you will not. Simplification will not help you. Simplification will mean falsification of the real difficulty. It is only by a long process of experience and patient experiment that you can deal with situations such as these.

Take my own continent with its problems of colour and race in west Africa, in east Africa, in south Africa. Everywhere you have great differences of culture and conditions generally, and in all these cases you can only proceed empirically, making experiments, trying to follow lines that suggest themselves as practicable and wise in the particular circumstances, and avoiding general preconceived standardized solutions.

Again, take the other danger I have referred to—the danger of following slogans and catchwords. Today we hear a great deal of democracy. We are fighting the battle of democracy. We are fighting for freedom. Of course we do. But these words become clichés, they become catchwords and vague slogans, which in the end do not lead you very far. Our opponents have another set of formulas. They fight for the leadership principle, the *führer* principle. With them the objective has also become a catchword, a cliché. It must be quite clear to anybody who thinks of the real problems that face us that you will only get to practical solutions in the end if you have a good mixture of both democracy and freedom on the one hand, and of leadership on the other. It is no use simplifying your problem and using one simple formula, and thinking that you will reach the solution in that way. Here in this country you are a great democracy, perhaps the most outstanding democracy of history; but here too we have learned what leadership means in a great emergency. Without leadership, freedom by itself will not help you. Freedom, like patriotism, is not enough.

I mention this simply as a case where you cannot blindly follow one general trend of thought alone. The world is much too complex, and the problems to be solved are much more complex too. In the difficulties before us we shall want both leadership and democracy. We shall want not only freedom but also discipline. Discipline is just as essential. We shall have to bear that in mind in the days before us.

I mention another case of one-sided simplification and of following one trend of thought: I remember before the last war, and during the last war, we were very much concerned with the danger of what was called the 'balance of power'. We wanted to get away from it because it was the old system in Europe that had led to wars before. We were determined to avoid the balance of power, and so we went in for another formula. We wanted a universal all-in system of security, a system of universality and of idealism; and we followed it in the League of Nations. We recognized equality, we brought all the nations together, and in the end there was a very large number of them. In that way we thought we would avoid the problem of the balance of power, but we fell into the opposite danger. This war has taught us not only that idealism is not enough, and that universality is not the solution for our security problem, but it has also taught us that we cannot get away from the problem of power.

That is where this greatest war in history had its origin. We have found that all our idealism, all our high aspirations for a better world and a better human society, stand no ghost of a chance unless we reckon with this fundamental factor, and we keep power well in our minds when we search for the solution of the problem of security. The question of power remains fundamental, and it is, I think, the great lesson of this war. Peace unbacked by power remains a dream.

Therefore, looking at the situation that faces us in the near future, I would say that in arranging for a new world organization for security, as we shall have to do, we shall have to provide not only for freedom and democracy, which are essential, but we shall also have to provide for leadership and for power. If we leave the future security of the world merely to loose arrangements and to aspirations for a peaceful world, we shall be lost. We shall have to attend to the lesson we have learned, and see to it that in the new organization to preserve peace for the future, we give a proper place to leadership and to power. To my mind that can be done much more effectively than in the covenant of the League of Nations, by giving a proper place to the three great powers that are now at the head of our United Nations.

Great Britain, the United States, and Russia now form the trinity at the head of the United Nations fighting the cause of humanity. And as it is in war, so will it have to be in peace. We shall have to see to it, that in the new international organization the leadership remains in the hands of this great trinity of powers. These three powers must retain the leadership in war and in peace, and be responsible in the first instance for the maintenance of security and for the preservation of world peace. And this primary responsibility will not be affected by any duties resting on the rest of the United Nations.

I think it was largely because in the League of Nations as constituted after the last war we did not recognize the importance of leadership and power that everything went wrong in the end. What was everybody's business in the end proved to be nobody's business.

Each one looked to the other to take the lead, and the aggressors got away with it. Leadership had not been firmly settled by the constitution of that organization, and it all went to pieces in the general hesitation and confusion. And that is why we are fighting this war now. To my mind we shall have to see to it that in the new organization there is leadership and there is power, both in their proper place and exercising their proper function among the United Nations.

Apart from this flaw, I should say, judging from my own reading of events, that there was nothing much amiss with the League of Nations in other respects. It was a well thought out scheme, and it worked well, and for the first ten years of the League it was a surprising success. Until aggression and the question of power turned up, the League of Nations functioned very well indeed. It looked after matters of social welfare, health, labour, and other social activities of mankind, in a way which could not be bettered, and from that point of view the League system remains, on the whole, a good and proper one to continue in the future. But when it comes to questions of world peace, security and aggression, for which we did not make sufficient provision, we shall have to revise the covenant on the lines I have suggested.

Just one word more about the League of Nations, and I pass on to other subjects. I think one other flaw or weakness in the League organization after the last war was the fact that we did not pay sufficient attention, or indeed any particular attention to the economic question. The covenant much too exclusively followed political lines. We looked too much to political solutions. We have learned our lesson there, too. Just as we have learned our lesson that power is fundamental in the international order, so we have learned our lesson that unless the new organization which we are going to erect after this war attends efficiently and well to the economic conditions among mankind, we shall again get into the troubles which ruined world recovery after the last war; and I hope that our new organization will have its economic activities as properly defined and regulated as its political activities.

I think that so far you will be inclined to agree with me. I now come to much more explosive things, for which I hope you will not hold me responsible hereafter. I am suggesting some new lines of thought. We have moved into a strange world, a world such as has not been seen for hundreds of years; perhaps not for a thousand years. Europe is completely changing. The old Europe which we have known, into which we were born, and in which we have taken our vital interest as our mother-continent, has gone. The map is being rolled up[1] and a new map is unrolling before us. We shall have to do a great deal of fundamental thinking, and scrapping of old points of view, before we find our way through that new continent which now opens up before us.

Just look for a moment at what is happening, and what will be the state of affairs at the end of this war. In Europe three of the great powers will have disappeared. That will be quite a unique development. We have never seen such a situation in the modern history of this continent. Three of the five great powers in Europe will have disappeared. France has gone, and if ever she returns it will be a hard and a long upward pull for her to emerge again. A nation that has once been overtaken by a catastrophe such as she has suffered, reaching to the foundations of her nationhood, will not easily resume her old place again. We may talk about her as a great power, but talking will not help her much. We are dealing with one of the greatest and most far-reaching catastrophes in history, the like of which I have not read of. The upward climb will be a bitter and a long one. France has gone, and will be gone in our day, and perhaps for many a day. Italy has completely disappeared, and may never be a great power again. Germany will disappear. Germany at the end of this war will have disappeared, perhaps never to emerge again in the old form. The old Bismarckian Germany may perhaps never rise again. Nobody knows. The Germans are a great people, with great qualities, and Germany is inherently a great country, but after the smash that will follow this war Germany will be written off the slate in Europe for long, long years and after that a new world may have arisen.

We are therefore left with Great Britain and with Russia. Russia is the new colossus in Europe—the new colossus that bestrides this continent. When we consider all that has happened to Russia within the last twenty-five years, and we see Russia's inexplicable and phenomenal rise, we can only call it one of the great phenomena in history. It is the sort of thing to which there is no parallel in history, but it has come about. These are questions of power which I say we should not neglect. Russia is the new colossus on the European continent. What the after effects of that will be nobody can say. We can but recognize that this is a new fact to reckon with, and we must reckon with it coldly and objectively. With the others down and out, and herself the mistress of the Continent, her power will not only be great on that account, but it will be still greater because the Japanese empire will also have gone the way of all flesh, and

---

[1] 'Roll up that map; it will not be wanted these ten years.' William Pitt, about a map of Europe, after hearing the news of Napoleon's victory at Austerlitz in 1805.

therefore any check or balance that might have arisen in the East will have disappeared. You will have Russia in a position which no country has ever occupied in the history of Europe.

Then you will have this country of Great Britain, with a glory and an honour and a prestige such as perhaps no nation has ever enjoyed in history; recognized as possessing a greatness of soul that has entered into the very substance of world history. But from a material economic point of view she will be a poor country. She has put in her all. This country has held nothing back. There is nothing left in the till. She has put her body and soul and everything into it to win the battle of mankind. She will have won it, but she will come out of it poor in substance.

The British Empire and the British Commonwealth remain as one of the greatest things of the world and of history, and nothing can touch that fact. But you must remember that the Empire and the Commonwealth are mostly extra-European. Those are the overflows of this great British system to other continents. The purely European position of Great Britain will be one of enormous prestige and respect, and will carry enormous weight, but she will be poor.

Then outside Europe you have the United States, the other great world power. You will therefore have these three great powers: Russia the colossus of Europe, Great Britain with her feet in all continents, but crippled materially here in Europe; and the United States of America with enormous assets, with wealth and resources and potentialities of power beyond measure. The question is how you are going to deal with that world situation. I am just painting before you the picture of the new world that we shall have to face, which will be something quite unlike what we have had to deal with for a century, or indeed for centuries.

Many people look to a union or closer union between the United States of America and Great Britain, with her Commonwealth and Empire, as the new path to be followed in the future in this world which I am describing as facing us. I myself am doubtful about that. I attach the greatest importance to Anglo-American collaboration for the future. To my mind it is, beyond all doubt, one of the great hopes of mankind. But I do not think that, as what I might call a political axis, it will do. It would be a one-sided affair. If you were to pit the British Commonwealth plus the United States against the rest of the world, it would be a very lopsided world. You would stir up opposition and rouse other lions in the path. You would stir up international strife and enmity which might lead to still more colossal struggles for world power than we have seen in our day. I do not see human welfare, peace, security along those lines.

So we come back to where we started, namely the trinity. We shall not act wisely in looking to an Anglo-American union or axis as the solution for the future. We shall have to stick to the trinity that I have referred to. I think we must make up our minds to that as the solution for the present and the near foreseeable future.

But then I am troubled with this thought—and this is the explosive stuff I am coming to. In that trinity you will have two partners of immense power and resources—Russia and America. And you will have this island, the heart of the Empire and of the Commonwealth, weak in her European resources in comparison with the vast resources of the other two. An unequal partnership, I am afraid. The idea has repeatedly floated before my mind, and I am just mentioning it here as something to consider and to ponder—whether Great Britain should not strengthen her European position, apart from her position as the centre of this great Empire and Commonwealth outside Europe, by working closely together with those smaller democracies in western Europe which are of our way of thinking, which are entirely with us in their outlook and their way of life, and in all their ideals, and which in many ways are of the same political and spiritual substance as ourselves. Should there not be closer union between us? Should we not cease as Great Britain to be an island? Should we not work intimately together with these small democracies in western Europe which by themselves may be lost, as they are lost today, and as they may be lost again? They have learned their lesson, they have been taught by the experience of this war when centuries of argument would not have convinced them. Neutrality is obsolete, is dead. They have learned the lesson that, standing by themselves on the Continent, dominated by one or other great power, as will be the future position, they are lost. Surely they must feel that their place is with this member of the trinity. Their way of life is with Great Britain, their outlook and their future is with Great Britain and the next world-wide British system.

We have evolved a system in the Commonwealth which opens the door for developments of this kind. Today in the Commonwealth we have a group of sovereign states working together, living together in peace and in war, under a system that has stood the greatest strain to which any nations could be subjected. They are all sovereign states, they retain all the attributes and functions and symbols of sovereignty. Other neighbouring nations, therefore, living the same way of life, and with the same outlook, can with perfect safety say: 'That is our group; why are we not there? With full retention and maintenance of our sovereign status, we choose that grand company for our future in this dangerous world.'

It is naturally a question for the states of western Europe to settle themselves. It is for them to say whether in the world as they have learned to know it, as history has proved it to be, it is safe for them to continue in the old paths of isolation and neutrality, or whether they should not help themselves by helping to create out of closer union with Great Britain a great European state, great not only in its world-wide ramifications, great not only as an Empire and a Commonwealth stretching over all the continents, but great as a power on this Continent, an equal partner with the other colossi in the leadership of the nations.

I think this trinity will be the stabilizing factor, the wall of power behind which the freedoms and the democracies of the world can be built up again. It will be the protecting wall. But I should like to have that trinity of equals. I should like to see all three of them equal in power and influence and in every respect. I should not like to see an unequal partnership.

I call this very explosive stuff, but we are living in an explosive world. I want you, ladies and gentlemen, to bear in mind that we are living in a world where we are forced to fundamental thinking and to a fundamental revision of old concepts. The old world that we knew has gone, and it will not return. To my mind it is a question whether those who think alike and feel alike, whose interests and whose safety rest on the same broad human political basis should not be together in building up that splendid trinity to which we look forward for the future leadership.

So much for Europe, and I am saying nothing about America and Asia. It is all very speculative, and I am saying nothing dogmatic, but I am sure we shall have to do a great deal of fundamental thinking. I shall not be surprised to find that not only in this country but elsewhere outside this island, and especially in western Europe, many thoughtful people are thinking in the same direction. They have learned much in this, the bitterest experience of their lives and the lives of their countries, and their minds are probably following some such line of thought as that to which I am giving expression.

Let me say a few words about the Commonwealth and Empire, because after all we remain a very great world community. It is not only the spiritual power which we command as no other group on earth commands. It is not only that we possess that strength of soul, that inner freedom which is greater than all the freedoms of the Atlantic Charter, but we are also a very powerful group, scattered though we are over the world. And we must look to our own inner strength, our inner coherence, our system, our set-up and pattern, to see that it is on safe lines for the future.

What is the present set-up in our group? We are an Empire and
a Commonwealth. We are a dual system. In that dual system we
follow two different principles. In the Commonwealth we follow
to the limit the principle of decentralization. In the Commonwealth
this group of ours has become wholly decentralized as sovereign
states. The members of the group maintain the unbreakable spiritual
bonds which are stronger than steel, but in all matters of government
and their internal and external concerns they are sovereign states.
In the colonial Empire, on the other hand, we follow quite a different
principle. We follow the opposite principle of centralization. And
the centralization is focussed in this country, in London. The
question that arises in my own mind, looking at the situation
objectively, is whether such a situation can endure. To have the
Empire centralized and the Commonwealth decentralized, to have
the two groups developed on two different lines, raises grave questions for the future. Is this duality in our group safe? Should we not
give very grave thought to this dualism in our system?

I hope you will forgive my doubts, Mr Chairman, but I do not
speak critically here. I am not a critic of the Empire. I am just
thinking objectively, and giving expression to my concern. I am not
out to criticize. But I know as a fact that wherever I have gone in the
colonial Empire I have found criticism of this situation. Your own
British people outside this island, living in crown colonies, are very
critical and restive under this system which is centralized in London.
It is not the nature of the beast, you know. The Britisher resents
being run by others and from a distance. The question is whether
there should not be an approach between the two systems so as
gradually to eliminate this dualism and have a closer approach
between the two, and bring Empire and Commonwealth closer
together.

Following that line of thought it has seemed to me that our
colonial system consists of too many units. If there is to be decentralization you will have to decentralize from the colonial office
in London, and give administrative powers of all sorts, and all
degrees, sometimes to very small units, or to some still in a very
primitive stage of development, and that might be a risky thing to
do. Our colonial system consists of a very large number of units in
all stages of development, and if there is to be decentralization and
devolution of power and authority, it becomes in my opinion
necessary to simplify the system, to tidy it up, to group smaller
units, and, in many cases, to do away with units which have simply
arisen as an accident by historic haphazard. They should never have
existed as separate units, and in many cases their boundaries are

quite indefensible. You know how this great show has grown up historically, by bits of history here and there, without any planning, and, of course, inevitably so. But the time has come, or the time may be coming now, when it is necessary to tidy up the show, to reduce the number of independent colonial units, to abolish a number of separate administrations scattered pell-mell over the colonial Empire, and to reduce the consequent expenditure which is a burden on the local peoples, many of them very poor, undeveloped and with very small resources. It is a heavy burden on them, and their slender resources might be devoted to better purpose than carrying on a heavy administrative machine, perhaps beyond their capacity.

As I say, it is a question whether we should not abolish a number of units, and group others, and so tidy up the show. Then in such a case you can decentralize, and you can safely give larger powers and greater authority to those larger groups that you will thus create. Where it might be unsafe and unwise to give larger authority to a number of small units, it might be safe and wise, and the proper course, to give authority and to decentralize administrative power in the case of larger units grouped under a better arrangement.

I do not wish to go into details, but the case I know best is my own African continent, which contains a large number of British colonies and territories. There it seems to me quite a feasible proposition to group the British colonies and territories into definite groups. You have west Africa, you have east Africa, and you have southern Africa. It is quite possible to group those colonies into larger units, each under a governor-general, and abolish not a few of them that need not continue to enjoy a separate existence. In that way you will overcome the difficulty of the highly centralized system centring in London, which is irksome to the local people, is perhaps not serving their highest interests and their best development, and gives outsiders the occasion to blaspheme and to call the colonial Empire an imperialist concern, run in the economic interests of this country.

As you will solve this problem of centralization in the colonial Empire you will also solve another equally important problem. And this brings me to the Commonwealth. In many of these cases of colonial reorganization where there will be new and larger colonial groups under a governor-general, you will find that it is quite possible to bring these new groups closer to a neighbouring Dominion, and thereby interest the Dominion in the colonial group. In this way, instead of the Dominions being a show apart, so to say, having little or nothing to do with the Empire, and taking very little interest in it, these regional Dominions will become sharers and partners in the Empire. You will tighten up your whole show; you will create fresh links between the Empire and the Commonwealth, and create a new interest and life in the system as a whole. You will create better co-operation, and you will bring to bear on the problems of these colonial groups the experience and resources and leadership of the local Dominions too. In this way you will tighten up your whole system, and instead of being two separate systems, the one decentralized and looking after its own affairs, and the other centralized and centred in London, you will have a much more logical, co-operative and statesmanlike arrangement. Perhaps I am now over-simplifying here, but I simply put this picture before you as it has developed in my mind, the picture of a larger, more co-operative world community. The time is coming when the colonial system will have to be simplified and tightened up, and to a large extent decentralized, and when the Dominions will have to be called in to play their part also in the new set-up.

Not only Great Britain and not only London, but the Dominions also should, by loose consultative arrangement, have a hand in this new colonial pattern, and the Dominions should also bring their resources and their experience to bear in the development of the colonies. I think the suggestion is very well worth considering. Perhaps the new link could best be introduced by means of a system of regional conferences, which would include both the local Dominion and the regional colonial group of the area concerned. Perhaps to begin with nothing more is needed than merely an organized system of conferences between them, where they could meet and exchange ideas, and by means of which they could settle common policies, discuss common interests, and in that way link up the Dominions and the colonies with the mother-country in a common, more fruitful co-operation.

These, in broad outline, are our future arrangements as I see them. Not only for our own future but for the future of the world do I want to see our group strengthened and co-ordinated and elements of risk and of danger removed from its path. I want to see it launched forth after this war on the new paths of history with a better prospect of co-operation and collaboration among all its parts. I want a common pride to develop on the basis of better co-operation and understanding. I want the Dominions to take both interest and pride in the colonies within their sphere, and in that way to create, in our great world-wide Commonwealth, a new *esprit de corps*, a common patriotism, and a larger human outlook.

Mr Chairman, these are some of the explosive thoughts that I have taken the liberty to mention here this afternoon. This is a very good and proper occasion for ventilating such ideas. I am speaking to very responsible men. I am speaking to an audience whom I greatly respect and honour. I am speaking to men who are responsible for what is probably the largest human community that has ever existed in this world. I see that we are moving to a point in history when there will be great changes in the world, when the new world situation will call for changes among all the nations such as they have never faced before, and I have asked myself whether this is not the time for us, too, to look into our own household a bit. It has done wonderfully well in this war. It has done very well both in peace and in war, but not least in this war. It has done miracles, and I want those miracles to continue. I want us on the future paths of history to have a fair clean run, because I think we mean a great deal to the world. I think this world needs our British system. I think we, in our group, play a part which is essential and vital to the future of mankind, and whatever we can do to put our own house in order, to remove anomalies, to remove the sources of internal friction or of misunderstanding, is a service not only to our group but to mankind at large, and must have its effect on the rest of the world. Surely people all over the world will look to this group of peoples comprising one-fourth of the human race, and see how they guide their destinies in peace and war along human lines of mutual helpfulness. Surely such a spectacle must have a far-reaching influence for good. I look upon this Empire and Commonwealth as the best missionary enterprise that has been launched for a thousand years. This is a mission to mankind of good will, good government and human co-operation, a mission of freedom and human helpfulness in the perils that beset our human lot.

Where we are helping ourselves in ways such as I have mentioned, putting our house in order on lines I have suggested, or on similar lines, we shall not only be serving our own cause and strengthening ourselves internally, but we shall be making our contribution to human destiny, and to the promotion of those ideals for which our young men are fighting and bleeding and dying today. I think we shall be serving that greater human cause which we all have at heart, and for which we are prepared to make such sacrifices in our day.

I utter no dogmatic conclusions; I have no set ideas; I am simply giving you the lines of thought that run in my mind when I survey the new situation facing us in the world. I want us not only to think about the other countries who are today labouring in dire trouble all over the world, but also to pay some attention to our own show, which I think also requires a little looking after, and especially at a time like this, when a new world is in the making.

625   To L. S. Amery   Vol. 72, no. 190

[London]
2 December 1943

My dear Amery, I find that my address to the E.P.A.[1] last week has stirred up a much greater interest in the topics discussed than I had expected. You heard my address and will see it when printed. Perhaps you will be interested in a short paper I had written earlier (of which no use has been made) in which the question of a larger Commonwealth (including the west European democracies with the British Commonwealth) is linked up with the question of future world security. I enclose for your information a copy of this paper,[2] of which a copy has also been given to Richard Law. The whole subject is most difficult, but also very important, and I know you are giving constant thought to it. You may therefore like to have the paper for your information.

I much enjoyed that wonderful birthday evening we spent with you and dear Mrs Amery[3] at your home. Now I am on the point of leaving on my return to South Africa, and can only send both of you my affectionate good wishes. Ever yours sincerely,

s. J. C. Smuts

626   From L. S. Amery   Vol. 70, no. 19

15 December 1943

My dear Smuts, I hope you had a good trip back and have not found too many things amiss on your return. Anyhow, I have no doubt that you will have a hectic week or two catching up with arrears.

I was glad to see that your minister of the interior[4] dealt with the Indian question in a sympathetic fashion and on a line which suggested that it was as members of the South African community permanently established and not as mere immigrants that their future would have to be considered. That should have helped to

---

[1] 624.

[2] Entitled 'The New Europe, the New Commonwealth and World Security' and dated November 1943 (Smuts Collection, Box K, no. 178).

[3] Born Florence (Bryddie) Greenwood; married Leo Amery in 1910.

[4] C. F. Clarkson.

some extent in India both to counteract the Indian notion that these are their people and not South Africans, as well as to soothe the intense racial sensitiveness of Indian public opinion. That and your help over food will I hope have prevented Wavell's advisers from doing anything precipitate and mutually damaging in pursuance of the policy of reprisals sanctioned by the Indian legislature.

Your speech to the E.P.A.[1] has created much sensation here and, subject to some criticisms of your rather hard words about France, has met with widespread approval. I am sure that it was on balance a thoroughly good thing that your views should be ventilated. I am also grateful to you for not troubling to press for a rectification of Attlee's not altogether accurate description of how it came to be published,[2] as Attlee made it after some remarks I had whispered to him on the front bench, and I should have been greatly distressed if I had thus indirectly been the source of embarrassment to you.

I have since read your most interesting memorandum to Dick Law,[3] giving greater precision in certain directions to what you said to the E.P.A. Broadly speaking I share your view, but am not sure that, in the form in which you put it in the memorandum, it isn't open to the criticism of 'over-simplification'. What I mean is this. Undoubtedly for a considerable period immediately following the war we shall have to keep the nations of western and southern Europe, as well as the northern democracies, together in the interests of their peace and of our own peace. The area in question is really very much Scandinavia plus the old Roman Empire west and south of the *limes*.[4] But here I would draw a certain distinction. Full membership of the British Commonwealth depends, I think, on several essential factors. There is the community of ideals of liberty and social justice; there is economic suitability and readiness for full co-operation; lastly, there is a reasonable measure of defensibility, i.e. the additional member must contribute as much to the common defence as he asks of it; finally, these must all be permanent and not temporary factors.

In my mind, the Scandinavian countries, and above all Norway and Iceland, fit into that picture. Their standards of life are ours. They make admirable settlers in every Dominion. They contribute

---

[1] 624.

[2] Arising out of a question in the house of commons about the views expressed in Smuts's speech, a supplementary question raised the point of who was responsible for its publication. Attlee at first replied that he had no information and then added: 'I understand the speech was printed at the desire of Field Marshal Smuts himself.' Subsequent contributions to the debate left the impression that the Empire Parliamentary Association had not sanctioned publication. But *see* 627. (*House of Commons Debates*, vol. 395, cols. 773–4.)

[3] *See supra*, p. 469, note 2. [4] The boundaries of the Roman Empire.

to our sea power and would fit in naturally to any scheme of developed Empire economic co-operation. Lastly, the Scandinavian peninsula itself and even Denmark are pretty defensible and, from the air point of view, would be a most effective outpost against a resurgent German menace.

On the other hand, with the exception of Holland and to some extent Belgium, the mentality of the other members of the west and south European group is very different from ours. It is by no means certain that they will continue to be democracies long after the war. On the contrary I think it is not unlikely that within twenty years most of continental Europe will be more or less totalitarian, whether by a reaction against the victorious Democracy of this war or by advance from it towards Communism—both come to much the same thing. Further, the natural economic interest of most of these countries lies in their trade with central Europe. Continental Europe west of Russia is a natural economic entity, and will, I have little doubt, gradually evolve its new economic order, together with its colonies, based on some system of inter-European preference, currency arrangements, etc. That will be much more to the interest of the western European countries, as well as to the rest of our Commonwealth, than trying to bring them into some scheme of inter-imperial economic preference.

Lastly, and this is really the critical point to my mind, the whole of the west and south European group by themselves are in the long run incapable of defence in the event of Russia and Germany coming together—the great danger of civilization which [Sir Halford J.] Mackinder predicted years ago. It is I think essential for the future that Germany, after due punishment and relative weakening, should be brought back into the main European fold, and that a European commonwealth should comprise the main European block of countries up to the Russian border. It is precisely from that point of view that I am anxious that continental Europe should constitute a definite world economic group, and while we should naturally begin by holding together the western and southern nations, we should also do so from the point of view of bringing Germany, the Danubian countries and Poland into the picture as parts of a single European commonwealth which, with its colonies, would then be a really viable group on the modern scale, and a group which, if differing somewhat in political outlook from ourselves, would still be based in the main on the old European civilization going back to Greece and Rome and western Christianity.

I do not regard such a European commonwealth as likely to be any danger to ourselves. The very temper of compromise which will make it possible is not likely to make for aggression. In any case, it has nothing to fear from us but may have more to fear from its eastern neighbour. In other words, as the minimum units of world power grow in size, the frontier round which the balance of power centres will, so far as we are concerned, shift from the Rhine and its estuary to eastern Poland, Persia and possibly the Russo-Chinese frontier.

Who is to take the leadership in the future European common-wealth is obviously still uncertain. But I am not so sure that it might not even yet be France. I doubt if she will have suffered anything like as much as Germany will suffer before this war is over. So far as area and natural resources go, France is of course a bigger country even than pre-1914 Germany and with bigger natural resources. What with all that Germany is likely to have to give over to the Poles she will be on a much smaller scale in everything except population and I wonder very much whether even there the disparity may not be greatly reduced by things that may happen before this war ends. All therefore depends on whether the French are capable of a new vital urge which may give them both the resources and the spirit of leadership within the next fifty years. On the other hand, *pace* [Sir Robert] Vansittart, it is not inconceivable that a chastened Germany[1]

627   From T. Drummond Shiels   Vol. 72, no. 24

Private   Westminster Hall
                                                         Houses of Parliament
                                                                    [London]
                                                            15 December 1943

Dear Field Marshal, In sending you the enclosed copies of your memorable speech, I wish to thank you very much for the message which you sent to South Africa House from Cairo, and for the generous attitude you took in regard to the slip which was made in the house in reply to a supplementary question.[2] While it would have been awkward to have raised it again, you had the right to request it, and I can assure you that your reply was regarded as very characteristic by those who were aware of what happened.

I dare say that Mr [B. G.] Fourie will have sent you copies of *The Times* publication of the speech. *The Times* has been enthusiastic in the matter, and, no doubt, you have seen the leading article supporting the publication. The press as a whole responded splen-

---

[1] Here the document in the Smuts Collection breaks off.
[2] *See supra*, p. 470, note 2.

didly, and the general public have been intensely gratified at the opportunity of reading what you said. Letters have been pouring into this office[1]—as no doubt they are now into *The Times* office—from all parts of the country for copies of the speech. I do not remember one which has made such a stir. Copies, as you requested, have been sent to His Majesty.

I have not myself escaped criticism from certain quarters in connection with publication, but I am quite certain that, in view of the large circulation of the enclosed pamphlets, not only to our own 800 members but also to members in Canada, Australia, New Zealand, South Africa, etc., a garbled report of the speech, or of parts of it, would have come out, and I think it was far better to publish the speech in full at the beginning.

May I thank you again for all your courtesy and helpfulness, and assure you that your visit will long remain in our memories as a happy and profitable one, both in its personal contacts and for its imperial and internal importance.

With kindest regards and all good wishes to you and Captain [J. C.] Smuts, I am, Sincerely yours,

T. Drummond Shiels
Deputy and Acting Secretary

628   To M. C. Gillett   **Vol. 72, no. 233**

Doornkloof
[Transvaal]
24 December 1943

Notice the date. And so my long interrupted correspondence with you is once more resumed. I missed the first week-end after my return as I was so rushed for time, but now the flood has somewhat abated. It has been a time of the most hectic activity I have known in my life.

But first a word about my return journey. The first night I could not leave London because of the weather and all our luggage had to be brought back, with another day in London. The second day we left for our airport, flying by places where in the happy past we had enjoyed great walks and bathes in the coves—a never to be forgotten time, and my heart went out to those places when I once more saw them. That night again the weather was too bad to venture over the sea, and so I spent another day inspecting aerodromes and air stations from which much of our deadly bombing and fighting

---

[1] The office of the Empire Parliamentary Association.

is done. The third night we set off and what a night it was! The worst of the lot. For ten hours we flew at a very great height using oxygen all the time and after 2,400 or 2,500 miles we arrived next morning at Tunis. Another plane that left immediately behind us was lost with all its valuable personnel and passengers. But I need not go into details. We got safely through, though of course there could be no sleep. We had a wonderful pilot to whom under Providence our safety was due. At Tunis I met Japie [Smuts] and General Frank Theron and could settle many matters. We stayed the night and flew off to Cairo next day along the old route of our advance and much of it so well known to me, and reached Cairo the afternoon. Japie in the meantime was going forward to join Eisenhower's headquarters on which he will act for the South African forces under that command. At Cairo I had much to do during the three days of my stay. I attended the final conferences where the resolutions for our future work were taken, dined alone with Roosevelt and discussed the future, saw much of Churchill with whom most of my time was spent, though I found time for many others—diplomats and army representatives. Finally I inspected our South African tank forces in the field taking the C. in C. Sir Henry Wilson and the C.I.G.S., Sir Alan Brooke, with me. A most useful function which everybody enjoyed. It was a grand sight to see those magnificent boys on parade, as fine a body of men as could be seen in this war. I stayed with the embassy people and had many talks with Eden and other men of note. I gave a press interview or rather conference which was much appreciated by the pressmen who had been kept very much in the dark while great conferences were held and decisions taken. And so off to the south, taking the crown princess of Greece to join her small family at the Cape. It was a pleasant three days in the air over scenes and sights already so familiar to me, but never too familiar to be enjoyed afresh. One night at Khartoum with the dear Huddlestones,[1] and the next night with the equally dear Moores at Nairobi. I met people at each place and could give them the news and receive local information. And so at 5 p.m. the next day at Pretoria where Isie and the family, and the government, and so many others met us at the aerodrome. It was a joyful homecoming, and I was indeed glad to be back and to find everybody in good form. That was Saturday and the following Sunday was quietly spent at home with the family, and little interruption by visitors who considerately spared me this first day of my homecoming. How glorious it was to walk the dear veld once more and to breathe that incomparable air. After the heavy recent rains the country was a picture and the cool

[1] Sir Hubert Huddleston and his wife, born Constance Eila Corbet.

summer air almost more than one could bear to breathe. But the following Monday I was in office and there I have been ever since. Of course the volume of work that awaited me was overwhelming, and the callers, and the letters and telegrams! Interviews, cabinet meetings, consultations, to pick up the threads once more. And so it has been continuing up to now. I shall not have a day off, and have my hands and time full to prepare for the coming session of parliament.

But enough so far. Happy Christmas and New Year.

Jan

629   To M. C. Gillett   Vol. 75, no. 196

Doornkloof
[Transvaal]
4 January 1944

...As I lie in bed writing the rain is again falling outside, and last night we had a great downpour, so you can see the season continues its blessings. I am afraid however that it is rather too much and the crops will soon begin to suffer from the excessive wet which starts all sorts of insects and crop diseases. Already we are warned that there may be a short crop this year owing to the phenomenal rains. It is curious that farther north conditions are just the opposite, and in Kenya and eastern Africa generally there is fear of famine this year owing to continued drought. We have been urgently asked to make provision for many territories to our north and we don't know whether the opposite conditions here will not place us in the same predicament. I notice from the papers that big crops are expected in America, north and south, and that may help the food situation in the world generally which promises otherwise to approach famine conditions at the end of the war. Owing to food shortage and the enfeebled power of resistance everywhere of the underfed populations I much fear that the end of the war may be just as calamitous for human life as the war itself. Very bad news comes from many parts.

The war itself appears to be going well. Rather slow in Italy where weather conditions must be horrible, but in Russia magnificent progress continues to be made in all directions. The sinking of the *Scharnhorst*[1] was a fine achievement and reduces very much the

---

[1] The battle-cruiser *Scharnhorst*, the only heavy German ship still in Norwegian waters, made an unsuccessful attack on a British convoy to Russia on 26 December 1943. She was reported by the convoy's escort ships, detected by the British battleship *Duke of York* (Admiral Sir B. A. Fraser) and sunk with the loss of her commander (Admiral Bey) and almost the whole crew.

already low power of the German navy. Berlin must be reduced to a dreadful mess, and I notice the statement of a neutral traveller that the place is quite unrecognizable owing to the vast destruction.

Our Allied troubles are not confined to the fighting fronts but as the war continues in its fifth year the effects of social and economic conditions in the great Allied countries will be felt more and more acutely. Prices rise, cost of living goes up, inflation comes adding to the other difficulties and losses, the temper of the people becomes more frayed owing to the long continued strain, labour troubles become more acute, and so the internal tensions become more and more of a problem. The high spirit with which we started, the spirit of dedication, becomes more faint, slackness and selfishness and general senselessness return and undermine the war effort and the will to victory in a very marked degree. Only the Russians can keep up the pace, owing to their Communist drill and the memory of what they have been through in a generation. With us life has on the whole been pleasant and the flesh-pots are a living memory with a strong appeal. In America the social and economic atmosphere appears to be very bad, and we are continually being warned that political conditions are worsening and that the repetition of the Woodrow Wilson *débâcle* is by no means out of the question. It is all very sad and discouraging. Meanwhile our own propaganda is not very good. There is no deep religious appeal producing a spirit of consecration and dedication, and the flame of the spirit burns low.

Here in South Africa people have almost forgotten the war. Africa is clear, our arms are making great progress in Europe and Asia. So why worry! That is the spirit. Money is plentiful, speculation is difficult to keep down; there is a general air of optimism owing to the plethora of money about and the removal of immediate danger. Recruiting is bad and people are only thinking of the new world of better conditions which is to follow the war. It is difficult for the responsible authorities to say that this is a fool's paradise —that conditions may be worse than they were before. The Nats would at once say: 'We told you so. We warned you to keep out of the war. This is the pass to which *you* have brought this country. Away with you, and advance the republic and secession!'

This week the cabinet will be dealing with our programme for the coming session in which all sorts of social and economic advances will have to play their part. It is going to be a difficult session, with a new parliament and one-third of the members new and undisciplined and expecting all sorts of things in the new order of things. My own mind is largely occupied with the troubles of the war, and the still great troubles of the peacemaking ahead of us, and it is difficult for me to concentrate on the vagaries connected with the parish pump. And yet that is my business and what I am in office and paid for! So there you are, at the beginning of a new year, with all its problems and tangles and hazards! It will at best be a difficult and dangerous year, but great prizes may be possible. Happy New Year to you. Ever lovingly,

Jan

630   To M. C. Gillett   Vol. 75, no. 198

Parliament
[Cape Town]
14 February 1944

You will be astonished to hear that I have had *one* letter from you since my return to South Africa and that was some time during this month. This will show you the difficulties of mail correspondence these days. I have had one other from Arthur. I have written you several, some of which I fear have not even yet arrived. If letters take such a time to arrive I may be in England before many others arrive from me. We are almost back in the time when Livingstone first heard of the Franco-Prussian war after it had been finished and peace had been made. I do not, however, think that this war and the coming peace will be as soon as all that.

We have now had almost a month of parliament and I have of course been very fully occupied. The opposition may not be so numerous as before—they are in fact about half of their former number—but they are just as vocal, and their policies have not changed. It is still the old, monotonous song which is being sung, and I am weary in my soul of it. Still the job goes on and one carries on even where one is not interested in it. Outside of parliament there is quite enough to engage one's interest to the full. Here we have a new education question and the Dutch Reformed Church is making a great push for separate schools in which children will be taught only through mother tongue mediums and the second language will only be taught as a language, that is, as a foreign language, and the gulf between English and Dutch will be still further widened.[1] Then there are again signs of labour troubles on the mines. You know what that means and has meant.

Abroad the war is not going well, except in Russia which now

[1] The Nationalists were resisting a government proposal for dual medium secondary schools where some subjects would be taught in English and some in Afrikaans. This proposal was never put into effect.

seems to be winning the war for us. We are stuck in south Italy and even our feeble attempt of a diversion at Anzio has done us no good.[1] Anzio sounds too much like the notorious Anzac.[2] If this happens in the Mediterranean where we have had such resounding successes what is going to happen when the European invasion comes? It is not a comforting prospect. In fact the whole war situation has changed enormously since I left London not so long ago. Then everything seemed to be going well for us everywhere. Now Russia alone advances and is much more the colossus than ever before. How will she use her immense power and unprecedented position when the war is over? That is more and more becoming a subject of thought to all thinking people. We must work together, but does co-operation work well in an unequal partnership? These are the points I made in my 'explosive' speech, and they are even more pointed now than three months ago...

631 To Moustafa el Nahas   Vol. 75, no. 27

Cape Town
28 March 1944

My dear Minister President,[3] I have received through your consul-general in the Union,[4] your message to me in reference to a statement made by me about a Jewish national home in Palestine.[5] I do not know whether Your Excellency had before you the actual terms of my statement but you will find from reading it carefully that it contained no more than is contained in the Palestinian mandate to the government of the United Kingdom. That mandate had no reference to the eviction or expulsion of the Arab population of Palestine, nor had my statement any such implication. It was the intention of the mandate, as it was and remains my hope, that within the confines of the old historic Palestine a place would be found for both Arab and Jew as had been the case throughout the ages. With good will and mutual accommodation I see no reason why this ideal may not yet be realized and the terms of the mandate carried out. Yours sincerely,

J. C. Smuts

[1] The Germans had been able to seal off the Anzio beach-head and prevent the Allied forces from advancing north to Rome.
[2] The unsuccessful Gallipoli campaign of April 1915–January 1916 in which the Australian and New Zealand Army Corps (A.N.Z.A.C.) were engaged.
[3] of Egypt.   [4] S. Aboulfetouh.
[5] See Smuts Collection, Box F, no. 69 for a statement by Smuts on 'Zionism' (1944).

632   To L. S. Amery   Vol. 75, no. 28

Telegram

To: L. S. Amery

From: Smuts

Dated [19] April 1944

I have just sent following message to Wavell contents of which I hope will please you:

At a meeting on 18 April between the prime minister and the minister of the interior and representatives of the Natal Indian Congress[1] it was unanimously agreed that legislation be immediately introduced into the Natal provincial council to provide for a joint board of five, consisting of two Europeans and two Indians with a European chairman, whose function it will be to license the occupation of dwellings in areas within boroughs and towns in Natal. On the passing of the ordinance the application of the Pegging Act[2] in Durban will be withdrawn by proclamation.

This agreement provides a fair solution of the trouble which has arisen in connection with the Pegging Act and will, I trust, be as welcome to your Excellency as it has been to me.

633   To J. H. Hofmeyr   Vol. 75, no. 34

Telegram

To: Mr Hofmeyr, Cape Town

From: General Smuts, Pretoria

Dated 21 April 1944

I thank you for much appreciated telegram from you and colleagues. I send my best wishes for you all in your heavy burdens, which I am sorry not to share with you. Whatever I can do by cable from the other side will be most gladly done.[3] Good-bye.

---

[1] Besides Smuts and C. F. Clarkson, minister of the interior, the following prominent Natalians were present: Senator D. G. Shepstone; G. Heaton Nicholls, then administrator of the province; D. E. Mitchell, then a member of the provincial executive. The seven Indian representatives were led by Abdullah Ismail Kajee, chairman of the Natal Indian Congress, which had been founded by Gandhi in 1894. The settlement arrived at was known as the Pretoria Agreement.

[2] *See supra*, p. 422, note 2.

[3] Smuts made his third war-time visit to London to attend the conference of Commonwealth prime ministers.

634   To J. H. Hofmeyr   Vol. 75, no. 40

Telegram

From: high commissioner, London
To: secretary for external affairs, Cape Town
Dated 1 May 1944
Following for Mr Hofmeyr from General Smuts:

Thank you and colleagues for kind message. I was able both at Cairo and Algiers to do useful work in reference to Greek troubles and our own defence contribution. In view of our man-power position and prospect of very heavy fighting in Italy where our 6th Division has gone, I have in principle agreed to Coloured Fighting Brigade being formed from our Coloured battalions in Middle East. That will largely solve our man-power problem in case war is unduly prolonged. Matter being examined by our defence department and I hope my colleagues will give sympathetic political consideration.[1]

Referring to discussion on Smith reprieve[2] I agreed to it largely on ground that he belonged to Allied British forces and this was first case. If it had been a purely South African matter my decision would have been different on merits. Defence of our action might ...(?) ...(?) [*sic*] on that high almost international courtesy level.

Our conference begins today and promises to be exhaustive examination of general war and post-war situation, without coming to rigid conclusions. I shall keep you informed so far as that is practicable. All good wishes to you and colleagues to whom I am deeply grateful for all the consideration you have constantly given me.

[1] The original document is annotated as follows in Hofmeyr's handwriting:
'Following for General Smuts from Mr Hofmeyr:

Colleagues unanimously and strongly of opinion that proposal to constitute Coloured Fighting Brigade should not be proceeded with. It is considered that we are bound by assurances given in parliament not to arm non-Europeans save in last resort of direct threat to Union itself. Political repercussions of going back on that would be serious and it would probably be necessary to secure approval of parliament for change of policy. Apart from that we feel that long-range consequences of Coloured men being asked to do fighting job for which we have been unable to find white men would be considerable. Any good done by making 5,000 more fighting men available would be out of proportion to ultimate harm to Union. We would rather explore other possibilities of dealing with man-power question. Lawrence anxious about effect on demobilization scheme. Sturrock advises that general staff are perturbed about proposal from defence organization point of view. We hope you will reconsider matter in light of above.'

[2] On 24 December 1943 an eleven-year-old girl had been raped, mutilated and murdered in Durban. A British soldier, Sidney Bernard Smith, had been found guilty of this crime after a unanimous verdict of the jury. Mr Justice Carlisle found no extenuating circumstances and sentenced Smith to death on 24 February 1944. In April 1944 he was granted a reprieve and his sentence was commuted to life imprisonment.

635   From L. S. Amery   Vol. 73, no. 12

The original document is annotated in Smuts's handwriting as follows: 'For keeping among my papers'.

India Office
Whitehall
8 May 1944

My dear Smuts, It might save time when we meet on Tuesday if I dictated one or two points now as they occur to me which we can then discuss more fully.

World organization. I fear the prime minister is much too sanguine about the possibilities of a coercive world structure. Is it really likely that we, Russia and the United States will for many years continue equally actively interested in preventing trouble anywhere. Are we going to be ready to coerce Russia if she intervenes in China on behalf of the Communists, or incorporates Outer Mongolia in the Soviet Union against China's protest?

Will either we or Russia be prepared to intervene actively if another South American war breaks out, as it easily may?

Let us suppose, however, that the Big Three continue to agree. If they do the enforcing, I fear the rest of the world will resent it. On the other hand, once we start a formal constitution, with a council, an assembly, etc., it raises endless questions: membership of the council, voting power, etc., and the whole thing ends in paralysis, as it did last time.

After all, such a coercive system is in effect a federation and only possible if individual nations are prepared to subordinate themselves to the new super state. We are not prepared to do so even within the Commonwealth so why should the nations at large do so? They may pretend to, but it will break down in practice.

I should think that it would be much wiser to make the future world organization, if there is to be one, avowedly consultative and for conciliation and leave it to the influence of the great powers, with moral support from others, to intervene diplomatically and if necessary by sanctions or by force in cases of obvious aggression—if their own sense of right and wrong and the general moral support of others justify it.

In any case, I hope you will bring out the importance of something like a regional sub-division of whatever world organization comes into being. European quarrels are much better settled among the European nations and the same applies to South American or Far Eastern ones. This is, of course, apart from the question of regional consultative councils on colonial administration or regional defence arrangements within the Commonwealth.

Europe west of Russia is obviously such a region and we should aim at encouraging it to build itself up in that capacity. The more closely it does so economically and otherwise, the better. At the outset we shall obviously have to take a leading part in building it up. To secure Russian agreement to our policy may not be easy and the whole thing may take time and may be complicated by European Communist revolution and subsequent violent reaction. All I would say is that we must make sure that Germany eventually is part of the European system and helps to give it strength. I am all for punishing Germany drastically now, but once that is over I would wipe the slate and do everything to bring her back into the circle of Western civilization and not let her become an outpost of Eur-Asiatic totalitarianism. When the stage of European coalescence comes we can stand aside, for its successful evolution will, I think, demand constitutional and economic developments in which we cannot well take part, not only because of our interests outside, but because of the jealousy that would arouse in Russia and elsewhere. There is this further advantage in building up a European Commonwealth, and that is that if Russia fails as a partner in world security, a restored and united Europe would be an effective counterpoise and the balance of power for us would oscillate round the Europe–Russia frontier, where it once used to oscillate round the Rhine.

Empire organization. I am sure the first argument we have got to meet is the idea that effective Empire organization is opposed to effective world organization. We can only play our part in the world system, whatever it may be, if we are united in outlook and purpose among ourselves. That need not imply a rigid constitution; but it does imply continuous close contact, and that seems to me the most essential thing to agree upon. You will remember that in the last war it was agreed that the imperial war cabinets should meet annually and then somehow it all petered out. I would suggest that the great thing to aim at is agreement now on effective annual meetings. Even if prime ministers cannot attend, distance is so short now in terms of time, and wireless telephony so perfect, that no external affairs minister attending a conference need be out of touch for twenty-four hours with his prime minister or his cabinet.

If a regular conference system is to work smoothly it should have its own secretariat. What it is essential to convince Mackenzie King of is that such a secretariat is not a policy-shaping body, but purely a post office and secretarial body looking after the distribution of information, agenda, etc. I don't think anyone's sovereignty was in the least touched by the existence of the collective secretariat at Geneva, but its efficiency undoubtedly kept the League alive.

I realize that there is always the fear that the secretariat may be dominated by Whitehall influence. Why that should be so more than a secretariat in the dominions office, I don't know. But the objection might be met by locating the secretariat outside London, say at Windsor or Hampton Court. You will remember that the Allied Supreme Military Council was located at Versailles for the very reason that if located in Paris it would have been supposed to be too completely dominated by Foch and the French general staff.

Economic organization. In the private memorandum I gave you on Friday I have put the fundamental objections in principle to schemes which have been worked out on the basis of out-of-date theories. There are of course plenty of detailed objections, which I need not go into. But I am sure that it would not pay any of us to sacrifice our freedom to develop definite trade agreements, firstly within the Empire and secondly outside, for the chance of standing in a queue with anybody and everybody simply because there was some lowering of world tariffs. After all, we of the Commonwealth are none of us the world's cheapest producers on a purely price basis. On the other hand, we each of us have rich markets which afford the basis of bargaining value for value. You will remember that when the old wine preference was dropped in 1860 the once flourishing Cape wine industry perished entirely. It has now been slowly building up for the last forty years and might yet become a really big thing as quality and vintages improve. It would be a pity to let that as well as your fruit and other similar industries fade out again.

There is also always the question of keeping up the strength of this old country and I am convinced we cannot possibly pay our way after this war unless we are in a position effectively to control our imports and to secure good markets by mutual bargaining.

Palestine. I doubt whether it would be advisable to raise this in full conference, remembering that my Indian colleague, Firoz Khan,[1] is a Muslim. But no doubt you will discuss this with Winston and with the other Dominion prime ministers from the point of view not only of peace in the Middle East, but of the restoration to prosperity of that vital region of the world. Yours ever,

Leo Amery

[1] Sir Firoz Khan Noon (q.v.).

636   To J. H. Hofmeyr   Vol. 75, no. 70

South Africa House
Trafalgar Square
London, W.C.2
8 June 1944

Dear Jantjie, Just a line to let you know that I shall be with you soon after the receipt of this, which goes by Forsyth who is preceding me. In another ten days I shall have wound up my affairs here and visit our men in Italy and then proceed south as soon as I can. I think it essential to see our troops at the front. They are now actually leading in the Eighth Army. I have had to remain here until Overlord[1] was well started and on its way, and this has now fortunately taken place. I think we may expect difficult moments as the enemy can build up faster than ourselves, but our air supremacy ought to counterbalance this advantage of his. Both here and in Italy our cause has prospered and if this progress can be maintained my optimism as to the end of the war in Europe this year may yet be justified.

Your session has lasted far beyond my worst anticipation as the opposition looked tired when I left. They must have got their second wind thereafter, and I felt sorry for you and my other colleagues who had to bear the brunt of this long session. However you got through all that lengthy programme of important measures and I cannot tell you how grateful I am for your patient endurance. I hope you will have a bit of a rest before plunging into the arrears of office work at Pretoria. I would have returned sooner but Churchill and other ministers appealed to me in such strong terms to stay longer that I did not feel it right to leave at such a moment. It has been indeed a critical time from weather point of view and a critical decision had to be made.

As regards the Sixth South African Division, I have just heard from Alexander that they are distinguishing themselves and have been pushed through the Canadians and United States troops to take the van in the further advance beyond Rome. I am told they are in the highest form.

Forsyth, who precedes me, can give you all the detailed business information. Everything so far has gone well in the settlement of outstanding questions.

Give my warm regards to all my colleagues and my love to Borrie. In spite of all troubles and the like, these are great days for us. Ever yours,

J. C. Smuts

[1] Code name for the Allied cross-Channel invasion of occupied France.

637   To M. C. Gillett   Vol. 75, no. 203

Doornkloof
[Transvaal]
26 July 1944

I am afraid that two weeks have passed since I last wrote to you. But I have never been more hard pressed for time than in recent weeks since my return from London. New work and problems keep crowding in, and there is a long list of conundrums that have accumulated in my absence. I know you will understand...

I was at Rooikop for a day a week ago and found everything in good order. The farm was teeming with game of all sorts; 500 acres under wheat made a wonderful sight. The house is as inviting as ever. As it was bitterly cold here I was glad to be for a day in that genial warmth of the Bushveld on a winter's day. What a dreamland that is—'a sleep and a forgetting'.[1] I could spend my old age, if ever it comes, in blessed retirement in some such surroundings where sense and soul are soothed and memories are softened, and all is gentle and benignant to the spirit. Gethsemanes and Golgothas may be the proper end for the great spirits of the world—but for such as me give me the Bushveld in the latter days. I should like to dream of the future and meditate on the past, and so merge into that all to which I belong.

The war news continues to be cheerful and to intrigue me. Why do the Germans keep the Anglo-Americans as in a vice in the west and allow the Russians to romp forward in the east? We are almost in a state of stalemate in Normandy—the thing I feared so much. But in Italy and the east we are doing very well. The last week has seen the abortive mutiny in Germany,[2] and for the moment it has enabled Hitler to kill off his difficult elements in the army. But a mutiny in the army like that shows that the army is beginning to despair and that the end of Germany is certain. The disasters in the east[3] give point to this coming fate. But the Nazi leaders are desperate men and will fight on until nobody will be inclined to show Germany much mercy. The senseless continuance of the war is certain to lead to extreme exasperation and worsen whatever fate

[1] 'Our birth is but a sleep and a forgetting.' Wordsworth, *Ode. Intimations of Immortality*, iv.

[2] An elaborate plot by a number of high-ranking German army officers to assassinate Hitler and take over the government had failed. The explosion of a bomb placed in his conference room at Rastenburg by Colonel K. P. S. von Stauffenberg only wounded him slightly.

[3] In their summer offensive the Russians had, by the end of July, reached the river Niemen; the Germans had lost twenty-five divisions and many more had been cut off in Courland. In the south the Russians had crossed the Vistula.

Germany may expect at the hands of her enemies. However are we going to make peace in such a situation? I find the position for a real peace infinitely more difficult than in 1919. I cannot find hate in my own heart, but I must confess that even so I am nonplussed by the peace problems which confront the world at the end of this war. And the fear remains in my mind that Germany will yet go with Russia—a bolshevized Germany turning her back on the West and seeking salvation in the embraces of Russia. 'Evil, be thou my God' as Milton has put it in the language of Satan.[1] It will be the great betrayal of Western culture which Germany herself has contributed so much to build up. But from the Hitlers and Himmlers with their blood-stained hands and blackened souls anything may be expected. If some such development should come about as the outcome of this war the future of Europe and of the world will be darker than ever. I should like to hear your and Arthur's reflections on this theme which continues to haunt my thoughts. Of course Russia herself may save her soul and take her place in the spiritual movement of the West. But the defection of Germany will be like the passing of a world. I fear we do not realize the tremendous movement in which we are engulfed. A whole world seems to be sagging and sinking. I read the Gospels to keep my foothold on the verities of our spiritual heritage. Otherwise my own mind will begin to reel. Happy those who are not oppressed with too much imagination! But good-night, dears. I have to finish other things as in a couple of days I leave for Natal on awkward problems.[2]

J. C. S.

638   To M. C. Gillett   Vol. 75, no. 204

Doornkloof
[Transvaal]
7 August 1944

I sit outside in the early morning sun. This is Monday, a public holiday with us, and before I take my morning exercise I shall write you a line. I am very pleased to have a day off, not only to read up papers for which there is no time in office hours but also to work off heavy arrears of correspondence; and later I shall take a good, long walk before the end of the day. It is a heavenly spring morning, bright sunshine following on a frostless night; the birds are singing,

---

[1] 'Evil be thou my Good.' *Paradise Lost*, book IV, l. 108.
[2] The Pretoria Agreement on the Pegging Act (*see supra*, p. 479, note 1) had come to grief. *See* W. K. Hancock, *Smuts—The Fields of Force*, pp. 463–5.

the sweet-smelling wattles are in bloom; the trainer aeroplanes are circling in the air in their involved dancing exercises. There is a spring and vibrancy all around as the spring bursts into life. There comes on one suddenly all this air of mystery and miracle which is nature on the move. In our souls too there is an elation, a deep sense of joy and of unity with all things good and fair. One senses divinity all around. One feels the inner drives of nature beyond and behind the reach of the differentiated senses. One absorbs it all without understanding the mystery of it. Surely it is God—that force behind and in all which makes it all real and worth while. Oh, if all life could be for ever like this—if dull moments would not interrupt it; if the sense of futility and frustration could be eliminated from our experience of the world and ourselves! I am reminded of Paul's description of the world suffering from the sense of the vain and the futile, and its intense yearning for the perfect—the coming of the Sons of God, as he calls it in *Romans* 8. I always look upon that great chapter of 8 *Romans* as stamping Paul as one of the great spirits of the world. And his insight, almost too great for language to express, seems to pierce to the very heart of the wonder of this world and what lies in it and beyond it. It is so much more than what the scientists call evolution. It is not only evolution, life on the march, but the inner sources from which all life flows forward. It is the straining towards perfection, towards maturity of form and of content. It is the spirit in its striving beyond the reach of the present, in its infinite progress from minimal beginnings to the glory and the grandeur of the future. And there is the glory of the march, the procession of the ages from unimaginably far-off beginnings in our astronomical past to some unknown goal. And the suffering, and the heroism, and all the hidden gold of the human soul which has become revealed in this Odyssey of the race. And oh, how the doves sing in the trees and the insects hum through the air! This is the Transfiguration, the moving Transfiguration which accompanies our procession through life and history. It is always there—in the seasons, in the aspirations which move us, in the infinite longings which no defeat can still. Here is immortality—here eternity in all its human meaning for us. And still the aeroplanes hum through the air, mingling their dull roar with the song of birds and hum of insects—to remind me that there is another side to this picture. There is strife, war, pain and sorrow as never before. The world beyond this idyllic scene at Doornkloof is saturated with human blood and tears. Millions of our race are in deep anguish and sigh and pray for release from nameless agonies of body and soul. And so mercy and sadism wrestle with each other and weave the web and build up the structure of this world of ours. Our minds are silent before this drama which man himself is playing on this theatre of history. August 1914–August 1944: what a period it has been, what a tragedy, such as only the world spirit could play out—for such a time and on such a scale! As I write the news from Normandy, Brittany, Russia and Poland, Burma and the Far Pacific is coming in fast, pointing to a great sudden change in the whole war situation. The enemy lines are wavering and breaking at last. And inside Germany Hitler has let the devil loose in a new purge greater than that of ten years ago. It does look as if the end is nearing, and evil is defeating itself after all its colossal successes of the last five years. But we should not be too optimistic. I still stick to my view expressed long ago that the end of this year will see the end of the war—at least so far as Germany is concerned. Some think now that it is much nearer, but the Devil is a determined fellow, and in this case he is really desperate, and will fight with desperate determination to stave off his doom. The Nazis know that they are beaten, but their doomed leaders will prefer dying fighting to the gallows which await them. And so I imagine we shall get to the end of this year before the 'cease fire' is sounded in the west. In the east it will certainly not before sometime in 1945.

Shall we have learnt our lesson? And are we certain what that lesson is? Will nationalism—which began so beneficently in the fight for freedom—continue to degenerate into a force for evil worse than the tyrannies and imperialisms of the past? Once alive, it has now become a spook, an obsession driving mankind to its doom. Unless we can make a peace which confines nationalism to a mere cultural level and robs it of its racial poison and imperialistic ambition, war will continue to destroy the civilization which the past has built up. Science and nationality cannot continue to live together. Unless we can plan our future on universal lines we are heading for the abyss. This to me is the lesson, not only of this war, but of all the immense advances on all fronts which the world has made in the last three or more generations. Are we big enough, and big-hearted enough to understand that this is the real outcome of this war, and courageous enough to act up to it? That test will be applied to us in the next few years. And I must confess that I am appalled at the prospect, and by the fear that once more we may fail—in insight, in magnanimity and in the courage called for in such a situation. May God have mercy on our stupidity and weakness, and give us strength of heart and mind.

Here all going well. I have my hands very full, more than full with problems—many again of race and colour. And the approach of the end brings forward a host of problems of reconstruction and the switch over to peace, of which you too in England have more than your full share. So I shall not go into details.

I have not yet heard from you since I left London in June. But I hope all goes well and that your news when it arrives will be good. Dear love to you both. Ever yours,

Jan

639   From a publisher   Vol. 74, no. 17
Telegram

From: C. Kearton, Jarrolds
To: Field Marshal Smuts
Dated 23 August 1944

Have you read Crafford's biography *Jan Smuts*[1] and if so do you object to anything in it concerning yourself? We plan to publish soon here. Some copies American edition available in South Africa.

640   To a publisher   Vol. 74, no. 17
Telegram

To: C. Kearton, Jarrolds
From: Smuts
Dated [24] August 1944

Have not read and no time to read Crafford. Friends who have consider it inaccurate.

641   To W. E. Vardy   Vol. 75, no. 107

Pretoria
30 August 1944

My dear Vardy, Although as a rule I do not intervene in provincial elections I feel that in your case an exception should be made, as the Germiston[2] election is being fought by the Nationalists not on provincial issues but as a matter of no confidence in the government.

---

[1] F. S. Crafford, *Jan Smuts: A Biography* (1945).

[2] The result of the provincial bye-election at Germiston (Transvaal) on 7 September 1944 was as follows: W. E. Vardy (United party) 3,367; C. A. Smit (National party) 1,671.

As a firm and active supporter of the United party you are entitled
to and have the full confidence and support of the party. I trust
that the Germiston constituency, which only last year expressed its
confidence in the government by an overwhelming majority, will
place the same confidence in you that it placed in Mr [J. G. N.]
Strauss.

Nothing has happened since to shake that confidence. I am aware
of minor grievances and irritations which are felt, and in regard to
them I can only say that I have full sympathy with the public, and
that the government are doing their best to remedy them as fast as
possible. These troubles spring out of war conditions beyond the
control of the government and are in fact less serious in this country
than in most others in or out of the war. They are being tackled and
will pass. In any case they form no excuse for withholding support
from the government.

The meat scheme[1] is one of these troubles which cause discomfort,
but will pass. In the end, and I believe before long, it will appear as
one of the best services the government have rendered this country.
We must have stability for producer and consumer alike, and when
certain obstinate difficulties have been ironed out the public will
bless the government for this and similar schemes intended to bring
about stable living conditions for all classes of our people. This meat
scheme is in line with our other policies of social improvement and
advance, such as the soldiers' demobilization scheme already
published, the social security, the housing, the health policies and
other projects now under close examination. These policies link up
with our war policy which was intended to stabilize justice and
democracy for all peoples, ourselves included. They constitute
a great programme for our human advance.

What was and is the alternative policy on which the Nationalists
have fought us? Their policy in the war has proved a disastrous
blunder which might have landed this country, as it has landed them,
in the Hitler camp. Their open and expressed contempt and hatred
for our soldiers, and for all who took their part loyally in the war,
will not be so easily forgotten or forgiven, and prove only too clearly
how they will deal with our faithful men and women if ever they
should get the chance. Fair words and promises now in their discomfiture will not cancel their deeds of the last five years.

Whether in reference to the war policy or the post-war policies
which flow out of it, the people of South Africa will judge the
Nationalists by their actions in the war and will not be influenced

---

[1] A scheme for grading meat and fixing the price paid to the producer. It became the
basis of a permanent system under the Marketing Act.

by their present professions of good will. They have shown no spirit of repentance for their past errors and misdeeds and continue to propagandize the old bitternesses. Where we as a party wish to foster equal rights for both languages and an educational system which make our people fully bilingual, they promise to fight us tooth and nail. Their policy remains one of racial exclusiveness and of making a divided house of this land and people. They do not deserve our confidence and will not soon get it after the experience we have had of them during the last five years. Let them first repent their errors and bring forth fruit meet for repentance.[1] Fair words and smooth promises will not do, nor will fishing in troubled waters succeed.

The people of South Africa are not a fickle people. They have memories and convictions which the experience of the last five years has made only stronger and deeper. They will continue to give their confidence to their proved friends in the years of the Great Test and to carry the standard of the United party. With all good wishes, Yours sincerely,

s. J. C. Smuts

642 To M. C. Gillett

Vol. 75, no. 208

Doornkloof
[Transvaal]
5 October 1944

Such nice letters come from you and Arthur, and in such good time—about fourteen days on the way—that I think this new air letter mail is a great success. You don't know how much I value you two's letters, even where they deal almost exclusively with domestic details. And why not? Why not family matters in these days when public affairs are so grim and one likes to get away to the intimacies of the personal life? Arthur's ancient aunts sound quite charming in their rural setting. And so all your news about Aston and the dear grandchildren. I am glad you are also smitten with the disease of grandchildren from which I have so enjoyably suffered for so many years...It sounds all so cheerful and comforting to the spirit. I believe the essence of life is displayed not in the great things but the small, just as the mysteries of matter are now being discovered, not in the molar masses, but in the atom and its infinitely small constituents. *All* your news is delightful to me, whether it is good or bad. And don't forget sometimes to say a word about yourself and Arthur, who after all are nearer to me than all the dear rest.

---

[1] 'Bring forth therefore fruits meet for repentance.' *St Matthew* iii.8.

Isie has returned from Natal coast,[1] much better. The tiredness has disappeared and she is more actively interested in everything. It was that perpetual fatigue which made Louis [MacIldowie] fear that some crisis might once more ensue. Now, however, she is her old cheerful self once more, and our only trouble is to keep her from plunging once more too deep into Gifts and Comforts and all that endless correspondence. It is a comfort to have Sylma [Coaton] staying in the house and thus taking much domestic affairs off her hands. She (Isie) is the real cement in this family and if she were to go the house would fall to pieces. And what would become of me in the latter days?

I was glad to read what you said about [Lord Robert] Cecil's eightieth anniversary and Gilbert's [Murray] fine speech. What great men they both are—great in spirit if not in stature. The new scheme worked out at Dumbarton Oaks[2] looks very much like the old League, but with more responsibility on the Big Three for security —as it should be. There is, however, a serious difference with Russia over the voting,[3] which has led to much searching correspondence in which I have taken a hand. I remain in great fear that Russia will not play and rely on her enormous strength in playing a lone hand. That may mean World War III and should be prevented at all costs. But she is a strange and difficult customer to deal with. There is always the air of reserve and mystery, with strange and unexpected outbursts which make one guess as to what is going on behind that bearish exterior. I suppose it is a case for infinite patience on our part. And yet always we have to hold on to essentials and decline to compromise on them and so compromise the future.

Arnhem has of course been a bad setback,[4] worse in its effects than its immediate importance. For Arnhem was the gateway to the Ruhr and perhaps to the end this year. Now I fear we may be delayed over the winter and only reach the end sometime before next summer. And the world's life is ebbing away and every month counts. I dare say the set-back was unavoidable in the weather and other conditions, but it is a very real one. The best thing for the Germans also is to end the war soon and before the frightful devastation which a pro-

[1] She had been resting at Botha House, an official residence on the south coast near Durban.

[2] A conference between representatives of the United States, Great Britain, Russia and China had been held at Dumbarton Oaks, near Washington, between August and October and resolutions had been taken which later formed the basis of the United Nations Organization.

[3] That is, the system of voting to be adopted in the security council. For Smuts's views on this see Winston Churchill, *The Second World War*, vol. vi, pp. 183–5.

[4] An attempt by Allied forces to seize a bridgehead on the north bank of the lower Rhine at Arnhem, which began on 17 September, was abandoned on 25 September.

longation means. And the world-wide suffering. Suffering may have a purifying effect but it has its awful brutalizing side, its aspect of mere senseless loss and agony—its meaninglessness, so to say. Jesus' suffering those last days and hours saved mankind. But what salvation does this horror over the world mean? Our sense and thought are baffled before this mystery of suffering as we see it today on a scale never known before. St Augustine could still write his *City of God* while Huns or Vandals were ravaging north Africa and sacking Rome.[1] But what City of God can be discerned in this murk of fiendishness? The question is forced on one: Is this a God's world or a Devil's world? Who is king? And this question itself is blasphemy and only makes things worse. One has to cling to faith beyond the very limits of faith, just as Shelley's *Prometheus* inculcates 'hope till Hope creates from its own wreck the thing it contemplates'.[2] But it is very hard and sounds like a mockery in conditions such as now cloud our human destiny.

I sent Jan's interesting letters[3] on to Joan [Boardman] as the first in the list of recipients. I hope the others will enjoy them as much as I have done. I can't guess what he is doing, but I suppose something worth while. I should be sorry if he goes for good to India. But he has the missionary spirit and one does not like to interfere. Besides it will have no effect. It is a rotten climate for one's family. And in the end India will show little gratitude to the English oppressors however well-meaning they may be. I am deep in another Indian tangle[4] and could only get out of it by great good sense which unfortunately Indians don't possess. They have lived too long under the shadow of the inferiority complex I fear. But I must not continue this political story. Good-bye, with love,

Jan

P.S. Thank you for Burtt[5] and Wilde's *De Profundis*.[6]

643   Speech (1944)   Box K, no. 186

This speech was made at the congress of the United party in Johannesburg on 11 October 1944.

You meet in fateful days to deal with very important problems. I wish you all success in your deliberations. You will consider your

---

[1] *The City of God* was written between 413 and 426. The Vandals appeared in the Roman province of Africa in 429. The Visigoths sacked Rome in 410.
[2] *Prometheus Unbound*, IV, l. 573.
[3] Written from India and, later, Burma where Jan Gillett was on active service.
[4] *See supra*, p. 486, note 2.
[5] E. A. Burtt, *Types of Religious Philosophy* (1939).
[6] First published in 1905.

work in a sense of heavy responsibility as the foremost party in this country, to whom, with your Allies, the task of leading South Africa through this crisis has been entrusted. South Africa is largely in your hands. You represent the United party. You are a united party, united and powerful, with a proud record behind it, with, we hope, a great future before it, to which you will move forward with courage and confidence. A careful survey conducted throughout the country shows that our party position remains sound and the spirit firm and solid. You know that from personal knowledge. Make it even more so. There are great tasks ahead. Let this congress strengthen our hands for those great tasks and so render a real service to the country.

Within the time at my disposal I must limit myself to certain points.

Let me begin with the war and our war work. It is a good story. Let us not forget that our task first and foremost is to help carry this war to a successful end as soon as possible. That thought dominates everything. To that everything else, however important, is subsidiary. Remember the best contribution we can make to the peace is to end the war as soon as possible. The world is bleeding and suffering to death. Now in the sixth year of the war the whole mechanism of civilized society is in danger, the very foundations of the future are cracking in the universal destruction.

I am thankful to say that in the last twelve months very great progress has been made on all the war fronts. I shall make no particular reference to the Russian and Far East campaigns, important as they are, and immense as has been especially the Russian performance. In the decisive campaigns in the West we have had the Allied victories in the Mediterranean, in which South Africa bore her share, and which opened the way for the still greater campaign launched in France last June. Its success has been spectacular, and brought the end in Europe very much nearer. Indeed the victory in Normandy has completely transformed the war situation. It has carried our armies from the Normandy beaches to the Siegfried line, and liberated France and Belgium within a couple of months, and is probably the greatest and most decisive single victory so far of the whole war. In addition, all Germany's satellites are dropping out, and most of them are already fighting with the Allies. The war is now everywhere at or near the doors of Germany itself, and the last phase has been reached in the West. It will be a terrible struggle, and all our thoughts and prayers and efforts should be concentrated on it. The German people are desperate and led by desperadoes who expect no mercy and to whom none will be shown. The bitterness and the horror of this final struggle in the West may well surpass anything that has so far happened in this war. Let our thoughts and efforts be concentrated on that final clinch in the West. Our own war effort has continued at its maximum and has been in large measure confined to the countries in the Mediterranean basin, and in the seas round Africa. Besides our armoured division, and other technical and engineering units, which have so distinguished themselves in Italy from Cassino onwards, we have our naval forces of more than sixty vessels, and an air force of thirty-four squadrons, besides many thousands of our men seconded to the British army, navy and air force. Everywhere our men have made their great military contribution, in proportion to our population equal to that of any other country. Their performance as fighters, their behaviour as men, has everywhere earned the highest praise and brought honour to the name of South Africa. The orange flash[1] is a badge of honour wherever it is seen.

Of our contributions in munitions and war supplies of all kinds I need not speak. You know how great it has been, how much above anything we have ever done in that line, or were thought capable of doing. Weapons and ammunition of all kinds, technical appliances, coal and other minerals, essential products of all sorts, services such as ship repairs, engineering and artisan services of all kinds—it is all an outstanding achievement and has been of first-rate importance for the carrying on of the war. When we entered the war five years ago we little thought how much we would be able—and would —contribute to this war. South Africa has made a real difference to this war. It has been an astonishing national effort, and its effect on our name and standing in this world and our future is far beyond anything that we had foreseen. We shall reap great dividends from this national investment. It was indeed an effort to be proud of, and it is being continued at its maximum.

Remember that this great work was undertaken and carried on in spite of very great difficulties. A divided public, a political situation which had always to be carefully watched, subversive movements, sabotage, the absence of transport and supplies from abroad on which we had been so dependent. Shortages cramped our style in all directions. But in spite of everything we carried on resolutely, proudly, with a high heart. In spite of the shortages in our own requirements we helped others in distress, we welcomed the refugee, we fed, housed, and clothed the hungry who were in greater need than ourselves. And we were proud to do so, even at some cost and discomfort to ourselves. South Africa behaved grandly and she acted up to the great spirit which is hers. And in spite of all difficulties and handicaps and threats we could preserve social and industrial

[1] *See supra*, p. 397, note 1.

peace. We were more free from strikes and other disturbances than ever before, and than most other countries in these times of universal unrest and upset. We could largely improve industrial and working conditions in all directions, and we could achieve a spirit of social and industrial co-operation and teamwork among our people such as we have seldom or never known before. I say it is a good story, a great story, of which every South African, however much he may have differed from our policy, can be justly proud. The future will be prouder still.

It is not in a spirit of boasting that I mention all this, although we could boast if we so wished. No, I mention all this for remembrance —to give you the whole picture, to remind you of much that is so easily forgotten in these days, to give you the wider perspective that we should ever keep before us when awarding praise or blame. Let us lift our hearts to that great scene of high resolve and of our own achievement as a people, as a party, as a government. Let us bear in mind the whole picture when today many troubles, food troubles, control troubles, and many others are with us, perhaps unduly much with us. We may not have all the meat or fish or potatoes or butter we wish or all the other good things which either do not exist or which we have shared with others in greater need or in our war effort. We do not wish to have behaved differently. Like other humans in general we have made and still make mistakes, both as a government and as a people. But through it all there has been good will, the will to do what is right and fair, to serve to the best of our ability, and to overcome difficulties—many of them new to us, many for which our social or administrative set-up was quite unprepared. We are all learning valuable lessons. Perhaps even the mistakes are a salutary experience. Let us not lose our tempers and talk or write wildly. We have to look around this suffering world and see how much we have to be thankful for. At least others tell us so. We have on the whole behaved greatly, let us continue to do so. We have nothing to apologize for, much to be thankful for. The memory of these great days and experiences through which we have been privileged to pass should ever be with us to sustain us, and to give us poise and serenity of mind in the minor troubles we may have or still meet. Let us also remember that we ourselves have set a high standard in this the greatest crisis of our lives and of world history, and that we should be just to ourselves and continue to act up to this standard to the end, and not get bogged in a quagmire of petty grievances and complaints and in a spirit unbecoming our grand performance and endurance as a people. That is our record as a people, and as a party carrying out a true national policy. By that record we are prepared to be judged. We certainly have not acted in any party spirit, or thought of party interest. In these tremendous days we have not bothered about popularity and have only aimed at what we thought right in the interests of the country and the world. In a measure we had our reward at the general election last year when the people with an overwhelming vote approved of what we had done. And a still greater reward awaits us when the great day of victory arrives to crown our policy and efforts with final success. I ask for no other, no greater reward. South Africa will have come unwounded, unscathed through the greatest struggle in her history, stronger and greater than when she entered it, and with a clear and open course to the future for the generations to come. What an addition has been made to our great national tradition![1]

So much for our own work as a party. Now a word about the attitude of our opposition. They are now asking for the confidence of the people. Their leader is again preparing for another election and is launching a big campaign against the government. He and his minions are rushing around the country making propaganda for party ends. We ask why the people should trust them. What was their policy and contribution during the greatest storm that ever struck us? And what are they still doing but making party propaganda and weakening and dividing the national will and creating a spirit of public disunion and dissatisfaction? Their course throughout the difficult years, and even now, is the complete answer to their request for public confidence. Their record speaks for itself. Their deeds condemn them.

Their policy was hopelessly wrong and misleading throughout. If their course had been followed, where would we have been today? How sure they were that the war was hopelessly lost for us! How sure they were of Hitler's victory and of the republic which they would get with Hitler's help! Did Dr Malan not even enter into negotiations with Hitler by way of Zeesen in order to get his co-operation? Today he accuses Pirow[2] of building upon a German victory. But what was his own attitude at that time? Today he attacks the *Ossewa-Brandwag*[3] for the same reason, but at that time he carefully took the O.B. under his wing and promised it protection. Today he trims his sails to quite another wind. He has even forgotten that he won Wakkerstroom[4] with O.B. votes.

---

[1] At this point Smuts began to speak in Afrikaans. For this portion of the speech in the original *see* pp. 502–4.

[2] *See supra*, p. 388, note 2.   [3] *See supra*, p. 172, note 4.

[4] In 1943 W. R. Collins won Wakkerstroom (in the eastern Transvaal) for the United party with a majority of 551. In the bye-election after his death J. G. W. van Niekerk won the seat for the National party with a majority of 221.

But gratitude, chivalry and steadfastness are not among his qualities. We ask: what has happened to that whole policy and what would have become of the country if it had been followed? Why, with all the facts before us, should we follow it now? If ever a party went hopelessly wrong it is the National party under the misdirection of its leaders; and South Africa will surely not forget it. And then they expect soon to take over the government of the country! On what do they build that expectation! Hitler and his victory have been given up for good. On what do they rely now? It is almost too childish to mention, but I repeat what Dr Malan himself announces.

In the first place, imagine it, they build upon my early disappearance and the rise of Mr [J. H.] Hofmeyr as my substitute. The divided United party will then be shattered and United Afrikanderdom will take over. There is, of course, no division in Dr Malan's Afrikanderdom! We do not now have Pirow or van Rensburg [J. F. J.] in mind, or the Calvinist fathers of the church who have no confidence in Dr Malan. We are merely thinking of the young Turks about him who all want his position. United Afrikanderdom! What an argument from a party leader! Of course I shall disappear from the scene one of these days. And a good thing too. I have been there long enough—for almost half a century, and almost half the history of the Transvaal. It is time for younger leaders. But let me warn Dr Malan not to belittle Mr Hofmeyr or any of the younger leaders in the United party. He and his young people must prepare for many disappointments.

And the Doctor makes another big miscalculation. He too often looks back instead of forward. A new South Africa is coming into existence, with new horizons and a new outlook. This outlook, the racial division of the past, the painful memories and bitter thoughts of the past vanish before the vision of the new, greater, better South Africa. The country is outgrowing the old clothes into which the Doctor and his friends again want to thrust it. Not in vain has our generation experienced three great wars and tasted the fruits of racial division. Not in vain have we lived through the amazing development of our generation. In all this South Africa has given proof that it will become a great country and people—united, fit for her calling and done with childhood, and with childish deeds and childish thinking. The new South Africa is not a country where the Doctor and his henchmen with their present outlook will easily or for long—if ever—enjoy leadership.

What I have said about the Re-united National party applies also to the various ramifications of that party, a party which is even afraid to choose a proper name. I regard the *Broederbond*[1] as one of these ramifications; it is in great measure the underground movement of the Re-united National party or People's party. It is unnecessary for me to expatiate on this. We are watching the *Broederbond*, just as we watched the *Ossewa-Brandwag* when it looked dangerous. As for the civil service, the government can at any time declare membership of the *Broederbond* a transgression of the Public Service Act,[2] with all the legal consequences for the *Broederbond* official concerned. The government will act in this way or some other way at the right time and according to circumstances. This is not the moment to pursue the matter further and I leave it at what I have said.

One more question to Afrikanders: Another foundation on which Dr Malan builds his hopes for the future is the colour question. On this question, he says, the National party won the election of 1929 and he asks why it cannot happen again. Can there be better proof of the political bankruptcy of the opposition than this open acknowledgment of and persistence in the crass deception which was practised on the public in 1929? The black peril of that election was a cry which nauseated every right-minded Afrikander, even among the Nationalists.[3] No—that horse will not run again. Even in the last election they did everything possible to refurbish and exploit that outworn lie. It was and will be of no avail. Once bitten, twice shy. White South Africa is big and strong and just enough to do right by all races and colours, and we shall indeed do this while taking into account and preserving our well-known standpoint of separateness[4] in social intercourse, housing and field of employment between the colours. The propagation of this lie is unworthy even of the Nationalists and will in future recoil on them like a boomerang and, alas, perhaps also on the country.

Now Dr Malan wants to exploit politically the Indian question in Durban although it is a question for which he personally bears a heavy responsibility in the past.[5] In spite of his present attitude

---

[1] The *Afrikaner-Broederbond* was founded in 1918. Members must be male, over twenty-five years of age, Afrikaans-speaking and Protestants. Membership is not disclosed and Broeders become such only by invitation. The avowed aim of the society is to advance Afrikaans culture but it has been suspected and accused of political activity and infiltration.

[2] In December 1944 civil servants were forbidden to become members of the *Broederbond*. The prohibition was lifted when the National party came to power in 1948.

[3] *See* vol. v, p. 395, note 1.

[4] Here Smuts used the word *apartheid*. This now notorious term, which the National party adopted in 1948 to epitomize its colour policy, had been in earlier use as a softer synonym for *segresasie* (segregation). *Apartheid*, in its turn, has given place, in National party parlance, to *afsonderlike ontwikkeling* (separate development).

[5] *See* vol. v, p. 368, note 2.

we hope to arrive at a satisfactory solution even of this thorny matter. The government, for its part, will do everything reasonable and possible to reach such a solution.

I now pass on to refer to some of the more important matters which will constitute our post-war programme, some of which are already being tackled by the government while others have to await the conclusion of the war in Europe. The end of the European war will probably reduce our munition programme by half, while it will increase our activities at our ports for transport to the Far East, and will make increased demands on our capacity for ship repairs. It may also be assumed at this stage that our share in the war against Japan will be limited chiefly to technical and engineering services and the like, and more especially to the air, and that the call on us for infantry will be comparatively small. The close of the European war will therefore bring about a large-scale demobilization of our fighting and auxiliary services beyond what may be temporarily required for garrison duties and lines of communication purposes during the Japanese war. Shortage of shipping and other transport will remain acute during that stage and may seriously limit the rate of our progress with demobilization and the return of our surplus forces from the north. Even so, however, it may be assumed that a large measure of demobilization will take place as soon as the fighting in the north comes to an end, and all the necessary preparations have now to be made to cope with that heavy task. Much in that direction is already being done. The government programme for benefits to the returned soldiers, their rehabilitation, training and education and their absorption into normal civil life, has already been published and widely welcomed by our fighting services. The machinery for this return to normal life is being created and extended all over the country, and will, I trust, be able to function at once when the occasion arises. Meanwhile, the cases of those already released from military service are being attended to. This enormous task of demobilization in all its aspects will tax the energies of the government and the country to the utmost, but there is a firm determination to do justice to our soldiers, and whatever can be done now already in preparing for the smooth working of the whole demobilization and resettlement scheme is being and will be done. I am sure the country and employers will co-operate most whole-heartedly with the government in making this great task a success. Industry will have to be expanded and set going all along the line, employment will have to be created on as large a scale as possible, and the switch-over from military to civilian products will have to be speeded up as much as possible. The consultations and planning necessary for these purposes have already begun, and can in any case not be delayed much longer, as next year will probably see demobilization in full swing.

Besides demobilization and the restoration of normal civil life other very heavy tasks await us. Most of these have already been surveyed and reported on. In fact our programme is already well advanced. The social security code is already before parliament and will, it is hoped, be passed into law in its next session. National health services have been the subject of an elaborate inquiry by the Gluckman commission[1] and a valuable report has been made to the government, which will enable us to make at least a commencement with a national health scheme next year. The national housing scheme has formed the subject of consultation and inquiry with the local authorities, the financial aspects have been agreed upon, and the programme for next year provisionally settled. The expansion of industry and of industrial employment calls for large-scale readjustment of our educational system in the direction of vocational and technical training. All these matters, so far as they fall within the provincial sphere, have been discussed with the provinces at an important conference last week, and the policy of the government has been published in a statement just issued by me. I am most grateful to the provinces and the local authorities for their ready response to the government's appeal, and their willing collaboration in these vast national undertakings.

You will agree that this is a very large programme to carry out in the immediate future—a programme which will demand an effort little short of that involved in the war itself. But it is not all. Agriculture, mining, secondary industry have all to be stimulated and pushed in a many-sided advance to keep up and increase the tempo of employment which we developed in war time. The price structure of the country will have to be such as to make local production hold its own fairly against the outside competition which is sure to follow as soon as international trade gets into its stride. The price structure again is closely affected by the wage structure, and all of them hang together with the scale of social services which the country can afford. All these aspects of our economic system as a whole are interdependent and have to be harmonized with each other if a breakdown and a slowing down of our progress are to be prevented. And beyond all will be the world economic situation after this devastating war, which is bound to have a profound effect on our local conditions and prospects. I just mention these important points as matters which will vitally affect the new South Africa after this war and will call for

---

[1] Report of the National Health Services Commission (U.G. 30 of 1944).

our thought and action. They all tend to show that if justice is to be done to our country in the new prospects which will open out before it in the near future we shall have little time and energy left for that sort of internal warfare which has been the stock in trade of our politics. The end of this war will present South Africa with economic problems and also with opportunities of advance such as she has never faced before. Let national teamwork such as we have never had before enable us to rise to our great opportunities and render a united nation-wide service to our country which will initiate a new era in our history. We have great natural resources, we have a sound financial system, and our credit stands very high in the world. We have thus the conditions for great economic advance, a much enlarged employment, greater production and larger national income, and for a higher standard of life. All that is needed is work, national team-work, and the will to realize our national destiny. Let us crown our great war effort with a still greater peace effort in which all sections of our complex population will join. Forward South Africa! *Suid-Afrika vorentoe!*

So ver oor ons eie werk as party. Nou 'n oomblik oor die houding van ons Opposisie. Hul vra nou om die vertroue van die volk. Hul leier maak al weer klaar vir 'n ander eleksie en loods 'n groot veldtog teen die regering. Hy en sy trawante storm rond deur die land en maak propaganda vir party doeleindes.

Ons vra waarom die volk hul sal vertrou. Wat was hul beleid en bydrae gedurende die grootste storm wat ooit oor ons gegaan het? En wat doen hul nou nog as alleen party propaganda maak en die nasionale wil verswak en verdeel en 'n gees van verdeeldheid en ontevredenheid onder die publiek te skep? Hul koers dwars deur die moeilike jare, en nou nog, is die volkome antwoord op hul versoek om publieke vertroue. Hul rekord spreek vir homself. Hul dade veroordeel hulle.

Hul beleid was dwarsdeur hopeloos verkeerd en misleidend vir die volk. Was hul koers gevolg, waar was ons vandag? Hoe seker was hul dat die oorlog vir ons hopeloos verlore was! Hoe seker was hul van Hitler se oorwinning en van die republiek wat hul met Hitler se toedoen sou kry! Het dr Malan nie selfs onderhandelinge oor Zeesen met Hitler aangeknoop om sy medewerking te verkry nie? Vandag beskuldig hy Pirow van bou op 'n Duitse oorwinning. Maar wat was sy eie houding destyds? Vandag val hy die O.B. om dieselfde rede aan, maar destyds het hy die O.B. sorgvuldig onder sy vleuel geneem en beskerming belowe. Vandag span hy sy seile na glad 'n ander wind. Hy het selfs vergeet dat hy Wakkerstroom met O.B.

stemme gewen het. Maar dankbaarheid, ridderlikheid, of koers hou tel nie onder sy kenmerke nie. Ons vra was is van al daardie beleid geword, en wat sou van die land geword het was dit gevolg? Waarom, met al die feite nou voor ons, sou ons dit volg? As ooit 'n party hopeloos verdwaal het was dit die H.N.P. onder die misleiding van sy leiers en Suid-Afrika sal dit seker nie vergeet nie. En dan verwag hul nog om die regering van die land spoedig oor te neem!

Waarop bou hulle daardie verwagting? Hitler en sy oorwinning is vir goed opgegee—waarop steun hul nou? Dit is byna te kinderagtig om dit te noem, maar ek herhaal wat dr. Malan self verkondig.

In die eerste plaas (begryp jou) bou hul op my verdwyning eersdaags, en op die opkoms van mnr. Hofmeyr as my plaasvervanger. Dan sal die verdeelde Verenigde Party uitmekaar spat en die Verenigde Afrikanderdom sal oorneem. Daar is mos geen verdeeldheid onder dr Malan se Afrikanerdom nie! Ons dink nou nie aan Pirow of van Rensburg nie, of aan die Kalvinistiese kerkvaders wat geen vertroue in dr Malan het nie. Ons dink maar net aan die jong Turke om hom wat almal sy plek wil he. Verenigde Afrikanerdom! Wat 'n argument van 'n party-leier! Natuurlik sal ek een van die dae van die toneel verdwyn. En 'n goeie ding ook. Ek is daar lang genoeg gewees—al byna 'n halwe eeu, en byna die helfte van die geskiedenis van Transvaal. Dit word tyd vir jonger leiers. Maar laat my dr Malan waarsku om mnr. Hofmeyr of enige van die jonger voormanne in die Verenigde Party nie te verkleineer nie. Hy en sy jongspan moet klaarmaak vir baie teleurstellings.

En die doktor maak ook 'n ander groot misrekening. Hy kyk te veel agteruit in pleks van vorentoe. 'n Nuwe Suid-Afrika is aan ontstaan—met nuwe horisonte en uitkyk. Die uitkyk, die rasseverdeeldheid van die verlede, die pynlike herinneringe en bitter gedagtes van die verlede verdwyn voor die visioen van die nuwe, groter, beter Suid-Afrika. Die land ontgroei die ou klere waarin die doktor en sy vriende dit weer wil steek. Nie verniet het ons geslag drie groot oorloë deurgemaak en die vrugte van rasseverdeeldeheid geproe nie. Nie verniet het ons die verbasende ontwikkeling van ons geslag beleef nie. Deur dit alles heen het Suid-Afrika bewys gelewer dat dit 'n groot land en volk gaan word—verenig, opgewasse vir haar roeping, met die kinderjare, kinder doen en kinder denkery agter die rug. Die nuwe Suid-Afrika is nie 'n land waar die doktor en sy handlangers met hul teenwoordige uitkyk gemaklik of lang —so ooit—die leiding sal geniet nie.

Wat ek van die H.N.P. sê geld ook van die verskeie vertakkings van daardie party, 'n party wat selfs bang is om 'n regte naam te kies. As so'n vertakking beskou ek die Broederbond, wat in grote

mate die ondergrondse beweging van die H.N.P. of Volksparty is.
Dit is onnodig vir my hier daaroor uit te wy. Ons hou die B.B. dop,
net soos ons die O.B. dopgehou het toe dit nog 'n gevaar gelyk het.
Wat die publieke diens betref kan die regering ter enige tyd die
lidmaatskap van die B.B. 'n oortreding van die Staatsdienswet
verklaar, met al die wetlike gevolge vir die betrokke B.B. amptenaar.
Ter regte tyd en op bevind van sake sal die regering op hierdie wyse
en op ander wyse reageer. Die is nou nie 'n geleentheid op die saak
verder in te gaan nie, en ek laat dit by wat ek gesê het.

Net nog 'n vraag aan Afrikaners: 'n ander grond waarop dr Malan
sy hoop vir die toekoms bou is die kleurkwessie. Op hierdie kwessie,
sê hy, het die Nasionale Party die eleksie van 1929 gewen, en vra
hy waarom dit nie weer kan gebeur nie. Kan daar beter bewys wees
van die politieke bankrotskap van die Opposisie as hierdie openlike
erkenning van en volharding by die growe bedrog wat in 1929 op die
publiek afgespeel is? Die swart gevaar van daardie eleksie was 'n
kreet waarvan elke weldenkende Afrikaner, selfs onder die Nasion-
aliste, gewalg het. Nee, daardie perdjie sal nie weer hardloop nie.
Selfs in die laaste eleksie het hul alles wat moontlik was gedoen om
daardie afgesaagde ou leuen weer op te fris en uit te buit. Dit het
niks gebaat nie en sal ook nie weer baat nie. *Once bitten twice shy*.
Blank Suid-Afrika is groot en sterk en regskape genoeg om reg te
doen aan alle rasse en kleure, en ons sal dit ook doen, met inagneming
en behoud van ons bekende standpunt van apartheid in omgang,
behuising en werkkring tussen die kleure. Die propageering van
hierdie leuen is selfs die Nattes onwaardig en sal in die toekoms as
'n boomerang op hul terugwerk, en helaas, miskien ook op die land.

Nou wil dr. Malan die Indiërkwessie te Durban politiek uitbuit
hoewel dit 'n kwessie is waarvoor hyself persoonlik 'n sware verantwoordelikheid in die verlede dra. Tenspyte van sy teenswoordige
houding hoop ons tot 'n bevredigende oplossing ook van hierdie
netelige saak te kan geraak. Van regeringskant sal alles redelik en
moontlik gedoen word om tot so'n oplossing te kom.

644   To D. Moore   **Vol. 75, no. 147**

Doornkloof
[Transvaal]
19 October 1944

My dear Daphne, This is a line of farewell on your leaving Africa
for pastures new (or rather old). We shall miss you. I don't know
what I shall do when on my African travels or tours to England I have

to touch at Nairobi and my friends are no longer there. It will not be the same place—even if Philip Mitchell reigns there.

But this is not so much to bewail my lot as to say good-bye to very dear friends whom we shall miss more than I can tell. You go so far away that there is not even the prospect of seeing you and Henry soon again. And time is passing, and not much of it may be left to some of us.

Good-bye, dear friends. You have become very dear to us, and this parting is a great pain. Our thoughts and living remembrances will always be with you.

I shall not write any news as [Princess] Katherine will be able to tell you all that you may be interested in. We are sorry to part with her and I am sure she is equally sorry to leave this good country. I hope she may soon be able or permitted to return to Greece. The path of royalty is a hard one in these days.

I hope Ceylon and its burghers and others will be kind to you. It does not sound very attractive, but you may meet there again some of the admiralty who occupied your house at Mombasa.[1] James[2] will not be there, and I am more likely to see him in the near future than you.

We have just been talking of you and Henry and the daughters[3] over late evening tea. They all send love and best wishes. You leave very warm hearts behind in this Smuts circle. God bless you all and bring us together again. Ever yours,

J. C. Smuts

645   To J. Hutchinson   Vol. 75, no. 151

Pretoria
24 October 1944

My dear Hutchinson, I was so glad to hear of your luck in finding a publisher for that new Burchell![4] It would be a pity to spoil so fine a work with a photo of myself. But if you persist I gladly give my permission for that Christ College painting.[5] I do hope, however, that your floral illustrations will be better to look at. The foreword I shall write as soon as you give me some notes for it. It has been a lucky strike for you to find such an enterprising man as Gawthorn

---

[1] Refers to an occasion when several British admirals of the Eastern fleet were lodged in the governor's house.

[2] Admiral Sir James Somerville (q.v.).

[3] Deirdre Moore, married D. O'Neill; Jocelyn (Jo) Moore, died 1952.

[4] J. Hutchinson, *A Botanist in Southern Africa* (1946). Smuts refers to W. J. Burchell, *Travels in the Interior of Southern Africa*, published 1822–4.

[5] By Arthur Pan.

[P. R.]. Perhaps his photo will be better than mine. I am also glad you will remember Pole-Evans. Tell Mr Gawthorn I shall be so happy to have a copy of his *Story of Livings Things*.

Your family news is good. I was glad to hear of them all. My wife was poorly from sheer overwork, but is well again after some weeks on the Natal coast, where in a week-end I collected copiously. Jannie [Smuts] is drilling his engineers, and the rest are all usefully occupied in war work. All except the poor father, whose preoccupations at this stage of the war are mostly political—alas! All Jannie's papers on prehistory have at last been published by the local Royal Society.[1] His researches were so revolutionary that the great pundits were at first frightened, but the Abbé Breuil, who is the great authority and now here, agreed generally with his findings and so he has pushed the history of this poor race of man at least another million years back into the past.

In some free months recently I have been dipping into palaeobotany in order to get away from the horrid present. How pacifying plants are, especially where they have been dead so many millions of years! The human element is becoming much too oppressive in this sixth year of the war.

I shall give Jannie your message. And to you, my dear friend, I send best wishes for yourself, your family, and your work. Ever yours,

s. J. C. Smuts

Tell Hubbard [C. E.] I have not quite forgotten his grasses.

646   To G. Heaton Nichols   Vol. 75, no. 153

Pretoria
25 October 1944

My dear Nicholls, Thank you for your note on the Indian draft ordinance[2] and all the information you impart. I have asked Mitchell [D. E.] to come up on Friday and put me *au fait* with what passed at his talks with Kajee [A. I.] since the issue of the report.[3] The

[1] Four articles in the *Transactions of the Royal Society of South Africa*, vol. 25, p. 343 and p. 367 and vol. 31, p. 39 and p. 69. The Society originated in 1877 as the South African Philosophical Society which was granted a royal charter and registered by act of the Cape Parliament in 1908.

[2] The Occupational Control Ordinance drafted by the Natal provincial executive to implement the Pretoria agreement on the Pegging Act. *See supra*, p. 479, note 1 and p. 486, note 2.

[3] Presumably the report of the select committee to which the provincial council had referred the Occupational Control Ordinance.

Indians have rejected the new ordinance[1] and asked me to meet them this week or secure a postponement of the ordinance. Mitchell could perhaps explain what is behind this.

I know of no document except the one we agreed to. At least I can remember nothing else. With kind regards, Ever yours,

s. J. C. Smuts

647   To C. Weizmann   Vol. 75, no. 160

Pretoria
14 November 1944

My dear Weizmann, I have read your memorandum on a settlement of the Palestine question, dated 16 October 1944.[2] It is a powerful document, and at the same time a poignant one. In spite of your cogent argument for a whole and undivided Palestine, I am afraid there will and must be partition. Too many chances were missed since 1919 in the carrying out of the spirit and intention of the Balfour declaration. Probably the chief failure was the limitation on immigration in the early years when a strong immigration policy was possible. If by now the Jewish population of Palestine were in the majority a far-reaching solution would be possible. Now, with a majority of Arabs, and the Arab world in uproar, and British policy afraid to antagonize Arabs and Muslims, the best one could expect is a partition which will do substantial justice to the Jews and create a viable Jewish state. The atmosphere has been worsened by the insane assassination of poor Moyne,[3] and a malign fate has done the Jewish cause great harm at a critical moment—one of the worst strokes of luck you have had to endure. I am not at all *au fait* with the present British proposals and speak only of the knowledge I have of the situation as it was six months ago.

I enclose a copy of a little statement I made at the request of a local Jewish paper on your approaching seventieth anniversary. I hope you will not resent what I have said, although it ends on a somewhat minor note.[4]

[1] The Residential Property Regulation Ordinance controlling acquisition as well as occupancy of property.

[2] The memorandum was a reply to a new partition scheme for Palestine suggested by the British government.

[3] Lord Moyne was murdered in a street in Cairo by two members of the terrorist Stern group on 6 November shortly after taking up his post as British minister of state in the Middle East.

[4] *See* Smuts Collection, Box F, no. 74. The last paragraph begins: 'The greatest Jewish leader before him failed to enter the Promised Land and died on the mountains of Vision and Disappointment.'

Victory is approaching and can now not be far off. But it will dawn over a bleak world, bled white with loss of life and treasure beyond anything in the history of the race. I am a firm believer in man—as I am in God—but I must admit that the prospect before the world, even with victory, appals me. And you as a scientist know what fate is in store for us if this is not the end of war itself. It is not only the Jewish cause which is at stake, but that of the whole human race. May the genius of our race which has accomplished so much in the past enable us to survive and surmount the dangers now facing us, even in this hour of coming victory.

My warm greetings and best wishes for you and Mrs Weizmann.[1] Keep up your hearts in faith in the Eternal. Ever yours,

s. J. C. Smuts

648   To Sir Shafa'at Ahmad Khan   Vol. 75, no. 161

Pretoria
15 November 1944

Dear Sir Shafa'at, I have your letter of 14 November[2] and note that the government of India recognize the right, which is of course beyond question, of free consultation and negotiation between the Union government and their Indian nationals. They do not, however, understand whose *bona fides* in such negotiations the government of India feel uncertain about—whether that of the Union government or of the Indian community. Nor do they concede the claim of the government of India to intervene in negotiations between them and their Indian nationals. They feel that this claim to come in between the Union government and the Indian community in questions arising in the Union can only produce confusion and uncertainty and in the end react on the relations between our two countries. I do not know of any other country which makes such claims to interfere in the affairs of their friendly neighbours. Such a position cannot be acceptable to the Union government—as you appear to assume. Yours sincerely,

s. J. C. Smuts

[1] Born Vera Chatzman, married C. Weizmann in 1906.
[2] Not in the Smuts Collection.

649   To M. C. Gillett   Vol. 75, no. 211

Doornkloof
[Transvaal]
22 November 1944

It is possible that I have somewhat fallen back in my correspondence.
I am not quite certain but have that guilty feeling. Your and Arthur's
letters still arrive regularly and are much enjoyed. The fact is that
I am so hard worked at present that after a long and hard day's work
there is really no energy except perhaps to look through some pictures in *Flowering Plants*[1] or the like. The days are spent in interviews
and conferences, in reading and answering urgent important despatches from everywhere, in purely political party business and in
preparing drafts and the like on many post-war projects. It is
a horrid undertaking—this last of making blueprints for a world
which may remain unborn. The better world, the new order, all the
visions which people see in the skies of the future. We are evidently
living in an era like that of Godwin[2] and Shelley in the early nineteenth century when people believed in the perfectibility of human
nature and thought the old order could be sloughed off like a skin
and hey presto! the new world of heart's desire would dawn. For
all this we have to prepare, for this public anticipation we have to
cater—we poor miserable public men—in a world already overcrowded with insoluble war and post-war problems. It is all rather
funny, but to tired bodies and minds very trying. The *practical*
problems and tasks are so enormous that one has really no time for
this artistry of the future. Look at the world today, at what is
happening in Europe, at a whole world order slowly sagging to
lower levels. How can one who desires to face facts and realities be
patient with all this pining after what is not[3] and may never be.
Look at unchanged human nature, look at the cost in an impoverished
war-exhausted world. It is all rather trying to my tired nerves and
brain. In Britain the authorities have simply succumbed to this
pressure, in the pious hope that all will be well with larger production,
flourishing foreign trade and rich sources for the tax-gatherer to tap.
I see the world differently, I am sorry to say. It is and will be a poor
world, with a bleak outlook. We shall have to live much more simply,

---

[1] *Flowering Plants of South Africa*, a quarterly publication, 1921–44; continued as
Flowering Plants of Africa 1945 . . . .
[2] William Godwin (1756–1836), English political philosopher, father-in-law of
Shelley.

[3]

We look before and after;
We pine for what is not.

Shelley, To a Skylark.

with fewer comforts and benefits and largesse from the public purse. People are tired and easy-going and will not work harder. It is all shorter hours and easier conditions of life people are after; and I don't see where the finance for paradise is to come from. Perhaps the Banker[1] can explain to a simple Boer who gets more and more puzzled over this gap between our wishes and our means. I suppose what all this tirade really means is that I am tired and long for rest. So be kind to me in your judgment!

In one of your letters you refer to my recantation about France. I am not conscious of having recanted anywhere on anything. I have never been against the French. All I have warned against is our leaning on the French and giving them the lead in the pious hope that they will see us through. That would be sheer illusion. They broke miserably in 1939 and almost ruined the world. And the same thing may happen again. French policy and pride and political rottenness almost were our undoing, and I don't know that it will not be the same again. I rejoice at any sign of their recovery, finding their lost soul and what is called repentance in the Gospels. They are doing grandly in Alsace just now.[2] But how deep has the inner national corruption gone? This leaning on France and letting France run Europe may be as fatal in future as it has been for the last generation or two. I wait and see. Now you see how far Churchill and Eden are already going to restore France to the old position which she so hopelessly forfeited. France is being put back in a position to claim leadership, as she certainly will. I would far rather see some other set-up in which France will play her legitimate part, without once more playing the *prima donna* in Europe. I see many indications among the smaller fry in favour of a set-up such as I advocated for western Europe in which moral and political leadership will be with Britain. But in Britain itself there is little response. People are tired, statesmen no longer feel a great mission, after the failure of imperialism and Liberal *laissez-faire*.

I think there is a great moral enthusiasm in the English which no longer finds expression in British policy. I long for the old courage and inspiration. But leaders are tired and cautious, or timid, and the wrong ones thus get the chance to lead or mislead the world. You will see this is all in my explosive speech,[3] which was really meant to explode public opinion but has only exploded myself! I don't complain. But I see a great leadership renounced at a critical time in world history. Britain has been the soul of resistance and should be

---

[1] Arthur B. Gillett.

[2] The French First Army, after a heavy battle, captured Belfort in southern Alsace on 22 November and reached the Rhine north of Bâle.   [3] **624.**

the soul of the new leadership in Europe. America is still very immature. Russia is brutal and a barbarian of the spirit, and has much,
very much, still to learn. France? No, I honestly doubt.

Arthur writes about 'Tsalta' and is on the whole pleased it is
sold. So am I. The place gave us infinite pleasure and joy. But the
building was poor workmanship and would have meant repeated
repairs. The price was good and nothing has been lost in fact. All
our joys and enjoyment were free, gratis, of the spirit, as they should
be. The Banker is happy, so am I, although the real pleasure was
really mine more than his.

The war. It seems a tremendous effort is being made to break
Germany this winter. And the signs look rather favourable. I don't
see how Germany can for many months continue to stand the hammering she is now getting in west and east. Unless the winter is such
as to render this increasing weight of attack impossible, she will
probably break up under the awful ordeal. In any case by spring the
end must come, if not earlier. What troubles me much more is the
sort of peace we are going to have this time. Can hatred make peace
—a real peace? And, however we express it, hatred is now in power
all over Europe. The slogan of 'never again' may find a devastating
application to which all will this time agree—the great antagonists
as well as all the small ones whose sufferings under German occupation have been unspeakable. Europe is coming up against a decision
at least as vital to her future as victory itself. I am deeply troubled,
as you can well imagine. In her present mood I fear the decision.
But I should not write more about this. And perhaps my forebodings may not materialize. But the forebodings are there all the
same.

You will have seen a good deal of the recrudescence of the Indian
trouble here. Some evil fate seems to dog our footsteps, and when
I think the matter has been settled it bursts out again like an internal
boil. I am busy with this trouble to see what can be done about it.
This has now gone on since shortly after the Boer War, and may
outlast me. But I must struggle with it to find some *modus vivendi*
even if a solution is not possible.

At home all goes well. Isie jogs along quietly...Japie [Smuts] is
planning operations for Alexander. He has been offered a majorship
but has refused because he thinks I am behind it, whereas I knew
nothing about it, and it came from Alexander's staff. Such is the
pride in this ridiculous Smuts family, with the Krige taint added.
I have my hands too full to bother about these things. We are too
much burdened with our troubles. We should be free and above it
all. After all, is this not the nature of man—what we call free will?

Let each find his own way and level, and let us view the effort with sympathy and good will. What a letter! Forgive me. Ever lovingly yours,

Jan

650   To W. S. Churchill   Vol. 75, no. 167

Telegram

To: Right Honourable Winston Churchill

From: Smuts

Dated 30 November 1944

My thoughts are today[1] much with you my friend, the one in all the world to whom so many owe so much. May God continue to bless you with strength of body as he has blessed you with strength of soul.

651   From L. S. Amery   Vol. 73, no. 23

[London]
1 December 1944

My dear Smuts, It may possibly interest you to read the enclosed brief appreciation[2] I wrote the other day for Winston's birthday. Naturally in a tribute of this sort I rather skated over some of our differences more particularly the difference of our outlook on Empire and economic questions. But I think it is a fair estimate and not too fulsome.

I am grateful to you for what you have been trying to do to straighten out the tiresome South African–Indian crisis. I know enough about South Africa to understand the problem from your end. On the other hand I also know enough about the Indian point of view and its long history to realize how passionately they feel out there. This is obviously one of those questions where no immediate solution is possible and where one can only move from one compromise to another in hope of reaching a final adjustment some day. Meanwhile I can only hope that we can turn this immediate corner without too serious damage to inter-imperial relations. It has been unfortunate that the new high commissioner[3] is not able to arrive

---

[1] Churchill's birthday.
[2] Not attached to the document in the Smuts Collection.
[3] M. R. Deshmukh.

till next month. I think you will find him more helpful than his predecessor.[1]

The falling back of the Germans upon the 'inner fortress'[2] is being skilfully and tenaciously conducted, and as a military proposition we may well be many months from the end. On the other hand you will remember that all our deliberations in the summer of 1918 were based on the assumption that the Germans would certainly hold out for another year, and then the end came with a run. Let us hope it may be so again. Yours ever,

Leo Amery

652   To G. M. Huggins   Vol. 75, no. 169

Pretoria
4 December 1944

My dear Prime Minister, I enclose for your information copy of a bill for a Dongola Wild Life Sanctuary which it is intended to introduce into the Union parliament at its following session next year.

I know that some private persons and members of the government of South Rhodesia are also interested in this project for the protection of wild life in the Limpopo valley and I therefore take the liberty to send you this draft bill. Yours sincerely,

J. C. Smuts

653   To M. C. Gillett   Vol. 75, no. 214

Doornkloof
[Transvaal]
17 December 1944

There is no particular letter to answer, but this being Sunday morning I write you before parties of guests arrive to engage us for the Sunday! I had a long almost three hours' walk yesterday (Dingaans Day)[3] so as to set this day free for visitors. I wish they would not come. I am harassed all the week with the public, and Sundays is the only free moment for browsing into a book and collecting one's scattered thoughts and impressions. But there is no release and the

---

[1] Sir Shafa'at Ahmad Khan.

[2] The belief that the German leaders had prepared a national redoubt (*Alpenfestung*) in the mountainous region south of Munich to which their forces would retreat proved to be unfounded.

[3] *See* vol. III, p. 147, note 1.

human tension continues all the time, except in sleep. I was very glad to be able to escape the fuss of Dingaan's Day functions yesterday and to roam over the green fields with my bodyguard. They have become part of the permanent environment and are no longer resented. But I look forward to the day of solitariness when nature alone will suffice for my simple needs.

Last week I spent partly at Port Elizabeth in connection with a visit which, as usual, became a racket of functions. You know how you are rushed from one body to another, and everywhere the interminable speeches to listen to, or to make! All so well meant on both sides but all so exhausting, at least to the principal victim. But it is more and more the lot of public men to work harder and harder, and all the time to make speeches, statements, propaganda, messages, congratulations and condolences as the occasion requires. I do not know how a man like Churchill manages it—the long harangues in parliament, the endless cabinet and other meetings, the interviews with important personages, and all the time in between the real, nerve-wracking, hard work. I suppose it is the job that carries and sustains us, and not we the job. It is like moving by the momentum of the job you are doing. The great thing is in all this not to become mechanical, but to keep on top of it all. That I find the hardest, especially when one is really physically exhausted and all the resilience is gone. Poor Churchill must be passing through a very bad time. The tiresome press attacks over Greece and Poland and what not. The coalition machine shakes and groans. The commons call for long orations over delicate international matters. And all the time the work has to be done, in between so to say. I admire his colossal patience, and the *appearance* of enjoying all this. For it can only be appearance. I fear we are ploughing the sands of the sea over Poland. The Poles have no political capacity, even at their best. And now that sufferings have almost demented them they mess up their affairs in a heart-breaking way. Meanwhile they quarrel with their friends and do not notice the Great Bear watching the scene. Britain is being driven into impossible expedients to appease Poland while not quarrelling with Russia, and the future of Europe may once more be loaded with a burden which it cannot bear. But why should you be troubled with these lucubrations. I was really only discussing the burdens on the poor Churchill. At the moment the Greek mess appears the worst of them all. Having spent our blood and treasure over the liberation of Greece and almost lost north Africa over it we are now being attacked by the liberated and are apparently involved in the absurd and indefensible task of evolving some government for Greece which will represent all the contrary elements! The liberated countries are full of private commandos and guerilla forces of resistance which obey no government and are now free to promote their own interests and aims. Unless they are disarmed there will be no peace for Europe after this war. Their governments are poor weak affairs, and the situation of disorder may degenerate into large-scale anarchy. That is the danger before Europe, and it is very widespread. Instead of merely keeping the peace while we are the occupying power we try to put up puppet governments and so interfere in the internal government of these territories, and are accused of behaving like the blessed Unholy Alliance[1] after Waterloo. Meanwhile the U.S.A. and Russia look on and grin at our discomfiture. It is an unpleasant spectacle, and if we are not careful it may degenerate into misunderstandings and fissures. Victory is coming, but it brings with it a most unholy brood of post-war problems and tangles. My fear is that we may, in trying to extricate ourselves from these temporary troubles, rush into far more long-term blunders which might burden the future of Europe. It is all very difficult and dangerous ground over which we are now beginning to move. So Happy New Year to you all! Ever yours,

Jan

654   To L. S. Amery

Vol. 75, no. 189

Pretoria
20 December 1944

My dear Amery, Last mail brought your latest welcome letter,[2] as well as your brilliant article in the *Daily Mail* on Churchill—quite the best thing on him I have recently seen.

My Indian trouble drags along,[3] and I agree with you that in itself it is insoluble, but short-term arrangements are perhaps possible, and I continue at the task which has already taken me most of my public life. I don't despair yet, and am glad to hear that the next high commissioner will be a more helpful person. The present one was more keen on gathering ammunition for his anti-British campaign in his contemplated role as an Indian party politician. But he won't go far.

Meanwhile the Greek boil has burst, and what an unpleasant

---

[1] *See* vol. IV, p. 63, note 2.   [2] **651.**

[3] Smuts had received a deputation from the Natal Indian Congress which asked that the government should refuse assent to the Residential Property Regulation Ordinance (*see supra*, p. 507, note 1). In February 1945 the law advisers of the central government found both ordinances to be *ultra vires* and assent to them was withheld.

bizarre situation!¹ I exchange occasional messages with Churchill which I fear he does not like. But I much fear our foreign office policy in that particular aspect has been faulty. We paid much too much attention to the brigands whom we built up for their nuisance value to the Germans, while they have now directed that value against us. Leeper [R. W. A.] never was big enough for the problem, and nobody else had much time for it. We are now landed in real meddling in rival parties. It is not a defensible or a pleasant position to be in. Fundamentally the Greeks are with us, and that makes the situation all the more ridiculous.

The war is lasting too long. We dispersed our forces after the battle of Normandy, and now can't pinch through anywhere. Air strategy the last six months has lacked the great touch. And so the malaise continues and the secret weapons have time to develop.

What a doleful letter! Let me end with cheerful good wishes to you and dear Mrs Amery and victory in the spring! Ever yours,

J. C. Smuts

655   To G. Heaton Nicholls   Vol. 75, no. 190

Telegram

From: secretary for external affairs, Pretoria

To: high commissioner, London

Dated 20 December 1944

Following from prime minister for high commissioner. Begins: Your 1509 fairly summarizes my attitude in this complicated matter. I don't believe that any party of Greeks is really anti-British, but they have a dog-fight among themselves out of which we should keep at all costs. We have got ourselves embroiled and should extricate ourselves and act simply as the friendly occupying military power, without getting mixed up with local party broils. I am dubious about the regency idea, and more so about Damaskinos, who may prove just another failure.² Greece is essentially friendly, we should also be friendly and tell E.L.A.S. that they must disarm first and we shall then give full opportunity to E.L.A.S. forces, and especially to their officers, to join under our command in the war against

¹ On 3 December internal war began in Greece when an attempt by the Communist E.A.M.–E.L.A.S. to seize power in Athens was opposed by forces of the British military mission.

² At this time the British government was considering a proposal from its representatives in Greece to recognize Archbishop Damaskinos (q.v.) as regent—a suggestion strongly opposed by the king.

Germany. The constitutional issues could be settled later and we shall hold the ring between the groups.

You are quite at liberty to show this to Cranborne, in whose good judgment I have great confidence. Ends.

656   To M. C. Gillett   Vol. 75, no. 215

Pretoria
28 December 1944

As the old year is speeding to its close I wish to send you a line of greeting and good wishes for the New Year. May it bring us good, and best of all, peace. We may say of 1944 what Shelley said of life —'The world is weary of the past, O may it die and rest at last.'[1] After most spectacular victories which led to high hopes for an early end we have been plunged in gloom and a prospect of longer battling and much more suffering. It is easy now to explain all this —after the event, when it is always easy to be wise. But this war is a series of big mistakes by both sides, and I suppose it will be won (and lost to the other side) by mistakes of which the end is not yet. I should guess that the worst mistake of all is the Germans letting the Russians in from the east while they waste all their reserves to keep us back in the west. They may have good reason for this, but to me it just looks a fatal blunder. Nor can one be thankful for it, considering the matter in all its far-off bearings.

What a daring, what a risky thing it was of the prime minister to go to Greece at this juncture! It shows the courage of the man and his anxiety not to spare himself in the dreadful pass to which we have been led in Greece. 'Wounded in the house of our friends' he wires to me.[2] But considering everything I am doubtful about this knight errantry, which might cost us very dear if he were to go ill again or suffer other mishap. He is the one essential man alive at this juncture, and one wonders if we were to lose him. The pattern of world affairs more and more disclosing itself is very disillusioning, almost frightening—not so much for the war as for the peace to follow. I am so afraid we may lose grip, and that the situation may pass out of our control. We are so much on a knife edge as regards the future, and any false step may mean disaster.

Still, 1945 may bring luck. Let us hope and pray, and remember

[1]   The world is weary of the past,
                          Oh, might it die or rest at last!
                                                   Hellas, l. 1100
[2] For this telegram *see* W. S. Churchill, *The Second World War*, vol. VI, p. 270. The quotation is from *Zechariah* xiii.6.

the many past mercies we have been vouchsafed. I feel tired in more ways than one, though I do my best not to look it! The best is to present a fair front to the world; it may mean half the battle, and is in any case good propaganda. But right inside I feel the strain and the discord and the pain of this dear old world. The mood will pass and the sun will shine again.

No reading worth mentioning because there is no time for it. Last night I could not sleep and so read again the last chapters of Fisher's *History of Europe*.[1] They are among the best in the whole book and well worth rereading. His picture of the fading out of liberty and the false new lights of Bolshevism, Fascism and Nazism coming in Europe is most powerful. And now we are once more fighting a great war for 'liberty'. Shall we ever rekindle that great light again? Is anything ever resuscitated from eclipse? It will never be quite the same, and I frankly confess I do not yet discern the lineaments of the new liberty, much as I have spoken about it. It must be something different, something deeper and more complex than the liberty of the nineteenth century. Holism is not a theory of liberty alone but of something more vital and organic, where units are not free but members of one another in the whole. The whole problem requires much more thinking than I have given it. And thinking is not enough. It must be *lived*. The truth must be *lived* to be realized and finally formulated. 'I am the Truth, and the Way, and the Life.'[2] Good-bye dears, ever lovingly yours,

Jan

657 To T. W. Lamont

Vol. 77, no. 129

Pretoria
4 January 1945

Dear Tom, Just a line of warm good wishes to you and Florence for the New Year. May it bring peace and rest for the world from this agony which is now lengthening beyond our worst anticipations.

This is not a letter but only a line of good wishes to show that you are still very much in our minds and our hearts. One finds little time for real letters nowadays, and more than ever friends are remembered in spirit and not on paper. Still it is a great pleasure to see the paper sometimes! I was very glad to get your interesting letter of last October[3] which reached me some six weeks later—such are the

[1] H. A. L. Fisher, *History of Europe* (1936).
[2] 'I am the way, the truth, and the life.' *St John* xiv.6.
[3] Smuts Collection, vol. 74, no. 38.

delays of correspondence nowadays. You spoke of victory perhaps before Christmas: As a matter of fact the letter arrived with the new German offensive against the First Army, and a big dent in our line.[1] No, the end is not yet, and we shall be lucky if we see it by next summer. Hitler's elimination has meant the return of the experienced generals to effective command, and the German war effort has gained greatly in consequence.[2] Then again our announced peace policy must have stiffened German resistance very considerably. I don't think our propaganda has been helpful from this point of view. Meanwhile all sorts of small differences are developing in our post-war programmes which distract our joint effort and encourage the enemy. The liberated countries again show little gratitude to their liberators, and Greece is keeping several British divisions pinned down to keep the peace between the contending factions. Meanwhile the footprints of the Russian giant are being made on the sands of time![3]

You ask about my ideas for the peace so far as Germany is concerned. Little that we could suggest would be of much value when the end comes. The Big Three, to whom France has now to be added, will parcel out Germany between themselves for occupation, and each will carry out his own policy in his own sphere of occupation. Large chunks will be torn off to satisfy those neighbours who have suffered under the Nazis. Germany itself as an entity will scarcely continue to exist. Only the German people will remain, concentrated into a smaller area to stew in their own juice. The Atlantic Charter will go the way of Wilson's Fourteen Points.[4] And a generation hence people will once more be wondering at the peacemakers of 1945–6! The new problem will be far more difficult to solve than that of 1919, because Nazism has been a far more awful scourge than Prussianism. And the statesmanship of 1945–6 will be no better, perhaps worse, than that of 1919. With our experience of 1919 I almost despair of a real statesmanlike peace this time, and sometimes think that a period of cooling off after the war may well be allowed before we attempt the peace in the right spirit. What is against that view is the fact that events are on the march, that the tempo of change is so intense that chaos may well ensue after this war if a stable peace is

---

[1] On 16 December 1944 the Germans had launched a massive attack on the American First Army in the Ardennes region and broken through towards the river Meuse.

[2] The Ardennes counter-offensive had been planned by Hitler against the advice of the generals.

[3]   And, departing, leave behind us
                 Footprints on the sands of time.
                            Henry Wadsworth Longfellow, *A Psalm of Life*.

[4] *See* vol. IV, p. 85, note 1.

not swiftly imposed on all. Even so there may be chaos, as there is now in the Balkans and elsewhere. The fact is that Nazism, Fascism, and Bolshevism are not mere political movements but new religions like Mohammedanism, and that mere political methods of coping with them are quite inadequate. What is *our* new religion to counter these counterfeits of religion? We are drifting on the tides, with no compass except the old liberal humane ideas which have so far guided our human advance. And so for me a big ? mark hangs over the future.

My love to you and Florence in which Isie most warmly joins. Her health has suffered from overwork but still she carries on. I am well and very busy, looking into an obscure world beyond. Ever yours,

J. C. Smuts

658   To M. C. Gillett   Vol. 77, no. 242

Groote Schuur
[Cape Town]
21 January 1945

I have yours of 28 December before me telling of skating on Port Meadow and of hard frost, and of Christmas trees and all the other occasions proper to this season. It warms my heart to see how you carry on in the usual way, with difficulties of servants and assistance and shortages of all sorts. Arthur also carries on as usual, and comes back late at night from London banking. It sounds all very gallant and in the true English tradition of not getting flurried...People carry on, and only the politicians appear to be unduly upset by events. The English press and parliament do not come well out of this attack on the government over Greece and similar matters. The mischief has been not only the strain on the government and much overworked men at the head of affairs, but also the opening given to American journalism to go one better and to magnify fissures between American and British policy. I have expressed my agreement with our Greek policy. From all I hear from the Middle East the policy of E.A.M.–E.L.A.S. constitutes one of the blackest chapters of this war, and the fiendish cruelties of these Communist blackguards on the Athenian population measure up with the worst told of German and Russian cruelties. If our army in Greece had allowed these cruelties to continue we would have deserved the condemnation of all mankind. Now, having done our unpleasant duty and saved Athens, the government are held up as royalist reactionaries. The politicians do not come well out of this, nor the press. Luckily this is now over, but it shows that the great war strain is being felt, and as the war lengthens out the risk of similar incidents increases.

Fortunately Russia appears to be speeding up the end in a way exceeding our best expectations. The new winter offensive has broken the whole German lines and promises to proceed at full blast along the whole vast eastern front. The Germans are letting the Russians overrun Germany from the east while keeping us out on the west. There seems some curious blunder over all this handing over of their country to the Russians rather than the English and Americans who, after all, have still some strain of mercy in them. Can it be that Hitler and Himmler prefer, in case of an Allied victory, to see Germany itself destroyed and made a funeral pyre for the Nazi war lords? It is a terrible thought—this idea of immolating your whole people for *your* spectacular death—but I can see no other rational explanation of this stonewalling against us in the west and running before the Russians in the east. When you receive this the Russians will be very far into Germany, while we may still be struggling against weather and what not before the Rhine. The victory will apparently be a Russian one, and we shall follow in their wake—with no particular credit for the end. Russian strategy is as much superior to ours as is their strength, and perhaps the superior strength allows of a better strategy. This is not as Napoleon viewed these matters. However, this is not a war letter and I apologize for this digression, which began with a tribute to the English national character.

Parliament has opened yesterday and the next three or four months will be spent in the ding-dong of the political struggle. Much to my regret, for all this noise of battle is quite immaterial to the struggle which is convulsing the world and settling our human destiny. Still, it must be endured with such grace as the Lord has given us. On the whole we have been highly favoured and our luck has been great. So why grouse over the irrelevant byplay of parliamentary debates? But it is very tiresome and adds very considerably to the time and trouble which one must devote to these irrelevancies. Much of our time will be taken up with the discussion of food and control troubles, as if we were a starving country, instead of being probably the best fed in the world. However it is probable that an unusual drought will affect our food position very much this year, and no doubt that will be put to the account of our war policy and our having to feed convoys and allies here and elsewhere.

I am glad the Big Three are going to meet.[1] Our policies appear to diverge on a number of points, especially in eastern Europe, and it would speed up the end if the Germans could be convinced that no division among the Allies will stand in the way of our victory. That and the V-bombs[2] seem to be the principal hopes of the Germans. The V-bomb has not been what was expected of it, and Allied policies should also undeceive them of their vain illusions...

Did I tell you that I am writing a foreword to Hutch's new book?[3] I have finished it and forwarded it to him. I have little time for these things, but am continually pressed for forewords which, of course, cannot be refused in all cases. Thus I have also written a foreword to Dr Broom's new book on Sterkfontein and Kromdraai ape-men[4] which opens up a most intriguing chapter in our human prehistory. It appears from his researches that manlike apes, very close to man, were living in the great Pluvials in South Africa—cheek by jowl with *Homo sapiens*, in the neighbourhood of Johannesburg. I have discussed the matter with Abbé Breuil and van Riet Lowe who on the whole agree with Broom's conclusions. My foreword discusses the prehistory aspects while Broom deals with the evolutionary aspects. All this involves labour for which I have no time, and yet one wishes to be helpful to a great researcher who is adding to South African science. Much of this sort of activity goes on all the time, in spite of my other preoccupations...

Think of our human march from those ancient times—a million years ago, if not more—up to today, with all our achievements in science and art and religion! Need we despair of the future, in the mess which troubles our human affairs today? Is there not something Godlike in us, in spite of all the devilries which are clogging our progress, like this war and the other social failures which surround us? Man is a revelation of the Divine. God reveals himself not only in the supreme characters of our race—in the Son and sons of God —but also in the human average, slowly rising beyond and above the sordid animal origins which we have not yet quite outlived. Man shows what Nature is capable of under favourable conditions. The foundations of the Divine are revealed by the footprints of man in prehistory. And so prehistory becomes a witness to the Divine character of this universe as a whole. Ever lovingly,

Jan

[1] A conference had been arranged between Roosevelt, Churchill and Stalin at Yalta in the Crimea.

[2] Apparently the V-2, a rocket bomb. The flying bomb was known as V-1.

[3] *See* **645**.

[4] R. Broom and G. W. H. Scheepers, *The South African Fossil Ape-men; the Australopithecinae* (1946).

659   From L. S. Amery   Vol. 76, no. 9

[London]
27 January 1945

My dear Smuts, I have seen Heaton Nicholls, who is an old friend
and a good fellow. Though no one can quite fill Deneys Reitz's
place I have no doubt that Nicholls will go down quite well here.[1]

He gave me your telegram about the Indian situation which I have
passed on to Wavell telling him that I have no doubt that your advice
is for the best. Naturally Wavell, too, will do what he can to steady
his council. The only trouble is that the legislature is meeting and
that intemperate speeches may be fired off by irresponsible members,
and that even [Dr N. B.] Khare, the member of council in charge,
may find it difficult to speak entirely out of consonance with the
general feeling of the assembly. If so I hope that South African
opinion will discount any undue ebullition of oratory and still enable
you to pursue your policy of gradual amelioration. There is a lot to
be said for what old Sidney Webb used to call 'the inevitability of
gradualness'. Whether it will lead to any ultimate social and racial
structure in South Africa no man can say today and it is no use
laying down definite blue-prints for the future. For all we know
science may one of these days concentrate on such modifications of
the human physical and mental structure as may make many of our
present problems out of date.

When are you going to have time to sit down to write another
book on philosophy? I went to my bookshelf the other day to look
up something in *Holism* but could not find the book. Whether it
has got lost in another shelf in the course of cleaning up the library
or has been lent and not returned I cannot say. From time to time
I accumulate occasional notes on the subject, fondly dreaming that
I, too, may some time or other have the leisure to put my own ideas
on paper, but the years pass and that may never be. Yours ever,

Leo Amery

660   From L. S. Amery   Vol. 76, no. 10

[London]
9 February 1945

My dear Smuts, Things are moving with a vengeance and I feel that
we are getting into pretty deep waters. If Clemenceau and Lloyd
George went pretty wild on the subject of reparations, they were

---

[1] G. Heaton Nicholls (q.v.) succeeded D. Reitz (q.v. vol. IV) as high commissioner.

moderation itself compared with what the Russians and the Americans look like forcing upon us, not only the drastic territorial reduction of Germany (which I would approve) but the wholesale looting of all her industrial plant, the carrying off of several millions of her able-bodied population into slavery in Russia and on top of that a long period of reparations payments entirely beyond the capacity even of an intact and unweakened Germany in 1939. The only outcome of it all would be the complete destruction of German economy to be followed by its reorganization on Communist lines under Russian auspices, in other words Russia on the Rhine. Meanwhile, by the time that becomes evident we here shall have swung round into a mood of pity for the Germans and of terror of the Russian menace.

As for Dumbarton Oaks, here again it seems to me—though you may differ—that we are repeating the mistake made when we tried to give to the League as such coercive powers. The moment you do that you raise the whole question of who is on the council, how many votes decide and all the rest of it, which in the end paralyses the whole organization and makes it a dangerous farce. To my mind one ought clearly to separate any world organization from the actual functions of diplomacy and the use of force. The object of a world organization is to create a world moral atmosphere and on occasion to help smooth out differences by conciliation. If the moral judgment of such a body condemns an act of aggression then the powers who are directly interested, or feel sufficiently strongly about it, can get together and act without waiting for others who may then very probably follow suit. If the thing is to depend on a formal vote there will always be enough members to delay or paralyse action and nothing will happen except the gradual creation of an anti-league bloc of aggressors.

Anyhow, it is the height of wishful delusion to imagine that a system of world peace can be based on Russian participation.

Forgive this outburst of pessimism. I daresay one way or another things may end up all right. But it looks to me as if there will be more and not fewer wars after you and I have joined our fathers. Yours ever,

Leo Amery

661 To A. B. Gillett   **Vol. 77, no. 249**

Groote Schuur
[Cape Town]
4 March 1945

Your last letter (17 February) has just reached me, most welcome and interesting...

I can understand Jan's [Gillett] upset over 'unconditional surrender',[1] and it is a mistake the term was ever used. It was quite unnecessary. It meant only that there was not going to be haggling over terms, but has now come to mean the severity of what our action will be. Yalta has defined its real meaning—destruction of Nazism, punishment of the chief criminals, prevention of future German rearmament by supervision of relevant industry, and labour reparation. Of course it may be applied in a way which will cripple Germany, economic and industrial, drastically. But that would be so ruinous for European recovery as a whole, that I doubt whether the great powers will be so unwise. Still, one cannot be certain, and I myself feel deeply concerned over the future of Europe. It is not only the fate of Germany which is involved, but that of all Europe, including Britain herself. Ourselves already exhausted, France suffering from inferiority and other obsessions, Europe broken as never before, Russia with a dangerous predominance—you have a situation there which one cannot contemplate without foreboding. May wisdom and moderation in victory prevail and save what can still be saved.

...I write no more. Within a month I shall probably be once more in London[2] and we can then compare notes in a better way than on paper.

The war goes extremely well, and the Germans are at last really cracking. Summer must see the end in Europe. Even the Japs seem to have used up their best men and armaments.

Here all well. Isie rejoices to think she is moving back soon to Doornkloof. My own tasks continue very heavy. Love from,

Jan

---

[1] The term was first used on 24 January 1943 by Roosevelt in a press interview immediately after the Casablanca conference. He said 'the elimination of German, Japanese and Italian war power means the unconditional surrender by Germany, Italy and Japan'. *See* Louis L. Snyder, *The World in the Twentieth Century* (1964), pp. 176–7.

[2] To attend the prime ministers' conference.

662   To M. C. Gillett   Vol. 77, no. 248

Groote Schuur
[Cape Town]
4 March 1945

I have just written a line to Arthur and now wind up with another
to you before we go out to the sea on this beautiful Sunday morning
...The sound of laughter and bright talk is heard all over the house
and there is gladness in the air. Yesterday afternoon Japie [Smuts]
and I took another long contour path[1] walk with our Gestapo.[2] And at
night I showed a film which the governor and party next door also
attended. So on the surface all goes well. But of course that is not
the whole story. We have just had a dreadful accident at Pretoria
where a munition magazine blew up with fearful losses of life and
material. At Durban a ship-repair strike is on which cripples our
war effort for the Far East. The food shortage continues to create
great political and social unrest. Parliament is more than usually
tiresome. Still the world revolves round her axis and the sun and
moves with the solar march towards some point in the constellation
Hercules! We must view our lot in its larger setting and not be unduly concerned over our immediate surroundings. And as Browning
says: God is in His Heaven, even if for the moment hell is on earth.[3]
But the end is nearing, and we hope and pray that it may also be the
end of our miseries, and not merely the beginning of new and larger
ones. I cannot say that I feel happy over the prospect. Roosevelt
wishes to remove our fears,[4] but I continue to fear for the future.

As I have written Arthur I shall probably be in London in about
a month so that I need not say too much on paper. From London
I shall move on to San Francisco.[5] I do not know where the ridiculous rumour has originated that I shall be president of the conference.
It is, of course, preposterous. Russia does not like me, France dis-
trusts me, even in British circles there is divided opinion, and South
Africa is too small fry for such exaltation. Indeed, it is only a sense of

---

[1] This runs along the southern slopes of Table mountain at a height of 1,000 to
1,400 feet.

[2] Smuts's police guards.

[3]
>   God's in his heaven—
>   All's right with the world!
>
>   *Pippa Passes*, part I.

[4] In his inaugural address on 20 January when Roosevelt entered on his fourth
presidential term he said, 'We can gain no lasting peace if we approach it with suspicion
and mistrust—or with fear.'

[5] The San Francisco conference met from 25 April to 26 June. It drafted the Charter
of the United Nations and the Statute of the International Court of Justice on the
basis of the decisions made at the Dumbarton Oaks and Yalta conferences.

duty that takes me to San Francisco at all, at a time when I am badly wanted in South Africa. But I feel I should be there, in case I could be needed as one of those who remember 1919. Issues may be raised where I could speak with some effect because of my past experience. Churchill has wired me to express his pleasure that I can and will go there. But it may be that when the conference comes, the play will already have been fully written and only the theatrical performance will take place; and in that I shall take little interest, and that probably with a sad heart. Without being a pessimist I must confess that I feel deeply concerned over the future. This has been a terrible war, and taken with the last, and what has happened in between the wars, it is only too evident that Europe, if not the world of man, is at its crisis of fate. Much as I think of the good in us, I have no confidence that we shall be wiser than in 1919. And bad mistakes now will be so much more ruinous than they were twenty-five years ago, when so much was still undestroyed. Now the crisis is graver, and the temper to deal with it worse; and so we face our problem with a double handicap. But mankind has survived so many misfortunes and repaired so many mistakes in such unforeseen ways that one should not be unduly depressed over what faces us. The trouble with me is partly that I cannot hate. Hatred simplifies the difficulty so much. You close your heart and your eyes to half the problem, and the solution is apparently so much simplified thereby. But when you can't hate, and you feel the poignancy of the situation as affecting not only yourself but also your enemy, the situation becomes exceedingly complicated and the way out all the more difficult to find. I don't hate Germans, and I feel deeply for Europe of which Germany remains an integral, if not a dominant part. I know how dangerous the predominance of any one power can be, and how liable such dominant power is to abuse. I remember British jingoism and the Boer War; and I know Russia has even less experience and human wisdom than the British. And so my faith in man does not extend to faith in Russia, with no check on her in Europe and Asia, and mistress of the continent of Europe. Such a position is too much of a temptation even to the wisest, let alone to an upstart power such as Russia. Our position in the world is therefore a very dangerous one, and one which permits of no mere optimism and exultation in victory...

Thank you for your last letters. They are a greater comfort to me than you know. You have that something of the spirit in you which appeals to the better in me, and so I derive strength and comfort from that dear voice which has been with me these last forty years. God bless you and yours.

All well and happy here, though all feel the strain of these days. Ever yours,

Jan

663   To Lord Wavell   Vol. 77, no. 147

Prime Minister's Office
Cape Town
6 March 1945

My dear Wavell, It was a pleasure to receive your note introducing your new high commissioner,[1] with the useful information about his background. I am favourably impressed by him at first sight.

I wish you to know that I personally do not take too pessimistic a view of our local Indian situation. It is difficult, and has been made more so by the retaliatory action in India[2] and the intemperate speeches in the Indian assembly. But even so I think that patient resolute action to mark progress step by step, will win through in the end. I hope that [we] shall keep personally in touch so that the last word may always be said as between friends.

My wife is well but much overworked, and the years roll on. Under doctor's orders she has had to curtail her excessive activities.

I received your *Other Men's Verse* with great pleasure and dip into it now and then with much interest. It is off the beaten track of anthologies and has many attractive features.

The war goes very well and is not far off the end in Europe. But what a hopeless mess it will leave behind in that continent! It may take generations before Europe recovers from this blow. With kind regards to you and Lady Wavell, Ever yours sincerely,

J. C. Smuts

664   To J. D. Smuts   Vol. 77, no. 158

Fairmont Hotel
San Francisco
24 April 1945

Liewe Japie, Ek was aangenaam verras 'n paar dae gelede 'n welkomme brief van jou te ontvang. Dit het maar twee weke geneem

---

[1] M. R. Deshmukh (q.v.).

[2] The Indian legislature had passed the Reciprocity Act which sought to impose similar disabilities on South Africans in India as were imposed on Indians in the Union. Its provisions came into force in November 1944.

my hier te bereik. Dankie daarvoor en vir al die goeie nuus en dinge daarin vervat.

Ek vrees die verlies van Roosevelt is 'n soort van nekslag vir ons en viral vir hierdie konferensie. Hy had sy hart in die sukses van die konferensie die belangrykheid waarvan hy duidelik gesien het. Nou is die konferensie niemand se baby, en ek vrees ons sal 'n baie moeilike en selfs gevaarlik toggie hier hê. Ek sal natuurlik doen wat ek kan, maar die stem van Suid-Afrika sal hier maar 'n gepiep onder die groot voëls wees.

Jannie en ek had 'n besige tyd in Londen soos gewoonlik, en 'n baie lange koue vlug oor die Atlantiese see—22 uur in die lug uit die 24 uur. In Newfoundland was die thermometer 11 grade onder o! In New York was ons baie aangenaam onthaal deur die Lamonts, waar Jannie goed kans had om N.Y. te sien. Toe weer voort by die mere en Chicago en die Middle West en die sneeu kruine van die Rockies tot hier. California is 'n juweel van 'n land en San Francisco 'n juweel in 'n juweel.

Ons werk begin morre, en ek voel ver van gerus oor die loop van sake. Die oorlog in Europa snel ten einde. Berlin is aan val en 'n wêreld sal daarmee val. Jul het 'n pragtige sukses in Italië gehad, en ek is bly dat die Springbokke so 'n pragtige bydrae tot die oorwinning gemaak het. Ek was baie bly om van Frank Theron te hoor dat Mark Clark en Truscott hoogst tevrede was met die prestage van die Afrikaners.

Ek het nog niks van Suid-Afrika gehoor nie, maar as daar iets biesonders is sal Hofmeyr my telegrafeer. Ek neem dus aan dat alles goed gaat. Ek hoop ook dat daar nou vrede en liefde op Doornkloof heers! Ek skryf aan Mamma om Cloete te sê dat hy die opmetings van Doornkloof en Rooikop moet bespoed. Cato haar volmag is van Londen aangestuur, en ek wil die transporte so gou moontlik na my terugkeer deursit. Hartelike groete en beste wense van

Pappa

TRANSLATION

Fairmont Hotel
San Francisco
24 April 1945

Dear Japie, I was pleasantly surprised a few days ago to receive a welcome letter from you. It took only two weeks to reach me here. Thank you for it and for all the good news and good things in it.

I fear the loss of Roosevelt is a sort of death-blow for us and especially for this conference. His heart was in the success of the conference the importance of which he saw clearly. Now the conference is nobody's baby and I fear we shall have a very difficult and even dangerous little run here. I shall, of course, do what I can, but the voice of South Africa will be a mere cheeping among the big birds.

Jannie[1] and I had a busy time in London, as usual, and a very long, cold flight over the Atlantic seas—twenty-two hours out of twenty-four in the air. In Newfoundland the thermometer was eleven degrees below zero! In New York we were very pleasantly entertained by the Lamonts and Jannie had a good opportunity of seeing New York. Then on again here by way of the lakes and Chicago and the Middle West and the snowy peaks of the Rockies. California is a jewel of a country and San Francisco a jewel within a jewel.

Our work begins tomorrow and I feel far from easy about the way things are going. The war in Europe is speeding to its end. Berlin is falling and a world will fall with it. You had a fine success in Italy and I am glad that the Springboks made such an excellent contribution to the victory. I was glad to hear from Frank Theron that Mark Clark and [General L. K.] Truscott were highly satisfied with the achievements of the Afrikanders.

I have as yet heard nothing from South Africa but if there is anything special Hofmeyr will telegraph me. So I assume that all goes well. I hope that love and peace will now reign at Doornkloof! I am writing to Mamma to tell Cloete[2] that he must expedite the surveys at Doornkloof and Rooikop. Cato's [Clark] power of attorney has been sent on from London and I want to put through the transfer as soon as possible after my return.[3] Hearty greetings and best wishes from

Pappa

665   To S. M. Smuts

Vol. 77, no. 160

Fairmont Hotel
San Francisco
5 May 1945

Liefste Mamma, Dit was my so'n vreugde om 'n paar dae gelede twee briewe van jou te ontvang, so vol nuus, en goeie nuus ook. Sylma skrywe ook dat alles goed gaan en dat jy daar goed en gerus uitsien. Dit is my innige verlange dat jou gesondheid goed sal bly en

---

[1] Captain J. C. Smuts accompanied his father as aide-de-camp.
[2] Dick Cloete, an attorney in Pretoria.
[3] Smuts at this time divided his farms among his children.

dat ons nog baie jare saam mag geniet. Ek kyk so uit na die tyd wanneer ek verlos sal wees van die politieke stryd en verknorsing, en in rus en stilte die aand van die lewe sal kan deurbreng. Jy weet ons het nog geen rus gehad van die dae toe ek Staatsprokureur geword het en ongekende laste op my geneem het. Dit is 47 jaar gelede. En nog duur dit voort. Maar nou dat die kinders al ons aardse besittings het kan ons terug gaan na die goeie oue dae, toe ons sonder sorg en kommer ons eie weg deur die wereld kon kies.

Ek was bly uit Sylma se brief te verneem dat die opmeting van Doornkloof nou plaas vind, en daarna Rooikop aan die beurt sal kom. Ek wil al daardie dinge nou in orde breng sodra ek thuis is. Ja, dit was 'n geval van 'touch and go' die nag met ons York in die blits. Maar gelukkig is alles goed afgeloop; mag dit so voortduur tot die einde.

Hier gaan dit maar straf, soos gewoonlik met my. Ek is President van die moeilikste en hardste kommissie—die oor die 'General Assembly' en vir die volgende 2 of 3 weke sal dit maar straf gaan. Maar ons sal in 'n maand klaar wees, en dan huis toe, oor Engeland en Italië waar ek ons seuns wil gaan besoek en dank vir die skitterende goeie werk wat hul verrig het. Van Alexander en ander bevelvoerders het ek boodskappe van gelukwense ontvang oor die magnifieke prestatie van die Springbokke. En ek moet hul daarvoor persoonlik bedank so gou moontlik. Dit sal nie baie tyd neem voor hul almal terug thuis is, en ek moet hul voor die tyd in Italië en Egypte gaan ontmoet. Hul sal die lang verblyf en oponthoud in die noorde baie vervelig vind, maar die transport kwestie is nou ons grootste moeilikheid. Ek wil ook graag vir Cato en die kleintjies in Engeland gaan sien met my deurreis. Dan sal Churchill ook baie graag my oor sake wil sien. Ons het 'n verbasende verpletterende oorwinning behaal. Maar ek verwag baie groot moeilikhede met ons Russiese vriende. Ek vrees Rusland gaan die groot oorwinning exploiteer vir eie doeleindes en 'n hel van Europa maak as ons dit nie verhinder nie. En hoe gaan ons dit verhinder? Hul is nou in 'n posiesie van baasskap oor Europa wat ek voorspel het in my "Ontplofbare Toespraak" 2 jaar gelede.

Ek was so bly dat met my aankoms in Engeland ek stappe op tou kon set wat Holland van hongersnood en hongerdood gered het. Ek had spesiale informasie waarop ek die Kabinet kon beweeg om dringende stappe te neem, en dit is toe deurgegaan. En nou is die ou nasie gered, en die vyand is daarheen.

Ek denk [ek] het al geskrywe van die heerlike dag en nag wat ons te New York kon deurbreng. Die liewe Lamonts was werklik te lief en die vloere was te koud vir ons. Hier is ons nog onder goeie

Amerikaanse en Engelse vriende. Jannie, wat baie gelukkig hier is en uitstekende goeie werk doen, sal seker alles aan Daphne skrywe van wie jy alles sal verneem. Ek is bly dat sy vir 'n maand by jou sal bly terwyl Sylma aan boer is. Nou soentjies aan almal en liefde van

Pappa

TRANSLATION

Fairmont Hotel
San Francisco
5 May 1945

Dearest Mamma, It was such a joy to me a few days ago to receive two letters from you, so full of news—and good news too. Sylma [Coaton] also writes that all goes well and that you look well and rested. It is my ardent desire that your health will remain good and that we may yet enjoy many years together. I so much look forward to the time when I shall be released from the plight and the struggle of politics and be able to spend the evening of life in rest and quiet. You know, we have had no rest since the days when I became state attorney and took upon myself unparalleled burdens. That was forty-seven years ago. And it still goes on. But now that the children have all our earthly possessions, we can go back to the good old days when we could take our own way through the world without care and anxiety.

I was glad to know from Sylma's letter that the surveying of Doornkloof is now taking place and that Rooikop will follow. I want to put all those things in order as soon as I am home.[1] Yes, it was a case of touch and go that night with our York in the lightning. But fortunately all went off well; may it so continue to the end.

The work here is heavy, as usual with me. I am president of the most difficult, most intractable commission—that on the general assembly, and for the next two or three weeks the going will be hard. But we shall be done within a month and then—home, via England and Italy where I want to visit our boys and thank them for the brilliant work they have done. I have had messages of congratulation from Alexander and other commanders on the magnificent achievements of the Springboks and I must thank them for this personally as soon as possible. It will not be long before they are all back home and I must go and meet them in Italy and Egypt before then. They will find the long stay and delay in the north very boring, but the transport problem is now our greatest difficulty. I should also like to go and see Cato [Clark] and the children in England when I pass

[1] *See supra*, p. 530, note 3.

through. And Churchill will want to see me about various matters. We have gained an amazing and shattering victory. But I expect great difficulties with our Russian friends. I fear Russia will exploit the victory for her own ends and make a hell of Europe unless we prevent it. And how shall we prevent it? They are now in that position of mastery over Europe which I predicted in my 'explosive speech'[1] two years ago.

I was so glad that I could, on arrival in England, set steps in train that saved the Netherlands from famine and death by famine. I had special information upon which I could persuade the cabinet to take urgent steps and it went through. And now that old nation is saved and the enemy has gone.

I think I have already written about the delightful day and night that we could spend in New York. The dear Lamonts were really too kind and nothing was too good for us. Here we are still among good American and English friends. Jannie [Smuts], who is very happy here and doing exceptionally good work, will probably write fully to Daphne from whom you will hear all. I am glad she will stay with you for a month while Sylma is farming. Now, kisses to all and love from

Pappa

666   To J. H. Hofmeyr   Vol. 77, no. 161

Fairmont Hotel
San Francisco
6 May 1945

Dear Jantjie, Just a few lines to tell you how we are getting on. We have taken a good while to get under way, but now the conference is speeding up and I have good hopes that another month may see the end. I am pressed very strongly to visit Canada on the way back, and think it good policy to do so. I shall thereafter be delayed for a week in London to fix up necessary business, and of course I shall have to visit our units in Italy and Egypt in order to thank them and to explain unavoidable delays in their return home and generally to try to keep up their morale in the weary waiting period. I may therefore not be back before the latter half of June—perhaps the end of June. I shall be very glad to be back, I assure you.

I have continually urged the speeding up of the conference work, as I fear events in Europe may soon distract much more the public attention and put the conference in the shade. Foreign ministers and other high authorities may have to hurry home to deal with the

[1] **624.**

bigger problems which the end of the war must bring. This is already happening. The Russian situation is ominous and I am glad the end of the war in Europe has come before serious rifts in the lute have developed. The Polish business is very bad and unfortunately Britain has become more deeply involved in it than I consider wise. Now the coming elections and political situation in Britain further complicates the problem of our Russian relations. Everywhere I find people in an anxious mood over the doings of the Great Bear. There is no doubt that Russia now occupies a position in the world which will give us all more thought and more headaches.

As regards the conference I find not only power politics well to the fore, but also a strong humanitarian tendency, finding expression in provisions for equal rights all round and other somewhat embarrassing proposals so far as we concerned. Trusteeships have become a bone of contention, and mandates are involved in this bigger issue. The idea about mandates is to continue the system under a new form of administration and to extend its scope to dependent peoples generally. The Americans are meanwhile insuring themselves by virtually excluding bases and similar titbits in the Pacific from the scope of these provisions on the grounds of security. Distributions of mandates, bases and similar territories will only take place at a later conference, and I am formally reserving our rights, including incorporation, as far as South West Africa is concerned. The conference has to be carefully and even anxiously watched, and I am doing my best in that respect.

You must have a good deal of trouble carrying your parliamentary and other heavy burdens. But as far as I can see, things are going on normally well, although much too slowly. I hope it will be possible to put through the important essential work and not delay too much over less important matters. With affectionate greeting to you and my other colleagues, Ever yours,

J. C. Smuts

667   To M. C. Gillett   **Vol. 77, no. 251**

Fairmont Hotel
San Francisco
8 May 1945

Your letter or rather letters duly arrived today and were very welcome. It did me good to read of you all happily at Aston...

That nice Quaker letter of which you send a copy[1] I quite

---

[1] A letter to Smuts from a member of the Society of Friends in South Africa.

remember receiving in South Africa and thanking the good writers. I was deeply moved by its wording which conveyed such a depth of sympathy and understanding.

Now about San Francisco. This is now in a third week here. The work is very slow, and the talking very copious. To me it is all a great trial, but I shall try to be patient. We have really done very little to the actual job in hand. I am doing my best to speed up the work for I fear the course of events in Europe is outstripping us here, and many of the most important delegates will have to return home and leave this conference a derelict rump of the smaller fry. People will not understand that they live and work amid tremendous events which may soon call many of us away, myself included. But I daresay to many it is a real holiday at their country's expense and in a pleasant beautiful place. It is a beautiful place in a most noble setting. Macchia hills all round, and some of them fairly high. I was on Sunday afternoon on the highest—2,600 ft. high Tamalpais, at the very moment (unbeknown to me) when the unconditional surrender was being signed at Rheims. I have seen the tall Red Woods nearby (*Sequoia sempervirens*) but on Sunday I hope to visit the Yosemite valley and there see the huge sequoias of enormous girth. It will mean a motor trip from here taking the whole day to and fro. It is cool weather here, mostly misty, but good to work in. I am president of the commission on the general assembly but do not feel overworked and can lend a helping hand in difficulties that turn up in other commissions. The Molotov troubles have been amusing to watch. He was determined to get the Lublin Polish government recognized before the story of the arrest of those Polish delegates to Moscow became known. But here events proved too fast for him, and the disclosure of the miserable facts has now put an end for the present to his efforts.[1] I am sorry we have got so deeply drawn into this Polish business. But really, the Russians are most difficult and appear determined to make obedient satellites of all their neighbours in spite of their protestations and undertakings at Yalta. How are you going to work the new plan with such partners?...

[1] One aspect of the Polish 'question' at this time was the rivalry between the Lublin ('Warsaw') government, sponsored by the Russians when they occupied Poland, and the Polish government in exile, with headquarters in London, which was protected by the Western powers. In March 1945 fifteen delegates of the Polish underground, representative of various political groups, went under Soviet safe-conduct to Moscow to discuss the formation of a united Polish government. They did not return. On 6 April the Polish government in London issued a statement on their disappearance. On 4 May Molotov, the Soviet foreign minister, admitted at the San Francisco conference that the men were being held in Russia. Next day Russian sources announced that they were to be tried on charges of 'diversionary tactics in the rear of the Red Army'.

668   To J. H. Hofmeyr   Vol. 77, no. 165

Telegram

From: South African delegation, San Francisco
To: secretary for external affairs, Cape Town
Dated 17 May 1945
For Mr Hofmeyr from General Smuts:

I have just read with deep emotion your beautiful victory broadcast to the nation last week. I congratulate you on a message which must have been as moving to our people as it has been to myself. It is all true and I trust its hopes and prayers will also come true. Thank you for it.

Note. Give this to press.

669   To S. M. Smuts   Vol. 77, no. 166

Fairmont Hotel
San Francisco
21 May 1945

Liefste Mamma, Wat 'n dag het ons gister gehad—Sondag! Seker een van die dae van my lewe wat ons nooit sal vergeet nie. Jannie sal jul seker alles volledig skrywe oor ons rit na Yosemite Canyon en die groot Sequoia boome, grootste en oudste van die wereld. Ons is hier 6 uur v.m. weg en 9 p.m. terug, en het 513 myl die dag afgery —oor die pragtige vrugbare California vlakte na die Rockies 8,000 tot 9,000 voet hoog met sneeuw bedekte kruine en hellings en watervalle in alle rigtings, een waarvan 1,400 voet hoog was. Dit was 'n heerlike warme sonnige dag en Jannie kon die Ciné met groot effek gebruik. As die prent 'n sukses is sal jul kan sien iets van die wonderlike natuurskou soos ek nog nooit in die wereld gesien het nie. Die grootste boom was 96 voet rond, maar had ook 'n skyn van gryse ouderdom wat werklik oorstelpend was—duisende jare in die verre verlede—voor Kristus en terug in die kindsheid van die geskiedenis. California is ryk, met vet grond, landerye en gras of koring of vrugteboorde of wingerde—soos ons nog nooit gesien het nie. Maar byna geen voëls, geen kerke in die dorpe, en geen mooi woonhuise op die plase soos ons in Suid-Afrika het. Almal een-voudige wonings van hout—shacks, soos ons hul sou noem. Die pragtige skoon van wonings op die ou plase soos aan die Kaap sien mens nêrens. Baker had my dit jare gelede vertel. Maar nou kon ek dit self sien. En dit in die rykste, vrugbaarse omgewing moontlik. Alles vir geld en geld maak en niks vir die oog en die siel. Maar California is baie jonger as die Kaap en is eers in en na 1850 ontwikkel en bewoon.

Ons werk vorder maar baie langsaam. Ek meen ons sal hier nog minstens twee weke wees. Ek het ook 'n uit noodiging van Pres. Truman na Washington as gas van die staat—dit beteken 1 of 2 dae daar, met dinners en 'n groot speech seker. Dan na Ottawa vir 'n dergelike programma. Dus nog drie weke in Amerika. En dan Londen, Italië, Egypte om ons seuns daar te ontmoet. Die twede helfte of selfs die einde van Juni bly dus nog my programma, en jy moet my nie voor einde van Juni verwag nie. Ek werk my nie dood nie en my gesondheid bly nog baie goed. Maar die lang programma voor maak my 'n beetje bang.

Saterdag namiddag is 'n plaque vir Roosevelt in die Muir Woods alhier onthul deur Stettinius, en ek was die voornaamste spreker daar. Baie het my daarna gelukgewens en gesê dit is die mooiste rede wat hul ooit gehoor het. Daarna, dieselfde aand had ek 'n kort uitsaai wat seker ook na julle Sondagaand gegaan het. Ek wonder of jul my goed kon hoor. Dit is so ver.

Van Japie had ek 'n interessante brief oor sy werk en toestande in Italië na die oorgawe. Ons Divisie het hom uitstekend gedra en baie lof in alle rigtings verdien.

Met ons gaan dit hier goed en ons het oor niks te kla behalwe die lange duur van die Konferensie. Die klimaat is goed en ons ondervind baie vriendskap in alle rigtings. Jannie is 'n groot sukses. Ek moet sê die res van my Delegasie is 'n flukse eersteklas geselskap waarop ek trots voel. Baie liefde en beste wense.

Pappa

TRANSLATION

Fairmont Hotel
San Francisco
21 May 1945

Dearest Mamma, What a day we had yesterday—Sunday! Certainly one of the days of my life that we shall never forget. Jannie [Smuts] will probably write to you fully about our drive to Yosemite Canyon and the big Sequoia trees, the biggest and oldest in the world. We left here at 6 a.m. and were back at 9 p.m. and covered 513 miles —over the lovely, fertile California plains to the Rockies, 8,000 to 9,000 feet high, with snow-capped peaks, and slopes and waterfalls in all directions, one of which was 1,400 feet high. It was a delightful warm sunny day and Jannie could use the ciné with great effect. If the film is a success you will be able to see something of this wonderful natural spectacle the like of which I have never yet seen in the world. The biggest tree was ninety-six feet round, but it also had an appearance of grey age which was really overwhelming—thousands of years in the far distant past, before Christ, and back in the infancy of history. California is rich, with fat soil, tilled fields and grass, or wheat, or orchards, or vineyards—such as we have never seen before. But almost no birds, no churches in the small towns, and no fine houses on the farms such as we have in South Africa. All simple dwellings—shacks, as we would call them. Nowhere does one see houses like those on the old farms at the Cape. [Sir Herbert] Baker told me that years ago. But now I could see it myself. And that in the richest, most fertile environment possible. All for money and money making and nothing for the eye and the soul. But California is much younger than the Cape and was first developed and inhabited in and after 1850.

Our work goes slowly forward. I think we shall be here at least two weeks more. I also have an invitation from President Truman to go to Washington as a guest of the state—that means one or two days there, with dinners and probably a big speech. Then to Ottawa for a similar programme. So three more weeks in America. And then to London, Italy, Egypt to meet our boys there. So the second half, or even the end of June remains my programme and you must not expect me before the end of June. I am not working myself to death and my health is still very good. But the long programme before me frightens me a little.

On Saturday afternoon a plaque for Roosevelt was unveiled here in Muir woods by Stettinius [E. R.] and I was the chief speaker. Many people congratulated me afterwards and said it was the finest address they had ever heard. Then I made a short broadcast that evening which probably went out to you as well on Sunday night. I wonder if you could hear me well. It is so far.

I had an interesting letter from Japie [Smuts] about his work and conditions in Italy after the surrender. Our division did exceptionally well and earned much praise in all quarters.

All goes well with us here and we have nothing to complain of except that the conference is lasting so long. The climate is good and we are befriended everywhere. Jannie [Smuts] is a great success. I must say the rest of my delegation is an able, first-class company of whom I feel proud. Much love and best wishes.

Pappa

670   To S. M. Smuts   Vol. 77, no. 171

Fairmont Hotel
San Francisco
4 Junie 1945

Liefste Mamma, Altyd as ek daardie datum sien of skrywe dan denk
ek terug na die treurige skeiding te Pretoria in 1900, 'n skeiding wat
vir 2 jaar geduur het en waarin so veel gebeur is wat ons lot en die
van ons land en volk diep geaffekteer het. In daardie twee jaar van
smart en verlies is tog die fondament gelê van al die groot werk en
vooruitgang wat in die geslag daarna gevolg het. En dit is 'n aan-
moediging om nooit moeg of neerslagtig te word nie wanneer moeilikhede byna oorstelpend is nie. Die pad van plig en gewete bly maar
die regte pad na die toekoms hoe donker dit ook mag lyk.

Ons werk hier talm baie en die vooruitgang van dag tot dag bly
klein. Maar 'n einde moet tog kom of gemaak word, en ons Groot
Base het nou die 15 Juni gestel as die eind datum van ons werksaamhede. Dus nog 10 dae van sukkel en sweet. Ons grootste moeilikheid nou is met die Russe, wat voorstelle oor die stemming van die
Groot Moondhede (die Veto) maak waarmee die res van ons nie
kan saamstem nie. Dit is dus nog moontlik dat ons nie sal ooreenkom
nie en dat die konferensie halfverrigter sake na huis sal terugkeer. Die
werk oor ander punte sal egter klaar gemaak word. Dit sal 'n skok vir
die wêreld wees, maar die Russiese houding is so onredelik en gevaarlik
dat dit die nuwe organisasie maklik 'n fiasco sou kan maak. Die plan
is dan van hier na Washington waar Truman my uitgenooi het; van
daar op uitnoodiging van Mackenzie King na Ottawa; en dan na
Londen waar Japie my sal ontmoet om my programma in Italië aan
my mee te deel. Met die alles sal dit nie moontlik wees om voor
einde van die eerste week in Juli thuis te wees nie. Jy sien die
afwesigheid word steeds langer, tot my spyt, maar omstandighede
laat my geen keuse. Ek wil baie graag ons troepe in Italië en Egypte
vaarwel sê en bedank vir al hul groot dienste. As hul nou eenmaal in
S.A. terug is versprei hul oor die heele land en sal dit nie moontlik
wees nie om hul persoonlik te ontmoet nie.

Vandag gaan dit persoonlik met ons baie goed. Jannie en ek en
andere lede van ons afvaardiging neem so veel oefening as ons werk
toelaat. Nog Saterdag was ons weer $2\frac{1}{2}$ uur in Muir Woods onder die
reuse boome waar mens vir ure kan rondwandel en berg klim. En
gister (Sondag) was ons vir lunch by die Meins (40 myl van hier)
waar ons 'n mooi Baker huis gesien het in die pragtigste omgewing.
Ek het jou al geskrywe dat Mrs Mein die suster is van Alpheus
Williams. Sy is 'n liewe aktiewe mens, baie nog aan S. Afrika geheg,

waar sy in Kimberley groot geword het. Die plek is vol Suid Afrikaanse plante en gedenkwaardighede. Die heele familie van kinders en kleinkinders was daar—'n aangename geselskap. Toe in die namiddag weer terug na 2 vergaderings en so na bed. Vandag weer etlike vergaderings en dan teen die aand 'n Cocktail vir die vernaamstes onder die Delegasies. Dis die gewoonte van sosial funksies alhier en die goedkoopste. Ons gesondheid bly goed en die klimaat hier is koel en heerlik vir werk. Min sonneskyn, gewoonlik mistige weer, maar aangenaam. Jou liewe briewe kom van tyd tot tyd en is baie welkom. Na ontvangs hiervan moet jy nie meer skrywe nie! Liefde en soentjies.

Pappa

TRANSLATION

Fairmont Hotel
San Francisco
4 June 1945

Dearest Mamma, Always when I see or write this date I think back to the sad parting at Pretoria in 1900—a separation that lasted two years in which so much happened that affected the fate of our country and people. Yet, in those two years of pain and loss the foundation was laid of all the great work and progress which followed in the next generation. It is an encouragement never to become weary or depressed when difficulties are almost overwhelming. The path of duty and conscience remains the right road to the future, however dark it may look.

Our work here is much delayed and progress from day to day is still small. But surely an end must come, or be made, and our Big Bosses have now set 15 June as the end date of our labours. So another ten days of struggle and sweat. Our greatest difficulty now is with the Russians who are making proposals about the voting of the great powers (the veto) to which the rest of us cannot agree. So it is still possible that we shall not come to terms and that the conference will return home with its job half done. The work on other points will, however, be finished. It will be a shock for the world but the Russian attitude is so unreasonable and dangerous that it could easily make a fiasco of the new organization.[1]

---

[1] At the Yalta conference of February 1945 it had been agreed that decisions of the Security Council of the future World Organization on matters of procedure should require an affirmative vote of seven of the eleven members, while decisions on other matters should be made by the affirmative vote of seven members *including the concurring votes of the permanent members* (the United States, Russia, Great Britain, France, China). At San Francisco an attempt was made by some of the lesser powers to exclude

My intention is to go from here to Washington to which Truman has invited me; from there, by invitation of Mackenzie King, to Ottawa; and then to London where Japie [Smuts] will meet me to give me my programme in Italy. With all this it will not be possible to be home before the end of the first week in July. You will see that my absence becomes longer and longer—to my regret; but the circumstances leave me no choice. I want very much to say good-bye to our troops in Italy and Egypt and to thank them for their great services. Once they are back in South Africa they will be scattered over the whole country and it will be impossible to meet them personally.

All is well with us today. Jannie [Smuts] and I and other members of our delegation take as much exercise as our work allows. Only on Saturday we were once more, for two-and-a-half hours, in Muir woods under the giant trees where one can wander about and climb for hours. And yesterday (Sunday) we went to lunch with the [W. W.] Meins (forty miles from here) where we saw a beautiful [Herbert] Baker house in the loveliest setting. I wrote to you that Mrs Mein is the sister of Alpheus Williams. She is a dear, active person, still much attached to South Africa where she grew up in Kimberley. The place is full of South African plants and mementos. The whole family of children and grandchildren was there— a pleasant company. Then back again in the afternoon to two meetings, and so to bed. Today more meetings and towards evening a cocktail party for the most important delegates. This is the usual social function here, and the cheapest. Our health remains good and the climate here is cool and delightful for work. Not much sunshine, usually misty weather, but pleasant. Your dear letters come from time to time and are very welcome. After receiving this you must not write again! Love and kisses.

Pappa

the veto of the permanent members 'from all arrangements relating to the peaceful settlement of disputes' or, at least, from discussions of disputes by the Security Council as distinct from investigation of such disputes. A crisis developed on 2 June when the Russian representative insisted that the permanent members must possess a veto over all matters before the Security Council. Eventually (13 June) the Yalta formula was adopted and included in the Charter of the United Nations (26 June). For Smuts's view on the veto see W. S. Churchill, *The Second World War*, vol. VI, pp. 183-4. *See also* **672**.

671   To M. C. Gillett   Vol. 77, no. 253

[San Francisco]
5 June 1945

Such a welcome letter arrived from you yesterday (written 20 May 1945). All its news was on the whole good and pleasant to me to read. Your movings about, Portway,[1] Hilda's [Clark] new home, the household at 102. To me all these items are like home news, and much better than war news and election news. By the way I was sorry to see dear Winston's wild explosion against the Labour party[2] with whom he has worked so well for so many all-important years. Somehow the attack sounds unreal, and will puzzle people, who will ask: if they are such bad company, however did he find them such good bedfellows all these years? It will cost him votes, not gain him more. I think his Conservative associates—Beaverbrook etc., have not served him well here. How much more seemly and also profitable would have been a nice friendly note, instead of these fulminations.

Here progress is slow and the going is hard all the way. I need not trouble you with details. Russia's attitude is difficult to understand, so different from Yalta and the other conference exchanges. As things stand at the moment, the conference itself is in danger, and I am doing my level best to prevent a crisis. I mean well by Russia although I am much afraid of her. But really she does make things very difficult even for those who wish her well. The old story of Poland, Rumania, Bulgaria, Hungary, Austria—is repeated here, and one is in doubt whether she is really intending to walk with us in the future. The world is so dangerous, people are so war weary, and we have so much to do in preventing utter wreck and ruin from overtaking poor Europe that one simply has not the heart to quarrel. And yet a policy of giving in and giving away and appeasement can have such disastrous results as recent history has shown, that one is bound to be careful and to be on one's guard.

According to present indications the conference will drag on to at least 15 June, perhaps longer. With visits to Washington and Ottawa still in my plan you can see that it is only late in June that I shall possibly be in London. Of course I shall not miss seeing you and

---

[1] A. B. and M. C. Gillett had bought a house in Portway, Street.

[2] The coalition government ended on 23 May and was replaced by a predominantly Conservative 'caretaker' government pending a general election on 5 July. In a broadcast speech on 4 June during the election campaign Churchill said, *inter alia*: 'Socialism is inseparably interwoven with totalitarianism...no Socialist government could afford to allow free...expressions of discontent. They would have to fall back on some form of Gestapo...This would gather all the power to the supreme party and party leaders...'

Arthur and the circle at Street. But dates and details must stand over for the present.

Jannie [Smuts] and I keep well, very well, considering. I still enjoy my weekly walk, two to three hours up and down these hills and valleys. If I had not these walks I would—like the Apostle Paul—be of all men the most miserable![1] Last Saturday I was once more in Muir woods among the giant Sequoias and could climb up the deep valley they inhabit to a height of over 2,000 ft. It was most refreshing—not merely the exercise, but the exercise in a real botanical paradise. The ranger there went some way with Jannie and me but turned back when the real business of the walk began. He was later heard to complain to a friend of mine that I almost killed him! The two Sequoias (the tall *sempervirens* and the thickset *gigantea*) grew everywhere, mixed with the giant Douglas Spruce and other monsters. Stettinius, who is very friendly to me, gave me a wonderful salad bowl hewn out of the giant Sequoia, a real gem of a gift. I love friends, and not less when they are rich and generous, like the dear Gilletts and the Stettinii. We are really very friendly, and I daresay he appreciates that I am helpful with the stiles and the hurdles on the way of the conference.

Sunday I went for lunch south (forty miles) to the Meins (old Johannesburg mining engineer) who lives in an interesting Herbert Baker house built for them in beautiful surroundings. A real bit of architectural Cape, rather incongruous in this American setting. But it shows how people love South Africa even when far and long away from her magic. But I must stop. Some conference people are here to consult me.

Ever yours,

Jan

672   To E. R. Stettinius

Vol. 77, no. 148

[San Francisco]
7 June 1945

Dear Mr Stettinius, When at our executive meeting today an appeal is to be made for speeding up our work I propose, unless you object, to make the enclosed statement, with the intention of inviting the Big Five to make some suggestion as to how we may proceed to finalize our work and wind up the conference at an early date. The answer might then be that the whole matter is under the considera-

---

[1] 'If in this life only we have hope in Christ, we are of all men most miserable.' 1 *Corinthians* xv.19.

tion of the Big Five, and meanwhile you appeal to delegates to speed up their committee and commission work as much as possible. Yours sincerely,

s. J. C. Smuts

ENCLOSURE

South African Delegation

We have arrived very near the end of our labours. Only a very few clauses of the draft Charter still remain to be dealt with, and they could be disposed of in a couple of days, but for a block which stops us and delays our work. In some way or other that block must be removed. I refer to the veto provision and its application.[1]

The clauses still standing over are all in one way or another affected by the interpretation of the veto recommendation. If that interpretation were settled we could finish our work in a few days and thereafter wind up this conference.

The representatives of the Big Five[2] were asked more than a fortnight ago what the veto meant and how far it was to be applied. No answer has yet been given. If it were given our work could be finished in a few days.

I would now appeal to the representatives of the Big Five to give us an answer, one way or the other. If they cannot, then we would ask them to suggest some way out, some procedure to remove the block and save the conference from failure, from being abandoned at this late stage.

We cannot face the world with a complete failure. The consequences would be too disastrous. We must have the answer of the Big Five so that, if necessary, we could devise some procedure which would enable us to complete our task and make a final report. If their answer should happen to be unfavourable, let us know it, so that we could shape our course accordingly. We must then wind up in a decent way and save the work that has already been done.

In making this request for an answer I am not only expressing my own strong feeling but feel sure I am also voicing the sense of many other delegates. We cannot drag out the conference much longer, and we must proceed to finalize our work as soon as possible.

[1] *See supra*, p. 540, note 1.
[2] The United States, Soviet Russia, Great Britain, France, Nationalist China.

673   To W. S. Churchill   Vol. 77, no. 169

Hyde Park Hotel
London S.W.1
3 July 1945

Dear Winston, Very warm thanks for your most kind message about my broadcast last Saturday.[1] I was not satisfied with it and it had to be written in a great hurry. But your commendation makes up for any feeling of inadequacy I may have.

I leave immediately after Victory Parade but shall certainly see you again before leaving. Meanwhile do not forget that I wish to take those two paintings with me—one for myself and one for the prime minister's house at Pretoria.[2] Ever yours,

s. J. C. Smuts

674   To L. S. Amery   Vol. 77, no. 175

Hyde Park Hotel
London S.W.1
4 July 1945

My dear Amery, Thank you very warmly for your invitation. I am however, due to leave here by air on Saturday morning for Italy where I have to visit my troops on the way to South Africa. Every moment of my time meanwhile is taken up with necessary but dreary engagements. I would have loved to come and discuss various matters with you. But that is how I am situated. You and Mrs Amery will understand. I must not delay my return to South Africa, where I left at the end of March and people will soon begin to forget me!

San Francisco was a difficult time, as you will no doubt hear in detail from Cranborne. On the whole a fair job of work has been done.

I had a discussion both here and there with Mudaliar [A. R.] over our Indian troubles, about which I am not entirely pessimistic. I also hope for the best from Wavell's move.

With warm good wishes for your son's and the government's success tomorrow.[3] Ever yours,

s. J. C. Smuts

[1] Entitled 'The Charter of the United Nations' and dated 26 June 1945 (Smuts Collection, Box K, no. 202).

[2] Paintings by Churchill. One of these was duly hung in the prime minister's house in Pretoria but later returned to the Smuts family and given by them to Smuts House at the University of the Witwatersrand.

[3] In the general election on 5 July both L. S. Amery and Julian Amery stood as Conservatives in Birmingham and Preston respectively and lost to the Labour party candidates.

675   To M. C. Gillett   Vol. 77, no. 256

Doornkloof
[Transvaal]
29 July 1945

What amazing things have happened since my last letter! There has been a political *débâcle* in Britain, greater if possible than that of 1906.[1] I hope this one will have equally beneficial consequences, though I am not certain. I don't think the internal policies will be much affected by the change. The social and other internal programmes of the coalition were largely influenced, if not worked out, by the Labour members, and the Labour government is not likely to diverge far from them, except in nationalization and banking, and even there they are not likely to go too far. The change is far more likely to be in the sphere of external affairs, where the hand of Churchill was most visible and his influence in the world enormous. No one can predict what the absence of his dominating position and prestige may have on British policy and British influence. It may be far-reaching. With the Labour government absorbed in internal policies, and the phenomenal rise of the U.S.S.R. and the United States in world affairs, the wise and experienced and moderating influence of the United Kingdom on world policies may become, not only relatively, but really less significant—much to the loss of the world. With the rise of the two colossi in the war and the new world, British influence could be so beneficial in its human, experienced, wise outlook. The world wants this wise broker between the new great powers whose outlooks are so very different. The world also wants British wisdom and sense of proportion in the new movements to the Left now becoming the world-wide fashion. I fear that the dropping of the pilot may have a bad effect in the stormy seas ahead. The country has not only got rid of the Conservatives, who were evidently discredited and distrusted, but they have by the same act lost the leader who really was not conservative but a great human, with vast experience and great breadth of sympathies. At the moment it is difficult to form a just opinion, but the international loss may yet be found to outweigh the national gain. I have publicly congratulated Attlee. Privately I have quoted to Churchill the lines from Mommsen on Hannibal's end which I have often quoted before: 'On those whom the Gods love they lavish infinite joys and

---

[1] The results of the general election, announced on 26 July, were as follows: Labour party 393; Conservative party 213; Liberal party 12; independents 22. Churchill resigned immediately and C. R. Attlee (later Earl Attlee) formed a purely Labour government. In 1906 the Liberal party had won a landslide election victory over the Conservative party.

infinite sorrows.'[1] What else could one say that is adequate to such a situation and such a fall after achieving the most colossal success in history? The Mountain of Transfiguration alternates with the shame of the Cross: such is the curve of the great ones, the favourites of the Gods. Like life and death, human destiny is of the essence of the mystery of this world, and the good and the wise maintain their sense of mystery whatever comes to them. After all, religion is based on this sense of mystery, but of a mystery which is essentially beneficent in its long-range effects. In spite of this philosophizing one cannot forbear sympathizing deeply with Churchill. To be so decisively rejected in the very hour of victory by the people whom he saved by his courage and stupendous exertions is truly the unkindest cut of all.[2]

Coming from the great to the small, I confess I am still basking in the sunshine of welcomes and public congratulations after my return from San Francisco. These tiring and tiresome functions are going on and will continue to do so for some weeks or longer. But I know my fate from what happened after the last war. Rejection and repudiation will once more close the chapter and end the glory. It will break no hearts. What is done is done and is part of the sum total of things, however insignificant a contribution. Nothing can add to or subtract from what is done and finished. And I shall face whatever may come with no wry face!

One thing I fear is that the Labour government will be no check on the wild career of Russia in eastern and central Europe. Their Leftist outlook and following will make such a check or break impossible for them. And yet that may be the most essential service to the world in the immediate future. One hears of wild doings in the Balkans, Hungary, Austria, Poland and eastern Germany. Russian policy is apparently completing the social and economic *débâcle* which the war started. And I see no one now to call a halt to this wild career of spoliation and disintegration. The United States is too far off and ill-informed on European matters to apply a brake. And in the next ten years the process of decay may continue instead of being reversed, and the new Europe beginning slowly to emerge. This is where I have most misgiving and fear in connection with what has happened. Bolshevism may have been a tonic to a serf Russia; it will be a poison to a more advanced and civilized world further west. The Left is the fashion, but it may end in a very naked world, and in sufferings of the more refined peoples and their educated middle classes, which would be a dreadful loss and set-back

[1] *See supra*, p. 269, note 2.
[2] 'This was the most unkindest cut of all.' Shakespeare, *Julius Caesar*, III.ii.188.

to the whole European system. As I have seen Italy a few weeks ago, a process of regeneration may start immediately, but not if it is to be preceded by a sad stage of bolshevization—and this I assume applies to many other countries in that region of Europe. I sense grave danger.

Unfortunately my official position closes my mouth, and I cannot give the warnings I think called for. And I may even take an exaggerated view of impending dangers. But I was not wrong in 1919–23, and I think the dangers today are, if possible, greater, as Russia is more ruthless and inexperienced in dealing with such situations than Britain and France were twenty-five years ago. All one can do is to put on one's thinking cap, and wait for such opportunities of being helpful as may occur in the future. Here in South Africa I shall be held up as one of the warmongers who helped to precipitate these evils on mankind! And the charge has a certain measure of plausibility which will go down, as it did in 1922–4.

Nothing else to report. A week has been spent here and at Lourenço Marques in entertaining Portuguese visitors of distinction. Ever yours,

Jan

676 To M. C. Gillett

Vol. 77, no. 257

Doornkloof
[Transvaal]
10 August 1945

This morning I received two letters from you and one from Arthur, all from Windermere, where you appear to have spent a very pleasant quiet holiday. How I do envy you! Since my arrival back in South Africa I have had a most busy time and have had to rush from one place to another to receive 'welcomes' and make reports of my doings abroad, and to all this has been added all the arrear business which awaited me here. This is a difficult time for those in authority and as you know people in South Africa are particularly exacting in their calls on the government. I have become even more than the government and am like a father to the people and all their complaints and prayers come to me *personally* in the hope or faith that I shall put them all right! I have had no free day except one Sunday at Rooikop where I took Bancroft and Cato [Clark] and enjoyed a good long walk, and the following Monday (bank holiday) when Bancroft and I walked from Irene to Pretoria over the hills. But I feel fit and well and have no complaints myself. If I had them nobody would hear but yourself! Problems *galore* on all sides, but I console myself with the thought that the burdens of other authorities are much heavier than my own. And I don't find them more successful than my erring self!

I am deeply disappointed with Potsdam.[1] The decisions and suggestions coming from that conference point to a set-up in Europe which alarms me. I see nothing ahead of Germany but a sunk area with lower production and lower standards and a centre of infection for the rest of the continent. Russia is being aggrandized into a really dangerous world power, and the British concern has been to come to agreements and eliminate discords, but the result is a world set-up which alarms me very much. Europe may well lapse to conditions which may frighten America once more into her shell and washing her hands of the old world. In this crisis U.N.N.R.A.[2] is resorted to as a palliative. But how much wiser it would be to make a peace which will set people on their feet instead of merely pacifying Russia and her satellites. I do feel that in Churchill Britain has lost her great hand and that her game will now be a most difficult and risky one. I have sounded a warning note, but we have reached a generation that knew not Pharaoh (or is it Joseph?),[3] and my influence has suffered a sad eclipse I fear. The new government is quite a good human team, but with more good will than experience and power. Churchill would in these times at the end of the war have been such a powerful standby for humane, far-sighted policies. I do not think American experience is adequate to this unprecedented situation, and Russia is more bent on building up her great state than in solving the problems of the outside world. We are in for very trying times. Her timing of her entry into the Japanese war—after the issue is already decided and the atomic bomb has appeared[4]— shows how much she is concerned with her own interests and future.

I never told you that for the last two years I had been deeply concerned with this atomic bomb business. Its success for war was already assured, but the question of future control has been my main preoccupation. How to control this new danger for man,

[1] Conference of representatives of the United States, Great Britain and Soviet Russia held in Berlin from 17 July to 2 August where the three powers agreed upon the terms to be imposed on defeated Germany, upon the cession of Königsberg and part of East Prussia to Russia and upon the Oder–Neisse line as the western frontier of Poland.

[2] United Nations Relief and Rehabilitation Administration. Established on 9 November 1943 to help war refugees and assist the economic recovery of war-damaged countries. Ceased its activities on 31 March 1949.

[3] 'Now there arose up a new king over Egypt, which knew not Joseph.' *Exodus* i.8.

[4] The first atomic bomb was dropped on Hiroshima on 6 August. Russia declared war on Japan on 8 August. Japan surrendered on 14 August.

incomparably greater than anything known before? The question is still unsolved and remains the greatest before us. Of course the industrial potentialities of the bomb are enormous, but that is a question for the future. Its destructive power is already clear...

677   To M. C. Gillett   Vol. 77, no. 258

Doornkloof
[Transvaal]
16 August 1945

This is written on the day following VJ day. We have a holiday today which enables me to write you my weekly letter, after taking a long walk this morning. What a sudden ending it has been to the Japanese war; I had expected another year of slaughter ending in the virtual extinction of Japan. And now the finale has come even more suddenly than in Germany. I look upon this as a double blessing—on us and on the Japs themselves.

I daresay this sudden collapse was largely due to the atomic bomb, the effect of which, both physical and psychological, must have been shattering. From that point of view its use has been justified. But it has been even more justified from the point of view of preventing war in future. Although much has been said in vague terms of the new weapons in preparation people were thinking of trifles like V1 and V2 bombs. And now they have, *before* the end of the war seen something infinitely more horrible and death-dealing. They would never have believed the warning about deadly weapons in future warfare unless there had been this actual display of them at the end of this war. We are now forewarned of what is coming if war is not ended for good. I knew all about it as I had been dealing with this matter for the last two years on my London visits. At last a discovery has been made which should put war out of court for good and all. The question of the control of sub-atomic energy now becomes the paramount international question. And something far more drastic has to be done than we have attempted at San Francisco. We could not, of course, use our secret knowledge there. But this new development is from every point of view, both national and international, both for war and industry, the most revolutionary that has ever been made.

I got your last letter a couple of days ago. It was written at the end of your visit to Edna[1] and Helen [Gordon] and also after the election

---

[1] Born Edna Brown; married, in 1905, Sir Hyde Clarendon Gowan (1878–1938) who was governor of the central provinces, India, 1933–8.

results had come out. I agree with you that nothing fearful will happen as a result. The Labour victory may be all to the good. I only fear that the loss of Churchill at this stage may seriously cripple British foreign policy. It is a dangerous world, now as much so as ever before; and the loss of a champion like Churchill cannot fail to be seriously felt in our dealings with colossi like the United States and the U.S.S.R. Attlee and his colleagues are good and honest men who will do their best, I have no doubt. But I would have preferred Churchill myself at the job. Unfortunately he had allowed himself to become Conservative leader, without being himself a Conservative in conviction. And this now is the result of that initial mistake. So our mistakes catch us out in the end! Fortunately internal politics are so well balanced in Britain that a change of government does not amount to much. And there are a number of necessary reforms which the Conservatives would never have made except under compulsion. Nationalization of power, transport, and the like has been our policy in South Africa for more than a generation and it has been all to the good. Our mining control is also such that the government is senior partner in gold and diamond mining. Finance is quite free with us, and I hope the Labour government will go slowly over that dangerous ground in view of the international position of Britain in finance. But why trouble you with these things of which you and Arthur know much more than I myself. It is foreign policy that troubles me.

And now it is peace, and we shall have the colossal problems of the switch over from war to peace, from war production and full employment to disorganized civilian industry and possible unemployment until things are normal again. Personally I could wish to be out of all this after the burdens I have had to carry these last years and at my age. But I have no general election to release me, and such a development here might (unlike in Britain) have catastrophic consequences. And so there is no mercy for this sinner, this old sinner, who will have to carry his burden—for the present at any rate. But I could have wished for a merciful release!...